West of the Rocky Mountains

Edited by

JOHN MUIR

Running Press   Philadelphia Pennsylvania

All rights reserved under the Pan-American and International Copyright Convention
Printed in the United States of America
Distributed in Canada by Van Nostrand Reinhold Ltd., Ontario
Library of Congress Catalog Card Number 75-37277
ISBN 0-914 294- 41-5 trade paper
ISBN 0-914 294- 42-3 library edition

3 4 5 6 7 8 9
First digit on left indicates the number of this printing.

Art direction by Jim Wilson
Cover Illustration by Charles Santore
Cover lettering by Peter Ruge

This book may be ordered directly from the publisher.
Please include 25¢ postage
Try your bookstore first.

Running Press, 38 South Nineteenth Street
Philadelphia, Pennsylvania 19103

CONTENTS.

JOHN MUIR

"I care to live", John Muir once wrote, "only to entice people to look at nature." This book, originally published in 1888 as **Picturesque California and the Region West of the Rocky Mountains, from Alaska to Mexico,** is undoubtedly the most spectacular example of how Muir put his credo into action. Still, it is only one of many remarkable efforts he made on behalf of the wilderness. An energetic lecturer, a tireless lobbyist and a prolific writer, Muir fought to preserve America's remaining wilderness from exploitation and destruction. He wanted Americans to adapt a less utilitarian attitude towards the wilderness. At the time, most of his fellow citizens looked upon the unsettled portions of the continents either as obstacles to progress or convenient repositories of exploitable resources.

John Muir was born in Dunbar, Scotland in April, 1838. "When I was a boy in Scotland", he once recalled, "I was fond of everything that was wild". He added that "all my life I've been growing fonder and fonder of wild places and wild creatures." In 1849 the Muir family emigrated to America, and settled in Wisconsin. Muir was an avid reader. As a young man he exhibited a talent both for mathematics and mechanical invention. The inventions he submitted to the 1860 Wisconsin Agricultural Fair were widely regarded as works of genius. Then, in 1867, while working as a machinist in a carriage factory, Muir suffered an accident that blinded him. He spent the next month in a darkened room, and his sight returned. But his injury had given him time to consider his future. His love of "all things wild" had never left him, and he determined upon his recovery to abandon his career as a machinist and fledgling inventor and to devote his life to observing closely nature in all its aspects.

His first project was a thousand mile walk from Indiana to the Gulf of Mexico. He next planned to trace the Amazon River to its source, but a severe attack of malaria forced him to give up the project. Having been advised to seek out a more temperate climate, Muir took passage to San Francisco. He kept traveling inland until he reached the Sierra Nevadas, which immediately captivated him. He spent most of the next eight years living by himself in the Sierras. "I am often asked", he noted in his journal, "if I am not lonely on my solitary excursions. It seems so self-evident that one cannot be lonesome where everything is wild and beautiful and busy and steeped with God that the question is hard to answer...".

He explored other wilderness areas, but the Sierra's remained Muir's spiritual home. There he found life serene. Men, he wrote, had shackled themselves to the "galling harness" of civilization. They ignored the yearnings for space, freedom and communion with nature —yearnings as old as mankind itself. Muir recognized in himself "a constant tendency to return to primitive wilderness", and believed that this was a desire active in all humans. "Going to the woods is going home."

"There is a love of wild nature in everybody, an ancient mother-love showing itself whether recognized or no, and however covered by cares and duties." To deny this is to encourage despair. Periodic journeys into the wilderness refresh and invigorate mind and body alike. "Climb the mountains and get their good tidings," he urged. "Nature's peace will flow into you as the sunshine into trees. The winds will blow their freshness into you, and the storms their energy, while cares will drop off you as autumn leaves." Only by contact with nature can man arrive at peace and discover his interior creative being. "In God's wildness lies the hope of the world —the great fresh, unblighted, unredeemed wilderness."

The Sierras provided the inspiration Muir needed to formulate his philosophy. Also, it was probably because of his early experiences in the Sierras that he became such a dedicated and energetic conservationist. For even in these wild mountains the depredations of sheep and cattle men and loggers were becoming evident: Meadows where for centuries grass flourished were simply devoured by the grazing herds. The soil soon followed the grass, and glades once lush became wastelands. Forests old when Columbus landed were ravaged by lumbermen. In a savage irony, man was everywhere destroying the very qualities that he so desperately needed in life.

For over thirty years Muir's was the most eloquent voice raised in nature's behalf. He was at once a tireless organizer, eloquent speaker and thorough, convincing writer. He led the seventeen year fight to have Yosemite declared a national park. He was instrumental in saving both the Grand Canyon and the Petrified Forest from destruction. And he was a prominent figure in the long battle to save the redwood forests. He was one of the founders of the Sierra Club and its first president, serving from 1892 until his death.

More important than the many battles he waged is his impact on the attitudes of his fellow citizens. John Muir helped to strengthen and confirm the then-emerging belief in the values of wilderness and the necessity of preserving it for future generations. He did so largely through his speeches and many articles.

While he was a prolific writer, this book is unique among his published works. Evidently, Muir hit upon the idea of putting together a series of articles for a national magazine, written by knowledgeable observers, in which the features and life forms of each of the regions west of the Rockies would be described. He convinced an editor to undertake the project, of which Muir became the enthusiastic overseer. He helped select illustrations, recruit writers and edit the contributions. He wrote six essays for the series, describing the Sierras and the Pacific Northwest region. The articles apparently enjoyed some success, for they were next collected and issued as a book, supplemented by over six hundred illustrations.

At the time of its original publication, there cannot have been anything quite like this book available. It was the first large-scale attempt to present to the American people a thorough description of the mountains, forests, deserts, wildlife and people of the western half of the nation.

Now, after being out of print for over seventy years, it is being reissued. It is some indication of the success of the original effort that the book remains largely as fresh and as capable of exciting wonder as it did eighty–seven years ago. It offers us a chance to recapture, fleetingly, the wild beauty that was once America. In so doing, it is hoped that the book will encourage us to appreciate, and to work to preserve, the wilderness, and the wildlife, that yet remain.

John Muir left a deep impression in the minds of his contemporaries. Through the example of his lifestyle, his writings and the national parks he helped establish, he continues to exert an influence today. Near the end of his life, he told a friend: "I have lived a bully life. I have done what I set out to do." On Christmas Eve, 1914, full of days, John Muir quietly died.

Richard E. Nicholls
for Running Press

PEAKS AND GLACIERS OF THE HIGH SIERRA.

LOOKING across the broad, level plain of the Sacramento and San Joaquin from the summit of the Coast Range opposite San Francisco, after the sky has been washed by the winter rains, the lofty Sierra may be seen throughout nearly its whole extent, stretching in simple grandeur along the edge of the plain, like an immense wall, four hundred miles long and two and a half miles high, colored in four horizontal bands; the lowest rose-purple of exquisite beauty of tone, the next higher dark purple, the next blue, and the highest pearl-white,—all delicately interblending with each other and with the pale luminous sky and the golden yellow of the plain, and varying in tone with the time of day and the advance of the season.

The thousand landscapes of the Sierra are thus beheld in one view, massed into one sublime picture, and such is the marvelous purity of the atmosphere it seems as near and clear as a painting hung on a parlor wall. But nothing can you see or hear of all the happy life it holds, or of its lakes and meadows and lavish abundance of white falling water. The majestic range with all its treasures hidden stretches still and silent as the sunshine that covers it.

The rose-purple zone rising smoothly out of the yellow plain is the torrid foothill region, comprehending far the greater portion of the gold-bearing rocks of the range, and the towns, mills, and ditches of the miners—a waving stretch of comparatively low, rounded hills and ridges, cut into sections by the main river cañons, roughened here and there with outcropping masses of red and gray slates, and rocky gold gulches rugged and rid-dled; the whole faintly shaded by a sparse growth of oaks, and patches of scrubby ceanothus and manzanita chaparral.

Specks of cultivation are scattered flats and hollows far apart—rose em-groves, vineyards and orchards, and of sight, and making scarce any in wide general views; a paradise purple skies during the spring parched, and bare all the from end to end of the zone in fertile bowered cottages, small glossy orange sweet-scented hay fields, mostly out appreciable mark on the landscape of flowers and bees and bland months—dusty, sunbeaten, rest of the year.

The dark-purple region of the giant silver-firs, forming erous forests on globe. They where vocal ning and blue zones are the pines and sequoia and the noblest conif- the face of the are every- with run- water

and c h e d delightful Miles of tan- are blooming and lily gardens, damp ferny glens in and richness, compelling beholder. Sweeping on extend a continuous belt from slightly interrupted at intervals tremendous cañons 3,000 to 5,000 dren- w i t h sunshine. gled bushes beneath them, and meadows, and endless variety of color the admiration of every over ridges and valleys they end to end of the range, only of fifteen and twenty miles by feet in depth.

Into these main river-cañons open, occupied by bouncing, dancing, the rivers, which, gray with foam, are the lowlands and the sea. All these waters to the onlooking forests, and to the stern, innumerable side-cañons and gorges rejoicing cascades, making haste to join beating their way with resistless energy to sounding together give glorious animation rocky grandeur of the cañon-walls.

There too, almost directly opposite our point of view, is the far-famed Yosemite Valley; and to right and left on the same zone many other valleys of the same type, some of them, though but little known as yet, not a whit less interesting, either in regard to the sublimity of their architecture, or the grandeur and beauty of their falling waters.

Above the upper edge of the silver-fir zone, the forest is maintained by smaller pines and spruces, that sweep on higher around lakes and meadows, and over smooth waves of granite and outspread moraines, until, dwarfed and storm-bent, the utmost limit of tree-growth is reached at a height of from 10,000 to 12,000 feet. While far above the bravest climbers of them all, rises the lofty, snow-laden, icy Sierra, composed of a vast wilderness of peaks, and crests, and splintered spires, swept by torrents and avalanches, and separated by deep gorges and notches and wide amphitheatres, the treasuries of the snow and fountain-heads of the rivers, holding in their dark mysterious recesses all that is left of the grand system of glaciers that once covered the entire range. During many years of faithful explorations in the Sierra, sixty-five glaciers have been discovered and studied, and it is not likely that many more will be found. Over two-thirds of the entire number lie between Lat. 36° 30′ and 39°, sheltered from the wasting sunshine on the northern slopes of the highest peaks, where the snow-fall on which they depend is most concentrated and abundant.

Nothing was known of the existence of active glaciers in the Sierra until October, 1871, when I made the discovery of Black Mountain Glacier and measured its

GLACIER BETWEEN MTS. RITTER AND LYELL.

movements. It lies near the head of a wide shadowy basin between Red and Black Mountains, two of the dominating summits of the Merced Group. This group consists of the highest portion of a spur that straggles out from the main axis of the chain near Mount Ritter, in the direction of Yosemite Valley. Its western slopes are drained by Illilouette Creek, a tributary of the Merced, which pours its waters into Yosemite in a fine fall bearing the same name as the stream.

No excursion can be made into the Sierra that may not prove an enduring blessing. Notwithstanding the great height of the summits, and the ice and the snow, and the gorges and cañons and sheer giddy precipices, no mountain chain on the globe is more kindly and approachable. Visions of ineffable beauty and harmony, health and exhilaration of body and soul, and grand foundation lessons in Nature's eternal love are the sure reward of every earnest looker in this glorious wilderness.

The Yosemite Valley is a fine hall of entrance to one of the highest and most interesting portions of the Sierra at the head of the Merced, Tuolumne, San Joaquin, and Owen's rivers. The necessary outfit may be procured here, in the way of pack animals, provisions, etc.; and trails lead from the valley towards Mounts Dana, Lyell, and Ritter, and the Mono Pass; also into the lower portion of the Illilouette Basin.

Going to the Black Mountain Glacier, only a few days' provision is required, and a pair of blankets, if you are not accustomed to sleeping by a camp-fire without them.

Leaving the valley by the trail leading past the Vernal and Nevada falls, you cross the lower end of Little Yosemite Valley, and climb the Starr King Ridge, from which you obtain a fine general view of the Illilouette Basin, with its grand array of peaks and domes and dark spirey forests—all on a grand scale of magnitude, yet keenly fine in finish and beauty; forming one of the most interesting of the basins that lie round about Yosemite Valley, and pour their tribute of songful water into it, swelling the anthems ever sounding there.

The glacier is not visible from this standpoint, but the two mountains between which it lies make a faithful mark, and you can hardly go wrong, however inexperienced in mountain ways.

Going down into the heart of the basin, through beds of zauchneria, and manzanita chaparral, where the bears love to feed, you follow the main stream past a series of cascades and falls until you find yourself between the two lateral moraines that come sweeping down in majestic curves from the shoulders of Red and Black mountains. These henceforth will be your guide, for they belonged to the grand old glacier, of which Black Mountain Glacier is a remnant, the only one that has endured until now the change of climate which has transformed a wilderness of ice and snow into a wilderness of warm exuberant life. Pushing on over this glacial highway, you pass lake after lake set in solid basins of granite, and many a well-watered meadow and thicket where the deer with their young love to hide; now clanking over smooth shining rock where not a leaf tries to grow, now wading plushy bogs knee deep in yellow and purple sphagnum, or brushing through luxuriant garden patches among larkspurs eight feet high and lilies with thirty flowers on a single stalk. The lateral moraines bounding the view on either side are like artificial embankments, and are covered with a superb growth of silver-firs and pines; many specimens attaining a height of 200 feet or more.

But this garden and forest luxuriance is soon left behind. The trees are dwarfed, the gardens become exclusively alpine, patches of the heath-like bryanthus and cassiope begin to appear, and arctic willows pressed into flat close carpets by the weight of the winter snow. The lakes, which a few miles down the valley are so deeply imbedded in the tall woods, or embroidered with flowery meadows, have here, at an elevation of 10,000 feet above sea level, only thin mats of carex, leaving bare glaciated rock bosses around more than half their shores. Yet amid all this alpine suppression, the sturdy brown-barked mountain pine is seen tossing his storm-beaten branches on ledges and buttresses of Red Mountain, some specimens over a hundred feet high and twenty-four feet in circumference, seemingly as fresh and vigorous as if made wholly of sunshine and snow. If you have walked well and have not lingered among the beauties of the way, evening will be coming on as you enter the grand fountain amphitheater in which the glacier lies. It is about a mile wide in the middle, and rather less than two miles long. Crumbling spurs and battlements of Red Mountain bound it on the north, the sombre rudely sculptured precipices of Black Mountain on the south, and a hacked and splintered *col* curves around from mountain to mountain at the head, shutting it in on the east.

You will find a good camp-ground on the brink of a glacier lake, where a thicket of Williamson spruce affords shelter from the night wind, and wood for your fire.

As the night advances the mighty rocks looming darkly about you seem to come nearer, and the starry sky stretches across from wall to wall, fitting closely down into all the spiky irregularities of the summits in most impressive grandeur. Then, as you lie by your fireside, gazing into this strange weird beauty, you fall into the clear, death-like sleep that comes to the tired mountaineer.

In the early morning the mountain voices are hushed, the night wind dies away, and scarce a leaf stirs in the groves. The birds that dwell here, and the marmots, are still crouching in their nests. The stream, cascading from pool to pool, seems alone to be awake and doing. But the spirit of the opening, blooming day calls to action. The sunbeams stream gloriously through jagged openings of the eastern wall, glancing on ice-burnished pavements, and lighting the mirror surface of the lake, while every sunward rock and pinnacle burns white on the edges like melting iron in a furnace.

Passing round the northern shore of the lake, and tracing the stream that feeds it back into its upper recesses, you are led past a chain of small lakes set on bare granite benches and connected by

Unclaim : 4/28/2022

Held date   : 4/18/2022
Pickup location : Outreach

Title   : Insidious
Call number   : FICTION COU
Item barcode   : 0000124441510
Assigned branch : Capitola

Notes:

Alias: MIL_MOG_EAS

Mount Emerson and the High Sierras. From Painting by W. Keith.

" This group consists of the highest portion of a spur that straggles out from the main axis of the chain near Mount Ritter, in the direction of Yosemite Valley . . . Visions of ineffable beauty and harmony, health and exhilaration of body and soul, and grand foundation lessons in Nature's eternal love, are the sure reward of every earnest looker in this glorious wilderness."

cascades and falls. Here the scenery becomes more rigidly arctic. The last dwarf pine is left far below, and the streams are bordered with icicles. The sun now with increasing warmth loosens rock-masses on shattered portions of the wall that come bounding down gullies and *couloirs* in dusty, spattering avalanches, echoing wildly from crag to crag. The main lateral moraines, that stretch so formally from the huge jaws of the amphitheatre into the middle of the basin, are continued along the upper walls in straggling masses wherever the declivity is sufficiently low to allow loose material to rest, while separate stones, thousands of tons in weight, are lying stranded here and there out in the middle of the channel. Here too you may observe well characterized frontal moraines ranged in regular order along the south wall of Black Mountain, the shape and size of each corresponding with the daily shadows cast by the wall above them.

Tracing the main stream back to the last of its chain of lakelets, you may notice that the stones on the bottom are covered with a deposit of fine gray mud, that has been ground from the rocks in the bed of the glacier and transported by its draining stream, which is seen issuing from the base of a raw, fresh looking moraine still in process of formation. Not a plant or weather-stain is visible on its rough unsettled surface. It is from 60 to more than 100 feet in height and comes plunging down in front at an angle of 38°, which is the steepest at which this form of moraine material will lie. Climbing it is therefore no easy undertaking. The slightest touch loosens ponderous blocks that go rumbling to the bottom, followed by a train of

GRANITE CONES ON THE UPPER MERCED.

smaller stones and sand.

Cautiously picking your way, you at length gain the top, and there outspread in full view is the little giant glacier swooping down from the sombre precipices of Black Mountain in a finely graduated curve, fluent in all its lines, yet seemingly as rugged and immovable as the mountain against which it is leaning. The blue compact ice appears on all the lower portions of the glacier sprinkled with dirt and stones imbedded in its surface. Higher, the ice disappears beneath coarsely granulated snow. The surface is still further characterized by dirt bands and the outcropping edges of blue veins, that sweep across from side to side in beautiful concentric curves, showing the laminated structure of the mass; and at the head of the glacier where the *neve* joins the mountain it is traversed by a huge yawning *bergschrund*, in some places twelve to fourteen feet in width, and bridged at intervals by the remains of snow avalanches. Creeping along the lower edge of the *schrund*, holding on with benumbed fingers, clear sections are displayed where the bedded and ribbon structure of glaciers are beautifully illustrated. The surface snow, though everywhere sprinkled with stones shot down from the cliffs, is in some places almost pure white, gradually becoming crystalline, and changing to porous whitish ice of varying shades, and this again changing at a depth of 20 or 30 feet to blue, some of the ribbon-like bands of which are nearly pure and solid, and blend with the paler bands in the most gradual and exquisite manner imaginable, reminding one of the way that color bands come together in the rainbow.

A Bergschrund in Black Mountain Glacier. Painting by W. Keith.

"Should you wish to descend into the weird ice-world of the Schrund, you may find a way or make a way by cutting steps with an ax. Its chambered hollows are hung with a multitude of clustered icicles, amidst which this subdued light pulses and shimmers with ineffable loveliness. Water drips and trinkles among the icicles overhead, and from far below there come strange, solemn murmurs from currents that are feeling their way in the darkness among veins and fissures on the bottom."

Should you wish to descend into the weird ice-world of the Schrund, you may find a way or make a way, by cutting steps with an axe. Its chambered hollows are hung with a multitude of clustered icicles, amidst which thin subdued light pulses and shimmers with ineffable loveliness. Water drips and tinkles among the icicles overhead, and from far below there come strange solemn murmurs from currents that are feeling their way in the darkness among veins and fissures on the bottom. Ice creations of this kind are perfectly enchanting, notwithstanding one feels strangely out of place in their cold fountain beauty. Dripping and shivering you are glad to seek the sunshine, though it is hard to turn away from the delicious music of the water, and the still more delicious beauty of the light in the crystal chambers. Coming again to the surface you may see stones of every size setting out on their downward journey with infinite deliberation, to be built into the terminal moraine. And now the noonday warmth gives birth to a network of sweet-voiced rills that run gracefully down the glacier, curling and swirling in their shining channels, and cutting clear sections in which the structure of the ice is beautifully revealed, their quick, gliding, glancing movements contrasting widely with the invisible flow of the glacier itself on whose back they are all riding. The series of frontal moraines noted further down, forming so striking a picture of the land-scape, correspond in every particular with those of this active glacier; and the cause of their distri-bution with reference to shadows, is now plainly unfolded. When those climatic changes came on that broke up the main glacier that once filled the amphitheatre from wall to wall, a series of residual glaciers was left in the cliff shadows, under whose protection they lingered until the ter-minal moraines under consideration were formed. But as the seasons become yet warmer, or the snow supply less abundant, they wasted and vanished in succession, all excepting the one we have just seen; and the causes of its longer life are manifest in the greater extent of snow basin it drains, and in its more perfect shelter from the action of the sun. How much longer this little glacier will last to enrich the landscape will of course depend upon climate and the changes slowly effected in the form and exposure of its basin.

But now these same shadows reaching quite across the main basin and up the slopes of Red Mountain, mark the time for returning to camp, and also hint the ascent of the mountain next day, from whose summit glorious views are to be seen far down over the darkening woods, and north and south over the basins of Nevada Creek, and San Joaquin, with their shining lakes and lace of silvery streams, and eastward to the snowy Sierras, marshalled along the sky near enough to be intensely impressive. This ascent will occupy most of your third day, and on the fourth, sweeping around the southern boundary of the Illilouette Basin, and over the Glacier Point Ridge, you may reach your headquarters in Yosemite by way of the Glacier Point trail, thus completing one of the most telling trips one can make into the icy Yosemite fountains.

The glaciers lying at the head of the Tuolumne and North fork of the San Joaquin may also be reached from Yosemite, as well as many of the most interesting of the mountains, Mts. Dana, Lyell, Ritter, and Mammoth Mountain,—the Mono Pass also, and Mono Lake and Volcanoes on the eastern flank of the range. For this grand general excursion into the heart of the High Sierra, good legs and nerves are required, and great caution, and a free number of weeks. Then you may feel reasonably safe among the loose crags of the peaks and crevasses of the glaciers, and return to the lowlands and its cares rich forever in mountain wealth beyond your most extravagant expectations.

The best time to go to the High Sierra is about the end of September, when the leaf colors are ripe, and the snow is in great part melted from the glaciers, revealing the crevasses that are hidden earlier in the season. Setting out with a pack-animal by the way of Vernal and Nevada falls at the lower end of Little Yosemite Valley, you will strike the old Mariposa and Mono Trail, which will lead you along the base of Clouds Rest, past Cathedral Peak, and down through beautiful forests into the Big Tuolumne Meadows. There, leaving the trail which crosses the meadows and makes direct for the head of the Mono Pass, you turn to the right and follow on up the meadow to its head near the base of Mt. Lyell, where a central camp should be established, from which short excursions may be made under comfortable auspices to the adjacent peaks and glaciers.

Throughout the journey to the central camp you will be delighted with the intense azure of the sky, the fine purplish-gray tones of the granite, the reds and browns of dry meadows, and the translucent purple and crimson of huckleberry bogs, the flaming yellow of aspen groves, the silvery flashing of the streams in their rocky channels, and the bright green and blue of the glacier lakes. But the general expression of the scenery is savage and bewildering to the lover of the picturesque. Threading the forests from ridge to ridge, and scanning the landscapes from every outlook, foregrounds, middle-grounds, backgrounds, sublime in magnitude, yet seem all alike—bare rock waves, woods, groves, diminutive flecks of meadow and strips of shining water, pictures without lines of beginning or ending.

Cathedral Peak, grandly sculptured, a temple hewn from the living rock, of noble proportions and profusely spired, is the first peak that concentrates the attention. Then come the Tuolumne Meadows, a wide roomy stretch lying at a height of about 8,500 feet above the sea, smooth and lawn-like, with the noble forms of Mts. Dana and Gibbs in the distance, and curiously sculptured peaks on either side. But it is only towards evening of the second day from the valley, that in approaching the upper end of the meadows you gain a view of a truly beautiful and well-balanced picture. It

A Bear Trap.

is composed of one lofty group of snow-laden peaks, of which Mt. Lyell is the centre, with gray, pine-fringed, granite bosses braided around its base, the whole surging free into the sky from the head of a magnificent valley, whose lofty walls are beveled away on both sides so as to embrace it all without admitting anything not strictly belonging to it.

The foreground is now aflame with autumn colors, brown, and purple, and gold, ripe and luminous in the mellow sunshine, contrasting brightly with the deep cobalt-blue of the sky, and the black and gray, and pure spiritual white of the rocks and glaciers. Down through the heart of the picture the young Tuolumne River is seen pouring from its crystal fountains, now resting in glassy pools as if changing back again into ice, now leaping in white cascades as if turning to snow, gliding right and left between granite bosses, then sweeping on through the smooth meadow levels of the valley, swaying pensively from side to side, with calm, stately gestures, past dipping sedges and willows, and around groves of arrowy pine; and throughout its whole eventful course, flowing however fast or slow, singing loud or low, ever filling the landscape with delightful animation, and manifesting the grandeur of its sources in every movement and tone.

WILD SHEEP OF THE SIERRA. DRAWN BY W. M. CARY.

"Even the wild sheep, the best mountaineers of all, choose regular passes in crossing the summits on their way to their summer or winter pastures . . . Rugged spurs and moraines and huge projecting buttresses begin to shut you in until, arriving at the summit of the dividing ridge between the headwaters of Rush Creek and the northmost tributaries of the San Joaquin, a picture of pure wildness is disclosed, far surpassing every other you have yet seen."

The excursion to the top of Mount Lyell, 13,000 feet high, will take you through the midst of this alpine grandeur, and one day is all the time required. From your camp on the bank of the river you bear off up the right wall of the cañon and on direct to the glacier, keeping towards its western margin, so as to reach the west side of the extreme summit of the mountain where the ascent is least dangerous. The surface of the glacier is shattered with crevasses in some places; these, however, are easily avoided, but the sharp wave-like blades of granular snow covering a great part of the upper slopes during most of the season are exceedingly fatiguing, and are likely to stop any but the most determined climbers willing to stagger, stumble, and wriggle onward against every difficulty. The view from the summit overlooks the wilderness of peaks towards Mount Ritter, with their bright array of snow, and ice, and lakes; and northward Mount Dana, Castle Peak, Mammoth Mountain, and many others; westward, sweeping sheets of meadow, and heaving swells of ice-polished granite, and dark lines of forest and shadowy cañons towards Yosemite; while to eastward the view fades dimly among the sunbeaten deserts and ranges of the Great Basin. These grand mountain scriptures laid impressively open will make all your labor light, and you will return to camp braced and strengthened for yet grander things to come.

The excursion to Mt. Ritter will take about three days from the Tuolumne Camp, some provision therefor will have to be carried, but no one will chafe under slight inconveniences while seeking so noble a mark. Ritter is king of all the giant summits hereabouts. Its height is about 13,300 feet, and it is guarded by steeply inclined glaciers, and cañons and gorges of tremendous depth and ruggedness, rendering it comparatively inaccessible. But difficulties of this kind only exhilarate the mountaineer.

Setting out from the Tuolumne, carrying bread, and an axe to cut steps in the glaciers, you go about a mile down the valley to the foot of a cascade that beats its way through a rugged gorge in the cañon wall from a height of about 900 feet, and pours its foaming waters into the river. Along the edge of this cascade you will find a charming way to the summit. Thence you cross the axis of the range and make your way southward along the eastern flank to the northern slopes of Ritter, conforming to the topography as best you can; for to push on directly through the peaks along the summit is impossible.

Climbing along the dashing border of the cascade, bathed from time to time in waftings of irised spray, you are not likely to feel much weariness, and all too soon you find yourself beyond its highest fountains. Climbing higher, new beauty comes streaming on the sight,—autumn-painted meadows, late-blooming goldenrods, peaks of rare architecture, bright crystal lakes, and glimpses of the forested lowlands seen far in the west.

Over the divide the Mono Desert comes full into view lying dreamily silent in thick purple light,—a desert of heavy sun-glare, beheld from a foreground of ice-burnished granite. Here the mountain waters separate, flowing

INDEPENDENCE LAKE FROM MT. LOLO.

HALF DOME, YOSEMITE: VIEW FROM MORAN POINT. ETCHED BY THOMAS MORAN.

"At the head of the valley, now clearly revealed, stands the Half Dome, the loftiest, most sublime and the most beautiful of all the rocks that guard this glorious temple."

east to vanish in the volcanic sands and dry sky of the Great Basin, west to pass through the Golden Gate to the sea.

Passing a little way down over the summit until an elevation of about ten thousand feet is reached, you then push on southward dealing instinctively with every obstacle as it presents itself. Massive spurs alternating with deep gorges and cañons plunge abruptly from the shoulders of the snowy peaks and plant their feet in the warm desert. These are everywhere marked with characteristic sculptures of the ancient glaciers that swept over this entire region like one vast ice-wind, and the polished surfaces produced by the ponderous flood are still so perfectly preserved that in many places you will find them about as trying to the eyes as sheets of snow. But even on the barest of these ice pavements, in sheltered hollows countersunk beneath the general surface into which a few rods of

MINARETS FROM THE WEST.

well-ground moraine chips have been dumped, there are groves of spruce and pine thirty to forty feet high, trimmed around the edges with willow and huckleberry bushes; and sometimes still further with an outer ring of grasses bright with lupines, larkspurs, and showy columbines. All the streams, too, and the pools at this elevation, are furnished with little gardens, which, though making scarce any show at a distance, constitute charming surprises to the appreciative mountaineer in their midst. In these bits of leafiness a few birds find grateful homes, and having no acquaintance with man they fear no ill and flock curiously around the stranger, almost allowing themselves to be taken in the hand. In so wild and so beautiful a region your first day will be spent, every sight and sound novel and inspiring, and leading you far from yourself. Wearied with enjoyment and the crossing of many cañons you will be glad to camp while yet far from Mt. Ritter. With the approach of evening long, blue, spiky-edged shadows creep out over the snowfields, while a rosy glow, at first scarce discernible, gradually deepens, suffusing every peak and flushing the glaciers and the harsh crags above them. This is the alpen-glow, the most impressive of all the terrestrial manifestations of God. At the touch

MT. LYELL GROUP FROM TUOLUMNE RIVER

of this divine light the mountains seem to kindle to a rapt religious consciousness, and stand hushed like worshippers waiting to be blessed. Then suddenly comes darkness and the stars.

On my first visit to Ritter I found a good camp ground on the rim of a glacier basin about 11,000 feet above the sea. A small lake nestles in the bottom of it, from which I got water for my tea, and a storm-beaten thicket near by furnished abundance of firewood. Sombre peaks, hacked and shattered, circle half way round the horizon, wearing a most solemn aspect in the gloaming, and a waterfall chanted in deep base tones across the lake on its way down from the foot of a glacier. The fall and the lake and the glacier are almost equally bare, while the pines anchored in the fissures of the rocks are so dwarfed and shorn by storm-winds you may walk over the tops of them as if on a shaggy rug. The scene was one of the most desolate in tone I ever beheld. But the darkest scriptures of the mountains are illumined with bright passages of Nature's eternal love, and they never fail to manifest themselves when one is alone. I made my bed in a nook of the pine thicket where the branches were pressed and crinkled overhead like a roof, and bent down on the sides. These are the best bed-chambers the Sierra affords, snug as squirrel-nests, well ventilated, full of spicy odors, and with plenty of wind-played needles to sing one asleep. I little expected company in such a place, but creeping in through a low opening I found five or six small birds nestling among the tassels. The night wind begins to blow soon after dark, at first only a gentle breathing, but increasing toward midnight to a gale in strength, that fell on my leafy roof in rugged surges like a cascade, while the waterfall sang in chorus, filling the old ice-fountain with its solemn roar, and seeming to increase in power as the night advanced—fit voice for such a landscape.

A REMINISCENCE OF EARLY DAYS.

How glorious a greeting the sun gives the mountains! To behold this alone is worth the pains of any excursion a thousand times over. The highest peaks burn like islands in a sea of liquid shade. Then the lower peaks and spires catch the glow, and long lances of light streaming through many a notch and pass, fall thick on the frosty meadows. The whole mountain world awakes. Frozen rills begin to flow. The marmots come out of their nests beneath the bowlders and climb sunny rocks to bask. The lakes seen from every ridge-top shimmer with white spangles like the glossy needles of the low tasseled pines. The rocks, too, seem responsive to the vital sun-heat, rock-crystals and snow-crystals throbbing alike. Thrilled and exhilarated one strides onward in the crisp bracing air as if nevermore to feel fatigue, limbs moving without effort, every sense unfolding and alert like the thawing flowers to take part in the new day harmony.

All along your course thus far, excepting while crossing the cañons, the landscapes are open and expansive. On your left the purple plains of Mono repose dreamy and warm. On your right and in front, the near Alps spring keenly into the thin sky with more and more impressive sublimity.

MULE DEER OF THE PASSES OF THE SIERRA. PAINTING BY W. M. CARY.

"Deer seldom cross over from one side of the range to the other. I have never seen the mule-deer of the Great Basin west of the summit, and rarely the black-tailed species on the eastern slopes, notwithstanding many of the latter ascend the range nearly to the head of the canyons among the peaks every summer to hide and feed in the wild gardens, and to bring forth their young."

DEER PASS INTO THE CAÑON OF THE MERCED, BELOW MOUNT LYELL. PAINTING BY JULIAN RIX.

"The more rugged and inaccessible the general character of the topography of any particular region, the more surely will the trails of white men, Indians, bears, deer, wild sheep, etc., converge into the best passes. Deer ascend the range nearly to the head of the cañons, among the peaks, every summer, to hide and feed in the wild gardens, and bring forth their young."

But these larger views are at length lost. Rugged spurs and moraines and huge projecting buttresses begin to shut you in, until arriving on the summit of the dividing ridge between the head waters of Rush Creek and the northmost tributaries of the San Joaquin, a picture of pure wildness is disclosed far surpassing every other you have yet seen.

There, immediately in front, looms the majestic mass of Mt. Ritter, with a glacier swooping down its face nearly to your feet, then curving westward and pouring its frozen flood into a blue-green lake whose shores are bound with precipices of crystalline snow, while a deep chasm drawn between the divide and the glacier separates the sublime picture from everything else. Only the one huge mountain in sight, the one glacier, and one lake; the whole veiled with one blue shadow—rock, ice, and water, without a single leaf. After gazing spell-bound you begin instinctively to scrutinize every notch and gorge and weathered buttress of the mountain with reference to making the ascent. The entire front above the glacier appears as one tremendous preci-pice, slightly receding at the top and bristling with comparatively short spires and pindacles set above one another in formidable array. Massive lichen-stained bat-tlements stand forward, here and there hacked at the top with angular notches and separated by frosty gullies and recesses that have been veiled in shadow ever since their creation, while to right and left, far as the eye can reach, are huge crumbling buttresses offering no invitation to the climber. The head of the glacier sends up a few finger-like branches through *couloirs*, but these are too steep and short to be available, and nu-merous narrow-throated gullies down which stones and snow are avalanched seem hopelessly steep, besides being interrupted by vertical cliffs past which no side way is visible. The whole is rendered still more terribly forbidding by the chill shadow, and the gloomy blackness of the rocks, and the dead silence relieved only by the murmur

MT. DANA GLACIER.

of small rills among the crevasses of the glacier, and ever and anon the rattling report of falling stones. Nevertheless the mountain may be climbed from this side, but only tried mountaineers should think of making the attempt.

Near the eastern extremity of the glacier you may discover the mouth of an avalanche gully, whose general course lies oblique to the plane of the front, and the metamorphic slates of which the mountain is built are cut by cleavage planes in such a way that they weather off in angular blocks, giving rise to irregular steps that greatly facilitate climbing on the steepest places. Thus you make your way into a wilderness of crumbling spires and battlements built together in bewil-dering combinations, and glazed in many places with a thin coating of ice, which must be removed from your steps; while so steep is the entire ascent one would inevitably fall to the glacier in case a single slip should be made.

Towards the summit the face of the mountain is still more savagely hacked and torn. It is a maze of yawning chasms and gullies, in the angles of which rise beetling crags and piles of detatched bowlders, made ready, apparently, to be launched below. The climbing is, however, less dangerous here, and after hours of strained, nerve-trying climbing, you at length stand on the topmost crag, out of the shadow in the blessed light. How truly glorious the landscape circled around this noble summit! Giant mountains, innumerable valleys, glaciers, and meadows, rivers and lakes, with the wide blue sky bent tenderly over them all.

Looking southward along the axis of the range, the eye is first caught by a row of exceedingly sharp and slender spires, which rise openly to a height of about a thousand feet from a series of short glaciers that lean back against their bases, their fantastic sculpture and the unrelieved sharpness with which they spring out of the ice

MT. DANA FROM THE WEST.

rendering them peculiarly wild and striking. These are "The Minarets." Beyond them you behold the highest mountains of the range, their snowy summits crowded together in lavish abundance, peak beyond peak, aspiring higher, and higher as they sweep on southward, until the culminating point is reached in Mount Whitney near the head of the Kern River, at an elevation of nearly 15,000 feet above the level of the sea.

Westward the general flank of the range is seen flowing grandly away in smooth undulations, a sea of gray granite waves, dotted with lakes and meadows, and fluted with stupendous cañons that grow steadily deeper as they recede in the distance.

Below this gray region lie the dark forests, broken here and there by upswelling ridges and domes; and yet beyond is a yellow, hazy belt marking the broad plain of the San Joaquin, bounded on its farther side by the blue mountains of the coast. Turning now to the northward, there in the immediate foreground is the Sierra Crown, with Cathedral Peak a few degrees to the left, the gray, massive form of Mammoth Mountain to the right, 13,000 feet high, and Mounts Ord, Gibbs, Dana, Conness, Tower Peak, Castle Peak, and Silver Mountain, stretching away in the distance, with a host of noble companions that are as yet nameless.

To the eastward the whole region seems a land of pure desolation covered with beautiful light. The hot volcanic basin of Mono, with its lake fourteen miles long, Owens Valley, and the wide table land at its head dotted with craters, and the Inyo Mountains; these are spread map-like beneath you, with many of the short ranges of the Great Basin passing and overlapping each other and fading on the glowing horizon.

At a distance of less than 3,000 feet below the summit you see the tributaries of the San Joaquin and Owens Rivers bursting forth from their sure fountains of ice, while a little to the north of here are found the highest affluents of the Tuolumne and Merced. Thus the fountain heads of four of the principal rivers of California are seen to lie within a radius of four or five miles.

WILD SHEEP IN THE PASSES OF THE SIERRAS.

Lakes, the eyes of the wilderness, are seen gleaming in every direction—round, or square, or oval like very mirrors; others narrow and sinuous, drawn close about the peaks like silver girdles; the highest reflecting only rock and snow and sky. But neither these nor the glaciers, nor yet the brown bits of meadow and moorland that occur here and there, are large enough to make any marked impression upon the mighty host of peaks. The eye roves around the vast expanse rejoicing in so grand a freedom, yet returns again and again to the fountain mountains. Perhaps some one of the multitude excites special attention, some gigantic castle with turret and battlement, or gothic cathedral more lavishly spired than any ever chiseled by art. But generally, when looking for the first time from an all-embracing stand-point like this, the inexperienced observer is oppressed by the incomprehensible grandeur of the peaks crowded about him, and it is only after they have been studied long and lovingly that their far-reaching harmonies begin to appear. Then penetrate the wilderness where you may, the main telling features to which all the topography is subordinate are quickly perceived, and the most chaotic alp-clusters stand revealed and regularly fashioned and grouped in accordance with law, eloquent monuments of the ancient glaciers that brought them into relief. The grand cañons

MOUNT RITTER. PAINTING BY W. KEITH.

"There, immediately in front, looms the majestic mass of Mount Ritter, with a glacier swooping down its face nearly to your feet, while a deep chasm drawn between the divide and the glacier separates the sublime picture from everything else. Only the one huge mountain in sight, one glacier, and one lake; the whole veiled with one blue shadow,—rock, ice and water, without a single leaf. The entire front above the glacier appears as one tremendous precipice, slightly receding at the top and bristling with comparatively short spires and pinnacles set above one another in formidable array."

likewise are recognized as the necessary results of causes following one another in melodious sequence—Nature's poems carved on tables of stone, the simplest and most emphatic of her glacial compositions.

Had we been here to look during the glacial period we would have found a wrinkled ocean of ice continuous as that now covering North Greenland and the lands about the South Pole, filling every valley and cañon, flowing deep above every ridge, leaving only the tops of the peaks rising darkly above the rock-encumbered waves, like foam-streaked islets in the midst of a stormy sea—these islets the only hints of the glorious landscapes now lying warm and fruitful beneath the sun. Now all the work of creation seems done. In the deep, brooding silence all appears motionless. But in the midst of this outer steadfastness we know there is incessant motion. Ever and anon avalanches are falling from yonder peaks. These cliff-bound glaciers seemingly wedged fast and immovable, are flowing like water and grinding the rocks beneath them. The lakes are lapping their granite shores, and wearing them away, and every one of these young rivers is fretting the air into music, and carrying the mountains to the plains. Here are the roots of the life of the lowlands with all their wealth of vineyard and grove, and here more simply than elsewhere is the eternal flux of nature manifested.

But in the thick of these fine lessons you must remember that the sun is wheeling far to the west, and you have many a weary and nerve-trying step to make ere you can reach the timber-line where you may lie warm through the night. But with keen caution and instinct and the guidance of your guardian angel you may pass every danger in safety, and in another delightful day win your way back again to your camp to rest on the beautiful Tuolumne River.

JOHN MUIR.

GLACIER ROCK, TUOLUMNE MEADOWS.   CATHEDRAL NEEDLES, SIERRAS, CAL.

THE PASSES OF THE HIGH SIERRA.

THE roads that Nature has opened through the heart of the High Sierra are hard to travel. So the sedate plodder of the lowlands would say, whether accustomed to trace the level furrows of fields, or the paved streets of cities. But as people oftentimes build better than they know, so also do they walk, and climb, and wander better than they know, and

so it comes, that urged onward by a mysterious love of wild beauty and adventure, we find ourselves far from the beaten ways of life, toiling through these rugged mountain passes without thinking of a reason for embracing with such ungovernable enthusiasm so much stern privation and hardship.

"Try not the pass" may sound in our ears, but despite the solemn warning, come from whom it may, the passes will be tried until the end of time, in the face of every danger of rock, avalanche, and blinding storm. And whatever the immediate motive may be that starts us on our travels,—wild landscapes, or adventures, or mere love of gain, the passes themselves will in the end be found better than anything to which they directly lead; calling every faculty into vigorous action, rousing from soul-wasting apathy and ease, and opening windows into the best regions of both earth and heaven.

The glaciers were the pass-makers of the Sierra, and by them the ways of all mountaineers have been determined. A

PASS THROUGH THE MINARETS.

short geological time before the coming on of that winter of winters, called "The Glacial Period," a vast deluge of molten rocks poured from many a chasm and crater on the flanks and summit of the range, obliterating every distinction of peak and pass throughout its northern portions, filling the lake basins, flooding ridge and valley alike, and effacing nearly every feature of the pre-glacial landscapes.

Then, after these all-destroying fire-floods ceased to flow, but while the great volcanic cones built up along the axis of the range, still burned and smoked, the whole Sierra passed under the domain of ice and snow. Over the bald, featureless, fire-blackened mountains glaciers crawled, covering them all from summit to base with a mantle of ice; and thus with infinite deliberation the work was begun of sculpturing the range anew. Those mighty agents of erosion, halting never through un-numbered centuries, ground and crushed the flinty lavas and granites beneath their crystal folds. Particle by particle, chip by chip, block by block the work went on, wasting and building, until in the fullness of time the mountains were born again, the passes and the summits between them, ridges and cañons, and all the main features of the range coming to the light nearly as we behold them to-day.

Looking into the passes near the summits, they seem singularly gloomy and bare, like raw quarries of dead, unfertilized stone,—gashes in the cold rock-bones of the mountains above the region of life, empty as when they first emerged from beneath the folds of the ice-mantle. Faint indeed are the marks of any kind of life, and at first sight they may not be seen at all. Nevertheless birds sing and flowers bloom in the highest of them all, and in no part of the range, north or south, is there any break in the chain of life, however much it may be wasted and turned aside by snow, and ice, and flawless granite.

Compared with the well-known passes of Switzerland, those of the south half of the Sierra are somewhat higher, but they contain less ice and snow, and enjoy a better summer climate, making them, upon the whole, more open and approachable. A carriage-road has been constructed through the Sonora Pass, the summit of which is 10,150 feet above the level of the sea—878 feet higher than the highest carriage-pass in Switzerland—the Stilvio Pass.

In a distance of 140 miles between lat. 36° 20′ and 38° the lowest pass I have yet discovered exceeds 9,000 feet, and the average height of all above sea-level is perhaps not far from 11,000 feet.

Substantial carriage-roads lead through the Carson and Johnson Passes near the head of Lake Tahoe, over which immense quantities of freight were hauled from California to the mining regions of Nevada prior to the construction of the Central Pacific Railroad through the Donner Pass. Miles of mules and ponderous wagons might then be seen slowly crawling beneath a cloud of dust through the majestic forest aisles, the drivers shouting in every language, and making a din and disorder strangely out of keeping with the solemn grandeur of the mountains about them.

To the northward of the memorable Donner Pass, 7,056 feet in height, a number of compara-tively low passes occur, through whose rugged defiles long emigrant trains, with foot-sore cattle and sun-cracked wagons a hundred times mended, wearily toiled during the early years of the Gold Period. Coming from far, through a thousand dangers, making a way over trackless wastes, the snowy Sierra at length loomed in sight, to them the eastern wall of the Land of Gold. And, as they gazed through the tremulous haze of the desert, with what joy must they have descried the mountain gateway through which they were so soon to pass to the better land of all their golden hopes and dreams!

Between the Sonora Pass and the southern extremity of the High Sierra, a distance of a hundred and sixty miles, there is not a single carriage-road conducting from one side of the range to the other, and only five passes with trails of the roughest description. These are barely prac-ticable for animals; a pass in this region meaning simply any notch with its connecting cañon and ridges through which one may, by the exercise of unlimited patience, make out to lead a sure-footed mule or mustang, one that can not only step well among loose stones, but also jump well down rugged stair-ways, and slide with limbs firmly braced down smooth inclines of rock and snow.

Only three of the five may be said to be in use—the Kearsarge, Mono, and Virginia Creek passes; the tracks leading through the others being only obscure Indian trails not graded in the least, and scarce at all traceable by white men. Much of the way lies over solid pavements where the

INDIAN CAÑON IN NORTH WALL OF YOSEMITE. PAINTING BY THOMAS HILL.

"Riding up the valley through stately groves, and round the margin of emerald meadows, the lofty walls
on either hand looming into the sky with their marvelous wealth of architectural forms, bathed in the purple
light of evening, and beating time to the tones of the falls, the whole seems a work of enchantment."

unshod ponies of the Indians leave no appreciable sign, and across loose taluses where only a slight displacement is visible here and there, and through thickets of weeds and bushes, leaving marks that only skilled mountaineers can follow, while a general knowledge of the topography must be looked to as the main guide.

One of these Indian trails leads through a nameless pass between the head waters of the south and middle forks of the San Joaquin, another between the north and middle forks of the same river, to the south of the Minarets; this last being about 9,000 feet high, and the lowest of the five.

The Kearsarge is the highest. It crosses the summit of the range near the head of the South Fork of Kings River, about eight miles to the north of Mt. Tyndall, through the midst of the grandest scenery. The highest point on the trail is upward of 12,000 feet above the sea.

GRANITE MOUNTAIN AND
SOUTH WALL OF KING'S RIVER CAÑON.

Nevertheless it is one of the safest of the five, and is traveled every summer from July to October or November by hunters, prospectors, and stock-owners, and also to some extent by enterprising pleasure-seekers. For besides the surpassing grandeur of the scenery about the summit, the trail in ascending the western flank of the range leads through a forest of the giant Sequoias, and through the magnificent Kings River Valley, that rivals Yosemite in the varied beauty and grandeur of its granite masonry and falling waters. This, as far as I know, is probably the highest traveled pass on the American Continent.

The Mono Pass lies to the east of Yosemite Valley, at the head of one of the tributaries of the South Fork of the Tuolumne, and is the best known of all the High Sierra passes. A rough trail, invisible mostly, was made through it about the time of the Mono and Aurora gold excitements, in the year 1858, and it has been in use ever since by mountaineers of every description. Though more than a thousand feet lower than the Kearsarge it is scarcely inferior in sublimity of rock-scenery, while in snowy, loud-sounding water it far surpasses the Kearsarge.

The Virginia Creek Pass, situated a few miles to the northward, at the head of the southmost tributary of Walker River, is somewhat lower, but less traveled than the Mono. It is used chiefly by

LAKE TAHOE AND MOUNT TALLAC. PAINTING BY JULIAN RIX.

"Drifted by the slightly moving air, we seemed suspended at a dizzy height, so clearly could we see the gamy fishes glide in and out of view at great depths below, casting shadows on the shining sandy bottom. Pine forests shelter the shy wild animals that frequent the lake borders, and the granite battlements of Mount Tallac stand guard over all."

"Sheep-men" who drive their flocks through it on the way to Nevada, and roaming bands of Pah Ute Indians, who may be seen occasionally in long straggling files, strangely attired, making their way to the hunting grounds of the western slope, or returning laden with game of startling variety.

These are all the traveled passes of the high portion of the range of which I have any knowledge. But leaving wheels and pack-animals out of the question, the free mountaineer, carrying only a little light dry food strapped firmly on his shoulders, and an axe for ice-work, can make his way across the Sierra almost everywhere, and at any time of year when the weather is calm. To him nearly every notch between the peaks is a pass, though much patient step-cutting is in some cases required up and down steeply inclined glaciers and ice-walls, and cautious scrambling over precipices that at first sight appear hopelessly inaccessible to the inexperienced lowlander. All the passes make their steepest ascents on the east flank of the range, where the average rise is nearly a thousand feet to the mile, while on the west it is about two hundred feet.

INDIAN PASS.

Another marked difference between the east and west portions of the passes is that the former begin between high moraine embankments at the very foot of the range, and follow the cañons; while the latter can hardly be said to begin until an elevation of from seven to ten thousand feet or more is reached by following the ridges, the cañons on the west slope being accessible only to the birds and the roaring falling rivers.

EMIGRANTS APPROACHING THE SIERRAS.

Approaching the range from the gray levels of Mono and Owens Valley the steep short passes are in full view between the peaks, their feet in hot sand, their heads in snow; the courses of the more direct being disclosed nearly all the way from top to bottom. But from the west side one sees nothing of the pass sought for until nearing the summit, after spending days in threading the forests on the main dividing ridges between the cañons of the rivers, most of the way even the highest peaks being hidden.

The more rugged and inaccessible the general character of the topography of any particular region, the more surely will the trails of white men, Indians, bears, deer, wild sheep, etc., converge into the best passes. The Indians of the west slope venture cautiously across the range in settled weather to attend dances and obtain loads of pine-nuts and the larvæ of a small fly that breeds in Mono and Owens lakes; while the desert Indians cross to the west for acorns and to hunt, fight, etc. The women carry the heavy burdens with marvelous endurance over the sharpest stones barefooted, while the men stride on erect a little in advance, stooping occasionally to pile up stepping-stones for them against steep rock-fronts, just as they would prepare the way in difficult places for their ponies. Sometimes, delaying their journeys until too late in the season, they are overtaken by heavy snow-storms and perish miserably, not all their skill in mountain-craft being sufficient to save them under

MULE TRAIN CROSSING THE SIERRA BY MONO PASS. PAINTING BY FREDERICK REMINGTON.

"The first white men that forced a way through its somber depths with pack animals were companies of eager, adventurous miners,—men who would build a trail down the throat of the darkest inferno on their way to gold. During the exciting times that followed the discovery of gold near Mono Lake, it frequently became a matter of considerable pecuniary importance to force a way through the cañon with pack trains early in the spring, while it was yet heavily choked with winter snow."

the fierce onsets of the most violent of autumn storms when caught unprepared. Bears evince great sagacity as mountaineers, but they seldom cross the range. I have several times tracked them through the Mono Pass, but only in late years, after cattle and sheep had passed that way, when they doubtless were following to feed on the stragglers and those that had fallen over the precipices. Even the wild

INDIANS PACKING ACORNS OVER THE MOUNTAINS.

sheep, the best mountaineers of all, choose regular passes in crossing the summits on their way to their summer or winter pastures. Deer seldom cross over from one side of the range to the other. I have never seen the Mule-deer of the Great Basin west of the summit, and rarely the Black-tailed species on the eastern slopes, notwithstanding many of the latter ascend the range nearly to the head of the cañons among the peaks every summer to hide and feed in the wild gardens, and bring forth their young.

Having thus indicated in a general way the height, geographical position, and leading features of the main passes, we will now endeavor to see the Mono Pass more in detail, since it may, I think, be regarded as a good example of the higher passes accessible to the ordinary traveler in search of

MONO PASS. — RED LAKE.

exhilarating scenery and adventure. The greater portion of it is formed by Bloody Cañon, which heads on the summit of the range, and extends in a general east-northeasterly direction to the edge of the Mono Plain. Long before its discovery by the whites, this wonderful cañon was known as a pass by the Indians of the neighborhood, as is shown by their many old trails leading into it from every direction. But little have they marked the grand cañon itself, hardly more than the birds have in flying through its shadows. No stone tells a word of wild foray or raid. Storm-winds and avalanches keep it swept fresh and clean.

THE HIGH SIERRA BETWEEN MOUNTS RITTER AND LYELL. PAINTING BY W. KEITH.

"Looking southward along the axis of the range, the eye is first caught by a row of exceedingly sharp and slender spires. These are 'The Minarets.' Beyond them you behold the highest mountains of the range, their snowy summits crowded together in lavish abundance, peak beyond peak, aspiring higher and higher as they sweep on southward, until the culminating point is reached in Mount Whitney, near the head of the Kern River, at an elevation of nearly 15,000 feet above the level of the sea."

The first white men that forced a way through its sombre depths with pack-animals were companies of eager adventurous miners; men who would build a trail down the throat of the darkest inferno on their way to gold. The name Bloody Cañon may have been derived from the red color of the metamorphic slates in which it is in great part eroded; or more probably from the blood stains made by the unfortunate animals that were compelled to slide and shuffle awkwardly over the rough cutting edges of the rocks, in which case it is too well named, for I have never known mules or horses, however sure-footed, to make their way either up or down the cañon, without leaving a trail more or less marked with blood. Occasionally one is killed outright by falling over some precipice like a bowlder. But such instances are less common than the appearance of the place would lead one to expect, the more experienced when driven loose picking their way with wonderful sagacity.

During the exciting times that followed the discovery of gold near Mono Lake it frequently

INDIAN SQUAWS GATHERING ROOTS AND BERRIES.

became a matter of considerable pecuniary importance to force a way through the cañon with pack-trains early in the spring, while it was yet heavily choked with winter snow. Then, though the way was smooth, it was steep and slippery, and the footing of the animals giving way, they sometimes rolled over sidewise with their loads, or end over end, compelling the use of ropes in sliding them down the steepest slopes where it was impossible to walk.

A good bridle-path leads from Yosemite through the Big Tuolumne Meadows to the head of the cañon. Here the scenery shows a sudden and startling condensation. Mountains red, black, and gray rise close at hand on the right, white in the shadows with banks of enduring snow. On the left swells the huge red mass of Mt. Gibbs, while in front the eye wanders down the tremendous gorge, and out on the warm plain of Mono, where the lake is seen in its setting of gray reflecting the light like a burnished disc of metal, volcanic cones to the south of it, and the smooth mountain ranges of Nevada beyond fading in the purple distance.

Entering the mountain gate-way the sombre rocks seem to come close about us, as if conscious of our presence. Happily the ouzel and old familiar robin are here to sing us welcome, and azure

FALL IN NORTH WALL OF BLOODY CAÑON. FROM DRAWING BY GEORGE SPIEL.

On the north wall of the cañon there is a long, narrow fall about two thousand feet in height that makes a fine, telling show of itself in contrast with the dull, red rocks over which it hangs. A ragged talus curves up against the cliff in front of it, overgrown with a tangle of snow-pressed willows, in which it disappears with many a surge and swirl and splashing leap, and finally wins its way, still gray with foam, to a confluence with the main cañon stream."

daisies beaming with sympathy, enabling us to feel something of Nature's love even here, beneath the gaze of her coldest rocks.   The peculiar impressiveness of the huge rocks is enhanced by the quiet aspect of the wide Alpine meadows through which the trail meanders just before entering the narrow pass.   The forests in which they lie, and the mountain-tops rising beyond them, seem hushed and tranquil.   Yielding to their soothing influences, we saunter on among flowers and bees scarce conscious of any definite thought; then suddenly we find ourselves in the huge, dark jaws of the cañon, closeted with Nature in one of her wildest strongholds.

After the first bewildering impression begins to wear off, and we become reassured by the glad birds and flowers, a chain of small lakes is seen, extending from the very summit of the pass, linked together by a silvery stream, that seems to lead the way and invite us on.   Those near the summit are set in bleak rough rock-bowls, scantily fringed with sedges. Winter storms drive snow through the cañon in blinding drifts, and avalanches shoot from the heights rushing and

HEAD OF SOUTH FORK, KING'S RIVER.

BLOODY CAÑON.—MONO TRAIL.

leaving no sign of their booming like water-falls. July they begin to blink Then are these sparkling eyes; sedges thrust up their short brown spikes existence.   In June and daisies bloom in turn, and the most profoundly and thaw out like sleepy about their shores, the snow-buried of them all is at length warmed and dressed as if winter were only the dream of a night.

Red Lake is the lowest of the chain and also the largest.   It seems rather dull and forbidding, at first sight, lying motionless in its deep, dark bed, seldom stirred during the day by any wind strong enough to make a wave.   The cañon wall rises sheer from the water's edge on the south, but on the opposite side there is sufficient space and sunshine for a fine garden.   Daisies star the sod about the margin of it, and the centre is lighted with tall lilies, castilleias, larkspurs and columbines, while leafy willows make a fine protecting hedge; the whole forming a joyful outburst of warm, rosy plant-life, keenly emphasized by the raw, flinty baldness of the onlooking cliffs.

After resting in the lake the happy stream sets forth again on its travels warbling and trilling like an ouzel, ever delightfully confiding, no matter how rough the way; leaping, gliding, hither, thither, foaming or clear, and displaying the beauty of its virgin wildness at every bound.

One of its most beautiful developments is the Diamond Cascade, situated a short distance below Red Lake.   The crisp water is first dashed into course granular spray that sheds off the light in

TOURISTS AMONG THE PASSES—MOUNT LYELL GLACIER IN THE DISTANCE. DRAWING BY A. J. KELLER.

"The roads that Nature has opened through the heart of the High Sierra are hard to travel. . . . Whatever the immediate motive may be that starts us on our travels,—wild landscapes, or adventures, or mere love of gain, the passes themselves will in the end be found better than anything to which they directly lead; calling every faculty into vigorous action, rousing from soul-wasting apathy and ease, and opening windows into the best regions of both earth and heaven."

quick flashing lances, mixed farther down with loose dusty foam; then it is divided into a diamond pattern by tracing the diagonal cleavage joints that intersect the face of the precipice over which it pours. Viewed in front, it resembles a wide sheet of embroidery of definite pattern, with an outer covering of fine mist, the whole varying with the temperature and the volume of water. Scarce a flower may be seen along its snowy border. A few bent pines look on from a distance, and small fringes of cassiope and rock-ferns grow in fissures near the head, but these are so lowly and undemonstrative only the attentive observer will be likely to notice them.

A little below the Diamond Cascade, on the north wall of the cañon, there is a long, narrow fall about two thousand feet in height that makes a fine, telling show of itself in contrast with the dull, red rocks over which it hangs. A ragged talus curves up against the cliff in front of it, overgrown with a tangle of snow-pressed willows, in which it disappears with many a surge, and swirl, and plashing leap, and finally wins its way,

still gray with foam, to a confluence with the main cañon stream.

Below this point the climate is no longer arctic. Butterflies become more abundant, grasses with showy purple panicles wave above your shoulders, and the deep summery drone of the bumble-bee thickens the air. *Pinus Albicaulis*, the tree mountaineer that climbs highest and blasts, is found in dwarfed,

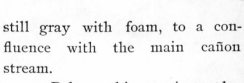

CATHEDRAL ROCKS.

braves the coldest wind-bent clumps

throughout the upper half of the cañon, gradually becoming more erect, until it is joined by the two-leafed pine, which again is succeeded by the taller yellow and mountain pines. These, with the burly juniper and trembling aspen, rapidly grow larger as they descend into the richer sunshine, forming groves that block the view; or they stand more apart in picturesque groups here and there, making beautiful and obvious harmony with each other, and with the rocks. Blooming underbrush also becomes abundant,—azalea, spiræa, and dogwood weaving rich fringes for the stream, and shaggy rugs for the stern unflinching rock-bosses, adding beauty to their strength, and fragrance to the winds and the breath of the waterfalls. Through this blessed wilderness the cañon stream roams free, without any restraining channel, stirring the bushes like a rustling breeze, throbbing and wavering in wide swirls and zigzags, now in the sunshine, now in the shade; dancing, falling, flashing from side to side beneath the lofty walls in weariless exuberance of energy.

A glorious milky way of cascades is thus developed whose individual beauties might well call forth volumes of description. Bower Cascade is among the smallest, yet it is perhaps the most beautiful of them all. It is situated in the lower region of the pass where the sunshine begins to mellow between the cold and warm climates. Here the glad stream, grown strong with tribute gathered from many a snowy fountain, sings richer strains, and becomes more human and lovable at every step. Now you may see the rose and homely yarrow by its side, and bits of meadow with clover, and bees. At the head of a low-browed rock luxuriant cornel and willow bushes arch over from side to side, embowering the stream with their leafy branches; and waving plumes, kept in motion by the current, make a graceful fringe in front.

From so fine a bower as this, after all its dashing among bare rocks on the heights, the stream leaps out into the light in a fluted curve, thick-sown with sparkling crystals, and falls into a pool among brown bowlders, out of which it creeps gray with foam, and disappears beneath a roof

EMERALD BAY.—LAKE TAHOE.

of verdure like that from which it came. Hence to the foot of the cañon the metamorphic slates give place to granite, whose nobler sculpture calls forth corresponding expressions of beauty from the stream in passing over it—bright trills of rapids, booming notes of falls, and the solemn hushing tones of smooth gliding sheets, all chanting and blending in pure wild harmony. And when at length its impetuous alpine life is done, it slips through a meadow at the foot of the cañon, and rests in Moraine Lake. This lake, about a mile long, lying between massive moraines piled up centuries ago by the grand old cañon glacier, is the last of the beautiful beds of the stream. Tall silver firs wave soothingly about its shores, and the breath of flowers, borne by the winds from the mountains, drifts over it like incense. Henceforth the stream, now grown stately and tranquil, glides through meadows full of gentians, and groves of rustling aspen, to its confluence with Rush Creek, with which it flows across the desert and falls into the Dead Sea.

At Moraine Lake the cañon terminates, although apparently continued by two lateral moraines of imposing dimensions and regularity of structure. They extend out into the plain about five miles, with a height, toward their upper ends, of nearly three hundred feet. Their cool, shady sides are evenly forested with silver-firs, while the sides facing the sun are planted with showy flowers, a square rod containing five to six profusely flowered eriogonums of several species, about the same number of bahias and linosyris, and a few poppies, phloxes, gilias and grasses, each species planted trimly apart with bare soil between as if cultivated artificially.

My first visit to Bloody Cañon was made in the summer of 1869, under circumstances well calculated to heighten the impressions that are the peculiar offspring of mountains. I came from the blooming tangles of Florida, and waded out into the plant-gold of the great Central plain of California while its unrivalled flora was as yet untrodden. Never before had I beheld congregations of social flowers half so extensive, or half so glorious. Golden compositæ covered all the ground from the Coast Range to the Sierra like a stratum of denser sunshine, in which I reveled for weeks, then gave myself up to be borne forward on the crest of the summer plant-wave that sweeps an-

INDIAN SQUAW AND PAPOOSE.

nually up the Sierra flank, snowy summits. At the I remained more than a izing, and climbing among ere the fame of Bloody

The mountaineer one of those remarkable in California, the bold have been brought into effects of the gold-period, landscapes. But at this tivities had subsided, and caused him to become a literally to lie down with meadows he could find. Highland instincts, he concerning Bloody Cañon, it. "I have never seen I never was so unfortunate I have heard many a I warrant you will find it

Next day I made tied my note-book to my the bracing air, every with eager indefinite hope, welcome to all the wild-

and spends itself on its Big Tuolumne Meadows month, sketching, botan- the surrounding mountains Cañon had reached me. with whom I camped was men so frequently found angles of whose character relief by the grinding like the features of glacier late day my friend's ac- his craving for rest had gentle shepherd, and a lamb, on the smoothest Recognizing my Scotch threw out some hints and advised me to explore it myself," he said, "for as to pass that way; but strange story about it, and wild enough." up a package of bread, belt, and strode away in nerve and muscle tingling and ready to give glad erness might offer. The

plushy lawns starred with blue gentians and daisies soothed my morning haste, and made me linger; they were all so fresh, so sweet, so peaceful.

Climbing higher, as the day passed away, I traced the paths of the ancient glaciers over many a shining pavement; and marked the lanes in the upper forests that told the power of the winter avalanches. Still higher, I noted the gradual dwarfing of the pines in compliance with climate, and on the summit discovered creeping mats of the arctic willow, low as the lowliest grasses; and patches of dwarf vaccinium, with its round pink bells sprinkled over the sod as if they had fallen from the sky like hail; while in every direction the landscape stretched sublimely away in fresh wildness, a manuscript written by the hand of Nature alone.

At length, entering the gate of the pass, the huge rocks began to close around me in all their mysterious impressiveness; and as I gazed awe-stricken down the shadowy gulf, a drove of gray, hairy creatures came suddenly into view, lumbering towards me with a kind of boneless, wallowing motion like bears. However, grim and startling as they appeared, they proved to be nothing more formidable than Mono Indians dressed in a loose, shapeless way in the skins of sage rabbits sewed together into square robes. Both the men and women begged persistently for whiskey and tobacco,

ILLILOUETTE BASIN ABOVE YOSEMITE.

"Leaving the Valley by the trail leading past the Vernal and Nevada Falls, you cross the lower end of Little Yosemite Valley, and climb the Starr King Ridge, from which you obtain a fine general view of the Illilouette Basin, with its grand array of peaks and domes and dark, spiry forests, all on a grand scale of magnitude, yet keenly fine in finish and beauty, forming one of the most interesting of the basins that lie round about Yosemite Valley, and pour their tribute of songful water into it, swelling the anthems ever sounding there."

and seemed so accustomed to denials, that it was impossible to convince them that I had none to give. Excepting the names of these two luxuries, they spoke no English, but I afterwards learned that they were on their way to Yosemite Valley to feast awhile on fish and flour, and procure a load of acorns to carry back through the pass to their huts on the shore of Mono Lake.

A good countenance may now and then be discovered among the Monos, but these, the first specimens I had seen, were mostly ugly, or altogether hideous. The dirt on their faces was fairly stratified in the hollows, and seemed so ancient and undisturbed as almost to possess a geological significance. The older faces were, moreover, strangely blurred and divided into sections by furrows that looked like some of the cleavage joints of rocks, suggesting exposure in a castaway condition for ages. They seemed to have no right place in the landscape, and I was glad to see them fading down the pass out of sight.

Then came evening, and the sombre cliffs were inspired with the ineffable beauty of the alpenglow. A solemn calm fell upon every feature of the scene. All the lower depths of the cañon were in gloaming shadow, and one by one the mighty rock-fronts forming the walls grew dim and

THE TWO LATERAL MORAINES OF THE BLOODY CAÑON GLACIER.—MORAINE LAKE IN THE FOREGROUND.

vanished in the thickening darkness. Soon the night-wind began to flow and pour in torrents among the jagged peaks, mingling its strange tones with those of the waterfalls sounding far below. And as I lay by my camp-fire in a little hollow near one of the upper lakes listening to the wild sounds, the great full moon looked down over the verge of the cañon wall, her face seemingly filled with intense concern, and apparently so near as to produce a startling effect, as if she had entered one's bed-room, forsaking all the world besides to concentrate her gaze on me alone.

The whole night was full of strange weird sounds, and I gladly welcomed the morning. Breakfast was soon done, and I set forth in the exhilarating freshness of the new day, rejoicing in the abundance of pure wildness so closely pressed about me. The stupendous rock-walls, like two separate mountain ranges, stood forward in the thin, bright light, hacked and scarred by centuries of storms, while down in the bottom of the cañon, grooved and polished bosses heaved and glistened like swelling sea-waves, telling a grand old story of the ancient glacier that once poured its crushing floods above them.

Here for the first time I met the Arctic daisies in all their perfection of pure spirituality,— gentle mountaineers, face to face with the frosty sky, kept safe and warm by a thousand miracles. I

The Lyell Glacier. From Painting by C. D. Robinson.

"From your camp on the bank of the river you bear off up the right wall of the cañon and on direct to the glacier, keeping toward the western margin. . . . The surface of the glacier is shattered with crevasses in some places; these, however, are easily avoided, but the sharp wave-like blades of granular snow covering a great part of the upper slopes during most of the season are exceedingly fatiguing, and are likely to stop any but the most determined climbers willing to stagger, stumble and wriggle onward against every difficulty."

leaped lightly from rock to rock, glorying in the eternal freshness and sufficiency of nature, and in the rugged tenderness with which she nurtures her mountain darlings in the very homes and fountains of storms.

Fresh beauty appeared at every step, delicate rock-ferns, and tufts of the fairest flowers. Now another lake came to view, now a waterfall. Never fell light in brighter spangles, never fell water in whiter foam. I seemed to float through the cañon enchanted, feeling nothing of its roughness, and was out in the glaring Mono levels ere I was aware.

Looking back from the shore of Moraine Lake, my morning ramble seemed all a dream. There curved Bloody Cañon, a mere glacier furrow two thousand and three thousand feet deep, with *moutonee* rocks advancing from the sides, and braided together in the middle like rounded, swelling muscles. Here the lilies were higher than my head, and the sunshine was warm enough for palms. Yet

the snow around the Arctic willows on the summit was plainly visible, only a few miles away, and between lay narrow specimen belts of all the principal climates of the Globe.

About five miles below the foot of Moraine Lake, where the lateral moraines terminate in the plain, there was a field of wild rye, growing in magnificent waving bunches six to eight feet high, and bearing heads from six to twelve inches long. Indian women were gathering the grain in baskets, bending down large handfuls of the ears, beating them with sticks, and fanning out the rye in the wind. They formed striking and picturesque groups as one caught glimpses of them here and there in winding lanes and openings with splendid tufts arching overhead, while their incessant chat and laughter proclaimed their careless joy.

I found the so-called Mono Desert, like the rye-field, in a high state of natural cultivation with the wild rose and the delicate pink-flowered abronia; and innumerable erigerons, gilias, phloxes, poppies and bush-compositæ, growing not only along stream-banks, but out in the hot sand and ashes in openings among the sage-brush, and even in the craters of the highest volcanoes, cheering the grey wilderness with their rosy bloom, and literally giving beauty for ashes.

CLIFFS OF CASTLE PEAK.

Donner Lake and vicinity of summit on Central Pacific Railroad.

Beyond the moraines the trail turns to the left toward Mono Lake, now in sight around the spurs of the mountains, and touches its western shore at a distance from the foot of the pass of about six miles. Skirting the lake, you make your way over low bluffs and moraine piles, and through many a tangle of snow-crinkled aspens and berry bushes, growing on the banks of fine, dashing streams that come from the snows of the summits.

Here are the favorite camping grounds of the Indians, littered with piles of pine-burrs from which the seeds have been beaten. Many of their fragile willow huts are broken and abandoned; others arch airily over family groups that are seen lying at ease, pictures of thoughtless contentment; their wild, animal eyes glowering at you as you pass, their black shocks of hair perchance bedecked with red castileias, and their bent, bulky stomachs filled with no white man knows what.

HEAD OF TUOLUMNE
CAÑON, NEAR CROSSING OF
VIRGINIA CREEK.

Some of these mountain streams pouring into the lake have deep and swift currents at the fording-places, and their channels are so roughly paved with bowlders that crossing them at the time of high water is rather dangerous.

That Mono Lake should have no outlet, while so many perennial streams flow into it, seems strange at first sight, before the immense waste by evaporation in so dry an atmosphere is recognized. Most of its shores being low, any considerable rise of its waters greatly enlarges its area, followed of course by a corresponding in-crease of evaporation, which tends towards constancy of level within comparatively narrow limits. Nevertheless, on the flanks of the mountains, drawn in well-marked lines, you may see several ancient beaches that mark the successive levels at which the lake stood toward the close of the glacial period, the highest more than six hundred feet above the present level. Then, under a climate as marked by coolness and excessive moisture as the present by devouring drouth, the dimensions of the lake must have been vastly greater. Indeed, a study of the whole plateau region, named by Fremont "the Great Basin," extending from the Sierra to the Wahsatch mountains, a distance of 400 miles, shows that it was covered by inland seas of fresh water that were only partially separated by the innumerable hills and mountain ranges of the region, which then existed as islands, forming an archi-pelago of unrivaled grandeur.

The lake water is as clear as the snow-streams that feed it, but intensely acrid and nauseating from the excessive quantities of salts accumulated by evaporation beneath a burning sun. Of course no fish can live in it, but large flocks of geese, ducks, and swans come from beyond the mountains at certain seasons, and gulls also in great numbers, to breed on a group of volcanic islands that rise near the centre of the lake, thus making the dead, bitter sea lively and cheerful while they stay. The eggs of the gulls used to be gathered for food by the Indians, who floated to the islands on rafts made of willows; but since the occurrence of a great storm on the lake a few years ago, that overtook them on their way back from the islands, they have not ventured from the shore. Their rafts were broken up and many were drowned. This disaster, which some still living have good cause to remember, together with certain superstitious fears concerning evil spirits supposed to dwell in the lake and rule its waves, make them content with the safer and far more important product of the shores, chief of which is the larvæ of a small fly that breeds in the slimy froth in the shallows. When the worms are ripe, and the waves have collected them and driven them up the beach in rich oily windrows, then old and young make haste to the curious harvest, and gather the living grain in baskets and buckets of every description. After being washed and dried in the sun it is stored for winter. Raw or cooked, it is regarded as a fine luxury, and delicious dressing for other kinds of food—acorn-mush, clover-salad, grass-seed-pudding, etc. So important is this small worm to the neighboring tribes, it forms a subject of dispute about as complicated and perennial as the Newfoundland cod. After waging worm-wars until everybody is weary and hungry, the belligerents mark off boundary lines, assigning stated sections of the shores to each tribe, where the harvest may be gathered in peace until fresh quarrels have time to grow. Tribes too feeble to establish rights must needs procure their worm supply from

PASS INTO THE TOULUMNE CAÑON FROM THE HEAD OF YOSEMITE CREEK BASIN.

their more fortunate neighbors, giving nuts, acorns or ponies in exchange.

This "diet of worms" is further enriched by a large, fat caterpillar, a

DOUBLE PEAK, TUOLUMNE CAÑON.— Elevation: 3,300 above the bottom of the Cañon.

species of silk-worm found on the yellow pines to the south of the lake; and as they also gather the seeds of this pine, they get a double crop from it,—meat and bread from the same tree.

Forbidding as this gray, ashy wilderness is to the dweller in green fields, to the red man it is a paradise full of all the good things of life. A Yosemite Indian with whom I was acquainted while living in the valley, went over the mountains to Mono every year on a pleasure trip, and when I asked what could induce him to go to so poor a country when, as a hotel servant, he enjoyed all the white man's good things in abundance, he replied, that Mono had better things to eat than anything to be found in the hotel—plenty deer, plenty wild sheep, plenty antelope, plenty worm, plenty berry, plenty sage-hen, plenty rabbit—drawing a picture of royal abundance that from his point of view surpassed everything else the world had to offer.

A sail on the lake develops many a fine picture;—the natives along the curving shores seen against so grand a mountain back-ground; water birds stirring the glassy surface into white dancing spangles; the islands, black, pink and gray, rising into a cloud of white wings of gulls; volcanoes dotting the hazy plain; and, grandest of all and overshadowing all, the mighty barrier wall of the Sierra, heaving into the sky from the water's edge, and stretching away to north and south with its marvelous wealth of peaks and crests and deep-cutting notches keenly defined, or fading away in the soft purple distance; cumulus clouds swelling over all in huge mountain bosses of pearl, building a mountain range of cloud upon a range of rock, the one as firmly sculptured, and as grand and showy and substantial as the other.

The magnificent cluster of volcanoes to the south of the lake may easily be visited from the foot of Bloody Cañon, the distance being only about six miles. The highest of the group rises about 2,700 feet above the lake. They are all post-glacial in age, having been erupted from what was once the bottom of the south end of the lake, through stratified glacial drift. During their numerous periods of activity they have scattered showers of ashes and cinders over all the adjacent plains and mountains within a radius of twenty and thirty miles.

Nowhere within the bounds of our wonder-filled land are the antagonistic forces of fire and ice brought more closely and contrastingly together. So striking are the volcanic phenomena, we seem to be among the very hearths and firesides of nature. Then turning to the mountains, while standing in drifting ashes, we behold huge moraines issuing from the cool jaws of the great cañons, marking the pathways of glaciers that crawled down the mountain sides laden with debris and pushed their frozen floods into the deep waters of the lake in thundering icebergs, as they are now descending into the inland waters of Alaska, not a single Arctic character being wanting, where now the traveler is blinded in a glare of tropical light.

Americans are little aware as yet of the grandeur of their own land, as is too often manifested by going on foreign excursions, while the wonders of our unrivaled plains and mountains are left unseen. We have Laplands and Labradors of our own, and streams from glacier-caves,—rivers of mercy sacred as the Himalaya-born Ganges. We have our Shasta Vesuvius also, and bay, with its Golden Gate, beautiful as the Bay of Naples. And here among our inland plains are African Saharas, dead seas, and deserts, dotted with oases, where congregate the travelers, coming in long caravans,—the trader with his goods and gold, and the Indian with his weapons—the Bedouin of the California desert.

JOHN MUIR.

GENERAL VIEW OF YOSEMITE OF SOUTH FORK, KING'S RIVER, LOOKING EASTWARD FROM TRAIL.

MOUNT HUMPHREY—VIEW FROM SOUTH FORK OF SAN JOAQUIN RIVER. PAINTING BY WM. KEITH.

"Notwithstanding the great height of the summits, and the ice and the snow and the cañons and sheer giddy precipices, no mountain chain on the globe is more kindly approachable."

CYPRESS GROVE. FROM AN EARLY SKETCH. BY JULIAN RIX.

"For about two miles it extends along the shore, then the Grove suddenly ends, and one may travel along the California coast to San Diego, and he will not find a score of indigenous cypress trees. . . . The imagination readily pictures strange forms in the twisted branches, which invariably leave the parent trunk at the sharpest of right angles. On bright sunny days its dense foliage casts a deep shadow, and its withered arms seem to reach out and point the ways to mysterious caverns or rocky cliffs, and high, rolling breakers."

EL CARMEL
ONE HUNDRED
YEARS AGO

A GLIMPSE OF MONTEREY.

By J. R. FITCH.

THROUGHOUT California the hand of improvement has swept away nearly all the peculiar adobe buildings that once made its towns as distinctively foreign as Guaymas or Mazatlan. One of the few places where may still be seen the low, small-windowed adobe houses, with their heavy tiled roofs and massive walls, is at the old town of Monterey, the original seat of government of the Spanish and Mexican territories, and the first capital of California under American rule.

Four generations have seen few changes in the Spanish quarter of the town; yet, in the last decade, Monterey has become one of the great popular resorts of the Pacific coast, and every year sees thousands of tourists enjoy its varied scenery and its equable climate. It is only one hundred and twenty miles from San Francisco, and is reached in three hours by a train that is the swiftest west of Chicago. It boasts of one of the finest hotels in the country; it prides itself on the magnificent seventeen-mile drive which has been laid out through the dark pine woods and along the shore of the Pacific. But these things touch not the old Spanish-Californian town, which is as far apart from all this modern life of pleasure as though it were planted in the heart of Andalusia. This trait has a piquancy to one's enjoyment of this bit of old world conservatism, set in the midst of the intensely modern life of California of to-day.   After the scenery—which seems to possess a perennial charm, giving the visitor fresh surprises every morning—there is nothing more attractive about Monterey than this dreamy Spanish life that takes no count of time or progress, the changes of governments or the new discoveries of science.   Sufficient unto the dwellers by this western sea, who have the old world sluggishness still unroused in their veins, are the few household wants, with music and the dance and the other simple pleasures of a life unvexed by care or greed. To get a taste of this life—so alien to everything American—is somewhat akin to the pleasure of sojourning in the remote villages of Canada.   It is equivalent to going abroad without crossing the ocean.

Sleepy as the old town looks in its mid-day siesta, it has had a stirring history.   It was founded by Junipero Serra, the leader of the Franciscan monks, who established a chain of missions along the Californian coast, and for fifty years created there the idyllic pastoral life, now seen only in the poet's dream of Arcadia.   The Bay of Monterey witnessed the arrival of stout Spanish troopers from Mexico, the building of a rude fort on the hill that overlooks the town, and the establishment of the seat of government of Alta California.

INTERIOR OF THE OLD EL CARMEL MISSION.

"CASSIANO."—THE MISSION INDIAN, SUPPOSED TO BE
136 YEARS OLD.

Then came the American adventurers under Fremont, the turmoil that preceded the Mexican war, the seizure of Monterey by the American troops and marines, and the conversion of the place into the capital of the new American territory. This was the heyday of Monterey's prosperity.   General Fremont made his headquarters in the low-browed log house on the hill, now so quaint in its ruin, and cannon bristled from the old fort— in these days given over to a sheep-fold.   Near at hand, on the very brow of the hill, is the ruined adobe fort, from which the Mexicans hoped to sweep away the hated intruder, but the guns that were to perform this gallant service never arrived, and the fort fell into decay.   Down in the town, one of the most curious objects is the old barracks, used at the time of the conquest for the soldiers of Stephenson's regiment.   It is one of the best specimens of Spanish-American architecture, and is graceful even in its ruins.   But prosperity soon deserted Monterey, for with the first news of the discovery of gold at Sutter's Mill the town was depopulated.   From that blow it has never recovered, and the finishing stroke was given by the removal of the county seat to a neighboring town. Within a few years, however, there has been a revival of prosperity, which has placed Monterey in the van of seaside resorts.

The town of Monterey lies on a gentle slope facing the beautiful bay, that sweeps in a perfect curve towards the north-west.   At the back it is protected from the harsh ocean winds by pine-crowned hills.   The streets straggle up the hill in picturesque confusion; the low, rambling Spanish houses are scattered about under live oaks and pines, while even decay and ruin are ren-

EL CARMEL MISSION.

"Built of a chalk stone, which took on with age the rich color of old parchment, the Mission was very impressive even in its ruin. I remember the impression it made upon me ten years ago, when the roof was gone and one of the side walls was crumbling into decay. Enough remained to show the architectural skill of the designer, and the loving care with which he had wrought the pillars of the door, the stairways and the great front window."

dered attractive by the roses, hollyhocks, and fuchsias, that clamber over the walls and run riot on the abandoned hearth-stones. Many small American cottages have been built of late years, but the prevailing style of architecture is Spanish, and the buildings erected by the early founders of the place still remain in fairly good preservation. These Spanish houses are of adobe,—sun-baked bricks of clay, mixed with dry grass. One can readily understand when he sees them the heavy task laid upon the Children of Israel—that of making bricks without straw. These Spanish houses have heavy walls, never less than two feet in thickness, with low ceilings, small windows and doors, a long, low roof, with eaves like those of the Swiss *chalet*, and an upper verandah, which generally runs around two or three sides of the house. The access to the verandah is by outside stairs, and both windows and doors in the second story opening on it give to the house an oriental appearance. With the

OLD CUSTOM HOUSE.—BUILT BY SPAIN, MEXICO AND THE UNITED STATES.
ADOBE BUILDINGS.—OCCUPIED BY GENERAL FREMONT DURING THE MEXICAN WAR.

whitewashed walls, green verandah and blinds, and red-tiled roof, these houses look like a bit out of Madrazo's pictures.

The illusion is made all the stronger by the brilliant color of the climbing roses and holly-hocks, and by the swarthy faces of the women and children that peep shyly from window or door-way at the stranger. Perhaps the features in the town that add most to its picturesqueness and give it a pronounced foreign flavor, are the tiling of the roofs and the high adobe walls that sur-round the few remaining gardens that are preserved in their original style. The tiles are earthen, each a semi-cylinder, and of great weight. When placed one within the other, they form a perfect protection against heavy rain, and no wind less than a Dakota cyclone could have power to lift them from their places. They give an appearance of great solidity to the houses, and the few remaining walls that show a coping of these tiles, present subjects which no artist could resist the temptation of transferring to his sketch book. These time-worn garden walls give the stranger the best idea of the construction of the adobe, as the bits of stubble show through the dark surface.

Another element of quaintness is furnished by the abundant traces of the whaling industry. The ribs of the sea leviathan form the gate-posts of many of the old residences, while the vertebræ have been used to pave the garden walks. These remains of a by-gone industry are bleached to the glittering whiteness of ivory, and stand out in strong relief against the deep green background of rose trees and cedar hedges.

Life goes on here in the open air. The residence streets are given over to the children and the domestic animals. Dirt and perfect health go hand in hand with these children of nature. They never wash, and yet they never need the services of a doctor. Even the American who settles in Monterey soon becomes Mexicanized. It takes strong moral force to resist the influence of this climate, so seductive in persuading one to put off to the morrow what ought to be done to-day. The old residents sleep and dream of the great future which is one day to come to their well beloved town, but they do nothing to hasten the day of prosperity, and their peculiar aversion to selling a foot of the land inherited from their fathers, checks all growth

POINT PINOS LIGHT HOUSE.

OLD CROSS.—SHOWING WHERE JUNIPERO SERRA LANDED IN 1770.
THE LAST GUN OF THE OLD FORT.

as effectually as Irish landlordism.

Turning one's back on the town, and looking out over the bay, what wonder is it that the dweller in Monterey is content with life. Italy has nothing fairer than this bay, with its perfectly rounded shore, its gleaming sand and its waters, blue and lustrous as those of the Ægean, sung by Homer. The shallow water near the shore is mottled with bits of lovely blue, but the breaker that rolls up on the snow-white beach is a brilliant green that is suddenly transformed into a long line of foam, which can scarcely be distinguished in color from the sandy stretch with which it plays hide and seek. Two old wharves break the placid surface of the bay, but they are seldom vexed with other business than that of the fishermen who return every morning with their catch. Further along is the wharf and the new bathing establishment of the Hotel del Monte—as modern and incongruous in this Sleepy Hollow of the West as is the neighboring railway depot and the impatient engine.

But Monterey has great attractions for the lover of the picturesque, aside from its marvelous bay and its many remains of quaint, eighteenth century Spanish life. It is built on the sheltered side of a neck of land that projects into the ocean. The shore line of this peninsula has been fashioned by the hand of old ocean into a succession of jutting headlands and secluded coves that make a panorama of marine views, each with some element of novelty to charm the eye and linger in the memory. The Pacific Improvement Company—a branch of the great Southern Pacific Company—saw the possibilities of this tour of the beach, and laid out a fine drive, now through the pine woods and now along the ocean shore. It extends for seventeen miles, and is declared by all tourists to be unexcelled, even on the Riviera. Starting out from Monterey on this road, one passes at the outskirts of the town the old red house which it is claimed was the first brick building erected on this coast, the material being brought from Philadelphia by way of Cape Horn. Near at hand is the headquarters of the Monterey Whaling Company, once the seat of a flourishing trade, now given over to complete desolation. The oak door, with its heavy panels and its old brass knocker, is a bit of antique elegance that

of whitewashed adobe wall. By the bridge, which Padre Junipero Serra erected and just above it, on the hill that com- cannon that frowned on intruders in held possession of the town. Round- eye is delighted with a series by bits of foam, while far dim horizon, is the blue suspicion of a breeze. road winds about the path, and if the his vehicle and and a half beach he paid by

looks sadly out of place in the present expanse which spans a little gulch, is the cross blessed here on a June day in 1770, while mands town and bay, is one of the the days when Fremont and Sloat ing the curve just beyond, the of little headlands, each marked away, stretching out to the Pacific, unruffled by the To the right as the shore, runs a foot- tourist here deserts walks for a mile around the will be re- some

novel The first remains whaling furnaces and some of the an- whose ribs alone re- gallant work they have Some of the kettles are bits of blubber, as recently that haunt this bay was tried carcass. All about the place lin- ground is saturated with the oil of foot like an asphaltum pavement on a the good fortune to see the royal sport of small boat venturing out near to the point is spouting; the quick pull near to the spot;

sights. is the of the old works—the kettles used, and cient whale-boats, main to tell of the done in years gone by. half full of grease and one of the basking sharks out for the oil in his huge gers the vilest of odors, and the many whales, and gives under one's hot day. Occasionally one may have whale hunting as it is practiced here: the where a thin column of mist shows the whale

marine monster rises to take breath, and then the wild dash of the maddened whale across the bay out toward the ocean, with the boat cleaving the water like an arrow shot from a bow; the firing of the bomb lance into the hunted animal every time he comes to the surface, and, finally, the return of the victors, towing the monarch of the deep to the place where his vast carcass is to be cut into pieces and rendered into oil. The latter work is now done on the shore of Carmel Bay, about six miles from Monterey, but the industry languishes, and whales may be seen on almost any clear day spouting undisturbed in the bay.

    A short walk from the whaling station brings one to the Chinese fishing village, which is

Lone Cypress—Midway Point, Monterey. Painting by Julian Rix.

"Down almost to the water grows the cypress, and on the extreme point a solitary tree has sunk its roots in the crevices of the wave-washed rock, and defies the battle of the elements that rage about it during the storms of winter. . . . A nearer view of the Cypress Grove shows that it forms simply the fringe of the pine woods and clings closely to the shore. Go back in the woods a hundred yards and not a single specimen of the cypress will be found."

worthy of study by any one who wishes to get a correct idea of the way the celestial lives when not governed by health boards and police. The place consists of a double row of shanties, built directly on the rocky shore, which here permits good-sized fishing boats to come to anchor at the owner's back door. Everything is unspeakably dirty and redolent with the odor of decaying fish. Swarthy women and little children who are tanned as black as negroes by sun and wind, swarm in the squalid cabins, and tumble about in the dust of the single street. On all the rocks about are arranged

CHINESE FISHING BOATS.

lattice-work frames that are covered with drying fish. The fish are mainly squid, about as long as one's hand, split and boned. After they have dried on the frames for two days they are tossed upon the ground, where the curing process is completed. Then they are raked up, and with the dry grass, weeds and dirt that adhere to them, all are placed in sacks, trodden down by the feet of the Chinese, care-fully packed, marked and shipped to China. Six or seven years ago it was no un-common sight to see fine cod, flounder and halibut, drying on these frames, but so destructive has been the custom of these fishermen in taking every-thing which came to their nets, that now the once de-spised squid is their main reliance. The long poles that adorn the fronts of most of the houses, the crazy balconies built out over the water, the flut-tering rags that hang from clothes-lines, the queer boats, with their lateen-sails, the children with their red and yellow garments, all these give to the squalid place a certain attraction. When viewed from the water, it is said by those who have traveled in China, to bear a striking resemblance to the native villages that line the Yangtse, and other great rivers of the Flowery Kingdom. Then Chinese have the Oriental disregard of the stranger, and calmly pursue all their avocations as though unobserved. It is seldom that the visitor will not find a group squatting about a small table in one of these hovels, eating with chop-sticks or wooden spoons from the common dish of fish, rice or unwholesome looking porridge that forms their staple diet.

About a half mile beyond the Chinese village one comes suddenly upon a collection of pretty cottages, built along the shore under the pines that clothe a rocky point. This is Pacific Grove, now one of the great popular pleasure resorts of California, with a large resident population, winter and summer. The grounds were laid out in 1875, on the plan of Ocean Grove, N. J. For several years it was a village of tents, but finally the Pacific Improvement Company secured control of the land, built a great hotel, brought fine water to the Grove, and now there are 300 pretty cottages, an increase of 100 within a single year. Avenues have been laid out through the dark, pine woods in the rear of the original grounds, and lots were recently sold at auction, the 1,000 lots aggregating $110,000. To give an idea of the wonderful growth of this place in popularity it may be said that lots, 30x60 feet, which three years ago were sold for $25, now command readily from $600 to $700,

CHINESE DRYING SQUID.

while as much as $1,500 has been paid for one of the business lots on the main street. As many as 3,000 people were regularly domiciled in the hotel and the cottages this season, yet the grounds were quiet and restful. No liquor is allowed on sale, and perfect order is maintained. The hotel which bears the pretty Spanish name of El Carmelo, has 114 large rooms, arranged in suites, with every modern convenience, and the table is famous for its excellence. From nearly all parts of the grounds magnificent views may be gained of bay and ocean, while the beach for bathing is warmer and more sheltered than any at Monterey. A long, high ridge of rock breaks the force of the ocean winds and makes of this sheltered cove an ideal bathing spot. Although the grove was originally founded by the Methodists, it is now non-sectarian, and it is worthy of remark that the first regular church building dedicated was a Protestant Episcopal Chapel. The grove has also been selected as the place of meeting of the California Branch of the Chautauqua Assembly, and every summer sees a large gathering from all parts of the State.

From Pacific Grove the road strikes through the heavy pine woods toward the ocean. Any one who visited Monterey ten years ago can recall this bit of road, at that time a waste of sand, through which horses plodded slowly and laboriously. Now the fine graveled highway permits of rapid trotting, and one bowls along under overarching boughs of the shadowy pines, which make delightful vistas, flecked with sunshine. A slight detour from the main road leads to the light-house on Point Pinos, named for the heavy growth of the Monterey pine, which bears a striking resemblance in its appearance and mode of growth to the spruce pine. Here one gets a superb view of the ocean from the light-house tower. The light station was established under the order of Secretary Thomas Corwin in 1853, and it has done good service in

CHINESE FISHERMEN GATHERING SHELLS.

warning mariners from a coast that is peculiarly dangerous to navigators. The light-house is built solidly of stone to resist the gales that sweep over the point, and its light is visible in clear weather from a vessel's deck sixteen and one half miles away.

Returning to the main road, this soon emerges from the pines, and then comes into view one of the prettiest scenes on this rare beach. To the right is the light-house with its back-ground of frowning pines—a sombre line that stretches away on both sides as far as the eye can reach. Near at hand, on the right, is a lovely little cove, with a beach as white and clear as the sanded floor of a Dutch housewife's kitchen. This is Moss Beach, famous for the delicate specimens of sea moss washed up every day at high tide. These are as infinite and as graceful in design as the coral, and one of the favorite pastimes of the dwellers at Pacific Grove is the floating out and preserving of these mosses. A little way to the right of this beach is the whirlpool—a rocky headland where several

GLIMPSE OF MONTEREY BAY.

currents meet and lash into foam the heavy rollers that come dashing in. When the flood tide is at its height, this angry conflict of the waters is a superb spectacle and reminds one of the seething rush of the waters through the narrow gorge of the Niagara River.

A few rods further and the chief curiosity of the beach is reached—the Seal Rocks, over which hundreds of ungainly seals are crawling. The rocks are much nearer to the shore than the celebrated seal rocks at the Cliff House, San Francisco, and one of them is worthy of the name of island, for it consists of many acres. The seals are mainly of a bright yellow color, much lighter than those by the Golden Gate, and several of the old sea lions are as large as a good-sized horse. Their bellowing is a strange sound, and when excited this varies from a short, sharp bark like that of a dog to the exact resemblance of the grunt of a hog. The huge fellows rule the roost, and one need remain here only a few minutes to witness some contest in which the smaller males are vanquished by the old sea lions.

Rounding a short curve on the beach, we approach Cypress Point, the boldest headland on the peninsula of Monterey. Down almost to the water grows the cypress, and on the extreme point a

HOTEL DEL MONTE AND GROUNDS—MONTEREY. FROM DRAWING BY HARRY FENN.

"One of the finest features of the grounds is furnished by the old oaks, many of which have been bent by the wind into the most fantastic shapes. Every resource of the landscape gardener has been lavished on the grounds, and artistic beds of choice flowers alternate with bits of rare shrubbery to make the place a paradise of dainty devices . . . To the invalid or to the tired brain-worker, it offers the supreme advantage of perfect rest. He must be ill indeed who can resist the spell of this atmosphere, charged with the salt of the sea and sweet with the balsam of the pine."

solitary tree has sunk its roots in the crevices of the wave-washed rock, and defies the battle of the elements that rage about it during the storms of winter. From a little distance this tree, with its nearest neighbor toward which it bends, bears a striking resemblance to a giant ostrich climbing up the rocks. A nearer view of the Cypress Grove shows that it forms simply the fringe of the pine woods and clings closely to the shore. Go back in the woods a hundred yards and not a single specimen of the cypress will be found. For about two miles it extends along the shore, then the Grove suddenly ends, and one may travel along the California coast to San Diego, and he will not find a score of indigenous cypress trees. The tree grows to a height of thirty or forty feet, but many dwarf speci-mens may be seen here, stunted by wind and water. The peculiarity of the tree is the dense massing of foliage on the topmost branches, and the tendency of the lower limbs to die, and thus form gnarled, uncanny looking arms. So very dense and even is the upper surface of the skyward foliage, that the tree might well be named the umbrella cypress. To properly appreciate this curious tree one must get it in silhouette against the horizon. Then these dead arms are etched sharply against the sky, and the whole tree seems endowed with a kind of malignant living spirit. The imagination readily pictures strange forms in the twisted branches which invariably leave the parent trunk at the sharpest of right angles. On bright, sunny days its dense foliage casts a deep shadow, and its withered arms seem to reach out and point the ways to mys-terious caverns or rocky cliffs, and high, rolling breakers. The ex-treme headland of Cypress Point is bare

PREPARING FISH FOR MARKET.
OLD TAN YARD.
HOTEL DEL MONTE DEPOT.

of trees or vegetation, a wild and stormy spot where the heavy swells of the ocean beat and break in terrible grandeur. A half mile from here the road reaches a rocky point, from which one catches a sudden glimpse through the frame-work of twisted cypress boughs, of Point Lobos and the more distant coast. It is a magnificent outlook—the stern and rocky points jutting far out into the ocean and serving as shelter for the beautiful Carmel Bay, whose waters are more deeply blue than those of Monterey. Again we note the perfect crescent sweep which seems to be a charac-teristic of the bays on this part of the California coast, the dazzling whiteness of the sand that brings into greater relief the blue line of the water, and the background of mountains that completes the picture. One bit of this bay is worth passing notice. It is known as Pebble Beach, because of the myriads of pebbles that take the place of the ordinary sand. The waves come in with a peculiar swish on these loose pebbles, and their constant action results in beautifully rounded specimens of all kinds and of every shade of color. The Beach is a favorite resort for collectors of pebbles, but the search usually proves disastrous to clothes and shoes, since the waves come up with great rapidity, and yet so noiselessly that the incautious seeker after pebbles, finding too late that he cannot escape in this yielding mass, is overcome by the water and receives a thorough drenching.

The road back to town from this beach presents no marked characteristics. It climbs a steep hill, passes through a fine grove of pines and finally ends in the main county road that soon brings the tourist back into Monterey after a drive which, for variety and beauty of scenery, it would be difficult to parallel in this country or Europe.

Another excursion that no visitor to Monterey can afford to miss, is that to the old Carmel Mission and Point Lobos. The road is not like the beach drive. It is the ordinary country road, with patches of sand, alternating with the hard *adobe* soil that becomes like flint in summer and like putty in winter. A drive of a few minutes brings you to the crown of the hill back of Monterey. From this coign of vantage a fine panoramic view can be secured of the crescent bay, and the mountains beyond on one side, while, by turning to the west, the broad expanse of the Pacific may be seen through the cañon that lies at the foot of the western slope of the hill. There is little that is striking for the next three miles on this road. It winds about among the pines, climbing and descending hills, with occasional glimpses of the ocean. Just as the road rounds the corner of the hill overlooking the Carmel Valley and Bay and Point Lobos, the tourist gets his first glimpse of old Carmel Mission—a picturesque structure, mellowed by time, standing in the midst of a field of tawny grain. A few minutes brings one to the branch road that leads to the mission. Here is the gar-Fathers den that the Franciscan planted more than one hun-

SCENES IN AND ABOUT MONTEREY.

trees that day, now as the padres dred years ago, and here are the huge pear they were wont to sit under in the heat of the heavy with fruit as they used to hang when preached to the Indians from the neighboring church. The mission church is surrounded by the ruins of an *adobe* wall and of the huts built for neophytes. The building, as originally designed, was of noble and graceful proportions. Built of a chalk stone, which took on with age the rich color of old parchment, the mission was very impressive, even in its ruin. I remember the impression it made upon me, ten years ago, when the roof was gone and one of the side walls was crumbling into decay. Enough remained to show the architectural skill of the designer, and the loving care with which he had wrought the pillars of the door, the stairways and the great front window. Nothing then remained of the roof save two shattered rafters, but these were perfect in curve, and allowed fancy to restore the church, and people it with devout worshipers. Upon the floor of hard packed earth were lying fragments of the adobe walls, which the unwise economy of the builders had substituted for the enduring stone of the front of the church. Now everything is changed. The church was restored two years ago, and a formal celebration of the event was held on the hundredth anniversary of the death of its founder, Padre Junipero Serra.

What the mission was in the zenith of its prosperity, when its 60,000 sheep and 87,000 cattle fed on the neighboring hills, may be learned from Mrs. Helen Hunt Jackson's papers, now gathered in "Glimpses of Three Coasts." She gives a vivid picture of the heroism and patience of these old fathers, which no one can realize fully who has not traveled over the chaparral-covered hills and along the dreary leagues of dusty mountain trails that separate these Franciscan Missions.

From the old mission to Point Lobos, the road passes some fine dairy ranches, but the buildings are mainly poor and the places give no indication of the wealth of their owners. Just on the farther edge of Carmel Bay is a small cove called Fisherman's Bay, rock-rimmed and gloomy, which no plummet has ever sounded. Here is the present headquarters of the whale fishing industry, the mere ghost of its former prosperity. A few Portuguese vegetable gardens find a foot-hold on the landward slope of Point Lobos, but the summit is formed of basaltic rock, seamed and rent by some great volcanic convulsion. From this point one commands the coast for many miles. After leaving the point the shore becomes more wild and rugged, and here is presented the curious spectacle of

LAWN VIEW.
HOTEL DEL MONTE GROUNDS.

the perforated rock, through which at high tide the waves break in showers of foam. The same formation is seen in even greater perfection at Santa Cruz, where a Natural Bridge has been formed by the constant erosion. The drive may be prolonged for miles down the coast, giving a succession of superb marine views of a bold, rocky shore line, scarred by the numerous canyons that form the beds of the mountain streams that rush down to the sea.

Seven years ago it was decided by a number of energetic Californians, with Charles Crocker, the railroad magnate, at their head, to make Monterey a great popular resort for the winter as well as the summer. The first desideratum was a fine hotel, and this was secured in the Hotel del Monte, which was constructed in the center of a large natural park of live oaks and pines, about a mile from the old town. The hotel was built in the best style, and with its grounds and facilities for the amusement of guests, was unequalled on the Pacific Coast. No less than 127 acres was laid out in pleasure walks and drives about the hotel. The Monterey cypress and pine were planted thickly, and these with the venerable oaks added greatly to the beauty of the numerous lawns. In places these lawns bore a striking resemblance to the parks in English domains, the turf being as brilliantly green

ALONG THE DRIVE—MONTEREY. DRAWING BY VICTOR PERARD.

"From Pacific Grove the road strikes through the heavy pine woods towards the ocean . . . The fine graveled highway permits of rapid trotting, and one bowls along under over-arching boughs of the shadowy pines, which make delightful vistas, flecked with sunshine."

A BIT OF OLD MONTEREY.

in December as in August. One of the finest features of the grounds is furnished by the old oaks, many of which have been bent by the wind into the most fantastic shapes. Every resource of the landscape gardener has been lavished on the grounds, and artistic beds of choice flowers alternate with bits of rare shrubbery to make the place a paradise of dainty devices. A novel sight to an eastern tourist is the Arizona garden, in which more than a score of different species of the cactus are growing, with other plants from the land of the Apache. It is worth taking a long journey to see these cactus plants in bloom, the colors being the richest in nature. An artificial lake, a race-track, lawn tennis, archery and croquet grounds, billiard and club rooms, unite to make this resort full of resources for recreation and amusement. Down on the beach, only a short walk from the hotel, are the large bathing-houses, with four enormous tanks of salt water, graduated in temperature, for the use of bathers. A few hardy bathers enjoy a plunge in the surf outside, even in the cold, windy days of fall and winter, but the majority prefer to disport in the tepid water of the tanks, which is constantly replenished with the pure water of the ocean. On April 1, 1887, at midnight, the Hotel del Monte was burned to the ground. In one hour the fine structure was in ashes. All the guests escaped without injury, but the majority lost wardrobe, jewels and baggage. The work of rebuilding was at once begun and pushed rapidly forward, reproducing the main structure, greatly enlarged by the new annexes. The new dining-room promises to be one of the most spacious and elegant in the country.

Monterey has one of the most equable climates in California or in the world, and this, together with the fact that the atmosphere is especially conducive to sleep, constitutes the great climatic charm of the place. The mercury seldom falls below 24° in midwinter, or rises above 80° in midsummer. The difference between the mean temperature of January and July is only six degrees. Flowers bloom in the open air the whole year round, and hard frost is unknown. Sheltered by the thick pine woods, it is almost entirely free from the heavy fogs that sweep over the fields not two miles away. To the invalid or to the tired brain-worker, it offers the supreme advantage of perfect rest. He must be ill indeed who can resist the spell of this atmosphere, charged with the salt of the sea and sweet with the balsam of the pine.

CHINESE SHELL MERCHANT.

J. R. FITCH.

INDIAN SQUAWS GATHERING STRAWBERRIES IN THE VALLEY.

THE UPPER YOSEMITE FALL.

THE
YOSEMITE VALLEY.

THE far-famed Yosemite Valley lies well back on the western slope of the Sierra, about a hundred and fifty miles to the eastward of San Francisco. It is about seven miles long, from half a mile to a mile wide, and nearly a mile deep, carved in the solid granite flank of the range.   Its majestic walls are sculptured into a bewildering variety of forms,—domes and gables, towers and battlements, and sheer massive cliffs, separated by grooves and furrows and deep, shadowy cañons, and adorned with evergreen trees.   The bottom is level and park-like, finely diversified with meadows and groves, and bright, sunny gardens; the River of Mercy, clear as crystal, sweeping in tranquil beauty through the midst, while the whole valley resounds with the music of its unrivalled waterfalls.

It is a place compactly filled with wild mountain beauty and grandeur,—floods of sunshine, floods of snowy water, beautiful trees of many species, thickets of flowering shrubs, beds of flowers of every color, from the blue and white violets on the meadows, to the crimson pillars of the snow-flowers glowing among the brown needles beneath the firs.   Ferns and mosses find grateful homes in a thousand moist nooks among the rocks, humming-birds are seen glinting about among the showy flowers, small

HUMMING BIRDS GLINTING AMONG
THE FLOWERS.

singers enliven the under-brush, and wide-winged hawks and eagles float in the calm depths between the mighty walls; squirrels in the trees, bears in the cañons; all find peaceful homes, beautiful life of every form, things frail and fleeting and types of enduring strength meeting and blending, as if into this grand mountain mansion Nature had gathered her choicest treasures, whether great or small.

Three good carriage roads enter the valley by way of Big Oak Flat, Coulterville, and Raymond, the greater part of the journey from San Francisco being made by rail. Each of the three roads, according to the measurements of rival agents, is the shortest, least dusty, and leads through the finest scenery. No one, however, possesses any great advantage over the others. All are dusty and, to most people, monotonous throughout their lower courses in the foot-hills, and all necessarily pass through belts of the noblest coniferous trees to be found in the world, so that a journey to Yosemite by any possible route, even with Yosemite left out, would still be worth the exertion it costs a thousand times over.

In May, when the travel to Yosemite begins, the snow is still deep in the upper forests through which the roads pass, but the foot-hill region is already dry and forbidding. The whole country, soil, plants, and sky seems kiln-dried, most of the vegetation crumbles to dust beneath the foot, the ground is cracked, and the sky is hot, withered, dim, and desolate though glowing, and we gaze through the white, hazy glare towards the snowy mountains and streams of cold water with eager longing, but not one is in sight. Lizards glide about on the burning rocks, enjoying a constitution that no drought can dry, and small ants in amazing numbers seem to be going everywhere in haste, their tiny sparks of life only burning the brighter with the sun-fire however intense. Rattlesnakes lie coiled in out-of-the-way places, and are seldom seen. The noisy magpies, jays, and ravens gather beneath the best shade trees on the ground, with wings drooped and bills wide open, scarce a sound coming from any one of them during the mid-day hours. These curious groups, friends in distress, are frequently joined by the large buzzard, or California condor as it is sometimes called, while the quail also seeks the shade about the tepid alkaline water-holes in the channels of the larger streams, now nearly dry. Rabbits skurry from shade to shade beneath the ceanothus bushes, and the long-eared hare may be seen now and then as he canters gracefully across the wider openings where there is a sparse growth of oaks. The nights are about as dry as the days, dewless and calm, but a thousand voices proclaim the abundance of life notwithstanding the desolating effects of the fierce drought. Birds, crickets, hylas, etc., make a pleasant stir in the darkness, and coyotes, the small despised dogs of the wilderness, looking like rusty bunches of hair, bark in chorus, filling the air with their keen, lancing notes, and making it hot and peppery, as if filled with exploding fire-crackers.

CALIFORNIA FOREST IN MERCED CAÑON. FROM A SKETCH BY THOMAS MORAN.
ETCHING BY M. NIMMO MORAN.

"These giant conifers wave in the open sunshine, rising above one another on the mountain benches in most imposing array, each species giving forth the utmost expression of its own peculiar beauty and grandeur, with inexhaustible variety and harmony. All the different species stand more or less apart in groves or small irregular groups, through which the roads meander, making delightful ways along sunny colonnades and across openings that have a smooth surface strewn with brown needles and cones."

On the upper edge of this torrid foot-hill region the curious Sabine pine is found, the first of the mountain conifers met by the traveler in ascending the range. Nobody at first sight would take it to be a pine or conifer of any kind, it is so loose and wide-spread in habit, and its foliage is so thin and gray. The sunbeams sift through even the leafiest trees with scarce any interruption, and the weary, heated traveler finds but little protection in their shade. It grows only on the dry foot-hills, seeming to enjoy the most ardent sunshine like a palm, springing up here and there singly or in scattered groups among scrubby white-oaks and thickets of ceanothus and manzanita.

The generous crop of sweet, nutritious nuts it yields renders it a favorite with the Indians and bears. Indians gathering the ripe nuts make a striking picture. The men climb the trees and beat off the magnificent cones with sticks, while the squaws gather them in heaps, and roast them until the scales open and allow the hard-shelled seeds to be beaten out. Then, in the cool evenings, men, women, and children, smeared with resin, form circles around their camp-fires on the bank of some stream, and lie in easy independence, cracking nuts, and laughing and chatting as heedless of the future as bears and squirrels.

"CROSSING THE CHOWCHILLA RIDGE."—A COYOTE HOWLING

Fifteen to twenty miles farther on, at the height of from 2,000 to 3,000 feet above the sea, you reach the lower edge of the main forest belt, composed of the gigantic sugar-pine, yellow-pine, incense-cedar, Douglass-spruce, silver-fir, and sequoia. However dense and sombre the woods may appear in general views, neither on the rocky heights or down in leafiest hollows will you see any crowded growth to remind you of the dark malarial selvas of the Amazon and Orinoco with their boundless contiguity of shade, nor of the monotonous uniformity of the Deadar forests of the Himalaya, or of the pine woods of the Atlantic States. These giant conifers wave in the open sunshine, rising above one another on the mountain benches in most imposing array, each species giving forth the utmost expression of its own peculiar beauty and grandeur with inexhaustible variety and harmony. All the different species stand more or less apart in groves or small irregular groups, through which the roads meander, making delightful ways along sunny colonnades and across openings that have a smooth surface strewn with brown needles and cones. Now you cross a wild garden, now a ferny, willowy stream, and ever and anon you emerge from all the groves and gardens upon some granite pavement or high bare ridge commanding glorious views above the waving sea of evergreens far and near.

The sugar-pine surpasses all the other pines in the world, not only in size, but also in kingly majesty and beauty. It towers sublimely from every ridge and cañon of the range at an elevation of from three to seven thousand feet above the sea, attaining most perfect development at a height of about five thousand feet. Full-grown specimens are commonly about two hundred and twenty feet high, and from six to eight feet in diameter near the ground, though some grand old patriarch is occasionally met that has enjoyed five or six centuries of storms and attained a thickness of ten or even twelve feet, living on undecayed, sweet and sound in every fibre. The trunk is a smooth, round, delicately tapered shaft, mostly without limbs to a height of one hundred feet. At the top of this magnificent bole the long, curved branches sweep gracefully outward and downward, sometimes forming a palm-like crown sixty feet in diameter, or even more, around the rim of which the magnificent cones are hung. When ripe, in September and October, the cones are commonly from fifteen to eighteen inches long, and three in diameter, green, shaded with purple on their sunward sides, but changing to a warm, yellowish brown after the seeds are discharged. Then their diameter is nearly doubled by the spreading of the scales, and they

INDIAN SQUAWS GATHERING PINE CONES.

remain pendant on the ends of the branches, producing a fine ornamental effect all winter. The wood is fine-grained, fragrant, and is considered the most valuable of all the Sierra pine.

From the heartwood, where wounds have been made, the sugar, from which the common name is derived, exudes in crisp, candy-like masses. When fresh, it is white and delicious, but inasmuch as most of the wounds on which it is found have been made by fire, the exuding sap is stained on the charred surface, and the hardened sugar becomes brown. The Indians are fond of it, but because of its laxative properties only small quantities may be eaten.

The most constant companion of this species is the yellow-pine, and a worthy companion it is. The Douglass-spruce, libacedrus, sequoia, and the silver-firs are also more or less associated with it, but on many deep-soiled mountain sides, about five thousand feet above the sea, it forms the bulk of the forest. The majestic crowns approaching each other in bold curves make a lofty canopy through which the tempered sunbeams pour, silvering the needles, and gilding the boles and flowery ground into a scene of enchantment. On the warmest slopes the chamœbatia, a small shrub belonging to the rose family, is spread in a continuous growth like a carpet, brightened in the spring with the crimson *sarcodes*, or snow plant, and the wild rose. On the northern slopes the boles are more slender, and the ground is mostly occupied by an under-brush of hazel, ceanothus, and flowering dogwood, but never so dense as to prevent the traveler from sauntering where he will.

The yellow or silver-pine (P. ponderosa) ranks second among the Sierra pines as a lumber tree, and almost rivals the sugar-pine in size and nobleness of port. Seen in winter laden with snow, or in summer when its brown staminate clusters hang thick among the shimmering needles, and its large purple cones are ripening in the mellow light, it forms a magnificent spectacle. But it is during cloudless wind-storms that these colossal pines are most impressively beautiful. Then they bow like willows, their leaves streaming forward all in one direction, and when the sun shines on them at the required angle they glow as if every needle were burnished silver. The fall of sunlight on the royal crown of a palm as it breaks upon the glossy leaves in long lance-like rays, is a truly glorious spectacle, like a mountain stream breaking upon bowlders. But still more impressively beautiful is the fall of the light on these lofty silver-pines; it seems beaten to the finest dust, and is shed off in myriads of minute, glinting sparkles that hide all the green foliage and make one glowing mass of white radiance.

The famous big tree, *sequoia gigantea*, extends from the well-known Calaveras Grove to the head of Deer Creek, near the big bend of Kern River, a distance of nearly two hundred miles, at an elevation of about five to eight thousand feet above the sea. From the Calaveras to the south fork of Kings River it occurs only in small, isolated groves among the pines and firs, and is so sparsely and irregularly distributed that this portion of the belt is not easily traced. Two gaps nearly forty miles wide occur in it between the Calaveras and Tuolumne groves, and between those of the Fresno and Kings rivers. From Kings River the belt extends across the broad, rugged basins of the Kahweah and Tule rivers to its southern limit on the head of Deer Creek, interrupted only by deep, rocky cañons, the width of this portion of the belt being from three to nearly eight miles, and the length seventy miles.

In the northern groves few young trees or saplings are found promising to take the places of the failing old ones, giving rise to the notion that the species is doomed to speedy extinction, as being only an expiring remnant of an ancient flora once far more widely distributed. But careful study has shown that the Big Tree has never formed a greater part of these post-glacial forests than it does at the present time, however widely it may have been distributed in the pre-glacial forests.

To the southward of Kings River no tree in the woods appears to be more firmly established in accordance with climate and soil. For many miles they occupy the surface almost exclusively, growing vigorously over all kinds of ground,—on rocky ledges, along water-courses, and on moraines and avalanche detritus, coarse or fine, while a multitude of thrifty seedlings and saplings, and middle-aged trees are growing up about the old giants, ready to take their places and maintain the race in all its grandeur. But, unfortunately, fire and the axe are already busy on many of the more accessible portions of the belt, spreading sure destruction, and unless protective measures be speedily adopted and applied, in a few decades all that may be left of this noblest of trees will be a few hacked and scarred monuments.

There is something wonderfully telling and impressive about sequoia, even when beheld at a distance of several miles. Its dense foliage and smoothly rounded outlines enable us to recognize it in any company, and when one of the oldest patriarchs attains full stature on some commanding ridge it seems the very god of the woods. Full-grown specimens are about fifteen and twenty feet in diameter, measured above the swelling base, and about two hundred and fifty feet high. Trees twenty-five feet in diameter are not rare, and one is now and then found thirty feet in diameter, but very rarely any larger. The grandest specimen that I have measured is a stump about ninety feet high, which is thirty-five feet eight inches in diameter, measured inside the bark, above the bulging base. The wood is dull purplish red in color, easily worked, and very enduring; lasting, even when exposed to the weather, for hundreds of years. Fortunate old trees that have passed their three thousandth birthday, without injury from lightning, present a mound-like summit of warm, yellow-green foliage, and their colossal shafts are of a beautiful brown color, exquisitely tapered, and branchless to a height of a hundred and fifty feet. Younger trees have darker, bluish foliage, and shoot up with tops comparatively sharp.

The Calaveras Grove is the northmost, and was discovered first of all. It may be visited by tourists to the valley by way of Milton, Murphy's Camp, and Big Oak Flat, though it is not on any of the roads leading directly to Yosemite. The flowery leafiness of this grove is one of its most charming characteristics. Lilies, violets, and trientales cover the ground along the bottom of the glen, and carpets of the blooming chamœbatia are outspread where the light falls free, forming a beautiful ground of color for the brown sequoia trunks; while rubus, dogwood, hazel, maple, and several species of ceanothus make a shaggy underbrush in the cooler shadows.

Most of the larger trees have been slightly disfigured by names carved and painted on marble tablets and countersunk into the bark, and two have been killed; one of them by removing the bark in

THE TWO GUARDSMEN.—CASCADE FALL.—LOOKING DOWN THE MERCED FROM FOOT OF
YOSEMITE VALLEY. PAINTING BY THOMAS HILL.

"Its majestic walls are sculptured into a bewildering variety of forms,—domes and gables, towers and
battlements, and sheer massive cliffs, separated by grooves and furrows and deep, shadowy cañons, and adorned
with evergreen trees . . . . the River of Mercy, clear as crystal, sweeping in tranquil beauty through the midst,
while the whole valley resounds with the music of its unrivaled waterfalls."

sections to be set up in the London exposition, the other felled because somebody wanted to dance upon the stump, and the noble monarch now lies a mass of ruins. With these exceptions, the grove has been well preserved, that is, let alone, the underbrush and smaller plants in particular retaining their primitive wildness unimpaired.

Travelers to the valley, by way of Big Oak Flat, pass through the small Tuolumne Grove of Big Trees on the dividing ridge between the waters of the Tuolumne and Merced rivers. Those who take the Raymond route may visit the Mariposa and Fresno groves, by stopping over a day at Clark's Station. While those who choose the Coulterville route will pass through the Big Tree Grove of the Merced. These groves on the different routes are not equally interesting to most people, but all contain giants that are worthy representatives of their race. The traveler, however, who would see *sequoia gigantea* in

BURNT SECTION
80 FEET FROM STUMP.

all its glory, must visit the forests of the Kahweah and Tule rivers.

"THE GRIZZLY GIANT."—33 FEET IN DIAMETER.

From the Big Tree groves the roads conduct for a few hours through forests of sugar-pine and silver-fir which become yet more beautiful and interesting as you advance. Then, looking and admiring as best you can while being rapidly whirled onward through dust in a coach drawn by six horses, Yosemite Valley comes suddenly into view, and in an hour you are down the nerve-trying grade,—out of the shadows from the noblest forest trees in the world, into the midst of the grandest rocks and waterfalls.   Riding up the valley through stately groves, and around the margin of emerald meadows, the lofty walls on either hand looming into the sky with their marvelous wealth of architectural forms, bathed in the purple light of evening, and beating time to the tones of the falls, the whole seems a work of enchantment.

The first object to catch the eye on entering the valley is the Bridal Veil Fall, 900 feet in height,—a soft, delicate-looking thing of beauty, as seen at a distance of a mile or two, pouring its snowy folds and irised spray with the utmost gentleness, while the wind sways it from side to side like a downy cloud.   But on a near approach it manifests the speed and wild ungovernable energy of an avalanche.

On the other side of the valley, almost immediately opposite the Bridal Veil, there is another

SEQUOIA FOREST HEAD WATERS OF THE KAWEAH

fine fall, considerably wider at times when the snow is melting, and more than a thousand feet in height from the brow of the cliff where it first leaps free into the air to the head of a rocky talus, where it strikes and is broken up into ragged cascades.   It is called the Ribbon Fall or Virgins' Tears.   During the spring floods it is a magnificent object, but the suffocating blasts of spray that fill the recess in the wall which it occupies prevent a near approach.   In autumn however, when its feeble current falls in a shower it may then pass for tears with the sentimental onlooker fresh from a visit to the Bridal Veil.   Just beyond these two falls are the grand outstanding masses of the Cathedral and El Capitan rocks, 2,700 and 3,300 feet in height, the latter making a most imposing display of sheer, enduring, unflinching granite, by many regarded as the most sublime feature of the valley.   Then the Three Brothers present themselves,—a vast mountain building of three gables, the highest nearly 4,000 feet above the valley floor.   On the south side, opposite the Brothers, the Sentinel Rock, 3,000 feet high, stands forward in bold relief like some special monument, gracefully adorned with a beautiful cascade on either side and fringed at base with spruce and pine.

The general masses of the walls between the more prominent rocks thus far mentioned, are sculptured into a great variety of architectural forms, impossible to describe separately, each fitted to its place in this grand harmony.

Beyond the Three Brothers the Yosemite Fall is at length seen in one grand view throughout its entire length, pouring its floods of snowy rejoicing waters from a height of 2,600 feet down to the groves and green meadows of the valley, bathing the mighty cliffs with clouds of spray, and making them tremble with its deep, massy thunder-tones.

At the head of the valley, now clearly revealed, stands the Half Dome, the loftiest, most sublime and the most beautiful of all the rocks that guard this glorious temple. From a broad, sloping base, planted on the level floor of the valley, it rises to a height of 4,750 feet in graceful flowing folds, finely sculptured and poised in calm, deliberate majesty. Here the main valley sends out three branches, forming the Tenaya, Merced, and Illilouette cañons. Tracing the Tenaya Cañon from the valley up Tenaya Creek, you have the Half Dome on the right, and the Royal Arches, Washington Column, and the North

CALIFORNIA PARTRIDGES.

MEASURING A BIG TREE MARIPOSA GROVE.

Dome on the left. Half a mile beyond Washington Column you come to Mirror Lake, lying imbedded in beautiful trees at the foot of Half Dome. A mile beyond the lake the picturesque Tenaya Fall is seen gleaming through the rich leafy forest that fills this portion of the cañon, and to the left of the fall are the Dome Cascades, about a thousand feet in height, filling the cañon with their deep booming roar.

Just above the Tenaya Fall, on the left side, rises the grand projecting mass of Mt. Watkins, with a sheer front of solid granite like El Capitan, and on the right, the lofty wave-like ridge of Clouds' Rest, a mile in height.

A little farther up the cañon, you come to the Tenaya Cascades, 700 feet in vertical descent, gliding in a showy plume-like ribbon down a smooth incline of bare granite. Above the cascades, you pass a succession of less showy cascades and falls, and many small filled up lake-basins, with charming lily gardens, and groves of pine and silver-fir, set in the midst of waving folds of shining glacier-planed granite and rocks of every form, until, at a distance of about ten miles from the valley, the cañon opens into the beautiful basin of Lake Tenaya, and the noble Cathedral Peak with its many spires on the east, towers above it.

The Illilouette Cañon, through which the beautiful Illilouette basin is drained, is about two miles long. From different standpoints in its rough, boulder-choked bottom, a series of most telling and strangely varied views of the head of the valley may be obtained. The Illilouette Fall, near the head of the cañon, is one of the most interesting in the valley. It is nearly 600 feet high, but is seldom visited on account of the roughness of the way leading to it over the rocks. The canon of the main

AMONG THE BIG TREES OF CALIFORNIA — THE TRUNK OF WAWONA. — ROAD TO YOSEMITE.
DRAWING BY HENRY IHLEFELD.

"The wood is dull purplish-red in color, easily worked and very enduring, lasting even when exposed to the weather for hundreds of years. Fortunate old trees that have passed their three thousandth birthday, without injury from lightning, present a mound-like summit of warm yellow-green foliage, and their colossal shafts are of a beautiful brown color, exquisitely tapered and branchless to a height of a hundred and fifty feet. Younger trees have darker, bluish foliage, and shoot up with tops comparatively sharp."

THE THREE BROTHERS.—3,818 FEET HIGH

middle branch of the river extends back to the axis of the range in the Lyell Group, and contains so many waterfalls, cascades of every kind, lakes, and beautiful valleys with walls that are sculptured like those of Yosemite, that nothing like a complete description of it can be given here.

About a mile up the cañon from the main valley, along the margin of wild dashing rapids charmingly embowered, you come to the beautiful Vernal Fall, 400 feet in height. At the head of the fall lies the small Emerald Pool, and a mile beyond the snowy Nevada Fall is seen, which, next to the Yosemite, is the grandest of all.

It is about 600 feet in height, and on account of its waters being so tossed and beaten before reaching the brink of the precipice it is intensely white; while all the way down to the head of the Vernal Fall the river forms a continuous chain of cascades and rapids, hardly less interesting to most travelers than the falls.

The majestic rock called, from its shape, the Liberty Cap, rises close along side the Nevada, adding greatly to the grandeur of the view.

Tracing the river back from the head of the fall, you pass through the Little Yosemite Valley. It resembles the main Yosemite, though formed on a smaller scale. Then you find a long train of booming, dancing cascades, alternating with rapids and lakes and short, tranquil reaches, and a grand variety of smaller Yosemite valleys, garden patches and forests in hollows, here and there, where soil has been accumulated, until at length the icy fountains of the river are reached among the Alpine peaks of the summit.

The Yosemite Valley was discovered in the spring of 1851, by Captain Boling, who then, with two Indians as guides, led a company of soldiers into it from Mariposa to punish a band of marauding Indians who occupied the valley as their home and stronghold.

The regular Yosemite pleasure travel began in 1856, and has gradually increased until the present time. Considering the remoteness of many of the fountains of this current of travel, its flow has been remarkably constant. The regular tourist, ever in motion, is one of the most characteristic productions of the present century; and however frivolous and inappreciative the poorer specimens may appear, viewed comprehensively they are a hopeful and significant sign of the times, indicating at least a beginning of our return to nature; for going to the mountains is going home. Perhaps nowhere else along the channels of pleasure travel may so striking and interesting a variety of people be found together as in this comparatively wild and remote Yosemite. Men, women, and

MIRROR LAKE.

children of every creed and color come here from every country under the sun; farmers, men of business, lawyers, doctors, and divines; scientists seeking causes, wealthy and elegant loafers trying to escape from themselves, the titled and obscure, all in some measure seeing and loving wild beauty, and traveling to better purpose than they know, borne onward by currents that they cannot understand, like ships at sea.

Arriving in the valley most parties keep together and fall into the hands of the local guides, by whom they are led hastily from point to point along the beaten trails. Others separate more or less and follow their own ways. These are mostly members of Alpine Clubs, sturdy Englishmen and Germans, with now and then a cannie Scotchman, all anxious to improve their opportunities to the utmost. Besides rambling at will into odd corners of the valley, they climb about the cañons, and around the tops of the walls; or push out bravely over the adjacent mountains, radiating afar into the High Sierra among the ice and snow. They thread the mazes of the glorious forests, and trace the wild young streams in their courses down from the glaciers through grandly sculptured cañons, past garden hollows and lake basins, and down glossy inclines, sharing in all their exhilarating rush and roar.

Gentle, contemplative grandmothers, and a few fine-grained specimens of fewer years, spend most of their time sauntering along the banks of the river, and sitting in the shade of the trees; admiring sky and cliff, and falling water, in a quiet way, enriching their lives far more than their neighbors who keep themselves in perpetual motion, following each other along dusty trails, painfully "doing" the valley by rule.

Little children are, of course, the most delightfully natural of all the visitors, flashing around the hotel verandahs, or out beneath the trees, glowing in rainbow-hued ruffles and ribbons

GENERAL VIEW OF YOSEMITE VALLEY.

like butterflies and scarlet tanagers.   They consider the lilies and birds and bees, nor are they altogether unconscious of the glorious sublimities about them; for one may see them at times gazing silently with upturned faces at the mighty cliffs, and at the white water pouring out of the sky, their pure, natural wonderment offering a refreshing contrast to the mean complacency and blindness of the finished tourist, who has seen all, knows all, and is engulphed in eternal apathetic tranquillity.

The Yosemite Fall is partially separated into an upper and lower fall, with a series of smaller falls and cascades between them, but when viewed in front they appear as one, only slightly interrupted by striking on what seems to be a narrow ledge.   First there is a sheer descent of about 1,600 feet; then a succession of cascades and smaller falls nearly a third of a mile long, and making altogether a descent of 600 feet; then a final sheer fall of about 400 feet is made to the bottom of the valley.   So grandly does this magnificent fall display itself from the floor of the valley few

CRESCENT LAKE. FROM THE PAINTING BY THOMAS HILL.

"Crescent Lake is one of the many gems that abound in the great Yosemite Park, and is one of many glacial lakes that nestle at the base of the Merced group of snow-capped mountains, some eight thousand feet above sea-level. This wild and desolate region is the home of the grizzly, and also of 'Jim Duncan,' who has hunted and lived here for thirty-five years. He can boast of having killed a hundred bears; and, in company with Bob Whitman, of Buck Camp fame, still haunts the shores of this sylvan lake, an enemy to the brute creation and a friend to mankind. The picture represents Duncan and Whitman returning, as the sun goes down, from a hunt at 'Buck Camp.'"—THOMAS HILL.

visitors take the trouble to climb the wall to gain nearer views, unable to realize how vastly more
impressive it becomes when closely approached, instead
of being seen at a distance of from one to two miles.

The views developed in a walk up the zigzags
of the trail leading to the upper fall are as varied
and impressive, and almost as extensive, as those on the
well-known Glacier Point Trail.   One rises as if on
wings.   The groves, meadows, fern-flats, and reaches
of the river at once gain new interest, as if never seen
before, and all become new over and over again as we go
higher from point to point; the foreground also changes
every few rods in the most surprising manner, although
the bench on the face of the wall
over which the trail passes is very
monotonous and common-place in appearance as seen from the bottom
of the valley.   Up we climb with
glad exhilaration, through shaggy
fringes of laurel and ceanothus, and
glossy-leaved manzanita and live oak
from shadow to shadow across bars
of sunshine, the leafy openings
making charming frames for the
valley pictures beheld through them,
and for the glimpses of the high
alps that appear in the distance.
The higher we
go the farther
we seem to be
from the sum-
mit of the vast
carved wall up
which we are
creeping. Here

THE ILLILOUETTE FALLS.
FROM PAINTING BY THOMAS HILL.

we pass a huge projecting buttress whose grooved
and rounded surface tells a wonderful story of the
time when the valley now filled with sunshine was
filled with ice, when a grand old glacier, flowing
river-like from its many fountains on the snow-laden
summits of the range, swept through the valley with
its crushing, grinding floods, wearing its way ever

WAWONA VALLEY IN YOSEMITE PARK. FROM PAINTING BY THOMAS HILL.

"Wawona" in the Indian dialect, means big, prodigious, grand. This name has been given to one of the grandest and loveliest of valleys in the great "Sierras." Its bald granite domes and massive walls, over which cataracts dash and tumble to the blue depths below, tower 3000 feet above the Valley. The Merced group of Mountains, the source of the Merced River, whose snow-capped peaks pierce the clouds, are a fitting background to the "Forest Giants" of the Mariposa grove at their base.

Wawona is the last resting-place before entering the portals of the great Yosemite. —THOMAS HILL.

deeper, and fashioning these sublime cliffs to the varied forms of beauty they now possess.   Here a white, battered gully marks the pathway of an avalanche of rocks, now we cross the channel of an avalanche of snow.   Farther on we come to a small stream clinging to the face of the cliff in lace-like strips, or leaping from ledge to ledge, too small and feeble to be called a fall, trickling, dripping, slipping, oozing, a pathless wanderer from the upland meadows, seeking a way century after century to the depths of the valley without having worn any appreciable channel.   Constant dropping has not worn away *these* stones.   Every morning, after a cool night, evaporation being checked, it gathers strength and sings like a bird, but as the day advances, and the sun strikes its thin currents outspread on the heated precipices, most of its waters vanish long ere the bottom of the valley is reached.   Many a fine, hanging garden aloft on these breezy inaccessible heights owe

to it their freshness and fullness of beauty; ferneries in shady nooks, filled with adiantum, woodwardia, woodsia, aspidium, pelleæ, and cheilanthes; rosetted and tufted and ranged in lines, daintily overlapping, thatching the stupendous cliffs with softest beauty, the delicate fronds seeming to float on the warm, moist air, without any connection with rock or stream.   And colored plants, too, in abundance, wherever they can find a place to cling to; the showy cardinal mimulus, lilies and mints, and glowing cushions of the golden bahia, together with sedges and grasses growing in tufts, and the butterflies and bees and all the small, happy creatures that belong to them.

After the highest point on the lower division of the trail is gained it conducts along a level terrace on the face of the wall, around a shoulder, and into the deep recess occupied by the great Upper Yosemite Fall, the noblest display of falling water to be found in the valley, or, perhaps, in the world.   When it first comes in sight, it seems almost within reach of one's hand, so great is its volume and velocity, yet it is still nearly a third of a mile away, and appears to recede as we advance.   The sculpture of the walls about it is on a scale of grandeur, according nobly with the fall, plain and massive, though elaborately

TENAYA CASCADES.—HEAD OF TENAYA CAÑON.

finished, like all the other cliffs about the valley.

In the afternoon an immense shadow is cast athwart the plateau in front of the fall, and far over the fields of chaparral that clothe the slopes and benches of the wall to the eastward, creeping upward upon the fall until it is wholly overcast, the contrast between the shaded and illuminated sections being very striking in near views.

Under this shadow, during the cool centuries immediately following the breaking up of the Glacial Period, dwelt a small residual glacier, one of the few that lingered on this sun-beaten side of the valley after the main trunk glacier had vanished.   It sent down a long winding current through the narrow cañon on the west side of the fall, and must have formed a striking feature of the ancient scenery of the valley; the lofty fall of ice and fall of water side by side, yet separate and distinct.

The coolness of the afternoon shadow and the abundant dewy moisture from the spray of the fall make a fine climate for ferns and grasses on the plateau, and for the beautiful azalia, which grows here in profusion and blooms in September, long after the warmer thickets down the valley have withered and gone to seed.   Even close to the fall, and behind it at the base of the cliff, a few venturesome plants may be found, undisturbed by the rock-shaking torrent.

The basin at the foot of the fall into which the current directly pours when it is not swayed by the wind is about ten feet deep, and fifteen to twenty feet in diameter. That it is not much deeper is surprising, when the great height and force of the fall is considered. But the rock where the water strikes probably suffers much less erosion than it would were the descent less than half as great, since the current is outspread, and much of its force is spent ere it reaches the bottom; being received on the air as upon an elastic cushion, and borne outward and dissipated over a surface more than fifty yards wide.

This surface, easily examined when the water is low, is intensely clean and fresh-looking. It is the raw, quick flesh of the mountain wholly untouched by the weather. In summer droughts, when the snow-fall of the preceding winter has been light, the fall is reduced to a mere shower of separate drops without any obscuring spray. Then we may safely go back of the fall and view the crystal

GLACIER POINT.

shower from beneath, which, when the sun is shining, is extremely beautiful, each drop wavering and pulsing as it makes its way through the air, and flashing off jets of colored light of ravishing beauty. But all this is invisible from the bottom of the valley, like a thousand other interesting things. One must labor for beauty as for bread here as elsewhere.

During the time of spring floods the best near view of the fall is obtained from a ledge on the east side above the blinding spray, at a height of about 400 feet from the base of the fall. A climb of about 1,400 feet from the valley has to be made, and there is no trail, but to any one fond of climbing, and who is at all stirred by a love of adventure, this will make the ascent all the more delightful. The ledge runs out back of the fall on the sheer front of the cliff, so that the fall may be approached as closely as we wish. When the afternoon sunshine is streaming through the thronging masses of down-rushing waters the marvelous firmness and variety of their forms are beautifully revealed. The whole fall is a majestic column of foaming, snowy water, ever wasting, ever renewed. At the top it seems to burst forth from some grand, throbbing heart of the mountain in irregular pulses, comet-like spurts succeeding one another in sublime rhythm. Now and then one mighty throb sends forth a mass into the free air far beyond the others, which rushes alone to the bottom of the fall with long, streaming, tail-like, combed silk, illumined by the sun, while the others, descending in clusters, gradually mingle and lose their identity. They rush past with amazing velocity and display of power, though apparently drowsy and deliberate in their movements when observed from the bottom of the valley at a distance of a mile or two. The heads of these comet-like masses are composed of nearly solid water, and are dense white in color, like pressed snow, from the friction they suffer in rushing through the air, the portion worn off forming the tail, between the white lustrous threads and films of which faint, grayish pencilings appear, while the outer, finer sprays of waste water-dust, whirling in sunny eddies, are pearl gray throughout.

At the bottom of the fall there is but little distinction of form visible. It is mostly a driving, boiling, upswirling mass of scud and spray, through which the light sifts in gray and purple tones, while at times, when the sun strikes at the required angle, the whole is changed to brilliant rainbow hues. The middle portion of the fall is the most openly beautiful; lower, the various forms into which the waters are wrought are more closely and voluminously veiled, while higher, towards the head, the current is more simple and compact. But even at the bottom, in the boiling clouds of spray, there is no confusion, while the rainbow light makes all divine, adding glorious beauty and peace to glorious power. The Upper Yosemite Fall has far the richest, as well as the most powerful, voice of all the falls of the valley, its tones varying from the sharp hiss and rustle of the wind in the glossy leaves of the live-oaks and the soft, sifting, hushing tones of the pines, to the loudest rush and roar of storm-winds and thunder among the crags of the summit peaks. The low bass, booming, reverberating tones, heard under favorable circumstances five or six miles away, are formed by the dashing and exploding of heavy masses of water and air upon two projecting ledges on the face of

LIBERTY CAP AND NEVADA FALL.

the cliff, 400 and 600 feet above the base of the fall. The torrent of massive comets is continuous at time of high water, while the explosive, booming notes are wildly intermittent, because, unless influenced by the wind, most of the heavier masses shoot out from the face of the precipice, and pass the ledges upon which at other times they are wrecked. Occasionally the whole fall is swayed away from the front of the cliff, then suddenly clashed flat against it, or vibrated from side to side like a pendulum, giving rise to endless variety of forms and sounds.

Once during a violent wind-storm, while I watched the fall from the shelter of a pine-tree, the whole ponderous column was suddenly arrested in its descent at a point about midway between the base and top, and was neither blown upward or turned aside, but simply held stationary in mid-air as if gravitation below that point had ceased to act. Thus it remained for more than a minute, resting in the arms of the storm-wind, the usual quantity of water meanwhile coming over the brow of the cliff and accumulating in the air as if falling upon an invisible floor, swedging and widening. Then, as if commanded to go on, scores of arrowy water-comets shot forth from the base of the suspended fountain,

CATHEDRAL ROCKS, YOSEMITE. ETCHING BY JAMES FAGAN. PAINTING BY W. M. CARY.

"The general masses of the walls between the more prominent rocks thus far mentioned are sculptured into a great variety of architectural forms, impossible to describe separately, each fitted to its place in this grand harmony."

and the grand anthem of the fall once more began to sound.   After bathing so long in the spray of the fall it is natural to look above and beyond it and say: "Where does all this chanting water come from?"   This is easily learned by going and seeing.

The Yosemite Creek is the most tranquil of all the larger streams that pour over the valley walls.   The others, while yet a good way back from the verge of the valley, abound in loud-voiced falls and cascades or rushing rapids, but Yosemite Creek, as if husbanding its resources, after the

descent of its main tributaries from the snowy heights of the Hoffman Range, flows quietly on through strips of level meadow and smooth hollows and flats, with only a few small cascades, showing nothing in all its course to suggest the grandeur of its unrivalled falls in the valley.

Its wide and shallow basin is so crowded with domes it seems paved with them.   Some castellated piles adorn its western rim, while the great Tuolumne Cañon sweeps past it on the north, and the cool, shadow-covered precipices of the Hoffman Range bound it on the east and northeast.   During winter and spring most of the waters of the basin are derived directly from snow, but in summer only two or three, and in the drier seasons only one of its many streams draws its source from perennial fountains of snow and ice.   Then the main dependence of

CAPT. BOLLING AND PARTY ENTERING THE YOSEMITE VALLEY.

NORTH WALL OF UPPER MERCED, YOSEMITE, BELOW MT. LYELL.

the many tributaries are moraines of the ancient glaciers, in which a part of the melting snows and rains are absorbed.

Issuing from their moraine fountains, each shining thread of water at once begins to sing, running gladly onward, over boulders, over rock-stairs, over dams of fallen trees; now groping in shadows, now gliding free in the light on glacier-planed pavements, not a leaf on their borders; diving under willows, fingering their red roots and low-dipping branches, then absorbed in green bogs; out again among mosaics of leaf, shadows and light, whirling in pools giddy and ruffled, then restful and calm, not a foambell in sight; whispering low, solemn in gestures as full grown rivers, slowly meandering through green velvet meadows, banks embossed with bryanthus and yet finer cassiope, white and blue violets blending with white and blue daisies in smooth, silky sods of the Alpine agrostis; out again on bare granite, flowing over gravel and sand mixed with mica and garnets and white crystal quartz, making tiny falls and cascades in rapid succession, until at length all the bright, rejoicing choir meet together to form the main stream which flows calmly down to its fate in the valley, sweeping over the tremendous verge beneath a mantle of diamond spray. Amid the varied foams and fine ground mists of the mountain streams that are ever rising from a thousand water-falls, there is an affluence and variety of rainbows scarce at all known to the careworn visitor from the lowlands. Both day and night, winter and summer, this divine light may be seen wherever water is falling in spray and foam, a silent interpreter of the heart-peace of Nature, amid the wildest displays of her power. In the bright spring mornings the black-walled recess at the foot of the Lower Yosemite Fall is lavishly filled with irised spray, which does not simply span the dashing foam, but the foam itself, the whole mass of it, seems to be colored, and drifts and wavers, mingling with the foliage of the adjacent trees, without suggesting any relationship to the ordinary rainbow. This is perhaps the largest and most reservoir-like accumulation of iris color to be found in the valley.

The lunar rainbows, or spraybows, are grandly developed in the spray of the Upper Fall. Their colors are as distinct as those of the sun, and as regularly and obviously banded, though less vivid. They may be seen any night when there is plenty of moonlight and spray.

Even the secondary bow is at times distinctly visible. The best point from which to observe them is on the upper ledge, 400 feet above the base

of the fall on the east side. For some time after moonrise the arc is about 400 to 500 feet span, set upright, one end planted in the spray at the bottom, the other in the edge of the fall, creeping lower, of course, and becoming less upright as the moon rises higher. This grand arc of color, glowing with such invincible peacefulness and mild shapely beauty in so weird and dark a chamber of shadows, and amid the rush and roar and tumultuous dashing of this thunder-voiced fall, is one of the most impressive sights offered in all this wonder-filled valley.

Smaller bows may be seen in the gorge on the plateau between the upper and lower falls. Once toward midnight, after spending a few hours with the wild beauty of the upper fall, I sauntered along the edge of the gorge, looking in here and there, wherever the footing felt safe, to see what I could learn of the night aspects of the smaller falls that dwell there. And down in an exceedingly black, pit-like portion of the gorge, at the foot of the highest of the intermediate falls, while the moonbeams were pouring into it through a narrow opening, I saw a well-defined spraybow. beautifully distinct in colors, spanning across from side to side of the pit.

In the pool at the foot of the fall pure white foam waves were constantly springing up into the moonshine, beneath the beautiful bow, like a band of dancing ghosts.

The leaping waves so foamy white, amid rocks and shadows so weird and black, and the mystic circle of colored light, made a scene in the

YOSEMITE FALLS.

general gloom of the night marvelously vivid and wild. Another marvelous night scene, but not a safe one, is a view of the full moon through the edge of the Upper Fall, from the narrow ledge that extends back of it, 400 feet above its base. But the ledge is less than a foot wide on the face of the wall at one place, and though considerably wider behind the fall, it is rounded on the edge by the action of the water, and the fall is liable to be swayed against it even in calm nights; therefore one is in danger of being washed off. My own experiences one night back of the fall, when it was booming in all its glory, were such that I shall never venture there again. But the effect was enchanting; wild music above, beneath, around. The moon appeared to be in the very midst of the rushing waters and struggling to keep her place, on account of the ever-varying density and forms of the masses through which she was seen; now darkened by a rush of opaque comets, now flashing out through openings of gaudy tissue, suffering a rushing succession of eclipses that lasted but a moment,—a rare astronomical phenomenon, a transit of a thousand comets across the disc of the moon.

LAMON'S CABIN.—FIRST HOME IN YOSEMITE.

A very telling excursion may be made to Glacier Point and Sentinel Dome, thence across the Illilouette and Little Yosemite Valley, and return to the valley past the Nevada and Vernal falls. On the trail leading up the craggy wall to Glacier Point, the main rocks and falls of the valley are seen in striking positions and combinations, developing marvelously grand and beautiful effects as you climb from point to point. At an elevation of about 500 feet, a wide sweeping view down the valley is obtained past the Sentinel, and between Cathedral Rock and El Capitan. At 1,500 feet the wide upper end of the valley comes in sight, bounded by the great Half Dome, that looms sublimely into the azure, overshadowing every other feature of the landscape.

From Glacier Point you look down over the edge of a sheer wall 3,000 feet high, upon soft green meadows and innumerable spires of the yellow pine, with the bright ribbon of the river curving through their midst. On the opposite side of the valley a fine general view is presented of the Royal Arches, North Dome, Indian Cañon, and Eagle Cliff; with Mt. Hoffmann and the dome-paved basin of Yosemite Creek in the distance. To the eastward, Cloud's Rest is seen beyond the Half

CHILNOOALUA FALLS, NEAR WAWONA. PAINTING BY THOMAS HILL.

"Amid the varied foams and fine ground mists of the mountain streams that are ever rising from a thousand water-falls, there is an affluence and variety of rainbows scarce at all known to the careworn visitor from the lowlands. Both day and night, winter and summer, this divine light may be seen wherever water is falling in spray and foam, a silent interpreter of the heart-peace of Nature, amid the wildest displays of her power."

Dome, and Mt. Starr King girdled with silver firs, the deeply sculptured peaks of the Merced Group, and the icy clustered summits about Mt. Lyell on the axis of the range, and broad swaths of forests growing on ancient moraines, while the Nevada, Vernal, and Yosemite falls, in full view, are as distinctly heard as if one were standing in their spray.

DESCENT FROM INSPIRATION POINT.
(From Painting by THOMAS HILL.)

Here the attentive observer will not fail to perceive that all this glorious landscape is new, lately brought to light from beneath the universal ice-sheet of the Glacial Period, and that the loftiest domes have been overswept by it as boulders are overswept by a flood. Hence the most resisting parts of the landscape are the highest. Every dome, ridge, and mountain in the fore and middle grounds are seen to have rounded outlines, while those of the summit peaks are sharp, the former having been *over*flowed by the heavy grinding folds of the ice-sheet, while the latter were *down*flowed, thus grinding them into sharp peaks and crests. Here you see the tributary valleys or cañons of the main Yosemite Valley branching far and wide into the fountains of perpetual ice and snow. Adown these wide polished valleys once poured the ancient glaciers that united here to form the main Yosemite Glacier that eroded the valley out of the solid, wearing its channel gradually deeper, crawling on, unhalting, unresting, throughout the countless centuries of the Ice Period.

The distant views from the summit of Sentinel Dome are still more extensive and telling, and many charming Alpine plants—phlox, telinum, eriogonæ, rock-ferns, etc.—are found there.

On the way to Little Yosemite a view of the Illilouette Fall may be obtained from its head, though it is much inferior to the view obtained at the foot of the fall by scrambling up its rocky cañon from the valley. The fall in general appearance most resembles the Nevada. Before coming to the brink of the precipice its waters are severely dashed and tossed by steps and jutting angles on the bottom and sides of its channel, therefore it is a very white and finely textured fall. When in full play it is columnar, and richly fluted from the partial division of its waters on the roughened lip of the precipice. It is not nearly so grand a fall as the Upper Yosemite, so symmetrical as the Vernal, or so nobly simple as the Bridal Veil; nor does it present so over-whelming an outgush of snowy magnificence as the Nevada, but in the richness and exquisite fineness

LOOKING UP THE VALLEY.—BRIDAL VEIL FALL, ON THE RIGHT.

"The first object to catch the eye on entering the valley is the Bridal Veil Fall, 900 feet in height,—a soft, delicate-looking thing of beauty, as seen at a distance of a mile or two, pouring its snowy folds and irised spray with the utmost gentleness, while the wind sways it from side to side like a downy cloud. But on a near approach it manifests the speed and wild ungovernable energy of an avalanche."

of texture of its flowing folds it surpasses them all. After crossing the Illilouette Valley the trail descends into the Little Yosemite near the lower end, and thence down past the Nevada and Vernal falls to the main valley. But before returning, a visit should be made through the Little Yosemite. It is about four miles long, half a mile wide, and its walls are from 1,500 to 2,500 feet in height, bold and sheer and sculptured in true Yosemite style. And, since its rocks have not been so long exposed

to post-glacial weathering, they are less blurred than those of the lower valley, large areas of the wall surfaces showing a beautiful glacial polishing that reflect the sunshine like glass.

The bottom of the valley is flat and covered with showy gardens, meadows, rose and azalia thickets, and beautiful

SUMMIT OF "THE THREE BROTHERS."

groves of silver-fir and pine; while the river, charmingly embowered, flows through the midst of them, softly gliding over smooth, shining sands in peaceful, restful beauty. At the head of the valley there is a showy cascade where the river flows over a bar of granite so moderately inclined that one may enjoy a climb close alongside the glad dancing flood, with but little danger of being washed away.

This used to be a favorite hunting ground of the Indians, where they found abundance of game, —mountain quail, grouse, deer, and the cinnamon bear,—gathered together as if inclosed in a high-walled park with gates easily guarded. But the noisy, destructive methods of tourist sportsmen have driven most of the game away.

As the river approaches the Nevada Fall after its tranquil flow through the valley levels, its channel is roughened with projecting rock-ribs and elbows, the object of which seems to be to fret the stream into foam and fit it for its grand display. And with what eager enthusiasm it accepts its fate, dashing on side angles, surging against round, bossy knobs, swirling in pot-holes, upglancing in shallow, curved basins, then bounding out over the brink and down the grand descent, more air than water, glowing like a sun-beaten cloud. Into the heart of it all any one with good nerve and good conscience may gaze from the end of a granite slab that juts out over the giddy precipice and is brushed by the flood as it bounds over the brink.

Blinding drifts of scud and spray prevent a near approach from below until autumn. Then, its thunder hushed, the fall shrinks to a whispering web of embroidery clinging to the face of the cliff, more interesting and beautiful to most observers than the passionate flood fall of spring.

The view down the cañon is one of the most wonderful about the valley,—the river, gathering its shattered waters, rushing in wild exultation down the Emerald Pool and over the Vernal Fall;

A FERNY NOOK.

the sublime walls on stupendous mass of the blocking the view in immense three-sided, 3,000 feet deep, re- roar of winds and waters, grand mill in which the ground to dust. A the head of the fall a small part of its scending a north of the fall, the Liberty Cap, cascade, and main stream below the fall. officers in charge to regard the waste water, employed an enterprising tleman to "fix the falls," building a dam across the it leaves the river, so as to tumble and sing together. done, however, by this dam provement. Mending the would seem to be about the either hand, with the Glacier Point Ridge front, forming an hopper-shaped basin sounding with the as if it were some mountains were being short distance above the river gives off waters, which, de- narrow cañon to the along the base of forms a beautiful finally joins the again a few yards Some time ago the of the valley seemed cascades as so much inasmuch as they and ingenious gen- as he said, by cascade stream where make all the water No great damage was or any other im- Yosemite water-falls last branch of in- dustry that even unsentimental Yankees seeking new outlets for enterprise would be likely to engage in. As well whitewash the storm-stained face of El Capitan or gild the domes.

The Vernal Fall is a general favorite among the visitors to the valley, doubtless because it is better seen and heard than any of the others, on account of its being more accessible. A good stairway leads up the cliffs alongside of it, and the open level plateau over the edge of which it pours, enables one to saunter in safety close to its brow and watch its falling waters as they gradually change from green to purplish gray and white, until broken into spray at the bottom. It is the most staid and orderly of all the great falls, and never shows any marked originality of form or behavior. After resting in Emerald Pool, the river glides calmly over the smooth lip of a perfectly plain and sheer precipice, and descends in a regular sheet about 80 feet wide, striking upon a rough talus with a steady, continuous roar that is but little influenced by the winds that sweep the cliffs overhead. Thus it offers in every way a striking contrast to the impetuous Nevada, which so crowds and hurries its chafed and twisted waters over the verge, which seemingly are glad to escape, as they plunge free in the air, while their deep, booming tones go sounding far out over the listening landscape.

VERNAL AND NEVADA FALLS. CAP OF LIBERTY ON LEFT. PAINTING BY THOMAS HILL.

"About a mile up the cañon from the main valley, along the margin of wild dashing rapids charmingly embowered, you come to the beautiful Vernal Fall, 400 feet in height. At the head of the fall lies the small Emerald Pool, and a mile beyond the snowy Nevada Fall is seen, which, next to the Yosemite, is the grandest of all. It is about 600 feet in height, and on account of its waters being so tossed and beaten before reaching the brink of the precipice it is intensely white; while all the way down to the head of the Vernal Fall the river forms a continuous chain of cascades and rapids, hardly less interesting to most travelers than the falls."

From the foot of the Vernal the river descends to its confluence with the Illilouette Creek in a tumultuous rush and roar of cascades, and emerges from its shadowy, boulder-choked cañon in a beautiful reach of rapids, stately spruces forming a wall on either side; while the flowering dogwood, rubus nutkanus, azalia, and tall, plumy ferns, well watered and cool, make beautiful borders. Through the open, sunny levels of the meadows it flows with a clear, foamless current, swelled by its Tenaya and Yosemite Creek tributaries, keeping calm and transparent until nearly opposite the Bridal Veil Fall, where it breaks into gray rapids in crossing a moraine dam. In taking leave of the valley, the river makes another magnificent stretch of cascades and rapids on its way down its lower cañon, a fine view of which may be had from the Coulterville road that runs across the bottom of a rough talus close alongside the massy surging flood, and past the beautiful Cascade Fall.

Climbing the great Half Dome is fine Yosemite exercise. With the exception of a few minor

RAPIDS BETWEEN THE VERNAL AND NEVADA FALLS.

spires and pinnacles, the Dome is the only rock about the valley that is strictly inaccessible without artificial means, and its inaccessibility is expressed in very severe and simple terms. But longing eyes were none the less fixed on its noble brow, until at length, in the year 1875, George Anderson, an indomitable Scotchman, succeeded in making a way to the summit. The side facing the Tenaya Cañon is an absolutely vertical precipice from the summit to a depth of about 1,600 feet, and on the opposite side it is nearly vertical for about as great a depth. The southwest side presents a very steep and finely drawn curve from the top down a thousand feet or more, while on the northeast, where it is united with the Cloud's Rest Ridge, one may easily reach the Saddle, within 700 feet of the summit, where it rises in a smooth, graceful curve a few degrees too steep for unaided climbing.

A year or two before Anderson gained the summit, John Conway, a resident of the valley, and his son, excellent mountaineers, attempted to reach the top from the Saddle by climbing barefooted up the grand curve with a rope which they fastened at irregular intervals by means of eye-bolts driven into joints of the rock. But, finding that the upper portion of the curve would require laborious drilling, they abandoned the attempt, glad to escape from the dangerous position they had reached, some 300

feet above the Saddle. Anderson began with Conway's old rope, which had been left in place, and reso-
lutely drilled his way to the top, inserting eye-bolts five to six feet apart, and making his rope fast to
each in succession, resting his feet on the last bolt while he drilled a hole for the next above. Occasionally some irregularity in the curve, or slight foothold, would enable him to climb a few feet without
the rope, which he would pass and begin drilling again, and thus the whole work was accomplished in
less than a week. Notwithstanding the enthusiastic eagerness of tourists to reach the crown of the

VERNAL FALLS.—343 FEET HIGH.

Dome, the views of the valley from
this lofty standpoint are far less
striking than from many other points
comparatively low, chiefly on account
of the foreshortening effect produced
by looking down from so great a
height. The North Dome is dwarfed
almost beyond recognition, the grand
sculpture of the Royal Arches may
not be noticed at all, and the whole
range of the walls on both sides
seem comparatively low and sunken,
especially when the valley is flooded
with noonday sunshine; while the
Dome itself, the most sublime feature
of all general views of Yosemite, is
beneath one's feet. Little Yosemite
Valley is well seen, but a better
view of it may be obtained from the
base of the Starr King Cone. The
summit landscapes, however, toward
Mounts Ritter, Lyell, and Dana, are
very effective and grand. My first
view from the top of the Dome, in
November, after the first winter snow
had fallen on the mountains, was
truly glorious. A massive cloud of
pure pearl lustre was arched across
the valley, from wall to wall, one end
resting on the grand abutment of
El Capitan, the other on Cathedral
Rock, apparently as fixed and calm
as the brown meadow and groves in
the shadow beneath it. Then, as I
stood on the tremendous verge overlooking Mirror Lake, a flock of
smaller clouds, white as snow, came
swiftly from the north, trailing over
the dark forests, and, arriving on the

brink of the valley, descended with imposing gestures through Indian Cañon and over the Arches and
North Dome. On they came with stately deliberation, nearer, nearer, gathering and massing beneath
my feet, and filling the Tenaya abyss. Then the sun shone free, painting them with rainbow colors
and making them burn on the edges with glorious brightness. It was one of those brooding, changeful
days that come just between the Indian summer and winter, when the leaf colors begin to grow dim
and the clouds come and go, moving about among the cliffs like living creatures; now hovering aloft
in the tranquil sky, now caressing rugged rock-brows with infinite gentleness, or, wandering afar over
the tops of the forests, touch the spires of fir and pine with their soft silken fringes as if telling

THE SENTINEL. PAINTING BY JULIAN RIX.

"The Sentinel Rock, three thousand feet high, stands forward in bold relief like some special monument, gracefully adorned with a beautiful cascade on either side, and fringed at base with spruce and pine . . . The yellow sunbeams falling on the ripe leaves, streaming through their countless thousands of small painted windows, makes an atmosphere of marvelous beauty over each glassy pool, the surface stirred gently in spots by bands of whirling water-beetles, or startled trout glancing from shelter to shelter beneath fallen trees or some overhanging portion of the bank."

the coming of the snow. Now and then the valley appeared all bright and cloudless, with its crystal river wavering and shimmering through meadow and grove, while to the eastward the white peaks rose in glorious array keenly outlined on the dark blue sky; then the clouds would gather again, wreathing the Dome and making a darkness like night.

On the crown of the Dome, notwithstanding its severely bare appearance, there are four clumps of pines representing three species; *Pinus albicaulis*, *P. contorta*, and *P. ponderosa*, var. *Jeffreyi*, all three repressed and storm-beaten. The alpine spiræa grows there also, and blooms freely with potentila, ivesia, erigeron, solidago, penstemon, eriogonum, and four or five species of grasses and sedges, like those of other granite summits of the same elevation.

When the all-embracing ice-mantle of the Glacial Period began to grow thin and form separate glaciers that flowed like rivers in the cañons, Half Dome was probably the first of the Yosemite rocks to emerge from the ice, burnished and glowing like a crystal. Centuries of storms have passed over it since first it came to light, but it still remains a telling monument of the glaciers that brought it into relief from the general mass of the range. Its flinty surface, scarcely at all wasted, is covered with glacial inscriptions from base to crown, and the meaning of these is the reward of all who devoutly study them.

The quick, smart visitor to the valley who buys his ticket early, determined to take the water-falls by the forelock, when their streaming manes are whitest, and when the flooded meadows are covered with mirrors, can have but dim conceptions of the beauties of the peaceful yellow

NEVADA FALLS.

autumn when these same Yosemite waters flow gently and calm in the thick golden haze of the Indian summer. The river then forms a series of pools united by gentle trickling currents that glide softly over brown pebbles and sand with scarce an audible murmur. In and out, in bay and promontory, their shore lines curve, giving to each pool the appearance of a miniature lake, with banks embossed with brier and azalea, sedge and grass; and above these, in all their glory of autumn colors, a mingled growth of alder and willow, dogwood, and balm of Gilead. Mellow sunshine over head, mellow shadows beneath flecked with dashes of free falling light; the yellow sunbeams falling on the ripe leaves, streaming through their countless thousands of small painted windows, makes an atmosphere of marvelous beauty over each glassy pool, the surface stirred gently in spots by bands of whirling water-beetles, or startled trout glancing from shelter to shelter beneath fallen trees or some overhanging portion of the bank. The falls, too, are quiet, no wind stirs, the whole valley floor is a finely blended mosaic of ripe, painted leaves, all in bloom every morning with crystals of hoar frost. Even the rocks seem strangely mellow and soft, as if they too had ripened, all their flinty strength hidden and held in abeyance.

In December comes the snow, or perhaps in November. The clouds descending clasp the mountains from base to summit. Then follows an interval of brooding stillness. Small flakes or single crystals at length appear, glinting gently in zigzags and spirals in the dull gray sky. As the storm progresses the thronging flakes darken the air, and soon the rush, and roar, and deep, muffled booming of avalanches are heard; but we try in vain to catch a glimpse of their noble currents until rifts occur in the clouds and the storm ceases. Then, standing in the middle of the valley, we may witness the descent of several of the largest size within a few minutes or hours, according to the abundance and condition of the snow on the heights. When the mass first slips on the upper slopes of the mountain a dull, rumbling sound is heard, which increases with heavy deliberation, seeming to come nearer and nearer with appalling intensity of

HEAD OF THE LITTLE YOSEMITE.

OLD CABIN NEAR REGISTER ROCK.

LADDERS ABOVE VERNAL FALLS.

tone. Presently the grand flood is seen rushing with wild, outbounding energy over some precipitous portion of its channel, long, back-trailing streamers fringing the main body of the current like the spray and whirling folds of mist about a water-fall. Now it is partly hidden behind fringes of live-oak, now in full view, leaping from bench to bench, spreading and narrowing and throwing out long fringes of rockets airily draped with convolving gossamer tissue of snow-dust.

Compared with water-falls, these snow-falls have none of the keen, kissing, clashing sounds so common in some portions of the currents of water-falls, but the loud, booming thunder-tones, the pearly whiteness of the mass, with lovely gray tones in the half shadows, the arching leaps over precipices, the narrowing in gorges, the expansions into lace-like sheets upon smooth inclines, and the final dashing into upswirling clouds of spray at the bottom are the same in both.

In winter the thin outer folds and whirling spray of the great Yosemite Fall are frozen while passing through the air freely exposed, and are deposited around the base of the fall in the form of a hollow, truncated cone, which sometimes attains a height of more than 400 feet.

In the building of this cone, part of the frozen spray falls directly to its place in the form of

minute particles like the dust of wind-beaten snow, but a considerable portion is frozen upon the face of the cliff along the edges of the fall, and attains a thickness of a foot or more during the night. When the sun strikes this ice-coating on the cliff it is cracked off in large masses and built into the walls of the cone, while in windy, frosty weather, when the fall is swayed from side to side, the whole surface is drenched, dinding the whole mass of loose blocks and dust firmly together. While in process of formation the surface is smooth, and pure white, the outlines finely drawn, the whole presenting the appearance of a beautiful crystal hill wreathed with clouds of irised spray, with the fall descending into the heart of it with a tremendous roar, as if pouring down the throat of a crater. In spring, however, while wasting and breaking up, it is strewn with leaves, pine branches, stones, sand, etc., that have been carried over the fall, making it look like a heap of wasting avalanche detritus.

After being engulphed and churned in the stormy interior of the cone, the waters of the fall issue from arched openings at the base, seemingly chafed and weary and glad to escape; while belching spray, spouted up out of the throat of the cone past the sides of the descending waters, is wafted away in irised drifts over the evergreen bushes and trees, making a most enchanting show when the sun is shining; the wet pines, warmly green, drenched with billows of rainbow-dust, waving with noble gestures, as if devoutly bowing their acknowledgments of the marvelous blessing.

During wind-storms, when the fall is blown aslant, one may look down the throat of the cone from the ledge above. The mouth is then seen to be an irregular oval about 100 and 200 feet in diameter, with heavy, uneven, forbidding lips, white and glowing in contrast with the gloomy depth of the abyss.

Once I scaled the side of the cone and held my ear close down upon it while it sounded like a huge, bellowing, exploding drum; but falling ice from the wall, and choking drifts of spray, when the wind wavered, prevented my reaching the summit.

The best general view of the fall, and the ice-cone, and their grand surroundings, may be obtained without danger from a standpoint about 200 yards from the base of the cone. On bright days in March or February, when the sunshine is streaming into the grand amphitheatre at the most favorable angle, the view from here is truly glorious. Out of the blue sky into the white

ICE CONE, FOOT OF UPPER YOSEMITE FALLS.

THE YOSEMITE FALLS. PAINTING BY C. D. ROBINSON.

"The whole fall is a majestic column of foaming, snowy water, ever wasting, ever renewed. At the top it seems to burst forth from some grand, throbbing heart of the mountain in irregular pulses, comet-like spurts succeeding one another in sublime rhythm. Now and then one mighty throb sends forth a mass into the free air far beyond the others, which rushes alone to the bottom of the fall with long, streaming tail, like combed silk illumined by the sun; while the others, descending in clusters, gradually mingle and lose their identity."

crater the vast torrent pours, irised spray rising and falling, steeping everything in rainbow colors, —gray cliffs, wet black rock, the white hill of ice, trees, brush-fringes, and the surging, roaring torrents escaping down the gorge in front, glorifying all, and proclaiming the triumph of Peace and eternal invincible Harmony.

The summit peaks of the Sierra decorated with snow-banners was the most sublime winter phenomenon I ever witnessed, far surpassing the most imposing effects of the water-falls, floods, or avalanches.

Early one winter morning I was awakened by the fall of pine-cones on the roof of my cabin. A noble storm-wind from the north filled the valley with its sea-like roar, arousing the pines to magnificent activity, swaying the most steadfast giants of them all like supple reeds, plucking off branches and plumes and strewing them on the clean smooth snow. The sky was garish white, without clouds, the strange glare being produced no doubt by fine snow-dust diffused through the air. The wild swirling and bending of the pine-trees, the dazzling light, the roar of the wind sweeping around the grand domes and headlands and eddying in many a rugged cañon and hollow, made altogether a most exciting picture; but afar on the summits of the range the storm was expressing itself in yet grander terms.

RAPIDS OF THE MERCED RIVER.

The Upper Yosemite Fall was torn into gauzy strips and blown horizontally along the face of the cliff leaving the ice-cone dry.

While making my way to the top of the overlooking ledge on the east side of it to seize so favorable an opportunity of studying the structure of the cone, the peaks of the Merced Group appeared over the shoulder of the Half Dome, each waving a resplendent banner in the blue sky, as regular in form, and as firm and fine in texture as if made of silk. Each banner was at first curved upward from the narrow point of attachment, then continued in long, drawn out, lustrous sheets for a length of at least 3,000 feet, judging from the known height of the mountains and their distances apart.

Eager to gain a general view, I pushed my way up through the snow by Indian Cañon to a commanding ridge beyond the walls, about 8,000 feet in height, where the most glorious storm-view that I had ever beheld awaited me. Every alpine peak along the axis of the range as far as the view extended had its banner, from 2,000 to 600 feet in length, streaming out horizontally, free, and unconfused, slender at the point of attachment, then widening gradually as it extended from the peak until it was a thousand to fifteen hundred feet in breadth, each waving with a visible motion in the sun glow, and clearly outlined on the dark blue sky without a single cloud to mar their simple grandeur.

The tremendous currents of the north wind were sweeping the northern curves of the mountain peaks just as the glaciers they once nourished were swept down, a supply of wind-driven, wind-ground, mealy, frosty snow being incessantly spouted upward over the peaks in a close concentrated current, owing to the peculiar sculpture of their north sides. Thus, ever-wasting, ever-renewed, these glorious banners, a mile long, waved in the gale, constant in form, and apparently as definite and substantial as a silken streamer at a mast-head.

The vast depth of the valley, and the sheerness of its walls and westerly trend, causes a great difference between the climates of the north and south sides, more so than exists between many countries hundreds of miles apart, because the south wall is constantly in shadow during the winter months, while the north is bathed in sunshine every clear day, which falls vertically or nearly so on a great portion of the bevelled rocks, making mellow spring weather on one side of the valley, while winter rules the other.

Far up the northern cliffs, even where they seem perpendicular, many a sheltered nook may be found, closely embraced by warm, sunny rock-bosses, in which flowers bloom every month of the year. Butterflies too swarm in these high winter gardens, and may be seen any day except when storms are in progress, and for a few days after they have ceased. In January, near the head of the Lower Yosemite Fall, I found the ant-lions lying in wait in their warm sand-cups, rock-ferns being unrolled, club-mosses covered with fresh growing points, the flowers of the laurel nearly open, and the honeysuckle vines abounding there were rosetted with bright, young leaves, every plant telling of the spring and tingling with vital sunshine. All the winter birds resort to the warm shelters of the north side, and make out to pass the short days in comfort, seldom suffering when the snow is deepest.

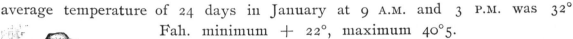

Even on the shadow side of the valley the frost is never severe. The average temperature of 24 days in January at 9 A.M. and 3 P.M. was 32° Fah. minimum + 22°, maximum 40°5.

Another specimen of January weather gave three days rainy, three cloudy, two snowy, and ten clear sunshine.

The winter birds sweeten these shadowy days with their hopeful chatter and song. They are not many, but a cheerier set never sang in snow. First and best of all is the water-ouzel, a dainty, dusky little bird about the size of a robin, that sings a sweet fluty song all winter,—all summer—in storm and calm— sunshine and shade—haunting the wild rapids and water-falls with marvelous constancy, building his nest in the cleft of a rock bathed in spray. He is not web-footed, yet he dives fearlessly into foaming rapids, seeming to take the greater delight the more boisterous the stream, cheerful and calm as any linnet in a grove. All his gestures as he flits about amid the loud uproar of the falls bespeak the utmost simplicity and confidence—bird and stream one and inseparable. What a pair, yet well related. A yet finer bloom than the foambell in eddying pool is this little bird. Like some delicate flower growing on a tree of rugged strength, the little ouzel grows on the booming stream, showing savage power changed to terms of sweetest love, plain and easily understood to human hearts. We may miss the meaning of the loud resounding torrent, but the flute-like

THE NORTH DOME.

DIFFICULT ASCENT OF THE HALF DOME.

voice of this little bird—only love is in it.   A few robins, belated on their way down from the upper meadows, linger in the valley and make out to spend the winter in comparative comfort, feeding on the mistletoe berries that grow on the oaks.   In the depths of the mountain forests, in the severest solitudes, they seem as much at home as in the old apple orchards about the busy habitations of man. They ascend the Sierra as the snow melts, following the green footsteps of Spring, until in July or August the highest glacier meadows are reached on the summit of the range.   Then, after the short summer is over, and their work in sweetening and cheering these lofty wilds is done, they gradually make their way down again in concord with the weather, keeping ahead of the snow, lingering here and there to feast on huckleberries and frost-nipped wild cherries growing on the upper slopes.   Thence down to the vineyards and orchards of the lowlands to spend the winter, and about the Bay of San Francisco, and along the coast; entering the gardens of the great towns as

RIBBON & HETCH-HETCHY-FALLS.

well as parks and fields, where the blessed wanderers are too often slaughtered for food,—surely a poor use for so fine a musical instrument : better make stove-wood of pianos to feed the kitchen fire.

The kingfisher winters in the valley, and the golden-winged woodpecker, likewise the species that lay up large stores of acorns in the bark of trees; wrens also; with a few brown and gray finches, and flocks of the arctic bluebird, which make lively pictures among the snow-laden mistle-berries.   About six species of ducks are found among the winter birds, as the river is never wholly frozen over.   Among these are the mallard and beautiful wood duck, though now less abundant than formerly on account of being so often shot at.

Flocks of wandering geese usually visit the valley in March or April, driven down by hunger, or weariness, or stress of weather while on their way across the range.   They come in by the river cañon, but oftentimes are sorely bewildered in trying to get out again.   I have frequently seen them try to fly over the walls until tired out and compelled to re-alight.   They would rise from the meadow or river, wheel around in a spiral until a height of 400 feet or thereabouts was reached, then form their ranks and fly straight toward the wall as if resolved to fly over it.   But Yosemite

"THE CASCADES."—LOOKING UP THE VALLEY WITH EL CAPITAN ON LEFT, BRIDAL VEIL ON RIGHT, IN BACK-GROUND.

"In taking leave of the valley, the river makes another magnificent stretch of cascades and rapids on its way down its lower cañon, a fine view of which may be had from the Coulterville road that runs across the bottom of a rough talus close alongside the massy, surging flood, and past the beautiful Cascade Fall."

magnitudes seem to be as deceptive to geese as to men, for they would suddenly find themselves in danger of dashing against the face of the cliff, much nearer the bottom than the top. Then turning in confusion, they would try again and again until exhausted. I have occasionally observed large flocks on their travels crossing the summits of the range at a height not less than 14,000 feet above the level of the sea, and even in so rare an atmosphere as this they seemed to be sustaining themselves without extra effort. Strong, however, as they are of wind and wing, they cannot fly over Yosemite walls, starting from the bottom.

Eagles hunt all winter along the northern cliffs and down the river cañon, and there are always plenty of owls for echoes.

Toward the end of March carex sprouts on the warmer portions of the meadows are about an inch high, the aments of the alders along the banks of the river nearly ripe, the libocedrus is sowing its pollen, willows put forth their silky catkins, and a multitude of happy insects and swelling buds proclaim the promise of spring.

KOCKS NEAR UNION POINT.

Wild strawberries are ripe in May, the early flowers are in bloom, the birds are busy in the groves, and frogs in the shallow meadow pools.

In June and July the Yosemite summer is in all its glory. It is the prime time of plant-bloom and water-bloom, and the lofty domes and battlements are then bathed in divine purple light.

August is the season of ripe nuts and berries,—raspberries, blackberries, thimbleberries, gooseberries, shadberries, black currants, puckery choke cherries, pine-nuts, etc., offering a royal feast to squirrels, bears, Indians, and birds of every feather. All the common orchard fruits as well as the cereals, grow well in the valley, and have been successfully cultivated there for many years by the old pioneer, Lamon, the first of all the Yosemite settlers who cordially and unreservedly adopted the valley as home. In the spring of 1859 he loaded an old horse with fruit-trees and a scant supply of provisions, and made his way into the valley from Mariposa, built himself a cabin beneath the shadow of the great Half Dome, cleared a fertile spot on the left bank of Tenaya Creek, and planted an orchard and garden; toiling faithfully as he was able, under hardships and discouragements not easily appreciated now that the valley has been opened to the world. His friends assured him that his trees would never bear fruit in that deep valley surrounded by snowy mountains, that he could raise nothing, sell nothing, and eventually starve. But year after year he held on undaunted, clearing and stirring the virgin soil, planting and pruning; remaining alone winter and summer with marvelous constancy. He was surprised to find the winter weather so sunful and kindly. When storms were blowing he lay snug in his cabin, pushing out now and then to keep the snow from his door and to listen to the thunder of the avalanches.

Late in the autumn, while Lamon thus lived alone, three Indians, who were hunting deer on the headwaters of the Bridal Veil Creek, killed a man by the name of Gould, who was on his way from Mono to Mariposa, and hid the body in a dense part of the forest beneath leaves and bark. The division of the spoils,—gun, blankets, and money,—brought on a quarrel, and one of the Indians confessed the murder. Lamon being the only white man known to be in the Yosemite region, it was feared that he was the victim, and two men were immediately sent into the valley to seek him. This was in January, and the appearance of the two weary messengers coming up the valley in midwinter was a grand surprise. After learning their errand, he assured his friends that nowhere else had he ever felt so safe or so happy as in his lonely Yosemite home.

After the fame of Yosemite had spread far and wide, and he had acquired sufficient means to enjoy a long afternoon of life in easy affluence, he died. He was a fine, erect, whole-souled man, more than six feet high. No stranger to hunger and weariness, he was quick to feel for others, and many there be, myself among the number, who knew his simple kindness that gained expression in a thousand small deeds. A block of Yosemite granite, chiseled and lettered, marks his grave, and some of his fruit-trees still live, but his finest monument is in the hearts of his friends. He sleeps in a beautiful spot among trees and flowers near the foot of the Yosemite Fall, and every crystal pressing on his coffin vibrates in harmony with its sublime music.

Before the Sierra was explored, Yosemite was generally regarded as a solitary, unrelated wonder. But many other valleys like it have been discovered, which occupy the same relative positions on the flank of the range, were formed

GLIMPSE OF THE YOSEMITE CHAPEL.

by the same forces in the same kind of granite, and have similar water-falls, sculpture, and vegetation. One of these, called "Hetch Hetchy" by the Indians, lies in a northwesterly direction from Yosemite, at a distance of about eighteen miles, and is easily accessible by a trail that leaves the Big Oak Flat road at Bronson Meadows, a few miles below Crane Flat.

As the Merced River flows through Yosemite, so does the Tuolumne through Hetch Hetchy. The bottom of Yosemite is about 4,000 feet above the level of the sea, the bottom of Hetch Hetchy is about 3,800 feet, and in both the walls are of gray granite, and rise precipitously from a level bottom, with but little *debris* along their bases.

Standing boldly out from the south wall, near the lower end of the valley, is the rock Kolana, considerably over 2,000 feet in height, and seeming still to bid defiance to the mighty glacier that once pressed over and around it. This is the most strikingly picturesque rock in the valley, forming the outermost of a group that corresponds with the Cathedral group of Yosemite. Facing Kolana, on the opposite side of the valley, there is a rock 1,800 feet in height which presents a sheer massive front like El Capitan, and over its brow flows a stream that makes, without exception, the most graceful fall I have ever seen. Tuccoolala it is called by the Indians. From the brow of the cliff it leaps clear and free for a thousand feet, then breaks up into a ragged foaming sheet of cascades among the boulders of an earthquake talus. Toward the end of summer it shrinks and vanishes, since its fountain streams do not reach back to the lasting snows of the summits.

When I last saw it in June, 1872, it was indescribably beautiful. The only fall that I know of with which it may fairly be compared is the Yosemite Bridal Veil, but it excels even that fall in floating, swaying gracefulness, and tender repose. For if we attentively observe the Bridal

Veil, even toward the end of summer, when the wind blows aside the finer outer folds of spray, dense, comet-shaped masses may be seen shooting with tremendous energy, revealing the stern fixedness of purpose with which its waters seek the new world below. But from the top of the cliff all the way down, the snowy form of the Hetch Hetchy veil is in perfect repose, like a plume of white cloud becalmed in the depths of the sky. Moreover, the Bridal Veil inhabits a shadow-haunted recess, inaccessible to the main wind-currents of the valley, and has to depend for its principal wind gestures upon broken waves and whirlpools of air that oftentimes compel it to rock and bend in a somewhat fitful, teasing manner; but the Hetch Hetchy Veil, floating free in the open valley, is ever ready to offer graceful compliance to the demands calm or storm. Looking across the calm day about the beginning of June, ingly glorious The Hetch Hetchy rising out of a dense growth of shining with sun-gold from its green grovy the blue air. At intervals along its venturesome pines are seen looking and before its sunny face, immediately

"KOLANA ROCK."
ON SOUTH SIDE HETCH HETCHY VALLEY.

and suggestions of valley, on a bright, the view is surpass-El Capitan is seen live oaks, glowing base to its brow in dizzy edge a few wistfully outward, in front of you,

Tuccoolala waves her silvery scarf, gloriously embroidered, and burning with white sun-fire in every fibre. In approaching the brink of the precipice her waters flow fast but confidingly, and at their first arching leap into the air a little eagerness appears, but this eagerness is speedily hushed in divine repose, and their tranquil progress to the base of the cliff is like that of downy feathers in a still room. The various tissues into which her waters are woven, now that they are illumined by the streaming sunshine, are brought out with marvelous distinctness. They sift and float down the face of that grand gray rock in so leisurely and unconfused a manner, and with such exquisite gentleness, that you may examine their texture and patterns as you would a piece of embroidery held in the hand. Near the bottom the width of the fall has increased from 25 to about 100 feet. Here it is composed of yet finer tissue, more air than water, yet still without a trace of disorder. Air, water, and sunlight are woven into a cloth that spirits might wear.

On the same side of the valley thunders the great Hetch Hetchy Fall, called Wapama by the Indians. It is about 1,800 feet high, and is so near Tuccoolala that both are in full view from one standpoint. Seen immediately in front it appears nearly vertical, but viewed in profile from farther up the valley it is seen to be considerably inclined. Its location is similar to that of the Yosemite Fall, but its volume of water is much greater.

No two falls could be more unlike to make one perfect whole, like rock and cloud, sea and shore. Tuccoolala speaks low, like a summer breeze in the pines; Wapama, in downright thunder, descending with the weight and energy of an avalanche in its deep rocky gorge. Tuccoolala whispers, He dwells in peace; Wapama is the thunder of His chariot wheels in power.

This noble pair are the principal falls of the valley. A few other small streams come over the walls with bird-like song, leaping from crag to crag too small to be much noticed in company so imposing, though essential to the

INDIAN CACHE.

Upper End of Hetch-Hetchy Valley. From Drawing by Harry Fenn.

"Before the Sierra was explored, Yosemite was generally regarded as a solitary, unrelated wonder. But many other valleys like it have been discovered, which occupy the same relative positions on the flank of the range, were formed by the same forces in the same kind of granite, and have similar waterfalls, sculpture and vegetation. One of these, called "Hetch-Hetchy" by the Indians, lies in a northwesterly direction from Yosemite, at a distance of about eighteen miles, and is easily accessible by a trail that leaves the Big Oak Flat at Bronson Meadows, a few miles below Crane Flat."

grand, general harmony. That portion of the north wall immediately above Wapama corresponds both in outline and details of sculpture with the same relative portion of the Yosemite wall. In Yosemite the steep face of the cliff is terraced with two conspicuous benches fringed with live-oak. Two benches, similarly situated, and fringed in the same way, occur on the same relative portion of the Hetch Hetchy wall, and on no other.

The floor of the valley is about three miles long, and from a fourth to half a mile wide. The lower portion is mostly level meadow, with the trees confined to the sides, and separated partially from the sandy, park-like upper portion by a low bar of glacier-polished granite, across which the river breaks in swift-gliding rapids. The principal tree of the valley is the great yellow-pine, attaining here a height of 200 feet. They occupy the dry sandy levels, growing well apart in small groves or singly, thus allowing each tree to be seen in all its beauty. The common pteris grows beneath them

INDIAN WIGWAMS, YOSEMITE VALLEY.

in rough green sheets, tufted here and there by ceanothus and manzanita, and brightened with mariposa tulips and golden-rods. Near the walls, on the earthquake taluses that occur in many places, the pines give place to the mountain live-oak, which forms the shadiest and most extensive groves of the valley. Their glossy foliage, densely crowded at the top, forms a beautiful ceiling, containing only a few irregular openings for the admission of sunbeams, while the bare gray trunks and branches, gnarled and twisted, are exceedingly picturesque. This sturdy oak, so well calculated for a mountaineer, not only covers the angular boulder slopes, but climbs along fissures, and up steep side-cañons, to the top of the walls and far beyond, dwarfing as it goes from a tree 30 to 40 feet high and 4 to 6 feet in diameter near the ground to a small shrub no thicker than one's finger.

The sugar-pine, sabine-pine, and two-leafed pine, also the Douglass spruce, incense-cedar, and the two silver-firs, grow here and there in the cool side-cañons and scattered among the yellow-pines, while on the warmest spots fine groves of the black-oak occur, whose acorns form so important a part of the food of Indians and bears. Bees and humming-birds find rich pasturage among the flowers,—mints, clover, honeysuckle, lilies, orchids, etc.

MIRROR LAKE, LOOKING UP TENAYA CAÑON—MOUNT WATKINS ON THE LEFT. PAINTING BY THOMAS HILL.

"Half a mile beyond Washington Column you come to Mirror Lake, lying imbedded in beautiful trees at the foot of Half Dome. A mile beyond the lake the picturesque Tenaya Fall is seen gleaming through the rich leafy forest that fills this portion of the cañon, and to the left of the Fall are the Dome Cascades, about a thousand feet in height, filling the cañon with their deep booming roar. Just above the Tenaya Fall, on the left side, rises the grand projecting mass of Mount Watkins, with a sheer front of solid granite like El Capitan, and on the right the lofty wave-like ridge of Cloud's Rest, a mile in height."

THE HETCH HETCHY FALLS.

On a stream that comes in from the northeast at the head of the valley there is a series of charming cascades that give glad animation to the glorious wilderness, broad plumes like that between the Vernal and Nevada of Yosemite, half sliding, half leaping down smooth open folds of the granite, covered with crisp, clashing spray, into which the sunbeams pour with glorious effect. Others shoot edgewise through a deep narrow gorge, chafing and laving beneath rainbow mists in endless variety of form and tone.

Following the river from the head of the valley, you enter the great Tuolumne Cañon. It is 20 miles long, 2,000 to 4,000 feet deep, and may be regarded as a Yosemite Valley from end to end, abounding in glorious cascades, falls, and rocks of sublime architecture. To the lover of pure wildness, a saunter up this mountain street is a grand indulgence, however rough the sidewalks and pavements which extend along the cool, rushing river.

The new King's River Yosemite is larger, and in some respects more interesting, than either the Hetch Hetchy or the Yosemite of the Merced. It is situated on the south fork of King's River, about 80 miles from Yosemite in a straight line, and 40 miles from Visalia, the nearest point on the Southern Pacific railroad. It is about nine miles long, half a mile wide at the bottom, and 5,000 feet above the level of the sea. The walls are quite as precipitous as those of Yosemite, 3,000 to 4,000 feet high, and sculptured in the same grand style so characteristic of all the valleys of this kind in the Sierra. As to water-falls, those of the new Yosemite are less striking in form and in the songs they sing, although the whole quantity of water pouring into the valley is greater, and comes from higher sources. The descent of the King's Valley waters is made mostly in long, dashing cascades, and falls of moderate height, that are far less showy in general views than those of Yosemite.

My last visit to this magnificent valley was made with a small party in July, 1875, when the beauty of its wildness was still complete. We set out from Yosemite, pushing our way through the wilderness, past Clark's Station, through the Mariposa grove of big trees, and the luxuriant forests of upper Fresno, down to the dappled plain of the San Joaquin. Thence, skirting the margin of the foot-hills, we crossed the stately current of King's River near Centreville, and facing eastward, climbed again into the sugar-pine woods, and on through the grand Sequoia forests of the Kahweah. Here we heard the sound of axes, and soon came upon a group of men busily engaged in preparing a section of one of the big trees they had felled for the Centennial Exhibition. This tree was 25 feet in diameter at the base, and so fine was the taper of the trunk it still measured 10 feet in diameter at a height of 200 feet from the ground. According to the testimony of the annual wood-rings, it was upwards of 2,000 years of age.

Out of this solemn ancient forest we climbed yet higher into the cool realms of the Alpine pines, until at length we caught a long sweeping view of the glorious Yosemite we were so eagerly seeking. The trail by which we descended to the bottom of the valley enters at the lower or west end, zigzaging in a wild, independent fashion over the south lip of the valley, and corresponding both in position and direction with the old Mariposa trail of Yosemite, and like it, affording a series of grand views up the valley, over the groves and meadows between the massive granite walls. So fully were these views Yosemitic in all their leading features it was hard to realize that we were not entering the old Yosemite by Inspiration Point.

In about two hours after beginning the descent we found ourselves among the sugar-pine groves at the lower end of the valley; and never did pines seem more noble and religious in gesture and tone.

NORTH DOME, KING'S RIVER.

FALL KING'S RIVER CAÑON.

SENTINEL ROCK OR HALF DOME, SOUTH FORK, KING'S RIVER.

The sun, pouring down mellow gold, seemed to be shining only for them, and the wind gave them voice; but the gestures of their outstretched arms appeared wholly independent of the wind, and impressed one with a solemn awe that overbore all our knowledge of causes, and brought us into the condition of beings newly arrived from some other world. The ground was strewn with leaves and cones, making a fine surface for shadows; many a wide even bar from tapering trunk and column, and rich mosaic from leaf and branch; while ever and anon we came to small forest openings wholly filled with sunshine like lakes of light.

We made our first camp on the river bank, a mile or two up the valley, on the margin of a small circular meadow that was one of the most perfect flower gardens I have ever discovered in the Sierra. The trampling mules, whom I would gladly have kept out, fairly disappeared beneath the broad over-arching ferns that encircled it. The meadow was filled with lilies and orchids, larkspurs and columbines, daisies and asters and sun-loving golden-rods, violets and roses and purple geraniums, with a hundred others in prime of bloom, but whose names few would care to read, though all would enjoy their fresh, wild beauty. One of the lilies that I measured was six feet long, and had eleven open flowers, five of them in their prime. The wind rocked this splendid panicle above the heads of the geraniums and brier-roses, forming a spectacle of pure beauty, exquisitely poised and harmonized in all its parts. It was as if Nature had fingered every leaf and petal that very day, readjusting every curving line and touching the colors of every corolla; and so she had, for not a leaf was misbent, and every plant was so placed with reference to every other, that the whole garden had seemingly been arranged like one tasteful bouquet. Here we lived a fine, unmeasured hour, considering the lilies, every individual flower radiating beauty as real and appreciable as sunbeams. Many other wild gardens occur along the river bank, and in many a cool side dell where streams enter, but neither at this time nor on my first visit to the valley were any discovered so perfect as this one. Toward the upper end of the valley there is quite an extensive meadow stretching across from wall to wall. The river borders are made up chiefly of alder, poplar, and willow, with pines and silver-fir where the banks are dry, and the common fringe of underbrush and flowers, all combined with reference to the best beauty and the wants of the broad crystal river.

The first two miles of the walls, beginning at the lower end of the valley, are beveled off at the top, and are so broken and soil-besprinkled that they support quite a growth of trees and shaggy bushes; but farther up, the granite speedily assumes Yosemitic forms and dimensions, rising in stupendous cliffs, abrupt and sheer, from the level flats and meadows. On the north wall there is a rock like the El Capitan, and just above it a group like the Three Brothers. Further up, on the same side, there is an Indian cañon, and North Dome, and Washington Column. On the south wall counterparts of the Cathedral and Sentinel Rocks occur in regular order, bearing the same relations to each other that they do in the old

up the valley was perfectly en-
the river presenting reaches of
sunbeams streaming through the
in broad masses upon white rapids
Here and there a dead pine, that
flood-time, reached out over the

GRANITE TUSKS.

FALL.—SOUTH FORK, KING'S RIVER.

GLACIAL AMPHITHEATRE.

Yosemite. Our journey chanting, every bend of surpassing beauty, the border groves, or falling or deep, calm pools. had been swept down in current, its mosses and lichens contrasting with the crystal sheen of the water, and its gnarled roots forming shadowy caves for speckled trout, where the current eddies slowly, and protecting sedges and willows dip their leaves. Amid these varied and everchanging river views the appreciative artist may find studies for a lifetime. The deeply sculptured walls presented more and more exciting views, calling forth enthusiastic admiration. Bold, sheer brows, standing forth in a full blaze of light; deep, shadow-filled side-cañons and gorges, inhabited by wild cascades, groups of gothic gables, glacier-polished domes coming in sight in everchanging combinations and with different foregrounds. Yet no rock in the valley equals El Capitan, or the great Half Dome; but, on the other hand, from no part of the Yosemite walls could a section five miles in length be selected equal in beauty and grandeur to five miles of the middle portion of the south wall of the new valley.

We camped for the night at the base of the new Washington Column, where ferns and lilies reached to our heads, the lavish exuberance of the vegetation about us contrasting with the bare, massive fronts of the walls. The summer day died in purple and gold, and we lay watching the fading

WINTER IN YOSEMITE VALLEY. PAINTING BY JULIAN RIX.

"In December comes the snow, or perhaps in November. The clouds descending clasp the mountains from base to summit. Then follows an interval of brooding stillness. Small flakes or single crystals at length appear, glinting gently in zigzags and spirals in the dull gray sky. As the storm progresses the thronging flakes darken the air, and soon the rush and roar and deep muffled booming of avalanches are heard; but we try in vain to catch a glimpse of their noble currents until rifts occur in the clouds and the storm ceases."

sunshine and growing shadows among the heights.   Each member of the party made his own bed,
like birds building nests.   Mine was made of overlapping fern fronds, with a few mint spikes in the
pillow, combining luxurious softness and fragrance, and making the down beds of palaces and palace
hotels seem poor and vulgar.

The full moon rose just after the night darkness was fairly established.   Down the valley one
rock after another caught the silvery glow, and stood out from the dusky shadows in long, imposing
ranks like weird spirits, while the thickets and groves along the river were masses of solid darkness.
The sky bloomed with stars like a meadow with flowers.   It was too surpassingly beautiful a night
for sleep, and we gazed long into the heart of the solemn, silent grandeur ere the weariness of enjoyment closed our eyes.

Next morning we continued on up the valley in the sunshine, following the north bank of the

CASCADES HEAD OF LITTLE YOSEMITE.

valley to where it forks at the head.   The glacier-polished rocks glowed in the slant sunbeams in many
places as if made of burnished metal.   All the glacial phenomena of the new valley,—the polished
surfaces, *roches moutonees*, and moraines are fresher, and therefore less changed, than those of the old.
It is evidently a somewhat younger valley, a fact easily explained by its relations to the fountains of
the ancient glaciers lying above it among the loftiest summits of the range.   Like the old valley, this
is a favorite resort of Indians because it produces acorns, and its waters abound in trout.   They,
doubtless, have names for all the principal rocks and cascades, and many grotesque and ornamental
legends relating to them, though as yet I have not learned any of them.

This valley is already beginning to attract tourists from all parts of the world, and its fame may
yet equal that of the old.   It is quite accessible, the greater part of the distance from the railroad being
by a good wagon-road, and all the necessary supplies may be obtained at Visalia.   A good mountain trail
conducts out of the valley at the head along the edge of the cascading river, and across the range by
the Kearsarge Pass to Owens Valley, which we followed, and reached Independence on the east side of
the Sierra in two days.   From here we set out for the summit of Mt. Whitney.   Then turning north-

ward, we skirted the eastern flank of the range until we reached the Mono region. Thence crossing the range by the Bloody Cañon Pass, we entered the Yosemite Valley from above. Thus through the grand old forests, from mountain to mountain, from Yosemite to Yosemite we drifted free, making a round trip without wheels or tickets, that for grandeur and general interest can not be surpassed in all the Sierra, or perhaps in any other mountain range in the world.

JOHN MUIR.

SNOW BANNERS.

TOTOKONULA: A LEGEND OF YOSEMITE.

BY J. VANCE CHENEY.

Secure in native stronghold of the rock,
Commanding all his great untamable realm,
There sat, no pale-face on his tinsel throne
Could give and take with young Totokonula,
The idol chieftain. Invincible, sooth, he was
Until the day he met the spirit-maid,
Fair, matchless Tisayac, guardian of the vale.
Bright with infinitesimal jewels sprayed
From the long torrent-fall of golden hair,
Her wings like moonlit clouds in the still heavens,
The spirit—so the wild birds light to rest—
Paused on the granite dome. True to his tribe,
The young chief scorned his passion, stout willed back
The rebel blood ; but who did ever win
With love against him ? Both those iron arms
At last would clasp the spirit—vain the reach,
Vain, now, their knotted thews ; swiftly from sight
The vision soared, the jewelled mist was gone,
And pale daylight, like a wind-lifted shroud,
Shivered, and closed upon the ghostly dome.

No longer young Totokonula led
The chase, no longer strode the growing field :
His sole hope fixed upon the spirit-maid,
Forsaking home and tribe, he went his way.
Ere long, lost Tisayac once more sought the vale,
And looked upon it from the massive dome
Of granite. The land, missing the master's care,
Lay parched with drought : its gardens ran to waste ;
Wild beasts made their lairs there, and reared their young.
The gentle guardian, grieving sorely, prayed
To the Great Spirit : lo, the dome was rent
From base to summit—split in gaping halves,
And through its parted heart poured melting snows
From cisterns of the inexhaustible hills.
The gracious waters flowed, and soon the song
Of birds was heard ; again the clean grass sprang,
The trees put forth, the wayside blossoms woke,
While fields grew green with spears of finer grains,

And sunward shot tall stalks of glossy corn.
The spirit passed—unseen, but not unknown ;
When, with loud acclamation of the tribe,
They gave the dome her all-adored name.

By fruitless quest outworn, the chief returned.
" If somewhat of the olden love remain,"
He said, " I may again my people serve,
Biding at home, contented."

But when he looked
On the cloven dome, and heard the people's praise
Of her that saved the vale, once more his soul
Was like a fire within him, and anew
He took his wanderer's way ; this time to win
The spirit or to die. Forthwith he passed,
But, first, with his huge hunting-knife he graved
The lineaments of his face in the rock above
The valley gate ; so faithfully he wrought,
The tribe must see his sorrow there, forgive,
And think on him with pity. Nevermore,
The legend runs, did young Totokonula
Or lead the chase or stride the growing field ;
No more his people saw him, though they looked
Up to the rock with longing, and forgave
And wished him back.

Season to season, suns
And snows of many years have stained the walls
Of wild Yosemite ; water and wind
Have warred, the battle-bolts of heaven dashed hot
Against them—they are there ! The native tribes
Are scattered, vanquished, lost ; but oft, at night,
When the round moon is up, and stars are large,
And winds are still, dusk forms in fancy pass
From crag to crag, pointing with steadfast finger,
All with the same defiant gesture saying,—
" The white man's foot is on the red man's grave,
Yet yonder dome is white-winged Tisayac still ;
And that sad face turned toward her, at the gate,
Is her young lover's—Chief Totokonula."

FALLS IN ALUM ROCK PARK. FROM ETCHING BY GEO. SPIEL.

"The Alum Rock Road, seven miles long, lined with eucalyptus and cedar, leads by gradual ascent to the suburban park of four hundred acres, lying in a deep cañon and affording a rare succession of views of mountain and valley. There are mineral springs of soda and sulphur, famous for their efficacy in many complaints, and here is a gorge that seems to have been formed by the rending asunder of the great mountain by some volcanic outburst."

ON THE ROAD TO THE LICK OBSERVATORY.

A VISIT TO THE LICK OBSERVATORY.

BY EDWARD S. HOLDEN, LL. D.

President of the University of California and Director of the Lick Observatory.

IF we have a day to spare for a visit to the great Observatory on Mt. Hamilton, we should start from San José as early as nine o'clock in the morning. The stage leaves even earlier, to avoid the heat of the middle of the day. The first four miles of the drive is along a perfectly straight, nearly level avenue, bordered by sturdy pine trees, and passing between level, fertile fields. Suddenly we come to the end of this avenue and have our choice of ways. To the left hand (north) a pretty road leads up through a cañon to the Alum Rock Springs; while another breaks sharp off to the right along the face of the foot-hills which begin here. We choose the latter way, which leads to Mt. Hamilton along one of the finest mountain roads in the whole country. When Mr. Lick selected the site of his Observatory he made it a condition that Santa Clara county should construct the best mountain road in California to the summit. The county gladly accepted this condition and has built twenty-six miles of capital roadway, at a cost of $78,000, from San José to the Observatory. The steepest grade is six and one-half feet in the hundred, or about three hundred and forty-three in the mile. Most of the road is materially less steep than this, and a smart team can easily trot all the way without a break.

Almost immediately after commencing the ascent of the foot-hills, we begin a series of turnings

SHARP TURNS IN THE MOUNTAIN ROAD.

A REST.—ASCENT OF MT. HAMILTON.

LOVELT ROCK.—MT. HAMILTON ROAD.

and twistings, in and out of ravines and along the face of
the hills.　Every turn gives a new view of the exquisite
valley of Santa Clara which lies on our right.　It is
full of squared plats of cultivation relieved against the
yellow wheat fields, which again are dotted over with
the beautiful green of the California live-oak.　This is
the typical landscape of California—brown hills and

GENERAL VIEW OF THE LICK OBSERVATORY.—SUMMIT OF MT. HAMILTON.

yellow fields, with evergreen oaks—and nowhere else in the state is it seen in such beauty. By and by the vineyards will begin to encroach on the brown hills and make a fringe of cool green in the hot sunshine. Our road stretches on and on, with its constant ascent, until we are near the crest of the first line of foot-hills. Here someone with an eye for beauty has built a little inn and called it Grand View. It is worth our while to alight for a moment, while the horses are being watered, and turn our eyes once more towards the valley and the Santa Cruz mountains beyond it.

The sloughs at the end of San Francisco Bay are shining in the sun amid their borders of green tulés. We are already high enough (1,500 feet) to get something like a birdseye view of San José and its lovely valley. Towards the west and south is the Santa Cruz range, hiding the Pacific from us. Yonder goes the narrow-gauge railway, making straight for the hills, apparently, but really finding its sure but tortuous way up the valley of Los Gatos creek, between high summits. You cannot mistake the dome of Loma Priéta (Black Mountain), some thirty miles away and 3790 feet high.

Next, to the north, is Mt. Choual, 3,500 feet high, and then Mt. Thayer, 3,550 feet. From thence towards the north the crests are lower for a long stretch until the Sierra Morena (from 2,500 to 2,800 feet high) is reached.

But it is time that we should be off and climb a still higher divide that separates us from a small interior basin beyond, known as Hall's Valley. The road continues its windings and twistings, first in ascent until the divide is reached (1,750 feet above San José), and then in descent into the valley itself, (1,455 feet above the city). Here we take a wide sweep among magnificent trees and level fields and then begin once more climbing towards a second divide. When this is reached the scenery grows wilder and rougher, and from the turns of the road we see the glittering domes of the Observatory on the summit of Mt. Hamilton itself. We drive rapidly down the road built on the south wall of the cañon and see far below us a shining thread of water. In a moment we are at the Smith's-Creek Hotel, which stands in a little square of buildings and inclosures.   This is the nearest hotel to the summit.   We are 2,058 feet above San José and still 2,152 feet below the summit itself.   There is a group of loungers enjoying a kind of *dolce far niente*, and perhaps among them you may see old Grizzly Bill, the bear hunter, whose blind staring eye mark some terrific encounter of which he will tell you by hours together.   Bear hunters, bears, pioneers of the days before '49, veterans of the Mexican War—all these will soon be gone.   Grizzly Bill is one of the last survivors and a local celebrity.

We cross a pretty bridge with a sharp turn to the left and begin the final ascent.   We have seven miles to go, which will take us the 2,000 feet upward.   The way is all ascent now, and with more twisting and winding than before.   It is said, on the authority of some statistical tourist, that there are 365 turns in the road in these last seven miles.   It is an easy number to remember—365; and I am not disposed to doubt it, or to count the turns.   At all events the road is crooked enough, but always singularly beautiful.   The illustrations which accompany this chapter give an excellent idea of the country;   particularly that on page 94, showing the panoramic view "round about the Observatory."

It is by no means bleak and desolate, the fine trees relieving the landscape and making it gracious.   From an elevated point of view the expanse of country below gets wider and wider at each turn, and when Cape Horn is reached and you can see miles and miles away, across the ridges and valley, you begin to lose the sense of the everyday world and to feel the true spirit of the hills.   We plod on and on, passing the level "flat" ("flats" are not always flat, by any means) where stand the kilns which furnished the 3,000,000 and more of brick required for the Observatory buildings, and finally arrive just below the great dome of the Observatory itself.   We are passing around the flanks of Mt. Ptolemy, fittingly named after the great astronomer of Greece.

Another turn or two, and we emerge

FOG.—LOOKING NORTHWARD FROM OBSERVATORY.

DOME OF THE GREAT TELESCOPE.

on the flat below the Observatory, among neat, low cottages, the dwellings of the astronomers and of the mechanics of the establishment. The driver is caring for his horses; let us get out and look about for a moment.   Recollect that only a few years ago not even a trail led over these hills and mountains.   The nearest house was eleven miles away.   The bandit Joaquin Murietta had his cabin near here on the Observatory lands, a mile or so distant. Now all is peace, order and comfort immediately around us, and beauty, grandeur, strength, power are on the faces of the hills.   But we will see that afterwards.   We came here to see the greatest Observatory in the world.   Let us climb these stairs on to the level summit,

THE ALAMEDA—SAN JOSE TO SANTA CLARA. FROM PAINTING BY VICTOR PERARD.

"The two towns, San Jose and Santa Clara, are practically one, being united by the magnificent avenue known as "The Alameda," which is lined with residences throughout its entire length of two miles. Here on any pleasant day one may see a constant procession of turnouts of every variety, well illustrating the social life that springs from wealth and leisure."

where the Observatory buildings are, just above us.   The routine of the establishment requires that we should go first to the Visitors' Room and register our names among those of hundreds of other pilgrims.   Here we can find water to remove the dust from our faces.   A guide is ready to take us about the building.   What do we wish to see first?   The great telescope, of course; it is the greatest telescope in the world, and it is the most favorably situated.   It is the final arbiter on astronomical questions.

There is no quicker way of indicating the importance of this gigantic instrument than by giving a few statistics of the telescopes of the world.   Sixty years ago a five-inch telescope was the most powerful refractor in existence.   About 1830, there were several nine-inch object glasses made, and ten years later two fifteen-inch telescopes were constructed, one for St. Petersburg and the other for Harvard College, which long remained the largest in the world.   In 1861, the Clarks of Boston made

SAN JOSÉ, FROM DOME OF COURT HOUSE.

an eighteen-inch instrument which is now in Illinois.   A twenty-five-inch was made in England about 1870.   Two twenty-six-inch objectives were made by the Clarks in 1873, one for Washington, and one for the University of Virginia.   Then came a twenty-seven-inch for Vienna, a thirty-inch (by the Clarks) for St. Petersburg; one of the same size for Nice; and finally the thirty-six-inch for Mt. Hamilton.   This is the *ne plus ultra*.

The telescope is sixty feet long, the tube alone weighs four tons, and yet it is handled as easily as a spy-glass.   Everything is balanced to a hair, and all conveniences for observation are provided.   The astronomer sits before the instrument in a high chair, and looks out through the opening in the dome.   The floor itself moves up and down like an elevator.   That iron column which supports the tube is thirty-seven feet high.   In a few moments a photographic object-glass can be attached to the front of the other objective and photographs can be had of all the stars which before were visible.

You must pause a moment to remember that all this grand establishment is the gift of JAMES LICK, a private citizen of California, to his adopted state.   He is buried in the base of

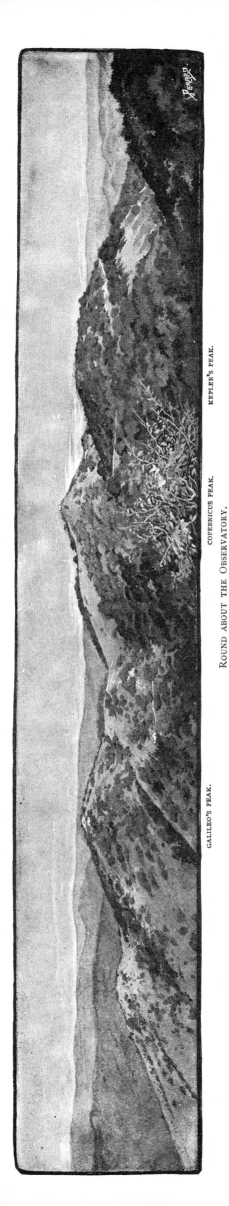

GALILEO'S PEAK.   ROUND ABOUT THE OBSERVATORY.   COPERNICUS PEAK.   KEPLER'S PEAK.

the great pier, and has such a tomb as no old-world monarch could have commanded or imagined.

But it is time to leave this instrument and to see the remaining rooms. Here is a library of mathematical and astronomical books. The astronomers must know what has already been done before they can add to knowledge. Study-rooms for the computers, instrument-rooms, clock-rooms, etc., are joined to the large dome. These stairs lead up to the dome for the twelve-inch equatorial, itself a noble instrument. Those separate houses yonder cover the Transit Instrument and the Meridian Circle. The brick houses near them are the private dwellings of the astronomers.

Let us go upon the roof of the building and see just where we are among these ranges of noble hills. First look to the west. There is San José in its valley and the Santa Cruz hills beyond. The bay of San Francisco shines in the strong light like pieces of a child's dissecting-map. There is Tamalpais (2,600 feet high, sixty-six miles away), which dominates the Golden Gate (of San Francisco). The deep cañon of Smith's Creek winds between us and the mountains which are ten and twelve miles distant. Counting from west towards north, they bear the names of Mts. Story, Lewis and Day. Between Story and Lewis rises the beautiful cone of *Monte Diablo*, 3,849 feet high, and more than thirty-nine miles distant. From thence towards the north there are no high mountains till we come to the near peak just across that profound cañon (Cañon Negro) below the Observatory hill. That is Mt. Galileo. The water supply of the Observatory is caught in the reservoir on its flank. Just beyond and above it, to the north east, is Mt. Copernicus, with a reservoir on its summit. The next peak with a reservoir is Kepler. Between Kepler and Copernicus is a high peak, not far off, called Hiparchus, after the father of Astronomy. Here is Mt. Huyghens near us, with a third reservoir and a wind-mill on its summit. We are now looking eastward across a deep cañon and towards a grand mountain mass, black with chaparral. This is Mt. Santa Isabel, so named by the Spaniards.

Mt. Hamilton (Observatory Peak) is 4,209 feet above the sea. Kepler is 4,257 feet and Copernicus, the loftiest of all, is 4,380 feet high. There is nothing above us within the range of vision save the summits of the Sierras, which you can just see on the eastern horizon, one hundred miles away. We look over the rugged San Anton Valley between Kepler and Isabel, across divide after divide, to Mt. Oso, eighteen miles away and 3,363 feet high, and to the ragged crests near it. To the south of Isabel and nearly in a line with it, are the Pachecho Peaks, Mariposa and Santa Aña. They are more than thirty miles away, and 2,845, 3,800 and 3,580 feet high respectively. Almost due south of us is Mt. Toro, fifty-five miles distant, 3,500 feet high, a very symmetrical land-mark; also Murphy's Peak, six miles off and perhaps 2,000 feet high. Look carefully near here and you may see the shining waters of Monterey Bay. Sweeping a little further towards the west we come again to Loma Priéta and Choual. Between Choual and Tamalpais we may see the ocean again in three different places. With a telescope, ships have been seen sailing off for distant ports. That shining edge of the sea horizon is eighty seven miles from us.

We have swept round the whole horizon now, and made ourselves acquainted with our neighbors. We are above countless smaller peaks, and look! far below there is an eagle circling round. He is high above the ground, and yet we are looking down almost on his broad back 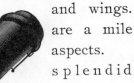 and wings. Let us use what remains of our time in walks to the near summits. They are a mile or so off, and from them we may see the now familiar scenes in new aspects.

Nothing could add to the beauty of this landscape except splendid cloud-effects. But there are no clouds. That is why the Obser-vatory was placed here. If we were here in the early morning we might see the fog lying in the valleys far below the summit. We must save an hour and a half of

THE GREAT TELESCOPE.

daylight for the drive down to the Smith's Creek Hotel. There is no hotel on the summit, and no one remains there at night save the astronomers who are minding the heavens. From below we may see their lamps shining like little stars all through the night, till daylight comes again and they go to their rest after a night of congenial toil. Every Saturday evening from seven to ten the great telescope is used to show the planets, the moon, and the brighter stars to visitors; but at ten o'clock it is closed and the work of the establishment begins again, to terminate with the next sunrise.

The drive down the mountain is, if any-thing, more interesting than the ascent. The pace is quicker and more exhilarating; the land-scape has grown more familiar and we discover new beauties; the long shadows bring out the contours of the hills; and we feel that we have been in the presence of a great and unique thing. Man has mastered this wilderness and has set a beacon here which shall shine for centuries

THE MERIDIAN INSTRUMENT.

"A Good Day for Mallards."

A bit of marsh near the old home of James Lick, in the Santa Clara Valley, and almost in sight of the house, furnished the subject of the above picture. Speaking of the home of the bachelor philanthropist, the strangeness of the place is worthy of mention. The "Old Curiosity Shop" would be an appropriate name for it. The house and grounds were in keeping with the barn, the inside of which was of polished mahogany. The fish ponds, swarming with strange aquatic birds, were hidden by a dense growth of weeping willows, which intensified the general gloom of the place.—Thomas Hill.

with the beneficent light of science. To our young country we have brought the aged science of the Chaldeans, and have ministered to it with the newest Arts. We have made for it a temple the like of which never was seen before.

The Lick Observatory has already passed out of its preliminary stage. It has ceased to be a museum of instruments and apparatus and has begun to be a busy laboratory where the inner secrets of the sky are studied. Our brief experience has proved to us that the position of the observatory is unique. We are bound to do our equal share in the work of such establishments, but we already see that the possession of the greatest of telescopes brings with it an immense responsibility. We find that each object looked at, no matter how familiar it may have been to us when observed through less powerful instruments, yields some new information if it is examined with a free and open mind. We are bound to prove all things, and at the same time to remember all things that have gone before. Every object must be examined as if for the first time, and yet we must bring to our scrutiny all the acquired knowledge of the great observers of past days. If we do not do both of these things we shall lose golden opportunities and fall below the standard which is set for us by our fortunate circumstances.

The observations already made with the large telescope in the few weeks that have elapsed since its installation have abundantly proved to us that there is nothing that we may not expect from it. The most difficult double-stars known to science have already been discovered here in the very regions most favorably situated for observation by other great telescopes of the world. Our examinations of the planets which have thus far been viewed, have resulted in important modifications of the conclusions reached by other competent observers with less admirable telescopes at their command. In the world of nebulæ we have already seen that there must be added to the hitherto known classes or kinds of nebulæ still another class of great complexity. Even in observations of the simplest character, like those of a lunar eclipse, the advantages of the size and situation of the telescope have enabled us to determine important questions till recently unresolved.

The applications of the photographic apparatus, which forms so important a part of our equipment, are most varied and we hope to solve some of the most important of astronomical problems by its use—such as the determination of stellar parallaxes, the automatic registration of the principal features of the moon and planets and other like things. The spectroscopic observations which will be made here ought to go far towards the solution of many questions as yet unresolved or at least imperfectly understood. We have carefully compared the performance of the great telescope with other large telescopes now in operation and with that of the famous telescopes of Lord Rosse and the great forty-foot reflector of Sir William Herschel. Such comparisons have shown us that there is no doubt whatever that Mr. Lick's wish has been carried out, and that the observatory which he founded does in fact possess, as he wished that it should, "the most powerful telescope in the world."

ABOUT THE BAY.

The magnificent Bay of San Francisco, in which all the navies of the world would find room to ride at anchor, is at once one of the largest and one of the most beautiful of all the harbors yet discovered on any coast. The shore-line, with its sinuous windings, measures perhaps two hundred miles, and, with rare exceptions, is one continuous circuit of quiet, restful beauty—continuous and yet so varied as to be wholly free from monotony. Most of the way, gracefully-rounded hills, grassy and garnished with trees, reach down to the very shore, their feet bathed in the rippling waves. Here and there little cañons are traced by meandering lines of dense foliage, the evergreen oaks commingling and harmonizing with many shades of deciduous growth. Now an open valley, teeming with the wealth of tillage, bursts on the view. Through the famous Golden Gate the broad ocean is seen, and at pleasant intervals as the round is made, the higher mountains of the coast-range loom grandly against the sky. Much

"Wildcat Cascades."—Near Berkeley.

of this panorama may be enjoyed from the decks of ferry and river boats, making regular trips on their various routes; but a complete tour by special boat amply repays those who make it. The present purpose, however, is not so much to indicate what may be seen during a day's yachting, as to give some hint of the beauty and interest of the belt of country about the bay, much of it not revealed to the mere voyager, but readily reached by easy jaunts.

In 1860 Oakland had scarcely more than a thousand inhabitants. Two small ferry-boats plied between the little city and its larger neighbor, and frequently ran aground in the creek. When the Oaklander did not reach his home in season it was understood that he was "stuck on the bar." But for years past Oakland and Alameda have had the most perfect ferry service in the world. Moles and piers have been extended into the bay, the creek has been deepened, large and swift

THE MOLE.—OAKLAND IN THE DISTANCE.

INTERIOR OF THE OAKLAND DEPOT.

ENTERING THE PIER.

ferry-boats ply on the routes, carrying daily some twenty-five thousand passengers, and the great freight-boats, like floating bridges, transfer an entire freight train at a single trip.

These transit facilities have contributed greatly to making Oakland one of the chief cities of California. It is a city of homes and schools, and as an educational centre people are drawn to it from all parts of the Pacific Coast. Like Brooklyn, it catches the overflow of a larger city; and it draws to it the best elements. The turbulent and disorderly are not attracted.

From the hills of Piedmont, a pleasant suburb, and destined hereafter to be dotted all over with villas, the observer looks down upon Oakland, stretching along the bay and estuary for five miles or more. The foreground is chequered with streets and avenues, with handsome residences, with school-houses and churches, and is brightened by long lines of evergreen trees. One sees the little parks for breathing spaces; the sheen of the water in Lake Merritt, flecked with white sails on holidays; the great city beyond, with fleets of merchant ships riding at anchor; the islands dotting

OAKLAND. LOOKING TOWARD THE GOLDEN GATE. FROM PAINTING BY C. D. ROBINSON.

"Oakland is a city of homes and schools, and as an educational center people are drawn to it from all parts of the Pacific Coast. Like Brooklyn, it catches the overflow of a larger city, and it draws to it the best elements. The turbulent and disorderly are not attracted . . . The city creeps back to the foothills, all the way on an upward grade, so that before the hills are reached there has been a gentle ascent of three or four hundred feet,—enough for the eye to take in the Golden Gate, the white-winged ships going to and fro, the islands standing like grim sentinels in the middle distance, the curve and sweep of the shore-line, and the bay which melts into the horizon on the south."

the bay, and a forest of tall masts skirting the numerous wharves. There are the city of Alameda, embowered with trees; the fruitful valley stretching southward, the background of hills, some of which rise to the majesty of mountains. The city over-runs its municipal lines on the north, so that one can hardly tell where Oakland ends or Berkeley begins.

This suburban breadth pleases the eye. Some one has said: "It is all suburb." So much the better; what is best in town and country life never comes amiss. Here are lots which are sometimes measured, not by the foot, but by acres, gardens and lawns; and sometimes the ambitious suburban resident indulges in a small orchard. If he does not always get the fruit, it may be because the small boy has been alert and too enterprising.

Berkeley, on the northern side of Oakland, has one of the most picturesque sites to be found, even in California. Sufficiently separated from San Francisco to escape the allurements of a large city, and near enough to get, under proper direction, advantage from its libraries and general facilities for culture, the town itself is large enough to afford society and temporary homes for students among its families; and is a thoroughly healthful place, with a good moral atmosphere. Having these and other advantages, Berkeley is pre-eminently adapted to be the seat of learning which it is becoming. Years

MASONIC TEMPLE AND FIRST CONGREGATIONAL CHURCH.

ago it was chosen as the site of the College of California, merged later into the State University, which now represents a property value of not less than three million dollars. Afterwards it was chosen also as the site of the Deaf and Dumb and Blind Asylum. The grounds of the University originally embraced one hundred and sixty acres, on the southerly side of which the town site was marked out. The profits of the sale of lots from the original plat, which was held as a college homestead, went to the maintenance of the institution until its absorption into the State University did away with the necessity of aid from this source; but a great many of these lots are held to this day by the original purchasers, numbers of whom have erected handsome residences. With clustering spires of churches and spacious school-houses and broad avenues and large residence lots, the little city stretching from the hills along the sloping ground sheer down to the sea, flanked by the University on the north and the asylum on the south, beautiful for situation beyond **any** other, has an assured future. It has room enough for one hundred thousand people. It may have to-day a population of five or six thousand. The wonder is that special attention has not long ago been turned to this bright and promising town. It has drawn to it a class of cultivated people who care less for rapid growth than for the good social and moral character of the place. The cluster of four University buildings, with the large corps of professors, afford facilities for a thousand students. They are not all there at present, but they will be at no distant day. The University Library, the Art Gallery, the Gymnasium, and the great Lick Observatory on Mount Hamilton are some of the accessories of this growing institution.

The asylum grounds comprise nearly one hundred acres, backed by the foot hills, which have been extensively planted with evergreen trees. The foreground is laid out for lawns and shrubbery. The buildings are new, substantial, and admirably arranged, both in the grouping and interior fitting, for the education of the deaf and dumb and blind. There is a model workshop, kitchen, and bakery; and the class-rooms and dormitories are well-nigh perfect. Berkeley is reached by ferry and railroad in the same time as Oakland, and tickets for the one place are generally good for the other. Three or four avenues connect these two charming suburbs. Looking from Berkeley the observer has Mount Tamalpais in the farther distance, the bay in the middle distance, while off in a southerly direction stands the great commercial city, its streets grooved over the hills, lighted by night with thousands of lamps.

The hills back of Berkeley are seamed with a network of deep ravines and mimic cañons, through which one may wander in wildness for hours without meeting a single human being or discovering a sign of any human habitation. The whole region is virtually untrodden by man, save an occasional botantist, a geologist or sportsman. Yet many a scene of rare beauty is prisoned within these walls. Three miles from Berkeley, accessible by what is known as the Berryman Road, is Wildcat Cañon, through which flows Wildcat Creek for more than a dozen miles, on its way to the bay. The two forks of the creek take their rise near the summit, in mountain springs, and, as they race down the hillside, a rich growth of vegetation springs up along their course, while their banks are overhung with tall trees. The scenery along the whole length of the cañon is extremely picturesque. Flanked by a steep, rocky wall on one side and sloping mountains on the other, carpeted with grass and flowers, with its groves of stately trees, the path of the stream is one of exquisite beauty. Every few rods the brook plunges into a deep pool, shrouded with moss-grown trees and bordered with delicate ferns. At one point the stream takes a leap of thirty feet over projecting ledges of rock, and the gap in the hills though which it passes is like a huge gateway hewn out of the solid rock. A charming little park lies beyond, completely walled in by hills, save where the water, a quarter of a mile below, like a tiny silver thread, seeks a passage to the sea. At the point where the road crosses the cañon is Cave Hill, a projection of the mountain-ridge to the west. Its cliff-like face fronts upon the cañon and almost overhangs it. About seventy-five feet above its base it is honeycombed with caverns, dome-shaped chambers a dozen or more in number, the largest of which is eighteen feet across, ten feet deep, and ten feet high to the center of its roof. The walls of the chambers are of solid rock, and are marked here and there with bright green stains and white incrustations. Several openings of like appearance can be seen at inaccessible points along the hill a hundred feet farther north, which may lead to extensive connecting chambers as yet unexplored.

Looking at Berkeley from the water, one sees a landscape gently reaching up to the hills, dotted with villas, cottages and public edifices. What Cambridge is to Boston, Berkeley will be to Oakland. The two may yet run together. But the great institutions, with the scholars who constitute their faculties, and the natural congregating of cultivated people about such institutions,— men and women devoted to art, science and letters,—will essentially mould the character of the place. One educational institution will often stimulate the founding of others. Thus the Roman Catholics have chosen in Oakland the site of St. Mary's College. Academies and seminaries are multiplied, and there is a constant creation of new educational facilities.

Beyond Oakland, on the east, is the Fruitvale suburb, long noted for its rural attractions, its orchards, and handsome country seats. Four miles beyond, and a mile or so from the main highway. is Mills College on the site chosen many years ago by Rev. Cyrus Mills and his wife as a **most** desirable place for a Young Ladies' seminary and college. More than eighty acres of lawn, garden, woodland, and recreation grounds are here dedicated to educational uses. The spacious edifice is admirable in all its appointments. Mrs. Mills is still working, planning, and giving for the enlargement of this prosperous institution. Dr. Stratton, a distinguished educator, is President, and nearly two hundred students are in attendance. It is a quiet and secluded place, the landscape made more beautiful by cultivation, living water running through the cool groves, and the hills towering up as sentinels on all sides. The college, the property of which is now worth about five hundred thousand dollars, has recently been given to the public, and the trustees manage it in that behalf.

Going south, the county road becomes a broad avenue, well watered for many miles, lined on either side with farms, gardens, orchards and homesteads. The great fruit-growing belt is reached in the vicinity of San Leandro, and extends for

THE CHABOT OBSERVATORY.

more than twenty miles. Where the orchards are less frequent, the vineyards begin. The cherry orchards hereabouts have long been famous, and apples, pears and plums are among the staple fruits of the district. Alameda fruit-growers are known in the markets of the Atlantic states through the car-loads of fruit sent forward long before eastern fruits have made their appearance.

COURT HOUSE.—OAKLAND.

San Leandro was once the county seat of Alameda County, and is not less important to-day. It is an orchard town with many beautiful homes. Haywards, just beyond, has long been famous as a summer and health resort. Looking from the hills near this town, the valley stretching out for miles beyond, and the bay as far as the eye can reach, the long succession of orchards, the tilth of many fields, and the blue hills in the distance,—all these harmoniously blended, make up a view of constant inspiration and gladness. Beyond Haywards is Niles, another picturesque little town, in the very mouth of the charming Alameda Cañon, having the tillable land and valley spread out before it.

The cañon—sometimes improperly called Niles cañon—pierces the foot-hills of the Coast Range, extending from Niles to Sunol, a distance of seven miles.

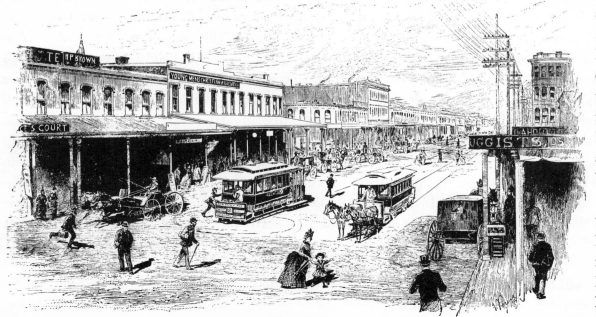

CORNER OF SEVENTH STREET AND BROADWAY.

DAM AT LAKE CHABOT.—PIEDMONT SPRINGS HOTEL.—ADAM'S POINT, LAKE MERRITT, LOOKING EAST.—ENTRANCE TO
UNIVERSITY GROUNDS OVER BRIDGE.

"This suburban breadth pleases the eye. Some one has said, "It is all suburb." So much the better, what is best in
town and country life never comes amiss. The sea and land, meadow and mountain, are incorporated into the landscape, and
all these harmoniously blended make up a view of constant inspiration and gladness."

It is christened after Alameda Creek, a sparkling stream which rises in the mountains and dances lightly along its rocky bed, singing softly to the hills and trees that line its course, cheerily greeting the little tributaries that join it at the mouths of deep ravines, now and then taking a wild plunge over a ledge of rocks only to recover its accustomed dignity the next moment, and at length to spread out, clear and placid, upon the breast of the valley.

At the entrance to the cañon the hills appear as if cleft asunder by some Titanic force. Every turn of the road discloses some new and striking effect. Here it winds along a narrow gorge whose rocky walls are a mosaic of green shrubs, clinging closely, as if aware of their precarious foot-hold. Now it opens upon a sunny glade, where cultivated fields and an old *adobé*, shaded by a giant cactus, bear witness to the industry of some early Mexican settler. Again it winds like a serpent along the close-knit bases of opposing hills, which recede a little farther on, to give place to a tiny lake. Many times the cañon twists and broadens into vast amphitheatres, encircled by towering cliffs which form a jagged line against the sky.

"THE OLD ADOBÉ," ALAMEDA CAÑON.

Passing slowly up Alameda Cañon, with his eyes open and appreciative, one may secure a gallery of mental pictures, which in richness of color, variety and beauty, will rival any collection of landscape paintings in the world. Many picturesque gorges and mimic cañons open into the Alameda, all of them richly rewarding exploration; but none among them compares with that of Stony Brook. It is hard for one who knows it well to share with the public the secrets of Stony-brook Cañon. Its memories are something to be hoarded as the miser hoards his gold; and, when the unwilling tongue is loosed, how difficult to speak of it in measured and temperate words! Never were such lights and shadows seen before, shifting and changing from dawn to even-tide; never such arches of living green, thickets of shrubs, mossy boulders, fern-grown hillsides, daintily-feathered out-cropping ledges, tiny cataracts, and deep, clear pools for light and shade to play among, while the seasons sweep down the cañon with their varying tints.

Alameda Cañon has long been a favorite resort for sportsmen. Its streams are stocked with

BOAT LANDING AT TWELFTH STREET.—LAKE MERRITT.

trout, and abound in pike and perch.   It is a favorite haunt for many sorts of wild fowl; while the hills which retreat from it on either side are the resort of larger game, including an occasional deer.   When we remember that this rare bit of rural beauty and wildness is almost on the threshold of a populous city, our appreciation is quickened and heightened.   The same is true of Wildcat Cañon. Either may be reached by all San Francisco and Oakland within an hour.

Years ago, the Beard orchard, near the old Mission San José, was famous for its wealth of rare fruits.   The present owner of the property, Mr. Juan Gallegos, has done everything that money and good taste could accomplish; and aided by an abundance of water, a perfect climate and other natural advantages of the locality, has succeeded in making his magnificent estate one of the most inviting places in California.   A vineyard of six hundred acres, stocked with the choicest varieties of Southern Europe, has superceded the orchard, and stretches in a picturesque and gentle slope toward the lower valley.   From its products the vaults of the wine company near by yearly store and age over half a million gallons of pure wines.   What has been done in this instance in the way of creating a beautiful estate has been accomplished in hundreds of other cases on a smaller scale. All about the Mission San José there are vineyards, gardens and orchards, fruitful and beautiful. Neither drought nor frost nor any blasting wind overtakes these valley gardens between the mountains and the sea.   The hills slope to the west and melt away in the valley carpeted with emerald in spring and with gold in the autumn.   Beyond the Mission are the Warm Springs, formerly a place of public entertainment, but now withdrawn to the use of private ownership.   Some of the wines produced in this vicinity have never been surpassed in delicacy of bouquet.

But in all these bay counties perhaps not more than half the area is valley.   Seen from the bay, a chain of hills, rising here and there to the dignity of mountains, extends longitudinally throughout the county.   Beyond these there are other low mountains, all belonging essentially to the same group.   Interspersed everywhere are picturesque valleys, such as the Morago Valley, just over the hills in the rear of Oakland, and the San Ramon, some miles beyond.   The Alameda Cañon is also the gateway to Livermore Valley, many hundred feet above the level of the sea, but hemmed in by mountains and hills.   Many of these are carpeted with vineyards, and together they constitute one of the most important wine districts of the State.   All the little valleys are dotted over with farm houses and country-seats, the vineyards creep up the mountain sides, and though the roads smoke in the dust of summer sometimes, the autumnal rains come, and all the brown hills are changed again to brilliant green.

The future villa-sites and country-seats will be among these hills, and often on their very tops.   Some day the plan, which has long been figured on paper, of a broad avenue from Berkeley to San Leandro, and thence for miles beyond, will find some enterprising men awaked to its advantages and ready for the work of construction.   A broad country road, winding along the foot-hills, watered and kept in repair but conforming to all the heights and depressions, would make accessible a thousand country-seats, each of which could be reached by a fine drive, and each having the advantages of one of the most charming outlooks in the State.   As sure as wealth and population increase these hills will be sought and occupied.   The wealthy citizen is willing to pay for both climate and prospect.   He is ambitious to make a picture of his country-seat.   He wants the broad, out-spreading landscape, softened and mellowed by distance, the scene-shifting of the water, and the sight of the busy city beyond, too far off to vex with its noise or chill with its ocean winds.   If he has a small orchard, a bit of green hillside for his Jersey cows, a sheltered nook where the magnolia blossoms and geraniums go aflame along the fences, where the border lines of town and country meet, his ideal home is as nearly realized as it ever can be in this world.   It is a place of great contentment and peace. All this region is constantly filling up with people who are making just such homes.   The city creeps back to

BOATING ON LAKE MERRITT.—THE RETURN.

MADISON STREET, OAKLAND.

the foot-hills, all the way on an upward grade, so that before the hills are reached there has been a gentle ascent of three or four hundred feet—enough for the eye to take in the Golden Gate, the white-winged ships going to and fro, the islands standing like grim sentinels in the middle distance, the curve and sweep of the shore-line, and the bay which melts into the horizon on the south.   The sea and land, meadow and mountain are incorporated into the landscape.   Those who must have the grandeur of snow-capped mountains, their sides furrowed by ancient glaciers, and cut asunder by yawning cañons, will look elsewhere.   But whoever is content with the quiet beauty of nature to which is superadded artistic and useful cultivation, a region well advanced in all the accessories of civilization, having schools, seminaries and colleges, with corresponding intelligence among the people at large, need not look beyond this foot-hill country around the Bay of San Francisco.   A vast deal of supplementary work remains to be done.   The hundred thousand or so of inhabitants are, to a large extent, busy with plans for future development.   Homes will be multiplied; scores of broad and beautiful country avenues will be made, connecting villa with villa and town with city; schools and churches will be quadrupled; additional railroads will be built; new lines of boats provided; local harbors

MILLS COLLEGE, NEAR OAKLAND. FROM PAINTING BY A. J. KELLER

"More than eighty acres of lawn, garden, woodland and recreation grounds are here dedicated to educational uses. The spacious edifice is admirable in all its appointments . . . The College, the property of which is worth about five hundred thousand dollars, has been given to the public, and the trustees manage it in that behalf."

LAKE MERRITT, LOOKING NORTH.

enlarged and improved; miles of wharves constructed; manufacturing stimulated and developed—all this and more with the inevitable growth of population, and the natural out-working of the energy to which this climate tends.

The attention of the stranger in crossing the Bay of San Francisco is pretty sure to be fixed on an isolated mountain which, as one approaches, seems to be lifted up from the plains. Seen from a distance, its outlines are softened, and its summit takes on a purple hue or is partly veiled in the soft gray tints of the mist which comes in from the ocean. The smaller mountains of the coast-range seem to be camping about Mount Diablo. But it stands alone like a grim and solitary sentinel, over-looking the great valleys, the magnificent bay, and the ocean, which through some atmospheric fiction seems at times to slide in nearly to the base of the mountain. It is not the highest mountain that gives one the grandest view. Tourists who have ascended some of the loftiest peaks of Europe have frequently noted that better views could be gained from moderate elevations.

The observer on Mount Diablo is at an elevation of a little less than 4,000 feet. Away to the south is Mount Hamilton, where the greatest telescope in the world has lately been lifted under its ample iron dome for the reading of the heavens. There is a wonderful nearness in these outlying and isolated peaks. Tamalpais, some thirty miles away from Diablo, seems only just across the bay, which appears to be narrowed to the breadth of a river. St. Helena, sixty miles north at the head of Napa Valley, looks as if the distance might be covered in a brisk morning walk. The mountains along the outer coast range, which divide the valleys from the sea, look like moderate hills falling away on the southern horizon until mist and cloud or golden haze furnish a vanishing point. They are gently taken within the veil. On a clear day with the mist of the ocean well banked up on the far horizon, the unaided vision sweeps a radius of more than a hundred miles. The two great rivers—the Sacramento and the San Joaquin—come together and empty into Suisun Bay at the foot of the great mountain. The valleys open, one to the north and the other towards the south; the serpentine courses of the rivers are finally lost fifty to sixty miles away, but the faint lines of smoke still beyond tell where the steamers are coming down from the upper valleys with barges in tow, laden with fruit and wheat. Distance minifies the valleys till they look like a succession of mere gardens. The immense wheat fields— often a thousand acres or more in one field—seem to be contracted to small squares, the orchards into still smaller ones; the nearest farm houses

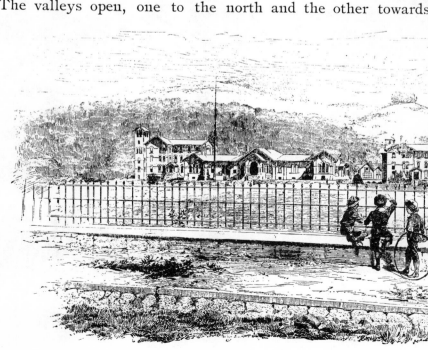

DEAF AND DUMB ASYLUM NEAR BERKELEY.

appear hardly larger than bird cages, and San Francisco is reduced to a picture; but with a powerful glass, the spars of the shipping that lines the water-front look like a forest of dead trees where a fire has lapped up every green thing.   By way of relief some ships, like toys, are seen coming in or going out with white specks of canvas which seem to kiss the water.   But the view which is printed as it were on the very soul is that beheld in looking across the great San Joaquin Valley, beyond all the towns and villages that dot the plain, interblending with tilth of fields and emerald squares of vineyard to the western slope of the Sierra, and beyond to the great domes and peaks lifted up from ten thousand to fifteen thousand feet above the sea, clad in eternal white, watching in serene majesty over all the peaceful and fruitful valleys.   The little threads of green which the eye sometimes follows sheer down into the center of the hot plains, define the living water that is constantly flowing down from these great heights.   A riverless plain will become a desert, but a plain walled up with snow-capped mountains becomes a garden, where vineyard succeeds vineyard, and orchards bend under the weight of ripening fruit.   The great pines wave and sough in the gales along the western flank of the

OAKLAND HARBOR.

Sierras; but best of all is the living water sent down leaping and singing to make glad these towns and cities of the plain.   No artist can paint the landscape which the eye takes in.   Its majesty and glory and sweet peace are reserved for those who ascend Mount Diablo, camping on the flank over night, and watching for the dawn on the top when the sun gilds these white crests and floods all the valleys with light.

Another view with less grandeur of sweep is that obtained from Mission Peak, just back of the little village of Mission San José.   From an elevation of about two thousand feet, the eye takes in the whole Valley of Alameda, the level land between the mountains and the bay for a distance of thirty or forty miles.   There is also the wide-off view; the city of San Francisco and the ocean beyond, the city of Oakland, small villages and towns, the spires of churches, long railway trains winding through gardens and orchards, the still water of the lower bay flecked with the white sails of market boats gliding out from the shore and the tide-water creeks.   Best of all is the pastoral scene — the one landscape where no single private domain can be defined, one extended garden touched with the repose of the soft and dreamy atmosphere, and from which there comes up the perfume of orchard and field, of ripening grain rippling in the summer breeze, and the wild flowers which have given a dash of color to all the hillsides. Going south from Mission San José, the hills in the foreground have hardly the dignity of mountains. They slope well down towards the bay, and culture is in many places carried to their tops. They are in the warm belt, alike beyond the reach of frost and the cold winds which come in from the ocean. Looking up these gentle declivities, one notes how the landscape has been toned by cultivation, and how without design these gradations of color blend and make up one harmonious rural picture. Even the salt-marsh is in some places rendered picturesque by great beds of salt made by the evaporation of shallow pools of ocean brine, the water having been let in from the bay and the solar heat of mid-summer completing the work.

THE VINEYARDS AT MISSION SAN JOSÉ. (VIEW FROM GALLEGOS' WINERY.)

At Alverado is the one successful beet-sugar manufactory in the United States. That single demonstration has been worth millions to the country. For if one establishment can make good sugar from beets and sell it at a profit, it is certain that others also, if well managed, can attain success. So well has the fact been demonstrated that one of the largest capitalized companies ever organized for sugar production has been formed in this State for the manufacture of beet-sugar. Many hundred tons of it have already been produced at Alverado. The sugar-beet covers hundreds of acres of rich valley land, and next to the vine, clothes the fields with the handsomest garment of green. When the hills are tawny, and the stubble fields have the color of old gold, these squares of living green set with golden borders form pictures that rest and delight the eye.

One turns also again and again to the vineyards along the hill-sides and away up the mountain slopes for refreshing views. What mysterious elements are in the soil that life should be always succeeding death? The wheat fields turn to russet, and later the stubble-fields are touched with dull brown tints; but just then the vine covers the parching earth and there is newness of life. One never tires of looking at these pictures which have been made by the hands of skillful industry in

Berkeley from the Hills. The Golden Gate in the Distance. From Painting by J. D. Robertson.

"Berkeley, on the northern side of Oakland, has one of the most picturesque sites to be found, even in California . . . With clustering spires of churches, spacious school-houses, broad avenues and large residence lots, the little city, stretching from the hills along the sloping ground sheer down to the sea, flanked on the north by the University, and on the south by the Asylum for the Deaf and Dumb, beautiful for situation beyond any other, has an assured future."

the valleys and along the mountain slopes. In some parts of the State where the forests have been destroyed and the hills torn up in the search for gold, the landscape has been sadly marred. But here it has been rendered more attractive by vineyards, orchards and gardens, and by homesteads, where rural taste and wealth have made country life as delightful as may be found in the world.

Many a quiet hamlet and minor town is in the process of transformation. Roads are smoothed and watered, trees are planted by the way-side, the villa replaces the pioneer farmhouse, the country hotel from which the guest was in a hurry to depart invites him now to tarry. In all these particulars there is a new departure. Villages are made attractive to strangers and tourists. Reference has been made to Oakland's water-park, made by a dam built across the estuary at Twelfth Street, the dam serving as a causeway. These two hundred acres, more or less, of water-surface, to-day constitute the most attractive feature of the city, which is a perpetual source of pleasure. Sail-boats are constantly skimming the lake, row-boats are darting here and there, while hundreds of pedestrians line the shore. The bounty of the State in giving all its rights to

A BIT OF ALAMEDA CREEK.

the city, has reduced the cost of this great improvement, which was constructed originally through the enterprise and liberality of a few citizens. The driveway on the eastern side may one day be extended around the entire shore, making a boulevard, an ornamental border and an avenue for a three-mile drive. Plans for the boulevard have already been made. Between the head of this beautiful lake and Piedmont there now exists a natural park—a broad stretch of intersecting hill and valley, beautiful with native oaks, picturesque and inviting. As the city grows in population and importance, other public improvements which will add to its attractiveness as a city of homes will doubtless be made. Something like half a million dollars has been expended by the Government already in making a navigable water-way up almost to the heart of the city. Ships come to the foot of Broadway between the solid retaining walls which line the banks of the estuary. When it is connected with the back bay, and Alameda becomes an island, as much so as New York

is to-day, the broad channel protected from storms will be not only a safe harbor, but the water-way for a commerce of which the present is hardly more than a suggestion.

The city of Alameda has already drawn thousands of visitors to the salt water bathing establishments on the bay side of the town. The novelty may be less now, but the easy access by rail, the broad avenues lined with cottages and villas, the large and well-kept bathing houses, and the water tempered by sunny days from spring to late autumn, will insure for this watering place a good degree of popular favor.

In all the sheltered vales and sunny

ENTRANCE TO MOUNTAIN VIEW CEMETERY.

"After a Good Day's Sport in the Sierras." From Sketch by F. O. C. Darley.

"All that wide and savage watershed of the Sacramento tributaries to the south and west of Mount Shasta affords good bear hunting at almost any season of the year—if you care to take the risks. It must be borne in mind that the grizzly bear of the Sierra is quite a different creature, so far as size, courage and ferocity are concerned, from his brother of the valley. It is said that the huge and blood-soaked stones of the Colosseum at Rome have generated many new flowers; and so we are permitted to hold that Mount Shasta, the savage guardian of this sublime heart of the Sierras, has brought forth and nourished a new, or at least a more terrible and monstrous order of beast than was ever encountered on the lower levels of California."

slopes hereabouts the climate approaches the semi-tropical.   Rare flowers, plants, shrubs and trees, from nearly all parts of the world, flourish here in the open air, giving no hint that they have been naturalized from far distant climes.   Australia, Japan and China, as well as all the Mediterranean countries, have made contributions.   Palms lift up their heads—even the date and cocoanut as well as the more familiar fan, royal, etc.; oranges put on their golden hue, lemons ripen throughout the year, pomegranates come to perfection, the Smyrna fig seems at home, tea plants thrive, camelias bloom in the gardens without the aid of hot-house stimulation, and roses imported from Southern France, and, for aught we know, from the plains of Sharon, are budding and blossoming all the year round.   The stranger noting all these is usually content with such witness for the climate.   There can be no frost-bound winter where summer melts into autumn and autumn into spring; where fragrant roses and white lilies are plucked in the gardens on Christmas morning, and all the brooks and rivulets go singing from the hills to the sea.

W. C. BARTLETT.

SOURCE OF THE SACRAMENTO RIVER.

GAME REGIONS OF THE
UPPER SACRAMENTO.

————

My mountains must be free,
They hurl oppression back;
They keep the boon of liberty.

————

WERE I asked to put a finger on the one most favored spot to be found on the map of the world for rod and gun and restful camp, I would indicate the tributary waters of the Sacramento, with Mount Shasta for a tent. And not because the first and best years of my life lay there, nor because I owe all I hope to be to this mighty, throbbing heart of roaring, white waters; but solely because there is gathered in and about this preëminent place more of the great things of earth than enter into the delights of a strong, healthful man in love with nature than can be found in any other one part of the world.

Back of all this lies the comfortable fact that this focus and centre of the sportsman's Eden is now quite as accessible as a city park. The Englishman in his journey around the world may arrive in San Francisco this evening, go to bed and be awakened next morning by the roaring waters from the melting snows of Mount Shasta, with the mountain lion and the grizzly bear on the overhanging crags for a background to the view as he looks from the window of his palace car. Thirty-five years ago it cost half a year, a small fortune, much patience, peril, often life itself to reach this paradise of the "mighty hunter." But now at last, and within this year, time, cost, peril,—all have been swept away together, while the mountains in all their black-white majesty remain—and ever must remain, thank God—as unchanged as the ocean. And the huge wild beasts are there in their fastnesses as of old. The trout in the sparkling waters are still eddying about under the overhanging rocks and beneath the gnarled and mossy roots that reach from giant trees, "bald with antiquity."

Go with me to this heart of the world's heart for an hour,—for who should know the haunts and the habits of all things here so entirely? In the first place few equipments are needed. You want your favorite gun, of course, good substantial boots, and that's about all. The best of hotel comforts, all the detail of fishing appurtenances, tents if you tire of the hotels and wish to penetrate farther than the farthest, all these things are on the ground and to be had at fair cost.   But there is one sort of outfit you must surely have before starting, and that is a kind of mental equipment.   You must catch the colors.   Do this and you will come away content.   Your catch of trout, your deathshot at the black, brown, or grizzly bear,—all this will to the end of life be mere detail in comparison of results.   This intensity and emphasis of color is due to the sapphire and purple of the skies and the mighty mountain of snow.   The vast and high-held world of whiteness above you, only a little below the sapphire of heaven, as it seems when you look up through the black immensity of trees overhead; this Mount-Shasta heaven and earth coming so close together—these two things make a new or at least a magnified and an intensified world of color.   And this element enters into all things there, even down to the fiery red blossom that bursts through the snow at your feet.   I implore you go prepared to see and comprehend, so far as possible, the indescribable calm of this colossal Shasta world.   The soul grows there.

Make your first, if not your final, stopping place at Lower Soda Springs.   This spring is of itself, to say nothing of its fabulously invigorating waters, a curious study.   Besides that, it is the first spot ever occupied by the white man in all its region.   And such men as Hastings, Lane, Frémont, made few mistakes in selecting camps.   Here too some battles were fought in the old days.   When "Mountain Joe" and myself owned the place the house was sacked and burned.   The Indians retreated across the Sacramento river with their plunder and climbed to near the summit of the almost inaccessible crags that pierce the clouds over against Mount Shasta.   And here on these gray and glorious heights we fought and vanquished them on the Fifteenth day of June, 1855. The deep cleft in the left side of my face is the work of an Indian arrow received in that deadly little engagement.

Do not pitch camp closer to Mount Shasta than Soda Springs.   It is a mistake to ram your head right up against a mountain, as if you were afraid you could not see it at a respectful distance.   There is an impertinence in that sort of doing, and it has its punishments, such as snow-

IN CAMP.

SPEARING SALMON.—McCLOUD RIVER FALLS. FROM PAINTING BY THOMAS HILL.

"On the east side of Shasta, in the deep and sombre gorge at its base, and in the shadow of its glacier-clad domes, flow the cold and crystal waters of the McCloud River, the source of which is found in the ice caverns of this "Monarch of Mountains." At the Falls, which are upwards of a hundred feet in sheer descent, the great emerald pools swarm with salmon, unable to pass the great barrier. Here they fall easy victims to the unerring spear of the Indian."

THE STORY OF THE MOUND.

blindness, rheumatism, and so on.   Mountains are like pictures; made neither to smell nor to eat.   And yet in the Vatican at Rome and in the Sierras of California you see herds of people who push themselves as far to the front as the bar of iron or the bank of snow will allow. The best in nature, like the best in art, is sacred.   Look upon it respect-fully, reverently, or not at all.   Even the wild beasts know that much.

The haunt of the bear changes somewhat with the season, although he is perhaps less of a nomad than any other inhabitant of these altitudes. The grizzly has been known to remain within an area of a few miles of dense wood and trackless rocks for a generation.   And that is the meaning of the little mounds of stones which you find on the old Indian trails that track from one tributary to another on the head waters of the Sacramento River.   It was the custom for each Indian as he passed the place where one of his people had been killed or maimed by one of these monsters, to pitch a stone or pebble onto the spot.   And thus from year to year the mound of stones was formed.   No doubt some sentiment of pity or respect lay at the bottom of the custom; but back of that lay the solid and practical fact of a warning to all unwary passers-by, that the grizzly bear had been there and probably at that moment was not many miles away.

I beg here to digress enough to state that the Indians, until taught better by the white man, would not harm a grizzly bear, even in self-defense.   For they held that the grizzly bear was the father of the Indian.   The mother of the Indian they asserted to have been the daughter of the Creator, who dwelt in Mount Shasta.   They held that the mountain was, of old, hollow like a tent; that they could see the smoke coming out from the top of the great wigwam.   And their story is to the effect that once when the wind was blowing fearfully from the ocean—which may be seen

A Herd of Elk.—Pitt River Cañon. From Painting by Thomas Hill.

"The haunt of this noble and high-headed creature is not far from the Modoc lava beds, or rather between the rocky fastnesses and the snow belt on the eastern and south-eastern base of the great snow peak. This large elk, certainly the largest in the world, seems to have been born of the thermal springs that burst from the savage and sublime mountain, along the lower edges of everlasting snow. He is a gregarious animal, more so than any other creature on the continent, save perhaps the buffalo, and you may have to search long before finding him. But in his undisturbed state he is a great lover of his kind and is to be found only in herds numbering from fifty to five hundred."

from the summit of the mountain on any day of exceptional clearness—the Great Spirit sent his daughter up to beseech the wind to be still; that he warned her not to put her head out for fear the wind would get into her hair, which was long as the rainbow, and blow her away. Being a woman, however, she put her head away out, and so was blown out and down to the very bottom of the snow where the chief of the grizzly bears was camped with his family. The Indians further insist that the grizzly bear at that time talked, walked erect, and even went hunting with bow and arrows and spear, and the story goes on to say that, in violation of all the laws of hospitality, the daughter of the Great Spirit was made captive and compelled to be the wife of the chief's son, and so became the mother of all good Indians. Finally, when the Great Spirit found out what had happened to his daughter, he came out and down the mountain in a great fury; and calling all the bears together he broke their hands and feet with a club and made them get down on their all-fours like other beasts. He made them shut their mouths so that they could talk no more forever, and then, going back and down into the hollow of Mount Shasta, he put out the fire in his wigwam and was seen no more. They point to the three great black spots on the south side of the mountain and say these are his footprints and explain that he descended the whole vast cone in three long strides, showing how very angry he was. And as evidence of the truthfulness of what they say about their origin, they point to the fact that the grizzly bear is even yet permitted to use his fists and stand up and fight like a man when hard pressed.

All the Indians believe to this day that the grizzly bear can talk, if you will only sit still when he comes up and hear what he has to say. But this may not be advisable. However, I know one wrinkled and leather-looking old woman, a century old perhaps, who used almost daily go out to a heap of rocks on the edge of a thicket and talk, as she said, with a grizzly bear. She was greatly respected.

Late Autumn or the very early Spring is the best time for hunting this king of the Sierra; the only safe time, indeed. For when the she-bear has young it is simply folly to be found in her vicinity. At other times this brute is not more to be dreaded than any other wild beast equally strong and reckless of danger.

All that wide and savage water-shed of the Sacramento tributaries to the south and west of Mount Shasta affords good bear hunting at almost any season of the year—if you care to take the risks. But he is a velvet-footed fellow, and often when and where you expect peace you find a grizzly. Quite often when and where you think you are alone, just when you begin to be certain that there is not a single grizzly bear in the mountains, when you begin to breathe the musky perfume of Mother Nature as she shakes out the twilight stars in her hair, and you start homeward, there stands your long-lost bear in your path! And your hair stands up! And your bear stands up! And you wish you had not lost him! And you wish you had not found him! And you start home! And you go the other way, glad, glad to the heart if he does not come tearing on after you.

More than thirty years ago in company with a cultured young man, Volney Abby by name, I went hunting for bear up Castle Creek, about a mile from the banks of the Sacramento. Pretty little dimples of prairie lay here and there, breaking the sombre monotony of pine and cedar, and, as we leisurely walked on, the waters sang among the mossy boulders in the bed of the creek with a singularly restful melody. My companion took out his Homer and as we sat on a mossy log he read aloud of the wanderings of Ulysses till twilight made him close the page. Our path, an old Indian trail, lay close by the singing waters that foamed down their steep way of rocks. To our right and up and away from the stream stretched a little crescent of wild clover. As my companion closed the book I caught sight of a pine tree dripping with rosin. The Indians peel off and eat the inner portion of pine bark at certain seasons of the year, and all through the Sierra you can to this day see evidences of this meagre means of subsistence. An Indian had been resting and feasting in this same sweet little clearing by the singing waters only a year or two before. I struck a match, touched it to the scarred and dripping white face of the pine—and such a light!

A grizzly! A grizzly! God help us! He came bounding down upon us like an avalanche, fat, huge, bow-legged, low to the ground, but terrible! He halted, just a second, to look at the fire perhaps, when my companion, bolder than I and more prompt to act, blazed away. The bear rolled over, being badly hit. But he kept rolling and tumbling straight in our direction, and not a tree or stump or stone at hand; only the old mossy log on which we had been sitting. I wanted to run. "We must fight!" yelled my friend. I jerked up my gun and he got at his knife, as the monster with his big red mouth wide open tumbled over the log full upon us, breaking my gun in two at the breech and taking the most of my companion's red shirt in his teeth as he passed. But he passed, thank heaven, passed right on. He did not pause one second. He did not even seem to see us. I think the fire may have blinded him and so saved our lives.

As to hunting this branch of the bear family in large parties, as proposed by some, and as I have seen hunting done in India, I cannot advise it. For one of these beasts could crush and mangle a dozen men as easily as one. All he desires when hurt is to get at you. The rest is merely detail with him. There is much said about the advisability of lying down and lying still when a bear is coming and you have no means of escape. This is a strain on the nerves, and

HUNTER'S BIVOUAC.—SHASTA FOREST.

it is not sure of adequate reward. I know one Indian, "Grizzly Dick,"—and who of the old moun taineers does not remember poor, simple Indian Dick with his triangular face and his one eye twisted upside down?—who had tried this method and barely got off with his life. It is safe to say that the majority of Indians, and white men as well, who thus far have tried this conciliatory method of lying down when they saw a grizzly coming, lay down the next time inside the monster's maw. I may, however, mention one white man, an Irishman, who escaped after close contact with a grizzly bear, but as by a miracle. And this is the only instance I can recall. This man was in the lead of a party of prospectors crossing a mountain, when he suddenly met the grizzly monster face to face. The man fell on his knees to pray. And then, as the beast shuffled forward, his big loose claws rattling and his big ungainly feet fairly shaking the ground, the poor man could no longer even support himself upon his knees, but fell forward on his hands; his companions in the rear meantime having clambered into trees. The bear paused at sight of this singular animal be fore him. It probably reminded him of his own fair image in childhood, which no doubt he had often seen mirrored in the glassy lake. Or this hairy and rugged miner may have reminded him of some one of his shaggy and ungainly little boys in his rocky home close at hand. At any rate he came up and smelled of the puzzling stranger, much after the fashion of a dog on meeting a strange fellow-canine. And I have heard the men, those who had clambered into the trees, solemnly assert that the Irishman responded in like simple inquiry; but of course this is not so. Be these things as they may, I am glad to record that in this single instance the terrified man escaped unhurt, and ever after ascribed his escape to his prayer and the Holy Virgin.

OLD GRIZZLY SURPRISED.

It must be borne in mind that the grizzly bear of the Sierra is quite a different creature, so far as size, courage and ferocity are concerned, from his brother of the valley. Frémont once told me of finding a great number of grizzlies under the oaks near Santa Barbara feeding on acorns which the young bears threw down from the branches overhead, where they were forced by their seniors to climb and break off the boughs. I observe that in his reports to the Government he speaks of having attacked a large family of grizzlies on one occasion of this kind and killed thirteen of them on the spot. I have myself seen this animal feeding under the oaks in Napa valley in numbers together, and that as composedly and as careless of danger as if they had been hogs feeding on nuts under the hickory trees of the Wabash. But, as said before, this was another order of bear, so far as size and savagery are concerned, than that of the region of Mount Shasta, the highest point and the real heart of California.

Botanists have found in the vicinity of San Diego a clump of trees entirely new to science. The Monterey cypress is peculiar to Monterey only. It is said that the huge and blood-soaked blocks of stone that make the foundations of the Coloseum at Rome have generated many new flowers. And so we are permitted to hold that the savage guardian of this sublime heart of the Sierras has brought forth and nourished a new or at least a more terrible and monstrous order of beast than ever was encountered on the lower levels of California. As found on the savage and almost inaccessible spurs of Mount Shasta he is certainly the king of all the beasts of America, if not of all the world; and in this fact I find excuse for having dwelt at some length on his habits and his haunts on the headwaters of the Sacramento River.

The next animal in rank, both in size and importance to the sportsman of this region, is the mountain elk. And he also is much larger than his brother in the valleys—like the grizzly bear, which often attains to the weight of two thousand pounds. He is also full of battle when pushed to the wall, his nature thus taking to itself something of the unconquerable splendor of his lofty environments. The haunt of this noble and high-headed creature is (or was, until driven farther up the savage spurs of Mount Shasta by the invasion of our armies and the shock of battle,) not far from the Modoc lava beds, or rather between these rocky fastnesses and the snow-belt on the eastern and south-eastern base of the great snow peak. This large elk, certainly the largest in the world, seems to have

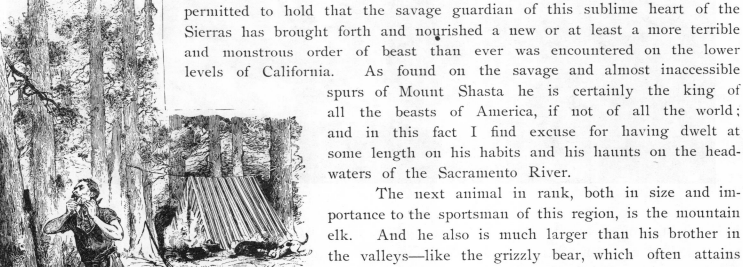

SUNDAY MORNING TOILET.

THE HOME OF THE EAGLE.—A SCENE FROM CASTLE CRAGS. FROM PAINTING BY THOMAS HILL.

"This wonderful group of castellated rocks rises abruptly from the deep gorge of the Sacramento, thousands of feet, piercing the clouds with thin rugged spires. It is truly the home of the Eagle."

been born of the thermal springs that burst from the savage and sublime mountain along the lower edges of everlasting snow.   To find him at home the hunter will have to change his base from Soda Springs, on the banks of the Sacramento, and move around the mountain about twenty-five miles to the eastward.   He is a gregarious animal, more so than any other creature on the continent, save perhaps the buffalo, and so you may have to search long before finding him.   True, if there have been invasions, as is not unlikely in the progress of civilization, you may find his large family broken up and scattered about through the dense wood and dimpled little valleys that prevail here.   But in his undisturbed state, as I knew him, he is a great lover of his kind, and is to be found only in herds numbering from fifty to five hundred.

In the Winter of 1856–7 I set out from the sweet little Now-ow-wa Valley (since named "Squaw Valley" by the coarse and common hunters who kill game as a source of livelihood) with two fine young Indian hunters from the McCloud River, in quest of a band of elk.   The winter had thus far been terribly severe and the large tribe of Indians encamped on banks of the McCloud, some ten miles distant, were starving.   The snow had been falling soft and continuously for a long time.   It lay from five to ten feet deep and was so wet and soft that the Indians even on their snow-shoes had been unable to move; hence their destitution.   But now clear, cold winter was

suddenly upon us, and this was their opportunity.   The snow was as hard as a floor.   The sky was sapphire.   The air keen and crisp and full of spice and energy.   The perfume of the frosted fir and spruce and pine and tamarack filled us with such an intoxicating delight as I never shall know again.   We struck straight up the mountain, right against the gleaming world of snow.   We must have made forty miles that day and encamped under one of "God's tents"—this is the name given them by the Indians.   They are formed entirely of the snow, with a huge and bushy fir-tree whose broad and low boughs reach out and over and down till pinned to the solid snow-

A CRITICAL MOMENT.

"THE MONSTER TUMBLED OVER THE LOG RIGHT UPON US."

bank. And thus is formed a perfect and most shapely tent of solid snow with dry quills for bed, and little dry, resinous and most fragrant cones for fire. And, oh! the perfume that fills this tent of snow, when the gentle flame starts and the indolent smoke lazily reaches up and loses itself in the lofty arches overhead!

The next day we came upon one of the warm springs, a bad, boggy hole in the side of the mountain containing perhaps two acres. The elk had been there only a few days before. Everything had been eaten to the earth, the vine maple, the birch, the alder, all things. There were stumps of willows here and there as large as my arm. The elk were evidently as hungry as the Indians and were eating solid wood.' We found where they had broken this corral of snow. It looked as if some huge saw-log had been drawn up the mountain by lumbermen; only this one deep track, and that leading sharp and steep up the world of solid snow. The Indians tightened their belts, tied their moccasins, loosened their arms, and with blazing eyes bounded forward. I followed as fast as I could.

The banks of snow on either side of this trench stood higher than my head. Now and then I could see where the big bull leader of the herd had rolled aside in the snow to fall into the rear while another took his place. On the crest of a cañon I came upon my Indians crouching down under the snow-bank in a blaze of suppressed excitement. Peering over them I saw a herd of many hundred elk, all lying down and ruminating under the dense trees on little hillocks that rose among the steaming warm springs.

The Indians conceded me the first shot, and I made my mark the shaggy tuft of hair that lay between a pair of most majestic horns. Over the knoll of snow and down into the corrall the Indians leaped, bows and bunches of arrows in hand, leaving their guns behind them; and before the poor cattle were yet fully on their feet their eager captors were sinking arrows up to the feathers in their sides.

And what a slaughter! Some of the bulls sullenly shook their stately horns, and struck out with their sharp and deadly hoofs, trying to fight. The

ON THE TRAIL OF THE ELK.

Indians, however, lost no time in hesitation.   They drove the elk into the crusted deep snow on every side, broke all discipline of the kingly camp, and darting around on the snow where the poor beasts wallowed helplessly, soon had the band in their power.   A tribe was starving.   There was no time for pity or sentiment; and they were equal to their bloody work.   And the wolves! the wild-cats! the California lions that night!   If you want a wild and a terrible sight, if you want to see savagery, to hear the howl of fiends, go high up Mount Shasta and put the scent of blood in the air on a mid-winter night!

In the early days the formidable antlers of these elk figured conspicuously as a means of defense in Indian warfare.   In this same winter of which I have spoken, even while I was out on the hunting expedition referred to, the Pitt River Indians rose up one night and massacred all the white settlers, nearly twenty in number, and re-claimed all that region lying below the Lava Beds down to near the Red Bluffs, and now known chiefly as the Fall River country.   As I was about the only white person left who was familiar with the country, I went out with the first expedition of volunteers as guide, and subsequently served with General Crook, who was then a lieutenant.   But

A MIDNIGHT PROWLER.

as we approached the scenes of the bloody massacre we found that the Indians had prepared great pits, or rather restored their old pits (which gives the name to that region), and had placed elk's antlers at the bottom of them.   We lost several horses in these deadly pitfalls and had some men badly hurt.   They were always placed in some narrow pass, entirely concealed by leaves and light sticks and branches, and were from ten to fifteen feet deep, with the sharp upturned antlers at the bottom.

The brown and black bear are found in numbers here, and in the early days they were as abundant as hogs on a farm, and quite as harmless.   They always hibernate, and generally in the hollow base of some stout tree.   The Indians have dogs trained to smell them out, when they have permitted themselves to be snowed under.   The Indians begin to dig down so soon as they find where bruin is hidden, and, strangely enough, so soon as the bear hears them he begins to dig out.   He comes crawling to the surface, blinking and blinded by the glittering snow, and falls an easy prey.   It is no uncommon thing for Indians to tie a rope around the mouth of a bear found thus and lead him into camp to amuse the children.   Contrary to the pretty and poetical notion, that the bear of the Sierras goes to sleep with the falling leaf and wakes with the Spring,

THE GAME REGIONS OF MOUNT SHASTA.—MOUNTAIN GROUSE. FROM PAINTING BY THOMAS HILL.

"The Grouse, in the summer months, inhabits the dense forests of Pine and Fir below the snow line of Mount Shasta. After the first fall of snow, they migrate to the warmer and better feeding ground of the foothills."

I happen to know that the whole bear family, from the imperial grizzly down to the dwarf black bear with big ears, does not sleep for the season, but dines not infrequently, and he dines without leaving his den. And yet the lazy, unclean fellow has laid by no store. The three kinds of deer found on the head-waters of the great river of California are nomadic, and move with the snow. Let the snow disappear and they disappear with it. The Mountain Sheep is found only on the farther and north-east side of Mount Shasta; sure-footed, gregarious, harmless and hard to capture.

The California lion abounds here, but he is a sneak and coward, and, were it not for his fine skin and claws, would hardly deserve mention. There is scarcely any fight in him, even when wounded. But at the Upper Soda Springs I saw only a short time since a sweet little girl with two great holes in the side of her neck. These had been made by this comely and supple coward. The beast had sprung upon her when only a few steps from the hotel door. He ran up the mountain dragging the poor little girl in his teeth by the throat, sucking her blood as he ran. Fortunately her grandfather happened to have his rifle near at hand. He pursued and killed the lion, and brought the child back to her mother.

For nearly half a century these cool and flashing head-waters of the great California river have been counted the best fishing grounds, even in a country celebrated as the very elysium of Izaak Walton's disciples. In them is to be found a new fish not known elsewhere in the world; as full of fight as it is possible for a fish to be with a hook in his mouth; proud too, disdaining small things, despising worms and warm pools and all shallow waters. This fish is of the trout family, and, as his great size and strength suggest, he is the king of all trout. He is to be found, so far as I can learn, only in the McCloud river, and that too only far up in the fresh snow-water, even laying his head and glittering sides against the icy banks of snow. His beautiful and varied colors have given him among the fishermen of this region the name of "Dolly Varden." But science knows him not and I think he has no other name save that of his Indian appelative, "Wi-la-da-it," or "Fighting Fish." I sent a skin of one of these fishes some years ago to Hon. R. B. Roosevelt, famous as an authority in such matters; but, as said before, this fish is, or was at that time, new to the learned. Only last season one of these bright beauties, after he had fought for half an hour and was apparently dead, pulled a man into the river and nearly cost him his life. He was saved from drowning by his companion, who plunged down the steep bank into the deep water where he had fallen and contrived to get him to the shore before he was carried over the falls only a short distance below—a rare instance of getting advantage from fishing in company with another, which, I must say, savors of profanity in a temple. Of course there are fishermen and fishermen; but the man who, to my mind, has any right to fish, fishes alone. The light, the peeps through the trees, the fragrance, above all the perfume of the cool and perfect temple of nature,—all these are lost with a crowd, are made less sacred with the sound of voices.

To take the ordinary trout,—and you will always have great respect for this spirited fish, till you have encountered the Wi-la-da-kit—you have only to visit these head-waters made from the melting snows of Mount Shasta, and then cast in your line. Under the shadows of the huge sugar pines, beneath the gnarled roots of ancient trees at the base of the steep red hills, you will find them eddying about by the basketful in almost any one of the thousand white streams that come tumbling headlong down from out the awful cañons—as if afraid of the grizzlies there. But go on up and up and up, find new grounds and take your trout skillfully and sparingly like a gentleman. There is a great difference in dollars. How much bigger and how much better is a dollar quietly made by the pen or the plow than a dollar obtained by selling beer and washing glasses for a garrulous mob! And so it is with your catch of trout. When the day's hard tramp is done let each crisp little trout taste of the perfumed woods, of the flashing white waters, the mossy brown rocks under foot, the emerald world of woods overhead, the gleaming snow beyond, and over all and still beyond, the fervid sapphire skies of California; and, although you may have disdained to take but the one trout, it will be enough—and the miraculous draught of Galilee was no more.

JOAQUIN MILLER.

THE HEART OF
SOUTHERN CALIFORNIA.

HE county of Los Angeles embraces so large an area and includes such diversity of climate and scenery, so wide a range of products and so much of the old dreamy life amid the new, that to describe it completely and yet concisely is extremely difficult. With ninety miles of coast; a range of mountains whose snowy summits rise above glowing orchards and verdant plains in winter, while cool sea-breezes temper the summer heat; with numerous beaches and picturesque mountain resorts, and all the variety of a country teeming with beauty and interest; the pen gives way to the camera and brush and the poet becomes the better historian. The scale is so large that a million mountain acres represent nothing in the estimate of values; the industrial and social development is so rapid that no account of it seems valid by the time the ink is dry.

Entering Southern California by either the San Gorgonio or the El Cajon Pass, the traveler experiences the charm of vivid contrast between lands of sun and lands of snow. The monotonous stretches of barren soil, the dim, confused outline of distant hills, the meagre, dust-covered vegetation suddenly give place to a vision of snow-capped and forested mountains through which the highways lead into regions of almost boundless fertility. To the naturalist, however, even the desert seems a garden. Here and there patches of abronia work miracles of beauty, and the bristling Cacti cheer his eye with their gay blossoms and awaken his curiosity by their strange armor and singular diversity of form. Glowing mats of *Opuntia* are varied by spaces of clean sand, on which the hateful "Chug" has scattered its dangerous joints; huge pillars stand covered with ivory hooks, and myriads of rosy pincushions bristle with barbed spines; every form is warlike in its expression and attitude. In contrast with various prostrate kinds, the giant *Pitihayas*, or torch-thistles, often grow to a height of forty feet, and distil from pure sunshine a delicious fruit, highly prized by the Mexicans. The bleached skeletons of these lofty torch-thistles, carved by the sand-blast of the desert wind, stand like sentinels among their lowlier fellows. The exquisite natural lace of their desicated stems was closely imitated by the Indian women who became skillful lace makers in the days of the missions.

The approach to Southern California by the Cajon Pass is through straggling forests of *Yucca brevifolia;* seen by moonlight, their wierd forms duplicated and magnified by the shadows cast upon the silvery sand, these forests afford one of the most fantastic sights in nature. The Franciscan missionaries, who entered the country at San Diego, also found what seemed an insurmountable barrier to their progress in the rank growth of the desert vegetation; but as they advanced into the richly wooded and fertile valleys of the interior, they were convinced that the cactus-covered *mésas* had been set to keep out intruders until the *messengers of the Lord* should come.

In the year 1771, Fathers Angel Somera and Benito Cambon reached the Santa Ana River, on their way to plant the mission of San Gabriel Archangel. They were amazed at the luxuriance of the wild oats, which grew taller than their horses, and the immense size of the oak and sycamore

THE YUCCA PALM.

trees; and they rejoiced greatly at the profusion of wild grape vines, and "Castilian" roses which adorned the cañons. In spite of this lavish beauty, the name "Rio de los Tremblores," which had been given to the river by a previous expedition, induced them to continue the journey some twenty miles to the northwest, where they reached the fertile uplands of the San Gabriel. There the Indian villages were most numerous, and there on the first day of September, 1771, the holy bells were rung, and the image of the virgin elevated in sight of a lofty mountain peak which they named San Bernardino, and all its dependent valleys were consecrated to civilization. After a few years of busy industry the mission was removed to its present site, eight miles from Los Angeles. Of its numerous buildings only two roofless *adobés* are standing, and the sheep herder and his flocks are to-day the only moving figures in the quiet landscape. It was near this spot that a famous little battle was fought between the Mexicans and the United States troops in 1847.

AN AIRY HOME.—OLD SAN GABRIEL.

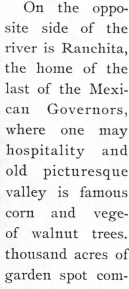

On the opposite side of the river is Ranchita, the home of the last of the Mexican Governors, where one may hospitality and old picturesque valley is famous corn and vege- of walnut trees. thousand acres of garden spot com-

still enjoy the ancient find many traces of the ranch life. Los Nietos for its immense yield of tables and for its groves Ranchita embraces four the tract, but is a mere pared with what it was before the "perfidious Yankees" outnumbered the original proprietors. Governor Pico is an octogenarian and a bachelor, but among the descendents of brothers and sisters who married into the most distinguished families is not often alone. The names of Concepcion, Estefana, Jacinta, Isidora, Tomasa, Feliciana and Josefa fall musically from his lips, and the bright faces of their owners are seen upon his walls; but they represent an intricate web of genealogy, for the fourth generation of Alvarados and Carillos is now on the stage. An aunt of the Governor died at the age of 74, leaving fifteen children, one hundred and sixteen grandchildren and ninety-seven great grandchildren.

The founders of the missions were wont to say that the difference of a single letter represented a difference of millions of souls. "All men will dare death for *Gold;* few are they who

Los Angeles. From Painting by Thomas Hill.

"Los Angeles, old and new, dense and straggling, growing out over a hundred hills, presents a shifting and bewildering panorama; for, like a rising tide, it is ever overflowing its boundaries, and hotels, cottages, churches, factories, schools and balconied villas spring to view in new places with magical rapidity. It occupies an area of about thirty square miles, while outside of its present limits are many embryo towns, villages and seaside resorts linked to it by fifteen lines of railroad."

will dare it for *God*."   All through Arizona and the lower peninsula, heaps of mining debris, slag, and the remains of rude furnaces mark the track of one class of pioneers; while olive and orange groves, ancient churches and peaceful occupations followed the path of the Franciscans in upper California, and made way for the romantic form of civilization under Mexican rule.   From Los Angeles to San Bernardino the country was one vast pasture for the flocks and herds of the San Gabriel Mission.   In 1834, there were 20,000 bushels of grain in its storehouses, 105,000 cattle and 20,000 sheep and goats grazed its plains, while 2,700 Indians were employed either as herdsmen, or in its orchards and vineyards.   At El Molino the *padres* ground their wheat into flour; their orange and olive plantations are found upon the Wilson and Cooper estates; Sunny Slope, Santa Anita, the Alhambra, and the site of Pasadina continued to be occupied as mission property many years after the grants were made.   The old Spanish maxim, "Plant a vineyard for your children, an orange grove

AMONG THE ORANGE GROVES—THE GOLDEN HARVEST.

for your grandchildren, and olive trees for posterity," was faithfully obeyed by the fathers wherever they went.   The industrial development of Southern California, with stock-raising at its base, was carried forward by them until the fitness of the land for the widest range of products had been demonstrated.

An edict having been issued by Felipo de Nevé, the Spanish Governor, authorizing the establishment of a *Pueblo* at the Indian village of Yangna on the banks of the river Porciuncula, there was planted, on the fourth day of September, 1781, the germ of a city under the protection of "*Nuestra Señora la Reyna de los Angeles*," both city and river thenceforth to be known by her name. The pioneers were twelve honorably discharged soldiers of the King of Spain, with their wives and children; in all forty-six souls.   All bore high sounding Spanish names: Moréno, Navarro, Villavicencia, Quintero, Rosas, Cañero, and others.   Each family had an outfit consisting of two oxen, two mules, two mares, two sheep, two goats, one calf, one ass, and for implements, *one hoe!*   Regular pay being continued to the soldiers, and the land a free gift under not very stringent conditions for its improvement, it is no wonder that the hoes were little used, and that not a trace of any possessory right descending from these families is to be found in the records of Los Angeles.

Never had so lovely a land so hopeless a beginning. Yet from a handful of soldiers trained to no useful labor, with hovels for houses, in a climate so seductive that only northern blood could resist its softening influence, the fathers by their indefatigable zeal and industry successfully replanted the old civilization on these extreme western shores. How the

OLD MISSION SAN GABRIEL.

missionaries labored with their own hands in teaching the neophytes the simplest arts and how they succeeded, is matter of history. By the Indians the bricks were baked, and the stones were hewn which went into the church edifices. The rafters were planed by dragging the logs down the mountain sides, until they were reduced to the proper size for supporting the tiled roofs.

What Indian labor was worth in laying the foundations of Californian civilization is best understood from the report of B. D. Wilson, the Government agent in 1852: "The Indians have built all the houses in the county and planted all the fields and vineyards. Under the missions there were masons, carpenters, plasterers, soapmakers, tanners, shoemakers, blacksmiths, millers, bakers, cooks, brickmakers and cart makers, weavers and spinners, saddlers and shepherds, agriculturists, horticulturists, *vignerons* and *vaqueros*—in a word, all the laborious occupations known to civilized society were carried on by them." In 1830 about thirty thousand Indians were employed in twenty-one missions. Three thousand Indians were constantly employed during eight years in building the mission of San Louis Rey. The old chieftain, Victoriano, who died in village of Saboba in 1887, was one of the workmen who built the mission of San Gabriel. An indescribable charm yet lingers around the scenes of this wonderful activity.

San Fernando, one of the youngest, was also one of the richest and most useful missions. In the first fifty years of its history there were recorded 3149 baptisms, 2140 burials, and 923 marriages. Its principal building was three hundred feet long, eighty feet wide, with walls four feet thick. This, with the church and other buildings of the mission, is now in ruins. Some of the olive trees are still alive and fruitful, and are the parents of many flourishing young orchards. A few of the old palm trees have survived in the gardens, and a pepper tree drops its coral berries into the broken fountain. They seem out of place in the near neighborhood of the new "San Fernando Mission Hotel," a Queen Anne structure with wide verandas, showy surroundings and modern appointments. The Theological School of the University of Southern California occupies temporary quarters near the site chosen for its permanent home, and the spell of silence and neglect which for a quarter century has kept San Fernando dormant is broken.

The San Fernando Valley is known for its fertility. A tract of four hundred and fifty acres has lately been planted with orange trees imported from Florida. Ninety thousand acres of wheat and barley covered the floor of the valley in 1887. Seen in the rich green of its young growth or in the gold of maturity it was a sight to be remembered; and not less so were the animated scenes which crowned

GIANT CACTUS—TORCH THISTLES.

the harvest. Bee ranches abound in the mountains, and one hundred thousand sheep feed in the upland pastures. It was here that General Andreas Pico first refined the petroleum which has since become one of the most important sources of wealth to this region, a thousand barrels being taken daily from the Pico and neighboring cañons. The various gold placers, worked at intervals since 1833, have yielded $8,000,000 during the last thirty years.

A large portion of the San Francisco ranch, often spoken of as the *locale* of scenes described in "Ramona," and also as the place where gold was first discovered, lies in Los Angeles County, and Camulos, another notable ranch, is but a short distance from Newhall, in Soledad township. This mammoth township, the Savoy of Southern California, covers an area of 1,200,000 acres and has several centres of population. It is settled principally by health-seekers because of its dry atmosphere. Grapes and other fruits are taken there by the car load for drying; and grape culture is likely to become its leading industry, though apples and small fruits flourish also. In the western part of this town lies Antelope valley, where the finest quality of wheat is produced at an altitude of nearly three thousand feet.

Near Lang's station are found ten thermal springs of varying temperatures, together with mud springs, which afford relief from rheumatism. The proprietor of these springs is the hunters' oracle, having killed the King of the Grizzlies, a formidable beast whose carcass weighed two thousand pounds, and whose feet and skin were exhibited at Woodward's gardens, San Francisco. The Los Angeleños still relate the exploits of Adams, the celebrated bear hunter and collector of wild animals, who made that city his base of supplies. He had trained "Lady Franklin," one of the most fascinating of grizzlies, to serve him as a decoy and also as a pack animal. Her appearance upon the Los Angeles plaza under a burden of camp equipage furnished greater entertainment than a bull fight to the *muchachos* of the old capital. Around Elizabeth Lake and four neighboring lakelets there is still excellent hunting, and the whole region is a fresh field for the botanist.

From Antelope Valley to Anaheim is a long step, but in taking it the observer has the advantage of meeting many of the strong contrasts which mark this imperial county.

It was a happy idea of some prominent Germans in San Francisco to convert a tract of land near the Santa Ana River into small homesteads for their countrymen. Out of this grew the "mother colony" of Southern California, one of the most contented and thriving communities in the State. Its fifty wineries are now manufacturing the product of more than 3,000,000 vines; but inasmuch as only one-third of each holding is devoted to grape culture, other fruits are cultivated, and grain-growing and sheep raising are not neglected.

Orange, Santa Ana and Tustin contain a greater wealth of products than any other equal portion of the county. Of these Tustin is the oldest and perhaps the most reposeful. In its depth of shade and long avenues of poplar trees it might be taken for a New England village. In March the orange groves are in their highest beauty. Each orchard seems finer than its neighbors, each tree more heavily laden than the last, as one moves along the shining rows from grove to grove. The air is filled with the mingled perfumes of orange and apricot blossoms, of poplar buds and sycamore tassels, of banks of sweet violets in the cottage gardens and fugitive odors of wild flowers from thousands of untilled acres. And, better still, the Tustinese have, as far as possible, spared every native tree, and are the wisest of their generation. These three villages are so closely connected by railroads, street cars and charming drives, that one is apt to regard them as one. They are also united in action for every public improvement and the adornment of their homes. Floriculture receives much attention, and is clearly more than a fashion since so many old favorites are seen among selected novelties from both hemispheres.

Raisin-making has became the chief industry at Orange, there being ten to fifteen square miles of vineyard in the neighborhood, planted almost wholly with the favorite raisin grape, the muscat of Alexandria. To this locality perhaps more than any other belongs credit for winning an enviable name for California raisins, leading Eastern dealers, long wedded to Spanish brands, having recently given the palm to the product of this place. As in the wine districts of France, Germany and Spain, there is here and there a little spot only which, from peculiarity and rare combination of climate and soil, comes to be known to the world by its choice vintage, so in California it is becoming apparent that certain products—raisins among them—can reach the highest excellence only in comparatively few and limited areas.

EUCALYPTUS AVENUE. FROM PAINTING BY W. C. FITLER.

"The town of Inglewood, where the pathfinder Fremont built a home for the evening of his days, commands a fine view of the city of Los Angeles and the Sierra Madre Mountains. The site was wisely chosen where grand avenues of eucalyptus and pepper trees are already grown, and citrus orchards are in full bearing."

SANTA ANITA RANCH, SAN GABRIEL.

COTTAGE AND LAKE, BALDWIN'S RANCH.

Though California vineyards lack as yet the picturesque peasant life which brightens those of Europe—like the pretty French girls in gay costumes; nevertheless connected with the picking and curing and packing even here is many a scene not altogether prosaic. The bamboo hats of the Chinese pickers show like enormous mushrooms along the fragrant rows; long lines of drying trays absorb the abundant sunshine; and finally, loaded wagons move slowly along the lanes to the sweating and packing houses, where skillful hands give artistic touches to the most beautiful of crops. Many of the vineyardists prepare for market their own grapes, the wife and children, after due training, packing the bloomful clusters in layers with excellent skill. At Orange there are four large estabishments for custom-packing. A single one of these put up and shipped thirty thousand boxes of raisins in 1885, sixty thousand in 1886 and ninty-seven thousand in 1887. The writer, wishing to be believed, hesitates to describe the corn and pumpkins and other vegetable crops of this delectable region. The reader is referred to the illustration, taken from veritable specimens on the field. Nor can one attempt to give any adequate idea of what the productive capacity may yet prove to be when the great ranches are divided. The rapid increase of population is seen in the numerous new settlements, and in the crowded condition of the hotels at Orange, Santa Ana, Tustin and Anaheim. The Hotel Palmyra at Orange, recently opened, has already made for itself a good name among tourists, from New York especially.

Near by is the Quaker Colony of El Modena, with six hundred inhabitants, a fine school house, a neat church, and restfully beautiful views of the Santa Ana Mountains and of the valley, reaching to the ocean.

The transition from the active to the passive phases of life are very sudden in Los Angeles County, especially as we near the southern limits. Tustin city is the gateway of the San Joaquin Ranch, which contains 48,803 acres; and the Lomas de Santiago, 47,516 acres more. The Cajon de Santa Ana ranch belongs to the numerous Yorba families, who still retain many of their old homesteads and habits.

VICTORIANO.

Ramona, a fair daughter of the first Spanish proprietor, was the wife of an American known and respected equally by his neighbors of different nationalities as Don Benito Wilson. Mrs. Jackson took the name of "Ramona," the heroine of her story, from this source, and first heard it at the house of a daughter of Ramona Yorba.

In the Santa Ana mountains are the most extensive apiaries. At the New Orleans fair of 1884 and other later Expositions the display of honey from the "Bee King" (Mr. I. S. Pleasants) attracted universal interest, not only for the intrinsic value and fine taste of the display, but for the consummate art by which the "blessed bees" were made to appear as exhibitors. In this vicinity is the home of Madame Modjeska, who has found diversion in managing a stock farm, and renewal of strength in surf-bathing at San Juan by the sea. A bold rider and a fearless swimmer, she explores the wild cañons, and with her husband makes her camps where she can enjoy the scenery of the summits.

WHERE VALLEY AND MOUNTAIN MEET—"KINNEYLOA" IN THE DISTANCE.

"H. H." once foretold the time when the native artists of Southern California would find their life and love in "picturing the cañons, the royal oak canopies, the herculean sycamores, the chameleon, velvety chaparral, and the water quarried gorges with their myriad ferns and flowers." But even "H. H." had never traversed the Santiago Cañon, one of the richest in all Southern California in groves and glades, in grape vine hammocks and bridges, in cataracts and trout pools. In the month of April a carriage trip from Tustin to San Juan Capistrano is a delightful experience, for the land is seen in a state of nature. There is hardly a sign of human ownership until the mission buildings are in sight and the billows of verdure are exchanged for a view of the peaceful ocean.

The San Juan mission, founded in 1776, was for many years the largest and richest of all in cattle, corn, oil, wine, and aguardiente. The main edifice was of stone with a dome and vaulted roof, surrounded by cloisters still sufficiently well preserved to show the former importance of the mission. In the earthquake of 1812, when the worshippers were gathered for the Sunday service, the dome

HOW THEY GROW AT TUSTIN.

fell, burying fifty-four persons beneath its ruins, and fatally injuring others. No attempt was made to rebuild it, other portions of the structure having been selected for sacred purposes. In 1842 the learned Father Geronimo Boscana officiated here, and wrote his work upon the custom and religion of the South California Indians. Here also Father Zalvidea passed the years of his exile from his beloved San Gabriel, and dying at San Juan, was buried near the altar of San Luis Rey.

Two and a half miles from San Juan village is the old embarcadero and a newly projected sea-side resort, San-Juan-by-the-sea. Fifty years ago, Richard H. Dana described this as "the only romantic spot in California." The grandeur of its cliffs and the charm of its delightful beach will never be forgotten by travelers on the old stage line to San Diego, especially if they saw it by moonlight. It is one of the richest portions of California coast scenery and is now on the direct line of southern trade. The Señoras will soon look from the windows of the old mission upon stranger sights than the tents of the railroad builders. The road is already an accomplished fact; and in the wake of these magicians will come white-winged yachts to the embarcadero, and cheerful villas will crown the cliffs at San-Juan-by-the-sea.

To lie among my orange trees
  That bloom by far Los Angeles;
To watch the lemon blossoms blow
  From out some fragrant, shaded spot,
Where dreaming with Boccaccio,
  The drowsy world is half forgot;
To hear the far-off summer sea;
  To scent the odorous southern breeze;

To catch the murmuring minstrelsy
  Of idly droning, gaudy bees;
To feel, though heaven is very near,
  That earth is fairer, and more dear;—
Ah! this is life's supremest gift.
  And, gazing through the purple haze,
One reads this legend in some rift:
  God's poems are such perfect days.

        —CHARLES H. PHELPS.

No book has been written, no song has been sung, which adequately represents the simple delight of living in old Los Angeles; the one city under our flag where one might bask in the sunshine for days or weeks, unreproved by his own conscience or the example of his fellow-men. The winter visitor who carried no time table, to whom no ride was long enough through pastures where myriads of wild geese were feeding, there found himself welcomed to some low-ceiled chamber of peace, opening upon a garden. If the mocking bird roused him from slumber, there was no rumble of trains, no cry of newsboy or milk-man, to break the spell of that perfect hospitality. If, waking late and refreshed, he looked forth through the trellised

OLD FOUNTAIN—SAN FERNANDO MISSION.

SANTA CATALINA ISLAND, LOS ANGELES COUNTY. FROM PAINTING BY J. IVEY.

"On no portion of the Pacific Coast is color and beauty in rock and in water so rampant as at Catalina. Caves, fissures and precipices offer endless sources of interest and admiration to those who leisurely pull around its coast, while the sea is a thing of enchantment. In corners under the cliffs it trembles like emeralds liquefied. Its moving wave masses reflect a color seen nowhere else, except on the shores of the Western Atlantic, while to look over your boat as it floats in some almost motionless recess of a cliff is to receive a revelation of beauty; for through more than ten fathoms of water your vision of rock or of fish is as clear as though it were the surface."—*J. Ivey.*

vines (where ruby-throated humming birds bathed in the spray of the fountain,) perchance he saw the hostess preparing his breakfast of coffee and tortillas, or the more appetizing "tomales." There was no hurry, no bustle—Angeleños might labor; they never toiled.

There was much informal visiting, and whatever the number of guests none lacked a cordial welcome. After the early dinner came the *siesta*. There was never a word about poor crops or bad investments; the sun was the bank, and had never failed. The family circle gathered on the wide veranda, where the guest was entertained with stories of pioneer experience, or took part in a dance to the music of the ever present guitar. The moon was their familiar friend and they made the most of her company.

Outside of the single business street and straggling lanes of the old *Pueblo*, one might easily lose himself for days or weeks in a wilderness of vineyards and groves of walnut and orange trees. The waters of the Los Angeles river were conveyed through every plantation by *zangas*, or distributing canals; flowing with a speed of five miles an hour, these streams were an important element among the homestead charms. The leafless walnut trees, with their silvery trunks and intricate net work of branches, relieved the monotony of the orange groves; and frequent patches of blooming almond trees were a foretaste of celestial gardens.

In Tustin one may still enjoy the delightful sense of solitude and society under corresponding natural conditions; but nowhere in Los Angeles is there a representative home of the period when it was the capital of California. Many of the old houses remain, full of interesting mementoes of the vanished social life, heirlooms brought from Spain and Mexico; but they have lost their setting. The Coronel and Wolfskill homesteads and orchards are impressively suggestive of the wonderful changes which have overtaken the city. The first orange trees in Los Angeles were planted by Louis Vignes, from trees obtained at the San Gabriel Mission. The Wolfskill orchard was started in 1841, and increasing year by year, soon became the largest in the country. In 1867 the orange crop of Los Angeles and San Gabriel was valued at over half a million dollars. In 1872 the average product of the oldest trees was two thousand to the tree; of the younger, eight hundred. The Wolfskill residence was typical. Its low roof was overhung with vines, and hedges of myrtle and pomegranate defined the private gardens. Certain orange trees which produced the choicest fruit were sacred to hospitality; so were the magnolias and other flowering exotics. No place in California

A VISION THROUGH THE TRELLISED VINE.

has a more fascinating story. After having furnished an important chapter in the industrial development of the country, it is numbered among departed blessings; and the Wolfskill railroad station is its monument.

The mother vine, *vina madre*, was also found at San Gabriel. To it the fathers had brought vine slips of a Spanish variety, now universally known as the Mission grape. While these were growing, *aguardiente* was manufactured from the wild grapes of the country. In 1831 this pioneer vineyard contained 50,000 vines, and 50,000 more had been distributed among the Indian *rancherias*. Little was known of these growing industries in the Atlantic States until 1857, when Mr. H. D. Barrows of Los Angeles presented President Buchanan with a representive collection of fruits and vines.

How these products spread and drew attention to the fertility of the country is shown by the fact that in 1883-4 there were 350,000 bearing orange trees in Los Angeles County, and 6,000,000 vines. San Gabriel had the largest vinery in the world, and the town of Florence the largest

ARCHED ENTRANCE TO SAN JUAN CAPISTRANO MISSION.

vineyard belonging to a single owner: the late Remi Nadeau having planted a solid block of five square miles with grapes, both mission and foreign. In San Gabriel, the centenarian orange trees and vines are still bearing fruit. Where nearly all the ancient landmarks have disappeared, in Los Angeles, a venerable sycamore tree spreads its branches over an area of two hundred and ninety feet. It has witnessed all the changes which transformed the Indian village of Yangna into a town, and the town into a modern city of sixty-five thousand inhabitants. This noble tree measures twenty-four feet in circumference and is ninety feet high, and like some of the old palm trees is likely to outlive the century.

A portion of "Sonora Town," the old *adobé* where Governor Pico once lived, and the church opposite the Plaza, illustrate the architecture of the first half century.

Among the old families one is constantly reminded of Dana's remark, that "should the Californians lose all else, they would yet be rich, in their pride, their manners and their voices." Joyous and generous to an extent which surprises those of cooler northern blood, a delicate reserve gives value to their simplest act of courtesy. They belonged to the land more than the land belonged to them, and for those who have had the happiness to know them well, it will have lost its greatest charm when they have passed away. But they will not entirely disappear. In the fusion of nationalities many new types are being evolved in California, among which the descendants of Spanish mothers and American fathers are distinguished for their fine social qualities. Among those of unmixed blood, the names of Coronel, Estudillo, Sepulueda and Del Valle, are known for important public services.

Los Angeles, old and new, dense and straggling, growing out over a hundred hills, presents a shifting and bewildering panorama; for like a rising tide it is ever overflowing its boundaries, and hotels, cottages, churches, factories, schools, and balconied villas, spring to view in new places with magical rapidity. It now occupies an area of about thirty square miles, while outside of its present limits there are many embryo towns, villages, and seaside resorts, linked to it by fifteen lines of railroad.

CONTENTMENT—A HOME NEAR THE MISSION.

Earlier in the century all the well-to-do citizens lived upon level streets, San Pedro, Alameda and Main streets being the most aristocratic. The less favored retired to the hills, whose narrow paths and zig-zagging stairways represented an ascending scale of poverty. These eyries, half hidden in curtains of scarlet geranium, with cascades of roses overflowing their walls, were very picturesque, and commanded views which in later days have proved fortunes to their possessors. All have been replaced by modern homes of rich and varied architecture which show the cosmopolitan character of the city and its wealth.

The Baker Block, the Catholic cathedral, and the Opera House, were the first buildings erected for public purposes which are worthy to outlast their century. In 1883–4, the Branch State Normal School building rose upon the Beaudry terrace, and in quick succession the Nadeau, Hollenbeck and other fine business blocks were built. Soon the old churches and school houses were replaced by

AFTER DINNER AT CORONEL'S.

larger and more beautiful edifices. The *Times-Mirror* Publishing house, the Fort Street Bank Building, the Clinton and Phillips blocks and the Westminster Hotel, are all admirable for their purposes and indicate a marked improvement in public taste.

There is no more enjoyable way of exploring this city of magnificent distances than by the numerous street-car and cable lines which connect widely-separated districts with its business centres. Nearly every visitor takes the three-mile trip upon the electric railway, and finds pleasant occupation for a day in riding through palm-tree avenues and long arcades of eucalyptus and pepper trees on the "bob-tail" car. From Boyle Heights, where many charming private residences are found, the orchards, vineyards and hamlets which fill the valley of the Los Angeles river open like a succession of pictures, and a comprehensive view of the city is obtained. There are several small but pleasant parks in and around Los Angeles, and picturesque outlying districts are reserved for pleasure grounds on a more extensive scale. Meanwhile Ellis and Figueroa streets, and other portions of the suburbs, are parks in effect, the unfenced private grounds, spacious and exquisitely kept as becomes the Angeleños, being open to orderly visitors.

Albert E. Sterner

"UNDER THE FAN PALMS."—TYPES OF EARLY DAYS IN LOS ANGELES. FROM PAINTING BY ALBERT E. STERNER.

"No book has been written, no song has been sung, which adequately represents the simple delight of living in old Los Angeles. . . . To look on such soul-filling scenes, to bask in such a genial, gentle air, and to feel that for the time all the world about one is making holiday and has put on holiday garb, is a most wholesome experience to contrast with the eager, driving life from which so many have temporarily escaped to indulge in the summer reverie."

Standing upon the Beaudry terrace, or any of the heights which overlook Los Angeles; scanning the network of railways which surround it, and the many fertile and populous valleys tributary to it; knowing that of its sixty-five thousand inhabitants two-thirds of them represent the wealth, culture and energy of the Atlantic seaboard and the interior States; we may easily believe that here will be developed one of the brightest centres of civilization to be found in the world.

The seat of the University of Southern California is at West Los Angeles, near the Agricultural Park. This unique institution is under the control of the Methodist Episcopal Church, which casting aside all precedents, takes the most direct road to the attainment of its leading object, the training of missionaries of Christian civilization. It is well endowed, and has an able corps of instructors. The Colleges of Letters and of Music are at West Los Angeles; the Medical College is in the centre of the city; the Theological School is at San Fernando, the Agricultural College at Ontario, and the Freeman College of Applied Sciences at Inglewood, near Redondo Beach. St. Vincent's College and other Catholic institutions of a high rank, and the excellent public schools, have been important elements in the recent growth of Los Angeles. The Eagle Rock Valley, Glendale, the Verdugo Settlement and Cañon,

THE GREAT PEPPER TREE.

OSTRICH FARM NEAR LOS ANGELES.

the Ostrich Farm, Ivanhoe and Burbank, are unincorporated suburbs which still further enhance the rural charms of the City of the Angels.

Throughout the southern counties of California the resurrection of the year is heralded by a procession of flowers, which, enlarging day by day, seems at last to enfold the earth in a garment woven of sunbeams. The sudden outburst of life and color is a surprise to the stranger and an ever-growing delight to the native, for the children of the sun are flower-lovers the world over. City and country share alike in this glorious benediction; even the beaches wear the gold and purple liveries of the Goddess of Spring. In the city, white lines of Callas divide the emerald lawns, scarlet Passion Flowers run over the buildings, and the Yellow Bignonia climbs from cornice to chimney-top. The poorest cottage has its flush of peach blossom, relieved by the rich green of orange leaves.

Later, as the Easter offerings fade, comes the festival of roses. In Los Angeles the annual Flower show, lasting from one to two weeks, maintains a "Home for Homeless Women," and enlists the entire population in its service.

The numerous seaside resorts of Los Angeles County are among its chief attractions. Among them Santa Monica is the best known, both as a watering place and an attractive town, not dependent upon birds of passage or given over to dulness for half the year. It has fine churches and schools, and though it has no harbor, the rebuilding of a pier where the coast steamers formerly stopped will restore its facilities for ocean transportation. The winters of Santa Monica are by many preferred to the summers; for the long drives upon the beach are then most exhilirating,

SAN ANTONIO CAÑON.—"OLD BALDY" IN THE DISTANCE. FROM PAINTING BY THOMAS HILL.

"'Old Baldy,' or the San Antonio Mountain, is snow-capped during most of the year, and stands exactly upon the line dividing San Bernardino and Los Angeles counties. Dispensing his lights and shadows and his radiant alpen-glow impartially, he feeds Pomona to repletion with artesian and brook water, and leaves Ontario to gather its supplies from his tributaries. The San Antonio Cañon leads into the heart of the range, where one finds the best of hunting and fishing, and the richest studies of rocks and waterfalls. What Shasta is to the northern counties, this noble mountain, along with its loftier neighbors, Grayback, San Bernardino and others, is to the south."

ARMY HEADQUARTERS, DEPARTMENT OF ARIZONA.

and the roads leading to Santa Fé Springs and other attractive places in the country are free from dust.

Few resorts can offer such a variety of recreation. The Sierra Santa Monica is a picturesque range where game is still abundant, and wild geese, ducks and pelicans are found in the lagoons. The camper may choose between Santa Monica proper, where the Los Angeles railroad terminates, Old Santa Monica, and the Heights, finding in each some special charm. Ocean Spray, a new settlement in the southern portion of the town, is already a favorite quarter for permanent homes. There are many cozy cottages scattered along the bluffs, and the Casino, modelled upon that in Newport, combines all the requirements for passing an agreeable leisure hour.

Long Beach is the favorite summer retreat of the Pasadenians, whose tents are giving place to cottages, as the spell of the ocean returns with season after season. This beach is like a continuous level floor for a distance of eight miles, making a most delightful road for driving, while a gently sloping bathing ground, with a breadth of from three to five hundred feet, lies along its course. In the height of the season a crowd of children may be seen rolling and tumbling like porpoises in the combing surf, or playing in the warm sands, quite unattended, for there is nothing to fear. Long Beach is a temperance colony, and offers many attractions to families as a permanent home. It has three churches and a good school; and the annual sessions of the Chautauqua circle bring together eloquent teachers and lecturers from all parts of the United States.

Redondo Beach also is connected with Los Angeles by a direct line of railroad, and has the advantage of deep water frontage, as well as a fine sandy and pebbly beach, and a salt-spring lake or lagoon, the waters of which are denser than those of the ocean.

The new town of Inglewood, where the path-finder Frémont is building a home for the evening of his days, commands a fine view of the city of Los Angeles and the Sierra Madre Mountains. The site was wisely chosen where grand avenues of eucalyptus and pepper trees are already grown, and citrus orchards are in full bearing.

More than twenty miles from the beaches there have been sleeping on the breast of the Pacific two islands which are destined to become of great importance in the future of Southern California. They are a *terra incognita* to most of the people, though Catalina has long been a rival of the beaches as a summer resort, and is thought to afford the finest camping and fishing place on the coast. Cabrillo, its discoverer, found it well peopled by a light-skinned Indian race, better clothed and more advanced in a few simple arts than any Indians he had seen. Like the islands of the Santa Barbara channel, Catalina abounds in earthen and stone memorials of a former age. There are many wild goats in the southern part of the island, and smaller game is plentiful. There is now a hotel on the island, and the round trip from Los Angeles via San Pedro, from which daily steamer trips are made, is one of the most inexpensive and pleasurable for the tourist.

The other island, San Clemente, is

A BIT OF OLD CHINATOWN.

more than twenty miles long, with an average width of two and a half miles, and has only one inhabitant during most of the time. Twice a year a band of sheep-shearers visit the island, returning with the semi-annual clip; once a year the solitary herder visits Los Angeles, receives his year's pay, and after a week's vacation goes back to his sheep. This way of life he has kept up for twenty years.

Nature has hidden away in many corners of California, for those who will come to see them, sights both wonderful and strange as well as grand and beautiful. Down on the coast, as well as in the wilder parts, she manifests herself in forms most unusual. The peculiar conditions of the atmosphere often produce a marked effect upon the view, and many a traveler through this region includes the mirage among the memorable things he has seen. This phenomenon still appears, but

PALM TREES ON SAN PEDRO STREET, LOS ANGELES.

it is not the modern traveler that sees and comprehends all there is in the landscape, for which his rapid, steam-driven course across country is ill-adapted. It was in the more leisurely days, before the land was criss-crossed with railroads, that the traveler saw the scene slowly unfold before his eyes and had time to note its strange peculiarities; and in the case of the mirage, to realize that there were vividly presented to his vision objects that his reason must reject as most certainly unreal. An old-timer, who frequently saw this weird manifestation, has thus described it.

Before the advent of the railroad in the Los Angeles valley the passage through the then thinly-settled country was by stage. The passengers, approaching the valley from the south, passed the night at San Juan Capistrano, and starting again at daylight soon reached the southern extremity of the valley. As the half-light of the dawn developed into the early morning haze, it seemed to bring into sight massive architectural works along the horizon. These shaped themselves to the eye as huge buildings, changing again into great arches, bridges and viaducts, that gave the appearance of an ancient country built up through centuries by uncounted generations, rather than an almost virgin land, scarcely touched, and as yet certainly untamed by the hand of man.

This phase of the vision continued until the atmospheric conditions were modified by the first rays of the rising sun, descending from over the range of mountains to the eastward. As the more massive forms disappeared they were succeeded by features more delicate and broken, and the distance was fringed with the scattered forms of spectral trees which reared their giant heads and out-reaching branches to heights not surpassed in the great forests of California; while underneath their spreading boughs huge animals were gathered, the whole like a vision of antediluvian life, in which the ghosts of prehistorical horses and cattle appeared to graze under the spectres of the primeval forest.

These visions were not in the imagination of drowsy travelers, awake in body but mentally asleep, nor did they appear in one form to one and differently to another; but they were sights as real as the myriads of wild geese, flocks of sheep, and grazing herds that wandered leisurely along the roadway.

The cool morning air, which retained its freshness until long after the sunlight had dispersed the early morning mirage, soon developed a keen appetite, and the hungry passengers were duly satisfied at one of those wayside stations that are so attractive and so necessary a feature of journeying by stage. After as little delay as possible they were presently speeding on their way in the full light and air of a glorious morning—one of those mornings when one is all enthusiasm with the abundance of animal spirits, when the whole body is aglow with life and every fibre tingles with animation. By this time every suggestion of haze and mirage had disappeared, and the most distant objects were distinctly visible through the transparent air. But with the approach of mid-day the increasing heat of the sun, warming both earth and atmosphere, once more produced strange effects. The heated air, fanned by the gentle breeze, rose from the ground in visible waves which became more and more decided to the view, until the far-off horizon was obscured and gave place to a billowy outline, the motion of which was wonderfully like that of the waters of the ocean. Indeed, the illusion was so complete, that instead of traversing an inland valley quite out of sight

SIERRA MADRE VILLA.

of the water, which was several miles away, the path of the stage coach appeared to lie along the shore of the sea. Passengers unfamiliar with the South were persuaded in their minds that this indeed was the fact, and commented on the wonderful beauty of this first sight of the sea. Along the apparent shore houses seemed to stand, and out of the waters rose groups of trees in effect not unlike those seen in the morning mirage. The lonely shepherd, standing with his dog not far from the valley road on one of the prominent observation-points which rise from the plain at irregular intervals, seemed to gaze out over the distant waters; and many a traveler, uninformed as to the locality, has reported at his journey's end that he had ridden for miles through the Los Angeles plain along the shore of the island-dotted sea.

These same visions may be seen by the traveler of to-day, but few modern sightseers are content to surrender the comfort and celerity of railroad travel to dwell upon the incidental mani-festations of nature, and either they do not see the strange mirage, or, seeing, they do not observe and understand it, and they too reach their journey's end perhaps thinking that from the windows of their train they have looked upon the sea.

"Entrance to Cajon Pass," San Bernardino County. From Painting by J. Ivey.

"No portion of the mountain range is more picturesque than that which overhangs and flanks the old city of San Bernardino, and this view is particularly charming, with its broken outlines, its wooded slopes, and refreshing creek full to overflowing after the early rains. It is only after the rains that such visions are seen in perfection, with an atmosphere clear as a dewdrop, and silvery mists floating out of the silent valleys like sweet-smelling incense."

The site of Pasadena was known in early days as *Llave del Valle*, "the *key* of the valley," through which the people of Los Angeles and the Verdugo settlement went to the San Gabriel Mission for their supplies. In 1874, when the "Indiana colonists" took formal possession of their lands, they changed the name to Pasadena, an Algonquin word, signifying "the *crown* of the valley." For already they saw upon its jewelled rim Santa Anita, a diamond in its loveliness of water and all the beauty that water develops; Sunny Slope, ruby-colored with the vintages of years; and emerald *Los Robles*, the cherished home of a distinguished soldier. Fair Oaks gleamed modestly through its leafy setting; and, supreme in their beauty and productiveness, were the old orchards and vineyards of the Wilson estate, seen from the windows of San Marino, the ranch house. This cluster of princely estates, and its nearness to Los Angeles, justified the choice of this tract for the colony's use—four thousand acres of wild land, watered by a tributary of the Los Angeles river. The wise selection was a prophesy of the success since achieved.

The founders of Pasadena were practical men, whose aim was to build up a community having a common interest in fruit-growing, free from debt, and sufficiently united in sentiment to secure social advantages and the benefits of co-operation. Their first care was to bring pure water from the mountains to every door. The next step was to build a school house and a place for religious worship. Without formal pledges, it was agreed that there should be "unity in essentials, in non-essentials liberty, in all things charity." This creed worked so well that in the first nine years there was no saloon, and neither lawsuit nor criminal prosecution in a population of one thousand inhabitants.

While many of the citizens were wealthy, there was no ostentation. Self-respect and cordiality were marked features of the social life. A natural live-oak park was the scene of frequent picnics, and the mountains and sea beaches furnished abundant recreation. Rivalry existed, even in this "Paradise," but it was between the orchards; and heated discussions, mostly upon the relative merits of seedling and budded orange trees, were of frequent occurrence. Thus earnestly was the miracle wrought. The colonists found their territory a vast seed-bed of weeds, and their soil everywhere honeycombed by gophers and squirrels; but during three years of persistent industry, they "beautified the place of their habitation and made their paths glorious" until many others also believed it a most desirable spot for a home. It had no hotel, but the hospitable doors of "Lock Haven" so often opened to lingering visitors that perforce it became one.

The fifth year of the colony was celebrated by a citrus fair, which drew crowds of visitors, but astonished none so much as the exhibitors, each of whom had been too busy with his own to estimate the collective value of the Pasadena orchards. During the following two years this colony took the highest premiums offered by the Southern district fairs. More truly was it morning-land in those days of joyous activity, shared alike by the young and by those who had reached the afternoon of life.

Three miles from Pasadena the Sierra Madre Villa, a favorite resort at all seasons and a winter residence for invalids, contributed greatly to increase the number of beautiful homes in its romantic neighborhood. For here the mountain range is most picturesquely broken with deep cañons and its peaks may be counted by scores between "Old Baldy" and the sea. The mountaineer no sooner conquers one summit than he is confronted with another apparently still higher, until standing upon Wilson's Peak, he has reached the rim of the local world. The floor of the Pacific with its shimmering islands seems very near; and the rich valley with its grain fields, pastures, Eucalyptus groves, orchards, vineyards, villages and villas, gives a human interest to the scene. This mountain is accessible all summer; and when there is no moon there is often a flaming camp-fire on the summit, lighted as a signal to watchers in the valley.

The cheerful isolation of the Sierra Madre Villa, its beautiful grounds and thrifty orange orchards, were fascinating to home seekers of cultivated tastes and not afraid of solitude with society so near at hand. Thus a world-wide traveler while a guest of the Villa selected a neighboring hill for his home. Having cut miles of mountain roads in order to reach it with building materials and planted other miles of broken country with orange and apricot trees, he saw that his work was good, in that he had both created and spared, and in memory of Polynesian days he named it "Kinney*loa*." Whereupon a neighbor, who had built his home on a still more elevated shoulder of the mountain, with a ready wit equal to the insight which discovers cities in all the cañon openings, christened it "Carter*hia*." The name given in jest now clings to it in earnest, and for the present generation it would be easier to change the name of a tree.

To many observers it seems a marvel that dwellers in the plains should build chambers in the sky; but an artist finds the grandest exercise of his power in giving new expressions to wild nature, especially in highlands. The mountains back of "Kinneyloa" rise like the bastions of a mighty fortress, and waves of chaparral reach to its very door; while the foreground slopes eastward in other waves of orchard bloom and brightness, not seen in detail but as masses of color against the liquid purity of the sky. Pasadena, the Raymond Hotel, and a dozen suburban villages lie cozily nestled at its feet. From "Carterhia" one cañon after another opens to the east; far away in the lowlands speed the railway trains, and westward lies the ocean, upon which the islands seem to float, like shadows of clouds. And if all these grander panoramas were wanting, the unexplored regions of mountain mystery in the background would quite suffice to make the place attractive. The originator of "Carterhia" has inspired many improvements in the San Gabriel Valley. Through his persuasion the Sierra Madre Villa, Arcadia and beautiful Monrovia—

CHINESE GATHERING GRAPES.

IRRIGATED ALFAFA FIELDS.

choice tid-bits of Santa Anita—were cut from the fifty-thousand-acre ranch.

Santa Anita contains the residence of the owner most picturesquely set near a lakelet which, though partly artificial, serves none the less as a beautiful mirror for a quiet, sylvan scene. It is reached through six miles of eucalyptus avenue, with many side avenues which subdivide ten thousand acres of orchards and vineyards. Here one may find a block of sixteen thousand orange trees, and another containing nearly as many almonds. The yield of the vineyards is enormous, and the wineries are built and furnished on a corresponding scale. La Puente contains sixteen thousand acres of grain and pasture land under the same ownership.

It would seem that the peculiarities of climate which multiplied the mission flocks and herds beyond all precedent are now developing the finest types of animal life in this locality. The horses upon which the missionaries entered the San Gabriel Valley in 1771, with a later acquisition of twenty from Lower California and a few starveling cattle, were represented as early as 1834 by 20,000 horses and 105,000 cattle. Sheep continued to multiply till they numbered about one-and-a-half million head. Among the admirable descriptions of "out-door industries of Southern California,"

by Mrs. Jackson, is one of sheep-shearing on the Puente Ranch, and a quaintly picturesque scene
it is, carrying even yet a decided flavor of the old Mission days. The passing traveler interested
in fast horses will doubtless turn aside while in the neighborhood to visit the Baldwin stables, the
home of so many famous racers.

Between Santa Anita and Sunny Slope are extensive orange and lemon orchards. All these
fruit-farms are reached by the California Central Railway and by a rapid-transit road from Los
Angeles. Monrovia, "the gem of the foothills," is less than four years old, and is now an incorporated city of about three thousand inhabitants, with
flowery homes and the usual ar-
ray of schools, banks, churches,
newspapers, and other institutions of a prosperous and civilized community. The rapid
growth has been accomplished
as if by magic, within a mile
of "the Duarte," one of the
quietest spots in the foot-hills.
Retired merchants and profes-

HOTEL ARCADIA.

ARCH ROCK,
SANTA MONICA BEACH.

sional men had
forgotten the
world and its
worries, and se-
cure in the pos-
session of their
living streams
and fruitful or-
chards, neither
desired nor wel-
comed a boom.
But it came in-
sidiously, in the
shape of a hand-
some hotel which
threw open these
blessings to the

world. The Azuza, lower down in the valley, and El Monte are experiencing a similar awakening.

The story of any one of the new settlements is the story of all. They were lighted in their
turns like the lamps of a great city, and before the spectators had ceased to wonder, the pleasant
slopes were bright with new homes. Lordsburg, La Verne, picturesque Glendora and its mate, Alosta;
Claremont, situated upon an elevated tableland, the site chosen by the Congregationalists for a college;
all these are links in the chain of thriving villages between Pasadena and Pomona. Each has its
own cañon and stream. The Big and Little Santa Anita and the Sawpit are wells for all the
western group; the San Gabriel River and its tributaries supply a lower section of the Valley.

"Old Baldy," or San Antonio mountain, is snow-capped during most of the year, and stands
exactly upon the line dividing San Bernardino and Los Angeles counties. Dispensing his lights and
shadows and his radiant alpen-glow impartially, he feeds Pomona to repletion with artesian and brook
water, and leaves Ontario to gather its supplies from his tributaries. The San Antonio cañon leads
into the heart of the range, where one finds the best of hunting and fishing, and the richest studies

ECHO MOUNTAIN, NEAR PASADENA.

WHITE CHARIOT PASSING ECHO MOUNTAIN HOUSE ON THE 48 PER CENT GRADE OF THE GREAT CABLE INCLINE, MOUNT LOWE RAILWAY.

"The climate of Echo Mountain is equable and delightful during the entire year. When clouds and fogs obstruct the vision and render residence somewhat uncomfortable in the valley, the mountain is invariably bathed in sunshine, and a dryness pervades the atmosphere. One of the most beautiful sights from Echo Mountain is to see the fog or cloud, like a white sea, hiding all but a few pinnacles and islands of the valley beneath, and, as the sun shines upon it, lighting it up into a fleecy brilliancy, and often revealing all the colors of the rainbow."

of rocks and waterfalls.   What Shasta is to the northern counties, this noble mountain, along with its loftier neighbors, Grayback, San Bernardino, and others, is to the south.   Its

> Mysteries of color daily laid
> By the sun in light and shade ''

are most impressive when the winter rains have purified the atmosphere ; but

> "The thief-like step of liberal hours,
> Thawing snow-drifts into flowers,''

may be heard from May to December.

The difficulties of making the ascent, which heretofore have rendered it impossible for all except the most hardy climbers to enjoy the enchanting views of the San Gabriel Valley and the Pacific Ocean, from the crests of the Sierra Madres, have been entirely overcome by the Mount Lowe Railway.   This road has included so many features in mountain railway construction as to entitle it to the proud distinction which has already been accorded to it by recent engineers, — " The most wonderful railway in existence."

Commencing at Altadena, with the Los Angeles Terminal Railway, for two and a half miles it is an electric trolley road, conveying passengers by fragrant flower gardens, orange groves and fruit orchards, over poppy fields named by Cabrillo's sailors Cape Floral, and into Rubio Cañon, which, with all the other cañons of the range, is filled with oaks, sycamore and the large-leaved maple, with the shining green of the wild cherry, and natural gardens of ferns and lilies.   Here in the heart of the cañon, where the surrounding rocks form a natural amphitheater of majestic proportions, Hotel Rubio is built.   This is a singularly interesting structure, being partially above and partially below an extensive platform, which spans the cañon at a height of over sixty feet.   For half a mile above Hotel Rubio, the cañon has been made accessible by plank walks and staircases.   It is one of Nature's choicest retreats.   Moss and fern grottoes, grand chasms, and eleven waterfalls, the last of the series, Thalehaha Falls, being an exquisitely beautiful stream of descending water. The smaller cañons and gulches in the immediate neighborhood become more interesting the more their depths are penetrated.   With each turn around some massive boulder new and charming views are revealed, and every foot of ground is covered with a profusion of wild-flowers.   In Castle Cañon days could be spent and something new discovered every hour.   The rocks are covered with lichens that give them a variety of rich colors, and through the trees glimpses of Mount Lowe can be seen.

Ascending from Rubio is the *Great Cable Incline*, the steepest mountain railway ever built.   It rises over 1,300 feet in a distance of about 3,000 feet, passing through Granite Gorge, over the MacPherson Trestle, and revealing a panorama of beauty, full of delight and charm, which engages the eye of the visitor until he stands on Echo Mountain, where there is a first-class hotel, a cozy Swiss *chalet*, and an astronomical and meteorological observatory, the latter under the direction of the eminent astronomer, Dr. Lewis Swift.   From this mountain radiate over thirty miles of the well-constructed bridle roads, reaching the highest summits of the range, and the numerous shady dells in the many cañons that seam the mountains.   Here, in the retreats of Nature's solitude, one may while away the pleasant hours in dreamy restfulness, listening to the hum of the bees, the warbling of the birds, and the singing of the various kinds of trees.

From the summit of Mount Lowe, one of the most extensive and beautiful panoramas of the world is revealed.   For nearly one hundred and fifty miles in every direction, scenes of grandeur, sublimity and pictur-esque beauty are opened up from the mountain ranges of Mexico, by San Jacinto, Santiago, San Bernardino and San Antonio, all clothed, during many months of the year, in robes of purest snow.   To the north and west the eye roams over mountain range after range, until in the far-away dreamy distance the Sierra Nevada chain is clearly distinguishable, with its offshoots which join the Coast Range near Santa Barbara.   On this lofty outlook the Mount Lowe Railway contemplates the erection of its "highest" hotel, built of granite quarried on the spot, and also of an astronomical observatory, which in equipment will be capable of doing the most efficient work for the advancement of science.

Switzer Camp is made in a sheltered nook on the main stream of the *Arroyo Seco*.   A central log cabin with its stone chimney is the common sitting room, around which are other cabins and tents.   An old-fashioned Dutch oven adds interest to the scene, and the sweetest of brown loaves and the brownest of baked beans issue from its capacious depths.   Here one may sleep on a bed of fragrant fir branches while the Arroyo sings over its rocky bed, and awake in a heaven of sylvan music made up of robin trills, the notes of linnets and finches, and sharper squirrel chirps strangely commingling.   The trail is superbly lighted with "Our Lord's Candlesticks," the stately

Yuccas. Sometimes one of these is seen standing alone, a symbol of purity and grace; oftener they are in companies like other social plants. The Yucca has not its equal among lilies and may be "considered" for a lifetime without satiety.

In early spring the cascades near Switzers are in full volume, and present the most spiritualized forms of water to be found in these mountains. There are other beautiful cascades in the foothills near Pasadena. Those of the Eaton and Millard's cañons are accessible by good roads and easy trails.

The Casitas Sanitarium is pleasantly situated on a curve of the mountains northwest of Pasadena. In the same neighborhood the sons of John Brown of Osawattomie live in a Log Cabin and guide excursionists through the wild scenery of the Casitas trail. Travel to these mountain resorts seems to be steadily increasing. The purest physical pleasure, renovation of body and spirit, every expression of the vitality of the earth, in rocks, water-falls, forests and the wealth of the valleys, are the harvest to be gathered upon San Antonio mountain.

The seasons of out-door recreation throughout all this region afford for those who can avail themselves of the opportunity a most idyllic experience. The accessibility of the numerous resorts, both the more popular and the less known, renders it an easy

A BEE RANCH.

matter for all who can leave behind the cares of business and the heated centres of population, to seek the comfortable and salubrious retreats where the temperature is delightful and the air like nectar. Indeed, the inhabitants of the coast are the beneficiaries, the year round, of the great ocean currents which temper both the winter blasts and the summer heat. In this region the wind currents are diverted by the high mountain barrier, which shields it like a wall. Yet the full benefit of the ocean breeze, coming pure and charged with vitality from the great water, is received unabated, and it gives a stimulus of its own which, added to the genial warmth by day and the refreshing coolness of the nights, renders life not only healthful but deliciously enjoyable.

Under such conditions do the Southern Californians seek the rest and relaxation of the summer season. From the populous districts excursion trains carry thousands daily to the shore or to the hills; and other thousands seek the remoter retreats in the mountains—all on pleasure bent which is seldom disappointing. There is a general consent to the lightening of business exactions, and wherever a railroad reaches or a trail leads there are found multitudes of those who at other times are buried among books of account and the affairs of the world. Along with them are other thousands who from all over the civilized globe are come to enjoy the celebrated pleasures of this occidental Eden; and American and foreigner, the denizen of the East and of the West, of the North and of the South, commingle in the enjoyment of rare days and perfect nights.

It is not alone the physical man that is served, with stimulating air to breathe and the

FALLS IN MILLARD'S CAÑON.

SWITZER'S CAMP, AND CASCADES.

freshest of food to eat, but the artistic senses are all ministered to. For wildness, as well as for gentle, peaceful, sensuous beauty, it would be difficult to surpass this entire region, which the world-making throes of the past and the atmospheric conditions of the present have conspired to endow with variety as well as rarity of beauty. To look on such soul-filling scenes, to bask in such a genial, gentle air, and to feel that for the time all the world about one is making holiday and has put on holiday garb, is a most wholesome experience to contrast with the eager, driving life from which so many have temporarily escaped to indulge in the summer reverie.

Among those who find their way to Southern California are many who, while they fully appreciate the quieter pleasures in store for quieter folk, are drawn thither by the hope of sport with rod or gun; and these are in no wise disappointed. From the wilder heights of the crags of Catalina to the coverts in the foothills, where small game abounds, they will find abundant opportunity of satisfying their desire for the pursuit of game of many kinds. Deer, wild goats, mountain lion, quail, water birds, cotton tail and jack-rabbit are plenty enough to satisfy the reasonable sportsman. Now and then a grizzly from the cañons makes his way within range of the Nimrod of the lower county and affords a kind of excitement that is *sui generis*. Hunting camps as well as facilities for more simple out-door life abound and guides whose services are recommended for those in quest of the larger game are numerous and skillful. Some of the wild denizens of this region, like the jack-rabbit, afford excellent sport to such as are fond of riding to hounds and like to vary their sport with an inspiriting ride across country; though these same agile, wily little beasts provide sport also for the hunter that goes afoot. At Wilmington, San Pedro and elsewhere on the coast there is also good sea-fishing, which pleasantly varies such sport with the rod as may be had along the up-country streams, where smaller fish abound.

These sports for those who love to go alone or in small parties are supplemented by the more general amusements that are open to all. About the hotels, among the camps and the small settlements, every variety of out-door exercise and in-door

EATON'S CAÑON.

GREAT CABLE INCLINE OF THE MOUNT LOWE RAILWAY.
VIEW FROM TERMINUS OF LOS ANGELES ELECTRIC ROAD.

"This Great Cable Incline is the wonder railway of the universe, and has already attracted more visitors than any other object of interest in California. It is the steepest railway and yet the safest ever constructed, and rises 1,300 feet in an ascent of nearly 3,000. At its foot is Hotel Rubio, 2,200 feet above the sea, higher than the Catskill hotels on the Hudson, and at its summit is Echo Mountain House, 3,500 feet above the sea, with an outlook over valleys, mountains, foothills, cities, towns, villages, sea-beach, ocean and islands nowhere else to be obtained. On Echo Mountain is a quiet Swiss *chalet* and astronomical and meteorological observatories under the direction of Dr. Lewis Swift, the celebrated comet discoverer."

recreation is indulged in under exceptionally favorable circumstances. A peculiar and important factor in all this recreative life is found in the general abandonment to it—the feverish restlessness which curses so many summer resorts and interrupts or abruptly terminates the city man's outing by dragging him to town whenever the present or the prospective market takes a new turn, being as remote as in human affairs it ever can be; and the sojourners in these summer communities surrender themselves freely to the relaxations offered.

CABIN OF JOHN BROWN'S SONS.

It would be difficult to suit a pleasure-seeker who could not be satisfied in this land—this veritable land of milk and honey, where Nature pours out her bounties and her beauties in lavish abundance, and the air of heaven conspires with the cunning of man to confirm health and to sanctify happiness.

Ten years ago, with Pasadena at one end of the line of settlements and Pomona at the other it was easy to foresee a change in the social condition of the San Gabriel Valley, and to predict that the vast estates would melt when touched by the iron road and electric wire. No country could be more inviting than the eastern portion of the valley, no lands exceeded those of Pomona in fertility. Raisins and oranges were the principal crops, and some of the old vineyards had produced eleven tons of grapes to the acre. The water supply was abundant from these unfailing sources, the San Antonio Cañon, the cienegas and artesian wells. Pomona is a town of churches and schools, and its banks and business houses indicate a substantial prosperity. The roads are well kept and beautifully shaded, and the "Palomares," the largest of its three hotels, is for Pomona what the "Raymond" is to Pasadena. Guests who stop during the sunny winter days oftentimes return to stay, and the tourist becomes a citizen.

To one returning to Pasadena after this flying trip to the eastern limits of the country, the Raymond Hotel is the most conspicuous object in the landscape. The opening of this hotel was also an historical landmark, indicating a point in the social evolution of the community; a time when the fusion of the populations of the Atlantic and Pacific coasts was taken up as a profitable contract by great railroad corporations. It is now so far systematized that when the hour strikes for the annual opening of the Raymond caravansery, a bevy of white-robed New-Hampshire girls drop into their appointed places in its service. The best society of the East and the interior fill it to over-flowing for six months. In April the season closes; and as quietly the manager, waiteresses and housekeepers vanish from Pasadena to reappear in the White Mountain resorts. A considerable percentage of the guests return to make permanent homes somewhere in the valley, which is seen in all its beauty from the Raymond Hotel. The Raymond and the railroads have stimulated the growth of Pasadena and made it a city. Beyond the corporate limits are many pleasant suburbs, which are linked to it by five lines of horse cars, fifteen miles of

FLOWING WELLS   POMONA.

track.   Hourly railroad trains run to Los Angeles, and special theatre trains three times a week.

The Pasadenians are justly proud of their schools and school buildings.   The Wilson Grammar school was built and furnished without cost to the citizens from the proceeds of a school lot in the heart of the city, the gift of Hon. B. D. Wilson, in 1875.

Old San Gabriel, still half Indian and half Spanish, is yet dreaming under its vines and pomegranate trees; while "the Alhambra," near by, is a wide-awake modern town.   But though the old Spanish school house is deserted the Mission church is well preserved, and what remains of its garden is carefully tended.   Under the stately palm and the orange and olive trees of Father Zalvidea's planting, one recalls interesting scenes enacted here early in the century.   Within the church, more than sixty years ago, the body of Josepha Coronel was buried with imposing ceremonies.   She was the first of her sex who taught school in California.   Beautiful and accomplished

THE RAYMOND HOTEL AT PASADENA.

herself, she gathered the daughters of Los Angeles into a school, lest they should grow up without what is even better than learning—the love of learning.   Many mothers of the best families were her pupils.   When she died a great crowd of mourners walked with the sorrowing family behind the bier whereon she lay, her white robes strewn with the fairest flowers.   Bearers constantly relieved each other for five long miles of the road to San Gabriel, when the mournful procession was met by the priests and a long train of Indians, who took up the precious burden and the solemn chant for the dead and moved on yet another five miles, when the church was reached and the last rites performed.   The father of this young lady was the first teacher in the State, and compiled a school book for the use of his pupils, which was printed at Monterey.

Within sight of the Old Mission the little church of the Holy Saviour was the first edifice of the Episcopalians in Southern California.   In the "God's acre" adjoining, a monument indicates the resting place of B. D. Wilson, the friend of the Indians and equally the friend of order and progress in the San Gabriel Valley.   But Wilson's Peak, which dominates the Sierra Madre mountains, will prove a more enduring monument to the memory of the useful pioneer and citizen.

As it was the homes of the Old city of Los Angeles which beguiled and enchanted the passing stranger in former years, so it is the homes of Southern California which attract the dwellers of less favored climes to-day — homes of almost infinite variety of aspect and situation; homes of

IN SANTIAGO CAÑON.

wealthy capitalists who hold the open sesame to speedy results, and the more modest yet equally attractive nests which seem to owe little to any cause but Nature and Time. The source of public security and social permanence being the "love of the freeholder for his home," that is the blessed land in which these are multiplied.

JEANNE C. CARR.

◉ Mt Shasta ◉

Mount Shasta rises in solitary grandeur from the edge of a comparatively low and lightly sculptured lava plain near the northern extremity of the Sierra, and maintains a far more impressive and commanding individuality than any other mountain within the limits of California. Go where you may, within a radius of from fifty to a hundred miles or more, there stands before you the colossal cone of Shasta, clad in ice and snow, the one grand, unmistakable landmark—the pole-star of the landscape. Far to the southward Mount Whitney lifts its granite summit four or five hundred feet higher than Shasta, but it is nearly snowless during the late summer, and is so feebly individualized that the traveler may search for it in vain among the many rival peaks crowded along the axis of the range to north and south of it, which all alike are crumbling residual masses brought into relief in the degradation of the general mass of the range. The highest point on Mount Shasta, as determined by the State Geological Survey, is in round numbers 14,440 feet above mean tide That of Whitney, computed from fewer observations, is about 14,900 feet. But inasmuch as the average elevation of the plain out of which Shasta rises is only about 4,000 feet above the sea, while the actual base of the peak of Mount Whitney lies at an elevation of 11,000 feet, the individual height of the former is about two and a half times as great as that of the latter.

Approaching Shasta from the south, one obtains glimpses of its snowy cone here and there through the trees from the tops of hills and ridges; but it is not until Strawberry Valley is reached, where there is a grand out-opening of the forests, that Shasta is seen in all its glory, from base to crown clearly revealed with its wealth of woods and waters and fountain snow, rejoicing in the bright mountain sky, and radiating beauty on all the subject landscape like a sun. Standing in a fringing thicket of purple spiræa in the immediate fore-ground is a smooth expanse of green meadow with its meandering stream, one of the smaller affluents of the Sacramento; then a zone of dark, close forest, its countless spires of pine and fir rising above one another on the swelling base of the mountain in glorious array; and over all the great white cone sweeping far into the thin, keen sky—meadow, forest and grand icy summit harmoniously blending and making one sublime picture evenly balanced.

The main lines of the landscape are immensely bold and simple, and so regular that it needs all its shaggy wealth of woods and chaparral and its finely tinted ice and snow and brown jutting crags to keep it from looking conventional. In general views of the mountain three distinct zones may be readily defined. The first, which may be called the Chaparral Zone, extends around the base in a magnificent sweep nearly a hundred miles in length on its lower edge, and with a breadth of about seven miles. It is a dense growth of chaparral from three to six or eight feet high, composed chiefly of manzanita, cherry, chincapin, and several species of ceanothus, called deer-brush by the hunters, forming when in full bloom one of the most glorious flower-beds conceivable. The continuity of this flowery zone is interrupted here and there, especially on the south side of the mountain, by wide swaths of coniferous trees, chiefly the sugar and yellow pines, Douglass-spruce, silver-fir and incense-cedar, many specimens of which are two hundred feet high and five to seven feet in diameter. Golden-rods, asters, gilias, lilies and lupines, with many other less conspicuous plants, occur in warm sheltered openings in these lower woods, making charming gardens of wildness where bees and butterflies are at home and many a shy bird and squirrel.

The next higher is the Fir Zone, made up almost exclusively of two species of silver-fir. It is from two to three miles wide, has an average elevation above the sea of some 6,000 feet on its lower edge, 8,000 on its upper, and is the most regular and best defined of the three.

The Alpine Zone has a rugged, straggling growth of storm-beaten dwarf pines (*P. Albicaulis*), which forms the upper edge of the timber line. This species reaches an elevation of about 9,000 feet, but at this height the tops of the trees rise only a few feet into the thin frosty air, and are closely pressed and shorn by wind and snow; yet they hold on bravely and put forth an abundance of beautiful purple flowers and produce cones and seeds. Down towards the edge of the fir belt they stand erect, forming small, well-formed trunks, and are associated with the taller two-leafed and mountain pines and the beautiful Williamson spruce. Bryanthus, a beautiful flowering heath-wort, flourishes a few hundred feet above the timber line, accompanied with Kalmia and spiræa. Lichens enliven the faces of the cliffs with their bright colors, and in some of the warmer nooks of the rocks, up to a height of 11,000 feet, there are a few tufts of dwarf daisies, wall-flowers and penstemons; but notwithstanding these bloom freely they make no appreciable show at a distance, and the stretches of rough brown lava beyond the storm-beaten trees seem as bare of vegetation as the great snow fields and glaciers of the summit.

Shasta is a fire-mountain, an old volcano gradually accumulated and built up into the blue deep of the sky by successive eruptions of ashes and molten lava which, shot high in the air and falling in darkening showers, and flowing from chasms and craters, grew outward and upward like the trunk of a knotty, bulging tree. Not in one grand convulsion was Shasta given birth, nor in any one special period of volcanic storm and stress, though mountains more than a thousand feet in height have been cast up like mole-hills in a night—quick contributions to the wealth of the landscapes, and most emphatic statements on the part of Nature of the gigantic character of the power that dwells beneath the dull, dead-looking surface of the earth. But sections cut by the glaciers, displaying some of the internal framework of Shasta, show that comparatively long periods

THE THREE ZONES OF SHASTA. FROM PAINTING BY THOS HILL.

"In general views of the mountain, three distinct zones may be readily defined. The first, which may be called the Chaparral Zone, extends around the base in a magnificent sweep of nearly one hundred miles in length on its lower edge, and with a breadth of about seven miles. The next higher is the Fir Zone, made up almost exclusively of two species of silver fir. The Alpine Zone has a rugged, straggling growth of storm-beaten dwarf pines which forms the upper edge of the timber line."

of quiescence intervened between many distinct eruptions, during which the cooling lavas ceased to flow, and took their places as permanent additions to the bulk of the growing mountain. Thus with alternate haste and deliberation eruption succeeded eruption, until Mount Shasta surpassed even its present sublime height.

Then followed a strange contrast. The glacial winter came on. The sky that so often had been darkened with storms of cinders and ashes and lighted by the glare of volcanic fires, was filled with crystal snow-flowers which, loading the cooling mountain, gave birth to glaciers that uniting edge to edge at length formed one grand conical glacier—a down-crawling mantle of ice upon a fountain of smouldering fire, crushing and grinding its brown, flinty lavas, and thus degrading and remodeling the entire mountain from summit to base. How much denudation and degradation has been effected we have no means of determining, the porous, crumbling rocks being

SUMMIT OF MT. SHASTA, AND THE GLACIER.

ill-adapted for the reception and preservation of glacial inscriptions. The summit is now a mass of ruins, and all the finer striations have been effaced from the flanks by post-glacial weathering, while the irregularity of its lavas as regards susceptibility to erosion, and the disturbance caused by inter and post-glacial eruptions, have obscured or obliterated those heavier characters of the glacial record found so clearly inscribed upon the granite pages of the high Sierra between latitude 36° 30′ and 39°. This much however is plain, that the summit of the mountain was considerably lowered, and the sides were deeply grooved and fluted while it was a centre of dispersal for the glaciers of the circumjacent region. And when at length the glacial period began to draw near its close the ice-mantle was gradually melted off around the base of the mountain, and in receding and breaking up into its present fragmentary condition the irregular heaps and rings of moraine matter were stored upon its flanks on which the forests are growing. The glacial erosion of most of the Shasta lavas gives rise to detritus composed of rough sub-angular boulders of moderate size and porous gravel and sand, which yields freely to the transporting power of running water. Several centuries ago immense quantities of this lighter material were washed down from the higher slopes by a flood

A QUIET NOOK ON THE UPPER SACRAMENTO.

of extraordinary magnitude, caused probably by the sudden melting of the ice and snow during an eruption, giving rise to the deposition of conspicuous delta-like beds around the base. And it is upon these flood-beds of moraine soil, thus suddenly and simultaneously laid down and joined edge to edge, that the flowery chaparral is growing.

Thus, by forces seemingly antagonistic and destructive Nature accomplishes her beneficent designs—now a flood of fire, now a flood of ice, now a flood of water; and again in the fullness of time an outburst of organic life—forest and garden, with all their wealth of fruit and flowers, the air stirred into one universal hum, with rejoicing insects, a milky-way of wings and petals, girdling the new-born mountain like a cloud, as if the vivifying sunbeams beating against its sides had broken into a foam of plant-bloom and bees. But with such grand displays as Nature is making here how grand are her reservations, bestowed only upon those who devotedly seek them. Beneath the smooth and snowy surface the fountain fires are still aglow, to blaze forth afresh at their appointed times. The glaciers, looking so still and small at a distance, represented by the artist with a patch of white paint laid on by a single stroke of his brush, are still flowing onward, unhalting, with deep crystal currents, sculpturing the mountain with stern, resistless energy. How many caves and fountains that no eye has yet seen lie with all their fine furniture deep down in the darkness, and how many shy wild creatures are at home beneath the grateful lights and shadows of the woods, rejoicing in their fullness of perfect life. Standing on the edge of the strawberry meadows in the sun-days of summer, not a foot or feather or leaf seems to stir; and the grand, towering mountain with all its inhabitants appears in rest, calm as a star. Yet how profound is the energy ever in action, and how great is the multitude of claws and teeth, wings and eyes, wide-awake and at work and shining. Going into the blessed wilderness, the blood of the plants throbbing beneath the life-giving sunshine seems to be heard and felt; plant-growth goes on before our eyes, and every tree and bush and flower is seen as a hive of restless industry. The deeps of the sky are mottled with singing wings of every color and tone,—clouds of brilliant crysididæ dancing and swirling in joyous rhythm, golden-barred vespidæ, butterflies, grating cicadæ and jolly rattling grasshoppers,—fairly enameling the light, and shaking all the air into music. Happy fellows they are, every one of them, blowing tiny pipe and trumpet, plodding and prancing, at work or at play.

Though winter holds the summit, Shasta in summer is mostly a massy, bossy mound of flowers colored like the alpenglow that flushes the snow. There are miles of wild roses, pink bells of huckleberry and sweet manzanita, every bell a honey-cup, plants that tell of the north and of the south; tall nodding lilies, the crimson sarcodes, rhododendron, cassiope and blessed Linnæa; phlox, calycanthus, plum, cherry, crategus, spiræa, mints and clovers in endless variety; ivesia, larkspur and columbine; golden applopappus, linosyris, bahia, wyethia, arnica, brodæa, etc.,—making sheets and beds of light edgings of bloom in lavish abundance for the myriads of the air dependent on their bounty. The common honey-bees, gone wild in this sweet wilderness, gather tons of honey into the hollows of the trees and rocks, clambering eagerly through

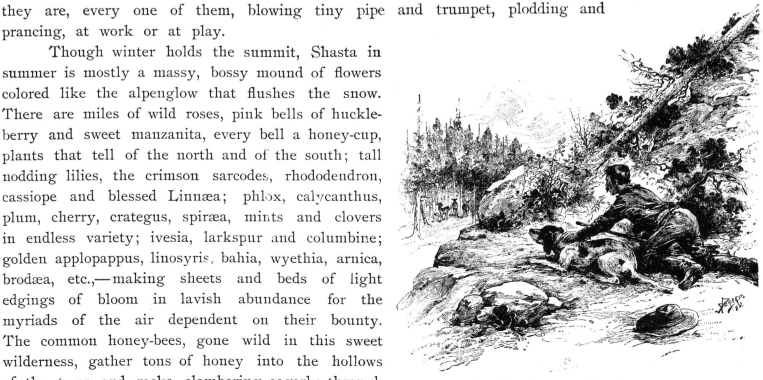

DEER STALKING—MT. SHASTA.

bramble and hucklebloom, shaking the clustered bells of the generous manzanita, now humming aloft among polleny willows and firs, now down on the ashy ground among small gilias and buttercups, and anon plunging into banks of snowy cherry and buckthorn. They consider the lilies and roll into them, pushing their blunt polleny faces against them like babies on their mother's bosom; and fondly, too, with eternal love does Mother Nature clasp her small bee-babies and suckle them, multitudes at once, on her warm Shasta-breast. Besides the common honey-bee there are many others here, fine, burly, mossy fellows, such as were nourished on the mountains many a flowery century before the advent of the domestic species—humble-bees, mason-bees, carpenter-bees and leaf-cutters. Butterflies, too, and moths of every size and pattern; some wide-winged like bats, flapping slowly and sailing in easy curves; others like small flying violets shaking about loosely in short zigzag flights close to the flowers, feasting in plenty night and day.

Deer in great abundance come to Shasta from the warmer foot-hills every spring to feed in the rich, cool pastures, and bring forth their young in the ceanothus tangles of the Chaparral zone, retiring again before the snow-storms of winter, mostly to the southward and westward of the mountain. In like manner the wild sheep of the adjacent region seek the lofty inaccessible crags of the summit as the snow melts, and are driven down to the lower spurs and ridges where there is but little snow, to the north and east of Shasta. Bears, too, roam this food-full wilderness, feeding on grass, clover, berries, nuts, ant-eggs, fish, flesh or fowl,—whatever comes in their way, with but little troublesome discrimination. Sugar and honey they seem to like best of all, and they seek far to find the sweets; but when hard pushed by hunger they make out to gnaw a living from the bark of trees and rotten logs, and might almost live on clean lava alone. Notwithstanding the California bears have had as yet but little experience with honey-bees, they sometimes succeed in reaching the bountiful stores of these industrious gatherers and enjoy the feast with majestic relish. But most honey-bees in search of a home are wise enough to make

McCLOUD RIVER—GOVERNMENT FISH-HATCHERY.

choice of a hollow in a living tree far from the ground, whenever such can be found. There they are pretty secure, for though the smaller brown and black bears climb well, they are unable to gnaw their way into strong hives, while compelled to exert themselves to keep from falling and at the same time endure the stings of the bees about the nose and eyes, without having their paws free to brush them off. But woe to the unfortunates who dwell in some prostrate trunk, and to the black bumble-bees discovered in their mossy, mouse-like nests in the ground. With powerful teeth and claws these are speedily laid bare, and almost before time is given for a general buzz the bees, old and young, larvæ, honey, stings, nest and all, are devoured in one ravishing revel. The antelope may still be found in considerable numbers to the north-eastward of Shasta, but the elk, once abundant, have almost entirely gone from the region. The smaller animals, such as the wolf, the various foxes, wildcats, coon, squirrels, and the curious wood-rat that builds large brush huts, abound in all the wilder places; and the beaver, otter, mink, etc., may still be found along the sources of the rivers. The blue grouse and mountain quail are plentiful in the woods and the sage-hen on the plains about the northern

"Among the Pines."   From Painting by Al Hencke.

Nowhere within the limits of California are the forests of yellow pine so extensive and exclusive as at the headwaters of the Pitt.   They cover the mountains and all the lower slopes that border the wide open valleys which abound there, pressing forward in imposing ranks, seemingly the hardiest and most firmly established of all the northern coniferæ.

base of the mountain, while innumerable smaller birds enliven and sweeten every thicket and grove.

There are at least five classes of human inhabitants about the Shasta region:—the Indians, now scattered, few in numbers and miserably demoralized, though still offering some rare specimens of savage manhood; miners and prospectors, found mostly to the north and west of the mountain, since the region about its base is overflowed with lava; cattle-raisers, mostly on the open plains to the north-east-ward and around the Klamath lakes; hunters and trappers, where the woods and waters are wildest; and farmers, in Shasta valley on the north side of the mountain, wheat, apples, melons, berries, all the best production of farm and garden growing and ripening there at the foot of the great white cone, which seems at times during changing storms ready to fall upon them —the most sublime farm scenery imaginable.

CASTLE LAKE.

The Indians of the McCloud River that have come under my observation differ considerably in habits and features from the Diggers and other tribes of the foot-hills and plains, and also from the Pah Utes and Modocs. They live chiefly on salmon. They seem to be closely related to the Thlinkits of Alaska, Washington, and Oregon, and may readily have found their way here by passing from stream to stream in which salmon abounds. They have much better features than the Indians of the plains, and are rather wide awake, speculative and ambitious in their way, and garrulous, like the natives of the northern coast. Before the Modoc war they lived in dread of the Modocs, a tribe living about the Klamath lake and the Lava Beds who were in the habit of crossing the low Sierra divide past the base of Shasta on free-booting excursions, stealing wives, fish and weapons from the Pitts and McClouds. Mothers would hush their children by telling them that the Modocs would catch them. During my stay at the Government fish-hatching station on the McCloud I was accompanied in my walks along the river-bank by a McCloud boy about ten years of age, a bright, inquisitive fellow, who gave me the Indian names of the birds and plants that we met. The water-ouzel he knew well and seemed to like the sweet singer, which he called "Sussinny." He showed me how strips of the stems of the beautiful maidenhair fern were used to adorn baskets with handsome brown bands, and pointed out several plants good to eat, particularly the large saxifrage growing abundantly along the river margin. Once I rushed suddenly upon him to see if he would be frightened; but he unflinchingly held his ground, struck a grand heroic attitude, and shouted, "Me no 'fraid; me Modoc!"

Mount Shasta, so far as I have seen, has never been the home of Indians, not even their hunting ground to any great extent, above the lower slopes of the base. They are said to be afraid of fire-mountains and geyser-basins as being the dwelling places of dangerously powerful and unmanageable gods. However, it is food, and their relations to other tribes that mainly control the movements of Indians; and here their food was mostly on the lower slopes, with nothing except the wild sheep to tempt them higher. Even these were brought within reach without excessive climbing during the storms of winter. On the north side of Shasta, near Sheep Rock, there is a long cavern sloping to the northward nearly a mile in length, thirty or forty feet wide and fifty feet or more

CASTLE LAKE.

in height, regular in form and direction like a railroad tunnel, and probably formed by the flowing away of a current of lava after the hardening of the surface. At the mouth of this cave where the light and shelter is good I found many of the heads and horns of the wild sheep, and the remains of camp-fires, no doubt those of Indian hunters who in stormy weather had camped there and feasted after the fatigues of the chase. A wild picture that must have formed on a dark night—the glow of the fire, the circle of crouching savages around it seen through the smoke, the dead game, and the weird darkness and half-darkness of the walls of the cavern, a picture of cave-dwellers at home in the stone age. Interest in hunting is almost universal, so deeply is it rooted as an inherited instinct ever ready to rise and make itself known. Fine scenery may not stir a fibre of mind or body, but how quick and how true is the excitement of the pursuit of game! Then up flames the slumbering volcano of ancient wildness, all that has been done by church and school through centuries of cultivation is for the moment destroyed, and the decent gentleman or devout saint becomes a howling, blood-thirsty, demented savage. It is not long since we all were cave-men and followed game for food as truly as wildcat or wolf, and the long repression of civilization seems to make the rebound to savage love of blood all the more violent. This frenzy, fortunately, does not last long in its most exaggerated form, and after a season of wildness refined gentlemen from cities are not more cruel than hunters and trappers who kill for a living.

Dwelling apart in the depths of the woods are the various kinds of mountaineers—hunters, prospectors, and the like—rare men, "queer characters," and well worth knowing. Their cabins are located with reference to game and the ledges to be examined, and are constructed almost as simply as those of the wood-rats made of sticks laid across each other without compass or square. But they afford good shelter from storms, and so are "square" with the need of their builders. These men as a class are singularly fine in manners, though their faces may be scarred and rough like the bark of trees. On entering their cabins you will promptly be placed on your good behavior, and, your wants being perceived with quick insight, complete hospitality will be offered for body and

mind to the extent of the larder. These men know the mountains far and near and their thousand voices, like the leaves of a book. They can tell where the deer may be found at any time of year or day, and what they are doing; and so of all the other furred and feathered people they meet in their walks; and they can send a thought to its mark as well as a bullet. The aims of such people are not always the highest, yet how brave and manly and clean are their

LOGGING IN THE MOUNTAINS.

lives compared with too many in crowded towns mildewed and dwarfed in disease and crime! How fine a chance is here to begin life anew in the free fountains and skylands of Shasta, where it is so easy to live and to die! The future of the hunter is likely to be a good one; no abrupt change about it, only a passing from wilderness to wilderness, from one high place to another.

Now that the railroad has been built up the Sacramento, everybody with money may go to Mount Shasta, the weak as well as the strong, fine-grained, succulent people whose legs have never ripened as well as sinewy mountaineers seasoned long in the weather. This, surely, is not the best way of going to the mountains, yet it is better than staying below. Many still small voices will not be heard in the noisy rush and din, suggestive of going to the sky in a chariot of fire or a whirlwind, as one is shot to the Shasta-mark in a booming palace-car cartridge; up the rocky cañon, skimming the foaming river, above the level reaches, above the dashing spray—fine exhilarating translation, yet pity to go so fast in a blur where so much might be seen and enjoyed.

The mountains are fountains not only of rivers and fertile soils, but of men. Therefore we are all, in some sense, mountaineers, and going to the mountains is going home. Yet how many are doomed to toil in town shadows while the white mountains beckon all along the horizon! Up the cañon to Shasta should be a cure for all care. But many on arrival seem at a loss to know what to do with themselves, and seek shelter in the hotel, as if that were the Shasta they had come for. Others never leave the rail, content with window-view, and cling to the comforts of the sleeping-car like blind mice to their mothers. Many are sick and have been dragged to the healing wilderness unwillingly for body-good alone. Were the parts of the human machine detachable like Yankee inventions, how strange would be the gatherings on the mountains of pieces of people out of repair! How sadly unlike the whole-hearted ongoing of the seeker after gold is this partial,

"Castle Crags," from Painting by Thos. Hill.

"The Shasta region is still a fresh, unspoiled wilderness, accessible and available for travelers of every kind and degree. Would it not be a fine thing to set it apart, like the Yellowstone and Yosemite, as a national park, for the welfare and benefit of all mankind, preserving its fountains and forests and all its glad life in primeval beauty? . . . No private right or interest need suffer, and thousands yet unborn would come from far and near and bless the country for its wise and benevolent forethought."—*John Muir.*

compulsory mountaineering; as if the mountain treasuries contained nothing better than gold. Up the mountain they go, high-heeled and high-hatted, laden like Christian with mortifications and mortgages of divers sorts and degrees, some suffering from the sting of bad bargains, others exulting in good ones; hunters and fishermen with gun and rod and leggins; blythe and jolly troubadours to whom all Shasta is romance; poets singing their prayers; the weak and the strong, unable or unwilling to bear mental taxation. But, whatever the motive, all will be in some measure benefited. None may wholly escape the good of Nature, however imperfectly exposed to her blessings. The minister will not preach a perfectly flat and sedimentary sermon after climbing a snowy peak; and the fair play and tremendous impartiality of Nature, so tellingly displayed, will surely affect the after pleadings of the lawyer. Fresh air at least will get into everybody, and the cares of mere business will be quenched like the fires of a sinking ship.

Possibly a branch railroad may sometime be built to the summit of Mount Shasta like the road on Mount Washington. In the meantime tourists are dropped at Sissons, about twelve miles from the summit, whence as headquarters they radiate in every direction to the so-called "points of interest;" sauntering about the flowery fringes of the Strawberry Meadows, bathing in the balm of the woods, scrambling, fishing, hunting; riding about Castle Lake, the McCloud River, Soda Springs, Big Spring, deer pastures and elsewhere. Some demand bears, and make excited inquiries concerning their haunts,—how many there might be altogether on the mountain, and whether they are grizzly, brown, or black. Others shout, "Excelsior," and make off at once for the upper snow-fields. Most, however, are content with comparatively level ground and moderate distances, gathering at the hotel every evening laden with trophies—great sheaves of flowers, cones of various trees, cedar and fir branches covered with yellow lichens, and possibly a fish or two or quail and grouse. But the heads of deer, antelope, wild sheep, and bears are conspicuously rare or altogether wanting in tourist collections in the "Paradise of hunters." There is a grand comparing of notes and adventures. Most are exhilarated and happy, though complaints may occasionally be heard—"The mountain does not look so very high after all, nor so very white; the snow is in patches like rags spread out to dry," reminding one of Sidney Smith's joke against Jeffrey, "D—n the Solar System; bad light, planets too indistinct." But far the greater number are in good spirits, showing the influence of holiday enjoyment and mountain air. Fresh roses come to cheeks that long have been pale, and sentiment often begins to blossom under the new inspiration.

The Shasta region may be reserved as a national park, with special reference to the preservation of its fine forests and game. This should by all means be done; but, as far as game is concerned, it is in little danger from tourists, notwithstanding many of them carry guns, and are in some sense hunters. Going in noisy groups, and with guns so shining, they are oftentimes confronted by inquisitive Douglass squirrels, and are thus given opportunities for shooting; but the larger animals retire at their approach and seldom are seen. Other gun-people, too wise or too lifeless to make much noise, move slowly along the trails and about the open spots of the woods like benumbed beetles in a snow-drift. Such hunters are themselves hunted by the animals, which in perfect safety follow them out of curiosity.

During the bright days of midsummer the ascent of Shasta is only a long, safe saunter, without fright or nerve-strain, or even serious fatigue, to those in sound health. Setting out from Sissons on horseback, accompanied by a guide leading a pack-animal with provisions, blankets, and other necessaries, you follow a trail that leads up to the edge of the timber-line, where you camp for the night, eight or ten miles from the hotel, at an elevation of about 10,000 feet. The next day, rising early, you may push on to the summit and return to Sissons. But it is better to spend more time in the enjoyment of the grand scenery on the summit and about the head of the Whitney Glacier, pass the second night in camp, and return to Sissons on the third day. Passing around the margin of the meadows and on through the zones of the forest, you will have good opportunities to get ever-changing views of the mountain and its wealth of creatures that bloom and breathe. The woods differ but little from those that clothe the mountains to the southward, the trees being slightly closer together and generally not quite so large, marking the incipient change from the open sunny forests of the Sierra to the dense damp forests of the northern coast, where a squirrel may travel in the branches of the thick-set trees hundreds of miles without touching the ground.

Around the upper belt of the forest you may see gaps where the ground has been cleared by avalanches of snow, thousands of tons in weight, which descending with grand rush and roar brush the trees from their paths like so many fragile shrubs or grasses.

HEAD OF IRON CAÑON.

At first the ascent is very gradual. The mountain begins to leave the plain in slopes scarcely perceptible, measuring from two to three degrees. These are continued by easy gradations mile after mile all the way to the truncated, crumbling summit, where they attain a steepness of twenty to twenty-five degrees. The grand simplicity of these lines is partially interrupted on the north subordinate cone that rises from the side of the main cone about 3,000 feet from the summit. This side cone, past which your way to the summit lies, was active after the breaking up of the main ice-cap of the glacial period, as shown by the comparatively unwasted crater in which it terminates and by streams of fresh-looking unglaciated lava that radiates from it as a centre.

The main summit is about a mile-and-a-half in diameter from southwest to northeast, and is nearly covered with snow and *névé*, bounded by crumbling peaks and ridges among which we look in vain for any sure plan of an ancient crater. The extreme summit is situated on the southern end of a narrow ridge that bounds the general summit on the east. Viewed from the north it appears as an irregular blunt point about ten feet high, and is fast disappearing before the stormy atmospheric action to which it is subjected. At the base of the eastern ridge, just below the extreme summit, hot sulphurous gases and vapor escape with a hissing, bubbling noise from a fissure in the lava. Some of the many small vents cast up a spray of clear hot water, which falls back repeatedly until wasted in vapor. The steam and spray seem to be produced simply by melting snow coming in the way of the escaping gases, while the gases are evidently derived from the heated interior of the mountain, and may be regarded as the last feeble expression of the mighty power that lifted the entire mass of the mountain from the volcanic depths far below the surface of the plain.

The view from the summit in clear weather extends to an immense distance in every direction. South-eastward, the low volcanic portion of the Sierra is seen like a map, both flanks as well as the crater-dotted axis, as far as Lassens Butte, a prominent landmark and an old volcano like Shasta, between ten and eleven thousand feet high, and distant about sixty miles. Some of the higher summit peaks near Independence Lake, one hundred and eighty miles away, are at times distinctly visible. Far to the north, in Oregon, the snowy volcanic cones of Mounts Pitt, Jefferson, and the Three Sisters, rise in clear relief, like majestic monuments, above the dim dark sea of the northern woods. To the north-east lie the Rhett and Klamath lakes, the Lava Beds, and a grand display of hill and mountain and gray rocky plains. The Scott, Siskiyou and Trinity mountains rise in long compact waves to the west and south-west, and the Valley of the Sacramento and the coast mountains, with their marvelous wealth of woods

HALTING FOR A VIEW—SHASTA.

and waters, are seen; while close around the base of the mountain lie the beautiful Shasta Valley, Strawberry Valley, Huckleberry Valley, and many others, with the headwaters of the Shasta, Sacramento and McCloud rivers. Some observers claim to have seen the ocean from the summit of Shasta, but I have not yet been so fortunate.

The Cinder Cone near Lassens Butte is remarkable as being the scene of the most recent volcanic eruption in the range. It is a symmetrical truncated cone covered with gray cinders and ashes, with a regular crater in which a few pines an inch or two in diameter are growing. It stands between two small lakes which, previous to the last eruption when the cone was built, formed one lake. From near the base of the cone a flood of extremely rough black vesicular lava extends across what was once a portion of the bottom of the lake into the forest of yellow pine. This lava flow seems to have been poured out during the same eruption that gave birth to the

LASSEN'S BUTTE.

cone, cutting the lake in two, flowing a little way into the woods and overwhelming the trees in its way, the ends of some of the charred trunks still being visible projecting from beneath the advanced snout of the flow where it came to rest; while the floor of the forest for miles around is so thickly strewn with loose cinders that walking is very fatiguing. The Pitt River Indians tell of a fearful time of darkness, probably due to this eruption, when the sky was filled with falling cinders which, as they thought, threatened every living creature with destruction, and when at length the sun appeared through the gloom it was red like blood.

Less recent craters in great numbers dot the adjacent region. Some with lakes in their throats, some overgrown with trees, others nearly bare—telling monuments of Nature's mountain fires so often lighted throughout the northern Sierra. And, standing on the top of icy Shasta, the mightiest fire-monument of them all, we can hardly fail to look forward to the blare and glare of its next eruption and wonder whether it is nigh. Elsewhere men have planted gardens and vineyards in the craters of volcanoes quiescent for ages, and almost without warning have been hurled into the sky. More than a thousand years of profound calm have been known to intervene between

"On the Big Bend." From Painting by W. C. Fitler.

Now that the railroad has been built up the Sacramento, everybody with money may go to Mount Shasta,—the weak
as well as the strong,—fine-grained, succulent people whose legs have never ripened, as well as the sinewy mountaineers'
seasoned long in the weather. This, surely, is not the best way of going to the mountains, yet it is better than staying below.

two violent eruptions. Seventeen centuries intervened between two consecutive eruptions on the island of Ischia. Few volcanoes continue permanently in eruption. Like gigantic geysers, spouting hot stone instead of hot water, they work and sleep, and we have no sure means of knowing whether they are only sleeping or dead.

Toward the end of summer, after a light open winter, one may reach the summit of Mount Shasta without passing over much snow, by keeping on the crest of a long narrow ridge, mostly bare, that extends from near the camp-ground at the timber line. But on my first excursion to the summit the whole mountain down to its low swelling base was smoothly laden with loose fresh snow, presenting a most glorious mass of winter mountain scenery, in the midst of which I scrambled and revelled or lay snugly snow-bound, enjoying the fertile clouds and the snow-bloom in all their growing, drifting grandeur. I had walked from Redding, sauntering leisurely from station to station along the old Oregon stage road, the better to see the rocks and plants, birds and people by the way, tracing the rushing Sacramento to its fountains around icy Shasta. The first rains had fallen on the lowlands, and the first snows on the mountains, and everything was fresh and bracing, while

ABOVE UPPER SODA SPRINGS.

an abundance of balmy sunshine filled all the noon-day hours. It was the calm afterglow that usually succeeds the first storm of the winter. I met many of the birds that had reared their young and spent their summer in the Shasta woods and chaparral. They were then on their way south to their winter homes, leading their young full-fledged and about as large and strong as the parents. Squirrels, dry and elastic after the storms, were busy about their stores of pine nuts, and the latest golden-rods were still in bloom, though it was now past the middle of October. The grand color-glow—the autumnal jubilee of ripe leaves—was past prime, but, freshened by the rain, was still making a fine show along the banks of the river, the ravines and the dells of the smaller streams. At the salmon-hatching establishment on the McCloud river I halted a week to examine the lime-stone belt, grandly developed there;

to learn what I could of the inhabitants of the river and its banks, and to give time for the fresh snow that I knew had fallen on the mountain to settle somewhat, with a view to making the ascent. A pedestrian on these mountain roads, especially so late in the year, is sure to excite curiosity, and many were the interrogations concerning my ramble. When I said that I was simply taking a walk, and that icy Shasta was my mark, I was invariably admonished that I had come on a dangerous quest. The time was far too late, the snow was too loose and deep to climb, and I would be lost in drifts and slides. When I hinted that new snow was beautiful and storms not so bad as they were called, my advisers shook their heads in token of superior knowledge and declared the ascent of "Shasta Butte" through loose snow impossible. Nevertheless, before noon of the second of November I was in the frosty azure of the utmost summit.

When I arrived at Sissons everything was quiet; the last of the summer visitors had flitted long before, and the deer and bears also were beginning to seek their winter homes. My barometer and the sighing winds and filmy half-transparent clouds that dimmed the sunshine gave notice of the approach of another storm, and I was in haste to be off and get myself established somewhere

QUAIL HUNTING, UPPER SACRAMENTO VALLEY. FROM PAINTING BY J. CARTER BEARD.

"There is no sound sweeter to the ears of a true sportsman than the *whir* of the wings of a quail, and no place where the sound can be heard as often as among the foothills of the Upper Sacramento. In this favored region the beautiful birds grow fat and hardy and make fine shooting; but he who would kill quail must be lively with the shotgun. The sport is most exciting. Suddenly the profound mountain stillness is broken by the sound of wings, and for an instant there is a flash of white plumage in the air. Then is the time to shoot; but, if the hunter's aim is not good, the birds will disappear in the nearest belt of timber.

SHEEP ROCKS, NORTH OF MT. SHASTA.

in the midst of it, whether the summit was to be attained or not. Sisson, who is a mountaineer, speedily fitted me out for storm or calm as only a mountaineer could, with warm blankets and a week's provisions so generous in quantity and kind that they easily might have been made to last a month in case of my being closely snow-bound. Well I knew the weariness of snow-climbing, and the frosts, and the dangers of mountaineering so late in the year; therefore I could not ask a guide to go with me, even had one been willing. All I wanted was to have blankets and provisions deposited as far up in the timber as the snow would permit a pack-animal to go. There I could build a storm-nest and lie warm, and make raids up and around the mountain in accordance with the weather.

Setting out on the afternoon of November first with Jerome Fay, mountaineer and guide, in charge of the animals, I was soon plodding wearily upward through the muffled winter woods, the snow of course growing steadily deeper and looser, and we had to break a trail. The animals began to get discouraged, and after night and darkness came on they became entangled in a bed of rough lava, where, breaking through four or five feet of mealy snow, their feet were caught between angular boulders. Here they were in danger of being lost, but after we had removed packs and saddles and assisted their efforts with ropes, they all escaped to the side of a ridge about a thousand feet below the timber-line. To go farther was out of the question, so we were compelled to camp as best we could. A pitch-pine fire speedily changed the temperature and shed a blaze of light on the wild lava-slope and the straggling storm-bent pines around us. Melted snow answered for coffee, and we had plenty of venison to roast. Toward midnight I rolled myself in my blankets, slept an hour and a half, arose and ate more venison, tied two days' provisions to my belt and set out for the summit, hoping to reach it ere the coming storm should fall. Jerome accompanied me a little distance above camp and indicated the way as well as he could in the darkness. He seemed loath to leave me, but being re-assured that I was at home and required no care, he bade me good bye and returned to camp, ready to lead his animals down the mountain at daybreak.

After I was above the dwarf pines, it was fine practice pushing up the broad unbroken slopes of snow, alone in the solemn silence of the night. Half the sky was clouded; in the other half the stars sparkled icily in the keen frosty air; while everywhere the glorious wealth of snow fell away from the summit of the cone in flowing folds, more extensive and continuous than any I had ever seen before. When day dawned the clouds were crawling slowly and becoming more massive, but gave no intimation of immediate danger, and I pushed on faithfully, though holding myself well in hand, ready to return to the timber; for it was easy to see that a storm was not far off. The mountain rises 10,000 feet above the general level of the country, in blank exposure to the deep upper currents of the sky, and no labyrinth of peaks and cañons I had ever been in seemed to me so dangerous as these immense slopes, bare against the sky. The frost was intense, and drifting snow-dust made breathing at times rather difficult. The snow was as dry as meal and the finer particles drifted freely, rising high in the air, while the larger portions of the crystals rolled like sand. I frequently sank to my armpits between buried blocks of loose lava, but generally only to my knees. When tired with walking I still wallowed slowly upward on all fours.

"THE CIRCLE OF CROUCHING SAVAGES AROUND THE FIRE.'

The steepness of the slope—thirty-five degrees in some places—made any kind of progress fatiguing, while small avalanches were being constantly set in motion in the steepest places. But the bracing air and the sublime beauty of the snowy expanse thrilled every nerve and made absolute exhaustion impossible. I seemed to be walking and wallowing in a cloud; but, holding steadily onward, by half-past ten o'clock I had gained the highest summit.

I held my commanding foothold in the sky for two hours, gazing on the glorious landscapes spread map-like around the immense horizon, and tracing the outlines of the ancient lava streams extending far into the surrounding plains, and the pathways of vanished glaciers of which Shasta had been the center. But, as I had left my coat in camp for the sake of having my limbs free in climbing, I soon was cold. The wind increased in violence, raising the snow in magnificent drifts that were drawn out in the form of wavering banners glowing in the sun. Toward the end of my stay a succession of small clouds struck against the summit rocks like drifting icebergs, darkening the air as they passed, and producing a chill as definite and sudden as if ice-water had been dashed in my face. This is the kind of cloud in which snow-flowers grow, and I turned and fled.

Finding that I was not closely

A SURE-FOOTED CLIMBER.

SHASTA, FROM EDGEWOOD.

pursued, I ventured to take time on the way down for a visit to the head of the Whitney Glacier and the "Crater Butte." After reaching the end of the main summit ridge the descent was but little more than one continuous, soft-mealy, muffled slide, most luxurious and rapid, though the hissing, swishing speed attained was obscured in great part by flying snow-dust—a marked contrast to the boring, seal-wallowing upward struggle. I reached camp about an hour before dark, hollowed a strip of loose ground in the lee of a large block of red lava where fire-wood was abundant, rolled myself in my blankets, and went to sleep.

Next morning, having slept little the night before the ascent and being weary with climbing after the excitement was over, I slept late. Then, awaking suddenly, my eyes opened on one of the most beautiful and sublime scenes I ever enjoyed. A boundless wilderness of storm-clouds of different degrees of ripeness were congregated over all the lower landscape for thousands of square miles, colored gray, and purple, and pearl, and deep-glowing white, amid which I seemed to be floating; while the great white cone of the mountain above was all aglow in the free, blazing sunshine. It seemed not so much an ocean as a *land* of clouds,—undulating hill and dale, smooth purple plains, and silvery mountains of cumuli, range over range, diversified with peak and dome and hollow fully brought out in light and shade. I gazed enchanted, but cold gray masses, drifting like dust on a wind-swept plain, began to shut out the light, forerunners of the coming storm I had been so anxiously watching. I made haste to gather as much wood as possible, snugging it as a shelter around my bed. The storm-side of my blankets was fastened down with stakes to reduce as much as possible the sifting in of drift and the danger of being blown away. The precious bread-sack was placed safely as a pillow, and when at length the first flakes fell I was exultingly ready to welcome them. Most of my firewood was more than half rosin and would blaze in the face of the fiercest drifting; the winds could not demolish my bed, and my bread could be made to last indefinitely; while in case of need I had the means of making snowshoes and could retreat or hold my ground as I pleased.

Presently the storm broke forth into full snowy bloom, and the thronging crystals darkened the air. The wind swept past in hissing floods, grinding the snow into meal and sweeping down into the hollows in enormous drifts all the heavier particles, while the finer dust was sifted through the sky, increasing the icy gloom. But my fire glowed bravely as if in glad defiance of the drift to quench it, and notwithstanding but little trace of my nest could be seen after the snow had leveled and buried it, I was snug and warm, and the passionate uproar produced a glad excitement. Day

MT. SHASTA, FROM McCLOUD RIVER.

after day the storm continued, piling snow on snow in weariless abundance. There were short periods of quiet, when the sun would seem to look eagerly down through rents in the clouds, as if to know how the work was advancing. During these calm intervals I replenished my fire—sometimes without leaving the nest, for fire and woodpile were so near this could easily be done—or busied myself with my note-book, watching the gestures of the trees in taking the snow, examining separate crystals under a lens, and learning the methods of their deposition as an enduring fountain for the streams. Several times when the storm ceased for a few minutes, a Douglass squirrel came frisking from the foot of a clump of dwarf pines, moving in sudden interrupted spurts over the bossy snow; then without any apparent guidance he would dig rapidly into the drift where were buried some grains of barley that the horses had left. The Douglass does not strictly belong to these upper woods, and I was surprised to see him out in such weather. The mountain sheep also, quite a large flock of them, came to my camp and took shelter beside a clump of matted dwarf pines a little above my nest.

FALLS OF THE PITT RIVER. FROM PAINTING BY GEORGE SPIEL.

"Tracing rivers to their fountains makes the most charming of travels, and not one dull passage is found in all their eventful histories. Tracing the McCloud to its highest springs, and over the divide to the fountains of Fall River, near Fort Crook; thence down that river to its confluence with the Pitt, on from there to the volcanic region about Lassen's Butte, through the forests of sugar pine to the fertile plains of Chico,—this is a glorious saunter and imposes no hardship."

The storm lasted about a week, but before it was ended Sisson became alarmed and sent up the guide with animals to see what had become of me and recover the camp out-fit. The news spread that "there was a man on the mountain," and he must surely have perished, and Sisson was blamed for allowing any one to attempt climbing in such weather; while I was as safe as anybody in the lowlands, lying like a squirrel in a warm, fluffy nest, busied about my own affairs and wishing only to be let alone. Later, however, a trail could not have been broken for a horse, and some of the camp furniture would have had to be abandoned. On the fifth day I returned to Sisson's, and from that comfortable base made excursions, as the weather permitted,—to the Black Butte, to the foot of the Whitney Glacier, around the base of the mountain, to Rhett and Klamath lakes, to the Modoc region and elsewhere,—developing many interesting scenes and experiences. But the next Spring, on the other side of this eventful winter, I saw and felt still more of the Shasta snow. For then it was my fortune to get into the very heart of a storm, and to be held in it for a long time.

On the 28th of April I led a party up the mountain for the purpose of making a survey of the summit with reference to the location of the Geodetic monument. On the 30th, accompanied by Jerome Fay, I made another ascent to make some barometrical observations, the day intervening between the two ascents being devoted to establishing a camp on the extreme edge of the timber-line. Here on our red trachyte bed we obtained two hours of shallow sleep broken for occasional glimpses of the keen starry night. At two o'clock we rose, breakfasted on a warmed tin-cupful of coffee and a piece of frozen venison broiled on the coals, and started for the summit. Up to this time there was nothing in sight that betokened the approach of a storm; but on gaining the summit, we saw toward Lassens Butte, hundreds of square miles of white cumuli boiling dreamily in the sunshine far beneath us, and causing no alarm.

CASTLE ROCKS,
EAST OF LOWER SODA SPRINGS.

The slight weariness of the ascent was soon rested away, and our glorious morning in the sky promised nothing but enjoyment. At nine A. M. the dry thermometer stood at 34° in the shade and rose steadily until at one P. M. it stood at 50°, probably influenced somewhat by radiation from the sun-warmed cliffs. A common bumble-bee, not at all benumbed, zigzagged vigorously about our heads for a few moments, as if unconscious of the fact that the nearest honey flower was a mile beneath him. In the meantime clouds were growing down in Shasta Valley,—massive swelling cumuli, displaying delicious tones of purple and gray in the hollows of their sun-beaten bosses. Extending gradually southward around on both sides of Shasta, these at length united with the older field towards Lassens Butte, thus encircling Mt. Shasta in one continuous cloud-zone. Rhett and Klamath Lakes were eclipsed beneath clouds scarcely less brilliant than their own silvery disks. The Modoc Lava Beds, many a snow-laden peak far north in Oregon, the Scott and Trinity and Siskiyou mountains, the peaks of the Sierra, the blue Coast Range, Shasta Valley, the dark forests filling the Valley of the Sacramento, all in turn were obscured or buried, leaving the lofty cone on which we stood solitary in the sunshine between two skies—a sky of spotless blue above, a sky of glittering cloud beneath. The creative sun shone glorious on the vast expanse of cloud-land; hill and dale, mountain and valley springing into existence responsive to his rays and steadily developing in beauty and individuality. One huge mountain-cone of cloud, corresponding to Mt. Shasta in these new-born cloud ranges, rose close alongside with a visible motion, its firm, polished bosses seeming so near and substantial that we almost fancied we might leap down upon them from where we stood and make our way to the lowlands. No hint was given by anything in their appearance of the fleeting character of these most sublime and beautiful cloud-mountains. On the contrary they impressed one as being lasting additions to the landscape.

The weather of the springtime and summer throughout the Sierra in general is usually varied by slight local rains and dustings of snow, most of which are obviously far too joyous and life-giving to be regarded as storms—single clouds growing in the sunny sky, ripening in an hour, showering the heated landscape and passing away like a thought, leaving no visible bodily remains to stain the sky. Snow storms of the same gentle kind abound among the high peaks, but in spring they not unfrequently attain larger proportions, assuming a violence and energy of expression scarcely surpassed by those bred in the depths of winter. Such was the storm now gathering about us. It began to declare itself shortly after noon, suggesting to us the idea of at once seeking our safe camp in the timber and abandoning the purpose of making an observation of the barometer at three P. M.,—two having already been made, at nine A. M., and twelve M.; while simultaneous observations were made at Strawberry Valley. Jerome peered at short intervals over the ridge, contemplating the rising clouds with anxious gestures in the rough wind, and at length declared that if we did not make a speedy escape we would be compelled to pass the rest of the day and night on the summit. But anxiety to complete my observations stifled my own instinctive promptings to retreat, and held me to my work. No inexperienced person was depending on me, and I told Jerome that we two mountaineers would be able to make our way down through any storm likely to fall.

Presently thin, fibrous films of cloud began to blow directly over the summit from north to south, drawn out in long fairy webs like carded wool, forming and dissolving as if by magic. The wind twisted them into ringlets and whirled them in a succession of graceful convolutions like the outside sprays of Yosemite Falls in flood-time; then, sailing out into the thin azure over the precipitous brink of the ridge they were drifted together like wreaths of foam on a river. These higher and finer cloud fabrics were evidently produced by the chilling of the air from its own expansion caused by the upward deflection of the wind against the slopes of the mountain. They steadily increased on the north rim of the cone, forming at length a thick, opaque, ill-defined embankment from the icy meshes of which snow-flowers began to fall, alternating with hail. The sky speedily darkened, and just as I had completed my last observation and boxed my instruments ready for the descent, the storm began in serious earnest. At first the cliffs were beaten with hail every stone of which, as far as I could see, was regular in form, six-sided pyramids with rounded base, rich and sumptuous

THE OREGON STAGE LEAVING COLES.

looking, and fashioned with loving care, yet seemingly thrown away on those desolate crags down which they went rolling, falling, sliding in a net-work of curious streams.

After we had forced our way down the ridge and past the group of hissing fumaroles, the storm became inconceivably violent. The thermometer fell 22° in a few minutes, and soon dropped below zero. The hail gave place to snow, and darkness came on like night. The wind, rising to the highest pitch of violence, boomed and surged amid the desolate crags; lightning-flashes in quick succession cut the gloomy darkness; and the thunders, the most tremendously loud and appalling I ever heard, made an almost continuous roar, stroke following stroke in quick, passionate succession, as though the mountain were being rent to its foundations and the fires of the old volcano were breaking forth again. Could we at once have begun to descend the snow-slopes leading to the timber, we might have made good our escape, however dark and wild the storm. As it was, we had first to make our way along a dangerous ridge nearly a mile and a half long, flanked in many places by steep ice-slopes at the head of the Whitney Glacier on one side and by shattered precipices on the other. Apprehensive of this coming darkness, I had taken the precaution when the storm began to make the most dangerous points clear to my mind, and to mark their relations with reference to the direction of the wind. When therefore the darkness came on, and the bewildering drift, I felt confident that we could force our way through it with no other guidance. After passing the "Hot Springs" I halted in the lee of a lava block to let Jerome, who had fallen a little behind, come up. Here he opened a council in which, under circumstances sufficiently exciting but without evincing any bewilderment he maintained, in opposition to my views, that it was impossible to proceed. He firmly refused to make the venture to find the camp, while I, aware of the dangers that would necessarily attend our efforts, and conscious of being the cause of his present peril, decided not to leave him.

Our discussions ended, Jerome made a dash for the shelter of the lava block and began forcing his way back against the wind to the "Hot Springs," wavering and struggling to resist being carried away, as if he were fording a rapid stream. After waiting and watching in vain for some flaw in the storm that might be urged as a new argument in favor of attempting the descent, I was compelled to follow. "Here," said Jerome, as we shivered in the midst of the hissing, sputtering fumaroles, "we shall be safe from frost." "Yes," said I, "we can lie in this mud and steam and sludge, warm at least on one side; but how can we protect our lungs from the acid gases, and how, after our clothing is saturated, shall we be able to reach camp without freezing, even after the storm is over? We shall have to wait for sunshine, and when will it come?"

The tempered area to which we had committed ourselves extended over about one-fourth of an acre; but it was only about an eight of an inch in thickness, for the scalding gas-jets were shorn off close to the ground by the over-sweeping flood of frosty wind. And how lavishly the snow fell only mountaineers may know. The crisp crystal flowers seemed to touch one another and fairly to thicken the tremendous blast that carried them. This was the bloom-time, the summer of the cloud, and never before have I seen even a mountain cloud flowering so profusely. When the bloom of the Shasta chaparral is failing the ground is sometimes covered for hundreds of square miles to a depth of half an inch. But the bloom of this fertile snow-cloud grew and matured and fell to a depth of two feet in a few hours. Some crystals landed with their rays almost perfect, but most of them were worn and broken by striking against one another, or by rolling on the ground. The touch of these snow-flowers in calm weather is infinitely gentle—glinting, swaying, settling silently in the dry mountain air, or massed in flakes soft and downy. To lie out alone in the mountains of a still night and be touched by the first of these small silent messengers from the sky is a memorable experience, and the fineness of that touch none will forget. But the storm-blast laden with crisp sharp snow seems to crush and bruise and stupefy with its multitude of stings, and compels the bravest to turn and flee.

The snow fell without abatement until an hour or two after what seemed to be the natural darkness of the night. Up to the time the storm first broke on the summit its development was remarkably gentle. There was a deliberate growth of clouds, a weaving of translucent tissue above, then the roar of the wind and the thunder, and the darkening flight of snow. Its subsidence was not less sudden. The clouds broke and vanished, not a crystal was left in the sky, and the stars shone out with pure and tranquil radiance.

Squaw Valley, near "Now-ow-wa" (Old Grizzly's Den Invaded). From Painting by Thos. Hill.

"Interest in hunting is almost universal, so deeply is it rooted as an inherited instinct, ever ready to rise and make itself known. Fine scenery may not stir a fibre of mind or body, but how quick and how true is the excitement of the pursuit of game."

During the storm we lay on our backs so as to present as little surface as possible to the wind, and to let the drift pass over us. The mealy snow sifted into the folds of our clothing and in many places reached the skin. We were glad at first to see the snow packing about us, hoping it would deaden the force of the wind; but it soon froze into a stiff, crusty heap as the temperature fell, rather augmenting our novel misery.

When the heat became unendurable, on some spot where steam was escaping through the sludge, we tried to stop it with snow and mud, or shifted a little at a time by shoving with our heels; for to stand in blank exposure to the fearful wind in our frozen-and-broiled condition seemed certain death. The acrid incrustations sublimed from the escaping gases frequently gave way, opening new vents to scald us; and fearing that if at any time the wind should fall, carbonic acid, which often formed a considerable portion of the gaseous exhalations of volcanoes, might collect in

A STORM ON SHASTA.

sufficient quantities to cause sleep and death, I warned Jerome against forgetting himself for a single moment, even should his sufferings admit of such a thing. Accordingly, when during the long dreary watches of the night we roused suddenly from a state of half consciousness we called each other by name in a frightened, startled way, each fearing the other might be benumbed or dead. The ordinary sensations of cold give but a faint conception of that which comes on after hard climbing with want of food and sleep in such exposure as this. Life is then seen to be a fire, that now smoulders, now brightens and may be easily quenched. The weary hours wore away like dim half-forgotten years, so long and eventful they seemed, though we did nothing but suffer. Still the pain was not always of that bitter, intense kind that precludes thought and takes away all capacity for enjoyment. A sort of dreamy stupor came on at times in which we fancied we saw dry, resinous logs suitable for camp-fires, just as after going days without food men fancy they see bread.

Frozen, blistered, famished, benumbed, our bodies seemed lost to us at times—all dead but the eyes. For the duller and fainter we became the clearer was our vision, though only in momentary glimpses. Then, after the sky cleared, we gazed at the stars, blessed immortals of light, shining with marvelous brightness with long lance rays, near-looking and new-looking, as if never seen before. Again they would look familiar and remind us of star-gazing at home. Oftentimes imagination coming into play would present charming pictures of the warm zone below, mingled with others near and far. Then the bitter wind and the drift would break the blissful vision and dreary pains cover us like clouds. "Are you suffering much?" Jerome would inquire with pitiful faintness. "Yes," I would say, striving to keep my voice brave, "frozen and burned; but never mind, Jerome, the night will wear away at last, and to-morrow we go a-Maying, and what camp-fires we will make, and what sun-baths we will take!"

The frost grew more and more intense and we became icy and covered over with a crust of frozen snow, as if we had lain cast away in the drift all

KEYSER'S—MUIR'S PEAK.

winter. In about thirteen hours—every hour like a year—day began to dawn, but it was long ere the summit's rocks were touched by the sun. No clouds were visible from where we lay, yet the morning was dull and blue, and bitterly frosty; and hour after hour passed by while we eagerly watched the pale light stealing down the ridge to the hollow where we lay. But there was not a trace of that warm, flushing sunrise-splendor we so long had hoped for. As the time drew near to make an effort to reach camp we became concerned to know what strength was left us, and whether or no we could walk; for we had lain flat all this time without once rising to our feet. Mountaineers, however, always find in themselves a reserve of power after great exhaustion. It is a kind of second life, available only in emergencies like this; and having proved its existence I had no great fear that either of us would fail, though one of my arms was already benumbed and hung powerless.

MUIR'S PEAK, LOOKING NORTH FROM SISSON'S LAKE.

At length, after the temperature was somewhat mitigated on this memorable first of May, we arose and began to struggle homeward. Our frozen trousers could scarcely be made to bend at the knee and we waded the snow with difficulty. The summit ridge was fortunately wind-swept and nearly bare, so we were not compelled to lift our feet high, and on reaching the long home-slopes laden with loose snow we made rapid progress, sliding and shuffling and pitching headlong, our feebleness accelerating rather than diminishing our speed. When we had descended some three thousand feet the sunshine warmed our backs and we began to revive. At ten o'clock A. M. we reached the timber and were safe.   Half an hour later we heard Sisson shouting down among the firs, coming with horses to take us to the hotel.   After breaking a trail through the snow as far as possible he had tied his animals and walked up.   We had been so long without food that we cared but little about eating, but we eagerly drank the coffee he prepared for us.   Our feet were frozen, and thawing them was painful, and had to be done very slowly by keeping them buried in soft snow for several hours, which avoided permanent damage.   Five thousand feet below the summit we found only three inches of new snow, and at the base of the mountain only a slight shower of rain had fallen, showing how local our storm had been notwithstanding its terrific fury.   Our feet were wrapped in sacking, and we were soon mounted and on our way down into the thick sunshine—"God's Country," as Sisson calls the Chaparral Zone.   In two hours' ride the last snow-bank was left behind.   Violets appeared along the edges of the trail, and the chaparral was coming into bloom, with young lilies and larkspurs about the open places in rich profusion.   How beautiful seemed the golden sunbeams streaming through the woods between the warm brown boles of the cedars and pines!   All my friends among the birds and plants seemed like *old* friends, and we felt like speaking to every one of them as we passed, as if we had been a long time away in some far strange country.

In the afternoon we reached Strawberry Valley and fell asleep. Next morning we seemed to have risen from the dead. My bedroom was flooded with sunshine, and from the window I saw the great white Shasta-cone clad in forests and clouds and bearing them loftily in the sky. Every-thing seemed full and radiant with the freshness and beauty and enthusiasm of youth. Sisson's children came in with flowers and covered my bed, and the storm on the mountain top vanished like a dream.

Arctic beauty and desolation, with their blessings and dangers, all may be found here, to test the endurance and skill of adventurous climbers; but far better than climb-

PITT RIVER CAÑON.

ing the mountain is going around its warm fertile base, enjoying its bounties like a bee circling around a bank of flowers.   The distance is about a hundred miles, and will take some of the time we hear so much about—a week or two—but the benefits will compensate for any number of weeks.   Perhaps the profession of doing good may be full, but everybody should be kind at least to himself.   Take a course of good water and air, and in the eternal youth of Nature you may renew your own.   Go quietly, alone; no harm will befall you.   Some have strange, morbid fears as soon as they find themselves with Nature even in the kindest and wildest of her solitudes, like very sick children afraid of their mother—as if God were dead and the devil were King.

One may make the trip on horseback, or in a carriage, even; for a good level road may be found all the way round, by Shasta Valley, Sheep Rock, Elk Flat, Huckleberry Valley, Squaw Valley, following for a considerable portion of the way the old Emigrant Road, which lies along the east disk of the mountain, and is deeply worn by the wagons of the early gold-seekers, many of whom chose this northern route as perhaps being safer and easier, the pass here being only about six thousand feet above sea-level.   But it is far better to go afoot.   Then you are free to make wide waverings and zigzags away from the roads to visit the great fountain streams of the rivers, the glaciers also, and the wildest retreats in the primeval forests where the best plants and animals dwell, and where many a flower-bell will ring against your knees and friendly trees will reach out

"SISKIYOU MOUNTAINS."—LOOP SHOWING THREE TRESTLES

"Many still, small voices will not be heard in the noisy rush and din, suggestive of going to the sky in a
chariot of fire or in a whirlwind, as one is shot to the Shasta mark in a booming palace-car cartridge: up the rocky
cañon, skimming the foamy river, above the level reaches, above the dashing spray,—fine, exhilarating translation,
yet pity to go so fast in a blur where so much might be seen and enjoyed."

their fronded branches and touch you as you pass. One blanket will be enough to carry, or you may forego the pleasure and burden altogether, as wood for fires is everywhere abundant. Only a little food will be required. Berries and plums abound in season, and quail and grouse and deer —the magnificent shaggy mule-deer as well as the common species.

As you sweep around so grand a centre the mountain itself seems to turn, displaying its riches like the revolving pyramids in jewelers' windows. One glacier after another comes into view, and the outlines of the mountain are ever changing, though all the way around, from whatever point of view, the form is maintained of a grand, simple cone with a gently sloping base and rugged, crumbling ridges separating the glaciers and the snow-fields more or less completely. The play of colors, from the first touches of the morning sun on the summit, down the snow-fields and the ice and lava until the forests are aglow, is a never-ending delight, the rosy lava and the fine flushings of the snow being ineffably lovely. Thus one saunters on and on in the glorious radiance in utter peace and forgetfulness of time. Yet, strange to say, there are days even here somewhat dull looking, when the mountain seems uncommunicative, sending out no appreciable invitation, as if not at home. At such times its height seems much less, as if crouching and weary it were taking rest. But Shasta is always at home to those who love her, and is ever in a thrill of enthusiastic activity—burning fires within, grinding glaciers without, and fountains ever-flowing. Every crystal dances responsive to the touches of the sun, and currents of sap in the growing cells of all the vegetation are ever in a vital whirl and rush, and though many feet and wings are folded how many are astir! And the wandering winds, how busy they are, and what a breadth of sound and motion they make, glinting and bubbling about the crags of the summit, sifting through the woods, feeling their way from grove to grove, ruffling the loose hair on the shoulders of the bears, fanning and rocking young birds in their cradles, making a trumpet of every corolla, and carrying their fragrance around the world.

In unsettled weather, when storms are growing, the mountain looms immensely higher, and its miles of height become apparent to all, especially in the gloom of the gathering clouds, or when the storm is done and they are rolling away, torn on the edges and melting while in the sunshine. Slight rain-storms are likely to be encountered in a trip round the mountain, but one may easily find shelter beneath well thatched trees that shed the rain like a roof. Then the shining of the wet leaves is delightful, and the steamy fragrance, and the burst of bird-song from a multitude of thrushes and finches and warblers that have nests in the chaparral.

The nights, too, are delightful, watching with Shasta beneath the great starry dome. A thousand thousand voices are heard, but so finely blended they seem a part of the night itself, and make a deeper silence. And how grandly do the great logs and branches of your camp-fire give forth the heat and light that during their long century-lives they have so slowly gathered from the sun, storing it away in beautiful dotted cells and beads of amber gum! The neighboring trees look into the charmed circle as if the noon of another day had come, familiar flowers and grasses that chance to be near seem far more beautiful and impressive than by day, and as the dead trees give forth their light all the other riches of their lives seem to be set free and with the rejoicing flames rise again to the sky. In setting out from Strawberry Valley, by bearing off to the north-westward a few miles you may

"See beneath green aisles in odorous woods
The slight Linnæa hang its twin-born heads,
And bless the memory of the man of flowers,
Which breathes sweet fragrance through the northern bowers."

This is one of the few places in California where the charming Linnæa is found, though it is common to the northward through Oregon and Washington. Here, too, you may find the curious but unlovable Darlingtonia, a carniverous plant that devours bumble-bees, grasshoppers, ants, moths, and other insects, with insatiable appetite. In approaching it, its suspicious looking yellow-spotted hood and watchful attitude will be likely to make you go cautiously through the bog where it stands, as if you were approaching a dangerous snake. It also occurs in a bog near Sothern's Station on the stage road where I first saw it, and in other similar bogs throughout the mountains hereabouts.

The "Big Spring" of the Sacramento is about a mile and a half above Sissons, issuing from the base of a drift-covered hill. It is lined with emerald algæ and mosses, and shaded with alder, willow and thorn bushes, which give it a fine setting. Its waters, apparently unaffected by flood or drouth, heat or cold, fall at once into white rapids with a rush and dash, as if glad to escape from the darkness to begin its wild course down the cañon to the plain.

Muir's Peak, a few miles to the north of the spring, rises about three thousand feet above the plain on which it stands, and is easily climbed. The view is very fine and well repays the slight walk to its summit, from which much of your way about the mountain may be studied and chosen. The view obtained of the Whitney Glacier should tempt you to visit it, since it is the largest of the Shasta glaciers and its lower portion abounds in beautiful and interesting cascades and crevasses. It is three or four miles long and terminates at an elevation of about 9,500 feet

MT. SHASTA AND CASTLE LAKE.

above sea-level, in moraine-sprinkled ice-cliffs sixty feet high. The long gray slopes leading up to the glacier seem remarkably smooth and unbroken. They are much interrupted, nevertheless, with abrupt, jagged, precipitous gorges, which, though offering instructive sections of the lavas for examination, would better be shunned by most people. This may be done by keeping well down on the base until fronting the glacier before beginning the ascent.

The gorge through which the glacier is drained is raw-looking, deep and narrow, and indescribably jagged. The walls in many places overhang; in others they are beveled, loose and shifting where the channel has been eroded by cinders, ashes, strata of firm lavas, and glacial drift, telling of many a change from frost to fire and their attendant floods of mud and water. Most of the drainage of the glacier vanishes at once in the porous rocks to reappear in springs in the distant valley, and it is only in time of flood that the channel carries much water; then there are several fine falls in the gorge, 600 feet or more in height. Snow lies in it the year round at an elevation of 8,500 feet, and in sheltered spots a thousand feet lower. Tracing this wild changing channel-gorge, gully or cañon, the sections will show Mount Shasta as a huge palimpsest, containing

SHASTA, FROM NEAR SISSON'S.

the records, layer upon layer, of strangely contrasted events in its fiery-icy history. But look well to your footing, for the way will test the skill of the most cautious mountaineers.

Regaining the low ground at the base of the mountain and holding on in your grand orbit, you pass through a belt of juniper woods, called "The Cedars," to Sheep Rock at the foot of the Shasta Pass. Here you strike the old emigrant road, which leads over the low divide to the eastern slopes of the mountain. In a north-northwesterly direction from the foot of the pass you may chance to find Pluto's Cave, already mentioned; but it is not easily found, since its several mouths are on a level with the general surface of the ground, and have been made simply by the falling in of portions of the roof. Far the most beautiful and richly furnished of the mountain caves of California occur in a thick belt of metamorphic limestone that is pretty generally developed along the western flank of the Sierra from the McCloud river to the Kaweah, a distance of nearly 400 miles. These volcanic caves are not wanting in interest, and it is well to light a pitch-pine torch and take a walk in these dark ways of the under-world whenever opportunity offers, if for no other reason to see with new appreciation on returning to the sunshine the beauties that lie so thick about us.

Sheep Rock is about twenty miles from Sisson's, and is one of the principal winter pasture-grounds of the wild sheep, from which it takes its name. It is a mass of lava presenting to the gray sage-plain of Shasta Valley a bold craggy front 2,000 feet high. Its summit lies at an elevation of 5,500 feet above the sea, and has several square miles of comparatively level surface, where bunch-grass grows and the snow does not lie deep, thus allowing the hardy sheep to pick up a living through the winter months when deep snows have driven them down from the lofty ridges of Shasta.

From here it might be well to leave the immediate base of the mountain for a few days and visit the Lava Beds made famous by the Modoc war. They lie about forty miles to the northeast-ward, on the south shore of Rhett or Tulé Lake, at an elevation above sea-level of about 4,500 feet. They are a portion of a flow of dense black vesicular lava, dipping north-eastward at a low angle, but little changed as yet by the weather, and about as destitute of soil as a glacial pavement. The surface, though smooth in a general way as seen from a distance, is dotted with hillocks and rough crater-like pits, and traversed by a network of yawning fissures, forming a combination of topographical conditions of very striking character. The way lies by Mount Bremer, over stretches of gray sage-plains, interrupted by rough lava-slopes timbered with juniper and yellow pine, and with

MOSSBRAE FALLS—SOURCES OF THE SACRAMENTO RIVER. FROM PAINTING BY THEOPHILUS REICHARD.

"It is lined with emerald algæ and mosses, and shaded with alder, willow and thorn bushes, which give it a fine setting. Its waters, apparently unaffected by flood or drouth, heat or cold, fall at once into white rapids with a rush and a dash, as if glad to escape from the darkness to begin their wild course down the cañon to the plain."

here and there a green meadow and a stream. This is a famous game region, and you will be likely to meet small bands of antelope, mule-deer and wild sheep. Mount Bremer is the most noted stronghold of the sheep in the whole Shasta region. Large flocks dwell here from year to year, winter and summer, descending occasionally into the adjacent sage-plains and lava beds to feed, but ever ready to take refuge in the jagged crags of their mountain at every alarm. While traveling with a company of hunters I saw about fifty in one flock. The Van Bremer Brothers, after whom the mountain is named, told me that they once climbed the mountain with their rifles and hounds on a grand hunt; but, after keeping up the pursuit for a week, their boots and clothing gave way, and the hounds were lamed and worn out without having run down a single sheep, notwithstanding they ran night and day. On smooth spots, level or ascending, the hounds gained on the sheep, but on descending ground, and over rough masses of angular rocks they fell hopelessly behind. Only half a dozen sheep were shot as they passed the hunters stationed near their paths circling round the rugged summit. The full-grown bucks weigh about 350 pounds. The mule-deer are nearly as heavy. Their long massive ears give them a very striking appearance. One large buck that I measured stood three feet and seven inches high at the shoulders, and when the ears were extended horizontally the distance across from tip to tip was two feet and one inch.

COASTING DOWN MT. SHASTA.

From the Van Bremer ranch the way to the Lava Beds leads down the Bremer Meadows past many a smooth grassy knoll and jutting cliff, along the shore of Lower Klamath Lake, and thence across a few miles of sage-plain to the brow of the wall-like bluff of lava 450 feet above Tulé Lake. Here you are looking southeastward and the Modoc landscape, which at once takes possession of you, lies revealed in front. It is composed of three principal parts; on your left lies the bright expanse of Tulé Lake; on your right an evergreen forest, and between the two are the black Lava Beds. When I first stood there, one bright day before sundown, the lake was fairly blooming in purple light, and was so responsive to the sky in both calmness and color it seemed itself a sky. No mountain shore hides its loveliness. It lies wide open for many a mile, veiled in no mystery but the mystery of light. The forest also was flooded with sun-purple, not a spire moving, and Mount Shasta was seen towering above it rejoicing in the ineffable beauty of the alpenglow. But neither the glorified woods on the one hand nor the lake on the other could at first hold the eye. That dark mysterious lava plain between them compelled attention. Here you trace yawning fissures, there clusters of sombre pits; now you mark where the lava is bent and corrugated in swelling ridges and domes, again where it breaks into a rough mass of loose blocks. Tufts of grass grow far apart here and there and small bushes of hardy sage, but they have a singed appearance and can do little to hide the blackness. Deserts are charming to those who know how to see them—all kinds of bogs, barrens, and heathy moors; but the Modoc Lava Beds have for me an uncanny look. As I gazed the purple deepened over all the landscape. Then fell the gloaming, making every thing still more forbidding and mysterious. Then, darkness like death.

Next morning the crisp, sunshiny air made even the Modoc landscape less hopeless, and we ventured down the bluff to the edge of the Lava Beds. Just at the foot of the bluff we came to a square enclosed by a stone wall. This is a graveyard where lie buried thirty soldiers, most of whom met their fate out in the Lava Beds, as we learn by the boards marking the graves—a gloomy place to die in, and deadly looking even without Modocs. The poor fellows that lie here deserve far more pity than they have ever received. Picking our way over the strange ridges and hollows of the beds we soon came to a circular flat about twenty yards in diameter, on the shore of the lake, where the comparative smoothness of the lava and a few handfuls of soil have caused the grass-tufts to grow taller. This is where General Canby was slain while seeking to make peace with the treacherous Modocs. Two or three miles farther on is the main stronghold of the Modocs, held by them so long and defiantly against all the soldiers that could be brought to the attack. Indians usually choose to hide in tall grass and bush and behind trees, where they can crouch and glide like panthers, without casting up defenses that would betray their positions; but the Modoc castle is in the rock. When the Yosemite Indians made raids on the settlers of the lower Merced, they withdrew with their spoils into Yosemite Valley; and the Modocs boasted that in case of war they had a stone house into which no white man could come as long as they cared to defend it. Yosemite was not held for a single day against the pursuing troops; but the Modocs held their fort for

months, until weary consists of numerous of the lava flow, and with salient and re-

MONSTER OAK—NEAR REDDING.

of being hemmed in they chose to withdraw. It redoubts formed by the unequal subsidence of portions a complicated network of redans abundantly supplied entering angles, being united each to the other and to the redoubts by a labyrinth of open and covered corridors, some of which expand at intervals into spacious caverns, forming as a whole the most complete natural Gibraltar I ever saw. Other castles scarcely less strong are connected with this by subterranean passages known only to the Indians, while the unnatural blackness of the rock out of which nature has constructed these defenses, and the weird, inhuman physiogomy of the whole region are well calculated

to inspire terror. Deadly was the task of storming such a place. The breech-loading rifles of the Indians thrust through chinks between the rocks were ready to pick off every soldier who showed himself for a moment, while the Indians lay utterly invisible. They were familiar with byways both over and under ground, and could at any time sink suddenly out of sight like squirrels among the loose boulders. Our bewildered soldiers heard them shooting, now before, now behind them, as they glided from place to place through fissures and subterranean passes, all the while as invisible as Gyges wearing his magic ring. Judging from the few I have seen, Modocs are not very amiable-looking people at best. When therefore they were crawling stealthily in the gloomy caverns, unkempt and begrimed and with the glare of war in their eyes, they must have seemed very demons of the volcanic pit.

Captain Jack's cave is one of the many sombre cells of the castle. It measures twenty-five or thirty feet in diameter at the entrance, and extends but a short distance in a horizontal direction. The floor is littered with the bones of the animals slaughtered for food during the war. Some eager archæologist may hereafter discover this cabin and startle his world by announcing another of the Stone-Age caves. The sun shines freely into its mouth, and graceful bunches of grass and eriogonæ and sage grow about it, doing what they can toward its redemption from degrading associations and making it beautiful.

Where the lava meets the lake there are some fine curving bays, beautifully embroidered with rushes and polygonums, a favorite resort of waterfowl. On our return, keeping close along shore, we caused a noisy plashing and beating of wings among cranes and geese. The ducks, less wary, kept their places, merely swimming in and out through openings in the rushes, rippling the glassy water, and raising spangles in their wake. The countenance of the lava beds became less and less forbidding. Tufts of pale grasses relieved on the jet rocks looked like ornaments on a mantel, thick-furred mats of emerald mosses appeared in damp spots next the shore, and I noticed one tuft of small ferns. From year to year in the kindly weather the beds are thus gathering beauty —beauty for ashes.

Returning to Sheep Rock and following the old emigrant road, one is soon back again beneath the snows and shadows of Shasta, and the Ash Creek and McCloud glaciers come into view on the east side of the mountain. They are broad, rugged, crevassed, cloud-like masses of down-

THE CHAPARRAL ZONE OF SHASTA.

grinding ice, pouring forth streams of muddy water as measures of the work they are doing in sculpturing the rocks beneath them; very unlike the long, majestic glaciers of Alaska that river-like go winding down the valleys through the forests to the sea. These, with a few others as yet nameless, are lingering remnants of once great glaciers that occupied the cañons now taken by the rivers, and in a few centuries will, under present conditions, vanish altogether.

The rivers of the granite south half of the Sierra are outspread on the peaks in a shining network of small branches, that divide again and again into small dribbling, purling, ouzing threads drawing their sources from the snow and ice of the surface. They seldom sink out of sight, save here and there in moraines or glaciers, or, early in the season, beneath banks and bridges of snow soon to issue again. But in the north half, laden with rent and porous lava, small tributary streams are rare, and the rivers, flowing for a time beneath the sky of rock, at length burst forth into the light in generous volume from seams and caverns, filtered, cool and sparkling, as if their bondage in darkness, safe from the vicissitudes of the weather in their youth, were only a blessing.

MOUNT SHASTA IN WINTER—NEAR SISSONS.

"Toward the end of summer, after a light, open winter, one may reach the summit of Mount Shasta without passing over much snow, by keeping on the crest of a long, narrow ridge, mostly bare, that extends from near the camp-ground at the timber line. But on my first excursion to the summit the whole mountain down to its low-swelling base was smoothly laden with loose, fresh snow, presenting a most glorious mass of winter mountain scenery."

Only a very small portion of the water derived from the melting ice and snow of Shasta flows down its flanks on the surface. Probably ninety-nine per cent of it is at once absorbed and drained away beneath the porous lava folds of the mountain to gush forth, filtered and pure, in the form of immense springs, so large, some of them, that they give birth to rivers that start on their journey beneath the sun, full-grown and perfect without any childhood. Thus the Shasta river issues from a large lake-like spring in Shasta Valley, and about two-thirds of the volume of the McCloud gushes forth in a grand spring on the east side of the mountain, a few miles back from its immediate base. To find the big spring of the McCloud, or "Mud Glacier," which you will know by its size (it being the largest on the east side), and making your way through sunny

GOD'S TENTS—SHASTA AFTER A SNOW STORM.

park-like woods of yellow pine, and a shaggy growth of chaparral, you will come in a few hours to the river flowing in a gorge of moderate depth, cut abruptly down into the lava-plain. Should the volume of the stream where you strike it seem small, then you will know that you are above the spring; if large, nearly equal to its volume at its confluence with the Pitt river, then you are below it; and in either case have only to follow the river up or down until you come to it. Under certain conditions you may hear the roar of the water rushing from the rock at a distance of half a mile, or even more; or you may not hear it until within a few rods. It comes in a grand eager gush from a horizontal seam in the face of the wall of the river gorge in the form of a partially interrupted sheet nearly seventy-five yards in width, and at a height above the river-bed of about forty feet, as nearly as I could make out without the means of exact measurement. For about fifty yards this flat current is in one unbroken sheet, and flows in a lace-work of plashing, upleaping spray over boulders that are clad in green silky algae and water-mosses to meet the smaller part of the river, which takes its rise farther up. Joining the river at right angles to its course, it at once swells its volume to three times its size above the spring.

The vivid green of the boulders beneath the water is very striking, and colors the entire stream with the exception of the portions broken into foam. The color is chiefly due to a species of algae which seems common to springs of this sort. That any kind of plant can hold on and grow beneath the wear of so boisterous a current seems truly wonderful, even after taking into consideration the freedom of the water from cutting drift, and the constancy of its volume and temperature throughout the year. The temperature is about 45°, and the height of the river above the sea is here about 3,000 feet. Asplenium, epilobium, heuchera, hazel, dogwood, and alder make a luxurious fringe and setting; and the forests of Douglass spruce along the banks are the finest I have ever seen in the Sierra.

From the spring you may go with the river—a fine traveling companion—down to the sportsman's fishing station, where, if you are getting hungry, you may replenish your stores; or, bearing off around the mountain by Huckleberry Valley, complete your circuit without interruption, emerging at length from beneath the outspread arms of the sugar-pine at Strawberry Valley, with all the new wealth and health gathered in your walk; not tired in the least, and only eager to repeat the round.

A MOUNTAIN BOUQUET.

Tracing rivers to their fountains makes the most charming of travels. As the life-blood of the landscapes, the best of the wilderness comes to their banks, and not one dull passage is found in all their eventful histories. Tracing the McCloud to its highest springs, and over the divide to the fountains of Fall river, near Fort Crook; thence down that river to its confluence with the Pitt, on from there to the volcanic region about Lassens Butte, through the Big Meadows among the sources of the Feather river, and down through forests of sugar-pine to the fertile plains of Chico—this is a glorious saunter and imposes no hardship. Food may be had at moderate intervals, and the whole circuit forms one ever-deepening, broadening stream of enjoyment.

Fall River is a very remarkable stream. It is only about ten miles long, and is composed of springs, rapids, and falls—springs beautifully shaded at one end of it, a showy fall one hundred and eighty feet high at the other, and a rush of crystal rapids between. The banks are fringed with rubus, rose, plum, cherry, spiræa, azalea, honeysuckle, hawthorn, ash, alder, elder, aster, goldenrod; beautiful grasses, sedges, rushes, mosses, and ferns with fronds large as the leaves of palms,— all in the midst of a richly forested landscape. Nowhere within the limits of California are the forests of yellow-pine so extensive and exclusive as on the head-waters of the Pitt. They cover the mountains and all the lower slopes that border the wide open valleys which abound there, pressing forward in imposing ranks, seemingly the hardiest and most firmly established of all the northern coniferae.

The volcanic region about Lassens Butte I have already in part described. Miles of its flanks are dotted with hot springs, many of them so sulphurous and boisterous and noisy in their boiling that they seem inclined to become geysers like those of the Yellowstone.

The ascent of Lassens Butte is an easy walk, and the views from the summit are extremely telling. Innumerable lakes and craters surround the base; forests of the charming Williamson spruce fringe lake and crater alike; the sun-beaten plains to east and west make a striking show, and the wilderness of peaks and ridges stretch indefinitely away on either hand. The lofty, icy Shasta, towering high above all, seems but an hour's walk from you, though the distance in an air-line is about sixty miles.

The "Big Meadows" lie near the foot of Lassens Butte, a beautiful spacious basin set in the heart of the richly forested mountains, scarcely surpassed in the grandeur of its surroundings by Tahoe. During the Glacial Period it was a *mer de glace*, then a lake, and now a level meadow shining with bountiful springs and streams. In the number and size of its big spring fountains it excels even Shasta. One of the largest that I measured forms a lakelet nearly a hundred yards in diameter, and in the generous flood it sends forth offers one of the most telling symbols of Nature's affluence to be found in the mountains.

The great wilds of our country once held to be boundless and inexhaustible are being rapidly invaded and overrun in every direction, and everything destructible in them is being destroyed. How far destruction may go it is not easy to guess. Every landscape low and high

A REMINISCENCE.

seems doomed to be trampled and harried. Even the sky is not safe from scath—blurred and blackened whole summers together with the smoke of fires that devour the woods.

The Shasta region is still a fresh unspoiled wilderness, accessible and available for travelers of every kind and degree. Would it not then be a fine thing to set it apart like the Yellowstone and Yosemite as a National Park for the welfare and benefit of all mankind, preserving its fountains and forests and all its glad life in primeval beauty? Very little of the region can ever be more valuable for any other use—certainly not for gold nor for grain. No private right or interest need suffer, and thousands yet unborn would come from far and near and bless the country for its wise and benevolent forethought.

JOHN MUIR.

OLD MISSION AT SAN DIEGO.

SOUTHERNMOST CALIFORNIA.

The great hills of San Bernardino County, seen from a distance, seem almost as dreary and bare as did the great plains around their feet before the mountain streams were led upon them, and the way through any of the deep cañons that open into them presents a succession of delightful surprises. The path winds along and across arcades of lofty alder that cover with dense shade a brook of clear cold water, rushing along between banks clad with maiden-hair and a dozen species of feathery ferns, above which the tiger-lily and columbine nod the long summer through. On either side tower lofty ridges with battlements of old gray granite, glowing in the sunlight that pours upon them the livelong day, or touches them with a soft, silvery hue through rifts in the clouds that tumble and roll over the crests of these ridges in long banks of fleecy white. Into these cañons come from side ravines little brooks hissing with speed or tumbling from rock to rock in showers of spray. The fragrance of the California lilac falls softly from the hillside where its bright lavender panicles rise above the red arms and bright-green leaves of the manzanita close beside it. The golden bells of the mountain mimulus and the scarlet trumpets of the wild gooseberry or the cream-colored ones of the honeysuckle fill up the intervals between the madroña, the wild cherry and the mountain sumac that robe a great part of the mountain slopes in everlasting green.

Higher and higher leads the brook, its waters clearer and colder, dashing down short cascades to sleep for a moment in some quiet pool, or foaming in green and white among boulders of granite or snowy quartz. The deep indigo of the larkspur still follows the winding stream and the lupin; the vetch and the wild pea sprawl in crimson and purple profusion over the white rocks beside it. And soon is heard the sighing of the breeze through the needles of the pine, and the sunlight sparkles on the shining leaves of the silver fir. Tall cedars stand massed in close brotherhood along the face of steep hills and guard the heads of side ravines that seem to stand almost on end.

SUMMIT OF MT. GRAYBACK.

The large live oak of the plains is seen no more, its place being taken by a deciduous tree resembling the eastern red oak, and occasionally by another live-oak of brighter green and whiter trunk. But these both soon disappear; the pines become smaller and the fir more abundant, the chincapin takes the place of the ordinary chaparral and the crimson torch of the snow-plant lights up the ground among the dark trunks of the cedar and sugar pine. Here and there the ravines widen into small meadows filled with long, rank grass, covering the ground in dense mats, beneath which little streams of icy water trickle eternally. The wild strawberry, gooseberry, raspberry, blackberry, choke-cherry, mountain elder, bear-berry and wild plum, appear where the ground opens out in tracts of good soil, and many of them flourish even among the rocks and shingle.

Almost from the time you enter the cañon until you reach the highest point where vegetation struggles for a footing, you may hear the mild complaint of the mountain quail over your intrusion as he surveys you from some rock along the path or vanishes with gently rustling foot over the dead leaves beneath the underbrush. Over your head the mountain pigeon clad in blue and lavender floats across the cañon or inspects you from some bare limb. Though his cousin the black squirrel is missing, as is also his little enemy the red squirrel, the gray squirrel is here, the same as the old friend of our boyhood, the same sly beauty as elsewhere. The common ground squirrel of the plains has disappeared and in his place is a large bob-tailed striped-sided chipmonk, playing among the rocks and scampering over the ground in very much his manner. Two other species of tree squirrels also appear—one about the size of the eastern red-squirrel and quite as active, and gray, but darker than the gray squirrel; the other scarcely more than half the size of the last, with dark gray coat bearing a black stripe on the back from tip of nose to tip of tail; a little jet of energy that flashes rather than springs from tree to tree and from rock to rock. The mountain jay, a gaudy rogue with a dark blue hood, keeps up an incessant clamor, together with half a dozen saucy little woodpeckers in gray jackets mottled with white and red; and the dolorous croak of the raven comes from above, where his glossy coat shines in the sun as he wheels through the openings among the tree-tops or drives the pine-hawk squealing to a place of refuge in some lofty pine.

The brook becomes a mere succession of falls between walls or large boulders so narrowly set that to reach the mountain top in comfort we must follow some of the ridges. Here the trees dwindle rapidly, and become distorted and gnarled; and soon after we find them carved into fantastic

BRANDING CATTLE—TYPES OF RANCH LIFE. FROM PAINTING BY FREDERICK REMINGTON.

"That the whole country back of San Diego Bay is desert is an orthodox and general belief. The greater part is indeed desert, as is far the greater portion of San Bernardino County, and more than half the remainder in both counties is un-arable mountain. Both San Bernardino and Los Angeles counties were for many years believed to be desert, fit only for stock range, and of little value even for that."

shapes by the sand-blast driven by the winds that often whistle around these higher peaks. At about eleven thousand feet above the sea nearly all vegetation disappears. The mountain quail, two or three kinds of wood-pecker, and the little squirrel attend us almost to the top, seeming reluctant to let go their claim upon all the primeval wilderness. But at last they vanish, leaving only the dark form of the condor wheeling in graceful curves far above all.

No other mountain commands such a view as that beheld from the highest peak of the San Bernardino range. Rising suddenly

ARTESIAN WELLS, SAN BERNARDINO.

more than two miles above the general level of the plains and valleys around its base "Old Grayback" looks down upon the rarest combination of the old and the new, the rugged and the soft, the wild and the cultivated. From where the antelope looms up like a stilted ghost through the mirage of the sunlit plain, to the great gorge full of dense chaparral where the grizzly bear dozes away the day, seems but a step; and scarcely another step from the live-oak grove in the valley where the deer gazes upon the settler's cabin, to the almost inaccessible crags from which the mountain sheep surveys undisturbed the world below.

From the top of this mountain the view is nearly all open, scarcely a ridge or belt of timber cutting off the view of the underlying panorama. Toward the east the great Colorado and Mojave deserts, each larger than the state of Massachusetts, lie gleaming beneath an almost eternal sun. Two little spots of green, one at Indio, the other at Palm Valley, fast brightening amid the broad waste of reddish gray, demonstrate that even these tremendous wastes are not wholly desert, but many of the large tracts of good soil which they contain will yet be reclaimed by water. Yet, barren as they look, these deserts seen from this height have an inexpressible power which riveting the eye holds it long, before it turns to more pleasant scenes. It is the grandeur of power superior to man and his works, like that of the ocean, that makes him feel his littleness as he never felt it before upon land. For those who know their value these deserts have a special charm and awaken feelings akin to pride and gratitude. They are a far greater blessing than if they had the rich soil and rain-falls of such states as Illinois. They are the great reservoirs of the pure, dry air that makes the climate which is the peculiar glory of California. The rising of the air under the heat of the sun causes most of the suction that causes the daily sea breeze to search every nook and corner of the land the long dry season through. Flowing over westward in a vast upper current, descending upon the ocean and mingling with the return current as it passes inland, it produces that dryness of the sea breeze which so distinguishes it from the sea air of the Atlantic coast. By making the whole upper stratum of air excessively dry, it permits that rapid radiation of heat from the earth which results in cool nights succeeding the hottest days,

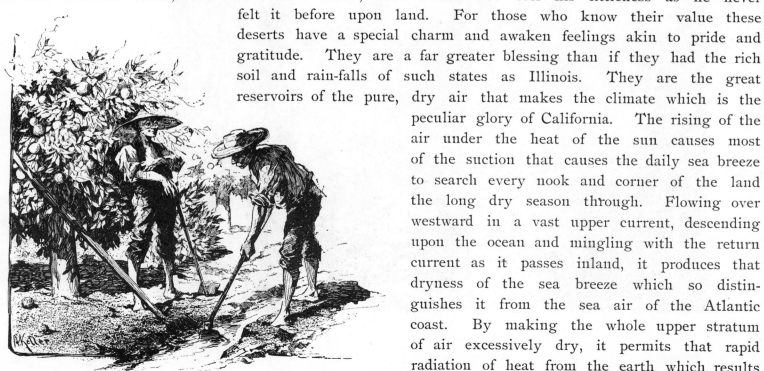

IRRIGATING.

and with the sea breeze turns the summer of this far southern land into a luxury instead of a terror.

On the north the mountain sinks suddenly thousands of feet into the upper valley of the Santa Ana river. Long winding lines of green alders mark the courses of the plunging streams that unite to form the river. Great scars gleam on the rugged hills beyond, where portions of the mountain side parted from the anchorage of ages and slid thousands of feet below, or where excess of water has cut its resistless way. Through the clear air little meadows of deep green look like gardens hung on high and the turreted crags above them like houses to which they belong. Six thousand feet above the sea a bright sheet of water, miles in length, covers the meadows of Bear Valley, the first of a series of great artificial lakes that are fast quadrupling what only three or four years ago were supposed to be the ultimate possibilities of the land. Beyond this the eye wanders away over ridge after ridge, dark with pine and fir, through which huge cliffs and crags of granite shine in the sun, then again over a hundred miles or more of desert, and rests upon the hazy blue of the great chain of the Sierra Nevada where it joins the coast range.

On the South yawns the pass of San Gorgonio, nine thousand feet deep, through which the Southern Pacific Railroad, looking like a spider's web dotted with gnats, winds out upon the Colorado desert. Just across the pass mount San Jacinto rises in one mighty sweep almost to a level with our feet, making it is said on the desert slope the most rapid rise of any known mountain in North America—ten thousand feet in five miles. Leading away from the rocky head and timbered sides of San Jacinto and extending southward, the high and rugged mountain chain shuts out the fiery breath of the desert from the inhabitable country west of it. Tumbling toward the coast in long lines of lower mountains, foot-hills and table-lands, until lost in the highlands of Mexico, the country presents a rolling confusion of blue, yellow, gray, brown, dark green and light green, arousing little suspicion of the rich valleys and slopes hidden amongst it all. Yet the settlement of San Jacinto at the mountain's base, Elsinore and Wildomar, nestled beside a sparkling lake, Murietta and Temecula, dotting with houses the great brown and yellow plains farther south, all warn the observer against deciding too hastily what those distant mountain chains may or may not enclose.

Far brighter the scene that, seeming almost at our feet, lies two miles below us on the west. The plains and slopes that stretch leagues away from the mountain's base, but a short time ago brown and sombre the summer through, with no tenants save sheep, cattle and horses, are now covered with large tracts of green, embroidered with miles and miles of silvery threads where the aqueducts that carry the drainage of these great hills wind through the abundance they have created, so dense in places as to hide the houses; where the area that once failed to maintain a wild steer now keeps a whole family in luxury.

A strange land this, that within less than a dozen years has reversed all opinions ever held concerning it, that scarcely ten years ago awoke from the sleep of ages and even now, notwithstanding its wonderful progress, is only rubbing its eyes. A wonderful progress, breaking at times into a pace necessarily too great to hold very long, yet whose course is ever onward. Where else have the rolling years looked upon such a change as a short time has wrought upon this wild cattle range? Where is there a greater development than on yonder spot upon the plain, scarce a dozen years ago hard, dry and bare as a brickyard, to-day a solid mass of green, with six thousand acres supporting in luxury a population of six thousand souls, yielding a million dollars worth of fruit each year?

In its appearance no less than in its products is Riverside unique. Perhaps no important point in the state has been developed amid conditions apparently so unfavorable, and yet there are few of them that to-day are more interesting and attractive. To fully realize the change which intelligence and energy have wrought here, one needs to remember that only a very few years ago where now are many thousand acres of shady orange orchards in the highest state of cultivation then was only a broad plain of reddish *mésa*, with neither tree nor shrub to cool the dry expanse. Except for a few months in winter and spring, there was not a particle of verdure to indicate that wealth of fertility which the application of water has since developed. Now, for miles in every direction stretch the orchards and vineyards the generous productions of which have made the name and fame of Riverside almost world-wide. Although scarcely more than a dozen years have passed since orange and raisin growing was here an experiment, the shipments of oranges and lemons already amount to about 225,000 boxes a year, and the raisin out-put to fully a quarter of a million boxes. The handling of this immense crop gives employment to a large number of people, and requires nearly a thousand cars to take it to its Eastern market.

Yet Riverside is only the pioneer; scores of similar places are rising out of the plains; the green is climbing the table-lands and over-spreading the slopes that lead up the mountain sides, and the end no man can tell. Right where the great slope joins the base of the mountain, where five years ago there was scarcely a house, a group of towns is now rising amid springing orchards of orange, lemon, prune and apricot trees and broad fields of deep-green alfalfa. Redlands and Lugonio, the central figures of the group, with their handsome homes, business blocks, school houses and churches, rising amid their thousands of green-acres, look down from their proud eminence over the whole great valley of San Bernardino. And beside these fair twin sisters and under the same splendid water system, Gladysta, Eastberne, Mentone, Terracina and Crafton are all following their lead, and the whole is fast becoming one settlement already close upon the heels of Riverside and Arlington in productive capacity.

Away beyond where Riverside and Arlington unite in a solid mass of green, South Riverside is dotting the slope of the Temescal mountains, springing from the desert under the water of Temescal creek, drawn by long tunnels from the earth in which but a short time since it was deemed forever lost. And far over these Temescal hills we can look down upon the great plains by the shining sea where Orange, Santa Ana and Tustin, Anaheim, Garden Grove and Westminster have risen in luxuriant beauty under the waters of the lower Santa Ana river which trickles from these snow-banks at our side. All along the base of the mountain chain that bounds the valley of

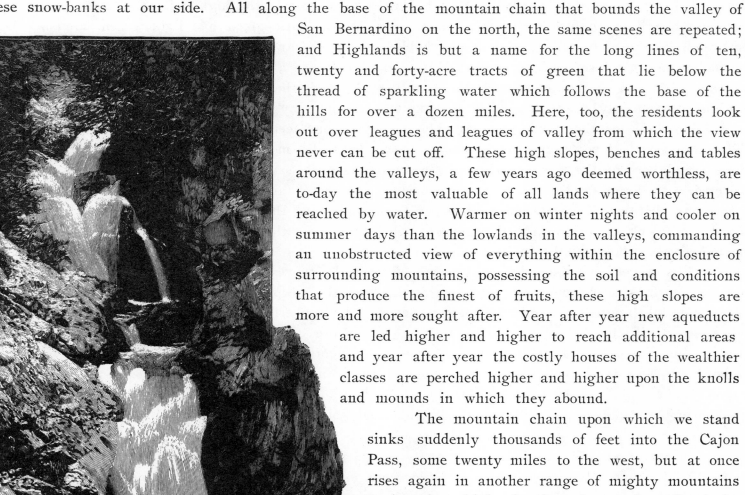

San Bernardino on the north, the same scenes are repeated; and Highlands is but a name for the long lines of ten, twenty and forty-acre tracts of green that lie below the thread of sparkling water which follows the base of the hills for over a dozen miles. Here, too, the residents look out over leagues and leagues of valley from which the view never can be cut off. These high slopes, benches and tables around the valleys, a few years ago deemed worthless, are to-day the most valuable of all lands where they can be reached by water. Warmer on winter nights and cooler on summer days than the lowlands in the valleys, commanding an unobstructed view of everything within the enclosure of surrounding mountains, possessing the soil and conditions that produce the finest of fruits, these high slopes are more and more sought after. Year after year new aqueducts are led higher and higher to reach additional areas and year after year the costly houses of the wealthier classes are perched higher and higher upon the knolls and mounds in which they abound.

The mountain chain upon which we stand sinks suddenly thousands of feet into the Cajon Pass, some twenty miles to the west, but at once rises again in another range of mighty mountains almost as high, forming the north wall of the San Gabriel Valley. Along the base of this range runs the new line of the Atchison, Topeka and Santa Fé Railroad, and beside it at frequent intervals lie numerous towns, all of the same character, all born of water and iron rails and shining in baptismal robes of green—Rialto, Cucamunga, Ettiwanda, Ontario, Claremont, and others, scarcely two years old yet seeming now

FALLS ON SAN JACINTO RIVER.

HEADWATERS OF THE SANTA ANA RIVER—HERE AND THERE ABOUT SAN DIEGO AND SAN BERNARDINO.

"On the north the mountain sinks suddenly thousands of feet into the upper valley of the Santa Ana River. Long winding lines of green alders mark the courses of the plunging streams that unite to form the river. . . . 'What a pity they have to irrigate' says the stranger. On the contrary, fortunate is the land, say we, where irrigation is necessary, provided abundant water is within reach; for the necessity of irrigation generally implies a climate that is a luxury in itself, a land in which production may go on during all the year."

to come into rivalry with Pomona and other older towns on the line of the Southern Pacific, which runs only a mile from the Santa Fé line, and parallel with it.

Almost in the center of the group below us lies the city of San Bernardino, surrounded by miles of deep-green meadow through which flow half a dozen mountain streams, while hundreds of artesian wells sparkle amid the foliage of the door yards, and gardens and orchards border the ditches that carry the waters above their native beds. A fortunate people they who inhabit this great valley. Little they care whether or not the winter brings rain. It always brings abundant snow upon the great hills, and these are reservoirs that never fail. A wonderful valley this; wonderful in its richness and extent of soil; wonderful in its adaptation of soil and climate to the choicest products of two zones; more wonderful still in having a water supply so ample and so easily carried to its highest lands.

Probably nowhere else in the world can such extensive and perfect water systems be found for such limited populations as those of Riverside, Redlands and Lugonio, where abundance of water for irrigation is carried to every farm in ditches or cement pipes, and the purest of mountain water for domestic use is conveyed to every home in iron pipes under pressure sufficient to throw it over the top of the highest house on the highest hill in the settlement. And yet Nature has eclipsed all this at San Bernardino, where all over the city and throughout an area of fifteen or eighteen thousand acres around it, artesian water of the purest quality is found in abundance less than two hundred feet from the surface, and almost every family has its own waterworks in the door-yard. A strange land this, where water wields a sceptre vastly more real and mightier far than the fabled wand of witch or fairy, literally transforming the very dust of the ground into gold.

"What a pity they have to irrigate," says the stranger. On the contrary, fortunate is the land, say we, where irrigation is necessary, provided abundant water is within reach; for the necessity of irrigation generally implies a climate that is a luxury in itself, a land in which production may go on during all the year.

Yet amid all this culture there is nothing so fine as some of the touches that nature in her more tender moods has laid upon the land. Civilization can only mar such pictures as that presented a few years ago in the *Potrero* of San Jacinto, which lies far below us in a girdle of bare, rugged hills. The thousands of acres of dark green alfalfa, the orchards and vineyards, and the hundred artesian wells whose pure waters sparkle in circular sheets over the edges of their pipes; the churches, school houses, stores and handsome dwellings in the main valley of San Jacinto, that in three years have risen from a desolate sheep-walk; have no such beauty as these wild gardens called *potreros* had before the axe and plough invaded their solemn shades. There shoulder to shoulder stood great live oaks that were old settlers before the missionaries landed on the Pacific, before the Aztec was driven from his capital, and before he robbed the Toltec of his land. Cold

ESTUDILLO HOUSE, OLD TOWN, SAN DIEGO, BUILT 1770.

PALM VALLEY, ON THE BORDER OF SAN DIEGO COUNTY. FROM PAINTING BY THOS. HILL.

"Two little spots of green, one at Indio, the other at Palm Valley, fast brightening amid the broad
waste of reddish gray, demonstrate that even these tremendous wastes are not wholly desert, but many of
the large tracts of good soil which they contain will yet be reclaimed by water."

water springing from the hillsides meandered through these shades to be lost again as soon as it reached the outer world of sunlit plain. The rippling brooks thus formed were hidden by dense ranks of alder and willow, sycamore and cotton-wood, and its banks were lined with ferns and perennial grasses. The wild rose and the sweet-briar covered many a low place with almost impenetrable green; the wild grape overwhelmed the elders with its drapery; the wild pea festooned the rocks from the chinks of which the red and cream-colored trumpets of the mimulus shone throughout the summer. Sun flowers large and small eclipsed the golden blaze of the primrose; while the wild-eyed iris smiled amid tall tulips and lilies. The sunlight glowing upon the hillsides above made these deep shades the more sweet; while the call of the quail, blending with the cooing of the dove and the songs of the oriole and mocking-bird, made one feel contempt for anything but the life of the lotus-eater.

The highest point in San Diego County is Mount San Jacinto, ten thousand five hundred feet above sea-level. The view from its top is nearly the same as that from Grayback, already described, which is only twenty-five miles away.

Forty miles back of San Diego the Cuyamaca range of mountains rises to a height of six thousand five hundred feet. This, like the other high chains in the southern part of the county, differs from the mountains of San Bernardino in an important respect. Instead of being elevated masses of rock and shingle and boulder, with a few incidental acres of good land scattered among them, they are simply vast elevations of rich arable land, where rock and boulder are the exception. Hence they may be crossed with a wagon, and are nearly all occupied by farmers, many of the best farms in the country lying at an elevation where one would find no trace of cultivation elsewhere in the southern counties.

The summit of the Cuyamaca range is an easily-climbed pyramid of rocks nearly three hundred feet high, reaching above the tops of the trees so that an unbroken view may be had. Encircling the mountain below this natural monument, the sugar-pine, yellow-pine, silver-fir, white cedar, mountain live-oak and red-oak stand densely massed, and the bark of the squirrel and the call of the mountain quail are heard among them. In a broad valley some two thousand feet below the summit the imprison-

BAY OF SAN DIEGO.

ed waters of winter shine over nearly a thousand acres in the Cuyamaca reservoir, ready to flow to the thirsty lands around San Diego Bay. From the pine-clad knoll by the lake comes the thunder of iron stamps in the mill where quartz is powdered to free the gold, and far and near over green meadows thousands of cattle are feeding. On the east the mountain falls abruptly more than a mile into the great sea of sand that reaches out of sight southward and far away to the east where Yuma lies broiling on its verge. Far away the snowy crown of our old acquaintance, Grayback, reaches two miles upward into the northern sky, with Cucamunga and San Jacinto, scarcely lower, beside it; while between them and us runs the lofty line of blue and gray mountains that bound the desert on the west. Dark with pine, or green with oak, the mountains wind away into the south, broken by valleys bright with grass or by ravines blue with chaparral, reaching far into Mexico, range upon range clad with timber or brush, or gray with ancient granite.

Below us on the north lie long rolling slopes, golden-hued with ripe wild-oats and grass, and scattered over them like a vast orchard are thousands of live-oaks. Upon these slopes are farms where the finest of fruits are growing without irrigation in a region where the rainfall is so great that nothing ever fails except from too much watering. Lower down are broad plains with thousands of acres golden with grain or tawny with stubbles, separated by high, boulder-studded hills, deep cañons filled with shade, or broad table-lands where the chaparral is fast vanishing as the tide of settlement advances. Lofty mountains rise on every hand; some, like Volcan and Palomar, almost level with our feet, crowned with forests and breaking away in long grass-clad ridges with timber gulches between; others lower and more rugged, like the great granite dome of El Cajon or Lyon's Peak. Everywhere toward the west the whole land is falling and falling, in long alternations of hill and slope and valley, away to where the great ocean lies like a cloud of gold beneath the sinking sun.

Far out into the sea runs a long promontory and almost touching it is the end of a long peninsula reaching up from the south. Within this the light shimmers upon a spacious bay where large ships are riding at anchor and outgoing and incoming steamers trail their sooty banners across the sky. Upon its shores lie San Diego and National City, fast merging into one, and on the peninsula that forms the harbor another city, Coronado, is growing fast. Just to the north lies False Bay, upon which Pacific Beach and Moreno are springing up in the freshness of youth, and

SAN DIEGO FLUME.

far away to the north Del Mar, Carlsbad and Oceanside stand fronting the sea. Towns and settlements are springing from the plains and valleys inland; a bright spot back of National City marks the great artificial lake lately completed; and winding over table-lands and along hillsides the water shines in the long flume that leads from the high mountains to the dry lands below.

One of the wonders of this region is its variety and diversity of climate. When the snow lies five feet deep among the pines of the mountain from which we behold this panorama, the guests are lounging on the verandas of the great hotel at Coronado only forty miles distant, or bathing in the surf that tumbles upon the shore beside it. And when this mountain lake is fettered in the bonds of the ice-king, oranges and bananas are ripening scarcely thirty miles away, and at Pacific Beach and Moreno, stretched upon the flowery sod that robes those lovely slopes, the people are basking beneath a semi-tropic sun. Scarcely less marked is the contrast in summer. For when the sun glares fiercely in many of the cañons and little valleys between this mountain and the sea, here the breezy shades are delightfully cool and there they know nothing of oppressive heat. Even San Marcos and Escondido faintly seen in their valleys fifty miles northward are near enough to the

coast to be blessed in this way; and so are
nearly all the settlements within ten or fifteen
miles of the sea. Truly a strange land! No
cold in winter; no heat in summer; yet all
you may wish of either within a few hours'
ride.

That the whole country back of San
Diego Bay is desert is an orthodox and general
belief. The greater part is indeed desert, as
is far the greater portion of San Bernardino
county, and more than half the remainder in
both counties is unarable mountain. But the
size of each county is so great that this pro-
portionally small remainder is really immense.
The same causes that limit it give it a value
such as no extent of acreage, richness of soil
or amount of rainfall could give. Both San
Bernardino and Los Angeles counties were for
many years believed to be desert, fit only for
stock-range and of little value even for that.
In like manner San Diego county has been
pronounced desert by thousands who have seen
only the bare table-lands of the coast-line, which
in their natural state seem as worthless as once
seemed the soil of Riverside and Pasadena.

LA JOLLA, SEA COAST NEAR SAN DIEGO.

Nevertheless it is fast filling up with people determined to see and test for themselves. Escondido,
San Marcos, El Cajon and other points easily visited by the hasty tourist are only examples of what
is going on at Santa Maria, Bear Valley, Fallbrook, and fifty other places more likely to escape
his notice. The county has a larger acreage of arable land than others which have comparatively
little mountainous area. But it is hidden away among hundreds of hills. It is the same with the
water. The mountains coax the water and snow from the clouds as liberally as elsewhere, and they
abound in springs and brooks and sites for reservoirs. But the tourist along the coast-line never
sees them, and few even of the inhabitants of the city of San Diego habitually talk of anything
but bay and climate.

This same little city is a curiosity for the political economist, a study for him who thinks
he knows human nature. In the adjacent county every town shows in an instant that it has been
built up by the surrounding country. Its streets are full of farm wagons and the carts and trucks
of business instead of real estate agents' buggies, and its backing is such that no stress of hard
times can greatly affect it. "Here are fine soil, climate and everything requisite for profitable production. Let's develop water and raise something." So say the people, and a city
arises necessarily—growing no faster than it is fed, a city on a substantial
basis. But in the case of San Diego quite a different notion has

prevailed. "Here is
a fine bay and climate.
Let's build a city,"
they said. "But is
there any land or
water back of it to
support a city?"
inquired some old-
fashioned ignoramus.
"Don't want any.
All the United States

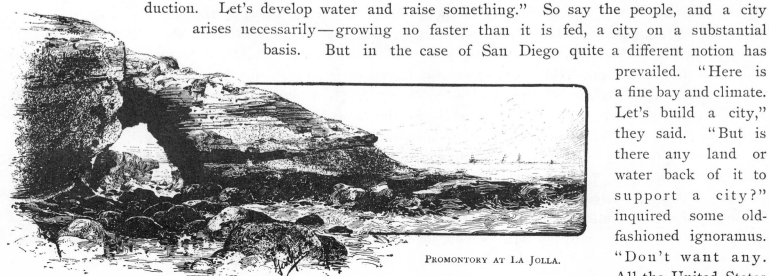

PROMONTORY AT LA JOLLA.

SAN JUAN-BY-THE-SEA.—VIEW FROM OLD MISSION OF SAN JUAN CAPISTRANO. FROM PAINTING BY J. IVEY.

"Two and a half miles from San Juan village is the old embarcadero and a newly projected seaside resort, San Juan-by-the-Sea. Fifty years ago Richard H. Dana described this as 'the only romantic spot in California.' * * * The señoras will soon look from the windows of the old mission upon stranger sights than the tents of the railroad builders. The road is already an accomplished fact; and in the wake of these magicians will come the white-winged yachts to the embarcadero, and cheerful villas will crown the cliffs at San Juan-by-the-Sea."

is our back country. Look at this map. Don't you see how this railroad has got to come here, and how that railroad can't afford to dodge us, and how this line of steamers must necessarily abandon San Francisco and come this way? Consider our divine climate, for want of which every sick man in the United States is dying. Why, there won't be room enough on these great slopes to hold them all when they find it out. Talk about back country and water! Why, a few such folks as you would soon spoil the whole business by implying that such things were necessary."

Twenty years ago San Diego was started on these two things, bay and climate. Under their influence it has grown to be a fine and wealthy city of twenty-five thousand inhabitants. If ever a people deserved destruction for willful indifference to the resources of their country the people of San Diego certainly do. But they have passed the point of destruction. They are saved in spite of themselves; saved by resources that for years they ignored and even despised. San Diego bids fair to become the third, possibly the second, city on the coast;

A MISSION INDIAN.

RUINS OF CLOISTERS, SAN LUIS REY MISSION.

but to the end of time the truest page of its history will be that which tells that its most rapid growth was artificial—caused by the expenditure of millions of money, not for any true development, but for mere conveniences for the people who were expected to come, and spent by men who neither inquired nor cared about any genuine and adequate resources, but with childlike faith believed that bay and climate alone would build and maintain a great city on the edge of a desert with only water enough to drink and wash in, without raising a thing to eat or wear and with no exports but money, sand and empty beer-barrels.

But here as elsewhere, however great the beauty that art and water have released from the bonds of ages, it is faint when compared with that of nature. Nor does this beauty consist alone of towering cliffs and pine-clad heights. There are scenes that can never be reduced to canvas. Many even of the lower hills that seem mere ramparts of boulders, rising tier upon tier for thousands of feet, have the rarest little parks and gardens upon their tops, groves of live-oaks enclosed in walls of bright green chaparral, with a spring at the upper edge and little meadows of long grass at the lower borders. Hundreds of these parks are large enough for farms and sometimes a dozen settlers find room in one; but hundreds of others are so small that the axe has not yet shorn them of their wild beauty, doubly intensified by their peculiar surroundings.

Nothing could be fresher and fairer than some of the winter scenes that but yesterday were common when the full bloom of mid-winter was upon the land, when the hills were aglow with orange and pink, and the valley with crimson, purple and gold; when thousands of bees and gay insects were humming through the bland sunshine, perhaps not fifteen miles from where the snow lay cold and shining amid dark regiments of pine. On every hand the plume of the valley-quail nodded among beds of golden violets; from far up the hillside rang his call, where the granite crags were almost covered with garlands of crimson and white; and from the tangle of wild rose and grape-vine on the low ground, from the masses of blue phacelias, that rivalled the arrow-grass in height, he darted up on whirring wings.

Out of the little ponds along the bottom-lands, the mallard with vigorous quack arose in a whirl of green and cinnamon, attended by a body of canvas-backs, widgeon and teal, sprigtails and red-heads, while scores of mud-hens, flapping and squealing, scattered among the rushes. There the sora-rail trotted along the shore and the large king-rail rose in flight for a few yards above the reeds; snowy egrets, bitterns and blue herons were eagerly fishing, while the glossy ibis stood pensive and stately at the water's edge where the snipe was probing the soft ground with his long bill and the kildeer running hither and thither with plaintive cry, all together making up a charming picture of glad wild life.

Even the door-yard of the ranch-house was then full of happy birds. From the orange tree where the ripened fruit hung beside the snowy blossoms of the future crop, the wild but tender notes of the mocking-bird filled the air. Among the blooming apricots dozens of crimson-headed linnets warbled joyously in anticipation of the fine times they would have when the fruit should be ripe enough to eat. Thrushes, mounted on the dense pink of the almond-tree, joined the chorus; wrens twittered; ruby-throated humming birds buzzed around the geraniums and roses; while hundreds of black-birds—some in glossy jet, some with crimson-barred wings, others with throat and wings banded with gold—sat chattering on the fence or garden walks or whirled with noisy wings around the roof of house or barn.

The whole landscape was then alive. Hares sprang from their hiding places, clearing a dozen feet at a bound, or crouched lower at one's approach, flattening their ears close to their heads. "Cotton-tails" scarcely larger than rats, peeped wonderingly out from among the crimson of the wild pea or the indigo of the larkspur; and toward evening they scampered by dozens over the greensward or sat along the spangled slopes leading into the hills. Hundreds of large gray ground-squirrels made for their holes at man's approach, while often the coyote or wild-cat sat upon the hillside watching you as if wondering whether it were worth while to run. The jetty coat of the raven glistened in the sun, and burrowing owls stood on every little knoll, bowing and twisting their heads to look at you. In the timbered shades snowy owls and others of soft brown with cheeks ribbed with fluffy feathers, stared from the leaves above; red-tailed hawks sat on the dead limbs of lofty sycamores; trim falcons of ashy white descended with hissing wing upon some luckless quail; and sparrow-hawks, scarcely larger than the meadow lark singing beside them, and little gray mottled hawks scarcely larger than the dove, sat upon the elder bushes calmly watching for their prey. The eagle might often be seen on some high crag of granite; the graceful lines of the sailing buzzard curved in every direction over the sky; dark dotted lines as converging strings were crossing the blue above from which came the mellow "houk" of the goose, or the penetrating "grrrrrr" of the sand-hill crane; while far above all, a mere speck in the zenith, soared with motionless wing the largest bird in America, the California Condor.

"But surely all this is changed when summer comes," one naturally thinks. Of course, yet not to any such extent as one would suppose; and few indeed are those that regret the change, for each season has its charms. Although there are three varieties of winter here there is but one summer—a long chain of sapphires in settings of ruby and gold. Weeks glide into months and months into seasons; yet the long procession of cloudless days rolls on so swiftly and smoothly that one forgets the day of the week and almost the name of the month itself. There is no such change in the appearance of the land as one would imagine must result from seven or eight months of dry warm weather. The fern-like leaves of the alfileria and its little pink stars and the gold and purplish flowers of the bright green clovers are indeed faded, but they lie in a thick mat of brown hay upon the plain, the best of fodder for your horse or cow. The yellow glare of the ripened fox-tail and wild oats lies along the slopes where the light lately rippled over wavy green.

The blaze of the cardinal flowers, shooting stars, poppies, buttercups, bellflowers, daisies and tulips has burnt out, and the glittering host of violets, pinks, phacelias, and penstemons that lately robed the land in prodigal splendor has furled its bright banners for a while. Nature has planted here a vegetation that might flourish upon the slope of Pluto's ash-heap, and with the exception of grass and small flowers much of the ground is almost as green as ever. The sycamore, cotton-wood, willow and alder are in the noon of life. Over them hangs perhaps in showers of foliage the wild grape, and the ivy twines around their trunks. In thick jungles the wild rose and sweet briar, now in full bloom, line the paths through the creek bottoms; on the more open flats the green wealth of the elder and its clusters of berries shine on every hand; several species of cactus are aglow with rose-like flowers, yellow, red and carmine; on the low ground the wild gourd and stramoniums spread their great green leaves; and still below these the wallow, the bull-rush, and a score of rank grasses struggle for the mastery. Even the dry, sandy places are relieved by the

SAN DIEGO AND BAY—FLORENCE HEIGHTS.

glistering leaves and whitish flowers of the ice-plant and the delicate pink of the *abronia* or sand verbena; while from the chinks in the granite rock-piles the cream-colored or crimson bugles of the mimulus shine as brightly as ever in the deep shade of the spreading live-oak.

The hills are less changed than the plains and cañons. The proud plume of the Spanish bayonet no longer nods in purple and white. The myriads of creepers, the silene and rock-rose, the painted-cup and the snap-dragon with their thousand gorgeous companions, have shed their brilliant attire. But the tall fuchsia is greener and more shining than ever; both varieties of the sumac are in the fullest glory of leaf and bloom; the white sage rears its tall spires full of blossoms of a delicate milky blue; the green of the wild buckwheat is drifted over with the reddish snow of its bloom; the cedar-like arms of the *adenostoma* are tufted with plumes of feathery white; the lilac, cherry, *cercocarpus*, *manzanita*, *baccharis* and all the other chaparral bushes, are in the heydey of life; and over the *ramiria*, the wild alfalfa and evergreen bushes, is twined in endless mazes the orange-colored, silken floss of that fairest of parasites, the California dodder.

INDIAN RANCHERIA, NEAR SAN LUIS REY MISSION. FROM PAINTING BY JULIAN RIX.

"All now speaks only of death and decay. Yet there was a time when busy life streamed daily through the portals of the Mission, when the dust of business whirled daily in its courts, . . . when thirty thousand cattle, ten thousand horses and as many thousand sheep belonging to this Mission roamed these hills around us."

Nor does Autumn bring any material change along the rolling hills; for it is only a palace car on the long train of summer days. On, and on, and on, the season rolls, until about the middle or end of December when, without jolt or jar, the traveller is suddenly whirled around a curve into spring; for such in fact is winter here. But all is done with scarcely any noticeable change. Nature dons no gorgeous funeral robes. No blood-red sun struggles down through smoky air. No bobolink pipes a sad farewell above our heads. No maple flames in crimson on the low-lands; no beech or hickory wears a golden crown, no oak a russet mantle, except on the mountains. No blustering scouts of winter overrun the land, and the scowling sky and chilly winds that in other lands too quickly arouse the Indian-summer dreamer are here unseen and unfelt. Here and

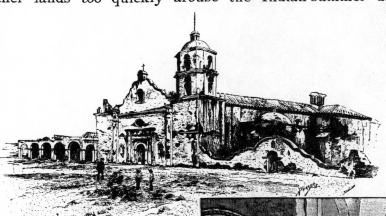

SAN LUIS REY MISSION.

there at the extreme end of the season the bright green of the sycamores and cotton-woods along the river-bottoms fades for a few weeks; but the hills display no standards of decay and their vests of chaparral show scarcely a trace of change. The serpentine trail of the cañons is still filled with glistening green; the grand old live-oaks shine as brightly as ever; the sun rolls daily through unclouded skies; the air grows drier and drier; the crimson of the sunset deepens in the valleys, and the granite peaks glow at evening with a deeper purple.

And such, more or

THE MISSION ALTAR.

less modified by distance from the coast and elevation, is the whole of southern and central California. What wonder then that it should be overrun by an immigration such as the world never has seen before, by immigrants in Pullman cars instead of "prairie schooners," by immigrants who build fine houses instead of log cabins, by immigrants who lay out broad gardens and orchards and avenues instead of corn and wheat fields. What wonder that handsome residences now line the road that has but lately taken the place of the old cattle-trail; that houses finished and furnished with all the refined elegance of modern art, embowered in roses, geraniums, heliotropes and lilies that bloom the year round, adorn

A MISSION CENTENARIAN AT HOME.

the high slopes where not long since the morning sun shone upon the glossy coat and polished antlers of the deer; that towns and villages rise amid a wealth of green where scarcely two years ago the whirring wings of myriads of quail beat the air above impenetrable jungles of cactus.

No sketch of Southern California could be complete without a glance at its remarkable development, of which no feature is more striking than the new vegetation that is taking the place of the old. Side by side are the products of two zones, each reaching the highest stages of development yet none of them natural to the soil. Great vineyards bearing five or six tons to the acre of the most delicate varieties of southern Europe, lie by the side of wheat fields of which the heads and grain far exceed in size and fullness the best of the famed fields of Minnesota or Dakota. Here the barley gives a return that no northern land can equal, and beside it the orange out-does its race in the farthest south, and keeps its fruit in perfection when that of other lands has decayed. Scarcely a tree or shrub or plant with which our northern childhood was familiar that does not reach the fullest perfection here, nearly all reaching a size that makes them hard to recognize. Alongside of them grow the feathery palm and banana, the aloe, the india-rubber tree and the tall white plumes of the pampas-grass; with the nutmeg and camphor-tree and a score of other foreign woods standing over lawns that shine with grasses unknown elsewhere in the United States. Instead of homely fences there are hedges of cypress, lime, pomegranate, *arbor vitae* or acacia, over which the broad head and drooping arms of the Mexican pepper tree fill up the sunny openings that the stately shaft of the Australian eucalyptus has failed to shade. Here and there are the guava, the Japanese persimmon, Japanese plum, the olive, nectarine and lemon; with groves of English walnut and orchards of prunes, figs, apricots, plums, pears, peaches and apples, meadows of alfalfa, gigantic corn, pumpkins and squashes that almost cover the ground, and gardens of vegetables that reach a fabulous size.

Even stranger than all this is the appearance of excellent hotels before there is a store in the place, and school-houses almost before there is a house in sight from which to send a pupil; to see railroads built before there is any produce for them to carry, and immense water-works before there is a settler to use the water, great boulevards before there are wagons to drive on them and electric lights almost before there are streets to light. Yet it is stranger still to see people flock to these new places, and to see what elsewhere would be an absurd venture yielding quick returns on the investment. With all these natural advantages there are some disadvantages, and many a settler suffers disappointment from financial miscalculation or otherwise. Overweening hope once dashed to earth generally embitters human nature, makes it querulous, unreasonable and blind to true merit. Many a newcomer here has built his air castle too high and based it on too slender a pecuniary foundation. Yet if he has been here a season he has no complaint to make of the country, and, though he may be anxious to sell, it is only in order to get money enough to repeat the experiment somewhere near by.

If there were anything novel in this extraordinary enthusiasm for the country we might well call it folly doomed to a speedy end. Such would be a just conclusion in almost any other land. But the "California Craze," that which the distant and partially informed observer has been inclined to laugh at as an hallucination, has been going on for ten years or more. It quickens its pace at times too much, but instead of stopping only slows down for a short breathing spell. Those who talk of collapsed "booms" because the crazy mob of speculators in twenty-five-foot lots let go after running prices up to a ridiculous figure, know little of the steady inflow of determined home-builders who want a few acres instead of a few feet, and who in their buying keep aloof from the centers of speculation. There is seldom a lull in the coming of these, and so it has been for a dozen years. And they never came much faster than at this very time, now that the brass-band and free-lunch have lost their whilom power and the auctioneer has thrown down his hammer and has gone to cultivating the soil. It is perhaps the highest praise of this land that a folly so stupendous and universal as to have set any other country back ten years in the race of progress has

OCEAN BEACH.

here had no effect except to make a few enthusiasts less rich than they thought themselves, and to bring down to their proper level a few who sought in a day to make fortunes out of nothing. The great tide of home-seekers pours steadily in and nothing now can stop it as long as the owners of land and water retain their senses and remember that too high prices would bar even the gate of Eden as effectually as the flaming sword. For those who have turned the last quarter in the race of life, as well as for those who, worsted in the struggle with barbarous climates, require some easy out-of-door life, no land nor clime in all the world is more inviting and none when tried satisfies so completely. Many other countries have as good soil and far more of it, but over it frowns an unfriendly sky. The world may have elsewhere as good winter climates, but in summer they are a torment. There may be elsewhere as good summer climates, but they are coupled with distressing cold and destructive blizzards in winter. The world is beginning to find this out and to act accordingly.

As the present civilization of this farthest west is superior to all that has preceded it in the great march of empire, so the older civilization was superior to any of that which moved northward from the old Aztec capital into what is now the United States. Even as the climate determines

the character of the immigration to-day, so it seems to have affected the nature of the earlier settlement and brought and kept here a more intelligent and cultivated class of missionaries and *rancheros* than those of the other Spanish-American colonies. The old missions were the richest of their kind; the old ranchos the wealthiest and most comfortable, probably the nearest approach to absolute comfort and contentment to be found on earth.

Standing, for example, within the ruins of the old mission of San Luis Rey but a slight knowledge of history is needed to see it in its

ROCK FORMATION—OCEAN BEACH.

past glory. Those lengthy colonnades and fretted arches, the long walls of *adobé* running in all directions, the rough mounds of earth that were once the walls of many houses, all speak of departed greatness. In one corner of the vast enclosure are the massive church and tower inside of which still stands, as in the olden time, the rudely painted altar before which thousands of dusky worshippers have bowed. High in the tower, where the cactus bristles in the rents made by time, still hangs the bell that called to prayer those who are now the tenants of the fallen tombs in the graveyard below. And the brain that sprung those arches and that dome, that laid out the great

walls and reared those columns, was trained only to the work of the cloister and the confessional, was thousands of miles from supplies or skilled labor, had no artizans to carry out its plans and no tools but those of the roughest sort, had only rawhide thongs instead of nails, no wagons, no modern appliances—nothing but the wild and lazy Indians, the raw earth at hand, and the timber on the mountains thirty miles away whence it had to be carried on Indian shoulders.

All now speaks only of death and decay. Yet there was a time when busy life streamed

Point of Rocks, San Diego Bay. From Painting by F. I. Heath.

"Nature has hidden away in many corners of California, for those who will come to see them, sights both wonderful and strange, as well as grand and beautiful. Down on the coast, as well as in the wilder parts, she manifests herself in forms most unusual."

daily through these portals, when the dust of business whirled daily in these courts, when all these buildings were thronged with dusky artizans alternating between work and prayer, when thirty thousand cattle, ten thousand horses and as many thousand sheep belonging to this mission, roamed these hills around us. Quietly this little world moved on without feeling the jars that shook the greater sphere. They scarcely knew of the war of American Independence until it was over, and when Napoleon was thundering at the gates of Europe the echo died away thousands of miles from these peaceful hearths. They lived, built, worked, taught, prayed and died, their lives one long, quiet summer day, until the secular power of Mexico eclipsed its peaceful sun; and then they hastened to put a barren sceptre into the invader's hand, tore up the vineyards, threw down the wine-press, dismantled the pictured shrine, and turned the Indians loose among the fattened herds.

The settlers who came in after the missionaries were from Spain or Mexico, generally of pure white blood and good family. To induce them to remain and settle the country they were given

THE PACIFIC FROM POINT LOMA.

extensive tracts of what was then considered the finest land. These "grants," which were merely Mexican homesteads on a grand scale, were made large to enable the owner to support the immense herds of cattle necessary for profit at that time, when hides and tallow were the only source of income, as well as to support the band of herdsmen needed to take care of them, and also to afford inducements for leaving home and friends and civilization to busy one's-self in what seemed as remote as the wilds of Africa seem to-day, and less likely to become civilized. These grants have been the source of much envy, hatred and quarreling, but they were as much open to the father or grandfather of the man who now thinks it an outrage that one family should own so much as they were to the Spaniard or Mexican. Viewed in the light of to-day they seem to have been a blessing rather than an evil in California, placing as they did the control of public improvements in the hands of a few instead of having thousands of petty landholders standing in the way, demanding exorbitant pay from railroads and irrigating canals, for right of way, on the ground that "they must be built, anyhow."

A Sand-storm on the Salton Desert. From Painting by Will. Sparks.

"A person who once passes through a sand-storm on the Salton Desert is not likely to forget the experience. The sky is usually free from clouds a few minutes before the storm commences, at which time they seem to spring into existence from nowhere. Far off in the distance small funnel-shaped columns of sand can be seen, that gradually grow larger and nearer until the sky is overcast and the sun blotted from sight. The darkness becomes intense, and the air is filled with myriads of fine particles driven by the wind with such force that they cut like a knife. Travel at such a time is out of the question, because it is not possible to see more than a few feet in any direction. The sand-storms generally last only a few hours, but often they will blow for days at a time and completely change the appearance of a piece of country by burying certain landmarks from sight."

The old settlers lived in large and massive houses of *adobé* or sun-dried brick, built often in the old Moorish style of a quadrangle with a court inside, having roofs of heavy red tile. They were superior to the *adobé* generally seen in New Mexico or Arizona, and for comfort in hot summer days or winter nights of comparative cold, their heavy walls made them far superior to the American's pretentious shell of clear-lumber, scroll-work, brackets, cornice and gable, just thick enough to get thoroughly heated through by five o'clock of a summer's day, requiring the whole night for cooling off; or badly chilled by dawn during the long winter nights, taking an all day's sun to warm up. In these they lived amid their numerous herds, healthy and happy. If they lounged on no silken sofas or gazed on no costly paintings, they took their ease in the saddle and their eyes wandered daily over pictures that art never can make on canvas. They had no railroads, but they could travel to the farthest northern settlement without spending a cent, exchange the tired horse for a fresh one at any ranch, or stop with a stranger as long as they pleased. They had no newspapers or telegraphs, but also no mining-stock reports to steal away their senses; no imposing school-houses with big cupolas, and only corresponding taxes; few novels or none, and but few lazy girls. They had no hammerless breech-loading guns, aristocratic dogs or repeating rifles; but they could lasso the largest grizzly and drag him, bound upon a rawhide, to fight the wild bull upon the plains. Rude was their system of justice. They had no tedious probate courts or public administrators; no doctors or lawyers; but they settled their troubles quickly, were gathered to their fathers without expensive assistance, and their families got their estates without waiting half a lifetime and then receiving only what the lawyers had left. Surrounded by plenty of the comforts of life, with plenty of servants that cost only their board, with nothing to do but look after their herds and flocks, attend fandangos, meriendas, bull-fights and horse races, and chatter in their beautiful language under their broad porches, most of them drifted down the stream of time without touching oar or rudder or striking snag or sand-bar. And something of the simplicity and peace and gladness of the old ranch life is and ever will be inherent in the very land and sky of California.

T. S. VAN DYKE.

MEXICAN BOUNDARY MONUMENT.

NORTH OF THE GOLDEN GATE.

STAND upon Telegraph Hill, in San Francisco, look northward across the glittering bay and gaze upon Mount Tamalpais rising twenty-seven hundred feet directly from the water, lying like a huge watch-dog beside the Golden Gate and holding the ocean winds at bay. Rearing its triple head toward the east as if to keep an eye upon the busy city opposite as well as upon the bustling steamers that speed across to Oakland, San Rafael and up the broad Sacramento River, Tamalpais extends its beautiful profile along the entire coast of Marin County. The bitter chemisal covers its heights, but below forest and chaparral contend for almost every inch of ground, while the graceful fleur-de-lis looks up to primeval redwoods. Many a rill sings its merry song as it dances over rock and pebble down, down, into the valleys to slake the thirst of man and beast and soil with water of marvellous purity. From mountain base to summit winds a well graded road, broad enough for carriages, varied enough in prospect to satisfy the most sated of travelers. Tamalpais is as unique as "Arthur's Seat," the crowning glory of Edinboro', and the time is not far distant when its signal charm will meet with fitting recognition. To-day it waits patiently for its poet.

Whence the name? One authority declares that it is taken from two words belonging to the Nicasio Indians who lived formerly within the shadow of the mountain; *Tamal* meaning "coast" and *pais* "mountain," collectively making "coast mountain." Another says that in the Aztec language *Tamal* means a boiled preparation of corn meal enclosing meat and wrapped in a corn husk. The similar Mexican dish of *tamales*, made of chicken, is to-day common in California. *Pais* in Spanish means "country," and whether Indian and Spanish have mingled to evolve euphonious "Tamalpais" is a mystery still unsolved and may ever remain so. Some maintain that there was an Indian tribe called Tamales, and that Tamalpais signifies "land of the Tamales;" but who knows? Whatever the origin of the name, this picturesque mountain constitutes the great beauty of Marin County. In fact it *is* Marin County, and this small corner of imperial California, surrounded on three sides by salt water, extending like a misshapen finger to the Golden Gate, plays no small part in the early history of the State. The name of this county is not from *mare*, "the sea," but from Marin, a famous chief of the Lacatuits who occupied the region prior to American settlement. From 1815 to 1824 he and his tribe successfully opposed Spanish invasion. However, the day came when Marin was captured and his people dispersed. Making his escape, Marin sought refuge on the small island in San Francisco Bay now called after him, and it was this fitting baptism that suggested the same nomenclature for the adjacent promontory. Taken prisoner a second time, Marin would have been shot but for San Rafael's mission priests, through whose intercessions he was set free. It was then that the chief became a convert to Christianity and retired to San Rafael, where he died in 1834. Many a time and oft he crossed the bay on his tule-float, and it was he who in 1822 assisted Comandante Arguelo in guiding the first raft of lumber from the Corte de Madera to the Presidio of San Francisco.

THE KEEPER OF THE LIGHT.

EXPOSED STAIRWAY,
POINT REYES LIGHTHOUSE.

But nearly three centuries before this Indian dreamed of living, Marin County sheltered the explorers Cabrillo and Francis Drake. Drake, the first Englishman "to plow a furrow round the earth," the first Saxon to visit the shores of California, was the pale-face who on June 17th, 1579, sought shelter under the lee of Point Reyes. There he discovered "a convenient and fit harbor," and there he tarried thirty-six days repairing and refitting "The Golden Hind," believing himself the first European to set foot on this western promontory, (not knowing that Cabrillo had landed in the self-same harbor in 1542,) and calling the land "New Albion," in honor of old England and because of the white cliffs lining the coast. Cabrillo and Sir Francis Drake! the first white men to approach the Golden Gate, the first to tread the sands of Marin County! There are those who believe that Drake discovered San Francisco Bay, but such faith is born of fancy. No navigator who had been beaten up and down the inhospitable Pacific coast could have entered so magnificent a bay without announcing the glad fact. Where in this bay are the "white cliffs" to recall far-distant Albion? They do not exist; but along the coast northeast of Point Reyes, on both sides of the harbor where Drake unquestionably dropped anchor, there are one, two, three, four, five, six, seven distant cliffs, whose sides, though not of chalk, suggest the whiter soil of England's coast.

POINT REYES LIGHT. FROM PAINTING BY JULIAN RIX.

" Built on an elevation three hundred feet above the sea, this beacon is reached by an exposed stairway of seven hundred and fifty steps. When storms are at their worst spray dashes up two hundred feet, falling upon the building that shelters the duplex 'siren' or fog whistle. The 'siren' of Point Reyes is heard twelve miles off the coast, and sings her mournful song eighty-three and one-third days in the year, the months of July and August being generally the most steeped in fog. The light, which owes its power to one thousand and thirty separate pieces of wonderfully adjusted glass, revolves every two minutes and flashes from the bull's eye at intervals of five seconds."

There are few snugger harbors than must have been that of Limantour Bay three hundred years ago. The bar across its mouth has grown apace since then, and the basin has become shallow, but even now vessels of one hundred tons—and Drake's ship measured no more—can float upon it. Drake's chaplain and historian, who complained of the weather farther north, would hardly have failed to note the trade-winds that make San Francisco Bay a trial to the flesh from May until September. It was during this period, in June and July, that "The Golden Hind" lay careened on American soil, yet winds are never mentioned. The chaplain takes pains to state that their ship was "secure from storms." Turn it which way one may, no candid person, having surveyed the coast, can believe that Drake or Cabrillo ever saw the Golden Gate. Marin County cannot be shorn of its laurels. The only port known until 1769 was the outside bay now bearing Drake's honored name. There José Gonzalez Cabrera Buenos, a Philippine pilot, learned in his craft, located the port of San Francisco in his book on navigation published at Manila in 1734. According to this pilot it lay in latitude thirty-eight and a half degrees, with Point Reyes on the north and the Farralones Islands on the south-southwest

By order of Phillip III. of Spain, General Sebastian Viscaino explored the coast of Alta California and, after discovering San Diego and the Bay of Monterey, anchored on January 7th, 1603, in the harbor that had protected Cabrillo and Drake. To the point of land behind which his vessel lay, the Spanish navigator gave the name of Punta de los Reyes—Point of the Kings—and there he descried the first known wreck on California's coast. Eight years before, in 1595, Sebastien Cermenon, while sailing from Manila to Acapulco, met his fate on the beach of Point Reyes.

OLD CHAPEL AND BEACH, AT FORT ROSS.

No wonder, then, that the United States Government should take pity on the neglected mariner and establish at Point Reyes a light-house of the first class, second only in size and importance to that of New York. Built on an elevation three hundred feet above the sea, this beacon is reached by an exposed stairway of seven hundred and fifty steps. When storms are at their worst spray dashes up two hundred feet, falling upon the building that shelters the duplex

"siren," or fog whistle, and the poorly-paid servants of a prosperous but ungrateful republic stand erect at the risk of their lives when going to and from their post of duty. Their only safety is in crawling on hands and knees up and down those seven hundred and fifty steps. Little does the anxious pilot realize, when listening intently for the voice that is to warn him of danger, how hard and ill-paid are the lives of those keepers on whose fidelity depends the commerce of the seas. The "siren" of Point Reyes is heard twelve miles off the coast, and sings her mournful song eighty-three and one-third days in the year, the months of July and August generally being the most steeped in fog. The light, which owes its power to one thousand and thirty separate pieces of wonderfully adjusted glass, revolves every two minutes and flashes from the bull's eye at intervals of five seconds.

When winds cease from bluster and fogs keep out of sight, Point Reyes is a delight to the senses. Below glitters the Pacific like molten silver, its waves lazily lapping the rocks where hair seals disport and lift up their bass voices in frequent chorus, and myriads of shags solemnly stand erect as though awaiting a revelation. Thirty miles to the south-west rise the solitary Farralones, where

MADRONA TREES, PAPER MILL CREEK—NEAR TAYLORVILLE.
FROM PAINTING BY JULIAN RIX.

"Here, too, are the ever welcome live oak and the Madrona with its magnolia-like leaves, reddish brown limbs and trunk, white wax-like flower and bright red berry. It is one of Nature's poems without words, that silences the irreverent and bends the knee of thankful fancy."

three men live year after year, only ten days out of three hundred and sixty-five being allowed to each one to visit the mainland and renew his acquaintance with the world. In case of necessity, however, leave is permitted without authority. Yet in spite of a loneliness varied only by the occasional appearance of a store-ship, there are those who seek the life because "it enables a fellow to save a little money." There they trim the light-house lamp day after day, lighting it with the setting of the sun, and look forward to the one excitement of the year, when the egg gatherers appear and carry off the harvest deposited by the murre. Gazing upon those specks upon the bosom of the sea, thought goes back to 1542, when Juan Rodriguez Cabrillo first discovered them, and, in their baptism, perpetuated the name of his pilot Farralo. And then thought turns to that July day, when, with singing of psalms and farewells to the simple and sad-hearted natives, who dreamed not what the white men signified to their race, Drake sailed away from Point Reyes, and the next morning, July 24th, anchored off the Farralones, which he called the Island of St. James. There he killed seals and birds; and thence he began his westward journey· round the world, little thinking that "the sea that was his glory" would be "his grave."

Northward for miles stretches the fine yet treacherous beach; eastward roll hills so rich in grasses as to make the brand of Point Reyes butter the envy of all farmers and the desire of every housekeeper. From high rocks back of the light-house there is a vision of Drake's old harbor and Tomales Bay which penetrates the Coast Range for sixteen miles, nearly to the centre of Marin County. Land-locked, sheltered from wind, with a mouth only half a mile wide, this pretty miniature of San Francisco Bay brings with it moisture that tells the reason why the average product of butter and cheese to the cow is greater in this small county than the average in the best dairy counties of New York, Ohio and other Eastern States. While, east of the Rocky Mountains, cattle are housed to shield them from inclement weather, and are fed with hay and corn meal to keep them in condition, the fortunate animals of Marin County breathe continually the pure air of sea and mountain and graze upon clover and native grasses.

Four leagues north of Point Reyes, where the county of Marin meets that of Sonoma, lies the little bay of Bodega, where Bodega y Quadra landed on October 3d, 1775. Thus within a coast line of twenty miles Cabrillo, Drake, Viscaino, and Bodega y Quadra made their discoveries in the new world, and left to Russia the honor of establishing the first settlement. Bodega Bay was originally taken possession of by Alexander Koskoff in 1811, on the plea that he had been refused a supply of water at Yerba Bueno, and that he had obtained by right of purchase from the Indians all the land lying between Point Reyes and Point Arena and for a distance three leagues inland. To work the Russians went with a will. Six miles from Bodega they built houses, fenced fields and grew grain, which they shipped from Bodega Bay in their own vessels. The sons of Spain looked on with scowling brows. To protect themselves from threatened attack the Muscovites explored the coast and north of Bodega found meadow and cove and beach well adapted for Russian headquarters. Here was Fort Ross established. In those days the fort consisted of a square enclosure one hundred varas each way. On diagonal corners, one facing the ocean and the other the mountains, were octagonal block houses of hewn logs with embrasures, each furnished with six eight-pounder pieces of artillery. A large building stood at the main entrance, where a sentinel was always on guard and where six cannon were stationed. Other cannon were kept at the house of the comandante, and at headquarters there were seventy stand of arms. Within the enclosure were fifty-nine buildings, including barracks, warehouses and a Greek Church. Walls and buildings were of wood, strong enough to resist Indian arrows. Beyond the walls were other structures, among them being two mills, one driven by water and the other by wind, a capital tannery, a blacksmith shop, and a ship-yard, where four vessels and many launches were built; indeed, here were launched the first sea-going craft constructed in California. East of the fort and across the gulch is said to have stood a church used by the humbler colonists, and near by lay the cemetery of never more than fifty graves. A farm of two thousand acres was under fence, and much more land was cultivated without being thus protected. One mile away from the coast forests abounded, and the first lumber ever made with a saw north of San Francisco Bay was produced by the Muscovite invader. Stumps of redwoods denote the early destruction, and around them shoots have sprung up to the height of fifty and sixty feet, with a diameter that fits them for the remorseless axe,

Russia's first intention was to obtain from California the cereals necessary for her people further north, and incidentally to still further prosecute the fur trade; but on account of complaints from the Comandante of San Francisco the attempt at agriculture was abandoned. On the mountain side, however, back of Fort Ross, an orchard of four hundred trees and a vineyard of seven hundred stocks were successfully planted. Officially, the Spaniards were always jealous of the Russians, and between 1816 and 1818 the expulsion of the latter was much discussed; but as the trade with the Russians increased yearly and benefitted the country, opposition took no active form, and the Muscovites sheltered ships of the Russian-American Company every winter. Better customers than the Russians the Pacific coast never had. They paid promptly for all purchases made, and gave to the Spanish Government one-half of the skins taken in hunting. Often as many as 80,000 seal-skins were collected at the Farralones in a single season. It was Russia, too, that sent the first scientists to the North Pacific. In 1816 the ship "Rurick" entered San Francisco Bay having on board

several distinguished naturalists, one of them being Dr. Eschscholz, after whom the yellow California poppy has been named *Eschscholzia*.

When hunting and trade ceased to be profitable Russia had no further use for her California colony, and on July 27th, 1841, Kostromitinoff sat in the house of Gen. Vallejo at Sonoma endeavoring to negotiate terms of evacuation. The Spanish took too high ground for the Russian. Vallejo insisted that inasmuch as the houses at Ross had been built of Mexican timber and stood on Mexican soil, they therefore rightly belonged to Mexico. The Russian refused to entertain such a romantic idea and straightway sold the entire property to Captain John A. Sutter for $31,000. On January 1st, 1842, after a sojourn of twenty-eight years, the Russians returned to our Alaska. Not long after their departure wild oats grew rank where grain once reared its head, and often stood ten feet high. This were the Indians wont to fire, and thus were destroyed houses, fences and the people's church. Nothing remains but the officers' quarters, the two forts, one fast crumbling to decay and leaning to the west, as though asking to be saved by those who had sailed away never to come back, the other transformed into a pig-sty and not to be approached by dainty shoes.

The chapel has been ruthlessly turned into a stable and not more than a dozen graves can be traced upon the hill. All are nameless! The orchard of five acres, containing apple, prune and cherry trees gray with neglected age, numbers to-day but fifty-nine trees. Of prunes not one is left, yet it is said that all the old California stock of German prunes came from seed produced at Fort Ross.

Thus have these best of foreign colonists passed away, leaving in their wake nothing but a memory. The American takes the Russian's place, scorns to preserve historic relics, turns "Timbertoe's" residence into an hotel and converts a fort into a profitable ranch!

No need to linger o'er the prosaic present, and turing southward the sentimental tourist is driven for six miles over the "coast grade road." Cut out of the mountain's side, with the sea not far below, it winds around

OLD RUSSIAN SAW-MILL, FORT ROSS.

the rock-bound coast, now down, now up, with here a gulch where Russians once grew wheat, and there a "Gunshot Point" where the notorious literary highwayman, "Black Bart," once plied his adopted calling. For six miles the picturesque road skirts the coast; for six miles the eye looks, first upon the Pacific Ocean with its breakers dashing over rocks whose only visitors are birds and seal, and then upon the precipitous sides of high hills inhabited solely by goats, coyotes and winged things. At last, ranch houses invade the solitude, and soon begins a beautiful descent that leads to the mouth of the Russian River, called "Slawianska" by the Muscovites and "San Sebastian" by old Californians. Thus no sooner is the ocean lost to view than this pretty stream, with its twists and turns, its islands and wooded hills, offers a balm to latest memory. Here the sportsman's holiday is spent. Here fish and game do congregate, despite the axe of the lumberman, that has levelled many a glorious redwood and will level many more. The voice of the saw sings the music of the century, and Duncan's Mills, the terminus of the stage route, owes its origin and prosperity to the noble redwoods that have been sacrificed for the benefit of ungrateful man. There, in a bend of the river, sit town and mill, and one has only to wade the not too deep stream to reach the "Moscow" of America, a pretty country-seat with such a full-length view of the river as can be excelled only still further east on the beautiful road to Guerneville. When beheld from a high point, mountain, sky and water seem to meet and mingle at this same sylvan "Moscow."

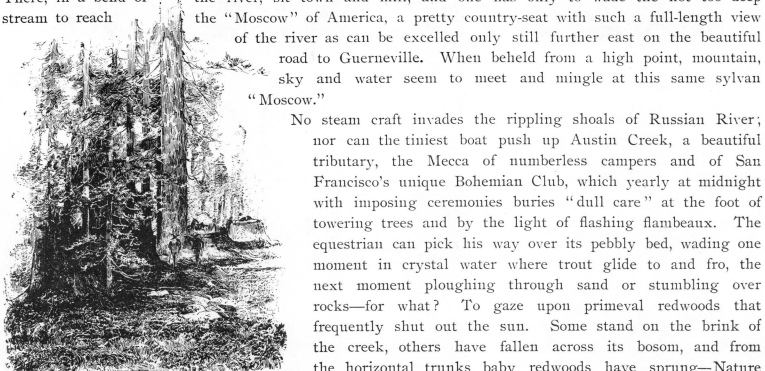

REDWOOD STUMPS AND NEW GROWTH.

No steam craft invades the rippling shoals of Russian River; nor can the tiniest boat push up Austin Creek, a beautiful tributary, the Mecca of numberless campers and of San Francisco's unique Bohemian Club, which yearly at midnight with imposing ceremonies buries "dull care" at the foot of towering trees and by the light of flashing flambeaux. The equestrian can pick his way over its pebbly bed, wading one moment in crystal water where trout glide to and fro, the next moment ploughing through sand or stumbling over rocks—for what? To gaze upon primeval redwoods that frequently shut out the sun. Some stand on the brink of the creek, others have fallen across its bosom, and from the horizontal trunks baby redwoods have sprung—Nature only knows how—standing as erect and self-reliant as though

MOUNT TAMALPAIS. FROM PAINTING BY JULIAN RIX.

"Rearing its triple head toward the east as if to keep an eye upon the busy city opposite as well as upon the bustling steamers that speed across to Oakland, San Rafael and up the broad Sacramento River, Tamalpais extends its beautiful profile along the entire coast of Marin County. The bitter chemisal covers its heights, but below forest and chaparral contend for almost every inch of ground, while the graceful fleur-de-lis looks up to the primeval redwoods. Tamalpais is as unique as 'Arthur's Seat,' the crowning glory of Edinboro', and the time is not far distant when its signal charms will meet with fitting recognition. To-day it waits patiently for its poet."

their roots were firmly planted in the ground many feet below.   Once or twice the big trees of
Mariposa are recalled by the sight of trunks thirty feet in girth.   Bush and brake form arches
overhead, and tiny streams add their musical mite to the creek as it courses to the sea, wild flowers
and berries bending low to kiss the waters in their flight.

Beside Austin Creek, ten miles from Duncan's Mills, stands the hunting box of Cazadero,
where redwoods come to an end.   Here is heard the snort of the iron horse that bears the forest
to the town, and here begins the journey of the North Pacific Coast Railroad from the redwoods
of Sonoma County to Sausalito by the sea.   Back to Duncan's Mills, through the same forest that
makes the glory of the region, the "narrow-gauge" speeds its tortuous way, crossing the Russian
River over a wooden bridge six hundred feet long; climbing, climbing, zigging and zagging, around
ravines, over spurs, across the highest trestle in California—one hundred and thirty feet above creek
and cañon—out of Sonoma County into Marin, through the first long tunnel, measuring two thousand
six hundred and twenty-nine feet, down, down to sea level, skirting the shore of Tomales Bay for fifteen
miles.   Near by Olema lies picturesque Bear Valley, running westward to the sea, once the home
of bruin and now the resort of bruin's worst enemy, man.   Never was foliage brighter than in
this secluded gorge, through which cool waters flow unceasingly.   Alders and laurels and live-oaks
make a veritable canopy, and wonderful ferns, from the most exquisite maiden hair to plumes several
feet high that nod with every breath of wind, carpet the emerald creek and grace the hill-sides.
Bower follows bower, and fauns and satyrs and pipes of Pan only are needed to complete the
romantic scene.

On again by the narrow-gauge, following a picturesque stream
that derives its modern name from California's pioneer paper-mill
still standing at Taylorville, past Camp Taylor with its merry-
voiced picnickers, along the sinuous creek of Lagunitas, the engine
tugs and puffs up the western slope of White's beautiful valley,
then for one thousand six hundred feet rumbles through
the bowels of a mountain.   Emerging five hundred
feet above the level of the sea, the narrow-gauge pursues
a steady downward grade through a series of elongated horse-shoe
curves, where at times the upper side of one curve lies fifty
and even a hundred feet above another, a hundred yards
across the deep ravine; while, in skirting the big toe of
the titanic horse-shoe, the train swings around three-quarters
of a circle and travels a long mile to gain nine hundred feet.
After passing along the sides and around the heads of cañons,
deep and steep and narrow, after
descending to the undulating parks
of Fairfax, pretty San Anselmo
Valley is reached.   Here begins
the easy ascent to Tamalpais and
to Lake Lagunitas, set like a great
diamond in the green enamel of
the mountain's side.   Here are inviting groves, and here are some
of the most beautiful residences in
Marin County.   Slough after slough
winds like a silver ribbon among
the low-lands that gradually lose
themselves in the bay, and in the
Corte de Madera del Presidio stand
the ruins of the first American
saw-mill that ever pierced the heart
of California's redwood.   Near by

"HIGH JINKS" AMONG THE REDWOODS.

LOGGING IN THE REDWOOD FOREST. FROM PAINTING BY A. HENCKE.

"But the real life of the redwood forest, the activity which gives it the stir and bustle of actually being alive, is that which comes from the logging industry. There is nothing in California that is more picturesque than one of these redwood logging camps. The low-roofed, open-sided mills, the long teams of stolid oxen with their clanking chains, the flannel-shirted drivers with their pistol-cracking whips and uninterrupted flow of high-keyed and objurgatory profanity, all combine to render the scene one that is novel and unusual."

sleeps in the sun the pretty settlement of Blithedale, and from its narrow valley is best seen the long scar upon the face of Tamalpais caused suddenly fourteen years ago by a cloudburst that came and went one October day, no one knowing of its advent until the mischief had been done. Ten miles farther along the shore of Richardson's Bay the narrow-gauge stops suddenly at the water's brink in pretty Sausalito (little willow copse), whence rapid ferry-boats convey passengers to San Francisco.

Sausalito, the rendezvous for all the yachting clubs of the Golden Gate, is a terrace of villas on one of the many hills that sit at the foot of Tamalpais. Here breezes ever blow, here ozone makes its home, and here anchored the first ships that entered the Golden Gate to find protection from storms and seek fresh water from the many springs. Here came the first settler in the township Captain John Reid, in 1826; here he built the first house in 1832, and from here he plied a small boat six miles across the bay to San Francisco, and thus became the pioneer ferryman.

Fortified with keys, the tourist on foot or on horseback passes over Sausalito's one level road skirting the sea, catches glimpes of yacht club houses to the left, slowly climbs a hill and halts before the inhospitable gate that the United States Government interposes between the public and its military reservation of seventeen hundred acres. The rusty lock yields to a less rusty key. Love's labor is not lost. Eye first finds delight and shade in the old grove of live-oaks that seem to cling desperately to the side of the wind-beaten hill, and then drinks in the wondrous panorama of the bay, which changes with every turn and grows finer with every ascending step. High above the bay are fortifications of earthworks more likely to serve their purpose than the ancient masonry of Fort Point, opposite. Below, in a little cove, are the Gravelly Beach batteries, where seven guns are in position. Beyond, under overhanging rocks that a slight convulsion of nature would quickly hurl to the sea, stands the fog signal station of Lime Point, built on a narrow ledge of rock and connected with the main land by narrow bridges. Tides ebb and flow unceasingly, river and sea meet and contend for the mastery, for the Golden Gate, only one mile and a quarter wide, is not far off. After climbing more hills covered with rich grasses, descending steep cañons and breasting the trade-winds of the Pacific, Point Bonito is the reward. Here is the mouth of San Francisco Bay, and here on "Land's End," attained only by a tunnel, stands a light-house of the second order, the beacon of which can be seen eighteen nautical miles out to sea. Prior to 1855 San Francisco Bay had no light-house. Then, at Point Bonita, a tower was reared three hundred and sixty feet above the sea that was often enveloped in fog, when none approached levels nearer the water. On the same bluff directly north of this tower was stationed a sixty-pound cannon, fired every half hour in foggy weather. Tower and cannon still remain much the worse for age and neglect, but are far more picturesque than their useful successors many feet below.

Point Bonita is well named; it is "beautiful." Across the narrow strait lies the Presidio, the cliffs and seal rocks. San Francisco's hills bound the southeastern horizon; vessels of every fashion sail or steam to and fro, laden with the wealth of nations, while the jagged coast stretches northward followed by breakers that form a long line of foam. The eye looks north as far as Bolinas and the reef below Duxbury Point, to reach which is a day's journey along a coast and mountain road of rare beauty. Bolinas with its pretty bay, the greater part of which at low tide is transformed into a great sand-bed, slumbers quietly the greater part of the year, content with its rich soil and gigantic clams until the summer solstice sends humanity to its beach for breath, of which there is abundance. Yet time was when Bolinas supplied San Francisco with its lumber. Unique and wild as is the coast-road from Sausalito to Bolinas, it hardly eclipses the mountain route between these points. Bolinas ridge reveals a noble vista of sea and harbor and undulating forest, and as the road winds down one wooded hill to ascend another, the eye that has had its fill of ocean, shore and smooth-faced mountains, revels in luxuriant foliage and its attendant light and shade. Here grows the California laurel, or bay, to a height of fifty feet, exhaling the aromatic odor so familiar in bay rum. Very hard and of yellowish gray color is the wood, which makes fine furniture and veneer. This beautiful evergreen has for its frequent companion the California nutmeg. Here too are the ever-welcome live-oak and the madrona with its magnolia-like leaves, reddish-brown trunk and limbs, white wax-like flower and bright red berry. It is one of nature's poems without words, that silences the irreverent and bends the knee of thankful fancy.

Who would see the madrona in its glory, let him visit that drinking cup of Tamalpais, Lake Lagunitas, and behold the two noblest specimens in the state. The buckeye, with its large-leaved foliage and great spikes of fragrant white flowers, together with the California lilac, scents the air. Here also thrives the manzanita, which rarely rises above twelve feet and is more shrub than tree. Poison-oak prefers shade to sunshine, like most evil-doers, and, climbing the white oak, bids sensitive skins beware. Pine looms up in every direction, and the California honeysuckle, half bush half vine, rises ten, twenty feet from the ground, its trumpet-shaped flowers peering out from the surrounding verdure like bits of bright color on nature's emerald palette. Mistletoe hangs and moss droops from many a tree. Those blessed herbs, sacred to Spanish medicine, *yerba buena* and *yerba santa*, grow close to the ground, while wild grapes, blackberries, gooseberries, whortleberries, raspberries, salmonberries and strawberries appear at discreet intervals and bid the traveler to an impromptu feast.

State Prison at San Quentin.

In dense thickets still live the California lion, wolf, mink, raccoon, wild-cat, deer, eagle and vulture, and even the obnoxious bear. At a turn in the steep road there is a trail still known as "Frémont's," by which "the pathfinder" and his men made a détour in early days to avoid Mexicans and Indians. Murmuring brooks and a pretty cascade not far away from the beaten track solace the thirsty soul. Farm succeeds forest. Wild oats, sometimes eight and ten feet high, burr-clover, alfileria and the ever-invading Scotch thistle tell of man's proximity and the end of a day's tour that has not its peer beyond the limits of the Yosemite.

East of Richardson's Bay and northeast of Sausalito lies the harbor of Tiburon, from which starts the broad-gauge railroad that pierces Marin County directly north to Petaluma and Sonoma. Following the coast it passes within a short distance of San Quentin, where the great State Prison indicates more sinners than saints. But San Quentin is misnamed. It was not generally known that the locality was once a battle-ground between whites and Indians, the latter being commanded by Quintin, a sub-chief under Marin. Hence in their ignorance people modified the French "Quintin" and applied the prefix "San," assuming the name to be Spanish and a holy man to be at the

SAUSALITO, FROM FERRY SLIP.

PAPER-MILL CREEK.

LAKE LAGUNITA.

bottom of it. Never was a penal institution more beautifully situated between bay and hills. If the contemplation of the beautiful in nature effected moral reform, San Quentin would be a blessing in disguise, but it is literally true that "the kingdom of God is within." Their nearest neighbors, the ruminating cattle, are no more oblivious to scenery than are the unfortunate prisoners whose lives have been passed in looking down, not up.

North of Point San Quentin extends the far nobler point of San Pedro, where Chinese fishermen ply their vocation so quietly and so remote from the beaten road as to be almost unknown. The artist will leave even the finest scenery to sketch the picturesque interiors and boat-life of this oriental colony. In San Pablo Bay lies the wealth these busy human bees are after, early and late. Their cone-shaped nets are set for shrimps, catching weekly from twenty to thirty tons. These little creatures are dried on hillsides bared of all semblance of grass, and are threshed by Chinese feet. After the hull has been removed in this primitive fashion, the shrimps are winnowed through a hand mill and sent to San Francisco, while the hulls are shipped to China and sold as a valuable fertilizer. Thus meet the old world and the new. Asia's most expert fishermen cross the Pacific Ocean to entrap along the shore of California crustacea with which to enrich themselves and the soil of the Celestial Empire. That a shrimp should produce such great results! Verily there is nothing so small in creation as to deserve contempt. The atom is but the unit of the universe.

Northward speeds the broad-gauge, catching inviting glimpses of San Pablo Bay, and northward lies Novato with fertile hills and valleys that

MOUNT TAMALPAIS, FROM ANGEL ISLAND. FROM PAINTING BY J. IVEY.

"This must rank as one of the prettiest of the many pretty corners of San Francisco Bay, and it would be difficult to conceive a fairer ideal of a suburban home than one of the villas which nestle among the leafage of the island-like promontory shown in the picture. Behind it is the picturesque outline of bold Tamalpais with its flanks of receding hills, then the placid, silvery water of Richardson's Bay, while at its feet plies the ferry which almost hourly makes trips to the City, and ever before them a measureless distance of beauty, embracing the City and hills of proud Berkeley, and vanishing into a glimpse of Mount Diablo."

need only the tickle of the hoe to laugh with a generous harvest of grain and fruit. At the foot of Olompali Hills is a wide and picturesque stretch of marsh with tule (reeds) several feet high. Time was, however, when glittering sandy beach preceded these salt marshes and a fine stream of living water sped into the bay. In that long ago a powerful tribe of aborigines called Olompalis lived in this region. Their existence is proved by the presence of acres of shell mounds in the depths of which are found stone implements unknown to later generations of Indians. Stone calumets and three distinct kinds of arrow have been excavated.

Facing the marshes of to-day stands the first house ever built in California north of San Francisco Bay. According to Catholic history as well as Indian legend, after the Presidio and before the Mission Dolores was established in San Francisco, an exploration of the interior was organized in 1775. Franciscan friars and Spanish soldiers visited among other rancherias that of the tribe settled under the hills of Olompali and taught them the art of making brick. Thus rose the two *adobe* buildings that have become historic. The first building, which measured only sixteen by twenty feet, with walls eight feet in height and three feet in thickness, was roofed with thatched tule, a hole in the middle supplying the place of chimney. In this one room lived the father of Camillo Yuinta, the last chief of the last tribe of this locality. The second building, probably erected by Camillo him- self, presented a much more inviting appearance, con- taining three good-sized rooms and to-day forming an interesting feature in the landscape of Olompali ranch. When the pioneer house was torn down, burr-clover, "filaree," and wild oats sprang from the heart of the brick immediately after rain had fallen! So it was not the Mission Fathers who introduced wild oats into California. Are they indigenous, or

LIME ROCK, NEAR GOLDEN GATE.

did Sir Francis Drake give them with other seed to his good friends at Point Reyes?

On the Olompali ranch fruits of all kinds, including even the orange, lemon and banana, grow in protected places, while the vine thrives and cattle roam the hills. Where once Frémont and his men fought an almost bloodless battle against the Mexicans and Indians, there flourishes a fine vineyard with never a trace of forty years ago. Then live-oaks covered the ground, and wherever a soldier fell at the foot of a tree a cross was cut upon the trunk. One tree still lives on which a cross is seen.

It was a white man that built the third *adobe* house in Marin County, and, strange to say, this too, was in Novato township. Fernando Fales received a grant for the Novato ranch in 1839, and in that year constructed an *adobe* building containing two rooms and a fire-place eight feet wide. Not one brick now stands upon another. American energy and thrift have reared a comfortable mansion where once the Spaniard smoked and vegetated, and Novato ranch, with its many dairies, its orchards and its vineyards, with its blooming valley and succulent hill-sides, is an epitome of the resources of Marin County.

Who would see "at one fell swoop" the region of Novato and San Pablo Bay will not grudge the toil of climbing Loma Alta. All things depend upon the point of view. The difference in observation between three thousand and one thousand feet above sea-level is the difference between the sublime and the beautiful. It is almost the difference between tragedy and comedy. Tamalpais inspires silence; Loma Alta sets the tongue wagging—it is human in its nearness to man and beast. The orchard of Novato ranch looks like a set of green chessmen drawn up for battle. The towns of Santa Rosa, Petaluma, Sonoma and Vallejo rise from the plains, Mount St. Helena bounds the north and the Sierras the east, while hills high and low wave at every point of the compass and the shimmering bay, with Black Point in the distance and with a coast line as undulating as the hills themselves, contributes the ever-changing element of water without which no scenery is complete.

OLD FORT ROSS, SONOMA COUNTY, CALIFORNIA.

To protect themselves from threatened attack the Muscovites explored the coast, and north of Bodega found meadow and cove and beach well adapted for Russian headquarters. Here was Fort Ross established. In those days the fort consisted of a square enclosure one hundred varas each way. On diagonal corners, one facing the ocean and the other the mountains, were octagonal block houses of hewn logs with embrasures, each furnished with six eight-pounder pieces of artillery. Within the enclosure were fifty-nine buildings, including barracks, warehouses and a Greek church. On January 1, 1842, after a sojourn of twenty-eight years, the Russians returned to our Alaska. Nothing remains but the officers' quarters, the two forts, one fast crumbling to decay, the other transformed into a pig-sty. Thus have these best of foreign colonists passed away, leaving in their wake nothing but a memory.''

And where are the people who roamed over this country fifty years ago? Come with me to the poor-house only a few miles away, at the entrance to beautiful Lucas Valley, and there you will see in a shanty, apart from the whites, an old Indian with an older squaw. She lies on the ground, a victim to rheumatism; he sits beside the fireplace, cooking and looking affectionately at the ancient bundle of bones that seems to be undecided whether to live or die. Neither speaks a word of English; both understand Spanish. "Never saw more devotion in my life than between those two Indians," says the superintendent. "Nobody knows how old she is—very near a hundred I think. Clean? Cleanest people on the ranch; wash themselves every day. No better workers, no more peaceable creatures than Indians if they let whiskey alone. Yes, these two are about all of them that's left, except a few collected on Tomales Bay, where they live by digging clams." Little thought Chief Marin, when dying at the Mission of San Rafael, that the last of his race would die in the white man's poor-house! If the survival of the fittest be the law of the universe, the red man's conquerer may yet be "hoist with his own petard."

OLD MILL AT TAYLORVILLE.

It was Chief Marin who aided Comandante Arguello in guiding the first raft of lumber across San Francisco Bay from Corte de Madera; "and thereby hangs a tale." Very dilapidated was the Presidio when, in 1822, Luis Antonio Arguello became Comandante. Lumber was necessary for repairs, so Arguello sent soldiers to Corte de Madera by the way of San José, crossing the strait of Carquinez on rafts, and then around by the way of Sonoma, Petaluma, and San Rafael—a distance of one hundred and twenty miles—to the timber region, which by water was only twelve miles off. Man could march but timber could not, so Arguello determined to build a launch for the purpose of necessary transportation. One carpenter only, an Englishman, happened to be in the country, to whom was confided the building of the first vessel in the bay, and after many trials and tribulations the small craft was launched, and turned to good account; but how dared the Comandante to build a vessel without consulting his imperious Excellency, Governor Sola? "It is insubordination!" exclaimed the infuriated Sola. "There are smugglers on the coast—may not this suspicious craft be intended for the same vile purpose? Or why may it not aid the piratical Russians at Bodega in killing seals and otters? Seize the vessel," ordered Sola, "and summon Arguello to my presence at Monterey." Surprised, but without a murmur, the patriotic soldier mounted his horse and travelled night and day until he reached the capital, weary, bruised, and lame, as his horse had stumbled and thrown him badly.

With a naked sword for a cane, Arguello hobbled before the Governor, whose temper was at boiling-point. How dared the Comandante to build a launch on his own responsibility? Because the houses of officers and soldiers were indecent, and all had agreed to help themselves as best they could without aid from the royal treasury. Running to seize his staff, for the purpose of using it in castigation, Governor Sola noted that Arguello, who had been leaning upon his sword, assumed a firmer position.

"What do you mean by that movement?" quickly asked Sola.

"I mean two things," replied Arguello. "First, convenience; second, because as a soldier and a man of honor I will not allow myself to be beaten without defending myself."

For the first time the bully found his master. Gazing fixedly at Arguello, the Governor put aside his cane, extended his hand, and going to his intended victim, said: "This is bearing worthy of a soldier and a man of honor. I solicit your friendship. Blows are only for the pusillanimous scamps who deserve them."

From that time forth Sola and Arguello were friends; but the launch, which had been brought to Monterey, was found so useful that it never got back to the Presidio, and Arguello sighed in vain for his timber.

What have Marin and his people left to tell their pathetic story? Mound after mound, few of

CAZADERO—LOOKING UP THE CREEK.

which have been excavated. According to Paul Schumacher, Marin County is richer in archæology than any other portion of California.

What Tamalpais is to the hills of Marin County San Rafael is to its valleys—as pretty a nook as Nature ever cudgelled out of her prolific brain. Surrounded on three sides by hills, Tamalpais towering in the southwest and San Francisco Bay glittering in the east, with Monte del Diablo as its majestic background, San Rafael blinks and purrs in the sunshine, the picture of beautiful content. Hills and hills and hills! many covered with evergreens, others shorn for pasturage, and others again laid out in vineyards, while below sits the charming town that, oddly enough, owes its birth to fear of the Russian eagle. The zealous Franciscans who watched over California looked with no favor on the advent of the Greek church at Fort Ross and Bodega. It boded ill to the true faith. The Russians had appropriated one of the Sandwich Islands; who could tell the length and breadth of their ambition? They were extending their settlements on the Pacific Coast and might perhaps claim sovereignty over the land by right of seizure and prior occupation. Something had to be done, so Father Mariano Vajeras, then resident of the missions, addressed a note of

DUNCAN'S MILLS.

warning to the King of Spain in May, 1817, and on December 18 of that year founded the mission of the archangel, San Rafael. They were wonderfully clever, were those missionaries. They knew where nature hid her plums, and always found them. There's not a mission in all California that is not the healthiest and prettiest spot in its neighborhood. If all pioneers had the same far-reaching brains, camps and villages never would be improperly located. Gradually the *adobe* buildings went up, first and foremost being the church roofed with tiles, but all were inferior to those of the older missions. That *bête noire*, the Russian eagle, never soared beyond the coast, so the archangel San Rafael devoted himself to the saving of savage souls. Long toiled the Franciscans with brain and muscle, and in 1834 the mission had an Indian population of twelve hundred and fifty, with a ranch of three thousand horned cattle, five hundred mules and horses, forty-five hundred sheep and goats, and a crop of fifteen hundred bushels of wheat and maize. That year the order of secularization went forth. Deserted by their neophytes, the monks were driven out, cattle and horses were scattered or carried off by greedy lay administrators. In 1845 the work of destruction was completed by the sale of the lands to private individuals. Between 1834 and 1842 the mission decreased from twelve hundred and fifty Indians to twenty.

Nothing remains of the mission but the ground on which stands the Catholic church with its school-house and rectory. Walk through San Rafael, however, and you will find pear trees set out by the fathers in what was once their orchard, which still bear heavily though planted nearly three-quarters of a century ago. You will find, too, in a vacant lot, a few overgrown, neglected grape-vines that could tell a wonderful story were there ears to hear. Though the Franciscans have long since passed away, they never can be forgotten, discovering as they did a valley deservedly proclaimed by them a "sanitarium;" and to-day invalids who cannot bear the harsh winds of San Francisco, merchants who cannot leave their business, make this spot their home and snap their fingers at the doctors. Very like Mentone in the south of France, San Rafael has more days that the invalid can spend out of doors, while the rides and drives are as numerous as they are varied. A sinuous river glides slowly to the bay only two miles distant, groves of laurel and live-oak abound, and forty miles of trails upon the northern hills disclose vistas that would delight the soul of Claude Lorraine. But look where one may, Tamalpais pervades the atmosphere and its ascent remains the crowning glory of the Golden Gate. Language grows puerile in the presence of God's mighty handiwork that sings the hymn of the ages. I do not marvel that all true devotees of nature hold mountains sacred and never profane their solemnity. I do not marvel that Christ went up into a high mountain to commune with the Father.

KATE FIELD.

EARLY CALIFORNIA MINING
AND THE ARGONAUTS.

———— •-•• ————

"WITH PICK, SHOVEL AND PAN WE STOLE CAREFULLY DOWN."

THE huge foundation stones of this vast state were, from the first, set in solid gold. As in the building of Solomon's Temple, the silver thereof was not accounted. Indeed, it was more than a dozen years later that the mountains of silver that lay within the lines of California, before she gave Nevada and other territories to the Union, were really discovered. The Spanish engineers had pierced Mexico to the heart, the miners of Spain had followed their veins of silver for miles up and down the Andes, but they never had touched the Sierras. And so the discovery of silver in California was as entirely an American discovery as was that of gold. And the stranger falls to wondering why silver was discovered so much later. Let us explain this. Gold had been washed and worn down from the mountains by centuries of attrition with boulders, gravel and *débris*, to where it was finally found in the lower levels of the foot-hills by the farmers and mill hands of General Sutter. Having found these particles of detached gold in this one spot at the base of the California Sierra, they searched and found it in thousands of other similar places, till finally they pursued it up the mountains to its very source and fountain-head on the mountain tops. Yet, in all this ardent search they found no silver. A million men came and went, searched the Sierras through, poured out life like water, worked as men never worked before, dug through and washed down mountains of silver, so to speak, but still silver remained practically undiscovered.

Yet, particles of silver had been washed and worn down from the mountains by flood and stream for centuries just the same as gold had been washed and worn down. But silver is perishable. It corrodes and resolves itself again into the elements that formed it. Diamonds, all precious stones, perish by flame and attrition; silver rusts and rots; but a particle of gold, even the smallest particle, whatever fortune overtakes it, remains as perfect to the end of time as when it was placed in its rocky bed by the finger of God. And this is the reason why we old miners found gold so readily and followed it to its source in the mountains; and this is the reason why we did not find silver till so many years later, and found it even then only by compulsion. That is, we found gold so mixed and charged with silver that an ounce of "gold" dust which was at first sold for sixteen dollars proved to be worth only seven dollars, the larger part being silver. And great was the lamentation of the miners at the supposed loss. Some of them abandoned their work in despair; others pushed on and pierced the earth deeper, till finally the grosser metal asserted itself almost entirely. And thus was laid bare, almost by accident, the shining silver foundations of a sister state. "Silver hath a vein, but gold the place where they find it."

It is worthy of note that all the gold of California, or rather all the gold mines of California, to be found on the surface, of any great account, were found almost at once. This fact strongly attests the valor, the daring, the superhuman endurance of the Argonauts. There was not a single mountain pass that was friendly to their approach. The plains were parched and arid; no maps, no foot-prints or marks of man—only the gleaming snow-peaks to guide them. A grave in the sand in the rear, two graves, three graves; then the mountains at last, and a shower of poisoned arrows from painted savages to receive the few haggard survivors! Never since the most magnificent conception of the siege of Troy has there been gathered together such a race of heroes as came here by land and by sea in the days of old. Time has leveled the graves of their innumerable dead. Romance has glorified and cast a glamour of mingled pathos and splendor over their fearful daring and self-denial. But the world will never know how many a poor Penelope wove and unwove her twenty years away and looked out with dimmed eyes each day and night for her unreturning wanderer.

California alone was broader in those days than all the storied world of ancient times. The best part of a year was consumed in reaching these shores. Peril and privation began when the journey began. And so it was that cowards did not start, and the weak and faint fell by the way. See what a situation! "In those days there were giants in the land, . . . mighty men of power and renown." Of such metal were the men who not only conquered an area of the earth larger than all the world of ancient times, but pierced the earth to the heart and wrung from her the precious secrets of her bosom. Not a gorge, not a gulch, not a peak was left unexplored. And yet a lingering tradition lay in the minds of some of these restless men in the region of Yreka, beyond Mount Shasta, as late as the season of 1853-4, that a portion of the Modoc was still unprospected. Frémont had met with serious trouble here. On one occasion he had left nearly one-half his detachment buried under some bay trees by the way; and but for Kit Carson neither the daring explorer nor one of his party would have survived the attack of this terrible and warlike tribe. Disaster even more fearful than this had overtaken many a daring party of Argonauts here; and so it came to be believed, from the very peril of it, that not only was the place entirely unprospected but surely rich in gold. A prospecting party was suddenly and secretly formed. It set out at midnight. The best men in Yreka were either of the party, arms in hand, or behind it with money and moral support. The writer, although but a lad, because of much experience with Indians was as a great favor let into the secret and permitted to share the perils and prospective fortunes of the bold and excited band. Three days, or rather three nights and the first half of a day, found us in a pleasant pine wood looking down into a deep gulch where water rippled and sang among mossy pebbles that lay at the roots of tiger lilies whose flaming heads tossed level with the shoulders of the tallest man in our party. Surely no wild man, no wild beast even, had ever passed this way. Surely no tame man—and this was the all-important thing to us—had ever struck a pick into this virgin lily land.

Guns in hand, our strongest-hearted men were stationed behind the pines on the hills round about. The weary mules and horses were tied fast in the thicket of dwarf tamarack hard by. And even the brown nose of one poor old and eloquent mule, old enough to want to be talkative, was tied as tight as a drum with a buckskin string from one of the men's leggings. And then with whisperings, cautious words of warning, with hope, with fear, but with hope largely dominant, the remainder of us with pick, shovel and pan stole carefully down to the cool, sweet stream and stood half hidden among the glorious wild lilies, looking for a place to begin.

And now let me note this fact—pardon the time and space, but I must write it down. As we go farther along you will know the reason why. The leader of our party among the lilies down there with the pick on his shoulder was a giant in stature and in strength, as I now remember him; the water singing there, the lilies nodding there, the long shadows of the pines pitching away across and up the steep hill beyond, tawny with its carpet of fallen quills, the men, muskets in hand, watching warily above! No one spoke. We waited for the strong man to begin, to make

MINERS PROSPECTING FOR GOLD. FROM PAINTING BY FREDERICK REMINGTON.

"The huge foundation stones of this vast State were, from the first, set in solid gold. Gold had been washed and worn from the mountains by centuries of attrition with boulders, gravel and debris, to where it was finally found in the lower levels of the foothills by the farmers and mill-hands of General Sutter. Having found these particles of detached gold in this one spot at the base of the California Sierra, they searched and found it in thousands of other similar places, till finally they pursued it up the mountains to its very source and fountain-head on the mountain tops. Diamonds, all precious stones, perish by flame and attrition; silver rusts and rots; but a particle of gold, even the smallest particle, whatever fortune overtakes it, remains as perfect to the end of time as when placed in its rocky bed by the finger of God."

HYDRAULIC MINING.

his choice of the spot where first to sink his pick, for so much depends on this; and no man, if the party is experienced in prospecting, ever intrudes a word upon the leader at such a moment. At length the man fixed his eyes on a little spot down the stream, and stepping briskly forward buried his pick to the handle in a place where he did not break a single lily or even disturb or soil the singing water. And that is all there is to say of this silent man, this Argonaut; he did not crush a single flower or disturb a single note in the long, lone melody of the waters, singing only for Him who divided the waters from the dry land. And there was one there who loved him as a brother for that. And how he wrestled then, and grappled with his work! He took the shovel from the man at hand, as he stood there, knee-deep in the loosened soil, and threw

ARGONAUTS EN ROUTE.

it hastily in a heap high up on the brown leaves on the bank. Then again the pick, and then again the shovel, till he stood breast deep. Then again the pick was buried to the eye. There was a dull, rusty, rasping and sullen sound, as if the man might have struck a coffin lid. He lifted up the pick slowly, held it up, and then with his left hand pushed off and down the long, sharp point of the pick, and with that same rusty, dull and rasping sound,—an old sardine box! Prospected? Why the place had been pierced as full of holes as a Tom Iron. Men had even sat here and placidly eaten sardines; and, as said before, vast and savage as the Argonauts first found California, they laid her secrets bare to the core, even before they sat down to rest.

May I record the fact that no man of our party murmured or spoke at all. Swear? Swearing was not as frequent then as now. Those early men, if we except the invasion from the penal colonies of Britain, were gentlemen.

The man with the pick threw down the sardine box, climbed out of the prospect hole, and pick on shoulder, plucking a single lily as he passed and breathing its languid perfume, climbed on up to where the wondering comrades were gathering around the horses preparatory to the return home. And I do not now recall that one word of explanation was given to those on the hill. They read our faces.

One more incident in this account of a single prospecting trip. Although it is but a single adventure, it is one of a thousand, of ten thousand, and ten thousand more not at all dissimilar. As we rode silently and warily back in single file through the long rustling rye grass, a shower of arrows struck us. We saw nothing more, heard nothing more. But one of our party fell dead from his horse, an arrow buried to the feathers in his breast; in fact, the point of the arrow came entirely through and out at the back, doubtless having passed through his heart, for the man never spoke. We carried the body back with us. And this made the first miner's grave in Yreka—the first, so far as I can find out, in all that part of northern California—the grave of the strong man who would not crush a tiger lily nor soil the singing water.

Hear some testimony other than that of rude and primitive writers for those earlier men. Is it because virtue is more picturesque in the convict from the penal colonies, or the unlettered Texan, that boorishness and outlawry have so conspicuous a part in the literature touching those early times? Bear in mind that a very notable

A "MUSHROOM" MINING TOWN.

proportion of the men of those days came from Harvard and Yale and many other institutions and centres of social advancement. Read the story of those who came to the surface as judges, legislators, governors, United States senators and so on, from swinging a pick in the mines. Let it be written down and never again forgotten in the deluge of cheap fiction, that the early men of California were often men of culture as well as courage.

It may not generally be known that those men built cities miles and miles in length in those days. Yet it is strictly true. It is to be admitted that those cities had but one street, that there were no street improvements, no sewers, no gas, no gas bills. But still the long, winding lanes of houses that wound up and down and beside the banks of the stream where lay the miner's "claims" have quite as much right to be called cities as have so many new stations and groups of houses to-day.

Last summer the writer returned to one of these wood-built cities, where he worked as a miner more than thirty years before. Pine trees had grown up in the lower end of the one long street, and an Indian woman with a miserable little babe asleep on her back was burning pine cones and hulling out the nuts with her black fingers for the San Francisco market. A little farther along two Chinamen were tearing out the stones that had formed the hearth of what had once been the most imposing house in this whilom populous "city." The briars were thick and rank over the heap of stones that once had been the "honest miner's" chimney. But the gnome-like little brown men crept close down to the earth and scraped up all the dust and ashes and *débris* to be washed in their "rocker" which sat on the edge of the once turbid but now peaceful stream close by. They were searching for the few imperishable little crumbs of gold which had fallen from the rich miner's hand into his fire-place

In the days of old,
In the days of gold.

Creeping up the bank amid briars and weeds and crooning to himself, came an old man with a beard like snow, as I neared the extreme end of this once famous mining town. He had a pan under his arm, and, with that old politeness and confidence of the genuine gold miner who made the days that are behind California splendid with glory, he set it down on a rock before me, shook his palsied old white head feebly at sight of the few grains of gold there, and muttering something about "striking it rich by and by," took up his pan and tottered on up to his old cabin, which, like himself, seemed sinking down very close to the bosom of our common mother.

———

The transition from placer or surface mining in California to tunnel underground mining was a slow but a very serious matter. No more warm, sweet sunlight for the strong brave man toiling his solid sixteen hours daily for his loved ones far away in the East. No more fervid skies for him forever, no more green trees moving in the wind on the steep hills above. No more birds, butterflies, lilies, buttercups; no more life, no more light, nothing—nothing at all now but the damp, dark, dismal, dripping mine with its creaking engines, crumbling walls, crashing timbers, disasters, death! And even hydraulic mining, a sort of half-way line between these two, was very perilous. But these bold and enduring men had come to California for a purpose, and when the gold had gone from the surface of the earth and down beyond the reach of the great hydraulics to some extent, they did not hesitate for a single day to

"DIGGINGS PETERED OUT"—TOWN DESERTED.

MONITORS AT WORK IN GRAVEL MINE.

"The method of working gold from rock and gravel is the same in all hydraulic mines in California. By a heavy stream of water thrown upon the bank from a nozzle called a "monitor," the gravel is broken up and washed down into the heads of the sluices, by which it is conveyed to the different places where the gold is collected. The monitors are cumbersome affairs, but so arranged as to be easily directed by one man, and are capable of throwing a stream of water from eight to nine inches in diameter. In many cases the water is conveyed nearly a hundred miles in flumes before it is used to wash out the precious metal. There is no grander sight in the world than half a dozen monitors at work in the early morning, each stream throwing off of a thousand rainbow tints in the bright sunlight."

follow it down, down, down to where the heat is so considerable to-day in some places that even the miner can hardly endure to lay his hand upon the rocky floors and walls of his sombre world. Of the thousands and tens of thousands who thus boldly descended into the earth, how few now survive! Only a solitary man in each ten thousand I should say ever came up and back to the world with the coveted gold on his broad shoulders. When you look you find such types of physical and mental strength as John Mackay, Senator Hearst, Senator Stewart, Senator Jones, all old miners who have come back to us up out of the earth, our old men now. Look upon them with your hat in your hand. They are our heroes, our very few survivors; they and a gray old comrade here and there along the foothills of the Sierras, or blown at rare intervals up and down the world, are all that is left to us now of our sixty times six hundred who descended into the

OLD-TIME TYPES.

earth a quarter of a century ago and battled there for years.

My own experience in the underground world of California was brief and bitter; so bitter that reason was almost overthrown, and I dwell upon it now only with pain and terror.

In the winter of 1854 I was employed to push a tub along a wooden track underground. It was a new tunnel; everything about it new, experimental. The mouth of the low, narrow tunnel opened out toward the sun and the swift, clear Klamath River. I was employed because I was so small. The two men worked on their knees and breasts. On the fifth day the hillside slid in and one of the men was crushed. The water came in. My head was caught up between two timbers, lifting my face above the water. I could hear the man groaning, till the water reached where he lay—then was the end. But as one of the men was out of the tunnel getting timbers and I happened to be near the mouth of the tunnel with my tub at the time of the slide, I was dug out by the man who escaped on the same day. I set this down as one example in a thousand that almost any surviving miner might narrate from his underground life in California. But it was from these small beginnings that the great hydraulics, tunnels, drifts, shifts, and underground cities of California and Nevada grew. It is some comfort however to know that experience and improved machinery have combined to make underground work far less perilous than of old.

There are several mining camps in the Sierras that claim the distinction of having had the first great tunnel. But no man can say certainly where and when we first went "underground." My recollection is that Grass Valley and the beautiful environs of Nevada City saw the miners first

APRONS FROM UNDERCURRENTS IN GRAVEL MINE.

"After some mines have been worked for a long time the bottom becomes so low that the water from the monitors cannot run off. To remedy this and still keep the mine working, tunnels are dug from the bottom of the mine to the river bed below. From the mouths of the tunnels sluices are built with openings at intervals through which the water escapes, and runs on to aprons that catch all the fine gold. The tunnels are all of a very large size, and many of them are hundreds of feet in length."

descend into the earth in any considerable bodies.   And as this fine region was about the first to
open the doors of the under-world and burst the rich coffers that had lain hidden there ever since
the finger of God set them down on the day of Creation, so it promises to be among the last to
show any signs of decay.   Indeed so far from declining in any way this place is walking right
along in the line, and almost if not quite at the head of the line of California progress and improvement.

But what mutations this place has seen, to be sure!   There was a world of wild flowers, birds
in abundance, glorious oak trees, grass.   Then the placer miner came, washing up the buttercups
by the roots; soiling cool, clear trout streams.   The fishes turned on their sides and died.   The
oak trees fell in a single season.   The birds disappeared.   For the first year after the pick-axe struck
in the grass roots of this region you would have said, "a cyclone has struck California!"

Then a woman came.   Then the baby.   Then a neat little cottage blossomed on the hillside,

PLACER MINING ON THE YUBA.

with some morning-glories growing about the door.   Then another woman came.   This one planted
a rose-bush.   The next year a man from New York planted some fruit trees.   The second year they
bloomed and actually bore fruit.   Then the birds came back.   The miners had now disappeared
underground.   The plough turned the soil above their heads and cows stood ruminating under
the few remaining oaks.   And now, when looking over this fair land only last month for the purpose of making these sketches, it was almost impossible to distinguish this portion of California from
the richest and oldest hill regions of Pennsylvania.   And singular as it may seem to the stranger,
I must set down the fact that the largest and most heavily-laden orange tree I have seen this side
of Sorrento on the Bay of Naples, is to be found in these same foothills of the Sierras, not very
far from the once flourishing mining town of Oroville.   It grows on an old mining claim.

Auburn is another mountain town that has more than held its own in the swift mutations
of time in California.   I recall this wooded and watered spot as a place of "flumes."   Whatever
Auburn may have seemed to others in the early days, I can think of it only as a place where
flume on top of flume encircled the pine-set hills from base to summit.   Many of these flumes

MINING IN THE BED OF THE FEATHER RIVER.

"The above view is looking down stream, and shows what a complicated amount of machinery is required in this method of getting gold from California rivers. It is impossible to explain the working of the many elevators, sluices and siphons in limited space, but the principle of the system is to wash the rock and gravel down into the river bed, and then force it up through the elevator, which appears in the center of the picture, by a powerful stream of water. This has so much force that rocks the size of a man's head are raised as easily as if they were pebbles. After being raised to the desired elevation, the sand and gravel is run into flumes or sluices that carry it to the different places where the gold is collected."

carried water to the rich gravel "claims" that lay in and about Auburn.   The larger number however were long deep "sluices," or flumes for conveying dirt, gravel, *débris* and so on *from* the gravel claims down to the great valley below.   The hydraulic roar was here in its day, the "dump," "slickings," law-suits ; sorrow enough for the poor miner and for the poor farmer in the valley below him as well.   "Time and I against any two," says the Spanish proverb.   And lo! to-day this once tumultous mining town of the Sierras is one of the very sweetest, rosiest, sunniest health-resorts west of the Rocky Mountains.

No traveler can afford to visit California without seeking out Placerville and Mariposa, digging down to their old life and contrasting that stormy old life with the new.   And the traveler should first understand that the geological history and make-up of all this mining region from Yreka to Mariposa was as stormy and tumultuous as were the lives of those who first possessed these rugged lands.   Beds of rivers, deep, wide and tortuous, heavy with nuggets of gold, were found by our miners almost on the very summits of the Sierras.   Mountains turned upside down!   Valleys set on edge!   Rivers stood on end!   Surely the Titans of old had battled here, hurling mountains and valleys in their fierce combat.   The great Columbia River, which draws its waters from far toward the north pole, once emptied into the Pacific Ocean through what is now called the Sacramento—at least this is the theory of observing and able engineers and miners who have, in their pursuit as gold seekers, tried to trace the dried-up and changed channels of our dead rivers.   Confusion on top of confusion is what confronted the miner of California from the first.   There was no order, no system, no law in the finding and following up of these old gold-bearing and dried-up river-beds.   Let us be thankful for the show of discipline and order that has at last asserted itself on the surface of the earth in the long and undulating lines of olive trees, orange trees, grape-vines and orchard trees of all kinds that reach from Oroville to Placerville, and on past the gleaming heaps of ground quartz on Frémont's Mariposa Grant, and farther yet to Governor Waterman's mines in the San Bernardino Range.

But the great, warm, rich bosom of California is torn to the heart no more now.   The transition from the placer mine to the vineyard and orchard is complete.   The placer mine with all its pathos has passed into history.   The dark and mysterious gnomeland under the earth is narrowing year by year.   Let us hope that the brave men there may come up to the light of day soon and to remain.   For California has so many things better than gold.   Were our mines in a land like that of Russia, life might not be so intolerable in their depths.   But in a clime like this of ours, man's place is surely on the surface of the earth, in his orchard, in his garden, in the path that leads back to Paradise.

JOAQUIN MILLER.

The Santa Clara Valley and Santa Cruz Mountains.

Los Gatos Creek.

TO describe the Santa Clara Valley and the Santa Cruz Mountains without making an overdraft on the superlatives requires rare self-control. Both by virtue of its natural features and its early settlement and splendid development the Santa Clara is the finest type of the Californian valley. To it must be given the palm for picturesque scenery, artistic homes, variety of fruit and other products; and devotion to religion, education and all the higher graces of life. To call it the garden-spot of California is no misnomer, as any one will testify who has ridden through the valley in April, when the air is heavy with the perfume of thousands of blossoming fruit trees; or in September, when the same trees are bending under a fruitage much of which has the rare flavor of the Orient — fig, apricot, nectarine, olive, pomegranate—all redolent of sacred story and all suggesting resemblance between the new western state and the Holy Land.

Santa Clara Valley, like most of California, was once the bed of a great inland sea. This is abundantly proved by the discovery of marine shells deep under the soil, of clay strata that are deposited only by quiet waters, and by water-worn pebbles and boulders. To this fact is due the enormous fertility of the land, a productiveness that has survived years of excessive cropping to the same cereal.

The Valley, which stretches from the lower part of San Francisco Bay down to the mountain barrier that shuts it off from San Luis Obispo County, a distance of about one hundred and twenty miles, is sheltered from the harsh sea winds and fog of the Pacific by the Santa Cruz Mountains, while on the east it is saved by the Coast Range from the hot winds that sweep across from Mojave Desert. These mountain walls ward off all sudden changes of temperature. But the crowning feature, which make this valley approach the poet's ideal of a lotus eater's land, is the sea-breeze from San Francisco Bay that tempers the heated air and makes August as full of life and vigor as those rare days of the New England June that Lowell has sung.

Nothing gives one a better idea of the Santa Clara Valley than a ride from San Francisco to Santa Cruz by the Southern Pacific Railroad in April. This is the blossoming time; when field and foot-hill and mountain-top rest the eye with their tender green, when the sky is as soft, as deeply blue, as free from clouds as the sky that Petrarch loved and mirrored in his verse; when distant orchards look like splashes of foam in the deep green of the valley's sea-like expanse, while those near at hand are a wondrous combination of pale pink and creamy white blossoms as exquisite in perfume as the magnolia or the orange—the paradise of the honey bee, whose droning music seems the fitting measure for these days, so full of the buoyant spirit of earth's busy spring.

The first ten miles from San Francisco one passes in review the unattractive suburbs of a great city, and thence proceeds through dreary lengths of marsh that skirt the shore of the bay. Here is the scene of Bret Harte's "A Blue Grass Penelope," a region cut by many lagoons, looking, with its miniature rivers and lakes when the sea comes in like a topographical map of a continent, but at low tide repulsive with slime and ooze. Upon the right one sees the beginnings of the Santa Cruz Mountains, where lofty wooded ridges serve as a natural barrier to the sea-fogs that sweep in from the Pacific. Millbrae, seventeen miles from San Francisco, marks the beginning of the great Valley. Here one gets the earliest glimpses of the park-like fields, dotted with native live-oaks which form so attractive a feature of the landscape for fifty miles; but it is not until Menlo Park is reached that the full beauty of the Valley is appreciated.

Nature has been prodigal of her gifts to Menlo, but man has aided in making it perhaps the finest type of the suburban villa-town to be found west of Chicago. Through broad avenues, lined with stately trees, the train flashes. Now we catch a glimpse of a superb house in Queen Anne style, almost hidden from view by the wealth of semi-tropical plants that grow so luxuriantly about it; now we come full upon a mansion built in the graceful style of the Italian renaissance and placed in the center of a great park which, with its soft velvety turf, its noble oaks and its trim hedge, makes one rub his eyes to see if he be dreaming of Surrey or Devon. To right and left extend long vistas of tree-lined avenues bordered with superb villas, where peaks and gables rise above the sea of deep green foliage. Upon the left is still to be seen the marsh-land that skirts the southern end of San Francisco Bay, but upon the right are the gently rolling foot-hills and above them the outlines of the mountains that form the eastern horizon. Soon one begins to notice low hills on the left, the first spurs of the Coast Range, and by the time Santa Clara is reached the valley has broadened to a width of perhaps fifteen miles and has a mountain wall on either hand.

This is the heart of the great valley. For thirty miles it is nearly as level as a barn-floor; the soil is a rich black loam; the foot-hills are cultivated as carefully as the low-lands; the plain is thickly settled, yet in both town and country the people have wisely left abundant elbow-room. There is no crowding. Even San Jose, which is something of a commercial city, has a spacious air that suggests comfort and leisure. Its streets are wide and tree-lined; its houses surrounded by ample grounds. Here one begins to take note of the fruit-tree and the vine which become the prevailing feature for more than twenty miles. Next to the fruit-tree stands the live-oak, and third in prominence comes the eucalyptus or Australian gum. Twenty years ago a ride through this section was practically a trip through an enormous wheat field, broken here and there by a vine-yard or a market garden. To-day one sees miles on miles of wheat, but even the very large fields are dwarfed by the thousands of acres in fruit and vines. The old order has changed; the great wheat ranch has given place to the small fruit farm; a hundred substantial homes now dot the plain where once the steam plow turned its ten-mile furrows and the great harvester marked its progress across fields as large as Eastern counties by long lines of well filled wheat sacks.

For fully twenty miles beyond San Jose the train seems to pass through a country that changes only from garden to orchard. The ground is everywhere as carefully cultivated and as free from weeds as a Connecticut onion bed; beyond the dreamy haze in which the fields lose themselves rise the foot-hills, here as green as emeralds, there glowing with the vivid yellow of the wild poppy. Acres of these wild flowers lie in masses on the hillsides and furnish charming contrasts of tint. The foot-hills and even the mountains show none of the roughness, none of the traces of great volcanic outbursts that make the mountain spurs of Southern California and of the high Sierra seem to have just emerged from the great conflict of earth's forces. Everything here is

FOOTHILLS IN THE SANTA CLARA VALLEY. FROM PAINTING BY W. R. SPARKS.

   "This is the heart of the great valley. For thirty miles it is nearly as level as a barn floor. The soil is a rich black loam. The foothills are cultivated as carefully as the lowlands . . . The effect upon the eye is very restful. Nothing can be imagined more charming than the nine miles' ride from San Jose to Los Gatos, a foothill town held in the keeping of the neighboring mountains " smooth and rounded like a water-worn rock on which the surf has beaten for centuries. For miles one may look in vain for any rugged peak to break this regularity. The effect upon the eye is very restful. These mountains seem like a collection of Titanic animals in repose, their rounded ridges suggesting the backs of sleeping monsters that were turned to stone when the earth was young. Each ridge is marked off by a cañon which is plainly traced by the line of oaks that cling to its steep sides, and high above all a rounded point that catches and gives back the strong sunlight is the dome of Lick Observatory on Mt. Hamilton, a landmark that man has placed among these everlasting hills.

After one has passed through the great orchards that lie below San Jose, he enters upon the richest farming land to be seen in the valley. The foot-hills draw nearer; the oaks are thicker; the train dashes between the spurs of a small mountain range and passes into the Salinas and Pajaro Valleys, which are famous even in California for their great crops of wheat.

IRRIGATING AT STRAWBERRY FARM.

But if you wish to see the beauties of the Santa Cruz Mountains, it is well to make the trip to Santa Cruz from San Jose by the Narrow Gauge Railroad. The Southern Pacific or Broad Gauge line passes down through the heart of the great wheat valleys and reaches the sea by a long détour; the other road is almost an air-line through the woods to the ocean at Santa Cruz. Nothing can be imagined more charming than the nine miles' ride from San Jose to Los Gatos, a foot-hill town held in the keeping of the neighboring mountains. Pretty villas perch on the steep slopes and grape-vines scramble clear to the tops of the hills. Here one sees benches of fertile land by the sides of the streams that strongly resemble the *mésa* of Southern California and Arizona, a formation that is seldom seen in any other part of the valley.

When the back is turned on Los Gatos, lo! the mountains appear. A few miles on and the clumps of live-oaks are left behind, giving place to the giant madrone with its pale-red trunk and large leaf; the dwarfed and gnarled manzanita, its wood having the color of fine old mahogany; the white and red oak; the laurel, alder, willow, cypress and pine. Soon the train whirls

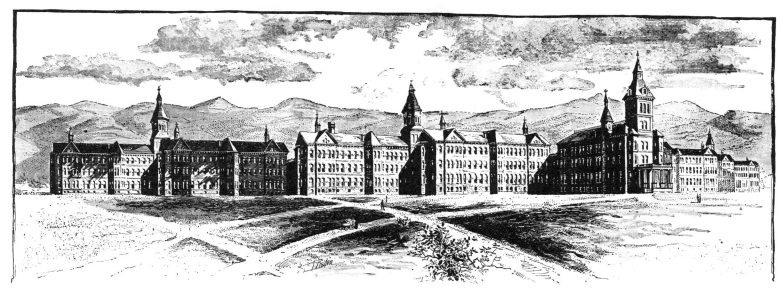

CALIFORNIA HOSPITAL FOR THE CHRONIC INSANE, AT AGNEW'S.

around a steep curve and the river bed appears far below, its sides lined with willow, out of which rise the young redwoods, their trunks as straight as a ship's mast, graceful and covered with feathery foliage of so deep a green that it makes all other vegetation appear faded beside it. These beautiful trees you have always with you during the twelve miles ride to the sea. Many are mere saplings; others are giants of the forest whose safety has been assured by their position in some inaccessible cañon. The train dashes through a half dozen tunnels; it crosses trestles, winds around cañons, runs along the banks of the wild San Lorenzo River; gives glimpses of lumbering mills, mountain ranches perched like Swiss *chalêts* almost in mid-air, hunters' camps that seem to answer the poet's yearning for a "lodge in some vast wilderness," a trout-brook that gurgles over the smooth stones and flashes back the sun's rays that shoot down through the overhanging redwoods. Now one catches sight of a long stretch of the river, hemmed in by mountains that seem as inaccessible as those of the Sierra; now the engine whisks the train into the sudden inky darkness of a long tunnel from which one emerges into a smiling little valley whose few acres furnish pasturage for a herd of sleek milch cattle. The river and its cañons seem far away, yet another turn brings the mountain stream again in sight; then one sees an occasional redwood of enormous girth and the brakeman shouts "Big Trees!" It is the Felton grove, five miles from Santa Cruz, which contains redwoods second in size only to the *giganteas* of the Calaveras and the Mariposa groves.

The road from this point to the sea is unsurpassed for wildness and beauty of scenery. It skirts the sides of the river, which are densely wooded; it runs along ledges of rock carved in the mountain side and one looks down a sheer descent of hundreds of feet upon the river that winds along below; at times it seems the train is imprisoned among these mountain fastnesses and cannot escape; then, presto! the whole world seems opened and the eye drinks in with delight the long stretch of shining river and the distant horizon that forms the background for the delicate tracery of foliage that frames in every picture. Soon a little valley appears, beautiful by nature; then come the gardens, orchards and vineyards of the Italians who reproduce here the beauty and squalor of their native Tuscany or Naples; and then the villas and church spires of Santa Cruz by the sea. The sun rests warmly on this pleasant sea-side town, but the salt air of the sea clears the atmosphere of all languor.

It may be well now to retrace our steps and note in some detail the features that make the Santa Clara Valley and the Santa Cruz Mountains worthy of the study of the seeker after the picturesque, as well as of the tourist who wishes to test the theories of Buckle and of Taine that the *milieu*, the environment, has a powerful influence in shaping men's lives and in molding their characters. Climate and occupation have done much to make the Santa Clara Valley what it is to-day. Harsh and cold must be the nature that would not respond to this genial climate in which the fierce heats of summer and the biting frosts of winter are alike unknown. In a climate where one may live comfortably out of doors throughout the year, and where nearly every month is marked by its distinctive fruits and flowers, one looks for the superb physical development of Italy and does **not** look in vain. No pallid cheeks, thin chests and meagre figures are to be seen among the natives of this valley. It is a delight to see these wholesome-looking young girls, with the promise of years, free from the prevailing weaknesses of less favored women; it is a pleasure to see these robust boys, with the lithe tread and sun-browned limbs of the Indian. It is a revelation of the possibilities of life in the open air, over which Thoreau or Theodore Winthrop would have grown eloquent, to behold women of tender nurture engaged in the light labor of rose garden or vineyard, getting thereby a warmth of color and a brightness of eye which nothing but this touch of nature can bring. The orchards and vineyards that form the chief attraction of this valley possess a deep significance to the students of race development, as they show how the American tendency to nervous disease may be counteracted or prevented, and how millions instead of thousands of families may draw health and comfort from labor in orchard and vineyard.

To the Eastern eye there is something strange and artificial about the Santa Clara orchards. The trees are planted with geometric regularity; the rows are as straight as a surveyor's line. Each tree is almost an exact duplicate of its neighbor, for in this exuberant soil and climate there is none of the desperate struggle for life which dwarfs the peach in colder climates and makes the apple tree a gnarled and twisted reminder of many a fierce winter storm. Everything here is beautifully symmetrical, with the well ordered regularity that would have pleased the

MRS. JOHN BROWN'S COTTAGE.

LICK PAPER MILLS.

AT PACIFIC CONGRESS SPRINGS.

makers of the gardens of Queen Anne's time. And what adds to the appearance of artificiality is the bareness of the ground. Not a weed, not a spear of grass intrudes upon this carefully kept domain. The grass-grown orchard so familiar in New England landscape is unknown. Yet, in spite of this made-up appearance there is something that strongly appeals to the artistic sense in these magnificent orchards. In blossoming time they are simply indescribable. Words are powerless to tell the eye's delight in beholding the great orchards of almonds, apricot, peach and cherry in full bloom. To these are added the occasional lemon or orange with its golden fruit peeping from among the mass of creamy blossoms, and the long rows of grape-vines with their vigorous young leafage of a tender green that is seldom reproduced in art save in the paintings of Madrazo and Fortuny. The California grape is never trained upon trellis or arbor or against the garden wall. The vine is a bush seldom more than three feet in height with thick leafage at the top and long graceful branches that wellnigh cover the ground. Where the rows climb the gentle slopes of the foot-hills and lend their vivid contrasts of color to the manzanita or *chemisal* of the mountain sides they give a charm to the landscape which suggests the storied Rhine or the slopes of Médoc and Burgundy.

The vine seems to give age and mellowness to the landscape. Planted on never so rude a mountain side, growing in a little clearing that is hedged about with the dense California chaparral, the vine brings with it somewhat of the Old World flavor of long residence and family industry

SANTA CLARA COLLEGE.—GENERAL VIEW FROM THE ALAMEDA. FROM PAINTING BY C. D. ROBINSON.

"Santa Clara seems like a part of San Jose, only here the bustle of the larger town is absent, and one appreciates more fully the magnificent shaded avenues that seem to end only in the distant mountains. Here is the old mission cross erected over one hundred years ago, and the fine buildings of the church and school of the Jesuit Fathers This famous institution of learning is one of the ancient landmarks of Santa Clara Valley. It is situated in the lovely little town of Santa Clara, a quiet spot which adds the charm of seclusion to the other advantages it affords to all without regard to creed. It was erected on the site of the old Santa Clara Mission, which was founded A. D. 1777, and is thus a connecting link between the past and the present."

passed down with the household traditions through many generations. The vineyardist must be a conservative. He loses much of that restlessness that is at once bane and blessing to the Californian. He becomes a lover of trees; he plants even the olive and the English walnut, although he knows that he may not live to enjoy the fruitage which comes but shyly after a decade and does not reach its full measure for a generation. It requires familiarity with California rural life to follow out the influences of vine-growing, but the observant stranger is struck with it in an indefinable way, just as he is impressed with the wide contrast of character and life between the wheat-rancher or cattle-man and the fruit-grower. Time was when in the very heart of the Santa Clara Valley great bands of cattle roamed the plains. The *vaquéro* was followed by the wheat-grower. Both led a life that starved the natural love of beauty and even of comfort. Their homes were *adobe* huts; they had not even kitchen gardens; no flowers save the tawdry hollyhocks which sprang up under their windows; trees they planted not. With the advent of the fruit-grower came

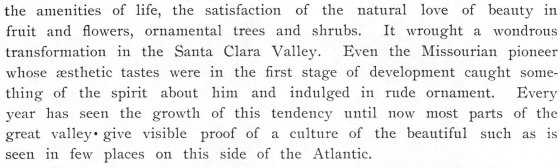

the amenities of life, the satisfaction of the natural love of beauty in fruit and flowers, ornamental trees and shrubs. It wrought a wondrous transformation in the Santa Clara Valley. Even the Missourian pioneer whose æsthetic tastes were in the first stage of development caught something of the spirit about him and indulged in rude ornament. Every year has seen the growth of this tendency until now most parts of the great valley• give visible proof of a culture of the beautiful such as is seen in few places on this side of the Atlantic.

The American artist has made little use of the California live-oak, yet it is one of the most picturesque of trees. Throughout this valley it grows to a size seldom equaled elsewhere. In sheltered places it is symmetrical, with rounded top and magnificent foliage, so dense that no patch of sky may be seen through its matted leafage; but in exposed, wind-swept cañons, or on rocky foot-hills it takes the fantastic shape of old New England apple-trees, with branches that seem endowed with uncanny life, and trunks that are bent almost to the ground. With scarred and gnarled bark and frequently with trailing streamers of moss, these trees have an individuality that makes them worthy of study. They lift into sublimity the cañons to whose rugged sides they cling and they save from commonplace monotony many a stretch of plain. They rest the eye in midsummer heat and dust, for when all else is sere and yellow the live-oaks preserve their deep green, seeming to draw life and color from sources beyond the reach of other trees. These oaks have been spared because they are not valuable for lumber, and the result is one for which all lovers of the picturesque may be devoutly thankful.

The eucalyptus, or Australian gum, is an alien tree that has done much to relieve the monotony of the level stretches of the valley. In some places it has been planted by the acre for timber, as it makes excellent wood for many purposes; but in most cases it serves for a hedge or wind-break or to mark off the boundaries of fields. At a little distance it strongly resembles the Lombardy poplar, having a straight trunk and close foliage; but seen near at hand it is like no other tree in this country. Its dark bluish-green leaves look heavy as though moulded of wax, and rustle in the wind with a sound not unlike that made by the strong foliage of the palmetto; its bark is smooth, and though it constantly sheds dead leaves, it is as green at the end of the long dry season as when washed by the winter rains.

No statelier driveway can be formed by the elm or oak than the eucalyptus makes when planted regularly and not exposed to severe winds. The occasional plantations of these trees make an oasis of vivid green on which the eye rests with pleasure.

It is necessary to pay many visits to the Santa Clara Valley, to stay for several days in its chief cities and to make excursions to the delightful suburban resorts that nestle under the shadows of the great mountains, before one gets any adequate conception of the scenic beauties or of the varied interests of this garden-spot of California. On the narrow gauge road between

Alameda and San Jose are several notable towns, among which may be mentioned Alvarado, the seat of a large beet-sugar factory and the center of a country where the sugar beet is extensively grown; Newark, noted for its car factories; Alviso, the shipping point for the great strawberry plantations that stretch away for miles on each side of the road, and Agnew's, the site of the new state asylum for the chronic insane.

At Alviso are the Lick paper mills, built on the site of the old flour mills of James Lick. Connected with this old mill is a reminiscence of this pioneer millionaire which is worth recalling. Lick came of Pennsylvania Dutch stock and in his early days wooed the daughter of a miller. The father refused her hand to the penniless young millwright and taunted him with his poverty. The young man, already burning with ambition to rise in the world, felt the rage that springs from wounded pride and unjust reproach and replied, "You will live to see the day when I will

HOTEL VENDOME, SAN JOSE.

build a mill so much finer than the house you live in that you will be ashamed ever to enter it again." A foolish boast of a hot-headed lover, the miller thought; but when the sand dunes in San Francisco that Lick bought for a few dollars became the business heart of the great city of the Golden Gate, then Lick remembered his vow, and at Alviso he erected a flour mill the like of which has never been seen in the world. It was lined with mahogany and California laurel, and cost over $250,000. For years it was one of the curiosities that tourists were eager to see, but one night fire reduced it to ashes. Yet the man who spent this large sum to gratify his pride, lived in a poor shanty in perfect contentment. Lick was a singular mixture of meanness and generosity. Up through his sordid nature blossomed the impulse that bore fruit in the great Observatory on Mt. Hamilton, while his passionate love of our national song, "The Star Spangled Banner," led him to leave $60,000 for a statue of its author, Francis Scott Key. The sculptor, Story, who received the commission, has made a noble work of art, and the statue now adorns Golden Gate Park, in San Francisco—one of the few memorials that the American people have raised to their own authors.

It is as difficult to describe San Jose as to picture with words a pretty woman. **The city reveals** some new charm at every visit. December finds it crowned with green; April, sweet with the perfume of flowers; and August, rich with the golden fruitage of all lands that finds a home here. It has none of the crudeness of many newly-built towns in California, for it is over one hundred years old. The pueblo called "San Jose de Guadaloupe" was built in 1777 by a company of Mexican soldiers, while a few months later the Franciscan *padres* established their mission near by, at Santa Clara. The old town led the sleepy life of all Spanish-American places until the Mexican war roused it from lethargy. Then came the gold discovery with its thousands of eager adventurers, the political excitement that led to the call of the State Legislature at San Jose before California was actually admitted to the Union, and then the new life that has stimulated its development and caused it to leap almost at a bound from village to city. Now it ranks fifth in the state in population, while in wealth and in social and educational advantages it is a worthy rival of Los Angeles and Sacramento. Its main features are its wide, well-paved streets, its handsome public buildings, its many churches and schools, its beautiful residences surrounded by lawns and rose-gardens, and its tree-shaded avenues that stretch away for miles across the level plain and climb the foot-hills to the mountains. The two towns, San Jose and Santa Clara, are practically one, being united by the magnificent avenue known as "the Alameda," which is lined with residences throughout its entire length of two miles. Here on any pleasant day one may see a constant procession of turnouts of every variety, for San Jose is noted for the number of its handsome equipages. There, too, one may see women and children bravely driving spirited horses, or a slip of a girl with bright eyes and hair

FALLS IN LOS GATOS CREEK, NEAR ALMA.

streaming in the wind dashing by on a pony as reckless and fearless as an Indian maiden. You note the fine development of all these children, their full chests, brown cheeks and supple limbs. The girls seem as much at home in the saddle as the boys; and they are so full of life and courage, so confident of their strength, that one has no fear for their safety. This procession that moves up and down the spacious Alameda under the checkered shade of its century-old trees, planted by the pious hands of the Mission Fathers, well illustrates the social life that springs from wealth and leisure. But nothing perhaps so well marks the social progress as the number and excellence of the schools and the variety of religious denominations that are represented by fine church buildings.

Santa Clara seems like a part of San Jose, only here the bustle of the larger town is absent and one appreciates more fully the magnificent shaded avenues that seem to end only in the distant mountains. Here is the old mission cross erected over one hundred years ago, the fine buildings of the church and school of the Jesuit Fathers, the University of the Pacific, supported by the Methodist Episcopal church, and the Home for Feeble-minded Children, a worthy state institution and the only one of the kind on this coast.

One of the most attractive features of San Jose, which endears it to every lover of the beautiful, is the great number of fine driving roads that have been laid out in every direction. It would be difficult in any part of the older-settled sections of the East to find drives of equal

REDWOODS ON BOULDER CREEK. FROM PAINTING BY JULIAN RIX.

"It is necessary to spend several days at a place like Wright's, Boulder Creek or Glenwood to appreciate the varied beauty of these woods and mountain streams. Sport with rod and gun may be found in almost every part of the mountains. The trout are gamy, the streams wild enough to suit the most exacting angler, and the man who would secure a full basket must not be averse to wading. Everywhere is the charm that comes of the wildness of Nature that even the vandal lumberman cannot destroy."

excellence. Formed of gravel and rock, they are little influenced by frosts and rain, while they are comparatively free from dust in the long dry season. The finest drive is the Alum Rock Road, seven miles long, lined with eucalyptus and cedar. It leads by gradual ascent to the suburban park of four hundred acres lying in a deep cañon, and affords a rare succession of views of mountain and valley. Here are mineral springs of soda and sulphur, famous for their efficacy in many complaints, and here is a gorge that seems to have been formed by the rending asunder of the great mountain by some volcanic outburst. Along the way one sees huge masses of volcanic rock piled in the most grotesque shapes, gleaming with brilliant colors and looking as though just cooled from the terrible convulsion that shot them forth from the bowels of the mountain. With a good hotel and mineral baths this park is a favorite resort of San Jose people.

Around San Jose is the best place for the study of the fruit industry that has grown to such enormous proportions within the last few years. Huge canneries may be seen on every hand, but there is scarcely an orchard which does not dry a large quantity of fruit every year. Nothing more picturesque can be imagined than the scenes about a large orchard during the drying season. The chief difficulty is to get sufficient labor and for this reason many school children are impressed into the service. The work is light, as most of the trees are small, and even the topmost limbs of the larger ones may be reached by a step ladder. Boxes holding almost fifty pounds are left by teams at regular intervals along the main avenues and into these the pickers empty their baskets. Most of the fruit is picked by hand, as to shake it upon the plowed ground would injure its appearance. Very pretty pictures are formed by the groups of pickers as they stand under the heavily-laden trees

SANTA CRUZ COTTAGES ON BEACH-HILL AND TERRACE.

gathering the golden apricot or the blushing peach. Here may be seen an entire family, from father to five-year-old boy, eagerly at work to save the fruit that in a few days will be too ripe for use; there is a party of men who grasp the supple branches of the apricot tree and strip leaves and fruit into their baskets with one dexterous sweep of both hands; in a neighboring orchard may be seen the squat figures of a gang of Chinese, with their huge umbrella-like straw hats that form so perfect a protection from the fierce sun, looking like so many machines. They seldom betray any curiosity at the appearance of visitors, and they labor in the same tireless way from early morning to nightfall.

When the apricot begins to turn yellow in the sun, then there is great scrambling to save the crop, for it is a peculiarity of this luscious fruit that the whole orchard appears to ripen in a day. Many of the apricots are sent direct to the cannery, while some growers dry them in the sun or in the huge artificial evaporators that have a capacity of several tons of fruit. The harvest of cherries, peaches and plums differs little from that at the East; but as the apricot, prune, almond and fig are almost unknown there no tourist who passes through this valley in July, August or September should fail to visit one of these great orchards and watch the process of fruit-drying. At Campbell, a suburb of San Jose, only four miles distant, may be seen the largest prune orchard in America. The prunes are of the choicest French varieties and hang in heavy purple clusters from the limbs. The tree is a beautiful one with its dark green foliage and its perfect oval shape. It seems to find in this valley a congenial home and is already so extensively grown in Santa Clara county that the exportation of prunes is a very considerable industry. The product is not inferior to the best imported varieties and the trees are so productive that the prune has been the favorite among orchardists for the last five years. The peach and the Bartlett pear also reach great perfection of form, color and flavor in this valley. The pear is one of the favorite fruits for shipment to the East, as it is gathered while green and, like the banana, is improved by ripening in the shade. The pear tree throughout California grows with astonishing vigor and in five years attains a size that it would not reach in colder climates in twice that length of time. All these fruits may be dried in the sun with perfect safety, as there is no fear of sudden rain. Every day the sun appears in a cloudless sky and his powerful rays soon cure the fruit. With some fruits, such as the peach and apricot, a fair color may be obtained in the artificial dryer or by the new process of evaporation, but the sun-dried fruit has a flavor that the other cannot equal.

All about San Jose the beautiful green of the vine adds its distinctive touch of color to the landscape in early spring; and in summer when the fields take on the tawny hue that they wear from June to November, then the deep green of the vine is shown in strong relief; later, in September and October the vine leaves show all the colors of the prism, rivaling the brilliant tints of the eastern maple and oak in Indian Summer. Perhaps the vine is seen at its best around Los Gatos, ten miles from San Jose. This is one of the pleasantest foot-hill towns in the state, and its beauties, long neglected, are now beginning to be appreciated by those in search of picturesque suburban homes. It lies at the base of a great spur of the Santa Cruz Mountains; around it is a natural amphitheatre of hills; first gently rolling foot-hills and then the dark and mysterious mountains. Ten years ago it was a dull country town, with little except a fine site to attract the tourist's attention. Now it boasts of scores of pretty villas scattered about the hills, each surrounded by orchard and

NATURAL BRIDGE.

COAST VIEWS NEAR SANTA CRUZ—ARCH ROCK.

MONUMENT POINT.

vineyard. The hillsides, which are too steep for planting in the usual manner, have been skillfully terraced, and there is no lovelier spot in California than these hillside homes, with their suggestions of the united advantages of town and country life. Back from the creek which winds through the town are orchards and vineyards, every available bit of ground having been planted to fruit-trees or vines. There is something in this volcanic soil which the choice wine-grape needs and the Los Gatos vineyardist can produce a wine unexcelled by any from the most favored parts of the Napa and Sonoma Valleys.

An easy drive of four miles from Los Gatos brings one to Saratoga, a queer old country town which has nothing to suggest its name save that it lies in a plain. The road is lined with fruit-farms and vineyards for its entire length. As one approaches Saratoga the mountains draw near and there is only a narrow fringe of foot-hills. Upon this fringe of very fertile land have been built many pretty cottages and the place known as Saratoga Park is already a favorite summer resort. A mile beyond the town is Pacific Congress Springs, with a fine hotel situated in a romantic cañon. The outlook from the hotel is superb, with half the Santa Clara Valley spread out at the left, while in front the thickly wooded mountains loom darkly against the clear blue sky. A walk through the woods from the hotel brings one to the mineral spring, whose waters were known to the Indians long before white men discovered their value. There is something peculiarly solemn and mysterious about these mountains. The night falls suddenly here and brings with it suggestions of utter solitude.   Perhaps it was this sense of remoteness from the world that led the widow of famous old John Brown to select a home in these secluded mountains.   Directly back of Saratoga village is a lofty mountain, reached by a winding wood road.   Near its summit is a homestead of about eighty acres with a small clearing planted to fruit-trees and vines and a common story-and-a-half house.   No glimpse of either house or orchard can be had from the main road.   One comes on it suddenly through a winding way, made dark even at midday by madrones and redwoods. A lonelier spot man never saw; it seems cut off from the world.   But turn your back on the house and you will see why the widow of old Ossawatomie Brown chose this spot as the home of her declining years.   Not fifty feet from the doorstep the mountain plunges down in sheer descent for hundreds of feet, and there, filling the whole horizon and framed in this border of everlasting hills, lies the whole Santa Clara Valley.   It is a magnificent bird's-eye view, for without a glass one may trace the railroads and see plainly the towns that are scattered along them like beads on

MAKING UP THE LOGGING TRAIN.

a string.   The valley resembles a huge checker board, with its green and yellow and black squares, while the mountains that hold all in their keeping reflect every color in the rainbow and are as clearly defined as though they were only two miles away instead of thirty.   One can fancy this white-haired woman, in whose eyes still lived the memory of the fierce anti-slavery conflict and the great crisis that robbed her of husband and sons, looking out on this peaceful scene and losing for the moment in the sunny joyousness of this fairest of California valleys the bitter recollection of her great loss.   Here she lived with her only daughter until growing weakness compelled her to move to the adjacent village, where, within the sound of the forest she loved so well, she passed away.   She lies buried in the little cemetery of Saratoga and her grave has become a pilgrim shrine to thousands.   Before her death a popular subscription was started and the mortgage on the ranch was lifted.   Something of the mother's passion for the wilderness is shared by her two sons, the last remnants of the family, who have made homes in the wildest part of the Sierra Madre Mountains, near Los Angeles.   Only a trail leads to their secluded ranch and months frequently pass without their appearance in the City of the Angels.

ON THE BEACH AT SANTA CRUZ. FROM PAINTING BY A. I. KELLER.

"The bathing beach is well sheltered, and on any pleasant morning or afternoon from May to November it presents a series of pretty pictures. From the long, low houses troop the bathers in every variety of costume. They plunge into the water, which is seldom too cold for a comfortable bath, and the more adventurous swim to the large float that tosses on the waves a hundred yards away. Near the shore the women and children cling to the ropes and enjoy the exhilarating contact of the breakers as they come dashing in. There is less tribute to conventionality at this beach than at most Eastern seasides, and more genuine pleasure. The Californian seldom takes his pleasures sadly, and here he seems to throw aside, for the time, the cares of business, and to enter thoroughly into the spirit of sport."

Even the utmost familiarity cannot rob the Santa Cruz Mountains of their impressiveness. Their ruggedness has preserved many parts in their primeval wildness, while the mountain ranches that one sees in lonely drives seem to be in harmony with their surroundings. Even near Saratoga, where one may catch glimpses of the busy outer world through leaf-fringed loopholes of the zig-zaz road, the solitude is startling. At long intervals the deep quiet is broken by the faint murmur of bells. Gradually the musical monotone grows louder, the bells jingle sharply and one catches the hoarse creak of wagon-wheels. A cloud of dust along the mountain side marks the approach of the wood-team. From around the sharp turn in the

"Giant" and "General Frémont."
Santa Cruz Big Trees, near Felton.

Ingersoll Group.

narrow road emerge three horses abreast, with two span of powerful animals behind. Mounted on the huge pile of wood, with one leg thrown over the great brake, is the driver. With instinct that seems almost human the three leaders crowd toward the bank, the driver tightens his reins, and the huge swaying mass goes by, the front wagon followed by another lashed to it by the tongue and both piled high with the evenly-split four-foot sticks of redwood. The great wheels almost graze the fragile carriage in which you sit, but you have confidence in the surpassing skill of these mountain drivers and your confidence is never misplaced.

The peculiar charm of the Santa Cruz Mountains is not revealed to one who simply dashes through them in an hour or two by train. It is necessary to spend several days at places like Wright's, Boulder Creek or Glenwood to appreciate the varied beauty of these woods and mountain streams. Sport with rod and gun may be found in almost every part of the mountains. The trout are gamey, the streams wild enough to suit the most exacting angler, and the man who would secure a full basket must not be averse to wading. Everywhere is the charm that comes of the wildness of nature that not even the vandal lumberman can destroy. It is a peculiarity of the redwood that it soon covers the scars of the ax. Around the stump of the giant tree that has fallen spring up a score of shoots, each a complete tree, and so rapid is growth under this

STOCK RANGES ON THE UPPER SAN JOAQUIN. FROM PAINTING BY SPIEL AND PERARD.

"The pastoral period of this valley was the time of large landholders. Pastoral life is the first step forward from subsistence by the chase. The aborigines lived by hunting, and their immediate successors by herding. Either pursuit requires that large tracts of country shall be controlled. Hence, when the herdsman took possession of the valley of California he did not content himself with small holdings. It required the natural feed upon a certain number of acres to raise a steer, or a certain number of steers to consume the feed on an acre, as the case might be; and so in the pastoral period a herdsman counted his steers to number his acres, or numbered his acres to count his steers."

semi-tropical sun, that five years will see the original heavy timber replaced by a young grove, with slender stately trunks and tops of feathery foliage. This second growth has none of the scrubby features that so often disfigure the offshoots of the oak or pine. In fact, a grove of these young redwoods, with their trunks as straight and smooth as a South Sea Island palm, is more beautiful than a forest of larger trees. The foliage of the redwood has an aromatic odor that brings suggestions of the Spice Islands of the Indies. It is wholly unlike the pine, being of darker green and more gracefully formed. Every shade of green is furnished in these forests by the foliage of the Monterey cypress, pines, and willows of many varieties, the laurel, alder and cottonwood.

Santa Cruz combines the attractions of the sea-shore and mountain. It has one of the finest bathing beaches on the coast and marine views unsurpassed for wild beauty, while at the same time it has a drive along the cañon of the San Lorenzo River which reveals glimpses of the heart of the mountains, where the salt air of the sea and the roar of the surf are unknown. Situated at the northern extremity of Monterey Bay, Santa Cruz has the ideal position for shelter and sunshine. It is cut off by a long wooded range from the harsh ocean breeze and fog, while at its back the mountains shelter it from the north and east winds. Italy has no place on which the sun rests fairer, where the roses bloom more luxuriantly, where the air is so warm and caressing yet freed from all that is enervating by the salt breath of the sea. There is a delicious mingling of the odor of the sea-weed and the balsam of the redwood; the ozone that one takes into the pulses make them leap like strong wine; the cloudless sky, the brilliant sun, the foam-lined crescent by the beach, the lustrous sea and the dark green mountains—these make up the ideal resting place where youth is renewed and strength comes from the touch of Mother Earth.

The city of Santa Cruz has one wide business street, finely paved with asphaltum rock that is found in the neighborhood; it has all the signs of being the center of a thriving trade, with unmistakable indications of wealth and culture in handsome homes, beautiful gardens, schools and churches. It is pre-eminently a pleasure resort, and for half of the year it wears the gay look of all sea-side places. But it is something more, as it has a large population of wealthy people who have chosen it as a permanent residence because of its equable climate and its educational and social advantages. Pacific and Mission Avenues, the principal streets for residence are handsomely built up, but the attraction of the place lies in the large number of neat cottages surrounded by rose-gardens.

Santa Cruz is a formidable rival to San Jose in the number and beauty of the drives in its vicinity. First must be placed the Cliff Road, which is laid out around the point on which the city is built. The peculiarity of the coast here is the succession of graceful headlands and crescent bays formed by the action of the water. The formation is sandstone, which is easily eroded, and the water frequently hollows out the harder ridges that are left, making miniature natural bridges through which one gets charming glimpses of sea and sky. For five miles one may drive around this beach on a perfect road. A singular effect is produced by the abundance of sea-weed in the water. It frequently lies in such thick masses just off shore that the herons stand on it, as on a raft, and spear the small fish with their sharp bills. When the waves come in they are darkened by the tangled bits of sea-weed, and when the breaker curls, a moment before it is shattered into foam, one may catch glimpses of this sea-weed looking like delicate forest foliage amid the clear green water.

Rounding a point one soon comes to the beach, marked by two long wharves. Around one wharf may be seen at most hours of day or night the Italian fishing

SAN LORENZO CREEK.

OLD SANTA CRUZ MISSION—FROM A PAINTING.

boats with their lateen sails, while in the morning the bay is dotted with quaint old-world craft that give the flavor of the Mediterranean to the scene.

The bathing beach is well sheltered and on any pleasant morning or afternoon from May to November it presents a series of pretty pictures. From the long, low houses troop the bathers in every variety of costume. They plunge into the water, which is seldom too cold for a comfortable bath, and the more adventurous swim to the large float that tosses on the waves a hundred yards away. Near the shore the women and children cling to the ropes and enjoy the exhilarating contact of the breakers as they come dashing in. On the beach is a crowd of the idle and the curious, watching for the unfortunate who shall be surprised and "rolled" by a big breaker. There is less tribute to conventionality at this beach than at most eastern seasides and more genuine pleasure. The Californian seldom takes his pleasures sadly and here he seems to throw aside, for the time, the cares of business and to enter thoroughly into the spirit of sport.

Upon the neighboring beach-hill, as well as along the terraces that rise in an amphitheatre from the business part of the town, are costly residences and neat cottages, all joined by the common band of flowers. Roses bloom here the year round, and in beauty and variety are equalled by those of few places even in this land of flowers. The salt air, which is fatal to nearly all fruits save the apple, seems to stimulate the rose and other flowers to lustier growth and the gardens have the freshness of perennial spring.

A romantic story of the early mission days lingers about Santa Cruz and has been made immortal by Bret Harte in his poem of "Portala's Cross." The Mexican Governor, with troops, Christian Indians and two Franciscan friars set out one hundred and twenty years ago from San Diego to find the Bay of Monterey which Viscairo had discovered and described more than a century and a half before. They failed to recognize the bay because they beheld it from the land, but they found and named the San Lorenzo River; and the "table land" near by, which delighted their eyes with its "variety of herbs and rose bushes of Castile," they christened Santa Cruz. The pious captain set up a cross on the shore, and when the party returned from their search for the great bay of San Francisco de Anis they found the Indians had decked the cross with flowers—a sign of good-will that they regarded as an omen of future missionary success. It was not until twenty-four years later that the first mission church was built. The only traces of the old mission that now remain are a few ancient pear trees that formed part of the *padre's* orchard, for the *adobe* ruins were cleared away some years ago to give place

PLAZA AND CATHOLIC CHURCH, ON SITE OF OLD MISSION.

to the modern church, and even the dust of the Fathers has been removed to other burying grounds.

Near Santa Cruz are many attractive resorts, which are almost as pleasant in February as in June. Seabright is a collection of Eastlake cottages just beyond the San Lorenzo River, with a perfect beach and a fine outlook on the bay; Aptos, Soquel and Camp Capitola are reached by a fine drive and each has its colony of summer visitors. North of the city about four miles is the great natural bridge, hollowed out by the ocean, over which a team may be driven. The most picturesque drive about Santa Cruz is the road to the big trees. This is cut in the face of the cañon, now plunging into the depth of a redwood grove, now emerging into the sunshine, now sweeping around a point that overhangs the valley three hundred feet below and that gives a magnificent outlook upon the shaggy mountains and the wild cañon. A portion of the way you are below the railroad and can detect the hoarse rumble of the train as it buries itself in a tunnel. Then the track appears, your road crosses it and you soon look down upon the locomotive and watch it sweep across the dizzy trestle that spans the great gulch.

The big trees of Santa Cruz are simply enormous redwoods; but they bear so close a resemblance to the true Gigantea of the Sierra that only an expert naturalist is able to distinguish between them. They are situated in a natural grove of twenty acres on the bank of a pretty

A GLIMPSE OF SANTA CRUZ.

creek, and give one who has never seen the Calaveras or Mariposa groves, a good idea of those giants of the forest. The largest tree here, styled the "Giant," is three hundred feet high and has a circumference of eighty-four feet at the ground. Forty feet of the top of this tree was broken off by a great storm several years ago. The most interesting tree in the grove is the "General Frémont," named after the Pathfinder, who is reported to have camped in this tree during his visit to the grove in 1846. This great tree is forty-eight feet in circumferance and two hundred and seventy-five feet in height, and the trunk is hollow to a height of fifteen feet, forming a good-sized room. This hollow has been fashioned into a comfortable apartment, with two windows and a door. Other notable trees are "General Grant," three hundred feet high and still growing; "Jumbo," a stately tree two hundred and seventy feet high with a large knot on the trunk bearing a close resemblance to an elephant's head and trunk; and "Bob Ingersoll," a giant two hundred and eighty feet high named in honor of the eloquent orator. The near neighbor of this tree is named "Ingersoll's Cathedral." At the time when the International Congress of the Young Men's Christian Association visited the grove the officers dedicated one of the trees to the Y. M. C. A. But one gets no

LOOKING UP THE VALLEY.—KINGS RIVER CAÑON. FROM PAINTING BY A. I. KELLER.

"The granite assumes Yosemitic forms and dimensions, rising in stupendous cliffs, abrupt and sheer, from the level flats and meadows. On the north wall there is a rock like El Capitan, and just above it a group like the Three Brothers. Farther up, on the same side, there is an Indian Cañon and North Dome and Washington Column. On the south wall counterparts of the Cathedral and Sentinel Rocks occur in regular order, bearing the same relations to each other that they do in the old Yosemite."

idea of these marvellous trees from the mere figures of height and girth. It is only when you sit or lie down a short distance from them and train the eye to note their proportions that you gain any conception of their vast size.

The mountains about Santa Cruz, which have always been a resort for those suffering with pulmonary complaints, are rapidly becoming the home of hundreds of fruit-growers. It has been found that the slopes of the mountains, and even the summits of all except the most lofty, are admirably adapted to fruits and the vine. Skyland and Vine Hill are good examples of what can

WATSONVILLE; MAIN STREET—ORPHANS' HOME.

be done on these mountain tops. From the summit of the mountain near Glenwood Springs one obtains a fine panoramic view of Skyland, covered with vineyards. Occasionally one may see the forest fires, that gain such fearful headway sweeping along the wooded ridges, marked by clouds of smoke by day and at night by fitful lines of flame that leap high in the air when a dead tree bursts into blaze. There are many pleasant hotels and camping grounds in the mountains, and each succeeding summer sees a larger number of visitors, attracted by the pure air and the superb views. The most prominent figure in the landscape is Loma Prieta, or "black mountain," a darkly wooded peak, with a peculiar flat top, which is worth climbing for the magnificent view its summit affords of the Coast Range and the sea. Here the eye may sweep for one hundred miles to the north and south, and on clear days the summits of the Sierra Nevada may be plainly distinguished. Another mountain that is worth a visit is Ben Lomond, 2,200 feet in height. The top of the mountain is rapidly being converted into vineyards and orchards, the soil having been found specially adapted to fruits.

Thirty miles below San Jose, on the broad gauge road, the valley changes its name but not its character. The soil, if possible, is richer, and the climate warmer, as the sea-breezes lose their force before they reach this sheltered region. First comes the Pajaro Valley, then the Salinas. The level, rich lands were sown for years with wheat and produced enormous crops, but of late attention has been given to fruit. Gilroy, Pajaro and Watsonville are all pretty towns, lying in the heart of this great wheat belt. The latter bids fair soon to be the seat of the most important beet-sugar manufactory in the country. Several years ago Claus Spreckels, the millionaire sugar refiner of San Francisco, became convinced that sugar could be produced more economically on the Pacific Coast from the sugar beet than from Hawaiian or Manila cane. He went to Germany and studied the subject. He imported sugar-beet seed and induced two hundred farmers about Watsonville to plant from five to twenty-five acres each to the beet. The beets are found to contain a large percentage of sugar and the new industry is probably destined to supersede both wheat-farming and fruit-growing in this valley.

The lower end of the Santa Clara Valley lies in San Bonito County. Hollister, the county seat, is a pretty town with a fine outlook on the Gabilan Mountains toward the west and the rugged Mount Diablo range on the east. Other attractive towns which lie in this extremity of the Santa Clara Valley are San Juan, the seat of one of the old missions; Tres Pinos and San Felipe. This region, which for many years has been famous for wheat-growing and stock-raising, promises soon to resemble the foot-hill country near San Jose, as the Gabilan mountain sides are being planted to orchards and vineyards.

GEORGE HAMLIN FITCH.

DUCK SHOOTING AMONG THE TULES.

THE SAN JOAQUIN VALLEY.

HIGH indeed on the calendar of saints stands the name San Joaquin, the name of the husband of Saint Ann, the patron saint of all seamen, and mother of the Virgin Mary.

Midway between San Francisco and the capital city of California the deep and sinuous San Joaquin River glides into the Sacramento River and in a little time, even before the differently colored waters are yet entirely blended, the two rivers debouch into Suisun Bay, thence into San Pablo Bay, thence into the glorious bay of San Francisco and on through the ocean of oceans.

the Golden Gate into

A wide and a which is made up of day's ride in almost any strong grass hangs heavily watery place is this deep still mouth of the San Joaquin, melting snows—tranquil and treeless. It would make a hard direction to reach either foot-hills or natural forests. The tall over the warm still waters, the round brown *tules*, ten, twenty feet in length wave gracefully in the waters, willows droop above the myriad water-fowls and now and then you see little puffs of smoke burst up from the vast level of brown grasses so far away that no sound reaches you. The sportsman is abroad here in the season, and not only is his game-bag filled but he will literally fill his boat with duck, geese, loon, brant, all sorts of bird indeed that are dear to the hunter's heart. And now and then you see a low, slow and primitive-looking boat with a mounted gun at bow or stern stealing meanly along the bank under the over-hanging willows. A flock of wild geese starts up from the still waters and, "*bang!*"—a row-boat puts out from the ugly little pirate and a dozen, twenty, thirty big fat geese are gathered up from the quiet bosom of the San Joaquin waters.

The soil here is rich, rich passing all power of description; and it is practically bottomless. Many stories are told of the costly attempts of railroad engineers in the early days to find the bottom of the loose alluvial soil. Trees of great altitude were cut down on the mountain tops, brought here on the cars and stood on end, only to disappear forever in the deep alluvial deposits near the mouth of the San Joaquin. And grangers who dig wells up and down and away out toward the far-away foot-hills will tell you of great redwood logs found lying soggy and solid one, two and even three hundred feet below the surface of the ground. A soil such as this must certainly endure while the world endures.

You can see small ships going up and down and in and out through the long strong grass and *tules* and willows here all the time. These little white sails seem to be walking through the grass. You do not see the water at all, and the sensation at seeing those quiet craft gliding about through the grass on the water that lies level with the grass roots at flood-tide is unique and even ghostly. For over all hangs a Sabbath-like stillness, save for the occasional boom from the ugly little pirate before described, an unbroken quiet, that is almost painful. And this continued quiet and sense of rest is not due at all to the vastness and room and large solemnity of these unpeopled sea-marshes. The secret of the profound silence is found in the fact that for more than a quarter of a century the only human beings hereabouts were hunters and fishermen. Chinamen, Portuguese, Italians, Kanakas, all nationalities indeed save Americans, ply their silent little ships here, about the mouth of this river, which may be navigated at some seasons of the year for near about three hundred miles. Our own people were building towns rather than seeking a living in the marshes.

It is estimated that the great San Joaquin Valley contains almost, if not quite, ten million acres of arable land. If, then, as many Californians argue with a good show of reason, a family of ten can be comfortably maintained on ten acres, we have before us here the home of ten million prosperous and happy people. Go with me up this great valley of ditches, of flumes, of artesian wells, of big trees, of boundless harvest fields, of fruit, of vines and flowers; of cities born but yesterday, of vast plains that are blossoming all about with villas as unique, as striking and as rich and beautiful in many cases as can be found at either Newport or Long Branch on the other great sea-board.

But let it be borne in mind all the time while taking a bird's-eye-view of this vast valley, that everything here is new, strangely new. The possibilities of this valley, this largest fertile valley west of the Rocky Mountains, were discovered only within the year. Yes, it was settled in a half-savage sort of way thirty, forty years ago. Yet all that time the resources of the region were literally prostituted. Men sat down here, as in the mines, for what they could make in a single season. The houses were rude sheds; fences there were none; no trees were planted. Men were even indifferent about any title other than that of temporary possession. In truth the land was held in such cheap estimation, largely because there was so much of it it seemed impossible it could ever be all settled up or claimed by any one, that we have to chronicle very few law suits or disputes about lines or titles or Mexican grants in all this region; fewer than in almost any other part of California.

And now, as we set our faces to the south-east for a three or four hundred miles' journey through this vast new Paradise, let it be borne in mind that always and forever to your left, high-hung against the restful blue of heaven is a continuous wall of snow. Let it be never so hot, never so sultry, there to the left, almost within reach as it would seem—so pure, so perfect is the air here—hangs your wide, white world of snow.

Another thing to charge your mind with and keep constantly before you in passing up this marvelous valley, as a sort of mental equipment for your personal comfort, is the fact of the super-abundance of water, of flumes, ditches, artesian wells—above all of artesian wells—for water comes up cool and fresh from the melting snows to the left, new and sacred from out of the hollow of God's hand. The history of artesian wells here would alone fill a most readable book; for here the artesian well in its perfection and full use and benefit to man was actually discovered. But we must hasten on. At the same time I ought to explain that the ancient *Artois*, now *Artesian*, in France, developed in a small way this fashion of finding and drawing water long before the pioneer farmers of California brought the system to perfection here in the San Joaquin Valley. Indeed, there are small oil wells and water wells in China of this order that are as old perhaps as the time of Alexander the Great. There is a well in Ohio deeper than any here, and a hundred years ago the Spanish and French settlers along the brackish banks of the Mississippi and the Gulf of Mexico made little artesian wells by the thousand. But what I mean to assert is that the artesian well never found its full value and benefit till this sudden and new development of the vast San Joaquin Valley.

To give some idea of its perfection, as well as its possibilities, let me briefly set down some

HUNTING WILD GEESE.—SAN JOAQUIN VALLEY. FROM PAINTING BY THOMAS HILL.

"The San Joaquin Valley, the paradise of the hunter, swarms with aquatic game. Wild geese are, at certain seasons of the year, so numerous that the farmer lives in terror of their periodical visits. They come in myriads, devouring the young growth of grain and every green plant in sight, leaving devastation in their path. The great difficulty of approaching this timid bird has taxed the ingenuity of the farmer to the utmost. A trained steer enables the hunter, armed with a formidable weapon, to approach within short range, and by this method hundreds have been killed at a shot."

incidents connected with the boring of an artesian well near Pixley, a sweet little town which has been newly planted and is prospering wonderfully far up the valley in the region of Tulare Lake. The writer had some commercial interest in this well and knows thoroughly the cost as well as all the incidental concern and excitement that attaches to the boring of a great artesian well.

In the first place, then, a contract is made, as a rule at so much per foot. Men, mules, derricks, long creaking wagons with enormous tubes of iron,—an army in fact, a curious, greasy, dusty, dirty old town on wheels to all appearances; with great strong men, greasy, dirty and dusty; braying mules, roaring drivers—these are the equipments. No foolish water-witch, with forked stick in two hands and eyes turned heavenward, is here. Very stern and very practical are the strong men who come to bore a well for us on the bare white plains of Tulare away off yonder toward the head of the San Joaquin.

A RABBIT DRIVE—SAN JOAQUIN VALLEY.

Day after day, week after week the thud and thump of the drill, the groaning of the greasy machinery, the grim solemnity of the greasy, great strong men! Then a drill would break or be lost for days in the dusty hollows of the world below. Then a tube would burst or bend. It takes pluck, patience, time, to do this work. Curious bits of stone, bits of shell now and then. The iron lips of the earth are forced open by these mighty men with their steel and she is yielding up the secrets of her creation.

At last a little moisture. Why, how thirsty has been this surface of the earth! Stratum after stratum has been passed, and all as dusty as dust can be. Ashes, alkali, sandstone, limestone, slate, pliocene and post-pliocene, as Lyell's Geology would put it, are passed as the warm and dusty summer runs by, and—"*water!*"

It has cost seven thousand dollars. It leaps out of the darkness down there twenty, thirty, forty feet into the air. It seems as glad to see us as we are to see it. The earth begins to drink all around. The very winds rise up everywhere in the fervid and parching valley and sweep past dipping their wings in the water, turning back, wheeling about, blowing the leaping, laughing waters in your face. The wind is very glad. The big and grim and greasy captain of the outfit lets his iron features relax. He too is glad, very glad and very grateful. It was a great day with us all.

Then away toward the lurid sunset some new settlers came out with their picks and shovels stealthily to dig a trench in their direction; for the water was flowing that way. They came cautiously as if afraid, as if waiting for the protection of darkness before they began to dig, as if afraid we would drive them away from the precious water. But when night fell we could hear the rattle of their tools on the hard and dusty soil till the night was far spent. Would the water reach them? Would it hold out till morning? And would we then go down and cruelly turn the cool sweet stream aside and keep it from flowing into the thirsty fields?

We arose with the early dawn and looked out and down after our flowing stream, and what did we see? A little lake! And seagulls had come and they lay like

DRYING.

RAISIN CULTURE.

GATHERING.

a snow-drift on a little island among the cattle and before the door of the thirsting settlers of the night before.

And this is the story of the sinking of an artesian well, the story of thousands. Some lands have been flooded to their ruin, some law-suits have come of it; but since water is quite as necessary as land in this region it is not hard to reach an equitable adjustment when all parties are so disposed.

Let us now return to the solid land. The San Joaquin Valley is, geographically as well as by natural endowment, the fervid heart of California. Ardent, fruitful, fertile as the Nile of old, she easily wears the white lilies of excellence on her wide, warm bosom. Begotten of an endless summer's sun, born of the everlasting snows of the Sierra Nevada Mountains, this tranquil river and this vast valley are to-day the glory of California and the wonder of the world. You can hear the mighty heart of this sunset Eden throb and beat and pulse away up yonder to the left as you journey along here with your face to the south; for the thundering waters of the Yosemite pay tribute only to the San Joaquin. In truth, the streams that pour down from the snow peaks which flash forever in the sun, giving fertility to this vast valley and making up the waters of this restful river, are not only very numerous but very, very beautiful. And these numerous rivers, fresh from the snows and forever clad in verdure, are not only very, very beautiful but they are, many of them, even now at this early date of our history, famous before the world in story and in song. The Mariposa, the Merced, the Tuolumne, the Stanislaus, the Calaveras, all these

(*a.*) ARTESIAN WATER-SPOUT.

famous little rivers, once as rich in gold as they shall yet be in beauty and tradition, are but tributaries of the San Joaquin. The great trees, the trees that people make the circuit of the world to see, they all stand here in eternal testimony of the fertility of the land and the salubrity of the elements. The "fountains of the deep" are broken here. Literally are the prophecies fulfilled to give additional floods of fresh water to the ten, twenty, thirty new cities born only yesterday to this marvelous land. Nothing like it has been since Moses smote the rock in the desert. As if the many strong mountain streams of melting snows were not enough, here are rivers rising up from the "fountains of the deep" and flooding the land for miles and miles, lakes are being formed, trees are taking root, forests are springing. From yonder snow bank thirty miles away and ten thousand feet in the air the cunning hand of man has drawn down the silver rivers to his valley of progress. And away deep down in the very bowels of the once arid earth, right here under foot he arrests the dark and silent rivers on their way to the sea and compels them to the surface to join force with the waters of the snow, to pay tribute to imperial San Joaquin. What marvel then that this heart of California, the heart of the world's heart, has suddenly come to be the wonder of civilization.

The story of this valley and its environs, larger than many German states and of vastly more importance in the coming welfare of the world, was a grand one from the beginning. Here for a quarter of a century lay the largest farms in all the world. Here to this day are the broadest fields of wheat, the biggest vineyards, orchards, irrigating ditches, gang-plows, reapers, threshers, all things indeed that lift up and help the world forward while man walks erect. For here no man puts his hand to the plow. The parable of our Saviour will here lose its meaning before the world is a generation older. The writer pauses here in the midst of these statements and wonders if he stands entirely alone in his estimation of this valley, its resources and achievments. No one is willing to be questioned as to his statements in matters of this kind, and turning to Charles Nordhoff's "California," I find this paragraph touching the San Joaquin valley: "Fields of two, three and four thousand acres make but small farms; here is a man with twenty thousand acres, here is another with forty thousand acres, and here is another with a still more preposterous area, all in wheat." Backed by this statement from one of the most trustworthy of all writers on California, I think I can now go forward and set down the fact that seventeen years ago I saw a gang-plow throwing a series of furrows said to be sixty miles in circuit!

Let it be borne in mind, however, that with rare exceptions, this, as well as the statements by the author above quoted, is all in the past. The sixty-mile furrow is no longer possible. More than thirty years ago, while crossing the lower end of this valley with Bayard Taylor, we saw wild horses but not a single house. Seventeen

(*b.*) FALLS ON KAWEAH RIVER.
SOURCES OF WATER SUPPLY FOR IRRIGATION.

EARLY MORNING AMONG THE TULES.—SAN JOAQUIN VALLEY. FROM PAINTING BY THOMAS HILL.

"The tall strong grass hangs heavily over the warm still waters; the round brown tules, ten, twenty feet in length, wave gracefully in the waters; willows droop above the myriad water-fowls; and now and then you see little puffs of smoke burst up from the vast level of brown grasses so far away that no sound reaches you. The sportsman is abroad here in the season, and not only is his game-bag filled, but he will literally fill his boat with duck, geese, loon, brant,—all sorts of bird, indeed, that are dear to the hunter's heart."

GRAIN WAREHOUSE—TRAVER.

WHEAT TEAMS, WAITING TO UNLOAD.

years ago, while on my way
to Yosemite with Grace Green-
wood, I saw and chronicled the fact that men and mules camped on the circuit of their sixty-
mile furrow. Nordhoff saw his forty-thousand-acre farms fifteen or sixteen years ago. As said
before, all things here were cast on a colossal scale in the beginning. Man seems to have been misled
by the magnitude, the majesty, of nature. Man is very tall, very strong, bold even to audacity,
but he has found out at last that he cannot touch the stars with his finger; he has learned that
his arm is not so long as the river nor his voice so loud as the voice of Yosemite.

Across the yellow plains here, where the wild horse less than half a century since threw his
mane to the winds, the obedient engine now draws an almost endless train of bread for the ships
of Europe that wait for the product of this valley within the Golden Gate. Where the sixty-mile
furrow made compass seventeen years ago, there are to-day probably sixty happy homes and many
school-houses. And still the great need of this valley is more people, multiplied homes. Let these
huge icebergs of desolation, these big farms that block the wheels of progress so entirely, pass
away as fast as possible. They are bad for the country, bad for those who have no land, and
still worse for those who own them. Singular as it may seem, the history of these big farms as
a rule is the history of final and complete overthrow of the owners. It has long been remarked
that in California a man richest in lands is poorest in all things else. Nature appears to resent
this inordinate greed, and few things seem to flourish on a scale so vast. California seems to be
peculiarly a garden land. Five, ten, twenty acres—farms of this or any reasonable size flourish.

A HARVESTER.

But where fields mount into the thousands,
disease, vermin of some sort, like a plague
of Egypt on the banks of the earlier Nile,
springs up out of the ground, as if to
compel the more fortunate to share a little
with the less fortunate. Year by year
the smaller farms lay siege around the
larger ones. The little grape fields are
cutting their way into the larger ones, and
there is coming to be a very healthful
conviction up and down the great San
Joaquin Valley that after all Eden may
possibly have been made up of a very few
acres. Back of this grows gradually the
conviction that California is the garden-
world; and that the San Joaquin Valley

is the garden of California. The man with more land than he can well handle is called a "speculator." He may be a good man and may be well respected; but somehow he is looked upon as something of a Shylock, as a man who is not doing any very good thing for his country.

The quest for quiet and pleasant little homes is notable all along here as we glide on up the valley, the great wall of snow continuously to the left. Some of the owners of these new little Edens are far away, even in the Eastern States. But this desire of so many of the best people of the land to build a little Paradise on earth, this effort to build little Edens of our own, this trying to get back into Paradise away out here in the great valley of California for the first time since the expulsion, there is a touch of tenderness in all this, a penitential desire to return to innocence and peace as of old, a thought that is too sacred for expression; and we dash on up the vast valley, cleaving new towns in halves at every station, meeting long and heavily laden trains of

Landing and Water-Front at Stockton.

grain, hay, lumber, grapes, fruit. Vineyards to the right and vineyards to the left, forest and farms. What would your wild horses do here to-day? Your sixty-mile furrow would be blocked by many a town. The roar of progress is in the air. The cities here are still smelling of paint. The long lines of lumber are yet green. Still the fragrance of fruit is in the fervid air.

Along with this continual march of civilization up the San Joaquin Valley is to be remarked a quiet earnestness among the people. All are thoroughly alert. The people have not yet had time to settle down to provincial ways. You do not feel that you are in a rural land at all. Perhaps the settlers on the small Edens that make up these half-finished cities are from cities in the East. These people are thoughtful, busy; they are building a new world. Here sits a man not ten feet distant who came last winter from New York. He has a new city away out yonder, thirty miles away on the brown foot-hills by one of the tumbling mountain torrents. His little city was born only last week. He has half a million of money and is going to build homes for invalid women of the East. He has no time for trivial word or act. Like nearly all the people along here he is nobly, grandly in earnest. No, he will not give his name or plans. He desires first to do his work and let it speak for itself. At his elbow is another able and earnest man. May be they are associated together, but most likely they are strangers. I think this man's name is Frazer, owner and proprietor of the great lumber yards at Selma, wherein I once saw a portion of a tree the whole of which yielded nearly 175,000 feet of clear lumber.

"Mercy on us! how many cities are they building along here, any how?" asks a stout man from the States, as he rubs his bald head and peers out at another new town smelling of paint and green lumber.

"Oh, don't know; about a hundred, I guess."

"And are they all going ahead like these along here?"

"Going ahead just as fast as they can get lumber to go ahead with, sir."

And yet, brisk and bright as are these cities here on the main line of travel, they are not alone in the march forward. Away out yonder, twenty, thirty miles away, toward the Coast Range to the right, on the lower and wooded foot-hills to the left, far below the line of snow, there too are life, prosperity, progress the same as here.

But what mean those little puffs of smoke that now and then burst above the scattered oaks and rise and melt away in the air? Almost any man familiar with war would say that these were batteries in action, and wait for the reverberation and sound of artillery. But no, these batteries are not mowing down men. They are reaping, heading, threshing; gathering bread on the banks of the San Joaquin River for the hungry world of Europe. Sixteen, twenty, thirty horses all abreast. Derricks, pulleys, ropes enough to rig a ship. And this huge machinery has lifted the load from the backs of men. Machines are doing the work that men and women do in other lands. In some places you see harvesters that are run by steam and the load is lifted not only from the backs of men but from the backs of horses also. Hands of steel are thrust out to grapple the grain, it is twisted into sheaves, borne back by iron arms, thrust into iron teeth, devoured. Look along the wake of the great groaning monster of steam and steel. You see only the leaning, gleaming stubble. This monster does not even stop to drop the bags of threshed and winnowed grain which he gathers in his course.

SECTION OF REDWOOD TREE, CUT AT FRAZER'S MILL.

And what is the temperature now at warmest time of year? It is warm, very warm. But it does not seem to me to be really hot, as it was here before the abundant inundation of water. I am constantly reminded of New Orleans, of New Orleans immediately after a summer shower. The atmosphere is humid, warm, sultry; but not hot, as it was a quarter of a century since.

It is hard for the observer to refrain from speculating as to the future of this vast valley which is only to-day newly discovered, rightly discerned. When the broad leaf of the banana holds back the heat of the sun, when the great trees of the earth that environ this valley shall descend from the mountains and stand by the artesian wells and lord the loftiest church spires, when you shall swing your hammock in the perpetually-laden branches of the rose tree, when birds of paradise fill the young forests that are only just now breaking through the earth, when these cities are all completed, watered and wooded, when all this arduous work of to-day is done, when we shall all sit down under our vine and fig-tree, when tranquil leisure and kindly love, religion and rest, when in short all these things now so nearly within our reach shall be ours, instead of the sweat and toil and concern of to-day—ah, my fellow world-builders, what a place, what a Paradise will San Joaquin Valley be then!

JOAQUIN MILLER.

OLD STEAMER LANDING, PETALUMA CREEK.

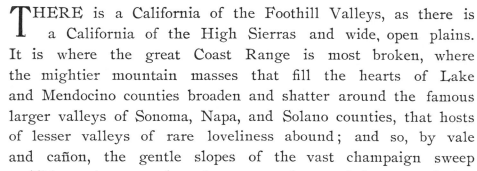

AT THE DRAWBRIDGE.

THE FOOTHILL REGION OF THE NORTHERN COAST-RANGE:

SONOMA, NAPA AND SOLANO VALLEYS.

THERE is a California of the Foothill Valleys, as there is a California of the High Sierras and wide, open plains. It is where the great Coast Range is most broken, where the mightier mountain masses that fill the hearts of Lake and Mendocino counties broaden and shatter around the famous larger valleys of Sonoma, Napa, and Solano counties, that hosts of lesser valleys of rare loveliness abound; and so, by vale and cañon, the gentle slopes of the vast champaign sweep down to the levels of marsh and bay. This region may be taken as a characteristic type of that sort of hill-country which, far more than the higher mountains, can be persuaded into alliance with human plans and be softened year by year into a land of orchards, vineyards, gardens, and beauty such as one finds to-day on the lower slopes of the Italian Alps and among the hills of Sicily. It contains hints of the levels and of the heights, of all soils, and of every climate. Even while it yields its proud strength to noblest use, it abides forever within the influence and freedom of the greater mountains, heaven-appointed interpreter of their peace.

The broad waterways from the Golden Gate inland, the Chesapeake of the Pacific Coast, extending past islands and oak-clad heights and limited areas of fertile plow-lands to the sea-green levels of Suisun, and the deserted wharves of many an ancient *embarcadero*, deep-hid in nodding *tules*, form the southern boundary of the champaign country of which I write. The sloping plain of the Western Sacramento lies to the east. North are the untilled mountain fastnesses, and west is the Pacific. A lessening fringe of redwoods extending southward from the superb Mendocino forests borders the ocean to within sight of San Francisco. When forest fires rage on Tamalpais and the hills beyond, the spicy fragrance of the burning cedar boughs sometimes can be distinguished twenty miles south. Inland, east of the redwoods, the country is a land of rolling and well-watered hills, with fertile valleys hidden between; it is partly a land of long and gentle ridges, partly one of single isolated peaks. Here, it is as much of a dairy country as the best of Switzerland; there, it is the home of the grape, the olive and, in favorable situations, even of the lemon and the orange. Everywhere from Tamalpais to St. Helena, and from the trout-streams of Northern Sonoma to the onyx quarries of Suisun, it is a free, wild, luxuriant land, abounding in great natural resources, and full of infinite variety.

Of a truth there are many other hill districts in the California Palestine, but nowhere else between San Diego and Siskiyou could a district as large as the whole State of Connecticut be mapped out so as to include so great an area of picturesque and valuable foothill-land, so many streams and springs, such large and important valleys, and so many rich and beautiful lesser vales and cultivated ravines. Four counties and parts of two others may be said to lie within its boundaries, and its area is upwards of three million acres. As a whole, its more characteristic features are repeated in many other districts, but not upon such a scale. One is not to forget that no part of California ever is free from the influence of the hills. Even the great valleys have their long, wave-like hollows and crests, nor is one ever out of sight of the blue mountains, east and west.

In the true champaign country the rolling hills, and the small valleys that they hide, are wonderful for beauty, for soil, and for climate. They seem but waste and barren hills, sometimes, too wild to be worth the taming and beaten down by years of use as a pasturage for sheep; yet they are sown deep with neglected sparkles of silver and dust of gold. Over hundreds of square miles of as yet uncultivated hillsides all the elements of successful horticulture are waiting to be utilized everywhere to the same extent as they already are in a few famous localities. Over all the valleys rise the uplands, the *mesas*, the broad and free champaigns. Throughout the whole district of which I write, the life of the hills gives form and color to the life of the lowlands. Even in its larger valleys the most striking natural features are the rolling hills that project far into the "bottoms," and the massive parks of oak, with their fine and stately charm—oaks planted by no human hands, white oaks in the valleys, evergreen oaks higher up and, still higher, a few scattered pines. The hills are so near, so much a part of even the valleys, that the region never can lose its wild charms. Wherever a house can nestle or an orchard be planted in the rock-shelters, men will come and make their homes between lowland and mountain. The subduing of these vast hillsides, slow and costly though it must prove, is really the problem before California now, and will be for many years to come. The level valleys are already known, already planted, fenced, and farmed. Railroads cross them, tourists visit them, towns are founded in the midst of them; their future is assuredly one of peace and smiling plenty, sheltered like vales of Tempe and Cashmere, in a land of summer. Nevertheless, it is only the full conquest of the whole beautiful and fertile "hill-country" which can harmonize and fulfill the possibilities of the champaign regions of California. To the glowing valley's superb abundance, the nuts and fruits, the oil and wine of the foothills, grown on hundreds of small homesteads, must add their finer flavors and their richer hues. Every available mountain acre must come under the yoke of careful tillage, even to the terracing of slopes that seem too steep to climb. And, though all this can be accomplished only after years of time and immeasurable labor, the ultimate result is the blending of valley and hill into a perfected whole, and we have such a country as Italy, Southern France, or the famous Rhine-lands.

The valleys of the champaign district, large and small, are thirty or forty in number, besides the many "flats," heads of ravines, and lesser vales that have as yet no distinct names, but are each of them occupied by a pioneer or two. The large valleys are already famous, and they open up and divide the whole region so as to make it easily accessible. It is through these eight or ten larger valleys that one begins to study the foothills; and the gateways of most of the large valleys are at the tide-levels. If one took a sailboat, or canoe, and skirted the northern shores of San Francisco, San Pablo and Suisun bays, he would obtain a far better general view of the great hill-and-valley region under consideration, than by any number of railroad journeys. Let us take an imaginary voyage along the sloughs and bay-borders, in one of the graceful, swift-sailed canoes, such as those that flit to and

COURT HOUSE, SANTA ROSA.

FOOTHILLS OF ST. HELENA. FROM PAINTING BY VIRGIL WILLIAMS.

"As one rides past orchard or vineyard he can hardly fail to note the cheerfulness of the laborers, for their work is clean and pleasant,—far different from the dust and heat of the harvest field. In some districts the fruit season lasts from April to December. June, July, August and September are, however, the months when all the world is on the hillsides, in the vines, or in the orchards of the valleys, gathering the bright, delicate, fragrant harvests."

fro like water-spiders on Oakland Creek or drift in fleets on summer tides of Casco Bay and Lake George.

Sailing under the lovely shadows of Tamalpais with all its clustering vales and streams and broken hills, we find the first great valley-basin fronting the bay—that of the Petaluma region, extending over an area of sixty or seventy miles of rich and moist lowlands and fertile adjacent slopes.   Schooners, small steamers and antique hay-barges ascend the winding sloughs to the old town of Petaluma.   As one looks north, over an almost imperceptible divide, and continuing in effect the same broad valley, the rim of the Santa Rosa basin is crossed.   Here is an undulating plain, dotted over with immense oak trees, and containing more than two hundred square miles of territory.   Along the western borders of this beautiful plain lies the picturesque Santa Rosa laguna, with its *tule*-covered islands and deep blue reaches of water.   Still farther north is the winding and

PETALUMA CREEK.

varied surface of the Russian River Valley basin, with its constant succession of hop-yards, orchards, vineyards, and alfalfa fields for twenty-five miles on either side of the broad river and its tributary streams.   From Petaluma to Cloverdale, across these three drainage basins, it is practically one sweep of valley, fifty miles in length from San Pablo Bay.   It is the largest valley in the whole region, and Petaluma, Santa Rosa, Headsburg and Cloverdale are its towns; but although it is the great valley of the Sonoma country, the name "Sonoma" belongs also to a small but not less famous valley of the same district.   Among the remarkable tributary villages that cluster about this great valley-plain, are the grape villages of Knights, Guillicos, Bennett and the Rincon, the famous apple valleys of Green and Alexander, and the lovely mountain valley of Dry Creek, which empties into Russian River.

Our canoe, creeping along the northern San Pablo shore, close to the headlands, east of Petaluma creek, comes next to the labyrinth of sloughs that lead to that ancient home of Spanish grandees, the rounded valley-plain of the Sonoma, the "Valley of the Moon," the land of the Bear Flag, the home of General Vallejo, and one of the centers of the grape-growing industry in California.   It is a curving valley some twenty-two miles long, and from two to eight miles wide.   On the west the hills are low and broken, so that connection is easy with the Santa Rosa region.   On the east are blue peaks, under whose shadows some of the earliest vineyards of Northern California were planted. The old Spanish buildings in the town of Sonoma mark the only point—excepting San Rafael—north of San Francisco Bay where any serious attempt was made to establish foundations for another Mission. If the reign of the priests had continued for a quarter of a century longer, all the larger valleys opening upon the bays from the north would have been occupied by Missions. Sonoma was already planned for; Santa Rosa and Vaca probably would have come next, for there were a few Spanish families in those valleys. Napa would probably have been the last of the fertile valleys of the north to be colonized by the *padres*, for they seem to have known less about it than about the others. After the secularization of the Missions, most of the lands of these valleys were granted to various persons, under the Mexican land laws, and here and there in the edge of the foothills, one will occasionally find the picturesque ruin of an old adobe built in the "forties." In Sonoma Valley the garden of General Vallejo is justly famous for its semi-tropical wealth, especially its orange groves. There are considerable orchards of young orange trees in this district, at El Verano and Glen Ellen. Beautiful vineyards, and clumps of fine redwoods curiously strayed this far inland from the coast, are to be seen in the Glen Ellen district and among the foothills surrounding it, linking it with emerald bands to both Santa Rosa and Sonoma.

The "Charleston" at Mare Island

Mare Island Navy Yard

Vallejo looking West to Mare Island

Mare Island Navy Yard on the right Vallejo opposite

Vallejo looking South to Mare Island

Still sailing east, along the San Pablo shore, now past oak-clad hills and bold red bluffs silver-white on top with acres of wild oats, now past marshes and sloughs, and golden banks of blossoming grindelias, one comes at last to the gateways of Napa, one of the famous grape valleys of the region. We have passed the Western Mayacamas Mountains with blue waterways sweeping against their bases, and beyond us lie the lesser Eastern Mayacamas range, on the other side of the valley. We can look straight up the rising valley-plain to Mount St. Helena, more than forty miles distant. East of Napa, and almost a part of it, lie two long, narrow, winding valleys, Pope and Chiles, "beautiful for situation," hidden in the foothills. Northeast, where notches in the mountain ranges show against the azure skies, are many clustering valleys, high and fair to see— valleys where the old pioneers yet dwell in the midst of flocks and herds. Capelle is one of the best known, Conn is another, Wooden is a third; largest of all, and furthest from Napa valley, is the great inland mountain-circled vale of Berryessa, famous for its cattle ranges and wheat fields, along the crystal waters of the Patch, and on the wooded spurs of the Blue Ridge. Between valley and valley, rising from the midst of foothills, and crowned with pines and redwoods, oaks and firs, the high ridge of Howell overlooks St. Helena, that pleasant vineyard-town of the upper Napa. At the very head of the valley, the grand mountain, St. Helena, looms up, the dominant feature in the landscape. Near its base is the town of Calistoga, with its summer resorts, its stage lines to the celebrated Geysers and the Petrified Forest, and its varied mining and horticultural interests. Calistoga is beyond the limits of Napa Valley, in its own mountain vale. Chrome, copper, iron, lead, silver, gold, and cinnabar are mined in the vicinity of Mount St. Helena; and old prospectors and stories of hidden treasures abound in the region. From one's canoe, by the green bay shores there are seen only the mountain ranges of the Mayacamas drawing nearer and nearer as they trend northward, growing more blue and faint in the misty distance about Howell's and St. Helen's. Still farther east, as one sails again along the shores past the Napa Valley, the foothills on which Vallejo and Benicia are built come down to the water's edge, and we pass through the Carquinez Straits, across which bands of elk have been known to swim as late as the year 1847, on their way from Livermore to the pastures around Clear Lake.   Beyond the straits, the hills retire

from the shore, leaving islands of marsh, half-tures. It is the north-gateway of the Coast the fourth great valley of Suisun, between the Green Valley ranges. of the finest fruit dis-included in its boun-than Napa if they were united a little more closely. First comes Suisun, only

wide lowlands and wandering sloughs, reclaimed, and broad salt-grass pas-ern shore of Suisun Bay. The inner Range is passed, and the mouth of group appears—the lovely semi-circle Montezuma hills and the Vaca and Here, in the heart of Solano, is one tricts of the state, and the valleys daries would form a larger valley

GRAPE ELEVATOR.

separated on the east from the Sacramento Valley plain by a low divide, and by the fertile Montezuma hills. West of Suisun, and parallel to it, over a low ridge of hills, is Green Valley, a perfect little gem of a mountain vale, with its winding river, its old ruined stone mill, and its fascinating waterfalls. North of Suisun, and opening upon it by winding roads through the hills, are Laguna, Vaca, Pleasant, and a group of glens and valleys devoted almost entirely to fruit-culture. Far beyond Pleasant Valley the hills drop to the Putah Creek Cañon, and there Putah flows cool and fresh from its

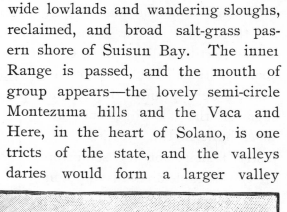

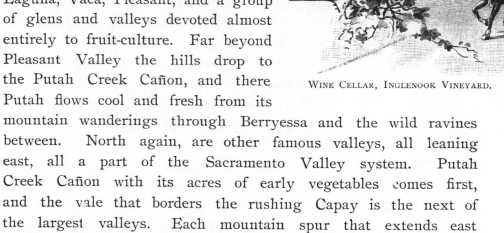

WINE CELLAR, INGLENOOK VINEYARD.

HYDRAULIC WINE-PRESS.

mountain wanderings through Berryessa and the wild ravines between.   North again, are other famous valleys, all leaning east, all a part of the Sacramento Valley system.   Putah Creek Cañon with its acres of early vegetables comes first, and the vale that borders the rushing Capay is the next of the largest valleys.   Each mountain spur that extends east towards the central plain or south towards the chain of bays and sloughs guards its own little valleys of oak and pine, its isolated peaks, its "flats" and plateaus, all fit for cultivation, but many of them nameless.

We have traced the shore-line from Marin to Solano, and have seen where the greater val-leys and hidden vales make their network of roadways into the heart of the mountains.   Before us, then, is the field of study at last—the vales and hills of the mountain peninsula that Tamalpais and Monte Diablo would look upon were the Sacramento-San-Joaquin Valley to be suddenly changed into a lake.   Disregarding lesser differences, one who looks northward from the summit of Monte Diablo sees the silver and emerald sweep of Suisun Valley as a Bay of Biscay projected from the Atlantic of the Sacramento plain; sees Napa's dark vines, the second great level expanse; sees, last of all, the Sonoma-Santa-Rosa districts, the largest of them, with islands of hills rising brown and high between, but nevertheless so distinctly united across the Glen Ellen ridges as to mark the essential unity of this third group of valleys.

RUSSIAN RIVER VALLEY.—MOUNT ST. HELENA FROM HEALDSBURG. FROM DRAWING BY THOMAS MOESSNER.

"Still farther north is the winding and varied surface of the Russian River Valley basin, with its constant succession of hop-yards, orchards, vineyards and alfalfa fields for twenty-five miles on either side of the broad river and its tributary streams. It is the largest valley in the whole region, and Petaluma, Santa Rosa, Healdsburg, Cloverdale and Ukiah are its towns; but, although it is the great valley of the Sonoma country, the name "Sonoma" belongs to a small but not less famous valley of the same district."

There is no part of California wherein so great a variety of crops is produced, chiefly without irrigation, as in the valleys and on the hillsides of the district of which I write, and which I have called the "Champaign Country" of the state. To those who know and admire the rolling hills of central Maryland and Virginia—the region above the dead levels and below the mountain fastnesses—the term has especial fitness. Men love such a land; they knit their hearts fast to the soil; their pioneer farms become ancestral homesteads and sacred possessions never to pass into alien hands. Leave the great Connecticut Valley, and wander among the Farmington hills, and you shall see how beautiful the vales of the uplands can become. Hills of northern Ohio, hills of central Michigan and of southern Pennsylvania, all have the same sweet, quiet charms that are so dear to art and literature. The great valleys of California have their twenty-thousand-acre wheat farms, their square miles of vineyard, the property of single owners; but the small foothill slopes, and even the large Coast-Range Valleys are not to be so managed. They seem to belong to the many, not to the few; they are set with colonies, and divided into small tracts; villages abound in every township, and a multitude of lesser industries thrive in the wake of the predominant industry of the whole district—horticulture.

Years ago, when the first American pioneers began to build their cabins in the valleys of the Coast-Range, they knew of but one art, caught second-hand from the Spaniards—the art of the herdsman. Wild oats grew everywhere, higher than the saddle-bows; grizzly bears were walking in plain sight over the valleys, twenty or more to be seen in any summer's day; fences there were none, except the occasional canals, and cattle-trails were the only roads. Yount and Wolfskill, and all the rest of the pioneers were, first of all, herdsmen. But the gold-camps were established, and cities rose under their impulse. Some of the old pioneers learned the art of wheat-raising, and broke up the soil of the valleys, while those who continued to be cattle-men retired into the foothills, then waste and thought to be worthless and barren. No one planted trees, except a few for shade around the house or for a little fruit for the family supply. The wheat went in long mule-trains of wagons to the *embarcaderos* on sloughs of the bays—Petaluma, Napa, Suisun, Cordelia, Bridgeport, and dozens of others—and thence by schooner to the metropolis. The valleys grew wheat over golden leagues for years and years—nothing but wheat, until the soil in many places was worn out, and farmers failed to find it any longer profitable, although the railroad ran past their doors, carrying the wheat to a market. The wheat era began to yield to the tree-and-vine period. Slowly, in a thousand places, at various times since 1849, small and feeble beginnings in horticulture had been made by men who were only experimenting for the future, and the results of the experiments encouraged others to greater risks. One of the largest orchardists of California gave up wheat, and began to plant fruit trees because he noticed that a pear tree in his garden yielded him a larger cash profit for three successive years than did ten acres of wheat. After a while many of the large wheat-growers began to divide up and sell their lands, which had grown too valuable for the cereals, and the reign of diversified products began; intensive horticulture took the place of mile-square grain fields and leagues of pasture lands which formerly occupied the fairest acres of the valleys. Everywhere, too, along the hill-borders of the valleys, and in the warmer mountain cañons, were spots of rich soil which the horticulturists seized upon as especially well adapted for fruit, vines, vegetables and flower-gardens. The most fruitful and profitable orchards and vineyards of Sonoma, Napa, and Vaca are on hillsides that face the larger valleys, or in the hearts of some of the lesser mountain vales.

The late B. B. Redding, one of the pioneers of California horticulture, used to say that the Coast-Range Valleys combined all the charms of lowland and upland. He was especially pleased with the views obtained looking southward from Cloverdale, down Santa Rosa Valley, and from Mount St. Helena, looking down the Napa Valley. While these valleys were as yet devoted almost wholly to wheat culture he prophesied that in twenty years the olive, the orange, the vine, the fig, the pomegranate, and all the deciduous fruits would largely supplant grain, and give a distinctive character to the industries of the valley as well as of the foothills. Year after year, he said, the line of cultivation will climb higher, and the mountain chaparral give place to fruits and nut-bearing trees. It has been as he predicted. The lands of this vast hill-region are as much the heritage of the horticulturist as are the hills of Provence and the slopes of Southern Italy.

The circle of the year is beautiful in an orchard land, and change melts into change so gently that the old eastern division of the seasons is quite lost. The trees, leafless in January, begin to bud and bloom in February, in miles upon miles of tinted almond flowers. The pink of the peach blossoms, the white of the plum, pear, and cherry, and the rosy apple-flowers, follow in succession. April is the month of orange blooms; the loquat blooms in winter, and its clusters of yellow, delicious fruit ripen and are gone before cherry time. The staple fruit-crops are apple, pear, plum, prune, cherry, apricot, peach, almond, fig, grape, quince, and the berries. The walnut, pecan, hickory, butternut, eastern and Italian chestnut, mulberry, pomegranate, Japanese persimmon, loquat, orange, and multitudes of rare fruits that seldom reach any markets, but are grown for home consumption, are to be seen on the foothill ranches. In the valleys are solid miles of orchards, with only country roads and divisions between; in the hills the pastures, rocks, and untilled slopes intervene, and give infinite variety to the picture.

GRAPE ARBOR.

A land of orchards and vineyards grows at last into a great number of small and highly improved holdings, giving employment to thousands of people and building up large and prosperous towns. The little farms in the course of time run to an endless variety of products—finer fruits, medicinal and dye plants, bulbs, flowers, and a thousand sorts of cultivated herbs, shrubs, vines and trees. One man grows tuberoses for perfume, another roses for the precious attar, a third the true Persian crocus for its dye-yielding pistils. Nurseries abound, and gardens old and famous, and lawns on which magnificent ornamental trees of rare species are to be found. Even the roadside trees, planted in long avenues, come at last to have ivy, wild grape, and climbing roses over them. It is only in the foothills that one can climb by winding roads from valley to plateau, and from plateau to ridge, looking down on still other valleys stretching out for miles, with hundreds of homesteads, set in the midst of pastures as yet uncultivated. It is only the foothill lands that are crowned with the gift and benediction of continual surprises. In the heart of the hills a strength not to be spoiled by words abides forever.

After the spring-tide of bloom in the orchards is past, after the rains have ceased and the last plowing is done, the stirring of the soil with cultivation begins. As one rides past orchard

NEAR SKAGGS SPRINGS.

or vineyard he can hardly fail to note the cheerfulness of the laborers, for their work is clean and pleasant, far different from the dust and heat of the harvest field. They stir the surface, destroy the weeds and aid the moisture to rise; they thin off the surplus fruit, so that what is left on the trees will be large and fine, bringing the highest market price; they pinch back too ardent shoots, and rub off the sprouts and suckers near the ground; they fight the insect pests with spraying machines, carried in a wagon from tree to tree or through the rows of vineyard. Long and busy days they occupy thus, in early summer before the main crop of fruit begins to ripen; then, suddenly the harvest days come, still more closely crowded with toil and responsibility. Along the creeks white tents are pitched in June, for the families of campers who gather fruit for the orchardists. They come up from the wheat-plains, out of the villages and towns, and even from the great city, to combine pleasure, health and profit, like the hop-gatherers of English Kent. Sometimes they work for day's wages, sometimes they rent the orchards on shares, but usually they are paid by the basket for gathering, or by the pound for cutting and drying fruit. The boys and girls come home from school, and put their books away in the garret; it is vacation, and they are needed in the orchards. For miles on miles the dusty roads are worn deep with great four-horse express wagons loaded with boxes of fruit going to the stations, to be shipped thence to San Francisco; or going to the packing houses to be assorted, packed, and sent on fast trains to eastern markets; or going to the canneries, where hundreds of boys and girls, men and women, are waiting with ready knives to receive them; or going to the drying floors, tables, or furnaces, to be prepared for market in still another form. There is vast energy everywhere; the harvests of the orchardist are ripening so fast under the hot summer sun that a day's delay may mean hundreds of dollars lost.

In some districts, if one begins with cherry plums, purple Guigne cherries, and Pringle apricots, and ends with the latest peaches, the fruit season lasts from April till December. June, July, August and September are, however, the months when all the world is on the hillsides, in the vines, or in the orchards of the valleys, gathering the bright, delicate, fragrant harvests. As yet there are only almond orchards among the nut-bearing sorts, but the English and Persian walnuts, the pistachio, the Italian chestnut, and the pecan, are likely to be planted in extensive orchards for profit. These will also belong to the late harvests of the horticulturist. The olive, too, is late in ripening, in the coast region, and like the best wine grapes, requires all the warmth and sunlight to be had. The orange and the lemon, which in this region are not grown extensively for market, but only in small family orchards, ripen their fruit all winter and spring. The Japanese persimmon, with its pointed and rounded fruits of rich golden red, is also one of the winter crops, seldom

IN THE PETRIFIED FOREST—11 FEET DIAMETER.

THE CALIFORNIA GEYSERS. FROM PAINTING BY JULIAN RIX.

Everybody who visits California wants to visit the Geysers, and the trip is one that no one will ever regret. Starting from San Francisco the scenery is one panorama of picturesque loveliness. It is only ninety-six miles, and the train runs through the Sonoma, Russian River and Napa valleys to Calistoga or Cloverdale, where stages are taken for the springs. The place is a great resort for pleasure-seekers, and thousands visit it annually for the benefit of the waters. The Geysers proper are in a canyon, and they spout up from the rocks on every side, throwing out every variety of water, and with temperatures varying from 40 to 212 degrees. For miles in the vicinity springs of different kinds can be found. The lowest is fifteen hundred feet above sea-level, and the highest about two thousand. The scenery around the Geysers is as grand and beautiful as any in the State. Mountain peaks can be seen on all sides, and the canyons and gorges are visions of wild grandeur. The hot springs themselves are beautiful to look at. The steam rises from a dozen rifts in the rocks, which might be called the safety valves of Nature, and fill the air, forming into the most fantastic shapes, and producing the most peculiar effects of light and shade where it partly obscures the trees and rocks. One of the springs is so hot that the steam has killed all vegetation near by, and the spot looks like a vision of the Inferno.

ON THE CREEK.

NAPA SODA SPRINGS.   INSANE ASYLUM, NAPA.

fit to gather
until after a
few light
frosts. In the
very orchards
where all these
sub-tropical nuts and fruits grow, some varieties of apples do well, the yellow Newtown Pippin
keeping till March or April. The full fruit harvest in the Californian foothills can easily be made
to cover the circle of the year.

The earliest fruit grown in all the vast region under consideration is in the Vacaville district.
This covers a large extent of country embracing the upper and lower Vaca Valleys, Pleasant Valley,
Putah Creek, the Winters region, Gates Cañon, Laguna Valley, Bassford Cañon, Miller Cañon,
Weldon Cañon, and some of the foothills bordering on Suisun. This very early fruit is mostly
shipped to eastern markets, and commands such high prices that an acre of warm, rocky hillside
is worth, as far as income goes, as much as half a dozen acres of the very richest bottom lands.
The fruit-growers of this early district rank among the most prosperous and intelligent orchardists
in California, and the region has become famous on account of their extensive enterprises. There
is a rivalry every season, among the different growers, as to which one shall first ship cherries,
apricots, or other fruit. Certain localities in the district excel in some fruits, some excel in
others; but all, as compared with valleys nearer the coast, have a much earlier season. To study
the early fruit region one can take a team at Suisun, and drive around the orchards of that
valley first, then follow the hill road to Laguna Valley, over other hills to Vacaville, and so on,
through a land of rolling hills and fertile valleys, set close with prosperous orchards, to the Putah
Creek and the outlook eastward past Winters in the Sacramento Valley. The high Blue Ridge
that separates this chain of valleys from Napa lies to the west, and aids to give them their especial
shelter and early season. The hills to the east are the last low outworks of the Coast Range, bordering the Yolo and Solano wheat-plains. The district is protected alike from the cold winds and sea-
coast fogs, and from the dry northers of the great interior valleys, but the nights are warm, and
hence the ripening of fruits is greatly hastened. One need not drive from Suisun to visit this
early district, for a railroad line passes through Vacaville and Winters; but the leisurely drive
from Suisun has its advantages. An orchard land with all its shade and fragrance, its fruitage,
and its scenes of joyous labor, should be studied in some such way; it cannot be rightly appreciated from the windows of a railroad car.

Green Valley of Solano is chiefly set in vineyards, as are Napa and Sonoma. The deciduous
fruits come to peculiar perfection in the valleys of the Santa Rosa group, where there are also
innumerable vineyards. At Cloverdale, Sonoma, and Calistoga, and in the Vaca valleys, the
orange and lemon thrive, and fruit excellently. Even as far seaward as San Rafael, under the
shelter of Tamalpais, the orange grows in many a garden. The date palm is one of the trees
that will reach perfection in many of the warmer valleys. The oldest and largest trees in Northern

California, and probably the best fruiting ones anywhere in the state, are the famous Wolfskill Palms near Winters, on the Putah. There are cork oak trees of large size in Sonoma, and carob trees in Napa. In Pleasant Valley there is a large Italian chestnut tree grafted on a wild scrub-oak of the hillsides, and the curious horticultural experiment is an entire success. Gradually, by dint of thousands of individual efforts and expenditures of time and money, new and rare plants and trees are introduced and tested, and the cultivation of the older sorts is developed on a more extensive scale. In such a land horticulture is constantly progressive.

In Napa Valley, next to the great expanse of vine-land through the golden and emerald sweep of the valley itself, the ridges that rise to that isolated height of Howell Mountain form one of the most picturesque regions of the state. Often one can stand in clear sunshine there while fog and cloud roll past, far below. Cool and quiet forests of pine and redwood are on the mountain-top; soft and fair are the hill-tints; sudden and splendid the sunbursts slanting down the rifts of cloud upon the clustering valleys of Conn, and Pope, and Napa; fresh and rain-sprinkled are the new vineyards and the gardens of cottage dwellers in the dim ravines underneath. One watches the clouds rise and climb over the Western Maya-camas, flowing again into the valley; then they lift, and move eastward like armies with their ad-vance guard and banners; shifting colors of faintest rose lie over Mount St. Helena's hood of pearly gray; northward, across the chaos of mountains, lie Mount Hall, Conoceti, and the realm of lakes and streams in the heart of the high Coast Range. Then a sudden rainbow spans the wilderness from battlements of sunlit cloud to purple Mount St. Helena, and a wind rises and scatters the cloud-armies into space. Boundaries there are none,

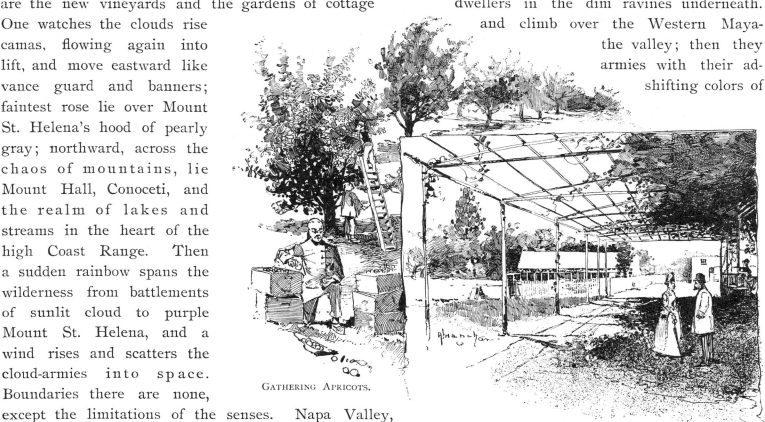

GATHERING APRICOTS.

A VINE-CLAD PORCH, MARK WEST SPRINGS.

except the limitations of the senses. Napa Valley, through its length and breadth shows all its farms outspread, its rambling old ranch-houses, its brick and stone wineries, its beautiful young city, Napa, its villages and churches, its roads and avenues and streams, clear to the shores of San Pablo. The country surveyor, on a summer's excursion, could seat himself at the base of the pine-tree flag-staff, on the highest point of Mount Howell, and gather grapes from the vines around him while he named and platted each farm in the valley for miles.

One of the most attractive spots on Mount Howell is on Anguin Creek, which issues forth from springs on almost the very summit of the mountain, and flows through deep ravines where fern brakes grow higher than one's head, and wild ginger, flags, spotted lilies, scarlet and yellow mimuli, and a great variety of moisture-loving plants congregate. Leaving the swampy and rocky ravines, it flows past woods and clearings, clumps of oaks, fringes of redwoods, slopes planted to vines and orchards, hill-pastures unchanged from the days when Yount the old pioneer settled in 1831 on his famous *La Jota* and Caymus ranches, and past trim summer cottages built for visitors from the valleys. It receives other rills and springs, and before long it approaches the precipi-tous verge of the high mountain plateau. Two long ridges descend from the height; between them lies a wild gorge that at last becomes a sheltered and fruitful valley, where vineyards and gardens lie at the base of the chaparral-clad hills. Into this gorge the stream suddenly plunges, after passing through a broken amphitheatre of black rock, fringed with giant trees and vast dra-peries of vines. This is *La Jota* Waterfall.

Summer days on the borders of all the Coast Range valleys are bright and good. Pioneers are clearing off the woods, burning the underbrush, breaking the soil, building rude cabins, hewing and blasting out roads. Health-seekers and campers are pitching tents, building summer cottages, following the trout streams or botanizing in the ravines. Beside the little flower-gardens where the settler's wife and children plant red roses and white lilies, great bushes of wild azaleas do sometimes grow by mountain springs, and add their glorious grace to the modest garden's blossoming; along the vineyard borders wild grape-vines climb to the utmost tops of the trees, and trail back in dark green curtains to the very ground. Boys gallop past on their tough mustangs; shy and sun-bonnetted little girls go by on their way to school; great wagons carry shakes and lumber from the upper mountain ranges to the valley towns below.

From Santa Rosa west, through the oaks and past grain fields and farm houses, to

NATURAL ARCH OF LAURELS, NEAR EL VERANO.

the hills by Sebastopol, then northward to the Russian River at Guerneville, and up the river to Healdsburg in the main valley, is one of the many delightful journeys in the California foothills, along the valley verges. Much of the way lies close to the margin line between the lands that are all so fertile that none is wasted, and the wilder lands from which men have to wrest a livelihood, hard enough, and yet none the worse for that. It is the peculiar charm of these border lands that they are never quite subdued. Wild flower seeds drift down from the mountains; springs trickle out, and make moist places that cannot be cultivated; song-birds nest in the trees of the foothills far more than in the valley; quails and rabbits dwell in the pasture copses and the sheltering ledges of rock. The man who owns his thirty or forty acres of such land has an infinite variety of uses folded up in his title deeds. He plants half a dozen small orchards in choice localities, no two alike for situation and consequent climate; he has a vegetable garden on the leaf-mould soil of some ravine's mouth; his vineyard, wine-cellars, barns, granaries and stables are on the hillside; his "wood-lot" yields pine and oak lumber for his fencing, tan-bark, fuel for his fire, the Christmas tree and Madrone berries for its garniture, pink urns of Manzanita blossoms for spring-time holidays; he can even stock a deer-park, or construct fish ponds at slight expense, or grow pond lilies by the thousand. All along the ranges of hills west of the Santa Rosa, all

NAPA SODA SPRINGS.

Napa Soda Springs are located on the mountain side, five miles north of Napa and one thousand feet above the valley. The climate is uniform and agreeable, and the waters that flow from the mountain sides are full of mineral salts,—iron and magnesia predominating. The surrounding country, from a scenic standpoint, is as beautiful as any in the State. One of the unique features of the Springs is the grand hotel and the surrounding buildings. They are built of solid masonry, quarried from one of the adjacent mountains. The rock is white and soft when first cut, and is easy to work, but after being exposed to the air a short time soon hardens and becomes softer in color. The main structure is circular in form, and is a magnificent piece of architecture. The grounds belonging to the Springs cover more than a thousand acres, and handsome buildings are picturesquely arranged over the hills and beside the beautiful streams of water. Nature has provided all the materials, and the hand of man has taken advantage of them and created a paradise. Thousands of people visit Napa Soda Springs every year for health and recreation.

PREPARING FOR THE VINTAGE—(KRUG'S).

along the hills between Sonoma and Napa, all along the Napa ravines, endless variety of situation is to be found. Here, a man chooses to build his house on some rounded, oak-covered hill, islanded in a vale; there, he nestles himself and all his belongings down into the shelters where the most tender of semi-tropic growths thrive, and even the leaves of the banana droop unbroken in safe shelter from the ocean winds.

The eastern slopes of the foothills from Sebastopol to the Russian River to which I have alluded, are full of sharp contrasts. In one district the soil is warm sand, in another black and strong adobe, in a third the red mountain soil that is so excellent for fruits and vines. In many of the ravines all these have been mingled ages ago, and form the best of garden soil. There are vales and uplands where a few homesteads are set, and all about them the higher steeps rise, the deeper cañons descend. Mountain flowers and valley flowers mingle by the roadside. A railroad is winding through the heart of the greater valley, linking this whole region with the rest of the state, and yet seeming a thing apart from the cloudy rim of the hills, so purple and golden at sunrise and sunset to the dwellers in the towns below. They look up to the mountains, while hunters and pioneers who move along those greater heights look down past the quiet foothills to the smooth floors of the misty valleys. Between them both, drawing strength from the mountain breasts and calm from the broad vales, the fortunate hill-dwellers have their abiding place.

In these rolling hills the very soil is more friendly and yet more free than elsewhere. The land ever eludes and escapes that close and brutal conquest which hurts men and soil alike. The valley-lands are crushed into subjection, until they yield complete submission, like olives thrice pressed for their oil. The foothill lands of the better sort return quickly to their native wildness if let slip for a few seasons from the dominion of plow and spade. The hillside vines and shrubs come back as of old; the oaks and pines spring up—it is too much a part of the mountains, after all, ever to forget the stock from which it sprang.

Sometimes a man wandering through the hills will find signs of a former garden in the woods and undergrowth. It always seems to harmonize perfectly with its surroundings; it has become a part of nature itself. The La Marque rose that some pioneer planted is high in the oak, or climbing up the rocky hillside; the apple and apricot trees appear a part of the forest already, though the blue-jays have found their fruits better than rose-hips and wild hazel nuts. They are mountain epicures, these chattering blue-jays, and having eaten the apricot pulp, they bore through the stone to get at the kernel. Over the fallen chimney of yellow limestone wild blackberry vines tangle, and mix with the roses run wild. The deserted and ruined place that would be weedy

PICKING HOPS.—RUSSIAN RIVER VALLEY.

The above picture shows a hop-field near Ukiah in the Russian River Valley. It is a characteristic bit of California landscape, and there is no more beautiful sight in the world. From the time the vines appear above the ground in the early spring until the blossoms are ready to harvest in September, a hop-field is an ever-changing picture. At first the vines are thin and scraggly, but in a week or so they lengthen out, and the growers twist them around the strings of the trellis. After that their growth is very rapid, they climb with astonishing speed, and soon the field is a vast image of avenues of verdant green. Late in the summer the blossoms appear, and the air is filled with a rich fragrant odor, while the green vines give place to the right of the blossoms. Gradually the flowers expand, and the green leaves and vines take on a somber hue. When picking time comes the field is a perfect symphony in green and white. Most of the picking is done by Indians, but as the work must be accomplished in a few weeks, all classes pitch in and help. People drop everything else for the work of picking hops, and the fields present the most remarkable activity. In picking hops the vines are torn from the trellis and stripped of the flowers, and it is really a work of devastation. When the harvest is over nothing remains but the bare trellis poles surrounded by the dead leaves of the formerly beautiful vines.

and ugly in the open valley, has slowly melted back into the wilderness of the hills once more, without a regret, and it is sweet and beautiful still.   Some of these days the old rancher who owns the land, and whose house is over the hill in another ravine, will sell this waste corner, and then the new owner will begin its reclamation over again, with the feeling, as he runs across signs of former occupancy, that a century or so has elapsed between.

CLOVERDALE, FROM THE HILLS.

Forgetting for a time the miles upon miles of tree and vine that yield their millions upon millions of dollars in annual vintage over this vast region; forgetting the forests that supply the valleys, and the mineral wealth of the mountain ranges overshadowing the valleys of which we have written, let us glance at the merely beautiful about it all, let us linger in places where, even centuries hence, no orchards can be planted and nature will hold her own forever.   The botanists and the pleasure seekers know something of the Coast Range in this wide region from the ocean to the Sacramento plain, and they are never tired of journeys thither.   Take it first at the extreme east, where Vaca Valley slants south and Utah Cañon descends towards Winters.   The rainfall is heavy and there are many annual flowers and a great abundance of trees—for a region so far inland.   The white oak of the valleys once grew in open groves, and groups of five or six in a place still remain to give a massive beauty to the landscape.   Along the streams are maples, white alders, willows of three or four species, cottonwoods and live-oaks.   On the foothills are mountain white-oaks, black-oaks, madronas, laurels, buckeyes, and a few digger pines.   Of shrubs, the manzanita and the California lilac are most common.   There are bush lupines, and varied species of compositæ, wild grasses, alfileria, wild poppies, buttercups, columbines, larkspurs, platystemons, wild peas, primroses, dodecatheons, sunflowers, gillias, Clarkias, and Collinsias, with asters, goldenrods, and hosts of brilliant yellow annuals for late autumn bloom.   Such native medicinal plants as the low, shrubby *Yerba Santa* and the golden-flowered *grindelia* grow in great abundance.   Another native medicinal plant, that curious vine, the " Big-Root," a member of the order

MOUNT ST. HELENA, FROM CALISTOGA.

" Cucurbitaceæ," is very common in the valley and on the hills.   The most attractive of the winter and spring blooming shrubs is the red-bud, with its rose colored, pea-shaped flowers, which appear before the leaves.   The California holly, or arbutus, with its December crop of bright, scarlet berries, and the lovely low bush of the snow-berry, are also conspicuous in the woods.   On the dry and gravelly ridges, unfit for cultivation, is the " *chaparral*," —a Spanish name for the thickets of scrub-oak —mountain mahogany, manzanita, chemisal, and other low shrubs, which often grow so close as to form dense and impenetrable barriers on the mountain side.   There are occasional paths and openings where cattle find some pasturage, and bees haunt the fragrant blossoming shrubs, but otherwise the chaparral ridges are wholly waste and useless.

If we turn to the moister uplands nearer the bays and the ocean, the open valleys that catch the fog-drift and sea-winds all summer, and are famous for dairies and hill-pasturage, we shall find very different sorts of growth. One can take, if he choose, that partly wooded and wholly charming region that lies north of San Rafael, —anywhere, in fact, between the Lagunitas and the verge of the Petaluma hills. Here, as I remember, there is a spring, and a rock-basin on the hillside above an old, abandoned railroad water-tank, about which wild shrubs have grown these many years. It is on the side of a deep ravine sloping north, and near the union of two other and still deeper ravines. Above it the red hills rise, set with clumps of shrubs, and on their summits are tan-bark oaks and scattered spruces; below it the bank descends gently to a wide stream, beautifully hidden with spring-blossoming shrubs. Far to the east are other hills of golden brown, ripening in the May sunlight, and signs of farms and bits of new orchards show in this direction. Northward, where the trend of the broader ravines is, the hills sink into darker shadows, and a tangled forest of mingled evergreens and deciduous trees. A few tall redwoods stand on the top, but for the most part the conifers have been cut down, and it is a deserted logging camp turned into a dairy farm, and just beginning to waken to the possibilities of horticulture, that we over-   look from the moist   hillside.

Blown from the top of the aban-doned water-

LOGGING IN HURLBURT CAÑON.

REDWOOD TREE-HOUSE, ON RUSSIAN RIVER.

tank, and far down the shrubbery of the winding ravine, the white spray keeps the slope green for many a rod. Purple asters, dark and glittering, bloom on the narrow brink of the stream, beaten into close mats by the soft, perpetual rain. Some day, perhaps, there will be a garden here, with a few acres of farm lands, up and down the ravine, and orchard trees planted where now the azaleas grow; these waste waters will flow in narrow fertilizing channels past almond and apricot, and all this exquisite wildness of copse and thicket must retire from the little mountain vale to linger just outside, on the steeper hills and in the rockier ravines.

The dull and barren look of the California hillsides is only in seeming. It is but a blundering botanist who misinterprets the lack of color along the paths and in the opens. Here, the choicest flowers have been gathered, or cropped by sheep and cattle, so that they were forced to retire to safer nooks. It is not on the pastured slopes or in the thickest woods that the most beautiful flowers grow, but in the old clearings run to waste and on rocky promontories that project into the air and light from vast mountain masses and are so difficult of ascent that a wild goat could hardly cling to their naked precipices. They are retiring farther and farther into the wilderness, where they can grow ungathered by careless hands, untrampled by cattle, uncropped by vandal sheep, sowing their seeds on the scanty soil caught in crevices of the rocks and blooming even more freely than when they grew on the valley borders, in the days before the conquest of California.

Out of the heart of the few acres of woodland, all that is left of the ancient forests of the region, an ice-cold spring trickles down, in the bewitching way that every mountain lad remembers. Masses of fern and lavender-hued ceanothus hide it, and beds of rushes fill the moist hollows be-

SONOMA CREEK, NEAR SOUTH LOS GUILICOS.

neath. Close by are tangles of blackberry and raspberry, white with bloom and red with ripening fruit, and on the hillside large pink wild roses grow. Where the sunlight shines on them all day they have the darkest imaginable of wild-rose flowers; in the shadows they are pale, faint-hearted daughters of the hidden wood-thickets, hard to find, and as quick to fade as the frail spring buttercups of New England. Far up on the broken banks, still in shade, growing from soft beds of fallen leaves, the beautiful pink lily, the Clintonia, holds up its clusters of slender tubes. The seed-pods already show on some stems, and soon will take on the rich blue color that makes them so handsome in late summer. Above the trees, where naked mountain tops rise, there are plant-growths of another sort, orange-hued erysimums, yellow echeverias, stems of cyclobotheras just gone to seed, and the brilliant crimson larkspurs in nodding clusters.

The story of the great foothill regions of the Northern Coast Range, beginning along the tide-waters of the *tule*-bordered bays, and extending across the fair valleys of vine and orchard into the middle slopes and ravines that are just yielding to the plow, ends, properly, in the midst of mountain lands that are too wild to be reclaimed and must ever remain camping grounds and pastures. Northward, clear to the Oregon line, some of the most characteristic features of the foothills I have described are repeated under infinitely varied surroundings. Fertile vales and plateaus

MIDWINTER FAIR BUILDINGS IN GOLDEN GATE PARK. FROM STRAWBERRY HILL.

Few of the many thousands of people who visited the Midwinter Fair realized what a beautiful sight the buildings and grounds made when seen from a distance. A great many visitors, of course, went to the top of the Electric Tower, or round the Firth Wheel, either of which afforded a bird's-eye view of the grounds, but only from the top of Strawberry Hill could a perfect idea be obtained. The above picture was taken from a point close to the top, and the buildings form into a beautiful composition like some Oriental city. Gilded spires and domes flash in the sun, and the many colors used in the decoration form a most harmonious combination. Between the buildings and trees glimpses of the beautiful Golden Gate Park can be seen, which, with its fine drives, beautiful pagodas and flower beds, is one of the finest public recreation grounds in the United States. The hills surrounding the Park are the admiration of all who see them. Far away in the distance the cross of Lone Mountain stands on a hill that rises high above the surrounding country.

lie underneath enormous crags and wildernesses of oak, redwood and pine. But the mountain peninsula between the Pacific and the plain of the Sacramento, and south of the fastnesses of Alpine Lake, contains within its varied districts the types of lowland, fruit-land, vineyard slopes, and all that is properly included in the requirements of a highly developed horticulture.

CHARLES H. SHINN.

THE NEW CITY BY THE GREAT SEA

Serene, indifferent of Fate,
Thou sittest at the Western Gate;

Upon thy heights so lately won
Still slant the banners of the sun;

Thou seest the white seas strike their tents,
O Warder of two Continents!

And scornful of the peace that flies
Thy angry winds and sullen skies,

Thou drawest all things small or great,
To thee, beside the Western Gate.

When forms familiar shall give place
To stranger speech and newer face;

When all her throes and anxious fears
Lie hushed in the repose of years;

When Art shall raise and Culture lift
The sensual joys and meaner thrift,

And all fulfilled the vision we
Who watch and wait shall never see,

Who in the morning of her race
Toiled fair or meanly in our place,

But, yielding to the common lot,
Lie unrecorded and forgot.

— *Bret Harte.* —

F ROM the day of its foundation, when its foundation stones were laid in solid gold—and that seems but yesterday to an old Californian—it has been the custom to contemplate the city of San Francisco from the Golden Gate and the Bay only. But this impetuous young lion of the sea has suddenly attained to the hill tops, descended, and set her swift feet in the waters of the sea of seas. To-day the city of San Francisco is forgetting to turn her face any longer towards the East. The Orient in the West, the waters of India, Japan, the world of waters, solicit her and kneel and woo forever at her feet.

San Francisco to-day is essentially, and almost as entirely as is Venice, a city of the sea. Let the traveler who comes this way by land only continue his westward flight a few moments after crossing the bay and touching the eastern border of our city, and he will be plunged into the Pacific Ocean.

No, at first sight as you approach it from the east, you would not say the "lion's whelp" is cradled in the sea waves, for huge hills heave up in shapely immensity right in your road and right in the heart of the city, as in the heart of Rome; but San Francisco is, for all the hills, essentially a city of the sea.

And yet this magnificent array of waters, grand, glorious, matchless, is overshadowed by the majestic environment of mountains as seen on your approach to San Francisco from your journey around the world by way of India:

Like fragments of an uncompleted world,
From bleak Alaska, bound in ice and spray,
To where the peaks of Darien lie curled
In clouds, the golden land looms bold and gray.
The seamen nearing San Francisco Bay
Forget the compass here; with sturdy hand
They seize the wheel, look up, then bravely lay
The ship to shore by rugged peaks that stand
The stern and proud patrician fathers of the land.

They stand white stairs of heaven,—stand a line
Of lifting, endless, and eternal white.
They look upon the far and clashing brine,
Upon the boundless plains, the broken heigh
Of Kamiakin's battlements. The flight
Of time in underneath their untopp'd towers,
They seem to push aside the moon at night,
To jostle and to loose the stars. The flowers
Of heaven fall about their brows in shining showers.

They stand a line of lifted snowy isles
High held above a toss'd and tumbled sea,—
A sea of wood in wild unmeasured miles;
White pyramids of Faith where man is free,
White monuments of Hope that yet shall be
The mounts of matchless and immortal song.
We look far down the hollow days; we see
The bearded prophets, simple-soul'd and strong,
That strike the sounding harp and thrill the heeding throng.

Serene and satisfied! supreme! as lone
As God! They lord the universal world,
They look as cold as kings upon a throne;
The mantling wings of night are crush'd and curl'd
As feathers curl. The elements are hurl'd
From off their bosoms, and are bidden go,
Like evil spirits, to an under-world.
They stretch from Cariboo to Mexico,
A line of battle-tents in everlasting snow.

The comely and but half-concealed figure of the "Sleeping Lady" in her chaste development of perfect womanhood crowns and makes most perfect the rounded hills within the city of San Francisco. For it is within the "watery walls" of the city that our work lies now, and we must forget, for a time at least, the far and fair environment of white mountains toward the east.

This restful figure of a woman in repose is the first thing that attracts attention as you approach the city by land from the east; and you have only to ascend these gradual hills, glide up and down by the feet of the Sleeping Lady and you will find the Pacific Ocean thundering in her ears only a bow-shot or two distant.

The good monks tell me, in connection with these sloping hills, that it was this half-hidden figure of the mother of men that first inspired the pious Jesuit Fathers to give the name of "Dolores" to their first consecrated mission in this part of California, which is still to be seen standing at the feet of the Sleeping Lady: "Dolores, our pitiful Mother of Pain."

But be this tradition true or false, I beg you stand before this little *adobe* place of prayer at the feet of the Sleeping Lady, with uncovered head. For surely this sloping mountain in the background was at least the battlement, if not the mother, of the Mission Dolores. And the Mission Dolores was the mother of San Francisco. And San Francisco, the wonder of the new world, with her consistency of contradictions, builded on lofty hills yet set in the sea, the greatest seaport in the world, yet solidly built and soberly sustained on foundations of gold and wheat—this singular city has never been unworthy her high origin and her pious founders.

Her mother, or at least her god-mother, is Dolores, and yet for three hundred and sixty-five days in a year San Francisco seems to be one colossal and continuous Newport in midsummer. And to the heart that beats in harmony with this environment, this larger world of things, life here offers an ever brimming, an ever exhilarating cup.

The tremendousness of the waters here—if the awkward word may be indulged, for it really seems as if we need a coinage of new words to pay tribute to these vaster things—the awful

The Golden Gate from San Francisco Bay. From Painting by Frederick S. Cozzens.

"To look down upon this rolling sea of clouds from the higher hills of San Francisco, or the far-away hills of Oakland or Santa Clara, to behold the snow-white fleet of air-built ships glide in through the Golden Gate in still and stately majesty! to see it widen away and move on up the great bay around the battlements of Alcatraz! to see the silent and magnificent procession pass on, rise up to meet the morning sun, and so lift heavenward under the touch of a golden scepter—oh, the color of cloud and sky and sun! the awful and imperial glory of it all! to see this is to see the garment's hem of the Most High."

environment of mountains, the sturdy and perfumed winds that have traveled nearly ten thousand miles to meet us face to face untouched save by the guiding finger of God—surely here is room and surely here is rest for the soul capable of such grandness

To see these long and uninterrupted regiments of waves march in continually! Such waves! Miles and miles and miles of unbroken waters tumbled mountain high or lost upon the land!

Go the girdle of the world, yet you will find no such glory of waters as those that thrash and thunder here. In other lands you may lay your "hand" on the Ocean's "mane," but not so here. The Pacific Ocean permits no familiarity in the region of San Francisco. This world of waters is sombre, gray, weary with its journey from the under world. Why, these long, lifting waves have journeyed for days and weeks and months from "far Cathay." And now they bend and break and kneel, they fall on their faces, they toss their white hands to Dolores on the hill begging her benediction as they sink at her feet and faint and die from very weariness.

MISSION DOLORES.

Here it surely seems that the hands on the dial plate of life should point forever to twelve o'clock. The roar of human progress keeps companionship with the roar of waters! Full tide! Flood tide! Onward and upward continually. You surely rise high above the plane of common life, absorbed in this ardor and this larger earnestness of all things animate and inanimate. But all this splendor of action, this tumult and uproar of elements, this world-building, by man and God together, means nothing or worse than nothing to the aimless and idle man. The weak and worthless clay from which a dull and indolent man is fashioned must be broken up and cast in a better mould before it can fit in here. Yet no well-born man who cares to keep his face to the front and truly live can ever leave this city to take up permanent abode in another land. For other lands and places are in comparison

"As moonlight is to sunlight,
As water is to wine."

It is a frequent saying in London and Paris that to belong to San Francisco is to belong to the nobility. And whatever there may be in this very common remark, it is certain that the man, or woman either, from San Francisco, or indeed from any part of the Pacific Coast, stands head and shoulders above his fellows from elsewhere; as if there might be a sort of special knighthood accorded to those who have crusaded and battled here.

And yet this singularly formed city has only now begun really to grow and really to know her boundless possibilities. True, we have for nearly forty years coined the larger half of the moneys of the earth; true, we have for a long time given gold and given bread to the world; true it is that to-day a countless fleet of foreign ships is waiting within the Golden Gate to carry away our harvest to the hungry millions. But for all that, this great city of churches and school houses and libraries and studios has hardly as yet had time to look in the glass and see how comely and how capable she really is.

But on some near tomorrow, when her hands are less loaded with continued toil in coining moneys and making bread for others, she will call in the services of her Sutros and other eminent engineers, and will thrust great tunnels through and through her innumerable hills, and will wash her hands and her feet and flush her sewers with the tumultuous waters that thunder in from India and Japan. And then the great, the greater, if not the greatest city, will look out and over the Pacific Ocean almost entirely. And then the islands that dot the busy bay will be made beautiful with trees and pleasant gardens, as at Constantinople. But a catalogue of what is to be is beyond my task, and I must content myself with the assurance that the ground is hardly yet broken on our great possibilities.

Less than forty years ago San Francisco was discovered sitting white-winged and weary like some lost bird down in the edge of the water of the bay. Lorn and dreary and storm-blown, she looked as if she would surely rise up and try to fly away so soon as the winds were done with their continual blowing. But the strange, strong bird, blown in from for-eign lands, did not rise up and fly away at all. The flattened white wings only widened out. The white tents turned to brick and stone. The cedars of a thousand

THE BAY AND ALCATRAZ.

Lebanons were hewn down in a day. You still may see the granite houses here that came to us by ships, all the way from China. They were fashioned and put together, like the Temple of Solomon, "without the sound of hammer."

Then fire and ashes! Then a greater city! Then fire and blackened ruins! Then a grander city still.

Then bad men seized the reins of government. And then her true lovers rose up in a day and took the reins in their own hands and hung the traitors as Haman was hanged.

Never since the siege of Troy have there been such brave men, such a gathering together of able, devoted and determined men of the world. Even the flower of Greece did not at all approach these modern Argonauts in loftiness of purpose or nobility of nature. For they went forth to destroy a city; while our heroes came to build a city. Look at a few names now famous in history that were once familiar on these shores—Grant, Sherman, Sheridan, Hooker, Crook in war; Mark Twain, Bret Harte, Stoddard in letters; while Bierstadt leads a list of artists that covers a page.

"NOB HILL," FROM THE BAY.

Rugged and glorious old Quebec, with her lofty battlements cemented together by the blood of Montcalm, Wolfe and Montgomery, is unique in the new world. She stands entirely alone. Romance and heroism are her history. Mexico City, with Cortez and his men smiling under their loads of gold while the gaudy flag of Spain fluttered from the temple to the sun—yes, here again are romance and audacious valor twined together, as in the old world; yet you search the United States in vain for their parallels. And you not only search this hemisphere but the whole world for a parallel story of courage, capacity, persistent endurance and splendid triumph like to this of the glorious city by the great sea.

Not the least of the difficulties encountered by these kingly pioneers was the character of the ground on which the city was to stand. Almost all the peninsula was covered with shifting sand-dunes. And these little heaving, rolling hills of sand seemed to be alive. They kept moving as if they were but a continuation of some long wave of the sea that rolled in, broke up and turned into sand.

There is a story told by an old man to the effect that when a boy he and his captain and the ship's crew walked out to where Golden Gate Park now stands; that the captain and his men fell asleep there and were buried fathoms deep in the rolling sea of sand-dunes.

But what a change! Golden Gate Park, once a sea of white sand, surpasses anything of the kind on this continent, if we may except the great Cypress Park of Chapultepec near Mexico City. It may read a little extravagant to the lovers of Central Park, or Fairmount Park in Philadelphia, to find Golden Gate Park set so entirely to

the front. But this is a matter not in the control of man. You may build and build for a thousand years and will not be able in all that time to produce in New York or any other northern city such beauty of color, such foliage and flowers as our climate gives us in a single decade of judicious care and management.

One of the curious sights here where the sand-dunes and San Francisco, and indeed the continent, conclude together, is the congregation of enormous and apparently innumerable sea-lions on some rocky islands that lift up suddenly and savagely in the roaring rim of the great sea. They moan as continually as the sea moans. They are as restless as the sea; and they are sometimes quite as loud and tempestuous of tongue. In truth I often hear these same sea-lions up at my

house on The Heights across the bay and a mile beyond Oakland, but I rarely hear the roar of the ocean there.

These stormy little islands called "Seal Rocks" are a part of San Francisco; but they are as free from invasion as they possibly could be if defended by all the guns of England. The ocean forbids all approach; and the ocean here is master. These great roaring creatures, be they beast or fish, are entirely unique in action, as in utterance. They are devoted to their young and they nurse them in their arms at the breast as a mother nurses her babe, and quite as tenderly. Here the whole day through, sun or shade, storm or calm, they climb the precipitous crags, toss their huge heads to heaven and howl most

HERE AND THERE IN GOLDEN
GATE PARK.

dismally. And yet in all this howling there is a deep undertone of harmony, a plaintive melody which you will miss for many an hour after you return to your hotel. These wriggling and roaring monsters are singularly intelligent, easily tamed and taught if taken when quite young, and are passionately devoted to home. Years ago one of these large creatures was captured and taken, at great cost, to one of the city "Gardens," or places of public resort, where a little lake, or rather a large tank, with a little rocky island such as he had been used to, had been prepared for his reception. But he was inconsolable and refused to eat or rest. One day when the wind blew in favorably from the ocean he heard the roar of the sea-lions and the thunder of the seas together. Suddenly he lifted his head in the air and howled an answer back that literally shook the rafters of the building and drove every one into the street with terror. Then he wriggled himself up to the top of his little pile of rocks and pointing his head to the sea sat there for days and days, till he died of starvation.

It is worth while climbing to Sutro Heights here to get a grander look at the sea; to say nothing of the semi-tropical gardens which the greatest planter of trees on the Pacific Coast has made on this summit of sand-dunes. For here, where an epitome of the Black Forest of Germany

BEACH AND SEAL ROCKS AT THE CLIFF HOUSE. FROM PAINTING BY C. D. ROBINSON.

"These stormy little islands called 'Seal Rocks' are a part of San Francisco; but they are as free from invasion as they possibly could be if defended by all the guns of England. The ocean forbids all approach; and the ocean here is master. These great roaring creatures, be they beast or fish, are entirely unique in action, as in utterance. Here the whole day through, sun or shade, storm or calm, they climb the precipitous crags, toss their huge heads to heaven and howl most dismally. These wriggling and roaring monsters are singularly intelligent, easily tamed and taught if taken when quite young, and are passionately devoted to home."

now tosses its sombre plumes, and banks of roses block the road at every turn, there was only a little time ago nothing at all but billowy, blowing sand.

The traveler should return to his hotel by the cars that wind in and about and above the Golden Gate; while the sea, the great white bounding sea, is leaping up like a happy dog that licks your hand. I speak of your returning to your hotel because you probably live in a hotel if you live in San Francisco. Not that we have no private houses here; for we have plenty of residences, and of the grandest on earth, as shall be presently shown; but in San Francisco the home is the exception, the hotel the rule. It would be tedious to tell how it first came to be the fashion to live continually in a hotel here; but it is probable that the excellence of the table had a deal to do with it. The fact is, New Orleans came here almost bodily at the first. This was when New Orleans was by long odds the most civilized city in the United States. And this French city of New Orleans brought with her her French cooks. This fact is the backbone of the reason why San Francisco is to-day a city of hotels. But of course beyond this is the dash and audacity of enterprise which compels the inhabitants together more than in other places, in order to transact

SUTRO HEIGHTS.

business and get about all there is to be had out of twenty-four hours in a day. And besides all that, as they have had all this time in their own hands the biggest half of all the gold on earth to pay for the best things of earth, these hotels have kept up to their high standard; established from the first, as said before, by the French cooks of New Orleans.

It is to be admitted that our remarkable markets have a bit to do with the excellence of our hotels also; but the epicure of Paris would hardly come here to wine and dine did we not have cooks. In London the English traveler will dilate long on the delights of the table in San Francisco as he welcomes you to his house. The tourist on his way around the world, if he is at all taught in the refinements of food, will linger long here and pass on with regret. For he well knows that nothing in all the girdle of the earth like the luxury of the San Francisco table can be had for a like sum of money.

And yet we have men still in our midst who saw the gaudy flag of Spain pulled down by the Republic of Mexico from their sea-beaten battlements whereon we have set so much luxury

The courtly Spaniard, with the dash of Moorish blood in his tawny face, is gone; the swarthy Mexican is no more, as a rule, among us. It is true, Spain and Mexico together have left some of their gay color of dress on our streets, just as New Orleans has left her cooks in our hotels; true, neither the Spaniard nor the Mexican is at all conspicuous above the Turkish merchant, the Armenian monk, or the Buddha priest. Indeed, this cosmopolitan and contradictory city is so full of queer people from the four quarters of the globe that the India silk merchant in black petticoat and red fez is of no more concern than is the keen-nosed gentleman of clocks from the verdant hills of Vermont.

SEAL ROCKS.

But the commingling of dress gives a color and a gaiety that is happy and most harmonious under our fervid blue skies. Our most staid and sober citizens have caught this cheerful infection of colors, and you see our best dressed ladies arrayed in emphasis of red and blue and gold that almost any other sky than ours would be out of patience with. Go to church and see what a glorious rainbow of bonnets! Go to the opera or theatre and see what a warm, rich harmony of red this fervid and emphatic city of ours has attained to in less than half a century. Go out on the compact streets any day in the three hundred and sixty-five and mark the roses, the California poppies, the flowers of emphatic color of all kinds which ladies wear at the girdle or breast. Such loads and loads of radiant hue, and harmony, and heavy perfume.

But above all this there is a larger, grander element of color and movement and animation and continual stir. The singular glory of sea-clouds that blow in from Japan and Alaska lends much, when matched with the blue skies above their fleecy whiteness, to this force and emphasis of color.

To look down upon this rolling sea of clouds from the higher hills of San Francisco or the far away hills of Oakland or Santa Clara! to behold the snow-white fleet of air-built ships glide in through the Golden Gate in still and stately majesty! to see it widen away and move on up the great bay around the battlements of Alcatraz! to see the silent and magnificent procession pass on, rise up to meet the morning sun and so lift heavenward under the touch of a golden sceptre— oh, the color of cloud and sky and sun! the awful and the imperial glory of it all—to see this is to see the trailing garment's hem of the Most High.

An untrained savage knows no difference between the color, or the value, of brass and gold. And there are millions of untrained and untraveled men and women, not at all savages, who are colorless enough to call this indescribable benediction of cloud and color and poetry of movement merely a fog. Out upon such blindness and savagery!

For more than forty years the writer of this page has from time to time made his home in and about this city and its environs. And he is free to say that in all that time he has never once seen a fog or even the semblance of a fog in San Francisco if that which they call fog in London and Liverpool is really fog. For, I repeat, as brass is to gold so is the fog of London and Liverpool to the movement and color and indescribable glory of the sun-clouds that blow in upon San Francisco on a sparkling, sunlit summer morning.

To descend from the clouds and get back to the color that emphasizes our streets, it may be observed that my little brown man who burns away his sins on a bit of red paper before a huge and hideous Joss of his own

THE GOLDEN GATE FROM POINT LOBOS.

building is the most curious and uncanny.   He is an intrusion, an impertinence; and yet he is the meekest and the quietest creature born.   He is asleep.   And he has been asleep for thousands of years. And while he slept we stole the secret of making "villainous gunpowder" from him.   We stole the mystery of the mariner's compass from him and by its help discovered America.   We stole the very spectacles from off his ugly little nose as he slept.   The kingly Persian stole his peaches

over the big garden wall and gave them the name of his own vale of Cashmere.   The sailor of Portugal brought home the orange from China and planted it and called it his own.   So that to this day in Italy or Spain an orange is "*un Portugalo.*" We have here the Pekin duck, the Shanghai hen, the China pig.   And if Charles Lamb has "writ from chronicles true," we owe this sleepy, dreamy, dreary idol worshiper, with eyes as bright and black and almost as small as

SURF AT FORT POINT.

PRESIDIO ENTRANCE.

those of a rat, for the costly discovery of the mystery of roast pig.

And yet with all this wisdom of his, here he stands on our cobble stones in paper shoes, silk pantaloons, and a short cotton petticoat!

ALCATRAZ.

IN THE PRESIDIO.

If you walk will see the silent and at many a door precisely ways of Rome or Con- silent here as he is there; garrulous and gay, here, the Orient is broken off and lodged and bit of the Past.   A good the unclean streets, rocking and clothes gorgeously col- through one of their streets you solitary little shoemaker sitting as you see him in the door- stantinople.   This shoemaker is while all the folk about him are same as there.   In fact a bit of the here at our door; a bit of the Orient many little children toddle up and down along in little paper shoes, and silk caps ored.   In fact a Chinese child is of itself

a sort of animated flower-pot in silk.   Oftentimes you see a fat Chinese father holding his dear little flower-pot by the hand.   And to see this toddling little flower-pot stop and suddenly turn around and throw its little bundled arms around one of its papa's legs and embrace that leg so far and fondly as it can for the superabundance of petticoat is curious, if not affecting.   They, father and child, are certainly fond of one another.

The Chinese theatre is a confusion of colors and of hideous harmonies.   The musicians (?) all sit on the stage behind the actors.   The entrances are the same as those in fashion at the

Interior of a Chinese Restaurant. From Painting By John Durkin.

"It is interesting to go to a first-class restaurant here and take tea. You buy all you want, and he puts it in a thin and beautiful porcelain cup. Then another little fellow toddles along with a brass kettle full of boiling water. And this little fellow will pour hot water on your tea till twelve o'clock at night, and it costs you nothing. The tea is good, of course, but the bread is bad, the fish is worse; and indeed everything is good to let alone, except perhaps the tea and candy. If you are a person of distinction, the cup and saucer and porcelain spoon are carefully wrapped up and presented to you. But you are expected to present the man who deals out the tea a five-dollar gold piece in return. If you are not a person of distinction you can buy the pretty porcelain cup and saucer and pay your bill also for fifty cents and go your way."

time of the destruction of Herculaneum; no curtains, but the actors make their entrances from the right and left of the musicians. Like the Greeks of old, they do not allow women on the stage. And even the women in the audience are set apart and back in the corners of the top gallery. The play is merely a record of their history, and I am told that one play may be fifteen years long! You buy a ticket for half a dollar, go in and sit till lunch time, then go out and come back again and sit till dinner time, then you come back and stay till midnight. About this time your ticket is supposed to be exhausted, and, if still alive, you had better go home.

It is interesting to go to a first-class restaurant here and take tea. One little man in red cap and paper shoes rocks about the room with tea. You buy all you want, and he puts it in a thin and beautiful porcelain cup. Then another little

IN CHINATOWN.

fellow toddles along with a brass kettle full of boiling water. And this little fellow will pour hot water on your tea till twelve o'clock at night, and it costs you nothing. The tea is good, of course, but the bread is bad, the fish is worse; and indeed everything is good to let alone except perhaps the tea and candy. If you are a person of distinction, the cup and saucer and porcelain spoon are carefully wrapped up and presented to you. But you are expected to present the man who deals out the tea a five dollar gold piece in return. If you are not a person of distinction you can buy the pretty porcelain cup and saucer and pay your bill also for fifty cents and go your way.

A "Joss."

May I be permitted to say that outside of the theatre and the Joss house, almost all you should care to contemplate in this quarter is to be encountered in the open streets? I feel it a sort of duty to insist upon this suggestion, and not at all because of the danger of infectious diseases, but because of a sort of moral disease, a sickness of mind which has put the depraved part of this quarter on exhibition. If you must see depravity, why, see it among your own kind and at less risk from small-pox, leprosy, and the like.

When living in Damascus I heard a story to this effect : a prince of that city went out into the Public Gardens to see the flowers that stood in pots on the marble steps that led to the fountains. But a miserable and dyspeptic old king who had preceded him took a pot that contained a rare and fragant rose and turning it upside down emptied out the earth, and there in the roots displayed to the prince a disgusting worm. And so the old king continued; at the root of every flower in the rich and nourishing soil he found grubs and bugs and worms and slugs.

Keeping this story in mind—for there is no flower without the hideous worm or slug at the root of it—you may be able to see some color, possibly even extract some sort of pleasure here

from this ancient heathen. But enough and more than enough of this people, to whom low politicians continually call the attention of the State and Nation. There are a thousand better things to behold in the growth and grandeur of this young city.

But to say that San Francisco owes all that she is and is to be to her own stout heart and steady march forward over many dangers, would be to say more than she would desire said of her.

Far back in the dawn of our nation's history you see dimly outlined the figures of Thomas Jefferson, Thomas H. Benton and other great world-builders. You see Benton rising in his place in the Senate and pointing to the future birth-place of San Francisco, as he cries:

"Yonder lies the East:

"Yonder lies the road to India."

When Jefferson purchased Oregon of France and first set the stars of our flag to blaze above these Pacific Seas he was compelled to explain to Congress that the purpose of an expedition to Oregon was "to open up overland commercial relations with Asia!"

You may frequently see reference to the Golden Gate in connection with the discovery of gold in California. The impression is popular that the one took its name from the existence of the other. Not so. The Golden Gate received its name from John C. Frémont long before gold was found by Marshall at Sutter's Mill. This intrepid explorer explained to the writer that the gold and glory of the sunset as seen from the hills to the east of the Golden Gate simply compelled that name. The Golden Gate got its name from its own gold.

If you should visit the old Frémont Springs in the direction of Mount Diablo from San Francisco and almost half way to the summit of the Contra Costa Mountains and sit down there at sunset, you would see the name "Golden Gate" written in gold on every gate-post, hillside or sea wave in sight.

Stand here where this young traveler pitched his tent nearly fifty years ago and watch the sun go down as he watched it for so long, looking away out and over "the road to India" and you will understand. You may sometimes see black storm-clouds, you may see banks of clouds that are as white as wool, clouds with a silver lining, all sorts of mobile elements of the

CHINESE MARKET.

CHINESE MERCHANT
AND BAZAAR.

air, but still always the dominant hue of the horizon here at that hour is gold! Old gold! New gold! Beaten gold! Molten gold! Mountains and seas of mobile and of massive gold! Behold the sun roll down the golden beams and lodge right in the Golden Gate, block it, fill it full! The gates take fire! The sea is gold, the sun is melted down as it sinks out of sight and speeds away out towards India with ten thousand miles of molten gold! See this and you will then not only understand why the place bears its name but will also understand why this spot to the man who loves color and the majesty of nature is above all on earth. But let us quote from Frémont:

"The Bay of San Francisco has been celebrated, from the time of its discovery, as one of the finest in the world, and is justly entitled to under the seamen's view of a mere harbor. But when all the accessory that character even advantages which belong to it—fertile and picturesque dependant country; mildness and salubrity of climate; connection with the great interior valley of the Sacramento and San Joaquin; its vast resources for ship timber, grain and cattle—when these advantages are taken into the account with its geographical position on a line with Asia, it rises into an importance far above that of a mere harbor, and deserves a particular notice in any account of maritime California.

"Its latitudinal position is that of Lisbon; its climate is that of Southern Italy; settlements upon it for more than half a century attest its healthfulness; bold shores and mountains give it grandeur; the extent and fertility of its dependant country give it great resources for agriculture, commerce, and population.

"The Bay of San Francisco is separated from the sea by low mountain ranges. Looking

U. S. Mint

Union Square.

Hall of Records

Market and Kearney Sts. Lotta Fountain

Polytechnic School

City Hall.

CHARACTERISTIC BITS OF SAN FRANCISCO.

The above collection of pictures represents different portions of San Francisco. They are, in fact, views of the most unique and characteristic bits of the city. Lotta's Fountain is one of the landmarks. It was presented to the city by the famous actress, and stands at one of the busiest spots in the whole world. It is in a certain sense the center of San Francisco, as people get in the habit of calculating all distances from that point. It is also the city's flower market, and during certain hours of the day is a perfect blaze of color. The United States Mint is a fine old doric structure, of most imposing appearance and architectural grandeur. Union Square is the down-town park of the city, and at all seasons of the year is a restful spot of green. The Hall of Records is the eastern end of the New City Hall, and as a piece of architecture is one of the most unique creations in the United States. The other view of the City Hall proper is taken from the Park-street side and shows the tower. The Polytechnic School is very much like other institutions of learning in the city. It is artistic in appearance, and is built in accordance with the needs of teachers and pupils. As a whole this collection of views makes a good showing, and gives an idea of the basis of San Francisco, or for that matter California, architecture.

from the peaks of the Sierra Nevada, the coast mountains present an apparently continuous line, with only a single gap, resembling a mountain pass. This is the entrance to the great bay, and is the only water communication from the coast to the interior country. Approaching from the sea,

the coast presents a south, the bordering in a narrow ridge of in a precipitous point, breaks heavily. On the tain presents a bold few miles to a height of

bold outline. On the mountains come down broken hills terminating against which the sea northern side, the moun- promontory, rising in a two or three thousand feet. Between these points is the strait—about one mile broad in the narrowest part, and five miles long from the sea to the bay. To this gate I gave the name of *Chrys- opylæ*, or *Golden Gate;* for the same reasons that the harbor of Byzantium (Constantinople afterwards), was called *Chrysoceras*, or *Golden Horn.*

"Passing through this gate, the bay opens to the right and left, ex- tending in each direction about thirty- five miles, having a total length of more than seventy, and a coast of about two hundred and seventy-five. It is divided by straits and projecting

points into three separate bays, of which the northern two are called San Pablo and Suisun Bays. Within, the view presented is of a mountainous country, the bay re- sembling an interior lake of deep water, lying between parallel ranges of mountains. Islands, which have the bold character of the shores—some mere masses of rock and other grass-covered, rising to the height of three and eight hundred feet—break its surface, and add to its picturesque appear- ance. Directly fronting the entrance, moun- tains a few miles from the shore rise about 2,000 feet above the water, crowned by a forest of lofty cypress (redwood), which

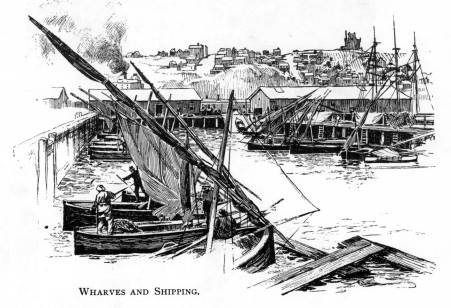

WHARVES AND SHIPPING.

is visible from the sea, and makes a conspicuous landmark for vessels entering the bay. Behind, the rugged peak of Mount Diavolo, nearly four thousand feet high, (3,770), overlooks the surround- ing country of the bay and San Joaquin.

"The immediate shore of the bay derives, from its proximate and opposite relation to the sea, the name of *Contra-costa* (counter-coast or opposite coast). It presents a varied character of rugged and broken hills, rolling and undulating land, and rich alluvial shores backed by fertile and wooded ranges, suitable for towns, villages, and farms, with which it is beginning to be dotted. A low alluvial bottom-land several miles in width, with occasional open woods of oaks, borders the foot of the mountains around the southern arm of the bay, terminating on a breadth of twenty miles in the fertile valley of San José, a narrow plain of rich soil, lying between ranges from two to three thousand feet high. The valley is openly wooded with groves of oak, free from underbrush, and after the spring rains, covered with grass. Taken in connection with the valley of San Juan, with which it forms a continuous plain, it is fifty-five miles long and one to twenty broad, opening into smaller valleys among the hills. At the head of the bay it is twenty miles broad; and about the same at the southern end, where the soil is beautifully fertile, covered in summer with four or five varieties of wild clover, several feet high. In many places it is overgrown with wild mustard, growing ten or twelve feet high, in almost impenetrable fields, through which roads are made like lanes. On both sides the mountains are fertile, wooded, or covered with grasses and scattered trees.

CASTLES IN THE AIR—IMPRESSIONS OF "NOB HILL."

On the west it is protected from the chilling influence of the northwest winds by the *Cuesta de los gatos* (Wild-cat ridge) which separates it from the coast. This is a grassy and timbered mountain, watered with small streams, and wooded on both sides with many varieties of trees and shrubbery, the heaviest forests of pine and cypress occupying the western slope. Timber and shingles are now obtained from this mountain; and one of the recently discovered quicksilver mines is on the eastern side of the mountain near the Pueblo of San José. This range terminates on the south in the *Anno Nuevo* point of Monterey Bay, and on the north declines into a ridge of sloping hills about five miles wide, between the bay and the sea, and having the town of San Francisco on the bay shore, near its northern extremity."

It is to be noted that the cold and precise lines of a government officer's report to his Department at Washington loses somewhat their dullness and stupidity when reciting the singular advantages and attributions of this spot where San Francisco now stands.

Nearly twenty years ago the writer drew into the Bay of Naples with a romantic notion of its beauty which the travelers of twenty centuries had heightened beyond measure. But there is no comparison between the two places. You have Vesuvius at Naples, but there is no other sign of like in the whole surroundings. You miss the clouds and the color of San Francisco Bay almost entirely. Instead you have the blue of the bay, the blue of the sky of Naples, the blue of all things about, yourself included if you attempt to remain there. Yes, Vesuvius is a constant comfort to lift your face toward and see its perpetual banner of smoke flutter and fly away; but Vesuvius is small, a strangely small affair to have such a name, especially to a man on terms of intimacy with the peaks of snow on the Pacific.

It may be mentioned here, if not digressing too widely, that on the third night I was hurled from my hard bed to the floor by an earthquake. I searched the newspaper early next morning to get the details. Not a word. I went to the editor. He neither knew nor cared anything about it.

"But do you never report these things?"

"*Certe, Signor*," smiled the polite child of the "twelve Cæsars;" "Whenever anybody is killed we never fail to report the earthquake." According to this man's way of looking at it, we can say that we have thus far almost entirely escaped such things as earthquakes in California. Indeed, the houses of San Francisco are, every one, standing witnesses against the occurrence of earthquakes in San Francisco. One of our many hills is crowned by edifices so airy and so light in their matchless elegance that they surely could stand but a little time in any part of Italy or Greece. Write it down from the testimony of these ten thousand unimpeachable witnesses that such a thing as an actual earthquake was really never known in San Francisco.

On the top of this hill—accessible by the cable cars, a San Francisco invention—some of

LONE MOUNTAIN, FROM GOLDEN GATE PARK.

the most enterprising and prosperous men of this age have grouped together and built palaces that surpass anything to be found on the banks of Como or the shores of the Adriatic. From their immense accumulations they have given back to the state and city great splendor and much that adds to the commonwealth. It may read extravagantly to strangers, but here on this height overlooking both bay and ocean is built the largest and costliest "brown stone front" in the world. Indeed it is vastly more than a brown stone front. It is an entire block. From the palaces of splendor let us go down to their market.

"You are to estimate the civilization of a city by the excellence and quantity of its markets," cried old Dr. Johnson one day with delight as he made the rounds of the stalls. If you will estimate the refinement of San Francisco by the same standard, it will be found that she stands far ahead of the whole world. But here the Californian is careful again to not arrogate all this surpassing excellence to his own enterprise and attainment. He frankly concedes that he no more created the juices of the countless varieties of grape or the flavor of our rare fruits than he created the gold which his energy wrung from the rock-ribbed hills. Yet all this unapproachable excellence of fruit and meat and milk and honey is as surely the staple of our market as was ever the existence of such a person as Dr. Johnson.

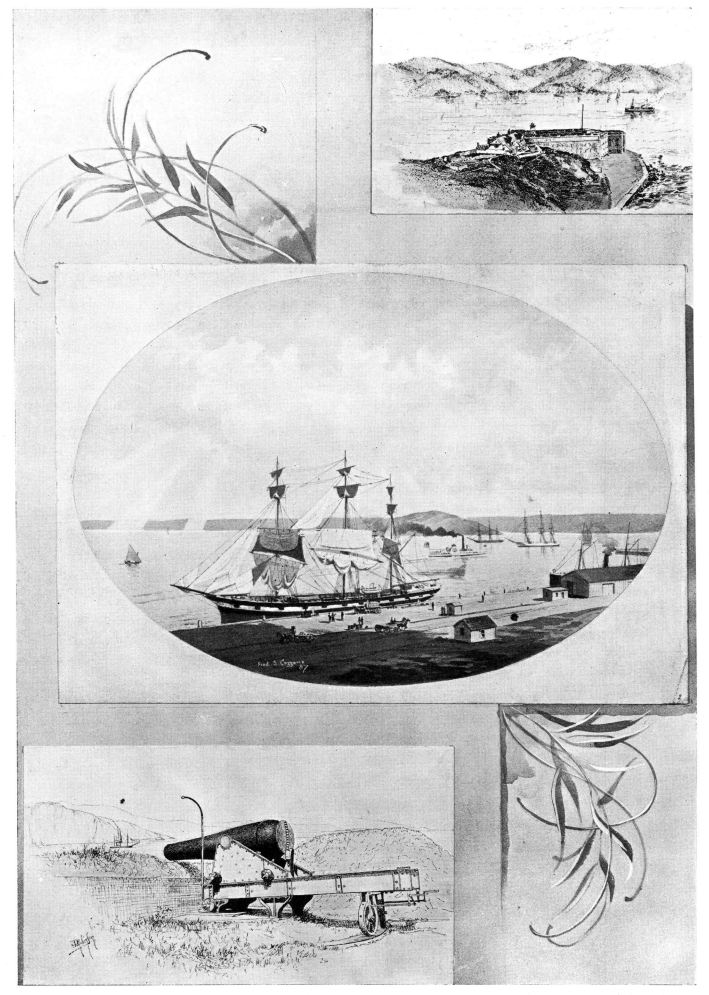

AROUND SAN FRANCISCO BAY.

FORT WINFIELD SCOTT—ALONG THE SEA-WALL—EARTHWORKS ABOVE FORT POINT (SHOWING A GUN WHICH WELCOMED
GENERAL GRANT HOME IN THE FALL OF 1879).

"Passing through this gate, the bay opens to the right and left, extending in each direction about thirty-five miles,
having a total length of more than seventy, and a coast of about two hundred and seventy-five.   *   *   *   Within,
the view presented is of a mountainous country, the bay resembling an interior lake of deep water lying between parallel
ranges of mountains.   Islands, which partake of the bold characters of the shores—some mere masses of rock, and
others grass-covered, rising to the height of three and eight hundred feet—break its surface, and add to its picturesque
appearance."

Bear in mind that California is to-day furnishing Europe with bread, meat, wine, fruit and many of the delicacies. In many parts of this State such things as rabbits, squirrels, quail, and in fact a dozen creatures that might be of great esteem for food in all other parts of the world, are here destroyed by the car-load to keep them from the fields of the farmer.

Such fish! Ducks the year through; five kinds of remarkably fine ducks.

"San Francisco?" said the Princess Louise at her table in the Citadel of Quebec to the writer, "San Francisco not only can live better, but she certainly does live better, than any other city in the world."

This of course is entirely true; and it may be a sort of necessity. For surely the people here are the most tireless and continuous workers to be found on the globe. Take for example the men who make the books and papers. Statisticians tell us that we publish in comparison with other cities almost ten papers to one! Of course these papers are read or they would not be published. It is told of a famous singer on her first appearance here, that on retiring from the front of the stage, where she had been called by tremendous applause, she suddenly heard a singular rustle and rattle of papers; and, on looking back over her shoulder, she saw that every man, woman and child had instantly dug up a paper and buried a nose in it. It may be because there is a constant inquiry toward this part of the new world, but a California newspaper is a pretty good passport to an Englishman's heart every day in the year. And if these same papers could give the world a little more of California and a little less of China, a little more about Californians and a little less about Chinese, the world would be a bit better pleased and a great deal better off. The same papers could do better work with the better theme, surely.

It was the custom of Rome to send forth and destroy every rival. And this is the old-new story of "the survival of the fittest." The rod of Moses must devour all other rods. There can be but one great city on this sea coast. The five prosperous republics to the south must pay tribute to us. The five railroads, no matter much where they terminate, must pour their produce and their people in at our gates. San Francisco is, and to the end must remain, the New York of the broader and better side of this continent; and the Orient must pay her continual court and tribute.

"Yonder lies the East:
"Yonder lies the road to India."

"All things are his," says the Spanish proverb, "who has the courage to wish." I cannot prove to you that this new city by the great sea will some day soon be the greatest city on the globe. We must have some faith. For I cannot even prove to you that the sun will rise to-morrow; but I surely think the sun will rise. You see it takes a little faith, even in so ordinary an office as the rising of the sun.

So here she sits at the Golden Gate,
  The city of Gold and of Destiny,
Nor uttering loud but daring to wait
  With high face held to the ultimate sea.

JOAQUIN MILLER.

ON THE HEIGHTS.

While round the rock where bask the seal
The gulls in sunny circles wheel,
The waters of the Golden Shore
Lave her fair sands, and fret no more.

A charm is on the sea, the bay,
The glist'ning whitecaps melt away:
Between the brown walls silently
The dipping ships are steering by.

A shape unseen, of might unguess'd,
Sits at this gateway of the West;
Smiling, she waits here by the sea,
Beck'ning our glories yet to be.

J. VANCE CHENEY.

The Sacramento Valley

T HE inexhaustible beauties of California seem to be only just undergoing discovery by the unfortunate millions who had not seen them face to face. The world that reads of the picturesque and longs for it, but has to be satisfied with the picture only, has been slow to comprehend that here is every conceivable beauty that nature can paint in valleys and frame with mountains.

The second largest of the states, there is no spot on its surface from which one may not look from a valley up to many mountains or from the mountain down upon many valleys. Fancy an area three times as large as Iowa, so pervaded by mountain ranges that the traveler is never out of sight of their ridges, escarpments and summits. These mountains begin at the ocean side, and as they recede landward the walls of each succeeding range rise higher and the valleys between them are wider and longer, until the great valley of California is crossed and with your face to the sunrise you confront the final wall, the Sierra Nevada, the mountain of the saw of snow, that barrier more than eight hundred miles long, with all its gates and passes in the region of perpetual snow, by which for centuries California was held unapproachable from the east. This mountain fortification and the great valley which it guards, and the wide ocean beyond, are the three physical facts which give to the state its singular climatic individuality. The fervent sun beating upon the valley heats so great a surface that quick evaporation follows, and as the mountains are highest to the east, the vacuum caused thereby must be filled by air that has been cooled by the sea. So it comes to pass in the long summer days that high insolation in the valley causes at evening the grateful and bracing breeze from the sea, and as this rolls inland it lifts the burden of the day off the tired spirits of those who have borne it, and they sleep blanketed, on pillows that are cooled by the breath of the unsleeping ocean. As the sun returns to pay his vertical respects to the Southern Hemisphere, evaporation ceases to lift the moisture into the upper air for transportation to distant regions. Land and water are nearer the same temperature and the clouds from the sea roll up the Sierra Nevadas, from plain to pinnacle, precipitating a rain-fall that increases one inch to each hundred feet of rise, until at the summit of the mighty wall it becomes snow which falls and falls from October till March until sometimes it is forty feet in depth, and men and horses cross its hard crusted surface on snow shoes.

At exceptional times the lower ranges that lie between the Sierras and the sea receive a snow-fall which lies upon their summits for weeks, and then is seen a panorama that no other land can hope to equal until God's hand shall have refashioned the world and what is now beneath shall be above the waters and what is now above shall sink beneath. Between the white ranges lie the green valleys, brightened by masses of wild flowers, as big as a principality, with the bloom of orchards and the blush of roses and the aroma of violets all about, and the same sunset kisses to sleep the spicy blossoms of the plain and the unfeeling lichens far above that rest under their blanket of snow. The deep snows that lie perpetually on the high Sierras above the timber-line and melt continually but never disappear, have nourished the mighty forests that outline the valley on the east, which are so rich in the resinous woods, the conifers and the oaks around whose feet bloom the flowers that love the cathedral-like solitude of the woods.

On this westward slope, under the shelter of these noble trees and the dense chaparral that clothes the sides of the cañons, in crystal springs fed by the snow, originate the rivers which carry back to the sea the water that it sent to the mountains in the clouds. This great upraise is the reservoir that stores the water which makes the rich valley fruitful. Remove the mountains, or deforest them, and the valley would be a desert, hopeless and hapless. Fitful rains would give its favored spots a short-lived verdure; but without the springs which now lie far above it, neither plant nor animal would long exist where now flourish both forms of life. But this mountain frame of the valley is not only the footing for eight hundred miles of forest and the source of many rivers and thermal and mineral springs; it is a vast safe-deposit where nature has stored mineral treasures of greater value and importance than have been found elsewhere upon the earth. Here are mines of gold and silver, and cinnabar and copper, of iron and of onyx, granite, marble and porphyry; diamonds, rubies and amethysts have been found in its mass of minerals; so it is not wonderful that a Californian abroad should be hailed in the words of the Prophet to the Prince of Tyros:—"Thou hast been in Eden, the garden of God; every precious stone was thy covering, the sardonyx, the topaz and the diamond, the beryl, the onyx and the jasper, the sapphire, the emerald and the carbuncle and gold: the workmanship of thy tabrets and thy pipes was prepared in thee on the day thou wast created."

This prelude to the description of a part of the picturesque area of the state seems necessary to prevent the mind of the reader from receiving a narrow impression from contemplation of a part of the scene which makes the mighty entirety of California. Of course there can be no valley without enclosing walls, and the impression made by these belongs to the valley itself. When these walls are such proud, grand and impressive battlements as are about the valleys of California, let description try in vain to do them justice. While the valley changes with seed-time and harvest below, above, between it and the clouds, the pines stand guard over the fountain; waterfalls and cascades sing without ceasing, the mountain lion and the great bear dispute the primacy of the forest, the doe hides her young and the brown pheasant drums at day-break to rouse the army of living things which dwell amongst the trees.

NIGHT IN THE SACRAMENTO VALLEY.

The moon hangs white and high
As 'twere in Winter sky;
The large stars dim her light,
And rule the noon of night.

The heavens! not one cloud there,
No mist in all the air;
The white Sierras keep
Their watch, the lowlands sleep.

The windmill round and round
Turns on with drowsy sound;
Deep in her dreams she lies
This vale of Paradise.

—J. Vance Cheney.

A desire for accuracy of detail has confirmed the custom of dividing the valley of California into two parts. In like manner San Francisco Bay, that greatest of our inland seas, is locally divided into a half dozen bays, but it is all one water, and the evidences of geology are that it once filled the valley whose streams now enter it by a common delta. In that far time picturesque California was like another world. The peaks of the Sierras, from Whitney to Shasta, were active volcanoes, raising pillars of cloud by day and of fire by night, making lurid the waters that rolled from Tehama to the Tehachapi. Those great volcanic torches lighted that age to its close, and where that sea had been their mighty mirror there is now a valley. This great trough is elevated at the ends, and sags in the middle where the two streams that flow from either extreme and give a name to

FARALLONE ISLANDS AND LIGHT-HOUSE. FROM PAINTING BY JULIAN RIX.

A group of volcanic rocks in the Pacific Ocean about thirty miles west of San Francisco constitute the Farallone Islands. At all seasons of the year they are most forbidding in appearance, and storm-clouds and fog hover over the peaks. There is a light-house on the highest peak of the largest island that is considered one of the most important stations in the world. All ships entering San Francisco have to pass these islands, and they are always dangerous on account of the tides and waves. The ocean around the islands is never quiet, and the light-house tender that takes supplies out two or three times a year is often compelled to "lay to" for days before a landing can be made. There is only one small cove that answers for a harbor, and in there the waves are always rolling. To make a landing is a difficult matter. The islands are almost devoid of vegetation, but millions of sea-birds make their homes on the barren rocks, and rear their young. The waters on the bar near the islands are the finest fishing-grounds on the coast, and fishing-steamers take out large parties, who generally catch more of the finny tribe than they can carry.

each half escape into the bay. These two watersheds are alike in soil, climate and productions, except that the San Joaquin is naturally more arid and in its upper part was actual desert, where extensive irrigation now induces a production that is tropical in its variety and value.

Over the north end of the Sacramento Valley Mount Shasta stands guard under a gleaming helmet of snow that is never lifted, even to salute the sun. In the southwest, nearly three hundred miles away, Mount Diablo may be seen from the summit of Shasta, as you look down the median line of the valley that stretches its length from this snow peak of the Sierras toward that sinister sentinel which overlooks the Contra Costa range.

The Sacramento River issues from the base of Mount Shasta in mighty springs, the streams from which brawl under the shade of the piney woods until they are confluent in the cañon of the Sacramento, down which the river goes roaring between narrow walls of rock and still narrower walls of bloom of the wild azalea, dogrose, calycanthus and other sweet flowering plants and shrubs.

GOVERNOR'S MANSION.

The yew tree bends to touch its foam and the pines echo its song. Springs of medicinal waters, the blend of minerals stored away in the volcanic age of Shasta, issue from the cliff on the left bank, and other springs burst out in torrents many rods in width that leap to join the river over a background of evergreen moss. Sometimes the foliage is drawn apart like a curtain, exposing walls of columnar basalt or large faces of malachite and azurite; for these everlasting cliffs between which the river runs from its prison under Shasta to freedom on the far plains are highly mineralized, the stream passing between mines of gold and silver and copper. But its waters here are as stainless as a star and so clear that the fisherman may almost select the trout to which to offer his fatal attentions.

The beauties of this cañon deserve protection as much as the more famous charms of the Yellowstone and Yosemite valleys. If its forest-clad slopes are left as nature dressed them it will be one of California's pleasant places; therefore commerce, with conquering axe and saw, should be forbidden here. These trees would make lumber? Yes, and the few pieces of Greek statuary and architecture that have survived the ages would break up into stones to wall a well or build a sewer, but we do not degrade them to such uses, albeit they are the creation of merely human genius. Joaquin Miller has said, "No architect that ever lived could build a tree." Nature built these trees, selected their wonderful variety, planted them in the groups that hide or foil the rocks, gave to one the charm of verdure only and to another added bloom. Let us give her handiwork in this place as much respectful care and shelter as we do to that which men wrought in ages long gone by. Then to this spot will many come and listen to the song of the river as it begins its journey, typical of life. At first cradled in flowers, sporting and leaping in the sun; later on toiling commercially by turning wheels, washing gold, aiding tillage and carrying boats and barges; and after defilement by cities, as they do defile us all, to sink in the ocean eternal.

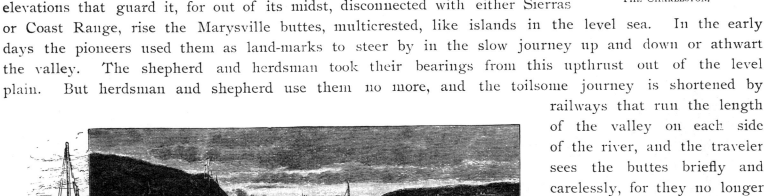

Between its mountain birthplace and its meeting of the tides, it has fallen four thousand feet and has traversed a valley which was baptised in its name and is destined to baptism in its waters.

The mountain summits which overtop its extremes are not the only elevations that guard it, for out of its midst, disconnected with either Sierras or Coast Range, rise the Marysville buttes, multicrested, like islands in the level sea. In the early days the pioneers used them as land-marks to steer by in the slow journey up and down or athwart the valley. The shepherd and herdsman took their bearings from this upthrust out of the level plain. But herdsman and shepherd use them no more, and the toilsome journey is shortened by

THE CHARLESTON.

STRAITS OF CARQUINEZ.

railways that run the length of the valley on each side of the river, and the traveler sees the buttes briefly and carelessly, for they no longer lift their pinnacles like pointed fingers to guide his journey. The eastern boundary of the valley is the Sierra Nevada range, the American Himalayas; its western boundary the Coast Range. Within these boundaries the pioneers saw it when in the season of verdure it rolled like an emerald sea, its billows breaking in voiceless surf at the feet of the mighty mountains which towered above it, glistening with snow or opalescent with the foliage of the manzanita or the chaparral. As the season changed and the sun shone with greater fervor they seemed to see the emerald evaporate as the grasses ripened like a field of wheat, and as the heat shimmered along the lion-colored earth the mirage gathered vley and willow copse and tawny dune, with fantastic finger changing them into homes and temples, parks and lakes, and lifting them into the air to foretell the towns and cities that were to be.

Once given over to pastoral occupation entirely, the 6,645 square miles area of this valley was like the Chaldean plains. Sheep and cattle on foot and herders and shepherds on horseback were its only living tenants. The land had only a grazing value for the pasture plants it produced, and for the possession of these rival stockmen struggled. The evolution of its utility furnishes a history that is common to all California. The men of Spanish blood who came here, with that knack of all the Latin races for taking pot-luck with the aborigines which is a survival of the Roman genius of adaptation that made the imperial eagles at home equally upon the Euphrates and the Mersey, counted their wealth not in the land but in the stock that grazed it. When one of those olive-skinned shepherd-kings of early California died, he willed his sheep and cattle and horses to the children whom he loved for their obedience and thrift; but to those who were prodigal and unforgiven he willed lands, the equivalent of cutting them off with a shilling. Alas,

STORE-SHIP AT MARE ISLAND.

for the practical forces of nature which will not be kept in bonds to help the dead hand give and with-hold! The flocks and herds and horses are not, and the children of those who inherited them in poverty execrate the unwise wisdom of their fore-elders, while the children of the prodigals who were punished with real estate are moved to thank heaven that their fathers were scapegraces worthy only to in-herit land. The evolution of its nobler utilities has passed from the pastoral stage through the cereal period, until now on these despised acres the vine and fig tree flourish; the palm, king of vegetables, spreads its fronds; the olive, with one side of its leaves silvered by the tints which it took from the dove's wing when the waters were receding, yields its oil; and that which one gen-eration rejected has grown to be the mighty inheritance of its successor.

Eight great counties share between them the Sacramento Valley. Some span it and rest each side upon its mountain boundaries, like a scroll unrolled with its edges raised. Others have one

MARYSVILLE BUTTES, FROM BOGG'S RANCH.

A GLIMPSE THROUGH THE TREES—SACRAMENTO RIVER.

side upon the mountain walls and one flung like a banner upon the plain below. Of the whole number Sutter alone reaches neither the Coast Range nor the Sierras. But to compensate it the Marysville *buttes* rise from its midst like that "arm clad in white samite, mystic, wonderful," that waved the "brand Excalibur." The other seven counties are Tehama, Butte, Colusa, Yuba, Yolo, Sacramento and Solano. The very names have the flavor of a land in which men live not by bread alone. They might have been assigned to duty in Vallambrosa or the Vale of Cashmere, where genius would have gathered them on its rainbow and lifted them up as the seven colors of its mighty arch. Then indeed would have been a rainbow that would have turned fable into fact and under all its span would be the pots of gold which have been hunted by the children of many lands. Only one of this group of counties has been christened by the name of a man. Sutter keeps green the memory of a pioneer. Within its borders is the home he built, in the midst of fig trees that have formed a temple many acres in extent, roofed by their broad leaves, and divided into colonnades by their trunks which are many feet in circumference. Here Sutter lived—patriarch and prodigal by turns, the owner of a principality in this valley, but with his Swiss temperament roused to unceasing sensibility by the far grandeurs and the near charms that were above and around him—he reigned here, a pastoral prince, lacking that thrift of pruning hook and plow which, with eye less sensitive to inspiring proportions and exterior beauty of tint and form, regards them all as skin-deep only, and sees under the poppy-spangled surface of the valley the earth's flesh, the soil where life is latent and waiting to be invited forth in the wheat and grape and olive, as bread and wine and oil.

Only one other county in California is named for a pioneer—Peter Lassen, a Norwegian, of that family which gave to philology the greatest orientalist yet produced in western Europe. It is

STATE CAPITOL BUILDING AT SACRAMENTO.

The Capitol building at Sacramento is beyond doubt the finest structure in the State. It was completed in 1869 at a cost of over three million dollars, and the result shows that the money was well expended. In design the structure is a sort of modified Doric with a touch of Corinthian. A native stone, soft in color, is used in the construction; and, now that the signs of age appear, the effect is most pleasing. The dome is a magnificent piece of architecture, and is pronounced to be one of the finest in the country. It rises considerably over a hundred feet, and can be seen for miles around. One of the chief charms of the State Capitol are the beautiful grounds surrounding the building. They are laid out in terraced lawns, planted with graceful shade trees, and preserve a quiet dignity in keeping with the building.

not without interest to record that he, like the Swiss Sutter, who called his Sacramento-Valley domain New Helvetia, was attracted to California from his far glaciers by the romantic fame of this land, and after hardy explorations of its great area selected a spot in the Sacramento Valley as the gem for which the rest of the state was only the setting. Lassen's choice was the tract now covered by the Vina Ranch in Tehama county, on which the grapes purple every year in the largest vineyard under single ownership in the world. Here were planted the first grape vines that were ventured in northern California. The cuttings were brought on horseback from Los Angeles, nearly six hundred miles away. Lassen, under the spell of that destiny which is upon pioneers who can spy out a land but cannot permanently conquer it for themselves, lost his possessions as did Sutter and, resorting to the lofty region crowned by the peaks that bear his name, left that alone as evidence that he had been. But this valley when it was virgin had these two men as lovers at the time when their ardent fancy, or such judgment as they had, could have made choice from all the untouched beauties between the Colorado and the Columbia.

When Thomas Carlyle was introduced to the ancient corporation of Edinburg University as Lord Rector and delivered that remarkable address which tingles yet like the pricking of a Scotch thistle, he cast about for a synonym of remarkable and immeasurable wealth that should offset or foil the riches of scholarship which he was about to explain. He found and expressed the treasury of material wealth in this sentence: "There is a greater ambition than gaining all of California would a thirst for learning which in rare and

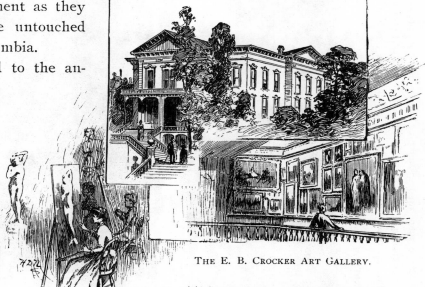

THE E. B. CROCKER ART GALLERY.

be." This was the ambition for letters, infrequent souls is a master motive, stronger than the desire for riches. It is an ambition which the material resources of California are elected to serve, a thirst which this valley is destined to quench. Peter Lassen's location, expanded into a vast domain, was at last acquired by Leland Stanford, by whom it has been dedicated in perpetuity as a part of the landed endowment of the memorial University which he has founded and is directing toward completion as an instrumentality in the new education which will blend art and science, theory and practice, philosophy and dynamics, to the end that students shall not lose the sturdy quality of self-support by over-polish, nor find it with no polish at all. Land and learning are the only enduring things. Men die to reach immortality; these live in immortality. Eight and three-quarter scores of years ago, a ruler of Madras, President of the British East India Company, a man of millions, went to and fro with armed escort, and possessed a great treasury. Princes were the puppets of his will in the East and Parliaments were in his train at home. Who was he? Alas! he has passed with the vanities, and proof of his station would be lost in the long perspective of time, if he had left his name attached only to his titles and his honors and his splendor; but he allied it to learning and by a gift, small though sufficient, for it was only $2,500, he founded Yale College, and the name of Elihu Yale, quite forgotten in England and Asia, is yearly known by more and more millions in America.

From this immortal land where Lassen built his cabin will issue the support of learning in a greater Yale. This soil of the Sacramento Valley, assigned by its far-seeing owner to so refined a function, will by his act project into the future of this side of the continent influences that may not now be seen from the hither end of the far-reaching path which lies before the Stanford University.

Commerce and culture love the same air. When the Italian Universities were eminent, commerce sought that land. The East, the cradle of the human race, and the source of wealth easiest won, saw the Attic beacon on the Calabrian peninsula and gave its spoil to freight the argosies that made Venice the proudest commercial city of her day. When trade abandoned the Adriatic, leaving behind colossal fortunes that are not yet exhausted and monuments of art and architecture that are yet unmatched, it was loath to leave learned Italy. True, in its wake had been Shylocks and Antonios, but there were also learned doctors of Parma and Padua. Passing into the Mediterranean, commerce cast anchor at Genoa, there training the navigators from whose ranks issued the discoverer of a new world, and remained until the profits of trade that centered upon learning had gilded both sides of Italy with greater riches than Rome had brought when she was mistress of the world. Then commerce noted the rising lustre of Leyden and Utrecht and passed the Pillars of Hercules to rest in Holland. Culture and commerce at Venice had built a city on the water, and in the Low Country they gathered the wealth that advanced dyke and dam against the ocean, reclaimed provinces from the water and built cities where fleets had floated. Then trade followed learning to the Thames and the world's commercial centre has abided there for centuries.

The commerce of coasts and continents follows the same law, and who shall say that out of

SACRAMENTO BY NIGHT.

the soil of this valley may not spring all that this founder, more generous than Elihu Yale, has planned to follow the institution which is to fill its treasury from these tens of thousands of acres? When his hand put in trust these millions for higher culture it actuated a web of wires unseen, running to myriad consequences that embarrass the fancy which is lifted to reflect them. The erection of this University, admitting the integrity of natural laws to stand unbroken, was an act that widened the glebe-lands of the future, that seeded virgin acres, and enlarged upon this round globe the gilding of the harvest. It opened new mines and stripped fresh quarries to flux noble ores. It heated the cupola and gave impulse to the flow of molten iron and steel into cunning molds to be shaped to useful purpose. It inspired the brawny arm that smites music from the anvil and the cunning hand that guides plane and chisel. It laid the keels of ships and sent them to wed the waters. It threw the shuttle through the warp and woof of wool and silk and cotton, gave distant shepherds dreams of plenty and cheered the toiler who plucks the bolls of cotton or winds silk from the cocoon. It was an act that will be at the planting of vine and olive tree, and when its remotest impact is felt, the source of its energy will be traced back to this valley whose fertility makes possible the scholastic facilities which are to be an attraction for the commerce of the Western Hemisphere.

FISHING
ON THE SACRAMENTO RIVER.

Descending the valley, at first, the pines and other mountain forest trees are seen to have turned towards the plain, but like men these are largest in the mountains and their march into the valley is soon abandoned, and the oaks appear in park-like groves which quite range to range. These are not but a deciduous tree, of which drooping viney limbs and reaches and beauty of form. These being quite indifferent for fuel, thrift, that can be wrought into coin, has left to give grateful shade and beauty ill spare their attractions. Passing the cross its upper end from the live-oak of our coast, the variety most numerous has noble dimensions, with great grace unfit for lumber and timber and which willingly spares nothing passed them by and they are to ennoble a landscape that could southern frontier of this oak belt, the valley lies in front with horizon unbroken except where towns and cities have redeemed the promise of the mirage, and groves and orchards have been planted. On the Western Continent it has no analogue. The valley of California, of which this is the upper half, has not only a potentiality of wealth unrivaled by any equally large area within our dominion, but as you look upon it there comes the inspiration that seems to see the promise of empire written on its face. This mirage of the fancy is irresistible, for the scene gives every beholder the glad feeling of a discoverer. We speak of the valley of the Mississippi, as we see it, without emotion. As it is only a vast watershed, with one boundary invisible from the other and each invisible from its center, the eye does not rouse the mind to sustained sensibility concerning it, and the imagination retires from the task of ascending the mount of vision when the substance thereof is lacking. But here is a valley vast in extent, the area of this half nearly equalling the entire area of Massachusetts, exceeding that of Connecticut and Delaware combined, and yet so clear are the atmosphere and sunshine that the eye discerns its lateral boundaries, and its length also may be seen from the accessible mountain peaks above it. It is a winterless valley. The soil never freezes, but from its vineyards and orange groves may be seen the snow on Lassen Butte until far into the summer, and that on Mount Shasta which defies the seasons. The pastoral period of this valley was the time of large landholders. Pastoral life is the first step forward from subsistence by the chase. The aborigines lived by hunting and their immediate successors by herding. Either pursuit requires that large tracts of country shall be controlled. Hence, when the herdsman took possession of the valley of California he did not content himself with small holdings. It required the natural feed upon a certain number of acres to raise a steer, or a certain number of steers to consume the feed on an acre, as the case might be; and so in the pastoral period a herdsman counted his steers to number his acres or numbered his acres to count his steers.

LIVE-OAK WITH ROOTED BRANCH.—SACRAMENTO VALLEY.

"Descending the valley at first, the pines and other mountain forest trees are seen to have turned toward the plain ; but like men these are largest in the mountains, and their march into the valley is soon abandoned, and the oaks appear in park-like groves which quite cross its upper end from range to range. These being unfit for lumber and timber, and quite indifferent for fuel, thrift, which willingly spares nothing that can be wrought into coin, has passed them by, and they are left to give grateful shade and beauty to ennoble a landscape that can ill spare their attractions."

The population was not much greater then than it had been when the aborigines were the landholders and lived by bow and spear. The wheat-raiser succeeded the man of flocks and herds, and then the valley of the Sacramento felt the improving influence of the plow. Here were the first great wheat-fields of the state, for the fashion of large landholders inherited by the herder from the hunter did not readily pass away. Perhaps in those days every man who owned land in this valley felt toward every other as Othello did when he believed Desdamona false. It was the valley beautiful; and if ever plain and mountain, soil and sky, snowy summit and verdant glebe were kissed into passion by the sun till they inspired the lust of sole possession, here was the scene.

One wheat farm of 60,000 acres and others of less but large area demonstrated the capacity for producing wheat in California, and argosies sailed thither around the great circles of the earth to carry away the wheat of the Sacramento valley to make bread for Europe. The arid parts of the valley are now being brought under irrigation. The waters of the Sacramento are to be deflected into canals that will carry them around the foothills to be tapped at intervals for the baptism of the land into more reliable fruitfulness. As this change comes to agriculture the land takes its last step in evolution and reaches its ultimate and noblest utility. At first given over to the hunter, then to the herder and then to the great wheat-rancher, irrigation finally fits it for a variety of crops and for division into small holdings upon which high farming only will be practiced. But no matter what high fortune befall the rest of it, Sutter County will always at harvest time look like a gold piece dropped from the skies. That part of the valley has all the moisture required to bring grain without failure, and the happy rural homes adorned with simple refinement testify to the profit won in raising the world's bread-corn.

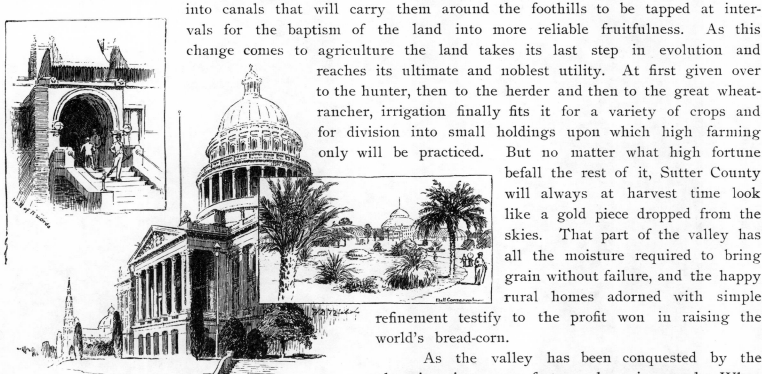

FRONT OF CAPITOL BUILDING.

As the valley has been conquested by the plow its picturesque features have increased. When it was all in glebe, as the plowmen drew their long furrows across it the color changed to brown, and seen from the summits it appeared as if an army of painters were busy with brush and pigment giving it a sad shade. Next the planted grain quickened and over the darkened fields spread its verdure, broken here and there by islands of poppies on the wheat. After seed time, the harvest, and with it the third change in color, for now the gilders seem to follow the painters and the green brightens into gold. At this season one could well fancy the valley one continuous riffle-box, over two hundred miles long, into which had been washed the gold from the mountains. The river and its confluents are land builders, and they find their materials in the mountains whence came the gold that was sought on their bars and in their channels by the early placer-miner. Along with the gold they brought the disintegrated rocks, which had once held it, and in this material, crushed by ancient glaciers or worn off by recent erosion, the very marrow of the great mountains has been spread by overflow upon the valley. So the farmer is a sort of placer-miner, but he mines with the plow and fills this great sluice with yellow grain which is transmuted into yellow gold.

During one year 1,630 square miles of wheat alone were sown and harvested in the eight counties of the Sacramento valley. This was a wheat field nearly twice as large as the State of Rhode Island. It yielded 11,739,182 centals of grain and at the export price of mid-August it was worth $16,669,638.44. At the close of the Mexican war our Federal Government paid $16,000,000 for California, Nevada, Utah, part of Colorado and Kansas, New Mexico and Arizona, and was denounced for making a foolish investment in a land speculation. But who then foresaw that one year's wheat crop of the Sacramento valley would be worth the price paid for all our conquests north of the Rio Grande? The barley, oats, rye and hay for the same year covered half the area occupied by wheat and had about half the total value. So that in these crops 2,440 square miles, or about one-third of the floor of the valley, yielded a market value of $25,004,457. These figures are not picturesque; they are pecuniary. They throw into startling relief the proposition to irrigate this valley, to increase its production by diversifying its crops.

What this may mean is foreshown at many points between tide-water and the mountains. Near Winters the Arabian date, grown from seeds planted by a pioneer, ripens its fruit every year. In Marysville the favorite shade-trees are the orange and lemon, and their fruit is offered to the visitor fresh from the trees. At Colusa raisin plantations and stone-fruit orchards appear like islands in an ocean of wheat. At Oroville the orange orchards are growing in area every year, and here, during Christmas, is held the Northern California citrus fair. It occurs during the orange-harvest, and the exhibit is in a great tent pitched in an orchard over trees that hang full of the fruit. This is in latitude 40°, nearly that of Chicago, New York and Boston, where at that season of the year the furies of the wind and winter are abroad, and the people who have toiled all summer to keep the heat out of their homes are toiling harder yet to keep it in. At Chico great almond orchards cast hundreds of bushels of nuts per acre, where the Indians used to *cache* acorns and think them pretty good.

At Davisville sub-irrigation has created a raisin plantation through which the overland railway runs, giving many a traveler his first sight of the process of turning grapes into raisins. At Woodland the vineyards already fill the landscape in all directions. Here are plantations of forty acres in vines whose owners pay annually $50 per acre in wages to labor and $1,000 per acre in railway freights to carry their products to market. Around the town of Willows and at many local centers in the midst or upon the borders of the valley these examples of high farming may already be seen. The river will not miss the water required to make them possible wherever irrigation is desirable.

The diversified qualities of the valley would not be seen without exhibiting also the tillage which depends upon drainage. The marrow of the mountains which was the first freight carried by the streams that thread the valley was not all deposited to make wheat fields. Some of the finest soil was carried on toward the bay where the current of the Sacramento feels the resistance of tides, and there it was deposited where drainage by ditches and sometimes protection by dikes is needed in order that it may be tilled. Here are the river-shore and delta lands, which furnish a commerce notably picturesque and profitable. The plantations are from a half mile to a mile in width on each side of the stream. In the season for shipping fruits and vegetables four steamboats ply up and down the river exclusively in this trade. Leaving San Francisco during the forenoon they go in pairs up the bay, through the fleets of fishing boats, where the Chinese junk and the lateen-sailed craft of the Greek fisherman spice the scene with a flavor of older lands. They pass Mare Island light, where tired ships of the line come from squadron duty to draw their fires and rest and, steaming under the peaceful sunset guns of Benicia Arsenal, enter the Sacramento in time for the next day's duty. The companion boats have been met on the way, freighted full and speeding to market. If you are a passenger you may sit in the wheel house with the pilot, provided your ways are winning, and from that high perch may witness what cannot be seen on any other river. The boat is a sort of aquatic express, stopping wherever a flag flies. Each farmer has a landing, and his produce is there ready for loading. The landing is usually in the shade of a wide-spreading sycamore tree. The foliage ashore is tropical in its forms and luxuriance. The freight sends up the aroma of orchard and vineyard, for it is largely fruit—peaches, prunes, pears, cherries, grapes—luscious all. Occasionally a landing is piled with melons, watermelons, muskmelons, and that cross between the two, the casaba, which has come to us from the far Orient. Here the Chinese laborer has his strongest hold, and there is no denying that he seems to fit the surroundings as perfectly as if this were the Hoang Ho and Cathay, not California. The river has lost its early sprightliness and brisk mountain spirits and sings and leaps no more. Its waters are as placid as a sheltered lake. No cities are in sight. Railroads brawl far away. It is delicious isolation in which Nature empties her Horn of Plenty.

The Asiatic illusion is perfected by the presence of the Chinese, who move silently and quickly at their duties in transferring the fruity freight from the landing to the steamer. Looking on, one thinks of Webster's seventh of March speech on the admission of California into the Union, in which he soothed the slaveholding Whigs for their loss of territory south of the Missouri Compromise line, by the assurance that slavery had been outlawed by Nature in California. "For," he said, "I hold slavery to be excluded from California and New Mexico by a law superior to that which admits and sanctions it in Texas. I mean the law of Nature, of physical geography, the law of the formation of the earth. California and New Mexico are Asiatic in their formation and scenery, composed of vast ridges of mountains, of great height, with broken summits and deep valleys. These mountain tops are covered by perpetual snow. I do not regard it necessary to prohibit slavery to California, and I would not take pains uselessly to re-affirm an ordinance of Nature nor to re-enact the will of God."

The physical likeness of this region to Asia appears to a marked degree in the valley of Cal

FIG ORCHARD, SUTTER FARM.

ifornia, and these Asiatics who swarm on the fruit-piled banks of the lower Sacramento seem at home under their wicker hats. These river-bank farms are not accessible to railroads and their exports must always seek an outlet by the river, so that this most picturesque commerce is safe from invasion. As the laden boats pass down the bay the breeze carries to the people on shore the perfume of the muskmelons and the sweet scents of peaches and berries; and when the cargoes are discharged on the wharf at San Francisco for distribution by the shouting and jostling and cosmopolitan crowd of merchants and peddlers, who bargain and blaspheme in every language from ancient Hebrew to modern Greek, the bracky breath of the bay and the rank smells of commerce are overcome for a time by these aromas of the orchards and gardens that have followed to market the sweet spoils of this gateway of the valley.

This river traffic began thirty-five years ago, with one sloop of thirty tons. Within a year from that time a schooner of thirty tons was added. The articles shipped were potatoes, cabbages, watermelons, pumpkins and squashes. The first fruit was produced and shipped in 1860, when peaches were first sent from the delta lands to market. Next apples and then pears appeared in the freight-list, and by 1866 the trade had grown so that the good steamer Reform took the place of the two sailing vessels. Since then the steamers Pioneer, Relief, Constance, Washington, Onward, Pride of

SUTTER'S MILL (AS IT APPEARED IN 1851; SITE OF MARSHALL'S DISCOVERY OF GOLD IN 1848). FROM PAINTING BY GEORGE SPIEL.

"Only one of this group of counties has been christened by the name of a man. Sutter keeps green the memory of a pioneer. Within its borders is the home he built, in the midst of fig trees that have formed a temple many acres in extent, roofed by their broad leaves, and divided into colonnades by their trunks, which are many feet in circumference. Here Sutter lived, patriot and prodigal by turns, the owner of a principality in this valley."

A RELIC OF THE FIFTIES.
OLD WHARF BRIG AT SACRAMENTO CITY.

the River, Sonoma and Aurora have been built by the company which started so long ago with the two small sailing crafts. Of these the Reform, Pioneer and Washington are departed. The others still walk the waters. The sloop and schooner made two trips a week and the traffic lasted from new-potato time in May to pumpkin-picking in December. The total business was 1,000 tons per year. Now the traffic lasts the year round, though it is heaviest in the fruit season, lasting four months when the steamers load 250 tons per day, every day in the week. They make one hundred and fifty landings in thirty miles. This trade started thirty-five years ago in such a way will be going on thirty-five years hence and more, and will be then, as now, one of the picturesque features of the valley of California which will attract the tourist, the artist and the student of commerce. Captain Nelson, who has charge of it now, commanded the good sloop Virginia, which made the first voyage after new potatoes in 1855, and though he is now Fleet Admiral to a squadron of steamers he is no prouder than when he first sailed up San Pablo bay and beat against the current through the Strait of Carquinez.

The many bays which are part of the great bay of San Francisco have been spoken of. A valley resembles a bay in having numerous smaller valleys which, opening into it, are its estuaries and part of its general system. So, penetrating the Coast Range and opening into the Sacramento valley are Suisun, Vaca and Capay valleys, the names of which have been carried abroad by the renown of their productions, for they ripen the earliest fruit in the state and have an expanse of orchards and vineyards which produce a great commerce. In these spurs of the main valley grows much of the fresh fruit that has its flush and flavor kissed into it by the sunshine of the Sacramento Valley and they may follow it with the walnuts and the wine that grew in the same soil. In these fruit-raising tracts may be followed, step by step the season through, the most picturesque of all the rural industries. April brings the cherries; May the early apricots and peaches; June more peaches, nectarines and apricots; July peaches, plums, prunes, and grapes; August pears, peaches, grapes in profuse variety—and so on, until December, when the peaches are still coming, plums

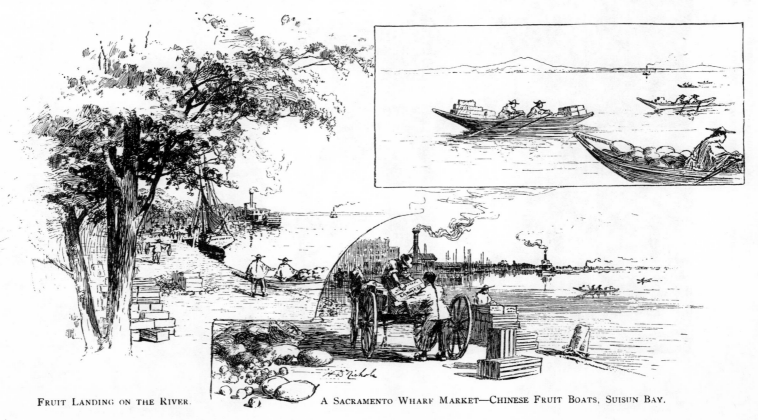

FRUIT LANDING ON THE RIVER.   A SACRAMENTO WHARF MARKET—CHINESE FRUIT BOATS, SUISUN BAY.

are plentiful, and raspberries, strawberries, blackberries, oranges, grapes, and that delicious globe of custard called in the gardens of Shimosa "the fruit of the gods," but here known prosaically as the Japanese persimmon, garnish the closing year.

The climate and soil capable of such a variety of productions are intended to invite a dense population, and when the valley of California has received the millions that it can support in comfort, the world will turn to it as an illustration of the happiness of man enjoying the bounties of God.

Its commerce is provided with transportation by a railway which enters the San Joaquin valley through the loop at Tehachapi, and makes its exit from the Sacramento valley by the cañon of the Sacramento, to climb the Siskiyou Mountains into the clouds and descend into the chain of valleys which lead to the Columbia River, connecting its waters with the mouth of the Mississippi by a continuous rail which makes a belt-route between the two great rivers whose head waters interlace, but which flow to different oceans separated by many thousands of miles. This railroad, which enters and leaves the valley by a mountain flight that would tire a bird, affords to the traveler a view of rural industries engaged in a greater and more gainful variety of productions than can be found together in any other part of the world. It runs through raisin vineyards where the waxy white grapes are jellied and browned in the sun, and it is bordered by almond-orchards which bloom in February and seem like fields of snow; the pomegranate and medlar, the orange and sweet things that grow on trees and are strange to the rest of the world, follow here in their season the bloom that lights the winter months of this winterless land.

"The Outlet by the River"—Steamer Landings.

After the wheat is tall enough to make waves in the wind, the wild flowers light their torches and flash upon the trains that go this way northward, and at last the blossoming borders end far up the mountains, and the passenger who has within an hour plucked a dog-rose or found a spray of purple lilac steps out into the snow and hears the pines soughing their winter song. Then down again, down toward the "emerald land" until the flowers report for duty again and the summer sun lights the verdure of Oregon. It is fairer than the passage of the Alps from France into Italy, and may be compared only to some of the Himalayan passes that lead from the plains of India into the mysterious Thibet. The railway is of the highest strategic value, and as it connects the Gulf of Mexico with the Puget Sound and is intersected by many lines from the interior of the continent it may play a formidable part in some future war, in the concentration and distribution of armies, and subject this valley of peace to the cries of strife.

Other railways are running or projected across it and soon all the points of observation from which its surroundings are seen to advantage will be accessible by rail. They will become familiar, but commonplace they never will be. The mountain barrier which shuts the valley in at all points except where its river runs into the bay, will forever feed the fancies of men with its inscrutable countenance which neither invites nor repels familiarity. In the forests that blacken its sides the wild deer will be at home, and the eagles that whirl in great circles on tireless wing above the valley will go to their inaccessible homes upon the summits. The mountain lion will cry like the banshee through the cañons and the great bears will shamble through the chaparral; for the civilization and refinement, the rich cities and many homes that are to be in the midst of

AZALEA FALLS.　　　　GREAT PALMS AT WINTERS.

orchards and vineyards and granaries filled with bread and cellars full of wine, will always have above them, on the road to the stars, the forest primeval and the unconquered mountains.

When the waters ripple in their appointed channels over the vast stretches of the valley, irrigating it in the dry season and draining it in the wet, then will be brought together those physical conditions in which primitive civilization took root. The arts and sciences passed their archaic age in irrigated countries where instead of four seasons there were only two. Egypt passed her culture and philosophy to Greece, and with Attic refinements they were bestowed upon Rome, and the human intellect took up its line of march along the zones where the soil yielded its best only when irrigated. Art and Science pitched their moving tents by the fountains and history has told its story under the trees that drink their waters, while poetry has sung of love and war from the time that Miriam chanted her hymn of adoration when Israel turned toward the irrigated valleys of the Promised Land, and David strung his harp and chanted: "The Lord is my Shepherd: I shall not want. He maketh me to lie down in green pastures: He leadeth me beside the still waters. He restoreth my soul."

In this valley man finds another Promised Land, flowing with milk and honey, rich in wine and oil, and the majesty of its surroundings must inspire those who people it to noble ways and great actions.

JOHN P. IRISH.

THE TULE REGION.

The topographical engineers in their surveys of California find that one of the most remarkable natural features of the state is the "hollow land," the "heart of its tule region," that lies between the great Sacramento and San Joaquin valleys, belonging in some degree to both, and yet in many respects different from either. Here is the waste and surplus of the two vast drainage basins from Shasta to Tehachapi; here, in the midst of broad sloughs, are the beginnings of another Belgium. In these green levels of wonderfully fertile soil, for the most part as yet unreclaimed, lie hidden all the potentialities that the Flemings and Hollanders have found in their dyke-protected swamps. Here, in this region, which is hardly explored or known to the world at large, are to be the great dairies of the coming California. The railroads only skirt its borders, and the river steamboats keep to their customary water-lanes; and hardly a duck-hunter or yachtsman knows half the sloughs and islands by name.

MOUNT DIABLO AND THE 'TULE REGION. FROM PAINTING BY H. D. NICHOLS.

"The inexhaustible beauties of California seem to be only just undergoing discovery by the unfortunate millions who had not seen them face to face. The world that reads of the picturesque and longs for it, but has to be satisfied with the picture only, has been slow to comprehend that here is every conceivable beauty that Nature can paint in valleys and frame with mountains. There is a wild sort of strength dormant here in this region; it has its perils and its heroes, no less than the high Sierras. Lonely, terrible, beautiful, are the real 'fenlands' of history, and this 'tule country' is of them."

The "Holland of California" embraces the greater part of a district about fifty miles long, and from twelve to thirty miles wide. Fringes of tule extend much farther north and south, but the main body of submerged and half-reclaimed lands occupies about twenty-three townships, lying between Suisun and the mouth of the Mokelumne. If one counts all the "swamp and overflowed" lands along the axis of the valley, the total area will not be less than 1600 square miles. The most of it lies in either fresh or brackish water; it is between river and tide, and when properly dyked can be irrigated at will, and at nominal expense. Here, as nowhere else in California, we may expect the growth of seeds for market, of bulbs, and root crops such as have made the drained bottom of the Haarlem Meer famous throughout Europe, and highly profitable even at eight hundred dollars an acre.

One of the best things about the real tule district is that it has a wonderful variety of aspects and color, in which, indeed, it the more resembles Holland. There are islands after

THE SIERRAS, FROM SACRAMENTO VALLEY.

islands, but no two are alike. One sees green, glowing banks, with occasional fields of wild poppies like flashes of deep flame; terraced weeping-willows stand near mossy buildings and ancient fences and farm-houses with long slanted roofs; plowed fields, where men are planting corn and potatoes, reach out into the midst of the tules—brown and fertile peninsulas, with seas of nodding marsh-growth about them. You sail past, and look down on all this, peering over the broad levee to watch the planting or the harvest, according as the season is, and you perceive that as soon as one crop is gathered another crop is planted in the rich, moist soil, and springs up as in a night. You push your boat in among the dark tules, and suddenly discover, on some low island-bank or river margin, the huts of Italian salmon-fishers, set in the acres of short salt-grass. Their brown nets hang from black, weather-stained fences; their red shirts are spread on the pollarded willows; their white fishing-boats swing lazily on the yellow tide, under skies of clearest blue. Tall, against the horizon, white herons stand, and flocks of wild-fowl cross from pond to pond in their marshaled array. You sail on and on into other sloughs, past other islands, some flooded and desolate, some golden with ripening wheat. Heavy wood-barges from the Sacramento float slowly past; river steamboats, stern-wheelers and side-wheelers of every imaginable pattern, mingle in the panorama. Here, the spring-floods rise unchecked, and change untilled miles of tule into temporary lakes; there, they break suddenly across massive levees, and large areas of fertile soil lie ten feet under-sea, or are torn across, melted again into rivers and swept out towards the Golden Gate. Here, men are sowing barley, cutting hay, chopping willows, breaking sod with eight horses harnessed to a plow; there, it may be, they are standing waist-deep in the mighty current, piling sand-bags into some fierce crevasse. Thus one may sail on for miles, finding out all the while that no part of California is less monotonous than this land of many islands.

There is a wild sort of strength dormant here, in this lowland region; it has its perils and its heroes, no less than the high Sierras. Lonely, terrible, beautiful, are the real "fen-lands" of history, and this "tule country" is of them. The great everglades of Florida are not more impenetrable than some of these tule wastes; the Arkansas canebrakes are not more picturesque; the cypress swamps of Louisiana are not better fitted to deeds of daring adventure. These broad and rich tule expanses may yet play the same part in Californian history that the Frisian swamps and the English fen-lands have played in the story of Europe. They make a whole Holland or rich, moist levels, where the struggle with nature ever goes on, training men for dominion, as the Isle of Ely trained Hereward. The rivers drag the land downward; the slow wash from the mountains upbuilds it; in the heart of California a new and wonderful community of boatmen and island-dwellers is being developed under stress and strain. Here, indeed, one finds many a Belgian or Hollander already at work, and more coming every year; the blood of the dwellers by Zuyder Zee turns to such fertile lowlands as these, and devotes its unconquerable stubbornness to the task of permanent reclamation. As one sails day after day along the borders of the tule-lands, it is easy to prophesy that the time will assuredly come when they will be as thickly settled as are the famous Holland provinces. Painters will come here to study quaint old villages, slanting windmills, and lines of willows by the canals. All the long account of the centuries of war with the tides and the rivers will be ancient history, and some "Beowulf the dyke-builder" will be the legendary hero of the race of tule-dwellers. All that now appeals most to the visitor to the region will have disappeared—the silence, the loneliness, the exquisite sense of untrampled domains, wide, almost, as infinite distance, with their green levels melting into the clear skies. It will be a densely-peopled land, full of villages and towns, and acre-wide gardens in the highest state of cultivation. It will be amazingly different from the tule-region of the closing decade of the nineteenth century, and no Californian of the present time would recognize it. There is no part of the state that has greater capacity to support a dense population.

If one goes far enough to reach the places that lie away from the traveled track, the time will at last come when the islands seem to sink slowly into a wonderful expanse of tule, reaching as far as the faint white and golden horizon whose mists half hide the great mountains. Flowers of royal purple, and deep scarlet, and glorious golden hues bloom here in untold profusion; acres of brown-headed "cat-tails" glisten in the sun; old Indian mounds rise above the dead level, clothed with short grass, as rich in color and as soft to the tread as the grass that grows in June on the Farmington meadows. Sometimes, in a place like this, springs of fresh water flow from the grassy knolls, and willows and blackberry vines grow there, with the yellow grindelia and the graceful wild asters. Sometimes rushes and olive-green canes mingle with the tules, and tangle about old barges lying fast in the shallows, while all the air is loud with the singing of birds, and made sweet and fresh by the ceaseless passing of the soft sea-winds overhead. There is not a house or a sign of living men in sight anywhere above the clear rim of the horizon. West and east, north and south, widening out farther and farther, are islands of soft green melting into blue tides and winding bayous, for mile after mile to the far-off bay's expanses of silver, and the feet of the distant Coast Range.

CHARLES HOWARD SHINN.

OAKS, UPPER SALINAS VALLEY.

MONTEREY TO VENTURA.

NO PART of California of anything like equal importance is perhaps so little known to the tourist or to the general reader as that between the San Joaquin Valley and the sea, southward from Monterey Bay. The region referred to embraces five counties, having double the area of two of the smaller New England states. It comprises half a score of fertile valleys and as many ranges of rugged mountains. It affords as much variety of scenery and climate as all New England and the Middle States combined, and vastly greater variety of products. It has remained comparatively a *terra incognita* mainly because formidable mountain barriers separate its valleys, and till lately have frightened off railroad builders. There are still wide gaps between the iron bands that penetrate its open valleys from the north and the south; but there is promise that these ere long will not only make the entire region accessible by rail but will make it part of the great Southern Pacific route for overland travel between San Francisco and the East. The completion of this coast line will doubtless shorten the distance somewhat between the metropolis and Los Angeles, and will bring Santa Barbara probably one hundred and fifty miles nearer. Besides, it will give travelers the grateful breath of the ocean most of the way, instead of the sultry heat of the San Joaquin and the hot winds of the Mojave desert.

This Southern Coast Range may be regarded as embracing six natural divisions: The Valley of San Benito, the Salinas Valley, the San Luis series of Coast Valleys, the Santa Maria and Santa Ynez Valleys, those skirting the coast of Santa Barbara, and the Santa Clara Valley " of the South," each of course having its tributary vales and its setting of foot-hills and mountains. The limitations of this chapter forbid anything beyond the briefest survey of these sections, each worthy of more attention than all together can receive.

The first named is really a continuation of the Santa Clara Valley proper, and has already been represented somewhat in " Picturesque California." Here it need only be recalled that San Benito Valley

MORNING AT THE ANACAPAS.—SANTA BARBARA CHANNEL GROUP. FROM PAINTING BY H. C. FORD.

"Among the delightful excursions naturally made from Santa Barbara should be mentioned a sail to the Channel Islands, some twenty-five miles distant. Prof. Le Conte and other authorities tell us these islands are simply the culminating peaks of a submerged mountain-range, what is now the Santa Barbara Channel having been a valley ages ago. The island of San Miguel is the western link in the chain, and the three Anacapas the eastern, the larger islands of Santa Rosa and Santa Cruz intervening, * * * The chief charm of these islands, however, is in their rugged shores, the basaltic walls often rising in a nearly vertical line from 150 to 300 feet. Rocky promontories here and there have been pierced by the action of the waves, ceaselessly at work during the ages, forming arches gigantic and beautifully turned. In the softer volcanic outflow composing portions of the walls are vast briny caverns, easily entered by tourists' boats, carrying torches because of the deep darkness."

is naturally one of the most attractive in the state. Its adjacent grass-clad hills allure the stockman; its fertile soil wins the heart of farmer and fruit-raiser; its thrift draws the merchant and mechanic; its quiet beauty attracts the tourist; its genial climate invites the health-seeker; and all these qualities recommend it to those in quest of delightful rural homes. The nucleus of its early settlement was the Mission of San Juan Bautisto, one of the quaintest and most interesting of all the twenty-one Franciscan Missions in California, but at the same time one of the least appreciated of all.

The Salinas Valley, threaded by the river whose name it bears, is a hundred miles long, and has an average width of perhaps ten miles. The percentage of waste land is so very small that

SAN MIGUEL MISSION.

its actual area of grain and fruit land is set down at 600,000 acres. Till lately it has been used almost wholly for grazing purposes. The four Missions within its limits controlled its vast ranges, their myriad flocks and herds roaming at sweet will over hill and vale alike. It is not surprising that the annual income of these four missions reached nearly $400,000, and that almost wholly without effort on their part. 'Twas only necessary to allow the horses and cattle and sheep to multiply and grow and fatten in this herdsmen's Paradise.

What *rodéos* were held there in those early days! In fancy we can see them even now. The dark-visaged *vaqueros*, superbly

mounted and vying with each other in daring feats of horsemanship, dash here and there around the great herds of wild cattle, the beasts lowing lustily and flashing vengeance from their glaring eyes; rival herdsmen contend hotly for the ownership of some fat steer; the *juez del campo* quickly hears and promptly decides between them; a ringing shout hails the victor; his lariat is flung; the steer is on the ground and receives his owner's brand.

SHEEP-SHEARING.

When finally the Mexican Government broke up the missions by the confiscation of their property, the *vaqueros* lost their vocation, and for lack of something else to do, as they doubtless persuaded themselves, they turned to bandit life. The extreme ruggedness of the surrounding mountains was their ready ally, the deep and almost hidden *potreros* of the Santa Lucias affording places of refuge quickly reached, and about

SAN ANTONIO MISSION.

as secure from pursuit as the Dominion of Canada is for the defaulting bank officer of to-day. From the early Fifties until late in the Seventies, or for almost thirty years, there were Mexican outlaws somewhere in the mountains of this region, keeping the frontier officers of justice busy enough. They were in a sort of vast natural fortress in the midst of the wilderness; the valleys descending from the southern barrier of their hills opened the way for forays into the rich region about the town of San Luis; east they knew every path into the San Joaquin Valley and the San Benito district; north was the Salinas lowland, and beyond it another refuge in the dense forests of Santa Cruz. All the notorious desperadoes of the time found hiding-places on the San Luis border. Vasquez and Lopez, Chaves, Procopio, and many others whose names live in the wild tales of the outlaw region, knew every cañon from Frémont's Peak to Paso Robles, and from the Panoche and Peach-Tree Valley to *Piedras Blanca* and the giant pyramid of Morro Rock.

As already noted, the half-civilized, nomadic grazier life of the early mission days has well-nigh faded out in California, but more frequent vestiges of the genuine old type may still be found along the borders of the Salinas Valley than in almost any other portion of the state. Indeed it may fairly be said that the foothills mainly and a large share of the rolling plains toward the head of the valley are still held by horses and cattle. Sheep-raising on the old-time large scale has been almost wholly supplanted.

Stock ranges of course mean large tracts of land, and unfortunately for the general prosperity of this region, vast areas of its fertile acres are still held by a few men. But when we remember that only a few years ago the entire valley was embraced by such large holdings, it is something to know that there are to-day a score of villages and towns, and perhaps two thousand happy rural homes where so recently the only "population" that made any considerable showing in the census was reckoned by "hoofs and horns." An incorporated company with headquarters at San Luis Obispo has lately been doing a really humane work—though probably not organized as a "Humane Society"—in buying up some of the original Spanish grants, subdividing them directly, and selling

EAGLE RANCH.

at reasonable prices and on easy terms to actual settlers. The stock-raising of to-day is a compromise between primitive grazing (entire dependence upon native grasses) and stock-farming, great fields of alfalfa and other cultivated pasturage being important factors in the business now.

At present wheat and barley are the great products, wheat predominating in the upper portion of the valley and barley in the lower half. As early as 1888 the total grain crop of the Salinas was about two million five hundred thousand bushels—constant bread enough for 400,000 people. Monterey was the banner grain county of the state that year. As the writer lately passed over the ground it seemed one continuous field of wheat and barley from Castroville, near the mouth of the river, to Soledad, thirty-three miles farther south. I happened there on Independence Day. The grain being overripe, no holiday was taken. But the genuine patriotism of the farmers was shown in the hundreds of flags flying everywhere, from the great steam harvesters, from the header-wagons, from all the horses' heads as they pursued their work. These men do not forget their country's greatness, but they realize that their wheat and barley fields are also great!

The immense grain warehouses, which because of their size arrest the traveler's attention at every railway station, tell the story plainly enough. One of these wheat and barley bins at Salinas City is nearly a quarter of a mile long; and large as they are, the great piles of sacked grain on their outside platforms proclaim them yet too small. Nor is the wheat all shipped away. Local mills of large capacity reduce vast quantities of it to flour. The Central Mill at Salinas—one of several belonging to the same company—turns out 400 to 500 barrels of flour per day, using about 700,000 bushels of grain annually.

The vast scale on which farming is done here lifts it out of the commonplace. It is not extraordinary for one of these agricultural moguls to raise and harvest one thousand, two thousand, yes even five thousand acres of wheat! There may be seen as many as ten or fifteen gang-plows running on a single farm and turning a hundred to a hundred and fifty acres of glebe per day. Steam power is extensively used, and yet it is not uncommon to find from one hundred to two hundred work horses as part of the equipment of a large farm.

The lower valley is so almost perfectly level that the steam harvester and thresher combined can be successfully operated. As the great traction wheels are rolled slowly forward a twelve or fifteen foot swath is "headed" and carried automatically to the rapacious mouth of the thresher—part of the one giant machine, and next comes to view as it pours from the "separator's" spouts into sacks, cleaned and graded, ready for market. The sacks being dumped

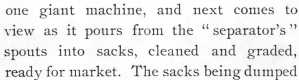

NAJOQUI FALLS.

at regular intervals, lie in rows convenient for hauling.

In the lower Salinas Valley the sugar beet is being tried and its cultivation will doubtless become a large industry. Those raised in the vicinity of Castroville and Salinas City are shown by tests to contain as high as 22 per cent —none less than 18 per cent—of saccharine, while 14 per cent is thought a good average in the beet-sugar districts of Germany. The sugar factory at Watsonville will probably be duplicated at Salinas and at other points southward.

It need hardly be said that vegetables of all sorts are of fine quality and yield immensely in all this region. And its comparative nearness to San Francisco, by ocean steamer as well as by rail, makes it especially available for profitable potato and onion and bean fields. It is well understood by this time that every locality of California has its big stories. The records of a recent

GAVIOTA PASS.

agricultural fair tell of Salinas Valley potatoes, thirty-one to the sack of a hundred pounds, onions of over five pounds apiece, and pumpkins of nearly three hundred pounds weight!

For several years various fruits have been raised in an experimental way with results so satisfactory that many orchards are now being planted in the foot-hills and small elevated valleys tributary to the Salinas. A typical one of these young fruit farms near Gonzales produces oranges, lemons, limes, figs, olives, almonds, English walnuts, apricots, grapes, peaches, pears, apples and cherries—the citrus fruits in a small way so far. All seem to be doing well. Much of the country however is in a transition state, parts of it just shifting from stock-raising to farming and other smaller portions from farming to horticulture. Here and there the change from grazing to fruit-raising is direct. This is true in the neighborhood of Paso Robles and Templeton, where the old Spanish "grants" have lately been sub-divided and immediately transformed into orchards of apricot, peach, pear, olive and prune trees. One

BATH HOUSE, EL PASO DE ROBLES.

SANTA BARBARA MISSION. FROM DRAWING BY J. P. ROBERTSON.

"As one strolls about the town which has grown up around the old mission buildings, or looks down upon all from one of the adjacent hills, he is sure to justify the reputation of the Franciscan fathers for rare good judgment and taste in selecting sites. It has long been taken for granted that wherever one of these missions was located the country is beautiful and fertile and healthful."

of the most extensive prune orchards in the world—if not indeed the very largest—is to be seen in this locality at Eagle Ranch near Templeton. The orchard covers a series of low knolls, embracing something over 200 acres, and contains about 25,000 bearing trees. A hot-air drying house on the premises cures the prunes, and they are carefully graded and packed in the same building. Samples from the first product of this orchard carried off the highest premium in the principal fruit exhibit of the state, and what is more to the purpose, the crop commands the best price in the New York market, in competition with the choicest foreign brands. This is mentioned only because of its bearing on the value of the experiment here made. Before improvement the place and its surroundings were doubtless quite as unpromising as could be found, and yet the highest success has

SAN LUIS MISSION.

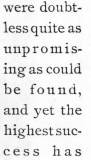

SAN LUIS OBISPO.

BISHOP'S PEAK.

been reached at once. The very inter-orchards can be multi-intelligent energy will higher foothills and till lately regarded as Eagle Ranch is Von Schroeder. It oc-which has an eleva-fifteen hundred feet closed by a rim of higher. A pretty cadéro Creek, runs ling over a precipice tiful waterfall, and embowered in shade.

esting point is that such plied wherever capital and join hands throughout the mountain vales—situations unavailable. the country home of Baron cupies a beautiful glen, tion of twelve hundred to above sea-level, and is en-hills rising a thousand feet mountain stream, the Etes-through the place, tumb-near its source in a beau-singing along its way,

Thousands of redwoods, raised on the premises from the seed, and various other desirable trees have been planted along the creek and in picturesque cañons. Artificial lakes, and a large grotto blasted out in the solid rock of a mountain spur, embellish the grounds. Several miles of well graded and macadamized roads have been made, one leading up past an orange orchard to a summit 2,500 feet above the ocean. From this point the view is broad and inspiring. Looking across the Upper Salinas Valley eastward, the Diablo Mountains, some fifty miles away, fill the horizon. To the south are the Santa Lucias, shattered into many interlacing spurs and stretching eastward until they join the Diablo range. Looking westward through a gorge in the higher mountains, the ocean comes into view, apparently so near that you listen for the sound of the waves. Northward one sees away beyond Templeton and Paso Robles over the undulating plains, dotted everywhere with live-oaks and white oaks. At another angle a series of minor valleys and cañons are seen opening into the Salinas from the west.

This far-reaching vista gives a hint of the wealth of mountain scenery belonging to this district. The Gablian and Diablo Mountains bound the valley on the east, and although of very moderate height, their summits afford fine views. From Frémont Peak a great sweep of the valley can be seen, a vast field of green from January to April; a little later it is golden with ripened grain, and finally it takes the lion's tawny hue. The summer phase is enriched and that of the autumn relieved by the ever-present live-oaks, which give a beautiful park-like appearance to all the upper valley.

For genuine mountain wildness however, one must penetrate the Santa Lucias, lying between the Salinas Valley and the sea. This exceedingly rough and billowy belt of mountains is twelve to twenty miles wide and extends from Carmel Bay a hundred miles southeastward. Strangely, this very interesting region, though less than one hundred and fifty miles from San Francisco, has been less explored than the High Sierras. Its vast wealth of wonder and beauty are almost unknown.

For miles the shore of the Pacific is a rock bluff 200 to 400 feet high. Here and there over this shore-line precipice mountain streams, of considerable size during the rainy season, pour their noisy torrents in a series of waterfalls. And so abruptly do the mountains rise that within a very few miles from this wave-washed base an elevation of 5,000 feet is reached. The gulches and cañons are clothed with redwoods, interspersed with oaks, madroñas, pines, and the usual wealth of undergrowth; flowering shrubs abound—ceonothus of several varieties, azaleas, etc.; and many rare mosses and ferns and wild flowers grow undisturbed in the deep solitudes. It is because this strong-hold of primitive nature is not easily reached that it is so little known; and its very inaccessibility adds to its charm. To be sure, travelers pass by rail and ocean steamer within twenty miles of its margins; but the coast is far too rough for safe landing, and the extreme ruggedness of the land forbids roads within its threshold. Portions of it indeed could hardly be pierced by the rudest trails for pack-animals. The United States Coast Survey has from time to time for several years been doing some work in this district, but they are obliged to make their survey from inland eminences, working by triangulation.

The headwaters of the Carmel, the whole length of the Sur with its tributaries, the upper San Antonio and Nacimiento rivers, indeed, all the streams of this region, afford the best of trout-fishing, and the forests are full of game. Old hunters predict that the last rendezvous of the California grizzly will probably be in the heart of this wilderness back of Point Sur.

The borders of the wilderness are reached by a wagon road from Monterey to the Tassajara Hot-Springs. Another way of reaching the district is by stage from King's City, on the Southern Pacific Railway, to Jolon (Holone), situated in one of a series of small valleys midway between the Salinas and the sea. From Jolon exploring parties may penetrate some of the wilder mountain fastnesses with pack-mules, following trails of the United States Coast surveyors; but whoever would see the region thoroughly would better adopt the methods of John Muir, swinging a blanket and a haversack of bread over his shoulders and sauntering wherever interest leads, reverently reading the while from Nature's book; receiving from the rocks beneath his feet, from the trees over his head, from plant and flower, from bird and beast and singing brook, lessons of living truth and lasting inspiration. Fortunately the beauty of this region is not likely to suffer the too-common fate of destruction. It is so hard to reach that the unappreciative are not apt to get within its sanctuaries, and its extreme roughness protects it alike from devouring herds and flocks, and from the devastating lumbermen. It is in this rare retreat of nature, and here alone in all the world, that the bracteate fir (*Abies bracteata*) is found.

If California had nothing of wonder beyond her mineral springs, these alone would in time make her famous. Many of the thousands who now make long journeys from America to the Spas of Germany will yet learn to prefer the healing waters which seem a natural part of our own "mineral resources." And this Southern Coast Range country has its full share of these springs. Of the score that could be enumerated, the Tassajara, the Paraiso, the Santa Ysabel, and the Paso Robles are perhaps the most remarkable. The latter with its famous "mud baths" is coming to have a national reputation.

Grouped about the hotel and cottages are the seven distinct springs, known as the "Hot Sulphur," the "Mud Spring," the "Soda Spring," the "Sand Spring" the "Garden Spring," the "Cold White Sulphur" and the "Iron Spring," the waters varying in temperature from 59° to 122° Fahrenheit. The Hot Sulphur Spring flows about 120,000 gallons per day. The main bath-house affords accommodation for something like a hundred bathers, there being sixty individual compartments and a large plunge bath.

A dome-shaped reservoir of solid masonry surmounts the spring itself, enclosing the hot water as it rises from nature's laboratory and holding the gases in solution. This "beverage" is constantly "on tap" for all the thirsty throng, and of course the water is conveyed to all the baths.

The Mud Springs, a mile and a half distant, cover a space of some six hundred square feet, and flow nearly 150,000 gallons per day. The temperature is 122° F. The bathing appliances are such that the prepared "moor" or mud which fills the individual vat is constantly surcharged with the hot water and bubbling gas as they boil up from the ground. These mud baths do not at first blush appear exactly cleansing in their effect, but undoubtedly they are curative of many serious ailments. For generations past they have been a great favorite with the Indians, perhaps partly because of the quality just named—not particularly antagonistic to dirt. Moor-bathing is, however, of late years being very generally introduced among the civilized throughout the world. The writer remembers that as far back as '71 people made long journeys to these springs, reached then by stage-coach only. The chronicles of the old mission priests have much to say in praise of the healing waters.

At Santa Ysabel remain the ruins of a dam across the cañon, where some forgotten race made their swimming pool of hot sulphur water.

LOS OSOS YALLEY.
(WARDEN'S DAIRY RANCH).

Of the old Spanish missions already referred to as connected with the Salinas Valley, that of San Miguel may be seen from the passing cars, Soledad (only a ruin now) is almost in sight from the railroad, Carmelo is an hour's drive from Monterey, and San Antonio is near Jolon. Each is richly worth a visit from all who feel interest in these vestiges of civilization's first steps along the great western shore.

The present terminus of the Southern Pacific Coast Division Railway is at Santa Margarita, about eight hours' run from San Francisco. A delightful stage ride of two hours intervenes between this and San Luis Obispo. If the traveler sympathizes with glorious Charles Dickens in the matter of public conveyance, realizing as Dickens did of England, that "the glory of the stage-coach is forever passing away," even here in California, he will enjoy this bit of coaching. The road first leads over beautifully wooded slopes; then up through a gap in the Santa Lucias, near the line of the long tunnel already surveyed for the promised extension of the railroad; then for a while in sight of the old road over which Frémont made his memorable march of nearly fifty years ago; and finally, descending rapidly through a pretty cañon, and among rounded hills, it brings the traveler suddenly in sight of Bishop's Peak, standing guard over the young city

DAIRY SCENE, SAN LUIS OBISPO COUNTY. FROM PAINTING BY CARL J. BECKER.

One of the most picturesque phases of life in California is found among the dairies, and particularly those of San Luis Obispo County. The business is very extensive in this part of the State, and is largely in the hands of Swiss people. No better milk or butter can be found any place in the world. The cattle are sleek and fat, and the people engaged in the industry are happy and contented. And why shouldn't they be? They have the most perfect climate, and live in a land like Paradise. The above picture is a most characteristic illustration of this locality. The weather is always warm and pleasant, and the milkmaid goes about her duties attired in garments that permit her to do the work with the greatest ease. She is the picture of health, and her every movement is full of grace. Cows, sheep, pigs and geese all look well-fed, and if they could speak would most likely give thanks that they had to spend their days among such delightful surroundings.

christened with its name. The town is fairly encircled with beautiful hills, San Luis Mountain and the one just named being the most conspicuous. From one point of view, the double summit of Bishop's Peak resembles a bishop's mitre; and from this resemblance the mission was named a hundred and thirty years ago, that is, Saint Louis of the venerated bishop "San Luis Obispo," the Bishop, in honor of Tolosa.

ZACA LAKE, 2,300 FEET ELEVATION.

As one strolls has grown up around ings, or looks down the adjacent hills, he reputation of the Fran-good judgment and It has long since been wherever one of these the country is beauti-

about the town, which the old mission build-upon all from one of is sure to justify the ciscan fathers for rare taste in selecting sites, taken for granted that missions was located, ful and fertile and healthful. Through the midst of the town flows a stream of water, which in the ante-urban days was doubtless as pure and clear as the hill springs which still feed it. Its banks were then shaded by beautiful oaks and sycamores, and trout leaped in its pools. But its poetry has departed. Its banks are now a busy mart of trade, for San Luis has been for years the chief commer-

cial town of all this Coast region. The upper Salinas Valley was one of its largest tributaries till pierced by a railway from the north, which stops short of this local metropolis. With good railroad service the increasing products of that fertile region—two hundred thousand acres of grain and fruit land as yet but little developed—will naturally seek tide-water by way of San Luis

SANTA YNEZ MISSION.

and Port Harford. Probably nowhere in California is there so large a body of excellent undeveloped lands as is comprised within the districts known as San Jose Valley, "the Cholame" and "the Huer-Huero," east of the Salinas. To the southeast and stretching along the western base of the Diablo Mountains for fifty miles, is the Carrisa Basin. It has an area of probably five hundred square miles, and is without drainage. Near the center is a bed of salt covering some 2,500 acres, evidently the residuum of a lake. Fifty or sixty years ago this valley was famous among the Spanish Californians for its vast herds of wild horses and antelope and elk. The southern portion of the basin is known as Elk Valley, from the abundance of elk horns found there. In the Carrisa Valley is the wonderful "Painted Rock," so full of interest to those who would study the ethnology of prehistoric California. It is nearly a hundred and fifty feet high and is hollow, forming an oval cylinder with a ground area of more than 5,000 square feet. On one side is a doorway, and the walls are pictured with curious devices in well preserved colors. These strange paintings may constitute the record, religious or historic, of some lost race of men, who perhaps worshiped in this natural temple of stone centuries ago.

It is believed that a cross railway will ere long penetrate that region, and extend through the mountains into the San Joaquin Valley, and still beyond to the great Sequoia lumber forests, bringing their products to the nearest port, and their people from the heat of interior summer to the grateful seashore.

As it is, the bathing beaches at Avilah and Pismo, near San Luis, attract throngs of visitors from the San Joaquin Valley every summer. Neither of these two places is exactly a Newport as yet; but if there is less of fashionable society and artificial gaiety, there is doubtless more genuine recreation. Pismo Beach is twenty-seven miles long and some four hundred feet wide. Rocky cliffs near Avilah afford interesting views, and indeed, most of the shore-line of San Luis Bay is rather picturesque. Some twenty miles northward, near the shore, stands up out of the sea one of the most notable landmarks of all this region, Morro Rock, a conical shaft of trachite, lifting its stately head nearly six hundred feet above the waves. In the early days it was a welcome guide to the mariner, and to the hunter and herder as well, for the land was then about as trackless as the sea. Morro Bay, lying at the foot of the great rock, is a beautiful sheet of water and is well sheltered.

ADOBE SANTA BARBARA.

OLD ADOBE OVEN.

The Santa Lucia range, extending through Monterey and San Luis Obispo counties, divides the latter into interior and coast valleys. The "Upper Salinas" and other valleys, already outlined, constitute the interior two-thirds, and the coast valleys the remaining third. Among these are the Nacimiento, the San Tablas, the Santa Rosa, the San Simeon, the Chorro and Los Osos, the San Luis and Laguna, the Verdi, Arroyo Grande, Los Berros, Nipomo and others, all beautiful and fertile vales. Among the ample and varied resources of this region, dairying and stock-raising are perhaps still the leading industries, but special farming and fruit-raising are rapidly coming to the front. Bituminous rock, one of the best paving materials in the world, crops out at many points in the hills and is being shipped in considerable quantities.

Pursuing the southward journey from San Luis one has railroad again for seventy or eighty miles, leading through the Arroyo Grande—a veritable cornucopia—and other coast valleys, past some of the bituminous mines, and finally across the great Santa Maria Valley and into that of Santa Ynez. The last two are the chief valleys of Santa Barbara County and, together with her smaller coast valleys, constitute a material resource often overlooked because of the poetic character which has long attached to "Saint Barbara's" realm. These two valleys might supply two hundred thousand people with the best that mother earth yields in nearly all of her various zones and climes; bread from the "finest of the wheat," meats from herd and flock, game from the outlying hills, butter and cheese from the numerous dairies, honey and olive oil, and fruit and nuts in superabundance. Los Olivos, the interior terminus of the Pacific Coast Railway, is named from the extensive planting of olive orchards in the adjacent Santa Ynez Valley. Though the settlement is very new, some 30,000 olive trees have been planted in the immediate neighborhood, many of them already quite productive. Since it has been demonstrated that California olive oil is second to none in the world, it seems almost certain that the industry will reach vast proportions here. Near the mouth of the valley which opens on the sea beach, is the flourishing temperance colony of Lompoc, with its vast fields of beans and English mustard, and extended orchards of choice apples. Really fine native apples are rarer by far in California than good oranges. It is therefore noteworthy that a limited strip of coast country here, including the Arroyo Grande Valley, lately mentioned, produces apples that compare well with the best product of New York and New England orchards. Indeed, Lompoc carried off the highest prize at the New Orleans World's Fair.

Near the village of Santa Ynez is another of the quaint old missions, lending its **name to**

"A GOOD CLIMATE IS NOT A BAD THING."

river and valley, mountain-range and town. Only a few miles drive from Los Olivos is Zaca Lake, a shining basin of silver set in an emerald rim, two thousand feet up the mountain side. The overlooking peaks afford broad views of land and sea, well worth the climb which is the price of beholding them. To the east and north and south is a wilderness of peaks and pinnacles and domes—one of the wildest and most interesting districts in this part of the state. For the topography of this region and an outline of general description the writer is indebted to Mr. Henry Chapman Ford, of Santa Barbara, who as landscape painter and amateur naturalist has explored the district pretty thoroughly :

"The Santa Ynez and San Rafael mountain ranges extend in lines nearly parallel with the coast through Santa Barbara and into Ventura County. The culminating peaks of the former rise to a height of 4,000 feet and those of the latter to 9,000 feet above the sea, the most elevated being crowned with coniferous forests which drop down their northern slopes to a considerable distance. From the higher altitudes of the San Rafael Mountains and those of Ventura flow unnumbered bright streams of water, the principal of which, like the Sisquoc, Santa Cruz, Indio, Mono, Santa Ynez, Coyote, Matilija, Santa Paula, Sespe and Piru, have during the later geographical ages worn deep cañons of striking grandeur and beauty. In nearly all these, charming cascades are frequent, interspersed with waterfalls of considerable height and volume. The most notable of the latter, rarely visited because not easily accessible, is near the head of a tributary of the Sisquoc on a slope of the San Rafael Mountains. By barometric measurement the waters leap 500 feet in a nearly perpendicular fall, broken only once by a projecting rock before they dash into the pool below. This waterfall is doubtless entitled to the distinction of being the highest in Southern California and one of the most beautiful in the state.

"The exploiting of any of the above named cañons will yield to the artist a wealth of picturesque motives, to the scientist subjects for thoughtful investigation, and to the tourist abundant sensations of delight. Each has its special attractions, but our limits forbid elaboration. The banks of the streams are fringed with willow, cottonwood, sycamore, alder and the fragrant bay, together with the rich variety of shrubs and wild flowers peculiar to the region; and this will apply to all the mountain brooks in the minor cañons on both sides of the Santa Ynez range, every one of which is overflowing with beauty. The united waters of these cañons form streams, four of which rise to the dignity of rivers, flowing through broad, rich valleys filled with fields of the cereals and orchards of the orange, lemon, olive, fig and English walnut, together with all kinds of northern fruit, while the hillsides are partly occupied by promising vineyards."

Of these four main valleys the Santa Maria and Santa Ynez have already been referred to. The San Buenaventura and Santa Clara of the South are not less fertile nor less beautiful.

As a rule the foothills and lower mountains of California as well as the valleys are so nearly bare of "woods" that strangers might go over most of the state on the beaten tracks of travel and, so far as observation is concerned, leave with the impression that it has no forests. This is especially true in the southern counties; when the writer was first told of anything that might properly be called a forest in Santa Barbara county, he was incredulous; yet it is true that within twenty miles, air-line, from Santa

DE LA GUERRA HOUSE, SANTA BARBARA.

SCENES IN SANTA BARBARA COUNTY.

The clear, deep, azure sky of California has a way of uniting every detail into the most artistic combination of form and color. Somehow any building that man can erect seems to harmonize with the surroundings and blend into the background as if it belonged there. The old Mexican adobe houses in the above group are specimens of the original architecture of the county. They are plain, box-like structures, but by some inexplicable law of *chiaroscuro* they always look quaint and picturesque, and seem as if they were built to make paintings of. Santa Barbara County contains some of the most beautiful road scenes to be found in the world. Magnificent trees grow on both sides and meet overhead, forming a natural arch of green leaves. The variety of scenery to be found in this favored spot is almost limitless, and on all sides the objects of the landscape form themselves into natural compositions, ready for the camera or the artist's pencil.

Barbara town, there are considerable areas densely wooded with the grandest of trees. In one basin on the northern slope of the San Rafael range, at an elevation of about 6,300 feet, as many as seven species of conifers are found: the sugar pine (*Pinus Lambertiana,*) the yellow pine (*P. ponderosa,*) the Coulter pine (*P. Coulteri,*) the Sabin pine (*P. Sabinana,*) the silver fir (*Abies concolor,*) the Douglas spruce (*pseudotsuda Douglasii*) and the incense cedar (*Librocedrus decurrens*). Specimens of the incense cedar reach twenty-four feet circumference, and yellow pines nineteen feet, the latter attaining a maximum height of 200 feet—not so large to be sure as in the Sierras, or even in the Northern Coast Range, but nevertheless stately trees.

These cañons of Santa Barbara are notable for their abundance of ferns, and more yet for the number of varieties and the extreme rarity of some of them. Mr. Ford gives a list of about twenty varieties, all beautiful and some of them exceedingly rare elsewhere. The peculiar charm of

CAÑON OF THE PIRU.

the Najogui (na-ho-weé) Falls consists largely in the wealth of ferns among which the cascade descends. Yielding to the spray or breeze, their delicate fronds sway back and forth with matchless grace, like sea-moss or fine kelp in the natural aquaria of the sea-shore. This beautiful cascade is near the Gaviota stage-road between Santa Ynez and Santa Barbara. The road leads through the Gaviota Pass, famous for its wild beauty, and then for forty miles along or near the ocean beach. Another stage line, connecting the same points, goes through the San Marcos Pass, equally interesting in a general way, and affording a fine distant view of Santa Barbara and its surroundings from the brow of the Santa Ynez Mountains.

The writer has asked himself the question, as doubtless many others have done: Why is the neighborhood of Santa Barbara so much preferred? Why singled out as the best climatically and notably attractive in a general way? Why is it known even more widely than California? A glance at the map answers part of the query. The general trend of California's coast is from northwest to southeast, and the harsher ocean winds sweep along in the same direction. Near the western boundary of Santa Barbara county, Point Conception, a bold promontory, stands out some twelve miles into the ocean, turning the wind away from the mainland and largely outside the Channel Islands, which extend eastward and with the mainland form the Santa Barbara Channel. From Point

Conception the coast-line runs fifty or sixty miles nearly due east, thus receding from the track of the wind and at the same time securing sunny exposure for the mainland. On the north the mountain wall is only a few miles inland. The small coast valleys referred to are really the low southern slope of the Santa Ynez range or of its foothills, separated by seaward spurs of the latter into five parts, as indicated by the names above, the entire group lying between the 34th and 35th degrees of latitude. All this promises a mild, equable climate, and the thermometer verifies the promise. The yearly average temperature is about 61° Fahrenheit; for January, 53.25°, for July 68.20°, difference between the average mean of summer and winter about 14°. The figures are based on careful records covering six consecutive years. The rainfall averages only about fifteen inches—usually 300 to 330 days of sunshine in the year. Southern California has been laughed at so much since the "boom" because of its alleged dependence on "climate," that there has been a decided inclination to blot out the word from its dictionaries. The writer, living in San Francisco, ventures to think that, after all, a good climate is not a bad thing. The above paragraph is not written for invalids alone. Everybody likes to be comfortable and to keep well.

The other query, as to the general attractiveness of this locality, has also been answered in part: a happy contiguity of mountain and sea, a pleasing combination of hill and dale, of beach and bay and isle; about the same elements which have drawn visitors from all the world to the shores of the Mediterranean.

The site of Santa Barbara is one of the most beautiful to be found anywhere—an unbroken gradual slope from the beach back to the old mission, three miles away, the upper part of the town having an elevation of about 300 feet. It is a city of homes, the business houses instinctively confining themselves to a single street. The finest of shade trees abound, and in the gardens flowers are blooming and fruits ripening in endless variety and prodigal profusion every month in the year. The beach affords a fine drive and fair bathing, there is no lack of interesting rambles in the various cañons, and Carpenteria, Montecito and the Patera are inviting points for excursions. After one has named many attractive features which are palpable to everybody at Santa Barbara, there seems yet to be a subtle something, an undefined and undefinable charm about the place that is pretty sure to win the heart.

Santa Paula Cañon.

Among the delightful excursions naturally made from Santa Barbara, should be mentioned a sail to the Channel Islands some twenty-five miles distant. Prof. Leconte and other authorities tell us these islands are simply the culminating peaks of a submerged mountain-range, what is now the Santa Barbara Channel having been a valley ages ago. The island of San Miguel is the western link in the chain and the three Anacapas the eastern, the larger islands of Santa Rosa and Santa Cruz intervening. The entire chain is some eighty-five miles long and has a total shore-line of near two hundred and forty miles. The highest portions rise about 1,000 feet above the waves, and are crowned here and there with conifers, and some trees and shrubs not found on the mainland at all. The chief charm of the islands, however, is in their rugged shores, the basaltic walls often rising in a nearly vertical line from 150 to 300 feet. Rocky promontories here and there have been pierced by the action of the waves, ceaselessly at work during the ages, forming arches gigantic and beautifully turned. In the softer volcanic outflow composing portions of the walls are vast briny caverns, easily entered by tourists' boats, carrying torches because of the deep darkness.

Many travelers going southward from Santa Barbara leave the railroad at Carpenteria, and by stage or private conveyance make a detour to the Ojai (O-hi) Valley, the road leading through the strikingly picturesque Cacitas Pass. From Nordhoff, in the lower Ojai, the Matilija cañon is easily reached—one of the most

WHITE CEDAR AND DOUGLAS FIR.

beautiful of those gorges which Helen Hunt Jackson said ought to become the subject of a book.

The town of Ventura—its name unpoetically shortened from San Buenaventura—is near the eastern extremity of the channel. Like Santa Barbara, it "sits in the lap of the mountains, its feet resting in the waves." *Xucu*, another of the Indian villages mentioned by Cabrillo, occupied part of the same ground only a half century after the discovery of America by Columbus; and doubtless these Indian villages were populous and thrifty long before the new world was known at all to Europeans. Ventura is also the seat of one of the ten missions embraced in the Southern Coast Region we have been outlining. The manifest thrift of the town gives instant evidence of tributary sources.

The valley of the Santa Clara River, mentioned at the beginning of this article, comprises the central portion of Ventura County, and opens on the sea with a width of about twenty miles. It is one of the largest and most productive valleys of Southern California, and also one of the most beautiful. Seen in early summer, its lower stretches are one vast field of green and gold—ripening wheat and barley and growing corn and beans, the vines

EL MORO ROCK.

of the latter covering the ground so that they look in the distance like great meadows. Beans in the bag are perhaps not exactly picturesque, but they are immensely profitable as produced here; and the growing crop as seen in this Ventura vista is a telling element in a beautiful picture. Back from the sea a few miles the valley is filled with orchards embracing nearly all kinds of northern and semi-tropical fruits. Even bananas are grown in certain sheltered nooks. The raising of apricots and English walnuts is already a large industry. Oranges and lemons are also grown to quite an extent, one of the earliest orchards, near Santa Paula, covering a hundred acres.

Other valleys of this county are the San Buenaventura, the Conejo, the Las Posas, the Simi and the Ojai, the last being a beautiful mountain-walled amphitheatre, garnished with groups of live-oaks and white oaks which make it one of nature's parks. The principal rivers are the Santa Clara and San Buenaventura. Among the tributaries of the one are the Piru, the Sespe and the Santa Paula; into the other flow the Coyote, Matilija, and the San Antonio. All of these are locally famous for the beauty and variety of their scenery.

Let Dr. Stephen Bowers, geologist and naturalist, describe one of them: "Piru Creek, flowing north into the Santa Clara, has cut its gorge through towering walls in the very heart of the mountains. The mouth of the cañon, thirty miles from the ocean, is nearly a thousand feet above sea-level. Conglomerate rocks rise on either side as one ascends the cañon for the first mile and a half. Then alternating shales, metaphoric and other sandstones, conglomerate and an occasional intercalation of granite or diarite or serpentine are met with. The strata are sometimes horizontal and again vertical, or folded, or heaved at every conceivable angle of inclination. This great variety of rock exposure continues for fifteen miles, the cañon widening in some places sufficiently for small farms until the 'narrows' are reached. Here the mountains close in on both sides and leave only a slender, tortuous, ribbon-like opening for the stream which flows between vertical or impending walls. At this point the creek-bed is more than sixteen hundred feet above sea-level, and here begins the most imposing scenery in all this region. Hitherto the course of the cañon has been nearly due north and south, but now it begins a tortuous course through a mountain of conglomerate

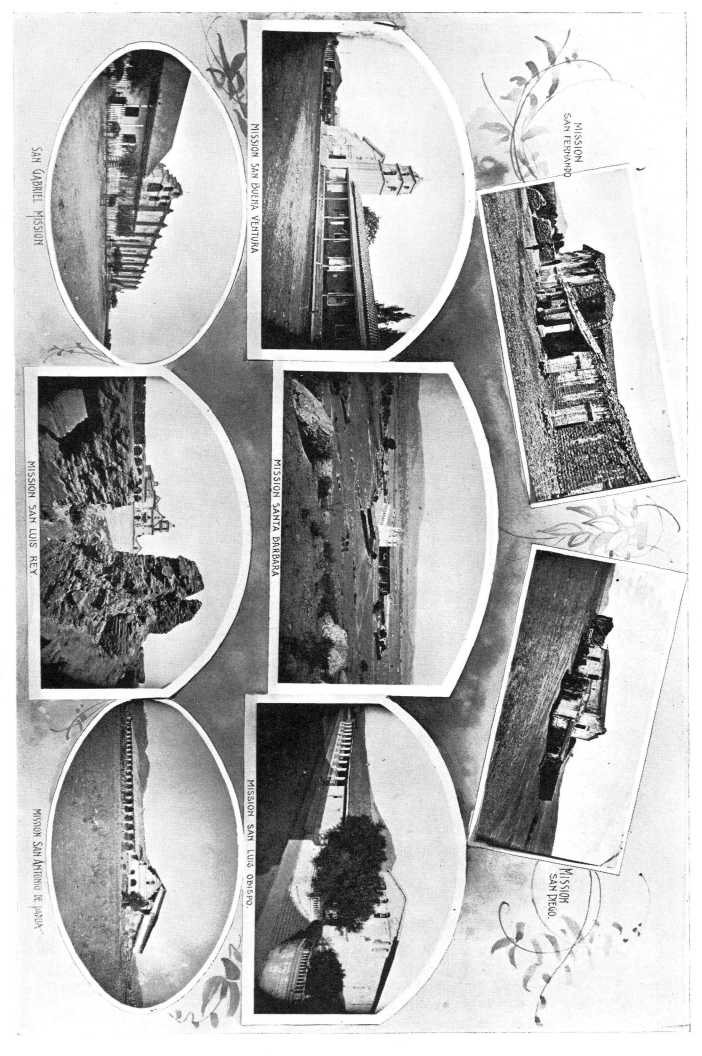

GROUP OF SOUTHERN CALIFORNIA MISSIONS.

The greater number of the missions of California are located in the vicinity of Santa Barbara and Los Angeles, and even at this late day throw a halo of romance over the landscape, that keeps green the memory of the padres who long ago braved the dangers of the wilderness to establish churches and spread the Christian faith. It is a fact beyond any doubt that all of the missions are located in a fertile country, with a climate like Paradise. Trees and flowers grow in profusion, and form the most perfect background for the crumbling adobe walls and tiled roofs. The architectural designs of the old churches depicted in the above group indicate a high order of ability, and it is a question that will perhaps never be decided whether the old monks created them in all their beauty by pure chance, or whether the work was done by a trained architect. But no matter how they were built, or by whom, their beauty has never been denied, and the destroying hand of time seems to give them an added charm.

SAN GABRIEL MISSION

MISSION SAN BUENA VENTURA

MISSION SAN FERNANDO

MISSION SAN DIEGO

MISSION SAN LUIS REY.

MISSION SANTA BARBARA

MISSION SAN ANTONIO DE PADUA

MISSION SAN LUIS OBISPO.

rock, leaving perpendicular walls from five hundred feet to more than a third of a mile high. In some places water percolates through interstices in the rock, from which ferns and flowering plants grow in rich profusion along the face of the walls hundreds of feet above the stream.

"Here are boulders of conglomerate rock as large as a dwelling-house. They are composed of pebbles and small boulders of granitic rocks, quartzite, red jasper, porphyry and other minerals, planed off and worn smooth by the water which has poured down the cañon for untold ages. A little farther on the gorge narrows to not more than twenty feet, with vertical walls on either side, causing the water to 'stand on edge,' as it were, when the stream is swollen by winter rains. At this place, far up on the mountain-side, a stream pours over the rocky wall in a beautiful cascade. The water is highly charged with lime carbonate and has built up a trough of calcareous tufa which projects several feet from the wall, and through which the water flows the entire year, reaching the stream below some distance from the mountain side.

"A little farther on the gorge widens and is filled with mottled conglomerate boulders of immense size and extending across the chasm. Half a mile from this point the conglomerate formation comes to an abrupt termination and granite begins. The transformation is very distinctly marked. A mountain of granite and another of conglomerate join without intervening space. Here nearly every shade of granite occurs, as quartzite granite, micaceous granite, feldspathic granite, gneissoid granite, black micaceous granite, red granite, pegmatitic or graphic granite, granite with large crystals of rose-colored orthoclase, etc. Farther on is a stratum of diorite nearly vertical and joined on either side by granite walls.

"The high cliffs that extend along the cañon were once the resort of the mountain sheep, and a pair of fine horns taken here lie beside me as I write. The frequent benches and small *mesas* along the course of the stream afforded them a place of refuge during the winter months.

"Wild and picturesque scenery still abounds as one continues the ascent of the cañon. For more than forty miles the stream of living water dashes through this rift in the solid mountain of granite, now hurling itself against the face of a perpendicular wall a thousand feet high, and then plunging at right angles toward a similar wall a few hundred feet distant to be again driven from its course with rush and roar. And thus it continues, falling more than four thousand feet from the time it leaves the gold mines of Fraser Mountain until it mingles its water with the Santa Clara River."

Not far from the mouth of Piru Cañon in the upper Santa Clara Valley, is the old Camulos Ranch where Mrs. Jackson located the home of Ramona. Passing there on a Southern Pacific train recently, the writer was somewhat amused to find the passengers crowding out onto the platform and steps of the cars and peering toward the ranch house as if expecting every moment to see Ramona and Alessandro emerge from the shadow of the great willow tree.

Altogether, this Southern coast-range region from Monterey to Ventura, with its wealth of natural scenery, its vast variety of interesting products, its superabundance of fruits and flowers, its genial and yet tonic climate, its romantic old missions and pre-historic relics, is well worth seeing and knowing.

WILLIAM L. OGE.

THE PLAIN OF OAKS.

PIONEER CAMP—LA HONDA CREEK.

"Oh Christ! it is a goodly sight to see
What Heaven hath done for this delicious land."

Childe Harold.

THE *Palo Colorado* at the summit had barely challenged the approach of day, as a small company of swarthy huntsmen scaled the western slope of the mountains that look down upon the distant Farallones —the faithful sentinels of the Golden Gate. Slowly and silently they pick their way under the shadow of the hills. No other foot perhaps had left an impress on the moss-grown slopes, so wild the spot. Nothing breaks the solitude, for even the very Indians have scarcely trodden these inhospitable paths or dragged their subtle forms through the well-nigh impenetrable cañons. Presently the hunters emerge from cañon and forest to find themselves upon the edge of a rocky outlook.

It is the beginning of November. The morn is perfect. The atmosphere is clear and buoyant; the sky and earth have only recently received their first refreshing bath, after many months of sunshine undisturbed. The distant hills and glossy slopes are still arrayed in all their autumn gowns, rich with velvet tans and russet furbelows, for as yet they await the more copious flow of the latter rains before changing to their winter's green.

As our hunters reach their present point of vantage, instinctively they turn their faces to the west. Before them lies the broad Pacific; beneath them wave after wave expends itself upon the weather-beaten crags of Point San Pedro or Corral de Tierra; to their right the Enseñada de los Farallones, terminating at Point Reyes, under which, at Drake's Bay, lies the port of the old San Francisco. Behind and above them are still seen the rolling hills that extend onward and upward toward the summit, here yellow with their late crop of oats, there green with clumps of manzanita or chaparral; there rugged and bare, or anon clothed with a depth of forest that seems to span the very chasms of the mountains with colossal redwoods.

Again the swarthy huntsmen renew their eastward climb over many a rounded knoll, through many a mountain gorge. Presently a joyful shout from one of the hunters brings all his companions to his side. The whole scene has changed, the summit has been passed, the curtain of foliage has been suddenly lifted, and from the rocky ledge on which they stand spreads out before them one of the loveliest valleys of the world; while to the north and to the south extends a new and unheard-of inland sea as far as the eye can reach, and to the east, beyond this noble "Brazo de Mar," rises a magnificent chain of mountains. History never will know the names of these brave and dauntless hunters, but there is no doubt that to the expedition of General Portolá must be credited the first discovery of the Golden Gate, and that, on the 2d of November, 1769, the summit was first crossed and the most perfect harbor of the world was first displayed to European eyes, and where now nestles the fairest city of the wondrous West, the most beautiful, by far, of all the daughters of Atlas. The writer is well aware that many careful historians would give this

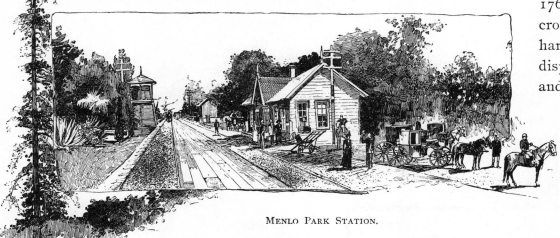

MENLO PARK STATION.

honor to Sir Francis Drake, but although he claims lineage with that renowned admiral and would gladly place so important a discovery to the family credit, it appears to him that the evidence is overwhelmingly in favor of Portolá. In 1769 no San Francisco graced the inner harbor; it was not till long afterwards that the old San Francisco of Drake's bay was safely housed within the Golden Gate.

The everlasting hills and tranquil bay, the glorious sky and balmy air, are the same to-day as when Portolá's bold retainers looked down this eastern slope that bright November morn; but otherwise how changed the outlook in this short space of time! There below us, the same long stretch of valley; there beyond, the same glistening "Brazo de Mar," and beyond again the bold front of Mount Diablo; to the right Mount Hamilton; to the left Mount Tamalpais, with the Coast Range meeting the eye the whole expanse between, the outline just the same; maybe, however, the Spanish soldiery could scarcely recognize in Tamalpais the sleeping beauty, now likened to Elaine, drifting feet foremost towards the ocean, her massive tresses loosened from their coils and floating downward to the vale below; her head and bust and clean-cut virgin bosom outlined in wondrous purple against the rosy setting of the evening sky.

But how different the valley, for here, to-day, for many a league, spreads out the fairy vale of Santa Clara—

" *   *   all rich with blossom'd trees,
And fields which promise corn and wine,
And scatter'd cities crowning these,
Whose far white walls along them shine."

There Mayfield and Mountain View; there the trim city of Santa Clara, while beyond, in the midst of the valley, half hidden by her own green avenues, coyly rests the garden city of San Jose.

The plain, in short, is one vast garden, the grapevines and fruit trees laden to the ground with their luscious burdens, whilst the homes are so thickly established that the whole expanse appears like one continuous cluster of intertwining villages overlapping each the other. Now turning to the left we note the upper valley contracting to a point where the line of hills meets the bay— the "Brazo de Mar" of Portolá. There, between the hills and the water, is the pretty town of San Mateo; there Millbræ; and there the San Bruno hills and Point Avisâdero; and beyond are the smoky environments and hazy outlines of the great metropolis of the Golden West. Here in the foreground, just beneath us, lie Redwood City, Belmont and San Cárlos, and a little to the right the beautiful valley of Portolá—a vale within a vale, while under the foothills that enclose that fairy glen we note the favored suburb of San Francisco,

PALO ALTO STABLES AND PADDOCKS.

White Oaks Near Menlo Park. From Drawing by James Fagan.

"The trees in this section of the country are simply magnificent. Here in this white-oak belt of Menlo, in very truth, is Dame Nature's Park. For miles and miles it seems as if some few score of the notable old country parks had been thrown together and transplanted bodily to this plain. We drive for hours over level, well-kept roads, the graceful white oaks meeting overhead, or now and again obtruding their gnarled trunks into the midst of the road and spreading out their arched limbs and drooping foliage till they form gateways that in their grace and elegance far eclipse the marble entrance to London's West End Park, or the crowning triumph of the Champs Elysée.

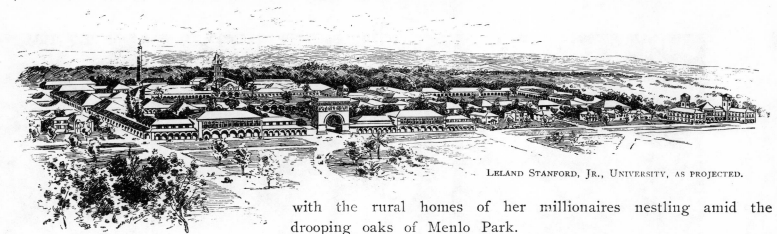

LELAND STANFORD, JR., UNIVERSITY, AS PROJECTED.

with the rural homes of her millionaires nestling amid the drooping oaks of Menlo Park.

Let us descend from our ærie height and inspect more closely the valley lying at our feet. It was here, so we are informed by the good Father Crespí, that Portolá's followers made themselves sick by eating too many acorns. We are not greatly surprised, for one oak alone, by a roadside inn in Portolá Valley, seems big enough to supply a whole brigade! The trees in this section of the country are simply magnificent. Here in this white oak belt of Menlo, in very truth, is Dame Nature's Park. For miles and miles it seems as if some few score of the notable Old Country parks had been thrown together and transplanted bodily to this plain. We drive for hours over level, well-kept roads, the graceful white oaks meeting overhead, or now and again obtruding their gnarled trunks into the middle of the road and spreading out their arched limbs and drooping foliage till they form gateways that in their grace and elegance far eclipse the marble entrance to London's West End Park or the crowning triumph of the Champs Elysées. Presently we pass the picturesque little depot lying so snug and cool under the shadow of its live-oak trees— trees that are green the year round and dense with the intensity of the growth of their small, dark, shining leaves. The station yard is bedecked with flowers and palms and well-trimmed lawns, and here and there, between the trees or over a wicket gate, we catch a glimpse of some half-hidden mansion and ornamental grounds that tell their tale of wealth and luxury and ease. Some distance from the track, we notice the giant redwood, "Palo Alto," that towers, a well-known landmark, for many a league and gives name to the far-famed rancho. Around the depot the scene is alive with glossy teams that paw the ground and champ the bit, impatient at the train's delay. A passing stranger may well wonder at the array of blooded horses and well-appointed carriages that he sees assembled in this station yard, for he would little dream that the adjacent woods could effectually hide the many sumptuous homes from whence they spring.

To be critical, we miss the freedom that surrounds the parks and mansions of our much-abused English aristocracy. There is scarcely a private park in any county in England that is not open to the public at all times; while, during the absence of "the family," the interior of the "Hall" or castle is always open to the inspection of any stranger on presentation of his visiting card. But in the atmosphere of Menlo Park there appears to be a certain reserve that is hard for us to understand—so many bolts, and bars, and gates, and locks. The mansions, moreover, are so studiously hidden from view behind impervious borders of shrubs and trees, that although the "woods are full of them," you may drive over miles of public roadway and catch scarcely a glimpse of the many beautiful houses and exquisite grounds that lie behind these walls of evergreen. But it may seem to the owners of these snug retreats that what they lose in beauty of landscape, they gain in seclusion and repose.

Let us turn from the public roadway for a time and invade some of these parks within a park that lie behind the triple barricades of flowering shrubs and well-trimmed evergreens. The best time, perhaps, to see the charming homes of Menlo Park is in the spring or early summer. We have a very vivid recollection of a pleasant time spent at a friend's house near Menlo towards the beginning of the "Merrie month of May." Whilst on this visit we had the opportunity of exploring a great many of the neighboring places. Nowhere else in the world did we ever see such a magnificent display of roses, banks and banks of them, tier on tier, of every kind and every color; the landscape brilliant with their gorgeousness, the atmosphere intoxicating with their perfume, whilst here and there the tallest oaks were bedecked from tip to base with wreaths of the most rare and exquisite varieties—the gay festoons hanging from the topmost branches and connecting tree with tree. There seems to be no end to these " parks within a park," as, one by one, we explore their hidden treasures. Here perhaps we enter at once from the highway into the very home of Flora, the carriage-drive winding around close-cut lawns and grassy borders, gay the whole extent with ornamental shrubs and rarest flowers, till at length the vista opens and we see before us a palace of spotless white in a setting of noble trees and sweeping lawns, relieved and beautified with flowers of every tint and color. Or perhaps we

A HILLSIDE VILLA.

enter from the highroad into a twisting, tortuous driveway, flanked on either side with a thick, maze-like hedge, till on a sudden turn there spreads out before us a veritable Gan'-Eden. Acres and acres of smooth, moss-like grass, with shady walks and sunny glades, incite us still further to explore these almost mystic groves. Trees and shrubs from every clime bedeck the lawns in exquisite taste of grouping and arrangement of color. Now we seek some quiet home nestling behind its luscious vineyards and thriving orchards, or now, perhaps, the more elaborate abode of some merchant prince or railroad magnate.

Presently, as we continue our drive, we stop before some unpretentious gateway to admire its perfect setting, though unadorned by any workman's skill. No keeper's lodge to bar the entrance or to challenge our approach, for here Dame Nature has exercised her own free will. A sturdy oak, in all its grace of limb and foliage, spreads forth a leafy portal, whose cavernous recesses and exquisite tracery men may try in vain to copy or excel. As we pass within the gates and follow the serpentine course of the sylvan roadway, we feel at once the charm surrounding a place whose owner is in touch with nature. Save that the road is hard-metaled, and well kept, we might almost imagine that the fairies and elves had, unassisted, planned these walks and drives and revelled in their fantastic dances under the silvered limbs of the majestic oaks, or picked the moonstone from the glittering leaves of the bright wild cherry trees. The birds chirp their lively welcome, nor try to hide themselves in this close sanctuary. The wary quail just nods his plume in saucy recognition, but scarcely struts from off the path; while the very hares and rabbits hop lazily along beside you. Nothing is afraid, for no gun awakes the echoes of Fair Oaks. Anon a green sward spreads before us; magnolia and other blossoms lend their fragrance to the air; the graceful palms and beds of gorgeous flowers give notice of a habitation near, and presently, almost hidden behind its network of sweetest roses, the quiet country home itself is found.

PORTOLÁ VALLEY.
MONTE BELLO VINEYARD AND WINERY.

But we must not longer dwell amid the avenues and fragrant bowers of Menlo Park; neither is ours the task to draw invidious comparisons of beauty or of style of residence.

" A tous oiseaux
Leurs nids sont beaux."

Suffice it to say that in and around this " Plain of Oaks "—so christened by Father Crespí and Gaspar de Portolá in 1769—are found to-day the suburban mansions of millionaires and railroad kings.

The climate of the White Oak Plain is exclusively its own—unique, even amid the perpetual sunshine of this glorious California.   Spring, summer, autumn, winter, it is never hot, never cold. In whichever direction you drive, you seem to meet one constant balmy breeze.   The ocean fogs, so prevalent on the coast, never enter this charmed circle ; whilst the piercing trade-winds are tempered and filtered down to the most refreshing and invigorating zephyrs.   This is doubtless due to the crescent shape, at this point, of the line of the Sierra Morena Mountains, that extend from the dim outlines just seen towards the south, where are situate the famous Mines of New Almaden, and sweep thence around toward the ocean, and thence again toward the east till they reach the other horn of the crescent at Belmont, where the heights and spurs of the peninsular range almost meet the very waters of the inner harbor of San Francisco Bay, thus obtruding a curved and almost pointed shield toward the ocean front, along the outer edge of which the trade winds are broken

A TYPICAL SUBURBAN HOUSE.

and diverted and the fog lifts or rolls away on either side as if by machinery.   "The Plain of Oaks " lies within this crescent.

In this most equable and perfect climate then, how delightful it is to spin along the broad and level " Camino Real" or King's Highway of the Spanish Dons, past the pretty towns of Redwood City, Belmont and San Mateo, on perhaps to San Bruno, or to the Mission Dolores of San Francisco itself ; or on the other hand, through Mayfield, Mountain View, Santa Clara, on to San José and Los Gatos on the south.   Another day, tiring of the level roads, we turn our horses' heads towards the hills, and visit the beautiful lakes of Spring Valley.   Or yet another day, we turn our attention to the rolling foothills that skirt the inner rim of the crescent of which we spoke.   On through the gentle valley of Portolá, where the orange and the pomegranate, the lemon and the lime, add their grace and beauty to its still more protected confines, and where many a lovely home nestles under its vine-clad hillside or spreads itself around some gurgling stream or cooling spring.   Or perhaps we mount the "Alpine Ridge," descend the beautiful cañon of the Pescadero, explore the charming little town of that name, collect our agates and carnelians, our amber and our opal from off the noted Pebble Beach, and return by the ravishing La Honda.   Now the road skirts the narrow ledge of some dizzy height ; now commands the distant panorama of rich valleys, the glistening bay, the line of mountains that lie beyond ; now threads some densely

A Bit of Mendocino Coast (Mouth of the Navarro River). From Painting by C. D. Robinson.

"Northward for miles stretches the fine yet treacherous beach, below glitters the Pacific like molten silver, its waves lazily lapping the rocks where seals disport and lift up their bass voices in frequent chorus, and myriads of shags solemnly stand erect as though awaiting a revelation. The mouths of these rivers are the starting points for the immense 'log-booms' which are floated from the lumber regions down to San Francisco, the voyage embracing, perhaps, the roughest coast to be encountered in California."

wooded gorge, where the redwood forests seem to point their giant fingers through the very dome of Heaven. The stillness is alone broken by the gurgling of the stream and the murmur of the trees— a very paradise for the sportsman and the camping party.

Or, should we tire of driving, we will walk across the fields from Menlo Park and visit the Palo Alto Rancho. Here we shall find the home and training-ground of some of California's most noted racers, as well as the training-ground of California's sturdy sons and daughters; for here are the noted Palo Alto stables, and here also, fast drawing toward the opening-day, is the Cambridge of the west, the truly magnificent Leland Stanford, Jr. University. If the Palo Alto Rancho succeeds in training young humanity half as well as she has heretofore trained her blooded horses and her thoroughbreds, she may indeed rest contented on her well-earned laurels.

Passing over the San Francisquito, whose clear sparkling waters gurgle at our feet, we presently find ourselves in the midst of a very labyrinth of paddocks, sheltered under the deep green foliage of the beautiful live-oaks. The tenants of these endless corrals are as great celebrities in their way, as is the worthy Senator, their owner. Now we inspect the miniature track, or kindergarten. Here the enterprising youngsters are taken in hand well-nigh before they can "stand alone," and are given their first lecture on physical culture, and other "lessons without tears." Presently we catch sight of the principal buildings, which form a large quadrangle, several acres in extent. There to the right are the homes of the sires, noble aristocrats puffed up with pride and with pedigrees equal to royalty itself. There is the stately "Piedmont," the valiant "Palo Alto;" and there the home of the majestic "Electioneer"—household words the world over. Now we approach the beautiful ladies of the seraglio. See how they thrust their inquisitive noses over the half-doors, curve their graceful necks and eye our approach with the innate curiosity of their sex. That large building in front of us is the hotel of the frolicsome yearlings, the pretty beauties. It is indeed a model stable, with model surroundings, in the midst of a model climate; small wonder that the horses too take rank as model horses. California has at least taught the world with clinching arguments, that she knows how to raise and how to train her horses, and we are satisfied—thanks to the unapproached generosity of one of her citizens—that she will show the world that she knows how to train her sons and daughters.

The Leland Stanford Junior University will by no means follow in the beaten track, for, in addition to the ordinary university studies, the plan of instruction will embrace the practical, technical study, not merely of the arts and sciences, but of the various trades, of farming, of mechanics and skilled labor of every description, under the most favorable conditions, so as "to qualify students for personal success and direct usefulness in life." California may indeed be proud of such an institution, and of a man who, while yet living, inalienably endowed it with the princely gift of $20,000,000.

The architecture is highly appropriate and characteristic of California, following as far as possible the style of the churches and buildings of the early missionary Fathers. The main court is already completed. The heavy red-tiled roofs overhang segregated, yet continuous, one story buildings of yellow sandstone, while the deep embrasures of the thick mullioned windows invite us to invade their cool recesses. As we enter through the eastern or the western archway, the eye is charmed with the rare display of exotics, graceful plants and sweet scented flowers. One continuous cloister— cool, shady and delicious—extends the whole length of the inner side of the quadrangle. The bright blue, cloudless sky, seen under the clean-cut yellow stone archways as one looks out from the quadrangle, is a sight not easily forgotten. To the north will rise, in due time, the lofty memorial arch, while facing it on the south will soon be built the beautiful chapel dedicated to the memory of the founder's only child.

As General Portolá stood upon the summit of the Sierra Morena and looked down upon this wide "plain of oaks," we wonder if his most exaggerated vision could have pictured the valley as it is to-day. What would he say could he judge of its future according to the advance shadows now cast by coming events!

ALBERT E. GRAY.

THE LAND OF THE REDWOOD.

CALIFORNIA contains a group of great and famous forests unlike any other forests known to man—the redwoods, remnants of an ancient and almost perished race of prehistoric giants of the vegetable world. They are the one most characteristic feature of the northern coast counties; they extend far inland to the heads of the larger valleys of the Coast Range; clumps of them crown mountains as far east as Howell and St. Helena, and when they are gone, unlike the cedars of Lebanon, they will leave no descendants.

In 1872 the late Asa Gray delivered an address upon "Sequoia and its History." It will be found in the second volume of his "Scientific Papers," and every person who is interested in the noblest coniferous forest in the world ought to read this fascinating study of a great subject. The two redwoods, the *Sequoia sempervirens* of the Coast Range and the *S. gigantea* of the Sierra, are the last representatives of a noble and numerous race of *sequoias* that once occupied a broad zone about the North Arctic circle. Their life history is so remarkable that it must interest every

TRANSFORMATION:
FROM FOREST TO MARKET.

intelligent reader. Briefly stated, then, all the best authorities agree that the oldest redwood trees now standing do not antedate the Christian era. Other trees are possibly older, and some of the Eucalyptus are taller. But the larger trees of the redwood forest, ranging in age from twelve hundred to eighteen hundred years, rank among the wonders of the vegetable kingdom. Science sees in them the last representatives of enormous forests; science sees that they were slowly perishing in their last strongholds, even before the lumberman discovered their economic value. They are the "sole and scant survivors of a race that has played a grander part in the past, but is now verging to extinction."

Redwoods have no near relatives among the living trees. They are distantly connected with the bald cypress of the swamps of the Atlantic and southern coasts—a large and long-lived tree; also with another conifer, the Glyptostrolus of China. Of the four related species, two are thus in California, one in China, and one along the Atlantic.

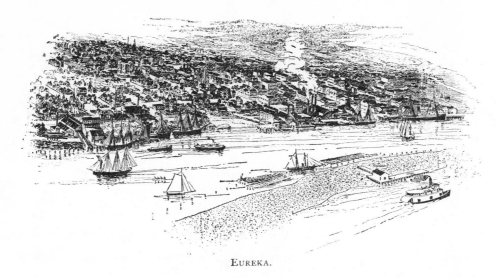

EUREKA.

In the tertiary period, however, there were species of Bald Cypress, of Glyptostrolus and of Sequoia in Europe. This is a curious condition of affairs, and points to the ancient occupation of the arctic and sub-arctic zones by an immensely varied vegetation, which, before the glacial age, contained the progenitors of the plants of China, Japan, the Pacific Coast, the Alleghanies and Europe. The advance of the glaciers moving southward drove the plants of the time before them in radiating lines of march, but they perished in many places where the new environment was unsuitable. The sequoias could only live on the Pacific Coast, where they found for ages a perfectly congenial home. The high inland basin between Sierra and Rockies, the Rockies themselves, the Mississippi valley, the Alleghanies, and the Atlantic shores were all found totally unsuited to the sequoias, though a hardier relative, the bald cypress, obtained a foothold. It was much the same in Asia, and especially in the insular climate of Japan, where the close relation of the flora with that of the Atlantic coast of the United States is very instructive—the sequoias could not live, but a distantly allied species flourished. The ancient sequoias, now fossils, are very abundant in northern Europe, in Iceland, Spitzbergen, Greenland, the Arctic shores of North America, Alaska, and Siberia. The most common of these fossil trees is similar to the redwood of the Coast Range; another fossil species was evidently the progenitor of the redwood of the Sierras, and it is also an interesting fact that before the glacial period the ancestor of our coast redwood was flourishing as far north as Oregon. Ages ago then, the two redwoods reached California, were cut off from their brethren, lived on and throve—the giants of an elder world. The three species of Torreyas, one of which is in California, have suffered reverses, and Dr. Gray uses the common yew as another illustration. Dr. Gray, in the study of the sequoias, which I have followed in this general view, says that "no account and no photographic representation of either species of the redwood gives any adequate impression of their singular majesty—still less of their beauty." Elsewhere he says that "the coast redwood—the most important tree in California, although a million times more numerous than its relative of the Sierra—is too good to live long. Such is its value for lumber and its accessibility that, judging the future by the past, it is not likely in its primeval growth to outlast its rarer fellow-species."

When the Americans conquered California the redwoods were, as now, confined to a narrow extent of coast line, but it extended farther inland, and over a much larger area than now, after forty years of lumbering. The growth of redwoods in the Sierra Madre Range of Los Angeles is the most southern outpost of the species. Scattered groups of poor redwoods, mixed with pines, extend from the southern end of Monterey County to the mouth of the Salinas, but there are no sawmills there, and the timber is used only for local purposes. Most of the trees stand in the bottoms of

FORT HUMBOLDT.

CAPT. U. S. GRANT'S RESIDENCE, GUARD HOUSE AND PARADE GROUND. 1853-4.

SURF CRATERS, MENDOCINO COAST. FROM PAINTING BY J. O. DAVIDSON, AFTER SKETCH BY C. D. ROBINSON.

For ages the giant surges of the Pacific have beaten in fury against the rock-bound coast of Mendocino County, seemingly in the effort to wash it out of existence. The rocks have resisted the unceasing attacks, but the waters are everlastingly taking them away, small portions at a time. The softer portions go first, to become a part of the beach at their base, leaving the cliff in the most fantastic forms. In some places the water has washed holes through the rocky walls, and during storms dashes upward with irresistible force. The immense weight of water gradually makes the hole larger, until at last the surrounding walls are unable to hold the outside portion, and it falls into the ocean with an awful roar. In some places the rocks show the action of water far away from the reach of the waves, and have been the cause of a good deal of controversy. The supposition is that they were of volcanic origin and were forced into their present position by earthquakes.

exceedingly inaccessible gulches.   The Santa Cruz forests begin on the Pajaro River, a few scattered trees lying in cañons south of that picturesque stream, and extend in a solid body well into San Mateo, with a fringe of scattered redwoods extending to within sight of the boundaries of San Francisco.   "Palo Alto," the landmark of the Stanford estate, is a redwood, one of whose giant trunks has fallen.   The Contra Costa forest, east of San Antonio, in the cañons that slope towards San Leandro Creek, and on the high ridges overlooking East Oakland, was only a small forest, but it was a very attractive one.   The Forty-Niners put mills there, and only a wilderness of suckers from the stumps is to be seen now.   With proper care this waste and twice-cut redwood district could be made a famous camping-park for San Francisco people.   The next group of redwoods was a small forest near Saucilito; then, after a region where no redwoods grew, the great forest of the State began, about the ravines of Tamalpais, and extended north to the Oregon line—*began*, I say, for now the line of merchantable timber forest has been pushed north, almost

SUNSET—COAST OF MENDOCINO.

to the mouth of Russian River.   There, at Duncan's mills and Guernville, begins the only redwood forest worthy of the name.

The best bodies of timber in the northern redwood forest will average 200,000 feet of marketable lumber to the acre.   It was estimated in the census report of 1880 that about 25,000,000,000 feet of accessible redwood lumber was standing in this great region, from Crescent City south to the Russian River.   Between 1880 and 1890 probably one-tenth of this standing and available timber has been cut.   The State Forestry Board in 1886 made a more liberal estimate.   Del Norte, Humboldt, Mendocino, and Sonoma were thought to have 1,002,100 acres of available redwood forests, which originally carried over 35,000,000,000 feet of marketable lumber, of which about 5,000,000,000 feet had been cut, leaving in round numbers 30,000,000,000 feet still standing.   The total cut from the upper belt of redwood, some 5,000,000,000 feet, as given above, extended over many years, but is increasing at a rate of from seven to ten per cent. a year; about 250,000,000 feet a year can be expected at the present time, and the export of redwood to other countries is capable of very great extension, as the peculiar value of the wood becomes better understood. The duration of the redwood forests of California can therefore be estimated at between eighty and one hundred years, allowing for the natural increase from young trees.   The view of the educated forester and of the scientific publications is that, with proper care, the redwoods need not be destroyed, but can continue to yield a great and increasing income to the State and to private owners for all time to come. If an efficient guardianship of the redwoods prevents fires and that close pasturage which has destroyed millions of seedlings, and also directs all cutting in accordance with scientific forestry, the timber-crop of the famous redwood belt of California will never slacken until some change of climate destroys the conditions which make the redwood possible. But the narrow, careless and ignorant policy of the present day is rapidly annihilating the finest forests of America.

The stories that old lumbermen tell of the size of some of the redwoods are worth recording. A Guernville tree was measured that was 349 feet high, and another was 19 feet in diameter. An acre of redwood when cut yielded 1,431,530 feet of marketable lumber. In 1855 a citizen of Arcata, Humboldt County, cut down a redwood which was 400 feet high. He sawed and split 60 feet of the trunk, and built two two-story houses, a garden fence and outhouses, from the lumber thus obtained. In 1856 a writer in *Hutching's Magazine* described a hollow redwood on the Trini-

ROCKPORT.

LUMBER CHUTES ON THE COAST—WESTPORT.

dad trail which measured 33 feet in diameter. Single trees that turn out 100,000 feet of good milling lumber are not uncommon in the redwoods. But the most careful estimates agree in placing the ratio of product at only about twenty-eight per cent; it takes three and a half of standing timber to produce one foot of salable lumber.

In California, as I have said, the term "Land of the Redwood" is used to distinguish the long forest strip beginning near Santa Cruz and skirting the line of hills between mountain and sea as far north as the Oregon line, which belt is the home of the *Sequoia sempervirens*. However close the alliance by nature may be, the redwood groups along the flanks of the Sierra are so far away and so different in their habits and environment that they have come to hold a distinctive and separate place in the public mind, and are commonly referred to as "sequoias."

NEWPORT.

To the eye the general effect of these groups of the *gigantea* is less especially distinctive. The great size of the trees would invariably attract the attention of even the most casual observer; but the final impression is very much the same as that given by the great pine forests in which they stand. There is the same sharp glare of sunshine, the same monotony of coloring in the reds and browns of the soil and bark. There is the same scarcity of animal and bird life, while the high altitude and lack of water combine to reduce the amount of brush and herbage beneath them to a minimum, and give the whole the air of barren—almost desolate—openness, which is so characteristic of the higher California forests. No such charge, however, can be lodged against the *sempervirens* forests. From beginning to end they have an individuality distinctively their own. Starting from the rich soil of the metamorphic limestone which escaped the floods of lava from the coast volcanoes, they harbor at their feet an almost riotous luxuriance of minor vegetation.

Individually the redwood is a striking but not altogether a picturesque tree. The full-grown specimens have somehow the appearance of having been made to order by a workman's hand rather than an artist's. They start from the ground without buttress or irregularity, and from the lowest space to the dizzy height of their crowns the turn is as true and the taper as perfect as if the work had been done by a lathe before they were stood on end. There is often something about the arrangement of the foliage, the stiff, crowded sequence of the branches with leaves only at their very tips, the entire cone-like regularity of form and leafage, which recalls involuntarily the toy trees that come in children's Nuremburg villages.

In the younger specimens this prosaic stiffness of outline is less noticeable. The branches run down almost, if not entirely, to the ground, and there is a feathery lightness about the tasseled

plumage which relieves the rugged hardness of their shape. Late in life again, when their tops have begun to be bald and ragged, when the infirmities of age have weakened a branch here and torn a rift in the foliage there, when the lightning has cut long seams in their smooth bark, and the forest fires have blackened their bases and dug out hollows in their sides, they take on the dignity and picturesqueness that accompanies old age, and with their patient sublimity and quiet strength are as picturesque as the most exacting observer could desire. There is no other

MILL AND WHARF AT FORT BRAGG.

class of trees which surpasses the redwoods in richness and vividness of coloring. There is a peculiar warmth in the yellow-green of the mature foliage that contrasts strikingly with the cinnamon-brown of the bark. In earlier life, and at the time when the newer leafage is unfolding, the color brightens to a perfect green. But the bark of the younger specimens is more dull and reddish. The constant moisture keeps the trees free from dust, and further affords a purity of atmosphere which brings out every detail both of form and color, with a startling distinctness and reality.

As might be expected, these beautiful woods are the home of a wide variety of both furred and feathered life; but the living genius of the redwoods is the great gray or Douglas squirrel. He is omnipresent in the forest, though in the regions most closely populated his numbers have been sadly lessened by the exterminating hand of man. Unconsciously this happy-hearted creature has become the protector of the redwood from some of its most ruthless and persistent enemies. Next to the forest fires nothing has done more toward injuring this forest tree than the depredations of the "seed-hunters." The demand for specimens of the redwood is so widespread and so great that each year large quantities of the seed are exported from California, and the collection

"SNAKING OUT."

CALIFORNIA GRIZZLY BEAR. FROM DRAWING BY F. O. C. DARLEY.

Of all the wild beasts of the wilderness that the explorers and prospectors had to fear none was so dangerous as the grizzly bear.   At one time it was quite common in the mountains of California, and was the cause of the death of many brave men. The grizzly bear as a general thing will not attack a man, but whenever compelled to defend itself will fight with the greatest ferocity.   The grizzly bear is so called from its color—a grizzled gray—but is very variable in this respect, some of them being blackish and brownish.   The above picture is a strong, characteristic drawing of this terror of the wilderness.

of this seed for the market has become a regular and a profitable business. For years the gatherer went through the forests singling out the trees that bore the largest quantity of cones. Careless of everything except his own selfish ends, he seldom hesitated at felling, without compunction, the choicest and most prolific trees. He had a color of right, however, in this vandalism, if one acknowledges the desirability of growing young redwoods, for with a hundred feet of smooth trunk towering above him before a single branch hung out its fringe of cones, it is scarcely to be wondered at that almost the only solution of the difficulty lay in bringing down the mountain to Mahomet, since in this case Mahomet could not climb.

Season after season the seed-hunter's destructive methods went on, till the Douglas squirrel unconsciously solved the problem, and offered himself in most unwilling martyrdom to the cause of these noble trees. Some wandering collector, too indolent to take upon himself the trouble which the process of cutting involved, bethought him of the collections laid up by the squirrels for their winter use. By dint of patient observation he was able to locate enough of these hoards to make up the desired "order for Europe." The method had so many advantages, both in point of the saving of labor and of mercy to the trees, that now the collector seldom or never fells a tree. As for the squirrels, the first and rightful owners of the burrs, they are either shot by their despoilers while chattering their indignant protests or left to starve in the rainy season coming on.

Most of the accessible portions of the redwoods have long since passed out of the hands of the government, and been "located" by private individuals by means of timber or other claims. As far back as the days of the Spanish occupation there were low adobe haciendas, in whose outlying corrals twice every year great herds of the wild Spanish cattle were driven in from these forests for numbering and branding. These establishments have given way to the less picturesque but more numerous cattle ranches of American days.

But the real life of the redwood forests, the activity which gives it the stir and bustle of actually being alive, is that which comes from the logging industry. There is nothing in California that is more picturesque than one of these redwood logging camps. The low-roofed, open-sided mills, the long teams of stolid oxen with their clanking chains, the flannel-shirted drivers with their pistol-cracking whips and uninterrupted flow of high-keyed and objurgatory profanity, all combine to render the scene one that is novel and unusual.

The camps are, for the most part, off from the line of road. They are established on difficult hillsides, and often in steep and almost inaccessible gulches. It is easy to tell when one is in their vicinity, by the intermittent rumblings, like distant thunder, that mark the downfall of the trees. Wherever an especially large and valuable group of redwoods is discovered there the camp is temporarily pitched. The lumberman is exceedingly particular about the size of the redwoods he fells. Nothing is too big for him, though he selects the largest merely for the commercial value of containing more feet of lumber than their smaller neighbors. He draws his line, however, at any tree that is under two or three feet in diameter at the least. The redwood is so extremely brittle that extra precautions have to be taken against the trees splintering and breaking in their fall. Specimens ten feet in diameter have been known to snap squarely off at unsuitable points, rendering them useless for certain purposes and making waste even for ordinary lumber.

The first thing done by the choppers in going to work on a given tree is to line the place of its fall. This being determined on, the space is cleared of logs and other debris, and often piles of brush and tree limbs are laid out to act as cushions for its fall. The next operation is the making of the "under-cut." Curiously enough, the lumberman in felling the redwood does not cut it close to the ground, but chooses to leave standing a stump from eight to ten feet high. There seems to be no really sensible reason for this practice. Theoretically, it is done because the portion of the tree near the ground is apt to be badly fire-hollowed or otherwise unsound. But as the same practice is observed in the case of perfectly sound trees, this theory can hardly be said to cover the whole case. It is probable that it results from the fact that the lumbermen are old hands at the business, and brought with them to California the habits acquired in the pine forests of Canada and of Maine. Hundreds of feet of valuable timber are thus left to waste uselessly in the stump. In making the "under-cut" the choppers stand on narrow pieces of iron-shod wood, driven into the tree about breast high. These "spring-boards," as they are called, are about three or three and a half feet long and about eight inches wide, and enable the axmen to make the cut at a point which otherwise would have been far beyond their reach. It is incredible almost how soon the heart of the tree can be laid bare by their swift, sure strokes. This done, the spring-boards are shifted, and the upper-cut is sawed on the opposite side. It is a delicate undertaking and one requiring close calculation, for a variation of a hair's breadth almost from a line at right angles to the chosen line of the bed prepared for it will cause the mighty tree to fall by so much to one side or the other, and increase the danger of breakage when it strikes.

As the cut approaches the center of the tree, before any distinct wavering of the trunk can be seen, the tree, as if conscious of its impending fate, begins to shiver and rustle its branches, with an uneasy sound that the quick ear of the woodsman recognizes instantly as the beginning of its overthrow. This increases until it becomes so violent that the dead limbs fall, and the air

NAVARRO.

is vibrant with the rustling of the leaves. Then the great head begins to swing and bend, the arc grows larger and larger, the sawyers spring from their boards to escape the final death-struggle, and with a rush like an avalanche and a noise like the roar of distant thunder, the redwood takes the final plunge and stretches its length obediently along the line laid out for it. So accurate do the choppers become in making these calculations that they can set a stake a hundred feet from the foot of a tree they are felling in the line of its proposed fall, and drop the tree so exactly that it will drive the stake down in its descent. Nothing could illustrate more clearly the great height of the redwood than the ruin wrought in it by its fall. As a rule, its scores of branches are crushed and broken into firewood, and lie in a confused heap under and along the trunk.

The next operation—that of clearing the trunk and cutting it into sections convenient for milling—is quickly done, and the awkward teams of oxen are driven in over a hastily constructed road, that is often almost no road at all, to assist in the process of "snaking out" the logs to the nearest shipping point. This is one of the most interesting features of the whole performance. An iron is driven into the butt of one of the logs, and by means of rope or chain attached to the yokes of the cattle. The other end of the log is joined in the same way to a second section of the tree, and so on, until sometimes five or six are thus connected together. Then the drivers

NOYO HARBOR.

LOG "CHUTING," CASPAR CREEK.

MENDOCINO HARBOR.

give the word to the ex-
long chains tighten, the
with the sound of un-
the oxen bend sturdily
is a moment of suspense,
lude of expectant effort,
line of logs begins to
its leafy bed, and follow
team toward the freer and
But the steam

pectant beasts, the
air grows resonant
restrained profanity,
to the pull, there
a breathless inter-
and then the long
move slowly out of
dustily after the
more open spaces.
"skidder," put in
operation on this coast within the past few years, is the wonder of the logging camp. It consists
of an upright, stationary engine, similar to those used in driving piles, but vastly more powerful.
It is moved from camp to camp along the "logging" railway on a low, strongly-built, flat car,
which is side-tracked when the skidder is at work. A steel-wire cable is made fast to a tree, and
stretched out through the forest, a quarter of a mile it may be, across rugged gulches and up
precipitous hillsides, and finally attached to another tree on the border of comparatively level ground,
reached by the logging teams. This cable serves as a tramway, over which a deeply-grooved pulley
is drawn, by a smaller cable winding on the great drum of the engine. A vertical cable, attached
also to the moving pulley, is made fast to an immense log, frequently twenty to thirty feet long
and eight or ten feet in diameter, weighing perhaps twenty to twenty-five tons. The engine gives
a few peremptory puffs, and up swings the great section of a redwood tree into mid-air, apparently
with as much ease as if it were a corncob, so mighty is the machinery. The power of the engine
is now applied also to the pulley, which moves along the tramway, the hoisting cable being at the
same time wound up proportionately on a separate drum, and so the pendant log is drawn home to
the railway-track, where a train of truck-cars stand ready, and by means of a few deft touches
from long pike-poles in the hands of stalwart loggers it is safely landed on the cars, without once
touching the ground.

Toward the upper end of a cañon the grade of the road is often so steep that a locomotive
cannot safely be used. The cars are in such places drawn up the heavy grades by a cable from
the stationary engine, the "skidder." The supremely exciting event is the turning loose of a train
of loaded cars on the down grade. When all is ready the brakes are loosened barely as much as
will admit of the train being started slowly by the long, strong push of all the men. Its tremendous weight, of course, soon tells on the grade, and the train is madly rushing across bridges and
around curves at a much faster rate than even the daring lumbermen would care to ride. The
locomotive stands side-tracked perhaps a mile or two below, at a point where the grade rises, and
reaching this the wild train sobers down gradually and finally stops, apparently willing enough
to submit to the usual régime of engine and brakes for the rest of the way to the mill.

Nor is the interior of the mill itself without interest and picturesque effects. The great
logs, as they come in, are eagerly seized by the powerful machinery, lifted rudely from the cars

A LOGGING TEAM IN THE REDWOODS NEAR FORT BRAGG.

Logging in the Mendocino redwoods is carried on very differently from similar operations in the East, or even in the Sierra Nevadas. Long hauls, *i. e.*, half a mile or more, are usually on "skid" roads. These are made by cutting logs of ten inches in diameter into lengths of eight feet, and placing them in the ground five feet apart, crosswise of the road, and protruding above the surface about four inches. They are then well greased so that the logs will slip easily along as they are dragged over them. One end of each log is "sniped"—rounded up a little so as not to catch against the roadbed. Steep, short ravines, and short hauls, are merely smoothed out and the ground kept wet under the advancing logs to facilitate easy movement. This scene shows the "landing" where the numerous log-ways concentrate at the railroad track for the mill. The load in this case is a large one, consisting of fourteen logs varying from twelve to twenty feet in length, and from two to five feet in diameter, and contains about 6,000 feet of lumber. Sometimes 5,000 feet are brought down in one log sixteen feet long.

that hauled them, and are soon brought face to face with the ravenous saws, hissing with spite and never for a moment concealing their savage teeth.

The smaller logs, those not exceeding six feet in diameter, are consigned directly to the circular saws, and transformed with amazing rapidity into boards as broad as the diameter of the log, less the slabs, and of varying thickness, as the timber is knotty or clear. The larger logs go to the "band" saw—an endless chain of finely-tempered steel, running with lightning speed over a drum above and one below, the continuous band being usually forty to fifty feet long, and having an available cutting length of ten to twenty feet. The full-width boards are carried from both the "band" and the circular saws by means of "live" rollers (practically endless chains) to the patent "edgers"—gangs of single-circle saws, quickly set to rip the boards, singly or several at a time, into any desired widths. Still carried forward by an automaton, they next come in contact with adjustable "trimmers," and are cut into proper lengths, dropping from these last saws upon cars that carry the lumber into the extensive yard to be piled, or out to the "chute" or wharf, if a ship be anchored for cargo. Surfaced stuff of several varieties—"rustic," ceiling, wainscoting, etc.— is usually made in these mills. The slabs and other waste-material are carried automatically along, cut into suitable lengths for fuel, and landed at the great furnaces beneath, or carried out farther and dumped from an elevated endless chain into not exactly a "lake of unquenchable fire," but certainly into a fire that is not usually quenched from month to month till the mill, from some cause, is "shut down" for a while—so great is the surplusage of fuel. Some of these mills, having all the recent improvements, cut as much as 120,000 feet of merchantable lumber in a day; the average for the largest mills, however, is hardly more than 100,000 feet per day.

The enormous waste of fuel, just referred to, turns our thoughts to an interesting feature of the lumber industry now being experimented with on this coast: the "booming" of logs to the metropolis, where all that is wasted, and is moreover a source of expense to destroy at the country mills, would be utilized. In the calm water of a river's mouth a floating enclosure is formed by what are known as "boom-sticks," each about thirty feet long, fastened together, end to end, by the strongest bar-link chains. Each boom-stick consists of four strong timbers very firmly bolted together, square blocks intervening at the ends and middle, so as to form large air-chambers, which give it great buoyancy in the water. All being ready the logs are floated through an open gateway into the enclosure till it is closely packed; the gate is closed and chained, and a long line from the towing steamer is attached to the apex of the great oval floating island of timber. As it glides out over the bar into the rough sea the conflicting waves, driven from either side by the rocky shores, seem eager to crush the giant intruder. Its sides are pressed inward, its edges are tipped up here and there, its prow rises and falls with the great swells. In such ordeals a log sometimes overrides the boom-stick that holds it in place. The construction is such, however, that the boom-stick, while partly capsizing, pushes the log back to its place on the inside, and then quickly rights itself. The Fort Bragg Redwood Company has so far brought to San Francisco about a dozen of these "bag-booms," as they are called, the largest containing nearly a million and a half feet of unsawn lumber. The mouth of the Noyo River, their starting-point, is one hundred and twenty miles distant, and the voyage embraces perhaps the roughest coast to be encountered in California. Redwood piles are similarly transported in immense rafts; one recently marketed consisted of twenty-eight sections, extending back from the towing steamer nearly three-quarters of a mile and containing over 50,000 lineal feet of wharf-piles.

Another very interesting feature of the redwood industry on the Mendocino and Humboldt coast is the ship-loading chute, employed where the shore is a high bluff, or where the approach is so rocky and the sea so rough that vessels cannot reach or lie alongside an ordinary wharf. The chute is usually an appendage of a short wharf, from the end of which it reaches out over the rocks and the seething waves that dash about them to a bit of open sea, where a ship may ride at anchor long enough to receive her cargo. The seaward end is suspended from a great crane, and is raised or lowered to suit the tide or the size of the ship to be loaded. The lumber, timber, etc., are brought on cars to the end of the wharf and transferred to the chute, either in compact piles or piece by piece. The writer has been most interested in watching the loading of railroad ties by this method. The incline of the chute is usually so steep that the ties fairly

ALBION.

whiz downward to the ship, smoking from friction as they go. Watching the operation for the first time one trembles for the ship and its crew, for the heavy darting missiles seem sure to crash like a cannon-ball through deck and hull. But while you hold your breath, quick as a flash the danger is averted. Upon a little platform beside the lower end of the chute stands a man, who holds in his brawny hands the lives of the men below. By means of a lever he works a powerful clamp-brake, bringing each flying timber to a standstill with an awful jerk. When stopped it hangs over the lip of the chute, and drops safely into the hands of the men who stow away the cargo. Should the brake-man press down his lever a half second either too soon or too late death and destruction would be the penalty of his very slight error. He must keep unremitting vigil over the chute, and must have eyes and muscles so perfectly trained and nerves so thoroughly steady as to be relied upon never to deviate a hairsbreadth from the right motion at precisely the right instant from morning till night, day after day. This being true, it is not surprising that he commands wages which exceed by far the usual income of an average college-graduate. And the skill and trustworthiness of this chute-brakeman is but a maximum example of the trained and faithful service required generally in these great redwood logging camps and mills. Especially in the larger mills, like that of the Fort Bragg Company, where machinery is multiplied and necessarily complicated, the utmost vigilance and accuracy and skill are essential at every point. Never was the writer more deeply impressed with the correlated character of society, the inter-dependence of every man upon his fellow-men in neighborhood, state and national relationship, than while watching the clock-like performance of duty by each man and group of men in one of these marvelous mills. Many foreigners find employment, but the clear-headed, large-muscled giants of Maine and Michigan are, and ever will be, in special request.

The vast extent of the redwood-lumber industry has already been referred to in this article. It hardly need be added that villages are born of it and often nurtured into towns of no mean importance, other industries springing up around the pioneer-pursuit—small farming, dairying, fruit and stock-raising, etc. The flourishing young city of Eureka, on Humboldt Bay, and an extensive chain of coast towns and villages, reaching southward to the mouth of the Russian River, are evidences of the commercial value of the redwood. Next to Eureka, Fort Bragg and Mendocino are perhaps the most notable examples of thrift. Tourists reach these larger and more interesting forests either by the small steamers from San Francisco or by stage from Ukiah.

Reverting again to the forests themselves, a word should be said about their probable permanency. It has been noted that the redwoods are a remnant of a species dating from the period immediately following the glacial epoch, and there is much speculation as to whether the area occupied by the redwoods has ever been greater than at the present time. The careful testimony of John Muir and other noted geologists would seem to show that they never occupied an area much more extended than at present. Had these limits been larger, it is almost impossible that some traces of the giants that formerly stood upon the land should not have survived to give us evidence of their existence. The redwood never decays. The trunks of standing specimens are never partly rotten, and even the

LOGGING CAMP.

fallen trunks, that have lain perhaps for centuries, are still as sound as on the day when they first came down. It is a regular business now to work up these old logs into fence-posts and other small lumber.

The great foe of the redwood is the forest fire. This is sometimes accidental, but too often deliberately set by the lumbermen to clear the ground of brush and debris after the trunks have been hauled away. Careless of the waste, these fires are allowed to spread unchecked, and sometimes burn for months before they are finally gotten under control. It would not be so bad if nothing but the underbrush were destroyed, because in the ground thus cleared the new sequoias would find their opportunity of springing from the seed, it being a well-established fact that the sequoia-seed will not germinate except in open ground. But the flames attack not only the herbage,

CLEAR LAKE.

but also the trunks of the great standing or fallen trees. Often the latter are burned entirely round and along their whole extent.

The redwood is not easily set afire, and does not burn quickly and with a heavy flame like pine. The smoke is thin and bluish, and not so acrid and irritating to the nostrils. The fire has a smouldering way of burning, however, which, once fairly begun, often continues for months and produces very curious results. Great hollows are eaten out from the sides of the standing trees, and often a hole is bored completely through the center of some fallen log from end to very end. Next to the fires, the greatest danger to the redwood comes from the trampling of the very young trees by the passing flocks of sheep. Every year in the spring the sheep-herders—those scenic vandals—drive their flocks broadcast through these leafy aisles. The sheep browse over miles of territory daily, and always in their wake is left ruin and destruction, both to plants and shrubs. It is not that they eat so much, but that they break and trample more, and they leave the soil so hard that seeds cannot grow there.

The trees themselves, on the other hand, are enormously prolific. The seed-bearing cone is remarkably small, considering the giant stature of the tree, being but an inch and a half to two inches in length. Hundreds of them, however, are borne on a single branch, and when the tree is in full bearing they lie so close together that they tint the whole dome of foliage their peculiar

HOME OF A PIONEER, MENDOCINO COUNTY. FROM PAINTING BY JULIAN RIX.

On the edges of the vast forests of Mendocino redwoods there are still standing many of the homes of the pioneers of the county,—the homes of men who had confidence in the future of the county, coupled with a love for the grand and beautiful in nature. The buildings, for the most part, are built of rough boards, and are not calculated to inspire one with their architectural beauty, but they proved a shelter to the brave men who had no fear of the howling wilderness; and many romantic and dramatic scenes have been enacted around their wide hearthstones. The interiors of the houses are all roomy and comfortable, and always make a visitor feel that it would be a pleasant thing to have a rainstorm raging outside so that he could sit in front of the fire and watch the flames curl up the wide chimney.

bluish-green. Were it not that the squirrels harvest nine-tenths of them, the ground would be sown more thickly than it could bear. As it is, enough escape so that, in a protected enclosure or wherever by the uprooting of a tree or the action of a fire an open space is formed, innumerable seeds take root and send up a crop of shoots which bid fair to prevent the redwood from ever dying out. There will come a time when the trees available for timber will be notably less; but there will probably be enough young saplings coming on to prevent the species from disappearing.

To appreciate fully the wondrous beauty and diversity of the redwood forests at least a year must be spent beneath their shades. They are probably most beautiful in the early spring, for then the air has lost the chill that came from the December winds, the flowers and greenery are at their freshest and brightest, the streams are fullest, and the birds, just returned from their migrations, are most cheerfully ubiquitous and full of song.

Later a little, when the days grow longer and the sun has parched the hillsides and sallowed the grasses even under the thicker foliage, there comes over the scene a shade of the same desolateness—the shadow of impending death—that renders the summer vistas of the interior California plains so painfully dead and barren. For days together there is no cloud in the sky, the wind stops blowing, the trees stand stiff and motionless in the heated air, the atmosphere loses its luminous quality of clearness, and over all things, drifting into every crack and cranny, thickening the air and tingeing everything with its yellow tones, floats the impalpable powder of the redwood pollen dust, a veritable golden shower.

Alternating with these sultry days come the periods when the fogs drift over the range, muffling the trees in their fleecy dampness, and distilling the moisture that keeps the life in the thirsty flowers.

As the fall months come on they bring the season of greatest dryness and the forest fires. These fires are not so picturesque as those in other forests. The small inflammability of the redwoods prevents the formation of those magnificent, fierce-burning columns of flame—veritable pillars of fire by night, like those of the Bible—which one sees when the flames take sudden hold of a large pine or cedar. The thick matting of needles, too, burns with a like slowness, and so, except when it reaches some pile of brush or invades some grassy slope which is set with other trees, it is not so grand and picturesque a spectacle as one has reason to expect. At night, however, when the flames creep waveringly along from point to point, when the long lines of fallen logs stand sharply defined in the sullen red of the embers, and when the sombre gray smoke drifts back with the wind till it mingles with the blacker vagueness of the shadows, there is enough of the weird and picturesque about it to fix the scene indelibly on the memory.

But the grandest season of the year is later on when the clouds begin to gather in the sky, the winds blow up strongly from the south, and the atmosphere is washed clear again by the heavy winter rains. There is something almost uncanny about a storm among these giant trees. One knows that the wind is blowing, because the ear is conscious of the loud, organ-toned symphonies that it makes in passing through their tops. But so great is the height of the trees, so stiff the branches, and so close the growth that they do not bend and give with the blasts like ordinary trees, but stand in that awful quiet while the roar and rush of the storm is passing over their heads.

CHARLES HOWARD SHINN.

THE REDWOODS OF MENDOCINO.

August of mien, tall, strong at heart,
The crown of Nature's art,
Earth's stateliest shapes—these kingly trees,
Who are their deities?

These giants that do scorn the oak—
Ay, scorn the storm-wind's stroke,
In all fair Greece no goddess stood
Could rule this western wood.

Under the shade of this great race,
On some new Buddha's face
Should break the truth's undying light,
And give his spirit sight.

Forsooth, the old Judean breeze
Should stir these solemn trees—
The spirit that forever thrills
Far on the Syrian hills.
—J. VANCE CHENEY.

WASHINGTON AND PUGET SOUND.

WASHINGTON Territory, recently admitted into the Union as a state, lies between latitude 46° and 49° and longitude 117° and 125°, forming the northwest shoulder of the United States. The majestic range of the Cascade Mountains naturally divides the state into two distinct parts, called Eastern and Western Washington, differing greatly from each other in almost every way, the western section being less than half as large as the eastern, and with its copious rains and deep fertile soil is clothed with forests of evergreens; while the eastern section is dry and mostly treeless, though fertile in many parts, and producing immense quantities of wheat and hay.   Few

states are more fertile and productive in one way or another than Washington, or more strikingly varied in natural features or resources. Within her borders every kind of soil and climate may be found. The densest woods and dryest plains, the smoothest levels and roughest mountains. She is rich in square miles—some 70,000 of them—in coal, timber and iron, and in sheltered inland waters that render these resources advantageously accessible. She is also already rich in busy workers, who work hard, though not always wisely; hacking, burning, blasting their way deeper into the wilderness, beneath the sky, and beneath the ground. The wedges of development are being driven hard and none of the obstacles or defenses of nature can long withstand the onset of this immeasurable industry.

CLIFF—HUNTING FOR EGGS AND YOUNG GULLS.

Puget Sound, so justly famous the world over for the surpassing size and excellence and abundance of its timber, is a long, many-fingered arm of the sea reaching southward from the head of the Strait of Juan de Fuca into the heart of the grand forests of the western portion of Washington, between the Cascade Range and the mountains of the coast. It is less than a hundred miles in length, but so numerous are the branches into which it divides, and so many its bays, harbors, and islands, that its entire shore-line is said to measure more than 1,800 miles. Throughout its whole vast extent ships move in safety, and find shelter from every wind that blows, the entire mountain-girt sea forming one grand unrivaled harbor and center for commerce.

The forest trees press forward to the water around all the windings of the shores in most imposing array, as if they were courting their fate, coming down from the mountains far and near to offer themselves to the axe, thus making the place a perfect paradise for the lumberman. To the lover of nature the scene is enchanting. Water and sky, mountain and forest, clad in sunshine and clouds, are composed in landscapes sublime in magnitude, yet exquisitely fine and fresh, and full of glad, rejoicing life. The shining waters stretch away into the leafy wilderness, now like the reaches of some majestic river and again expanding into broad roomy spaces like mountain lakes, their farther edges fading gradually and blending with the pale blue of the sky. The wooded shores with an outer fringe of flowering bushes sweep onward in beautiful curves around bays, and capes, and jutting promontories innumerable; while the islands with soft waving outlines lavishly adorned with spruces and cedars, thicken and enrich the beauty of the waters; and the white spirit mountains looking down from the sky keep watch and ward over all, faithful and changeless as the stars.

All the way from the Strait of Juan de Fuca up to Olympia, a hopeful town situated at the head of one of the farthest-reaching of the fingers of the sound, we are so completely inland and surrounded by mountains that it is hard to realize that we are sailing on a branch of the salt sea. We are constantly reminded of Lake Tahoe. There is the

TYPES OF CHINOOK INDIANS.

same clearness of the water in calm weather without any trace of the ocean swell; the same picturesque winding and sculpture of the shore-line and flowery, leafy luxuriance; only here the trees are taller, and stand much closer together; and the backgrounds are higher and far more extensive. Here, too, we find greater variety amid the marvelous wealth of islands and inlets, and also in the changing views dependent on the weather. As we double cape after cape and round the uncounted islands, new combinations come to view in endless variety, sufficient to fill and satisfy the lover of wild beauty through a whole life. Oftentimes in the stillest weather, when all the winds sleep and no sign of storms are felt or seen, silky clouds form and settle over all the land, leaving in sight only a circle of water with indefinite bounds like views in mid-ocean; then, the clouds lifting, some islet will be presented standing alone, with the tops of its trees dipping out of sight in pearly, gray fringes; or, lifting higher, and perhaps letting in a ray of sunshine through some rift overhead, the whole island will be set free and brought forward in vivid relief amid the gloom, a girdle of silver light of dazzling brightness on the water about its shores; then darkening again and vanishing back into the general gloom. Thus island after island may be seen, singly or in groups, coming and going from darkness to light like a scene of enchantment, until at length the entire cloud-ceiling is rolled away, and the colossal cone of Mount Rainier is seen in spotless white looking down over the forests from a distance of sixty miles, but so lofty and so massive, and clearly outlined, as to impress itself upon us as being just back of a strip of woods only a mile or two in breadth.

For the tourist sailing to Puget Sound from San Francisco there is but little that is at all striking in the scenery within reach by the way until the mouth of the Strait of Juan de Fuca is reached. The voyage is about four days in length and the steamers keep within sight of the coast, but the hills fronting the sea up to Oregon are mostly bare and uninviting, the magnificent redwood forests stretching along this portion of the California coast seeming to keep well back, away from the heavy winds, so that very little is seen of them; while there are no deep inlets or lofty mountains visible to break the regular monotony. Along the coast of Oregon the woods of spruce and fir come down to the shore, kept fresh and vigorous by copious rains, and become denser and taller to the northward until, rounding Cape Flattery, we enter the Strait of Fuca, where, sheltered from the ocean gales, the forests begin to hint the grandeur they attain in Puget Sound. Here the scenery in general becomes exceedingly interesting; for now we have arrived at the grand mountain-walled channel that forms the entrance to that marvelous network of inland waters that extends along the margin of the continent to the northward for a thousand miles.

Tatoosh Mountains, Looking West From the Camp of the Clouds. From Drawing by Victor Perard After Painting by W. Keith.

"The view we enjoyed from the summit could hardly be surpassed in sublimity and grandeur; but one feels far from home so high in the sky, so much so that one is inclined to guess that, apart from the acquisition of the knowledge and exhilaration of climbing, more pleasure is to be found at the foot of mountains than on their frozen tops. Doubly happy, however, is the man to whom lofty mountain tops are within reach, for the lights that shine there illumine all that lies below."

This magnificent inlet was named for Juan de Fuca, who discovered it in 1592 while seeking a mythical strait, supposed to exist somewhere in the north, connecting the Atlantic and Pacific. It is about seventy miles long, ten or twelve miles wide, and extends to the eastward in a nearly straight line between the south end of Vancouver Island and the Olympian Range of mountains on the mainland.

Cape Flattery, the western termination of the Olympian Range, is terribly rugged and jagged, and in stormy weather is utterly inaccessible from the sea. Then the ponderous rollers of the deep Pacific thunder amid its caverns and cliffs with the foam and uproar of a thousand Yosemite waterfalls. The bones of many a noble ship lie there, and many a sailor. It would seem unlikely that any living thing should seek rest in such a place, or find it. Nevertheless, frail and delicate flowers bloom there, flowers of both the land and sea; heavy, ungainly seals disport in the swelling

IN THE CASCADE RANGE—APPROACH TO MT. BAKER.

waves, and find grateful retreats back in the inmost bores of its storm-lashed caverns; while in many a chink and hollow of the highest crags, not visible from beneath, a great variety of water-fowl make homes and rear their young. But not always are the inhabitants safe, even in such wave-defended castles as these, for the Indians of the neighboring shores venture forth in the calmest summer weather in their frail canoes to spear the seals in the narrow gorges amid the grinding, gurgling din of the restless waters. At such times also the hunters make out to scale many of the apparently inaccessible cliffs for the eggs and young of the gulls and other water-birds, occasionally losing their lives in these perilous adventures which give rise to many an exciting story told around the camp fires at night when the storms roar loudest.

Passing through the strait we have the Olympian Mountains close at hand on the right, Vancouver Island on the left, and the snowy peak of Mount Baker straight ahead in the distance. During clear weather, or when the clouds are lifting and rolling off the mountains after a storm, all these views are truly magnificent. Mount Baker is one of that wonderful series of old volcanoes that once flamed along the summits of the Sierras and Cascades from Lassen to Mount St. Elias. Its fires are sleeping now, and it is loaded with glaciers, streams of ice having taken the place of streams of glowing lava. Vancouver Island presents a charming variety of hill and dale, open sunny spaces and sweeps of dark forest rising in swell beyond swell to the high land in the distance.

But the Olympian Mountains most of all command attention, seen tellingly near and clear in all their glory, rising from the water's edge into the sky to a height of six or eight thousand feet. They bound the strait on the south side throughout its whole extent, forming a massive sustained wall, flowery and bushy at the base, a zigzag of snowy peaks along the top, which have ragged-edged fields of ice and snow beneath them, enclosed in wide amphitheatres opening to the waters of the strait through spacious forest-filled valleys enlivened with fine dashing streams. These valleys mark the courses of the Olympian glaciers at the period of their greatest extension, when they poured their tribute into that portion of the great northern ice-sheet that over-swept the south end of Vancouver Island and filled the strait with flowing ice as it is now filled with ocean water.

The steamers of the sound usually stop at Esquimalt on their way up, thus affording tourists an opportunity to visit the interesting town of Victoria, the capitol of British Columbia. The Victoria harbor is too narrow and difficult of access for the larger class of ships, therefore a landing has to be made at Esquimalt. The distance however is only about three miles and the way is delightful, winding on through a charming forest of Douglas spruce, with here and there groves of oak and madrone, and a rich undergrowth of hazel, dogwood, willow, alder, spiræa, rubus, huckleberry and wild rose. Pretty cottages occur at intervals along the road, covered with honeysuckle, and many an upswelling rock, freshly glaciated and furred with yellow mosses and lichen, telling interesting stories of the icy past.

Victoria is a quiet, handsome, breezy town, beautifully located on finely modulated ground at the mouth of the Canal de Haro, with charming views in front, of islands and mountains and far-reaching waters, ever changing in the shifting lights and shades of the clouds and sunshine. In the back-ground there are a mile or two of field and forest and sunny oak openings; then comes the forest primeval, dense and shaggy and wellnigh impenetrable.

Notwithstanding the importance claimed for Victoria as a commercial center and the capitol of British Columbia, it has a rather young, loose-jointed appearance. The government buildings and some of the business blocks on the main streets are well built and imposing in bulk and architecture. These are far less interesting and characteristic however than the mansions set in the midst of spacious pleasure grounds and the lovely home-cottages embowered in honeysuckle and climbing roses. One soon discovers that this is no Yankee town. The English faces and the way that English is spoken alone would tell that; while in business quarters there is a staid dignity and moderation that is very noticeable, and a want of American push and hurrah. Love of land and of privacy in homes is made manifest in the residences, many of which are built in the middle of fields and orchards or large city blocks, and in the loving care with which these home-grounds are planted. They are very beautiful. The fineness of the climate, with its copious measure of warm moisture distilling in dew and fog, and gentle, bathing, laving rain, give them a freshness and floweriness that is worth going far to see.

Victoria is noted for its fine drives, and every one who can should either walk or drive around the outskirts of the town, not only for the fine views out over the water but to see the cascades of bloom pouring over the gables of the cottages, and the fresh wild woods with their flowery, fragrant underbrush. Wild roses abound almost everywhere. One species, blooming freely along the woodland paths, is from two to three inches in diameter, and more fragrant than any other wild rose I ever saw excepting the sweet briar. This rose and three species of spiræa fairly fill the air with fragrance after a shower. And how brightly then do the red berries of the dogwood shine out from the warm yellow-green of leaves and mosses. But still more interesting and significant are the glacial phenomena displayed hereabouts. All this exuberant tree, bush and herbaceous vegetation, cultivated or wild, is growing upon moraine beds outspread by waters that issued from the ancient glaciers at the time of their recession, and scarcely at all moved or in any way modified by post-glacial agencies. The town streets and the roads are graded in moraine material, among scratched and grooved rock-bosses that are as unweathered and telling as any to be found in the glacier channels of Alaska. The harbor also is clearly of glacial origin. The rock-islets that rise here and there, forming so marked a feature of the harbor, are unchanged *roches moutoneers*, and the shores are grooved, scratched, and rounded, and in every way as glacial in all their characteristics as those of a new-born glacial lake.

Most visitors to Victoria go to the stores of the Hudson Bay Company, presumably on account of the romantic associations, or to purchase a bit of fur or some other wild Indianish trinket as a memento. At certain seasons of the year, when the hairy harvests are gathered in, immense bales of skins may be seen in these unsavory warehouses, the spoils of many thousand hunts over mountain and plain, by lonely river and shore. The skins of bears, wolves, beavers, otters, fishers, martins, lynxes, panthers, wolverine, reindeer, moose, elk, wild goats, sheep, foxes, squirrels, and many others of our "poor earth-born companions and fellow-mortals" may here be found.

Vancouver is the southmost and the largest of the countless islands forming the great archi-

LOGGING SCENES—FROM FOREST TO RAFT.

pelago that stretches a thousand miles to the northward. Its shores have been known a long time, but little is known of the lofty mountainous interior on account of the difficulties in the way of explorations—lakes, bogs, and shaggy tangled forests. It is mostly a pure, savage wilderness, without roads or clearings, and silent so far as man is concerned. Even the Indians keep close to the shore, getting a living by fishing, dwelling together in villages, and traveling almost wholly by canoes. White settlements are few and far between. Good agricultural lands occur here and there on the edge of the wilderness, but they are hard to clear, and have received but little attention thus far. Gold, the grand attraction that lights the way into all kinds of wildernesses and makes rough places smooth, has been found, but only in small quantities, too small to make much motion. Almost all the industry of the island is employed upon lumber and coal, in which so far as known, its chief wealth lies.

Leaving Victoria for Port Townsend, after we are fairly out on the free open water, Mount Baker is seen rising solitary over a dark breadth of forest, making a glorious show in its pure white raiment. It is said to be about eleven thousand feet high, is loaded with glaciers, some of which come well down into the woods, and never, so far as I have heard, has been climbed, though in all probability it is not inaccessible. The task of reaching its base through the dense woods will be likely to prove of greater difficulty than the climb to the summit.

In a direction a little to the left of Mount Baker and much nearer, may be seen the island

SNOQUALMIE FALLS. FROM PAINTING BY GEORGE H. GAY.

"From the hotel at the ranch village, the road to the fall leads down the right bank of the river through the magnificent maple woods I have mentioned elsewhere, and fine views of the fall may be had on that side both from above and below. It is situated on the main river, where it plunges over a sheer precipice about two hundred and forty feet high in leaving the level meadows of the ancient lake-basin. In a general way it resembles the well-known Nevada Fall in Yosemite, having the same twisted appearance at the top, and the free plunge in numberless comet-shape masses into a deep pool seventy-five or eighty yards in diameter. The pool is of considerable depth, as is shown by the radiating, well-beaten foam and mist, which is of a beautiful rose color at times, of exquisite fineness of tone, and by the heavy waves that lash the rocks in front of it."

of San Juan, famous in the young history of the country for the quarrels concerning its rightful ownership between the Hudson Bay Company and Washington Territory, quarrels which nearly brought on war with Great Britain. Neither party showed any lack of either pluck or gunpowder. General Scott was sent out by President Buchanan to negotiate, which resulted in a joint occupancy of the island. Small quarrels, however, continued to arise until the year 1874, when the peppery question was submitted to the Emperor of Germany for arbitration. Then the whole island was given to the United States. San Juan is one of a thickset cluster of islands that fills the waters between Vancouver and the mainland, a little to the north of Victoria. In some of the intricate channels between these islands the tides run at times like impetuous rushing rivers, rendering navigation rather uncertain and dangerous for the small sailing vessels that ply between Victoria and the settlements on the coast of British Columbia and the larger islands. The water is generally deep enough everywhere, too deep in most places for anchorage, and the winds shifting hither and thither or dying away altogether, the ships, getting no direction from their helms, are carried back and forth or are caught in some eddy where two currents meet and whirled round and round to the dismay of the sailors, like a chip in a river whirlpool.

All the way over to Port Townsend the Olympian Mountains well maintain their massive, imposing grandeur, and present their elaborately carved summits in clear relief, many of which are out of sight in coming up the strait on account of our being too near the base of the range. Turn to them as often as we may, our admiration only grows the warmer the longer we dwell upon them. The highest peaks are Mount Constance and Mount Olympus, said to be about eight thousand feet high.

In two or three hours after leaving Victoria, we arrive at the handsome little town of Port Townsend, situated at the mouth of Puget Sound, on the west side. The residential portion of the town is set on the level top of the bluff that bounds Port Townsend Bay, while another nearly level space of moderate extent, reaching from the base of the bluff to the shore line, is occupied by the business portion, thus making a town of two separate and distinct stories, which are connected by long ladder-like flights of stairs. In the streets of the lower story, while there is no lack of animation, there is but little business noise as compared with the amount of business transacted. This in great part is due to the scarcity of horses and wagons. Farms and roads back in the woods are few and far between. Nearly all the tributary settlements are on the coast and communication is almost wholly by boats, canoes and schooners. Hence country stages and farmers' wagons and buggies, with the whir and din that belong to them, are wanting. This being the port of entry, all vessels have to stop here, and they make a lively show about the wharves and in the bay. The winds stir the flags of every civilized nation, while the Indians in their long-beaked canoes glide about from ship to ship, satisfying their curiosity or trading with the crews. Keen traders these Indians are, and few indeed of the sailors or merchants from any country ever get the better of them in bargains. Curious groups of people may often be seen in the streets and stores, made up of English, French, Spanish, Portuguese, Scandinavians, Germans, Greeks, Moors, Japanese and Chinese, of every rank and station and style of dress and behavior; settlers from many a nook and bay and island up and down the coast; hunters from the wilderness; tourists on their way home by the sound and the Columbia River or to Alaska or California.

The upper story of Port Townsend is charmingly located, wide bright waters on one side, flowing evergreen woods on the other. The streets are well laid out and well tended, and the

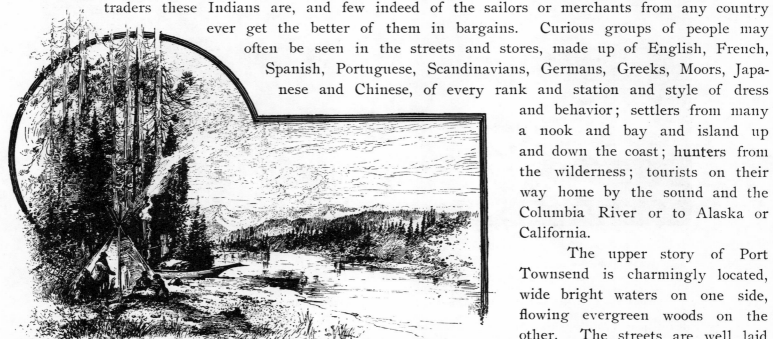

CAMP AMONG ALPINE FIRS—OLYMPIAN MOUNTAINS.

houses, with their luxuriant gardens about them, have an air of taste and refinement seldom found in towns set on the edge of a wild forest. The people seem to have come here to make true homes, attracted by the beauty and fresh breezy healthfulness of the place as well as by business advantages, trusting to natural growth and advancement instead of restless "booming" methods. They perhaps have caught some of the spirit of calm moderation and enjoyment from their English neighbors across the water. Of late, however, this sober tranquility has begun to give way, some whiffs from the whirlwind of real estate speculation up the sound having at length touched the town and ruffled the surface of its calmness.

A few miles up the bay is Fort Townsend, which makes a pretty picture with the green woods rising back of it and the calm water in front. Across the mouth of the sound lies the long narrow Whidby Island, named by Vancouver for one of his lieutenants. It is about thirty

"THE GORGE"—NEAR VICTORIA.

miles in length, and is remarkable in this region of crowded forests and mountains as being comparatively open and low. The soil is good and easily worked, and a considerable portion of the island has been under cultivation for many years. Fertile fields, open park-like groves of oak, and thick masses of evergreens succeed one another in charming combinations to make this "the garden spot of the territory."

Leaving Port Townsend for Seattle and Tacoma, we enter the sound and sail down into the heart of the green aspiring forests, and find, look where we may, beauty ever changing, in lavish profusion. Puget Sound, "the Mediterranean of America" as it is sometimes called, is in many respects one of the most remarkable bodies of water in the world. Vancouver, who came here nearly a hundred years ago and made a careful survey of it, named the larger northern portion of it "Admiralty Inlet" and one of the long narrow branches "Hood's Canal," applying the name "Puget Sound" only to the comparatively small southern portion. The latter name, however, is now applied generally to the entire inlet, and is spoken of by the people hereabouts simply as "The Sound." The natural wealth and commercial advantages of the sound region were quickly recognized, and the cause of the activity prevailing here is not far to seek. Vancouver, long before civilization touched these shores, spoke of it in terms of unstinted praise. He was sent out by the British Government with the principal object in view of "acquiring accurate knowledge as to the nature and extent of any water communication which may tend in any considerable degree to facilitate an intercourse for the purposes of commerce between the northwest coast and the country on the opposite side of the continent," vague traditions having long been current concerning a strait supposed to unite the two oceans. Vancouver reported that he found the coast from San Francisco to Oregon and beyond to present a nearly straight, solid barrier to the sea, without openings, and we may well guess the joy of the old navigator on the discovery of these waters after so long and barren a search to the southward.

His descriptions of the scenery—Mounts Baker, Rainier, St. Helens, etc.—were as enthusiastic as those of the most eager landscape-lover of the present day, when scenery is in fashion. He says in one place, "To describe the beauties of this region will, on some future occasion, be a very grateful task for the pen of a skillful panegyrist. The serenity of the climate, the immeasurable pleasing landscapes, and the abundant fertility that unassisted nature puts forth, require only to be enriched by the industry of man with villages, mansions, cottages, and other buildings, to render it the most lovely country that can be imagined. The labor of the inhabitants would be amply rewarded in the bounties which nature seems ready to bestow on cultivation." "A picture so pleasing could not fail to call to our remembrance certain delightful and beloved situations in old England." So warm

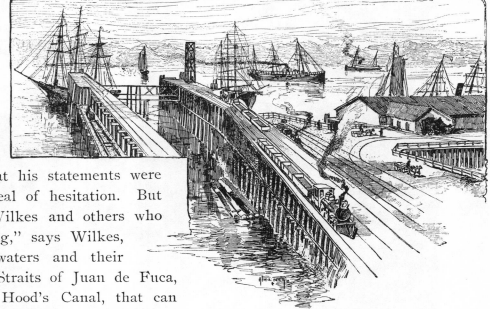

COAL BUNKERS AND WHARVES, SEATTLE.

indeed were the praises he sung that his statements were received in England with a good deal of hesitation. But they were amply corroborated by Wilkes and others who followed many years later. "Nothing," says Wilkes, "can exceed the beauty of these waters and their safety. Not a shoal exists in the Straits of Juan de Fuca, Admiralty Inlet, Puget Sound or Hood's Canal, that can in any way interrupt their navigation by a 74-gun ship. I venture nothing in saying there is no country in the world that possesses waters like these." And again, quoting from the United States Coast Survey, "For depth of water, boldness of approaches, freedom from hidden dangers, and the immeasurable sea of gigantic timber coming down to the very shores, these waters are unsurpassed, unapproachable."

The sound region has a fine, fresh, clean climate, well washed both winter and summer with copious rains and swept with winds and clouds that come from the mountains and the sea. Every hidden nook in the depths of the woods is searched and refreshed, leaving no stagnant air; beaver meadows and lake-basins and low and willowy bogs, all are kept wholesome and sweet the year round. Cloud and sunshine alternate in bracing, cheering succession, and health and abundance follow the storms. The outer sea-margin is sublimely dashed and drenched with ocean brine, the spicy scud sweeping at times far inland over the bending woods, the giant trees waving and chanting in hearty accord as if surely enjoying it all.

Heavy, long-continued rains occur in the winter months. Then every leaf, bathed and brightened, rejoices. Filtering drops and currents through all the shaggy undergrowth of the woods go with tribute to the small streams, and these again to the larger. The rivers swell, but there are no devastating floods; for the thick felt of roots and mosses hold the abounding waters in check, stored in a thousand thousand fountains. Neither are there any violent hurricanes here. At least, I never have heard of any, nor have come upon their tracks. Most of the streams are clear and cool always, for their waters are filtered through deep beds of mosses, and flow beneath shadows all the

THE NISQUALLY GLACIER.—SOUTH SIDE OF MOUNT RAINIER. FROM PAINTING BY W. KEITH.

"By night of the third day we reached the Soda Springs on the right bank of the Nisqually, which goes roaring by, gray with mud, gravel and boulders, from the caves of the glaciers of Rainier, now close at hand.   *   *   *   The first part of the way lies up the Nisqually Cañon, the bottom of which is flat in some places, and the walls very high and precipitous, like those of the Yosemite Valley.   The upper part of the cañon is still occupied by one of the Nisqually glaciers, from which this branch of the river draws its source, issuing from a cave in the gray, rock-strewn snout."

way to the sea. Only the streams from the glaciers are turbid and muddy. On the slopes of the mountains where they rush from their crystal caves, they carry not only small particles of rock-mud, worn off the sides and bottoms of the channels of the glaciers, but grains of sand and pebbles and large bowlders tons in weight, rolling them forward on their way rumbling and bumping to their appointed places at the foot of steep slopes, to be built into rough bars and beds, while the smaller material is carried farther and outspread in flats, perhaps for coming wheat fields and gardens, the finest of it going out to sea, floating on the tides for weeks and months ere it finds rest on the bottom.

Snow seldom falls to any great depth on the lowlands, but in glorious abundance on the mountains. And only on the mountains does the temperature fall much below the freezing point. In the warmest summer weather a temperature of eighty-five degrees or even more occasionally is reached, but not for long at a time, as such heat is speedily followed by a breeze from the sea. The most charming days here are days of perfect calm, when all the winds are holding their breath and not a leaf stirs. Then the surface of the Sound shines like a silver mirror over all its vast extent, reflecting its lovely islands and shores; and long sheets of spangles flash and dance in the wake of every swimming sea-bird and boat. The sun, looking down on the tranquil landscape, seems conscious of the presence of every living thing on which he is pouring his blessings, while they in turn, with perhaps the exception of man, seem conscious of the presence of the sun as a benevolent father and stand hushed and waiting.

SITE OF SEATTLE, 1850.

YESLER'S COOK HOUSE.

REMINISCENCES OF EARLY SEATTLE.

When we force our way into the depths of the forests, following any of the rivers back to their fountains, we find that the bulk of the woods is made up of the Douglas spruce, (*Pseudo tsuga Douglasii*,) named in honor of David Douglas, an enthusiastic botanical explorer of early Hudson Bay times. It is not only a very large tree but a very beautiful one, with lively bright green drooping foliage, handsome pendant cones, and a shaft exquisitely straight and regular. For so large a tree it is astonishing how many find nourishment and space to grow on any given area. The magnificent shafts push their spires into the sky close together with as regular a growth as that of a well tilled field of grain. And no ground has been better tilled for the growth of trees than that on which these forests are growing. For it has been thoroughly plowed and rolled by the mighty glaciers from the mountains, and sifted and mellowed and outspread in beds hundreds of feet in depth by the broad streams that issued from their fronts at the time of their recession, after they had long covered all the land. The largest tree of this species that I have myself measured was nearly twelve feet in diameter at a height of five feet from the ground, and as near as I could make out under the circumstances, about three hundred feet in length. It stood near the head of the Sound not far from Olympia. I have seen a few others, both near the coast and thirty or forty miles back in the interior, that were from eight to ten feet in diameter, measured above their bulging insteps; and many from six to seven feet. I have heard of some that were said to be three hundred and twenty-five feet in height and fifteen feet in diameter, but none that I measured were so large, though it is not at all unlikely that such colossal giants do exist where conditions of soil and exposure are surpassingly favorable. The average size of all the trees of this species found up to an elevation on the mountain slopes of, say, two thousand feet above sea-level, taking into account only what may be called mature trees two hundred and fifty to five hundred years of age, is perhaps, at a vague guess, not more than a height of one hundred and seventy-five or two hundred feet and a diameter of three feet; though of course, throughout the richest sections, the size is much greater. In proportion to its weight when dry, the timber from this tree is perhaps stronger than that of any other conifer in the country. It is tough and durable and admirably adapted in every way for ship-building, piles and heavy timbers in general. But its hardness and liability to warp render it much inferior to white or sugar pine for fine work. In the lumber markets of California it is known as "Oregon

Pine" and is used almost exclusively for spars, bridge timbers, heavy planking and the framework of houses. The same species extends northward in abundance through British Columbia and southward through the coast and middle regions of Oregon and California. It is also a common tree in the cañons and hollows of the Wasatch Mountains in Utah, where it is called "Red Pine" and on portions of the Rocky Mountains and some of the short ranges of the Great Basin. Along the coast of California it keeps company with the redwood wherever it can find a favorable opening. On the western slope of the Sierra, with the yellow pine and incense-cedar, it forms a pretty well defined belt, at a height of from three thousand to six thousand feet above the sea, and extends into the San Gabriel and San Bernardino Mountains in Southern California. But though widely distributed, it is only in these cool, moist northlands that it reaches its finest

LUMBER SHIPPING AT PORT BLAKELEY.

development, tall, straight, elastic, and free from limbs to an immense height, growing down to tidewater, where ships of the largest size may lie close alongside and load at the least possible cost.

Growing with the Douglas we find the white spruce, or "Sitka Pine," as it is sometimes called. This also is a very beautiful and majestic tree, frequently attaining a height of two hundred feet or more and a diameter of five or six feet. It is very abundant in southeastern Alaska, forming the greater part of the best forests there. Here it is found mostly around the sides of beaver-dam and other meadows and on the borders of the streams, especially where the ground is low. One tree that I saw felled at the head of the Hop-Ranch meadows on the upper Snoqualmie River, though far from being the largest I have seen, measured a hundred and eighty feet in length and four and a half in diameter, and was two hundred and fifty-seven years of age. In habit and general appearance it resembles the Douglas spruce, but is somewhat less slender and the needles grow close together all around the branchlets and are so stiff and sharp-pointed on the younger branches that they cannot well be handled without gloves. The timber is tough, close-grained, white and looks more like pine than any other of the spruces. It splits freely, makes excellent shingles and in general use in house-building takes the place of pine. I have seen logs of this species a hundred feet long and two feet in diameter at the upper end. It was named in honor of the old Scotch botanist, Archibald Menzies, who came to this coast with Vancouver in 1792. The beautiful hemlock spruce with its warm yellow-green foliage is also common in some portions of these woods. It is tall and slender and exceedingly graceful in habit before old age comes on, but the timber is inferior and is seldom used for any other than the roughest work, such as wharf-building.

The Western arbor vitæ (*Thuja gigantea*) grows to a size truly gigantic on low rich ground. Specimens ten feet in diameter and a hundred and forty feet high are not at all rare. Some that

I have heard of are said to be fifteen and even eighteen feet thick. Clad in rich glossy plumes, with gray lichens covering their smooth tapering boles, perfect trees of this species are truly noble objects and well worthy the place they hold in these glorious forests. It is of this tree that the Indians make their fine canoes.

Of the other conifers that are so happy as to have place here, there are three firs, three or four pines, two cypresses, a yew and another spruce, the *Abies Patoniana*. This last is perhaps the most beautiful of all the spruces, but being comparatively small and growing only far back on the mountains, it receives but little attention from most people. Nor is there room in a work like this for anything like a complete description of it, or of the others I have just mentioned. Of the three firs, one, (*Picea grandis*), grows near the coast and is one of the largest trees in the forest, sometimes attaining a height of two hundred and fifty feet. The timber, however, is inferior in

SEATTLE.

quality and not much sought after while so much that is better is within reach. One of the others, (*P. amabilis, var. nobilis*), forms magnificent forests by itself at a height of about three thousand to four thousand feet above the sea. The rich plushy, plume-like branches grow in regular whorls around the trunk and on the topmost whorls, standing erect, are the large beautiful cones. This is far the most beautiful of all the firs. In the Sierra Nevada it forms a considerable portion of the main forest belt on the western slope and it is there that it reaches its greatest size and greatest beauty. The third species (*P. subalpina*) forms together with *Abies Patoniana*, the upper edge of the timber-line on the portion of the Cascades opposite the Sound. A thousand feet below the extreme limit of tree-growth it occurs in beautiful groups amid park-like openings where flowers grow in extravagant profusion. The pines are nowhere abundant in the state. The largest, the yellow pine, (*Pinus ponderosa*), occurs here and there on margins of dry gravelly prairies and only on such situations have I yet seen it in this state. The others (*P. monticola* and *P. contorta*), are mostly restricted to the upper slopes of the mountains, and though the former of these two attains a good size and makes excellent lumber, it is mostly beyond reach at present and is

Types of "Free Trappers."—Indians Begging Tobacco. From a Drawing by Victor Perard.

"It was in those early beaver days that the striking class of adventurers called 'free-trappers' made their appearance. Bold, enterprising men, eager to make money and inclined at the same time to relish the license of a savage life, would set forth with a few traps and a gun and a hunting-knife, content at first to venture only a short distance up the beaver streams nearest to the settlements, and where the Indians were not likely to molest them. * * * In a few months their pack animals would be laden with thousands of dollars' worth of fur. Next season they would venture farther, and again farther, meanwhile growing rapidly wilder, getting acquainted with the Indian tribes, and usually marrying among them. * * * Oftentimes they were compelled to set their traps and visit them by night and lie hidden during the day, when operating in the neighborhood of hostile Indians. Then returning to the trading stations they would spend their hard earnings in a few weeks of dissipation and 'good times,' and go again to the bears and beavers, until at length a bullet or arrow would end all. Some men of this class have, from superior skill or fortune, escaped every danger, lived to a good old age, earned fame, and by their knowledge of the topography of the vast West then unexplored have been able to render important service to the country. From the Columbia waters beaver and beaver men have almost wholly passed away, and the men once so striking a part of the view have left scarcely the faintest sign of their existence."

not abundant. One of the cypresses (*Cupressus Lawsoniana*), grows near the coast and is a fine large tree, clothed like the arbor-vitæ in a glorious wealth of flat feathery branches. The other is found here and there well up toward the edge of the timber line. This is the fine Alaska cedar, (*C. Nootkatensis*), the lumber from which is noted for its durability, fineness of grain, beautiful yellow color and its fragrance, which resembles that of sandal-wood. The Alaska Indians make their canoe paddles of it and weave matting and coarse cloth from the fibrous brown bark.

Among the different kinds of hard-wood trees are the oak, maple, madrona, birch, alder, and wild apple, while large cottonwoods are common along the rivers and shores of the numerous lakes.

The most striking of these to the traveler is the Menzies Arbutus or madrona, as it is popularly called in California. Its curious red and yellow bark, large thick glossy leaves, and panicles of waxy-looking greenish-white, urn-shaped flowers render it very conspicuous. On the boles of the younger trees and on all the branches, the bark is so smooth and seamless that it does not appear as bark at all, but rather

SOURCE OF NISQUALLY RIVER.

the naked wood. The whole tree, with the exception of the larger part of the trunk, looks as though it had been thoroughly peeled. It is found sparsely scattered along the shores of the Sound and back in the forests also on open margins, where the soil is not too wet, and extends up the coast on Vancouver Island beyond Nanaimo. But in no part of the state does it reach anything like the size and beauty of proportions that it attains to in California, few trees here being more than ten or twelve inches in diameter and thirty feet high. It is, however, a very remarkable looking object, standing there like some lost or runaway native of the tropics, naked and painted, beside that dark mossy ocean of northland conifers. Not even a palm tree would seem more out of place here.

The oaks, so far as my observation has reached, seem to be most abundant and grow largest on the islands of the San Juan and Whidby Archipelago. One of the three species of maples that I have seen is only a bush that makes tangles on the banks of the rivers. Of the other two one is a small tree crooked and moss-grown, holding out its leaves to catch the light that filters down through the close set spires of the great spruces. It grows almost everywhere throughout the entire extent of the forest until the higher slopes of the mountains are reached, and produces a very picturesque and delightful effect; relieving the bareness of the great shafts of the evergreens, without being close enough in its growth to wholly hide them, or to cover the bright mossy carpet that is spread beneath all the dense parts of the woods. The other species is also very picturesque and at the same time very large, the largest tree of its kind that I have ever seen anywhere. Not even in the great maple woods of Canada have I seen trees either as large or with so much striking picturesque character. It is widely distributed throughout western Washington, but is never found scattered among the conifers in the dense woods. It

ALPINE FIRS, TATOOSH MOUNTAINS.

keeps together mostly in magnificent groves by itself on the damp levels along the banks of streams or lakes where the ground is subject to overflow. In such situations it attains a height of seventy-five to a hundred feet and a diameter of four to eight feet. The trunk sends out large limbs toward one another, laden with long drooping mosses beneath and rows of ferns on their upper surfaces, thus making a grand series of richly ornamented interlacing arches with the leaves laid thick overhead, rendering the underwood spaces delightfully cool and open. Never have I seen a finer forest ceiling or a more picturesque one, while the floor, covered with tall ferns and rubus and thrown into hillocks by the bulging roots, matches it well. The largest of these maple groves that I have yet found is on the right bank of the Snoqualmie River, about a mile above the falls. The whole country hereabouts is picturesque, and interesting in many ways, and well worthy a visit by tourists passing through the Sound region, since it is now accessible by rail from Seattle.

A FEAST OF SALMON-BERRIES.

Looking now at the forests in a comprehensive way, we find in passing through them again and again from the shores of the Sound to their upper limits, that some portions are much older than others, the trees much larger, and the ground beneath them strewn with immense trunks in every stage of decay, representing several generations of growth, everything about them giving the impression that these are indeed the "forests primeval." While in the younger portions, where the elevation of the ground is the same as to the sea-level and the species of trees are the same as well as the quality of soil, apart from the moisture which it holds, the trees seem to be and are mostly of the same age, perhaps from one hundred to two or three hundred years, with no gray-bearded, venerable patriarchs, forming tall majestic woods without any grandfathers. When we examine the ground we find that it is as free from those mounds of brown crumbling wood and mossy ancient fragments as are the growing trees from very old ones. Then, perchance, we come upon a section farther up the slopes towards the mountains that has no trees more than fifty years old, or even fifteen or twenty years old. These last show plainly enough that they have been devastated by fire, as the black melancholy monuments rising here and there above the young growth bear witness. Then with this fiery, suggestive testimony, on examining those sections whose trees are a hundred years old or two hundred, we find the same fire-records, though heavily veiled with mosses and lichens, showing that a century or two ago the forests that stood there had been swept away in some tremendous fire at a time when rare conditions of drouth made their burning possible. Then, the bare ground sprinkled with the winged seeds from the edges of the burned district, a new forest sprang up, nearly every tree starting at the same time or within a few years, thus explaining the uniformity of size we find in such places; while on the other hand, in those sections of ancient aspect containing very old trees both standing and fallen, we find no traces of fire, nor from the extreme dampness of the ground can we see any possibility of fire ever running there.

Fire, then, is the great governing agent in forest distribution and to a great extent also in the conditions of their growth. Where fertile lands are very wet one-half the year

IN SNOQUALMIE FOREST.

and very dry the other, there can be no forests at all. Where the ground is damp with drouth occurring only at intervals of centuries, fine forests may be found, other conditions being favorable. But it is only where fires never run that truly ancient forests of pitchy coniferous trees may exist. When the Washington forests are seen from the deck of a ship out in the middle of the Sound, or even from the top of some high commanding mountain, the woods seem everywhere perfectly solid. And so in fact they are in general found to be. The largest openings are those of the lakes and prairies, the smaller of beaver-meadow, bogs, and the rivers; none of them large enough to make a distinct mark in comprehensive views.

Of the lakes there are said to be some thirty in Kings County alone; the largest, Lake Washington, being twenty-six miles long and four miles wide. Another, which enjoys the duckish name of Lake Squak, is about ten miles long. Both are pure and beautiful, lying imbedded in the green wilderness. The rivers are numerous and are but little affected by the weather, flowing with deep steady currents the year round. They are short, however, none of them drawing their sources from beyond the Cascade Range. Some are navigable for small steamers on their lower courses, but the openings they make in the woods are very narrow, the tall trees on their banks leaning over in some places, making fine shady tunnels.

The largest of the prairies that I have seen lies to the south of Tacoma on the line of the Portland and Tacoma Railroad. The ground is dry and gravelly—a deposit of water-washed cobbles and pebbles derived from moraines—conditions which readily explain the absence of trees here and on other prairies adjacent to Yelm. Berries grow in lavish abundance, enough for man and beast with thousands of tons to spare. The woods are full of them, especially about the borders of the waters and meadows where the sunshine may enter. Nowhere in the north does Nature set a more bountiful table. There are huckleberries of many species, red, blue and black, some of them growing close to the ground, others on bushes eight to ten feet high; also sal-al berries, growing on a low, weak-stemmed bush, a species of gaultheria, seldom more than a foot or two high. This has pale pea-green glossy leaves two or three inches long and half an inch wide and beautiful pink flowers, urn-shaped, that make a fine, rich show. The berries are black when ripe, are extremely abundant and, with the huckleberries, form an important part of the food of the Indians, who beat them into paste, dry them, and store them away for winter use, to be eaten with their oily fish. The salmon-berry also is very plentiful, growing in dense prickly tangles. The flowers are as large as wild roses and of the same color, and the berries measure nearly an inch in diameter. Besides these there are gooseberries, currants, raspberries, blackberries, and in some favored spots strawberries. The mass of the underbrush of the woods is made up in great part of these berry-bearing bushes, together with white-flowered spiræa twenty feet high; hazel, dogwood, wildrose, honeysuckle, symphoricarpus, etc. But in the depths of the woods, where little sunshine can reach the ground, there is but little underbrush of any kind, only a very light growth of huckleberry and rubus and young maples in most places. The difficulties encountered by the explorer in penetrating the wilderness are presented mostly by the streams and bogs, with their tangled margins, and the fallen timber and thick carpet of moss covering all the ground. Notwithstanding the tremendous energy displayed in lumbering and the grand scale on which it is being carried on, and the number of settlers pushing into every opening in search of farmlands, the woods of Washington are still almost entirely virgin and wild, without trace of human touch, savage or civilized. Indians no doubt have ascended most of the rivers on their way to the mountains to hunt the wild sheep and goat to obtain wool for their clothing, but with food in abundance on the coast they had little to tempt them into the wilderness, and the monuments they have left in it are scarcely more conspicuous than those of squirrels and bears; far less so than those of the beavers, which in damming the streams have made clearings and meadows which will continue to mark the landscape for centuries. Nor is there much in these woods to tempt the farmer or cattle-raiser. A few settlers established homes on the prairies or open borders of the woods and in the valleys of the Chehalis and Cowlitz before the gold days of California. Most of the early immigration from the Eastern states, however, settled in the fertile and open Willamette Valley of Oregon. Even now, when the search for land is so keen, with the exception of the bottom lands around the Sound and on the lower reaches of the rivers, there are comparatively few spots of

After the Hop Harvest.—Indians Returning Home. From Painting by John Durkin.

"Most of the picking is done by Indians, and to this fine, clean, profitable work they come in great numbers in their canoes, old and young, of many different tribes, bringing wives and children and household goods, in some cases from a distance of five or six hundred miles, even from far Alaska. Then they too grow rich and spend their money on red cloth and trinkets. About a thousand Indians are required as pickers at the Snoqualmie ranch alone, and a lively and merry picture they make in the field, arrayed in bright, showy calicoes, lowering the rustling vine-pillars with incessant song-singing and fun. Still more striking are their queer camps on the edges of the fields or over on the river bank, with the fire-light shining on their wild, jolly faces; but woe to the ranch should 'firewater' get there."

cultivation in western Washington. On every meadow or opening of any kind some one will be found keeping cattle, planting hop-vines, or raising hay, vegetables and patches of grain. All the large spaces available, even back near the summits of the Cascade Mountains, were occupied long ago. The new-comers, building their cabins where the beavers once built theirs, keep a few cows and industriously seek to enlarge their small meadow patches by chopping, girdling and burning the edge of the encircling forest, gnawing like beavers, and scratching for a living among the blackened stumps and logs, regarding the trees as their greatest enemies—a sort of larger pernicious weed immensely difficult to get rid of. But all these are as yet mere spots, making no visible scar in the distance and leaving the grand stretches of the forest as wild as they were before the discovery of the continent. For many years the axe has been busy around the shores of the Sound and chips have been falling in perpetual storm like flakes of snow. The best of the timber has

MT. RAINIER—SODA SPRINGS.

been cut for a distance of eight or ten miles from the water and to a much greater distance along the streams deep enough to float the logs. Railroads, too, have been built to fetch in the logs from the best bodies of timber otherwise inaccessible except at great cost. None of the ground, however, has been completely denuded. Most of the young trees have been left, together with the hemlocks and other trees undesirable in kind, or in some way defective, so that the neighboring trees appear to have closed over the gaps made by the removal of the larger and better ones, maintaining the general continuity of the forest and leaving no sign on the sylvan sea, at least as seen from a distance. In felling the trees they cut them off usually at a height of six to twelve feet above the ground so as to avoid cutting through the swollen base where the diameter is so much greater. In order to reach this height the chopper cuts a notch about two inches wide and three or four deep and drives a board into it on which he stands while at work. In case the first notch, cut as high as he can reach, is not high enough, he stands on the board that has been driven into the first notch and cuts another. Thus the axemen may often be seen at work standing eight or ten feet above the ground. If the tree is so large that with his long handled axe the chopper is unable to reach to the farther side of it, then a second chopper is set to work, each cutting half way across. And when the tree is about to fall, warned by the faint crackling of the strained fibres, they jump to the ground, and stand back out of danger from flying limbs, while the noble giant that had stood erect in glorious strength and beauty century after century, bows low at last and with gasp and groan and booming throb falls to earth.

Then with long saws they are cut into logs of the required length, peeled, loaded upon wagons capable of carrying a weight of eight or ten tons, hauled by a long string of oxen to the nearest available stream or railroad and floated or carried to the Sound. There the logs are gathered into booms and towed by steamers to the mills, where workmen with steel spikes in their boots leap lightly with easy poise from log to log and by means of long pike-poles push the logs apart and

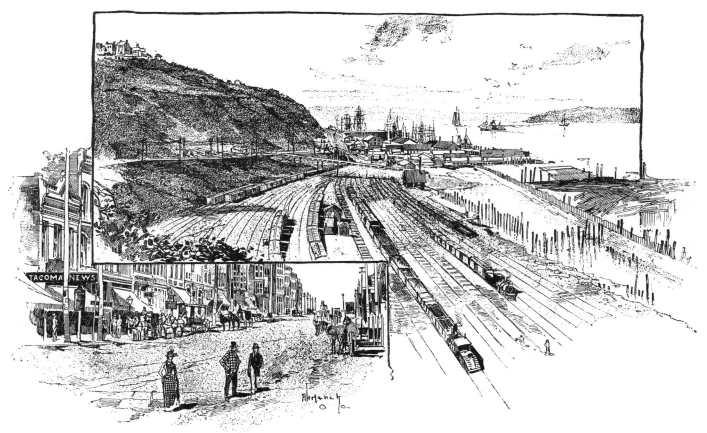

TACOMA: STREET SCENE—SHIPPING DOCKS.

selecting such as are at the time required, push them to the foot of a chute, drive dogs into the ends, and they are speedily hauled in by the mill machinery alongside the saw carriage and placed and fixed in position. Then with sounds of greedy hissing and growling they are rushed back and forth like enormous shuttles and in an incredibly short time the logs are lumber and are aboard the ships lying at the mill wharves.

Many of the long slender boles so abundant in these woods are saved for spars, and so excellent is their quality they are in demand in almost every ship-yard of the world. Thus these trees, felled and stripped of their leaves and branches, are raised again, transplanted and set firmly erect, given roots of iron and a new foliage of flapping canvas and sent to sea. On they speed in glad free motion, cheerily waving over the blue heaving water, responsive to the same winds that rocked them when they stood at home in the woods. After standing in one place all their lives they now, like sight-seeing tourists, go round the world, meeting many a relative from the old home-forest, some like themselves, wandering free, clad in broad canvas foliage, others planted head downward in mud, holding wharf platforms aloft to receive the wares of all nations.

The mills of Puget Sound and those of the redwood region of California are said to be the largest and most effective lumber-makers in the world. Tacoma alone claims to have eleven saw-mills, and Seattle about as many; while at many other points on the Sound, where the advantages are particularly favorable, there are immense lumbering establishments, as at Ports Blakely, Madison, Discovery, Gamble, Ludlow, etc.,—with a capacity altogether of over three million feet a day. Never-theless, the observer coming up the Sound sees not nor hears anything of this fierce storm of steel that is devouring the forests, save perhaps the shriek of some whistle or the columns of smoke that mark the position of the mills. All else seems as serene and unscathed as the silent watching mountains. Strolling in the woods about the logging camps, most of the lumbermen are found to be interesting people to meet, kind and obliging and sincere, full of knowledge concerning the bark and sap-wood and heart-wood of the trees they cut, and how to fell them without unnecessary breakage, on ground where they may be most advantageously sawed into logs and loaded for removal. The work is hard and all of the older men have a tired, somewhat haggard appearance. Their faces are doubtful in color, neither sickly nor quite healthy looking, and seamed with deep wrinkles like the bark of the spruces, but with no trace of anxiety. Their clothing is full of rosin and never wears out. A little of everything in the woods is stuck fast to these loggers and their trousers grow constantly thicker with age. In all their movements and gestures they are heavy and deliberate like the trees above them, and walk with a swaying, rocking gait altogether free from quick jerky fussiness; for chopping and log-rolling has quenched all that. They are also slow of speech as if partly out of breath, and when one tries to draw them out on some subject away from logs, all the fresh, leafy, outreaching branches of the mind seem to have been withered and killed with fatigue, leaving their lives little more than dry lumber.

ASCENDING MT. RAINIER.

Many a tree have these old axemen felled, but round-shouldered and stooping, they too are beginning to lean over. Many of their companions are already beneath the moss and among those that we see at work some are now dead at the top (bald), leafless, so to speak, and tottering to their fall.

A very different man, seen now and then at long intervals but usually invisible, is the free roamer of the wilderness— hunter, prospector, explorer, seeking he knows not what. Lithe and sinewy he walks erect, making his way with the skill of wild animals, all his senses in action, watchful and alert, looking keenly at everything in sight, his imagination well nourished in the wealth of the wilderness, coming into contact with free nature in a thousand forms, drinking at the fountains of things, responsive to wild influences, as trees to the winds. Well he knows the wild animals his neighbors, what fishes are in the streams, what birds in the forests and where food may be found. Hungry at times and weary, he has corresponding enjoyment in eating and resting, and all the wilderness is home. Some of these rare, happy rovers die alone among the leaves. Others half settle down and change in part into farmers; each, making choice of some fertile spot where the landscape attracts him, builds a small cabin, where with few wants to supply from garden or field he hunts and farms in turn, going perhaps once a year to the settlements, until night begins to draw near, and like forest shadows, thickens into darkness and his day is done. In these Washington wilds, living alone, all sorts of men may perchance be found, poets, philosophers, and even full-blown transcendentalists, though you may go far to find them.

Indians are seldom to be met with away from the Sound, excepting about the few out-lying hop-ranches, to which they resort in great numbers during the picking season.

Nor in your walks in the woods will you be likely to see many of the wild animals, however far you may go, with the exception of the Douglass squirrel and mountain goat. The squirrel is everywhere, and the goat you can hardly fail to find if you climb any of the high mountains. The deer, once very abundant, may still be found on the islands and along the shores of the Sound, but the large gray wolf renders their existence next to impossible at any considerable distance back in the woods of the mainland, as they can easily run them down unless near enough the coast

MOUNT RAINIER. FROM PAINTING BY W. KEITH.

"Ambitious climbers, seeking adventures and opportunities to test their skill and strength, occasionally attempt to penetrate the wilderness on the west side of the Sound, and push on to the summit of Mount Olympus. But the grandest excursion of all to be made hereabouts is to Mount Rainier, to climb to the top of its icy crown. The mountain is very high, 14,400 feet, and laden with glaciers that are terribly roughened and interrupted by crevasses and ice-cliffs. Only good climbers should attempt to gain the summit, lead by a guide of proved nerve and endurance. A good trail has been cut through the woods to the base of the mountain on the north; but the summit of the mountain never has been reached from this side, though many brave attempts have been made upon it."

to make their escape by plunging into the water and swimming to the islands off shore. The elk and perhaps also the moose still exist in the most remote and inaccessible solitudes of the forest, but their numbers have been greatly reduced of late, and even the most experienced hunters have difficulty in finding them. Of bears there are two species, the black and the large brown, the former by far the more common of the two. On the shaggy bottom-lands where berries are plentiful, and along the rivers while salmon are going up to spawn, the black bear may be found, fat and at home. Many are killed every year, both for their flesh and skins. The large brown species likes

higher and opener ground. He is a dangerous animal, a near relative of the famous grizzly, and wise hunters are very fond of letting him alone.

The towns of Puget Sound are of a very lively, progressive and aspiring kind, fortunately with abundance of substance about them to warrant their ambition and make them grow. Like young sapling sequoias, they are sending out their roots far and near for nourishment, counting confidently on longevity and grandeur of stature. Seattle and Tacoma are at present far

CAMP OF THE CLOUDS.

SUMMIT OF MT. RAINIER.

PARADISE FALLS, NEAR CAMP OF THE CLOUDS.

in the lead of all others in the race for supremacy, and these two are keen, active rivals, to all appearances well matched. Tacoma occupies near the head of the Sound a site of great natural beauty. It is the terminus of the Northern Pacific Railroad, and calls itself the "City of Destiny." Seattle is also charmingly located about twenty miles down the Sound from Tacoma, on Elliott Bay. It is the terminus of the Seattle, Lake-Shore & Eastern Railroad, now in process of construction, and calls itself "The Queen City of the Sound" and the "Metropolis of Washington." What the populations of these towns number I am not able to say with anything like exactness. They are probably about the same size and they each claim to have about twenty thousand people; but their figures are so rapidly changing, and so often mixed up with counts that refer to the future that exact measurements of either of these places are about as hard to obtain as measure-ments of the clouds of a growing storm. Their edges run back for miles into the woods among the trees and stumps and brush which hide a good many of the houses and the stakes which mark the lots; so that without being as yet very large towns, they seem to fade away into the distance.

But though young and loose-jointed, they are fast taking on the forms and manners of old cities, putting on airs, as some would say, like boys in haste to be men. They are already towns "with all modern improvements, first class in every particular," as is said of hotels. They have electric motors and lights, paved broadways and boulevards, substantial business blocks, schools, churches, factories and foundries. The lusty, titanic clang of boiler-making may be heard there, and plenty of the languid music of pianos mingling with the babel noises of commerce carried on in a hundred tongues. The main streets are crowded with bright, wide-awake lawyers, ministers, merchants, agents for everything under the sun; ox-drivers and loggers in stiff, gummy overalls; back-slanting dudes, well-tailored and shiny; and fashions and bonnets of every feather and color

GREEN RIVER.

bloom gaily in the noisy throng and advertise London and Paris. Vigorous life and strife are to be seen everywhere. The spirit of progress is in the air. Still it is hard to realize how much good work is being done here of a kind that makes for civilization—the enthusiastic, exulting energy displayed in the building of new towns, railroads, and mills; in the opening of mines of coal and iron and development of natural resources in general. To many, especially in the Atlantic states, Washington is hardly known at all. It is regarded as being yet a far wild-west—a dim, nebulous expanse of woods—by those who do not know that railroads and steamers have brought the country out of the wilderness and abolished the old distances. It is now near to all the world and is in possession of a share of the best of all that civilization has to offer, while on some of the lines of advancement it is at the front.

Notwithstanding the sharp rivalry between different sections and towns, the leading men mostly pull together for the general good and glory—building, buying, borrowing, to push the country to its place; keeping arithmetic busy in counting population present and to come, ships, towns, factories, tons of coal and iron, feet of lumber, miles of railroad—Americans, Scandinavians, Irish, Scotch, and Germans being joined together in the white heat of work like religious crowds in time of revival who have forgotten sectarianism. It is a fine thing to see people in hot earnest about anything; therefore, however extravagant and high the brag ascending from Puget Sound, in most cases it is likely to appear pardonable and more.

Seattle was named after an old Indian chief who lived in this part of the Sound. He was very proud of the honor and lived long enough to lead his grandchildren about the streets. The greater part of the lower business portion of the town, including a long stretch of wharves and warehouses built on piles, was destroyed by fire a few months ago, causing immense loss. The people, however, are in nowise discouraged and ere long the loss will be gain, inasmuch as a better class of buildings, chiefly of brick, are being erected in place of the inflammable wooden ones, which, with comparatively few exceptions, were built of pitchy spruce.

With their own scenery so glorious ever on show, one would at first thought suppose that these happy Puget Sound people would never go sightseeing from home like less favored mortals. But they do all the same. Some go boating on the Sound or on the lakes and rivers, or with their families make excursions at small cost on the steamers. Others will take the train to the Franklin & Newcastle or Carbon River coal-mines for the sake of the thirty or forty-mile rides through the woods, and a look into the black depths of the under world. Others again take the steamers for Victoria, Fraser River, or Vancouver, the new ambitious town at the terminus of the Canadian Railroad; thus getting views of the outer world in a near foreign country. One of the regular summer resorts of this region where people go for fishing, hunting and the healing of diseases, is the Green River Hot Springs, in the Cascade Mountains, sixty-one miles east of Tacoma, on the line of the Northern Pacific Railroad. Green River is a small rocky stream with picturesque banks, and derives its name from the beautiful pale-green hue of its waters.

Among the most interesting of all the summer rest and pleasure places is the famous "Hop-Ranch" on the upper Snoqualmie River, thirty or forty miles eastward from Seattle. Here the dense forest opens, allowing fine free views of the adjacent mountains from a long stretch of ground which is half meadow, half prairie, level and fertile, and beautifully diversified with outstanding groves of spruces and alders and rich flowery fringes of spiræa and wild roses, the river meandering deep and tranquil through the midst of it. On the portions most easily cleared some three hundred acres of hop-vines have been planted and are now in full bearing, yielding, it is said, at the rate of about a ton of hops to the acre. They are a beautiful crop, these vines of the north, pillars of verdure in regular rows, seven feet apart and eight or ten feet in height; the long vigorous shoots sweeping round in fine wild freedom, and the light leafy cones hanging in loose handsome clusters.

Perhaps enough of hops might be raised in Washington for the wants of all the world, but it would be impossible to find pickers to handle the crop. Most of the picking is done by Indians, and to this fine, clean, profitable work they come in great numbers in their canoes, old and young, of many different tribes, bringing wives and children and household goods, in some cases from a distance of five or six hundred miles, even from far Alaska. Then they too grow rich and spend their money on red cloth and trinkets. About a thousand Indians are required as pickers at the Snoqualmie ranch alone, and a lively and merry picture they make in the field, arrayed in bright showy calicoes, lowering the rustling vine pillars with incessant song-singing and fun. Still more striking are their queer camps on the edges of the fields or over on the river bank, with the fire-light shining on their wild jolly faces; but woe to the ranch should firewater get there!

But the chief attractions here are not found in the hops, but in trout-fishing and bear-hunting, and in the two fine falls on the river.

Formerly the trip from Seattle was a hard one, over corduroy roads; now it is reached in a few hours by rail along the shores of Lake Washington and Lake Squak, through a fine sample section of the forest and past the brow of the main Snoqualmie Fall. From the hotel at the ranch-village the road to the fall leads down the right bank of the river through the magnificent maple woods I have mentioned elsewhere, and fine views of the fall may be had on that side, both from above and below. It is situated on the main river where it plunges over a sheer precipice, about two hundred and forty feet high, in leaving the level meadows of the ancient lake-basin. In a

STAMPEDE OF INDIAN HORSES. FROM SKETCH BY F. O. C. DARLEY.

The Indian pony is an excitable and nervous creature and contains all the vices common to horse flesh. At times they are peaceable enough; but occasionally they take flight at almost nothing, and away they fly over the mountains. It is then the Indian's duty to go after them; but often the only ponies they can catch are almost as wild as the fleeing animals, and then the chase is a most exciting one. Often hundreds of ponies escape at a time, and it will take the Indians many days to bring them back to camp. But they all have to be brought back if it takes all summer.

general way it resembles the well-known Nevada Fall in Yosemite, having the same twisted appearance at the top and the free plunge in numberless comet-shaped masses into a deep pool seventy-five or eighty yards in diameter. The pool is of considerable depth, as is shown by the radiating well-beaten foam and mist, which is of a beautiful rose color at times, of exquisite fineness of tone, and by the heavy waves that lash the rocks in front of it.

Though to a Californian the height of this fall would not seem great, the volume of water is heavy, and all the surroundings are delightful. The maple forest, of itself worth a long journey, the beauty of the river-reaches above and below, and the views down the valley afar over the mighty forests, with all its lovely trimmings of ferns and flowers, make this one of the most interesting falls I have ever seen. The upper fall is about seventy-five feet high, with bouncing rapids at head and foot, set in a romantic dell thatched with dripping mosses and ferns and embowered in dense evergreens and blooming bushes; the distance to it from the upper end of the meadows being about eight miles. The road leads through majestic woods with ferns ten feet high beneath some of the thickets, and across a gravelly plain disforested by fire many years ago. Orange lilies are plentiful, and handsome shining mats of the kinikinik,

SNOQUALMIE HOP RANCH.

sprinkled with bright scarlet berries. From a place called "Hunt's," at the end of the wagon road, a trail leads through lush, dripping woods (never dry) of Thuja, Merten, Menzies and Douglas spruces. The ground is covered with the best moss-work of the moist lands of the north, made up mostly of the various species of hypnum, with some liverworts, marchantia, jungermania, etc., in broad sheets and bosses, where never a dust-particle floated, and where all the

HOP-PICKING.

HOP-DRYING KILN.

flowers, fresh with mist and spray, are wetter than water-lilies. The pool at the foot of the fall is a place surpassingly lovely to look at, with the enthusiastic rush and song of the falls, the majestic trees overhead leaning over the brink like listeners eager to catch every word of the white refreshing waters; the delicate maidenhairs and aspleniums with fronds outspread gathering the rainbow sprays, and the myriads of hooded mosses, every cup fresh and shining.

Ambitious climbers, seeking adventures and opportunities to test their strength and skill, occasionally attempt to penetrate the wilderness on the west side of the Sound, and push on to the summit of Mt. Olympus. But the grandest excursion of all to be made hereabouts is to Mt. Ranier: to climb to the top of its icy crown. The mountain is very high, 14,400 feet, and laden with glaciers that are terribly roughened and interrupted by crevasses and ice-cliffs. Only good climbers should attempt to gain the summit, led by a guide of proved nerve and endurance. A good trail has been cut through the woods to the base of the mountain on the north; but the summit of the mountain never has been reached from this side, though many brave attempts have been made upon it.

Last summer I gained the summit from the south side, in a day and a half from the timber line, without encountering any desperate obstacles that could not in some way be passed in good weather. I was accompanied by Keith, the artist, Prof. Ingraham, and five ambitious young climbers from Seattle. We were led by the veteran mountaineer and guide, Van Trump, of Yelm, who many years before guided General Stevens in his memorable ascent, and later Mr. Bailey of Oakland. With a cumbersome abundance of campstools and blankets we set out from Seattle, traveling by rail as far as Yelm prairie, on the Tacoma and Oregon road. Here we made our first camp and arranged with Mr. Longmire, a farmer in the neighborhood, for pack and saddle animals. The noble King Mountain was in full view from here, glorifying the bright sunny day with his presence, rising in god-like majesty over the woods, with the magnificent prairie as a foreground. The distance to the mountain from Yelm in a straight line is perhaps fifty miles; but by the mule and yellow-jacket trail we had to follow it is a hundred miles. For, notwithstanding a portion of this trail runs in the air where the wasps work hardest, it is far from being an air-line as commonly understood.

LACE FALLS.

"WE LINGERED IN THESE LOWER GARDENS OF EDEN."

By night of the third day we reached the Soda Springs on the right bank of the Nisqually, which goes roaring by gray with mud, gravel and boulders from the caves of the glaciers of Ranier, now close at hand. The distance from the Soda Springs to the Camp of the Clouds is about ten miles. The first part of the way lies up the Nisqually Cañon, the bottom of which is flat in some places and the walls very high and precipitous, like those of the Yosemite Valley. The upper part of the cañon is still occupied by one of the Nisqually glaciers, from which this branch of the river draws its source, issuing from a cave in the gray, rock-strewn snout. About a mile below the glacier we had to ford the river, which caused some anxiety, for the current is very rapid and carried forward large boulders as well as lighter material, while its savage roar is bewildering.

At this point we left the cañon, climbing out of it by a steep zigzag up the old left lateral moraine of the glacier, which was deposited when the present glacier flowed past at this height, and is about eight hundred feet high. It is now covered with a superb growth of *Picea amabilis;* so also is the corresponding portion of the right lateral. From the top of the moraine, still ascending, we passed for a mile or two through a forest of mixed growth, mainly silver fir, Paton spruce, and mountain pine, and then came to the charming park region, at an elevation of about five thousand feet above sea-level. Here the vast continuous woods at length begin to give way under the dominion of climate, though still at this height retaining their beauty and giving no sign of stress of storm, sweeping upward in belts of varying width, composed mainly of one species of fir, sharp and spirey in form, leaving smooth, spacious parks, with here and there separate groups of trees standing out in the midst of the openings like islands in a lake. Every one of these parks, great and small, is a garden filled knee-deep with fresh, lovely flowers of every hue, the most luxuriant and the most extravagantly beautiful of all the Alpine gardens I ever beheld in all my mountain-top wanderings.

We arrived at the Cloud Camp at noon, but no clouds were in sight, save a few gauzy ornamental wreathes adrift in the sunshine. Out of the forest at last there stood the mountain, wholly unveiled, awful in bulk and majesty, filling all the view like a separate, new-born world, yet withal so fine and so beautiful it might well fire the dullest observer to desperate enthusiasm. Long we gazed in silent admiration, buried in tall daisies and anemones by the side of a snow-bank. Higher we could not go with the animals and find food for them and wood for our own camp-fires, for just beyond this lies the region of ice, with only here and there an open spot on the ridges in the midst of the ice, with dwarf Alpine plants, such as saxifrages and irabas, which reach far up between the glaciers with low mats of the beautiful bryanthus, while back of us were the gardens and abundance of everything that heart could wish. Here we lay all the afternoon considering the lilies and the lines of the mountains with reference to a way to the summit.

At noon next day we left camp and began our long climb. We were in light marching order, save one who pluckily determined to carry his camera to the summit. At night, after a long easy climb over wide and smooth fields of ice, we reached a narrow ridge, at an elevation of about ten thousand feet above the sea, on the divide between the glaciers of the Nisqually and Cowlitz. Here we lay as best we could, waiting for another day, without fire of course, as we were now many miles beyond the timber line and without much to cover us. After eating a little hard tack,

SHIPPING AT TACOMA MILLS.

each of us leveled a spot to lie on among lava-blocks and cinders. The night was cold, and the wind coming down upon us in stormy surges drove gritty ashes and fragments of pumice about our ears while chilling to the bone. Very short and shallow was our sleep that night; but day dawned at last, early rising was easy, and there was nothing about breakfast to cause any delay. About four o'clock we were off, and climbing began in earnest. We followed up the ridge on which we had spent the night, now along its crest, now on either side, or on the ice leaning against it, until we came to where it becomes massive and precipitous. Then we were compelled to crawl along a seam or narrow shelf, on its face, which we traced to its termination in the base of the great ice-cap. From this point all the climbing was over ice which was here desperately steep but fortunately was at the same time carved into innumerable spikes and pillars which afforded good footholds, and we crawled cautiously on, warm with ambition and exercise.

At length, after gaining the upper extreme of our guiding ridge, we found a good place to rest and prepare ourselves to scale the dangerous upper curves of the dome. The surface almost everywhere was bare, hard, snowless ice, extremely slippery; and though smooth in general, it was interrupted by a network of yawning crevasses, outspread like lines of defense against any attempt to win the summit. Here every one of the party took off his shoes and drove stout steel caulks

MOUNTAIN SUPPLY TRAIN IN A STORM. FROM PAINTING BY A. I. KELLER.

Few people have any idea of the landslips that the mountaineers of Oregon and Washington are compelled to bear. In summer when the weather is pleasant their life is, in many ways, an enviable one; but when the winter "howls around" things change. The men who take supplies to the mines have, perhaps, the worst to bear. They must struggle through snow drifts and along the edges of precipices while the snow falls thickly and the wind cuts like a knife, so intense is the cold. Miners are often dependent for food on the arrival of these trains. Sometimes they never come, and the skeletons of men, horses and mules are found in the spring when the snow melts.

about half an inch long into them, having brought tools along for the purpose, and not having made use of them until now so that the points might not get dulled on the rocks ere the smooth, dangerous ice was reached. Besides being well shod each carried an alpenstock, and for special difficulties we had a hundred feet of rope and an axe.

Thus prepared, we stepped forth afresh, slowly groping our way through tangled lines of crevasses, crossing on snow bridges here and there after cautiously testing them, jumping at narrow places, or crawling around the ends of the largest, bracing well at every point with our alpenstocks and setting our spiked shoes squarely down on the dangerous slopes. It was nerve-trying work, most of it, but we made good speed nevertheless, and by noon all stood together on the utmost summit, save one who, his strength failing for a time, came up later.

We remained on the summit nearly two hours, looking about us at the vast map-like views, comprehending hundreds of miles of the Cascade Range, with their black interminable forests and white volcanic cones in glorious array reaching far into Oregon; the Sound region also and the great plains of eastern Washington, hazy and vague in the distance. Clouds began to gather. Soon of all the land only the summits of the mountains, St. Helens, Adams, and Hood, were left in sight, forming islands in the sky. We found two well-formed and well-preserved craters on the summit, lying close together like two plates on a table with their rims touching. The highest point of the mountain is located between the craters where their edges come in contact. Sulphurous fumes and steam issue from several vents, giving out a sickening smell that can be detected at a considerable distance. The unwasted condition of these craters, and indeed to a great extent, of the entire mountain, would tend to show that

THE FREE ROAMER
OF THE WILDERNESS.

Rainier is still a comparatively young mountain. With the exception of the projecting lips of the craters and the top of a subordinate summit a short distance to the northward, the mountain is solidly capped with ice all around; and it is this ice-cap which forms the grand central fountain whence all the twenty glaciers of Rainier flow, radiating in every direction.

The descent was accomplished without disaster, though several of the party had narrow escapes. One slipped and fell and as he shot past me, seemed to be going to certain death. So steep was the ice-slope no one could move to help him, but fortunately, keeping his presence of mind, he threw himself on his face and digging his alpenstock into the ice, gradually retarded his motion until he came to rest. Another broke through a slim bridge over a crevasse, but his momentum at the time carried him against the lower edge and only his alpenstock was lost in the abyss. Thus crippled by the loss of his staff, we had to lower him the rest of the way down the dome by means of the rope we carried. Falling rocks from the upper precipitous part of the ridge were also a source of danger, as they came whizzing past in successive volleys; but none told on us, and when we at length gained the gentle slopes of the lower ice-fields we ran and slid at our ease, making fast, glad time, all care and danger past, and arrived at our beloved Cloud Camp before sundown. We were rather weak from want of nourishment, and some suffered from sunburn notwithstanding the partial protection of glasses and veils; otherwise, all were unscathed and well. The view we enjoyed from the summit could hardly be surpassed in sublimity and grandeur; but one feels far from home so high in the sky, so much so that one is inclined to guess, that apart from the acquisition of knowledge and the exhilaration of climbing, more pleasure is to be found at the foot of mountains than on their frozen tops. Doubly happy, however, is the man to whom lofty mountain tops are within reach, for the lights that shine there illumine all that lies below.

The weather continued fine and we lingered in these lower gardens of Eden day after day, making short excursions of a dozen miles or so to lakes and waterfalls and glaciers, resting, sketching, botanizing, watching the changing lights and clouds on the glorious mountain until, all too soon, our Ranier time was done and we were compelled to pack our spoils and take the wasp-trail to civilization and Yelm.

JOHN MUIR.

COLUMBIA RIVER BAR

THE BASIN OF THE COLUMBIA RIVER.

OREGON is a large, rich, compact section of the west side of the continent, containing nearly a hundred thousand square miles of deep, wet, evergreen woods, fertile valleys, icy mountains, and high rolling wind-swept plains, watered by the majestic Columbia River and its countless branches. It is bounded on the north by Washington, on the east by Idaho, on the south by California and Nevada, and on the west by the Pacific Ocean. It is a grand, hearty, wholesome, foodful wilderness and, like Washington, once a part of the Oregon Territory, abounds in bold, far-reaching contrasts as to scenery, climate, soil and productions. Side by side there is drouth on a grand scale and overflowing moisture; flinty, sharply-cut lava beds, gloomy and forbidding, and smooth flowery lawns; cool bogs, exquisitely plushy and soft, overshadowed by jagged crags barren as icebergs; forests seemingly boundless and plains with no tree in sight; presenting a wide range of conditions, but as a whole favorable to industry. Natural wealth of an available kind abounds nearly everywhere, inviting the farmer, the stockraiser, the lumberman, the fisherman, the manufacturer and the miner, as well as the free walker in search of knowledge and wildness. The scenery is mostly of a comfortable, assuring kind, grand and inspiring without too much of that dreadful overpowering sublimity and exuberance which tend to discourage effort and cast people down into inaction and superstition.

Ever since Oregon was first heard of in the romantic, adventurous, hunting, trapping, Wild West days, it seems to have been regarded as the most attractive and promising of all the Pacific countries for farmers. While yet the whole region as well as the way to it was wild, ere a single road or bridge was built, undaunted by the trackless thousand-mile distances and scalping, cattle-stealing Indians, long trains of covered wagons began to crawl wearily westward, crossing how many plains, rivers, ridges and mountains, fighting the painted savages and weariness and famine! Setting out from the frontier of the old West in the spring as soon as the grass would support their cattle, they pushed on up the Platte, making haste slowly, however, that they might not be caught in the

"WE GO DOWN THE LONG, WHITE SLOPES."

storms of winter ere they reached the promised land. They crossed the Rocky Mountains to Fort Hall; thence followed down the Snake River for three or four hundred miles, their cattle limping and failing on the rough lava plains; swimming the streams too deep to be forded, making boats out of wagon boxes for the women and children and goods, or where trees could be had, lashing together logs for rafts. Thence crossing the Blue Mountains and the plains of the Columbia they followed the river to The Dalles. Here winter would be upon them, and before a wagon road was built across the Cascade Mountains the toil-worn emigrants would be compelled to leave their cattle and wagons until the following summer, and in the meantime with the assistance of the Hudson Bay Company make their way to the Willamette valley on the river with rafts and boats.

How strange and remote these trying times have already become! They are now dim as if a thousand years had passed over them. Steamships and locomotives with magical influence have well-nigh abolished the old distances and dangers, and brought forward the New West into near and familiar companionship with the rest of the world.

Purely wild for unnumbered centuries, a paradise of oily, salmon-fed Indians, Oregon is now roughly settled in part and surveyed, its rivers and mountain ranges, lakes, valleys and plains have been traced and mapped in a general way, civilization is beginning to take root, towns are springing up and flourishing vigorously like a crop adapted to the soil, and the whole kindly wilderness lies invitingly near with all its wealth open and ripe for use.

In sailing along the Oregon coast one sees but few more signs of human occupation than did Juan de Fuca three centuries ago. The shore bluffs rise abruptly from the waves, forming a wall apparently unbroken, though many short rivers from the coast range of mountains and two from the interior have made narrow openings on their way to the sea. At the mouths of these rivers good harbors have been discovered for coasting vessels, which are of great importance to the lumbermen, dairymen and farmers of the coast region. But little or nothing of these appear in general views, only a simple gray wall nearly straight, green along the top, and the forest stretching back into the mountains as far as the eye can reach.

Going ashore, we find few long reaches of sand where one may saunter, or meadows, save the brown and purple meadows of the sea overgrown with slippery kelp, swashed and swirled in the restless breakers. The abruptness of the shore allows the massive waves that have come from far over the broad Pacific to get close to the bluffs ere they break, and the thundering shock shakes the rocks to their foundations. No calm comes to these shores. Even in the finest weather, when the ships off shore are becalmed and their sails hang loose against the mast, there is always a wreath of foam at the base of these bluffs. The breakers are ever in bloom and crystal brine is ever in the air.

A scramble along the Oregon sea-bluffs proves as richly exciting to lovers of wild beauty as heart could wish. Here are three hundred miles of pictures of rock and water in black and white, or gray and white, with more or less of green and yellow, purple and blue. The rocks glistening in sunshine and foam are never wholly dry—many of them marvels of wave-sculpture and most imposing in bulk and bearing, standing boldly forward, monuments of a thousand storms, types of permanence, holding the homes and places of refuge of multitudes of sea-faring animals in their

SNOW-SHEDS ON OREGON SHORT LINE. FROM SKETCH BY JULIAN RIX.

In all points of the great northwest where snow is plentiful through the long winter months, the railroad tracks are in constant danger of being buried beneath the expansive white mantle, and interfering, if not entirely stopping, traffic. To overcome this great danger it is necessary to cover the track with wooden structures that have come to be known as "snow-sheds," although they are, in reality, a sort of trellis. These coverings are placed at such points where the snow is known to drift or to slide down in enormous avalanches. When the train passes through the snow-sheds in winter it is like going through an enormous tunnel, and the journey is made in total darkness. In summer some of the sheds become covered with creeping vines and form a most beautiful part of the grand landscapes.

keeping, yet ever wasting away.   How grand the songs of the waves about them, every wave a
fine, hearty storm in itself, taking its rise on the breezy plains of the sea perhaps thousands of
miles away, traveling with majestic, slow-heaving deliberation, reaching the end of its journey, striking
its blow, bursting into a mass of white and pink bloom, then falling spent and withered to give
place to the next in the endless procession, thus keeping up the glorious show and glorious song
through all times and seasons forever!

Terribly impressive as is this cliff and wave scenery when the skies are bright and kindly
sunshine makes rainbows in the spray, it is doubly so in dark, stormy nights, when crouching in
some hollow on the top of some jutting headland we may gaze and listen undisturbed in the heart
of it.   Perhaps now and then we may dimly see the tops of the highest breakers, looking ghostly
in the gloom; but when the water happens to be phosphorescent, as it oftentimes is, then both the
sea and the rocks are visible, and the wild, exulting, up-dashing spray burns, every particle of it,

CAPE BLANCO, OREGON COAST.

and is combined into one glowing mass of white fire.   While back in the woods and along the
bluffs and crags of the shore the storm-wind roars, and the rain floods gathering strength and
coming from far and near rush wildly down every gulch to the sea, as if eager to join the waves
in their grand, savage harmony; deep calling unto deep in the heart of the great, dark night,
making a sight and a song unspeakably sublime and glorious.

In the pleasant weather of summer, after the rainy season is past and only occasional refreshing showers fall, washing the sky and bringing out the fragrance of the flowers and the evergreens,
then one may enjoy a fine, free walk all the way across the state from the sea to the eastern
boundary on the Snake River.   Many a beautiful stream we would cross in such a walk, singing
through forest and meadow and deep rocky gorge, and many a broad prairie and plain, mountain
and valley, wild garden and desert, presenting landscape beauty on a grand scale and in a
thousand forms, and new lessons without number, delightful to learn.   Oregon has three mountain
ranges which run nearly parallel with the coast, the most influential of which, in every way, is
the Cascade Range.   It is about six thousand to seven thousand feet in average height, and divides
the state into two main sections called eastern and western Oregon, corresponding with the main
divisions of Washington; while these are again divided, but less perfectly, by the Blue Mountains

and the Coast Range. The eastern section is about two hundred and thirty miles wide, and is made up in great part of the treeless plains of the Columbia, which are green and flowery in spring, but gray, dusty, hot and forbidding in summer. Considerable areas, however, on these plains, as well as some of the valleys countersunk below the general surface along the banks of the streams, have proved fertile and produce large crops of wheat, barley, hay, and other products.

In general views the western section seems to be covered with one vast, evenly planted forest, with the exception of the few snow-clad peaks of the Cascade Range, these peaks being the only points in the landscape that rise above the timber line. Nevertheless, embosomed in this forest and lying in the great trough between the Cascades and coast mountains, there are some of the best bread-bearing valleys to be found in the world. The largest of these are the Willamette, Umpqua and Rogue River valleys. Inasmuch as a considerable portion of these main valleys were treeless, or nearly so, as well as surpassingly fertile, they were the first to attract settlers; and the Willamette, being at once the largest and nearest to tide water, was settled first of all, and now contains the greater portion of the population and wealth of the state.

"THESE WANDERERS ENJOY
THE FREEDOM OF GYPSY LIFE."

"PLODDING IN OLD '49 STYLE."

The climate of this corresponding portion of Washington, like the section, like the ton, is rather damp and sloppy throughout the winter months, but the summers are bright, ripening the wheat and allowing it to be garnered in good condition. Taken as a whole the weather is bland and kindly, and like the forest trees the crops and cattle grow plump and sound in it. So also do the people; children ripen well and grow up with limbs of good size and fibre and, unless overworked in the woods, live to a good old age, hale and hearty.

But, like every other happy valley in the world, the sunshine of this one is not without its shadows. Malarial fevers are not unknown in some places, and untimely frosts and rains may at long intervals in some measure disappoint the hopes of the husbandman. Many a tale, good-natured or otherwise, is told concerning the overflowing abundance of the Oregon rains. Once an English traveler, as the story goes, went to a store to make some purchases and on leaving found that rain was falling; therefore, not liking to get wet, he stepped back to wait till the shower was over. Seeing no signs of clearing, he soon became impatient and inquired of the storekeeper how long he thought the shower would be likely to last. Going to the door and looking wisely into the gray sky and noting the direction of the wind, the latter replied that he thought the shower would probably last about six months, an opinion that of course disgusted the fault-finding Briton with the "blawsted country," though in fact it is but little if at all wetter or cloudier than his own.

No climate seems the best for everybody. Many there be who waste their lives in a vain search for weather with which no fault may be found, keeping themselves and their families in constant motion, like floating seaweeds that never strike root, yielding compliance to every current of news concerning countries yet untried, believing that everywhere, anywhere, the sky is fairer and the grass grows greener than where they happen to be.   Before the Oregon and California railroad was built the overland journey between these states across the Siskiyou mountains in the old fashioned emigrant wagon was a long and tedious one.   Nevertheless, every season dissatisfied climate-seekers too wet and too dry might be seen plodding along through the dust in the old "'49" style, making their way one-half of them from California to Oregon, the other half from Oregon to California.   The beautiful Sisson meadows at the base of Mount Shasta was a favorite half-way resting place, where the weary cattle were turned out for a few days to gather strength for better climates, and it was curious to hear those perpetual pioneers comparing notes and seeking information around the campfires.

"Where are you from?" some Oregonian would ask.

"The Joaquin."

"Its dry there, ain't it."

"Well, I should say so.   No rain at all in summer and none to speak of in winter, and I'm dried out.   I just told my wife I was on the move again, and I'm going to keep moving till I come to a country where it rains once in a while like it does in every reg'lar white man's country; and that I guess will be Oregon, if the news be true."

"Yes, neighbor, you're heading in the right direction for rain," the Oregonian would say.   "Keep right on to Yamhill and you'll soon be damp enough. It rains there more than twelve months in the year; at least no saying but it will.   I've just come from there, plump drownded out, and I told my wife to jump into the wagon and we would start out and see if we couldn't find a dry day somewhere.   Last fall the hay was out and the wood was out, and the cabin leaked and I made up my mind to try California the first chance."

"Well, if you be a horned toad or coyote," the seeker of moisture would reply, "then maybe you can stand it.   Just keep right on by the Alabama Settlement to Tulare and you can have my place on Big Dry Creek and welcome.   You'll be drownded

IN YEW PARK, SALEM, OREGON.

there mighty seldom.   The wagon spokes and tires will rattle and tell you when you come to it."

"All right, partner, we'll swap square; you can have mine in Yamhill and the rain thrown in.   Last August a painter-sharp came along one day wanting to know the way to Willamette Falls, and I told him, 'young man, just wait a little and you'll find falls enough without going to Oregon City after them.'   The whole dogone Noah's flood of a country will be a fall and melt and float away some day."

And more to the same effect.

But no one need leave Oregon in search of fair weather.   The wheat and cattle region of eastern Oregon and Washington on the upper Columbia plains is dry enough and dusty enough more than half the year.   The truth is, most of these wanderers enjoy the freedom of gypsy life and seek not homes but camps.   Having crossed the plains and reached the ocean they can find no further west within reach of wagons, and are therefore compelled now to go north and south between Mexico and Alaska, always glad to find an excuse for moving, stopping a few months or weeks here and there, the time being measured by the size of the camp meadow, condition of the grass, game, and other indications.   Even their so-called settlements of a year or two, when they take up land and build cabins, are only another kind of camp, in no common sense homes.   Never a tree is planted, nor do they plant themselves, but like good soldiers in time of war are ever ready to

Mount Hood. From Painting by Julian Rix.

"That sharp, white, broad-based pyramid on the south side of the Columbia is the famous Mount Hood. Its upper slopes form the only bare ground, bare as to forests, in the landscape in that direction. It is the pride of Oregonians, and when it is visible it is always pointed out to strangers as the glory of the country,—the mountain of mountains. It is one of a grand series of extinct volcanoes, which extend from Lassen's Butte to Mount Baker, a distance of about six hundred miles, which once flamed like gigantic watch fires along the coast. Though it is 11,000 feet high, it is too far off to make much show under ordinary conditions in so extensive a landscape. Through a great part of the summer it is invisible on account of smoke poured into the sky from burning woods, logging camps, mills, etc., and in winter, for weeks at a time, or even months, it is in the clouds. Only in spring and early summer, and in what there may chance to be of bright weather in winter, is it or any of its companions at all clear or telling. From the Cascades on the Columbia it may be seen at a distance of twenty miles or thereabouts, or from other points up and down the river, and with the magnificent foreground it is very impressive."

march. Their journey of life is indeed a journey with very matter-of-fact thorns in the way, though not wholly wanting in compensation.

One of the most influential of the motives that brought the early settlers to these shores, apart from that natural instinct to scatter and multiply which urges even sober salmon to climb the Rocky Mountains, was their desire to find a country at once fertile and winterless, where their flocks and herds could find pasture all the year, thus doing away with the long and tiresome period of haying and feeding necessary in the eastern and old western states and territories. Cheap land and good land there was in abundance in Kansas, Nebraska, Minnesota and Iowa; but there the labor of providing for animals of the farm was very great, and much of that labor was crowded together into a few summer months, while to keep cool in summers and warm in the icy winters was well nigh impossible to poor farmers.

Along the coast and throughout the greater part of western Oregon in general, snow seldom falls on the lowlands to a greater depth than a few inches, and never lies long. Grass is green all winter. The average temperature for the year in the Willamette valley is about 52°, the highest and lowest being about 100° and 20°, though occasionally a much lower temperature is reached.

The average rainfall is about fifty or fifty-five inches in the Willamette valley and along the coast seventy-five inches, or even more at some points—figures that bring many a dreary night and day to mind, however fine the effect on the great evergreen woods and the fields of the farmers. The rainy season begins in September or October and lasts until April or May. Then the whole country is solemnly soaked and poulticed with the gray, streaming clouds and fogs night and day with marvelous constancy. Towards the beginning and end of the season a good many bright days occur to break the pouring gloom, but whole months of rain, continuous, or nearly so, are not at all rare. Astronomers beneath these Oregon skies would have a dull time of it. Of all the year only about one-fourth of the days are clear, while three-fourths have more or less of fogs, clouds or rain. The fogs occur mostly in the Fall and Spring. They are grand, far-reaching affairs of two kinds, the black and white, some of the latter being very beautiful, and the infinite delicacy and tenderness of their touch as they linger to caress the tall evergreens is most exquisite. On farms and highways and in streets of towns where work has to be done, there is nothing pictur-esque or attractive in any obvious way about the gray, serious-faced rain storms. Mud abounds. The rain seems dismal and heedless and gets in everybody's way. Every face is turned from it, and it has but few friends who recognize its boundless beneficence. But back in the untrodden woods where no axe has been lifted, where a deep, rich carpet of brown and golden mosses· covers all the ground like a garment, pressing warmly about the feet of the trees and rising in thick folds softly and kindly over every fallen trunk, leaving no spot naked or uncared for, there the rain is welcomed, and every drop that falls finds a place and use as sweet and pure as itself. An excursion into the woods when the rain harvest is at its height is a noble pleasure, and may be safely enjoyed at small expense, though very few care to seek it. Shelter is easily found beneath the great trees in some hollow out of the wind, and one need carry but little provision, none at all of a kind that a wetting would spoil. The colors of the woods are then at their best, and the mighty hosts of the forest, every needle tingling in the blast, wave and sing in glorious harmony.

"'Twere worth ten years of peaceful life, one glance at this array."

The snow that falls in the lowland woods is usually soft, and makes a fine show coming through the trees in large, feathery tufts, loading the branches of the firs and spruces and cedars and weighing them down against the trunks until they look slender and sharp as arrows, while a strange, muffled silence prevails, giving a peculiar solemnity to everything. But these lowland snow-storms and their effects quickly vanish; every crystal melts in a day or two, the bent branches rise again, and the rain resumes its sway. While these gracious rains are searching the roots of the lowlands, corresponding snows are busy along the heights of the Cascade mountains. Month after month day and night the heavens shed their icy bloom in stormy, measureless abundance, filling the grand upper fountains of the rivers to last through the summer. Awful then is the silence that presses down over the mountain forests. All the smaller streams vanish from sight, hushed and obliterated. Young groves of spruce and pine are bowed down as by a gentle hand and put to rest, not again to see the light or move leaf or limb until the grand awakening of the spring-time, while the larger animals and most of the birds seek food and shelter in the foothills on the borders of the valleys and plains. The lofty volcanic peaks are yet more heavily snow-laden. To their upper zones no summer comes. They are white always. From the steep slopes of the summit the new-fallen snow while yet dry and loose descends in magnificent avalanches to feed the glaciers, making meanwhile the most glorious manifestations of power. Happy is the man who may get near them to see and hear. In some sheltered camp-nest on the edge of the timber-line one may lie snug and warm, but after the long shuffle on snow-shoes we may have to wait more than a month ere the heavens open and the grand show is unveiled. In the meantime, bread may be scarce, unless with careful forecast a sufficient supply has been provided and securely placed during the summer. Nevertheless, to be thus deeply snowbound high in the sky is not without generous compensation for all the cost. And when we at length go down the long white slopes to the levels

PORTLAND—MT. HOOD IN DISTANCE.

of civilization the pains vanish like snow in sunshine, while the noble and exalting pleasures we have gained remain with us to enrich our lives forever.

The fate of the high-flying mountain snow-flowers is a fascinating study, though little may we see of their works and ways while their storms go on. The glinting, swirling swarms fairly thicken the blast and all the air as well as the rocks and trees are as one smothering mass of bloom, through the midst of which at close intervals come the low, intense thunder-tones of the avalanches as they speed on their way to fill the vast fountain hollows. Here they seem at last to have found rest. But this rest is only apparent. Gradually the loose crystals by the pressure of their own weight are welded together into clear ice, and as glaciers march steadily, silently on, with invisible motion, in broad, deep currents, grinding their way with irresistible energy to the warmer lowlands where they vanish in glad rejoicing streams. In the sober weather of Oregon lightning makes but little show. Those magnificent thunder storms that so frequently adorn and glorify the sky of the Mississippi valley are wanting here. Dull thunder and lightning may occasionally be seen and heard, but the imposing grandeur of great storms marching over the landscape with stream-ing banners and a network of fire is almost wholly unknown.

Crossing the Cascade range we pass from a green to a gray country, from a wilderness of trees to a wilderness of open plains, level or rolling or rising here and there into hills and short mountain spurs. Though well supplied with rivers in most of its main sections it is generally dry. The annual rainfall is only from about five to fifteen inches, and the thin winter garment of snow seldom lasts more than a month or two, though the temperature in many places falls from five to twenty-five degrees below zero, but only for a short time. That the snow is light over eastern Oregon, and the average temperature not intolerably severe, is shown by the fact that large droves of sheep, cattle and horses live there through the winter without other food or shelter than they find for themselves on the open plains or down in the sunken valleys and gorges along the streams.

When we read of the mountain ranges of Oregon and Washington with detailed descriptions of their old volcanoes towering snow-laden and glacier-laden above the clouds, one may be led to imagine that the country is far icier and whiter and more mountainous than it is. Only in winter are the Coast and Cascade Mountains covered with snow. Then as seen from the main interior valleys they appear as

FORDING SNAKE RIVER.

SNAKE RIVER, BELOW SHOSHONE FALLS.

FERRY AT SHOSHONE FALLS, IDAHO.

comparatively low, bossy walls stretching along the horizon and making a magnificent display of their white wealth. The Coast Range in Oregon does not perhaps average more than three thousand feet in height. Its snow does not last long, most of its soil is fertile all the way to the summits and the greater part of the range may at some time be brought under cultivation. The immense deposits on the great central uplift of the Cascade Range are mostly melted off before the middle of summer by the comparatively warm winds and rains from the coast, leaving only a few white spots on the highest ridges where the depth from drifting has been greatest, or where the rate of waste has been diminished by specially favorable conditions as to exposure. Only the great volcanic cones are truly snowclad all the year, and these are not numerous and make but a small portion of the general landscape.

Approaching Oregon from the coast in summer no hint of snowy mountains can be seen, and it is only after we have sailed into the country by the Columbia or climbed some one of the commanding summits that the great white peaks send us greeting and make telling advertisements of themselves and of the country over which they rule. So, also, in coming to Oregon from the east the country by no means impresses one as being surpassingly mountainous, the abode of peaks and

CASTLE ROCK ON THE COLUMBIA RIVER. FROM PAINTING BY JULIAN RIX.

"Between the Dalles and Cascades the river is like a lake, a mile or two wide, lying in a valley or canyon about three thousand feet deep. The walls of the canyon lean well back in most places, and leave here and there small strips or bays of level ground along the water's edge. But towards the Cascades, and for some distance below them, the immediate banks are guarded by walls of columnar basalt, which are worn in many places into a great variety of bold and picturesque forms, such as the Castle Rock, while back of these rise the sublime mountain walls, forest-crowned and fringed more or less from top to base with pine, spruce and shaggy underbrush, especially in the narrow gorges and ravines, where innumerable small streams come dancing and drifting down, misty and white, to join the mighty river."

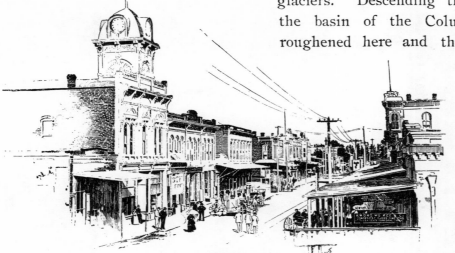

VIEW OF FIRST STREET, ALBANY, OREGON.

glaciers. Descending the spurs of the Rocky Mountains into the basin of the Columbia we see hot, hundred-mile plains, roughened here and there by hills and ridges that look hazy and blue in the distance, until we have pushed well to the westward. Then one white point after another comes into sight to refresh the eye and the imagination; but they are yet a long way off, and have much to say only to those who know them or others of their kind —how grand they are though insignificant-looking on the edge of the vast landscape, what noble woods they nourish and emerald meadows and gardens, what springs and streams and waterfalls sing about them, and to what a multitude of happy creatures they give homes and food. The principal mountains of the range are Mounts Pitt, Scott, Thielson, Diamond Peak, The Three Sisters, Mounts Jefferson, Hood, St. Helens, Adams, Rainier, Aiks and Baker. Of these the seven first named belong to Oregon, the others to Washington. They rise singly at irregular distances from one another along the main axis of the range or near it, with an elevation of from about 8,000 to 14,400 feet above the level of the sea. From few points in the valleys may more than three or four of them be seen, and of the more distant ones of these only the tops appear. Therefore, speaking generally, each of the lowland landscapes of the state contains only one grand snowy mountain.

The heights back of Portland command one of the best general views of the forests and also of the most famous of the great mountains both of Oregon and Washington. Mount Hood is in full view, with the summits of Mounts Jefferson, St. Helens, Adams and Rainier in the distance. The city of Portland is at our feet, covering a large area along both banks of the Willamette, and with its fine streets, schools, churches, mills, shipping, parks and gardens, makes a telling picture of busy, aspiring civilization in the midst of the green wilderness in which it is planted. The river is displayed to fine advantage in the foreground of our main view, sweeping in beautiful curves around rich leafy islands, its banks fringed with willows. A few miles beyond the Willamette flows the renowned Columbia, and the confluence of these two great rivers is at a point only about ten miles below the city. Beyond the Columbia extends the immense breadth of the forest, one dim black monotonous field, with only the sky, which one is glad to see is not forested, and the tops of the majestic old volcanoes to give diversity to the view. That sharp, white, broad-based pyramid on the south side of the Columbia, a few degrees to the south of east from where you stand, is the famous Mount Hood. The distance to it in a straight line is about fifty miles. Its upper slopes form the only bare ground, bare as to forests, in the landscape in that direction. It is the pride of Oregonians, and when it is visible is always pointed out to strangers as the glory of the country, the mountain of mountains. It is one of the grand series of extinct volcanoes extending from Lassen's Butte to Mount Baker, a distance of about six hundred miles, which once flamed like gigantic watch fires along the coast. Some of them have been active in recent times, but no considerable addition to the bulk of Mount Hood has been made for several centuries, as is shown by the amount of glacial denudation it has suffered. Its summit has been ground

OREGON CITY BRIDGE, AT WILLAMETTE FALLS.

to a point, which gives it a rather thin, pinched appearance. It has a wide-flowing base, however, and is fairly well proportioned. Though it is 11,000 feet high, it is too far off to make much show under ordinary conditions in so extensive a landscape. Through a great part of the summer it is invisible on account of smoke poured into the sky from burning woods, logging camps, mills, etc., and in winter for weeks at a time, or even months, it is in the clouds. Only in spring and early summer and in what there may chance to be of bright weather in winter is it or any of

its companions at all clear or telling. From the Cascades on the Columbia it may be seen at a distance of twenty miles or thereabouts, or from other points up and down the river, and with the magnificent foreground it is very impressive. It gives the supreme touch of grandeur to all the main Columbia views, rising at every turn, solitary, majestic, awe-inspiring, the ruling spirit of the landscape. But like mountains everywhere it varies greatly in im-

WILLAMETTE RIVER, BELOW PORTLAND.

A RIVER FISH-WHEEL.

pressiveness and apparent height at different times and seasons, not alone from differences as to the dimness or transparency of the air. Clear, or arrayed in clouds, it changes both in size and general expression. Now it looms up to an immense height and seems to draw near in tremendous grandeur and beauty, holding the eyes of every beholder in devout and awful interest. Next year or next day, or even in the same day, you return to the same point of view perhaps to find that the glory has departed, as if the mountain had died and the poor dull shrunken mass of rocks and ice had lost all power to charm.

Never shall I forget my first glorious view of Mount Hood one calm evening in July, though I had seen it many times before this. I was then sauntering with a friend across the new Willamette bridge between Portland and East Portland for the sake of the river views, which are here very fine in the tranquil summer weather. The scene on the water was a lively one. Boats of every description were gliding, glinting, drifting about at work or play, and we leaned over the rail from time to time contemplating the gay throng. Several lines of ferry-boats were making regular trips at intervals of a few minutes, and river steamers were coming and going from the wharves laden with all sorts of merchandise, raising long diverging swells that made all the light pleasure crafts bow and nod in hearty salutation as they passed. The crowd was being constantly increased by new arrivals from both shores, sailboats, rowboats, racing shells, rafts, were loaded with gayly dressed people, and here and there some adventurous man or boy might be seen as a merry

sailor on a single plank or spar, apparently as deep in enjoyment as were any on the water.   It
seemed as if all the town were coming to the river, renouncing the cares and toils of the day, determined
to take the evening breeze into their pulses, and be cool and tranquil ere going to bed.   Absorbed
in the happy scene, given up to dreamy, random observation of what lay immediately before me, I
was not conscious of anything occurring on the outer rim of the landscape.   Forest, mountain
and sky were forgotten; when my companion suddenly directed my attention to the eastward, shouting, "O, look! look!" in so loud and excited a tone of voice that passers-by, saunterers like ourselves, were startled and looked over the bridge as if expecting to see some boat upset.   Looking
across the forest over which the mellow light of the sunset was streaming, I soon discovered the
source of my friend's excitement.   There stood Mount Hood in all the glory of the Alpen glow,
looming immensely high, beaming with intelligence, and so impressive that one was overawed as if
suddenly brought before some superior being newly arrived from the sky.   The atmosphere was

WILLAMETTE FALLS.

somewhat hazy, but the mountain seemed neither near nor far.   Its glaciers flashed in the divine
light, the rugged, storm-worn ridges between them and the snowfields of the summit, these perhaps
might have been traced as far as they were in sight, and the blending zones of color about the
base.   But so profound was the general impression, partial analysis did not come into play.   The
whole mountain appeared as one glorious manifestation of divine power, enthusiastic and benevolent,
glowing like a countenance with ineffable repose and beauty before which we could only gaze in
devout and lowly admiration.

The far-famed Oregon forests cover all the western section of the state, the mountains as well
as the lowlands, with the exception of a few gravelly spots and open spaces in the central portions of the great cultivated valleys.   Beginning on the coast, where their outer ranks are
drenched and buffeted by wind-driven scud from the sea, they press on in close majestic ranks
over the coast mountains, across the broad central valleys, and over the Cascade Range, broken
and halted only by the few great peaks that rise like islands above the sea of evergreens.   In
descending the eastern slopes of the Cascades the rich, abounding, triumphant exuberance of the trees
is quickly subdued; they become smaller, grow wide apart, leaving dry spaces without moss-covering
or underbrush, and before the foot of the range is reached, fail altogether, stayed by the drouth

MULTNOMAH FALLS. FROM PAINTING BY JULIAN RIX.

"Many of these falls on both sides of the canyon of the Columbia are far larger and more interesting
in every way than would be guessed from the slight glimpses one gets of them while sailing past on the river,
or from the car-windows. The Multomah Falls are particularly interesting, and occupy fern-lined gorges of
wildest beauty in the basalt. They are said to be about eight hundred feet in height, and, at times of high
water when the mountain snows are melting, are well worthy of a place beside the famous falls of the
Yosemite Valley.

LUXURIANT FRUITS OF ROGUE RIVER VALLEY.

of the interior almost as suddenly as on the western margin they are stayed by the sea. Here and there at wide intervals on the eastern plains patches of a small pine (*P. contorta*) are found, and a scattering growth of juniper, used by the settlers mostly for fence posts and firewood. Along the stream-bottoms there is usually more or less of cottonwood and willow, which, though yielding inferior timber, is yet highly prized in this bare region. On the Blue Mountains there is pine, spruce, fir and larch in abundance for every use, but beyond this range there is nothing that may be called a forest in the Columbia River basin, until we reach the spurs of the Rocky Mountains, and these Rocky Mountain forests are made up of trees which, compared with the giants of the Pacific Slope, are mere saplings.

Like the forests of Washington, already described in this work, those of Oregon are in great part made up of the Douglas spruce or Oregon pine (*Abies Douglasii*). A large number of mills are at work upon this species, especially along the Columbia, but these as yet have made but little impression upon its dense masses, the mills here being small as compared with those of the Puget Sound region. The white cedar or Port Orford cedar (*Cupressus Lawsoniana-Chamæcyparis Lawsoniana*) is one of the most beautiful of the evergreens, and produces excellent lumber, considerable quantities of which are shipped to the San Francisco market. It is found mostly about Coos Bay, along the Coquille River, and the northern slopes of the Siskiyou Mountains, and extends down the coast into California. The silver firs, spruces, and the colossal arbor vitæ or white cedar (*Thuja gigantea*), described in the chapter on Washington, are also found here in great beauty and perfection, the largest of these (*Picea grandis*, Loud.; *Abies grandis*, Lindl.) being confined mostly to the coast region, where it attains a height of three hundred feet, and a diameter of ten or twelve feet. Five or six species of pine are found in the state, the most important of which, both as to lumber and the part they play in the general wealth and beauty of the forests, are the yellow and sugar pines, (*Pinus ponderosa* and *P. Lambertiana*). The yellow pine is most abundant on the eastern slopes of the Cascades, forming there the main bulk of the forest in many places It is also common along the borders of the open spaces in Willamette Valley. In the southern portion of the state the sugar pine, which is the king of all the pines and the glory of the Sierra forests, occurs in considerable abundance in the basins of the Umpqua and Rogue Rivers, and it was in the Umpqua hills that this noble tree was first discovered by the enthusiastic botanical explorer, David Douglas, in the year 1826. This is the Douglas for whom the noble Douglas spruce is named, and many a fair blooming plant also, which will serve to keep his memory fresh and sweet as long as beautiful trees and flowers are loved. The Indians of the lower Columbia River watched him with lively curiosity as he wandered about in the woods day after day, gazing intently on the ground or at the great trees, collecting specimens of everything he saw, but, unlike all the eager fur-gathering strangers they had hitherto seen, caring nothing about trade. And when at length they came to know him better, and saw that from year to year the growing things of the woods and prairies, meadows and plains were his only object of pursuit, they called him "The Man of Grass," a title of which he was proud. He was a Scotchman and first came to this coast in the spring of 1825 under the auspices of the London Horticultural Society, landing at the mouth of the Columbia after a long, dismal voyage of eight months and fourteen days. During this first season he chose Fort Vancouver, belonging to the Hudson Bay Company, as his headquarters, and from there made excursions into the glorious wilderness in every direction, discovering many new species among the trees as well as among the rich underbrush and smaller herbaceous vegetation. It was while making a trip to Mount Hood this year that he discovered the two largest and most beautiful firs in the world (*Picia amabilis* and *P. nobilis*—now called *Abies*) and from the seeds which he then collected and sent home tall trees are now growing in Scotland. In one of his trips this summer in the lower Willamette Valley he saw in an Indian's tobacco pouch some of the seeds and scales of a new species of pine, which he learned were gathered from a large tree that grew far to the southward. Most of the following season was spent on the upper waters of the Columbia, and it was not until September that he returned to Fort Vancouver, about the time of the setting in of the winter rains. Nevertheless, bearing in mind the great pine he had heard of, and the seeds of which he had seen, he made haste to set out on an excursion to the head waters of the Willamette in search of it; and how he fared on this excursion and what dangers and hardships he endured is best told in his own journal, part of which we quote as follows:

"October 26th, 1826. Weather dull. Cold and cloudy. When my friends in England are made acquainted with my travels I fear they will think that I have told them nothing but my miseries.

* * * I quitted my camp early in the morning to survey the neighboring country, leaving my guide to take charge of the horses until my return in the evening. About an hour's walk from the camp I met an Indian, who on perceiving me instantly strung his bow, placed on his

ROOSTER ROCK—INDIAN BLOCK HOUSE, COLUMBIA RIVER.

left arm a sleeve of raccoon skin and stood on the defensive. Being quite sure that conduct was prompted by fear and not by hostile intentions, the poor fellow having probably never seen such a being as myself before, I laid my gun at my feet on the ground and waved my hand for him to come to me, which he did slowly and with great caution. I then made him place his bow and quiver of arrows beside my gun, and striking a light gave him a smoke out of my own pipe and a present of a few beads. With my pencil I made a rough sketch of the cone and pine tree which I wanted to obtain and drew his attention to it, when he instantly pointed with his hand to the hills fifteen or twenty miles distant towards the south; and when I expressed my intention of going thither, cheerfully set about accompanying me. At midday I reached my long-wished-for pines and lost no time in examining them and endeavoring to collect specimens and seeds. New and strange things seldom fail to make strong impressions and are therefore frequently over-rated; so that, lest I should never see my friends in England to inform them verbally of this most beautiful and immensely grand tree, I shall here state the dimensions of the largest I could find among several that had been blown down by the wind. At three feet from the ground its circumference is fifty-seven feet nine inches; at one hundred and thirty-four feet, seventeen feet five inches; the extreme length two hundred and forty-five feet. * * * As it was impossible either to climb the tree or hew it down, I endeavored to knock off the cones by firing at them with ball, when the report of my gun brought eight Indians, all of them painted with red earth, armed with bows, arrows, bone-tipped spears and flint knives. They appeared anything but friendly. I explained to them what I wanted and they seemed satisfied and sat down to smoke; but presently I saw one of them string his bow and another sharpen his flint knife with a pair of wooden pincers and suspend it on the wrist of his right hand. Further testimony of their intentions was unnecessary. To save myself by flight was impossible, so without hesitation I stepped back about five paces, cocked my gun, drew one of the pistols out of my belt, and holding it in my left hand and the gun in my right, showed myself determined to fight for my life. As much as possible I endeavored to preserve my coolness, and thus we stood looking at one another without making any movement or uttering a word for perhaps ten minutes, when one at last, who seemed to be the leader, gave a sign that they wished for some tobacco; this I signified that they should have if they fetched a quantity of cones. They went off immediately in search of them, and no sooner were they all out of sight than I picked up my three cones and some twigs of the trees and made the quickest possible retreat, hurrying back to my camp, which I reached before dusk. The Indian who last undertook to be my guide to the trees I sent off before gaining my encampment, lest he should betray me. How irksome is the darkness of night to one under such circumstances. I cannot speak a word to my guide, nor have I a book to divert my thoughts, which are continually occupied with the dread lest the hostile Indians should trace me hither and make an attack. I now write lying on the grass with my gun cocked beside me, and penning these lines by the light of my *Columbian candle*, namely, an ignited piece of rosin-wood."

Douglas named this magnificent species *Pinus Lambertiana*, in honor of his friend Dr. Lambert, of London. This is the noblest pine thus far discovered in the forests of the world, surpassing all others not only in size but in beauty and majesty. Oregon may well be proud that its discovery was made within her borders, and that, though far more abundant in California, she has the largest known specimens. In the Sierras the finest sugar pine forests lie at an elevation of about five thousand feet. In Oregon they occupy much lower ground, some of the trees being found but little above tidewater. No lover of trees will ever forget his first meeting with the sugar pine. In most coniferous trees there is a sameness of form and expression which at length becomes wearisome to most people who travel far in the woods. But the sugar pines are as free from conventional forms as any of the oaks. No two are so much alike as to hide their individuality from any observer. Every tree is appreciated as a study in itself and proclaims in no uncertain terms the surpassing grandeur of the species. The branches, mostly near the summit, are sometimes nearly forty feet long, feathered richly all around with short, leafy branchlets, and tasselled with cones a foot and a half long. And when these superb arms are outspread, radiating in every direction, an immense crown-like mass is formed which, poised on the noble shaft and filled with sunshine, is one of the grandest forest objects conceivable. But though so wild and unconventional when full grown, the sugar pine is a remarkably regular tree in youth, a strict follower of coniferous fashions, slim, erect, tapering, symmetrical, every branch in place. At the age of fifty or sixty years this shy, fashionable form begins to give way. Special branches are thrust out away from the general outlines of the tree and bent down with cones. Henceforth it becomes more and more original and independent in style, pushes boldly aloft into the winds and sunshine, growing ever more stately and beautiful, a joy and inspiration to every beholder. Unfortunately, the sugar pine makes excellent lumber. It is too good to live, and is already passing rapidly away before the woodman's axe. Surely out of all of Oregon's abounding forest wealth a few specimens might be spared to the world, not as dead lumber, but as living trees. A park of moderate extent might be set apart

CASCADES OF THE COLUMBIA. FROM PAINTING BY JULIAN RIX.

"Thirty-five or forty miles below the Dalles are the Cascades of the Columbia, where the river, in passing through the mountains, makes another magnificent display of foaming, surging rapids, which form the first obstruction to navigation from the ocean, a hundred and twenty miles distant. This obstruction is to be overcome by locks which are now being made."

and protected for public use forever, containing at least a few hundreds of each of these noble pines, spruces and firs. Happy will be the men who, having the power and the love and benevolent forecast to do this, will do it. They will not be forgotten. The trees and their lovers will sing their praises, and generations yet unborn will rise up and call them blessed.

Dotting the prairies and fringing the edges of the great evergreen forests we find a considerable number of hardwood trees, such as the oak, maple, ash, alder, laurel, madrone, flowering dogwood, wild cherry and wild apple. The white oak (*Quercus Garryana*) is the most important of the Oregon oaks as a timber tree, but not nearly so beautiful as Kellogg's oak (*Q. Kelloggii*). The former is found mostly along the Columbia River, particularly about The Dalles, and a considerable quantity of useful lumber is made from it and sold sometimes for eastern white oak to wagon makers. Kellogg's oak is a magnificent tree and does much for the picturesque beauty of the

A ROGUE RIVER HOP RANCH.

Umpqua and Rogue River valleys where it abounds. It is also found in all the Yosemite valleys of the Sierra, and its acorns form an important part of the food of the Digger Indians. In the Siskiyou Mountains there is a live oak (*Q. Chrysolipis*), wide-spreading and very picturesque in form, but not very common. It extends southward along the western flank of the Sierra and is there more abundant and much larger than in Oregon, oftentimes five to eight feet in diameter.

The maples are the same as those in Washington already described, but I have not seen any maple groves here equal in extent or in the size of the trees to those on the Snoqualmie River.

The Oregon ash is not rare along the stream-banks of western Oregon, and it grows to a good size and furnishes lumber that is for some purposes equal to the white ash of the eastern states.

Nuttal's flowering dogwood makes a brave display with its wealth of showy involucres in the Spring along cool streams. Specimens of the flowers may be found measuring eight inches in diameter.

The wild cherry (*Prunus emarginata*, var. *Mollis*) is a small, handsome tree seldom more than a foot in diameter at the base. It makes valuable lumber and its black, astringent fruit furnishes a rich resource as food for the birds. A smaller form is common in the Sierra, the fruit of which is eagerly eaten by the Indians and hunters in time of need.

The wild apple (*Pinus rivularis*) is a fine, hearty, handsome little tree that grows well in rich, cool soil along streams and on the edges of beaver meadows from California through Oregon and Washington to southeastern Alaska. In Oregon it forms dense, tangled thickets, some of them almost impenetrable. The largest trunks are nearly a foot in diameter. When in bloom it makes a fine show with its abundant clusters of flowers, which are white and fragrant. The fruit is very small and savagely acid. It is wholesome, however, and is eaten by birds, bears, Indians, and many other adventurers, great and small.

COLUMBIA RIVER, OREGON.—DURING THE SUMMER FIRES.

Passing from beneath the shadows of the woods where the trees grow close and high, we step into charming wild gardens full of lilies, orchids, heathwarts, roses, etc., with colors so gay and forming such sumptuous masses of bloom they make the gardens of civilization, however lovingly cared for, seem pathetic and silly. Around the great fire-mountains, above the forests and beneath the snow, there is a flowery zone of marvelous beauty planted with anemones, erythroniums, daisies, bryanthus, kalmia, vaccinium, cassiope, saxifrages, etc., forming one continuous garden fifty or sixty miles in circumference, and so deep and luxuriant and closely woven it seems as if Nature, glad to find an opening, were economizing space and trying to see how many of her bright-eyed darlings she can get together in one mountain wreath. Along the slopes of the Cascades, where the woods are less dense, especially about the headwaters of the Willamette, there are miles of rhododendron, making glorious outbursts of purple bloom, and down on the prairies in rich, damp hollows the blue-flowered camassia grows in such profusion that at a little distance its dense masses appear as beautiful blue lakes imbedded in the green, flowery plains; while all about the streams and the lakes and the beaver meadows and the margins of the deep woods there is a magnificent tangle of gaultheria and huckleberry bushes with their myriads of pink bells, reinforced with hazel, cornel, rubus of many species, wild plum, cherry, and crab apple; besides thousands of charming bloomers to be found in all sorts of places throughout the wilderness, whose mere names are refreshing, such as linnæa, menziesia, pyrola, chimaphila, brodiæa, smilacina, fruitillaria, calochartus, trillium, clintonia, veratrum, cypripedidum, goodyera, spiranthes, habenaria, and the rare and lovely " Hider of the North" *Calypso borealis*, to find which is alone a sufficient object for a journey into the wilderness; and besides these there is a charming underworld of ferns and mosses flourishing gloriously beneath all the woods. Everybody loves wild woods and flowers more or less. Seeds of all these Oregon evergreens and of many of the flowering shrubs and plants have been sent to almost every country under the sun, and are now growing in carefully tended parks and gardens. And now that the ways of approach are open one would expect to find these woods and gardens full of admiring visitors reveling in their beauty like bees in a clover field. Yet few care to visit them. A portion of the bark of one of the California trees, the mere dead skin, excited the wondering attention of thous-

THE NEEDLES.

COLUMBIA RIVER ISLANDS, NEAR UPPER CASCADES.

ands when it was set up in the Crystal Palace in London, as did also a few peeled spars, the shafts of mere saplings from Oregon or Washington. Could one of these great silver firs or sugar-pines three hundred feet high have been transplanted entire to that exhibition, how enthusiastic would have been the praises ascribed to it! Nevertheless, the countless hosts waving at home beneath their own sky, beside their own noble rivers and mountains, and standing on a flower-enameled carpet of mosses thousands of square miles in extent, attract but little attention. Most travelers content themselves with what they may chance to see from car-windows, hotel verandas, or from the deck of a steamer on the Lower Columbia; clinging to the battered highways like drowning sailors to a life-raft. When an excursion into the woods is proposed, all sorts of exaggerated or imaginary dangers are conjured up, filling the kindly, soothing wilderness with colds, fevers, Indians, bears, snakes, bugs, impassible rivers, and jungles of brush, to which is always added quick and sure starvation. As to starvation, the woods are full of food and a supply of bread may easily be carried for habit's sake, and replenished now and then at outlying farms and camps. The Indians are seldom found in the woods, being confined mainly to the banks of the rivers where the greater part of their food is obtained. Moreover, the most of them have been either buried since the settlement of the country or civilized into comparative innocence, industry, or harmless laziness. There are bears in the woods, but not in such numbers nor of such unspeakable ferocity as town-dwellers imagine, nor do bears spend their lives in going about the country like the devil seeking whom they may devour. Oregon bears, like most

THE DALLES OF THE COLUMBIA.   FROM PAINTING BY JULIAN RIX.

"At The Dalles the vast river is jammed together into a long narrow slot of unknown depth cut sheer down in the basalt. This slot or trough is about a mile and a half long and about sixty yards wide at the narrowest place. At ordinary times the river seems to be set on edge and runs swiftly but without much noisy surging with a descent of about twenty feet to the mile. But when the snow is melting on the mountains the river rises here sixty feet, or even more during extraordinary freshets, and spreads out over a great breadth of massive rocks through which have been cut several other gorges running parallel with the one usually occupied."

others, have no liking for man either as meat or as society; and while some may be curious at times to see what manner of creature he is, most of them have learned to shun people as deadly enemies. They have been poisoned, trapped, and shot at until they have become shy, and it is no longer easy to make their acquaintance. Indeed, since the settlement of the country, notwithstanding far the greater portion is yet wild, it is difficult to find any of the larger animals that once were numerous and comparatively familiar, such as the bear, wolf, panther, lynx, deer, elk, and antelope. As early as 1843, while the settlers numbered only a few thousands, and before any sort of government had been organized, they came together and held what they called "a wolf meeting," at which a committee was appointed to devise means for the destruction of wild animals destructive to tame ones, which committee in due time begged to report as follows: "It being admitted by all that bears, wolves, panthers, etc., are destructive to the useful animals owned by the settlers of this colony, your committee would submit the following resolutions as the sense of this meeting, by which the community may be governed in carrying on a defensive and destructive war on all such animals:

"Resolved 1st.—That we deem it expedient for the community to take immediate measures for the destruction of all wolves, panthers and bears, and such other animals as are known to be destructive to cattle, horses, sheep and hogs.

"2d.—That a bounty of fifty cents be paid for the destruction of a small wolf, $3.00 for a large wolf, $1.50 for a lynx, $2.00 for a bear and $5.00 for a panther."

This center of destruction was in the Willamette Valley. But for many years prior to the beginning of the operations of the "Wolf Organization" the Hudson Bay Company had established forts and trading stations over all the country wherever fur-gathering Indians could be found, and vast numbers of these animals were killed. Their destruction has since gone on at an accelerated rate from year to year as the settlements have been extended, so that in some cases it is difficult to obtain specimens enough for the use of naturalists. But even before any of these settlements were made, and before the coming of the Hudson Bay Company, there was very little danger to be met in passing through this wilderness as far as animals were concerned, and but little of any kind as compared with the dangers encountered in crowded houses and streets. When Lewis and Clarke made their famous trip across the continent in 1804–5, when all the Rocky Mountain region was wild, as well as the Pacific Slope, they did not lose a single man by wild animals, nor, though frequently attacked, especially by the grizzlies of the Rocky Mountains, were any of them wounded seriously. Captain Clarke was bitten on the hand by a wolf as he lay asleep; that was one bite among more than a hundred men while traveling through eight to nine thousand miles of savage wilderness. They could have hardly been so fortunate had they stayed at home. They wintered on the edge of the Clatsop plains, on the south side of the Columbia River near its mouth. In the woods on that side they found game abundant, especially elk, and with the aid of the friendly Indians who furnished salmon and "wapatoo" (the tubers of *Sagittaria variabilis*), they were in no danger of starving. But on the return trip in the Spring they reached

THE GRIZZLY AND HIS PREY.

the base of the Rocky Mountains when the range was yet too heavily snow-laden to be crossed with horses. Therefore, they had to wait some weeks. This was at the head of one of the northern branches of Snake River, and their scanty stock of provisions being nearly exhausted, the whole party was compelled to live mostly on bears and dogs; deer, antelope, and elk, usually abundant, were now scarce because the region had been closely hunted over by the Indians before their arrival. Lewis and Clarke had killed a number of bears and saved the skins of the more interesting specimens, and the variations they found in size, color of the hair, etc., made great difficulty in classification. Wishing to get the opinion of the Chopunish Indians, near one of whose villages they were encamped, concerning the various species, the explorers unpacked their bundles and spread out for examination all the skins they had taken. The Indian hunters immediately classed the white, the deep and the pale grizzly red, the grizzly dark-brown—in short, all those with the extremities of the hair of a white or frosty color, without regard to the color of the ground or foil, under the name of *hoh-host*. The Indians assured them that these were all of the same species as the white bear, that they associated together,

TWIN FALLS—SHOSHONE.

had longer nails than the others, and never climbed trees. On the other hand the black skins, those that were black with white hairs intermixed or with a white breast, the uniform bay, the brown, and the light reddish brown, were classed under the name, *yack-ah*, and were said to resemble each other in being smaller and having shorter nails, in climbing trees, and being so little vicious that they could be pursued with safety.

Lewis and Clarke came to the conclusion that all those with white tipped hair found by them in the basin of the Columbia belonged to the same species as the grizzlies of the upper Missouri; and that the black and reddish brown, etc., of the Rocky Mountains belong to a second species equally distinct from the grizzly and the black bear of the Pacific Coast and the east, which never vary in color.

As much as possible should be made by the ordinary traveler of these descriptions, for he will be likely to see very little of any species for himself, not that bears no longer exist here, but because being shy, they keep out of the way. In order to see them and learn their habits one must go softly and alone, lingering long in the fringing woods on the banks of the salmon streams, and in the small openings in the midst of thickets where berries are most abundant.

As for rattlesnakes, the other grand dread of town-dwellers when they leave beaten roads, there are two, or perhaps three, species of them in Oregon. But they are nowhere to be found in great numbers. In western Oregon they are hardly known at all. In all my walks in the Oregon forest I have never met a single specimen, though a few have been seen at long intervals. When the country was first settled by the whites fifty years ago, the elk roamed through the wood and over the plains to the east of the Cascades in immense numbers, now they are rarely seen except by experienced hunters who know their haunts in the deepest and most inaccessible solitudes to which they have been driven. So majestic an animal forms a tempting mark for the sportsman's rifle. Countless thousands have been killed for mere amusement and they already seem to be nearing extinction as rapidly as the buffalo. The antelope also is vanishing from the Columbia plains before the farmers and cattle-men. Whether the moose still lingers in Oregon or Washington I am unable

CAPE HORN.

to say. On the highest mountains of the Cascade Range the wild goat roams in comparative security, few of his enemies caring to go so far in pursuit and hunt on ground so high and so dangerous. He is a brave, sturdy, shaggy mountaineer of an animal, enjoying the freedom and security of crumbling ridges and overhanging cliffs above the glaciers, oftentimes beyond the reach of the most daring hunter. They seem to be as much at home on the ice and snow-fields as on the crags, making their way in flocks from ridge to ridge on the great volcanic mountains by crossing the glaciers that lie between them, traveling in single file guided by an old experienced leader, like a party of climbers on the Alps. On these ice-journeys they pick their way through networks of crevasses and over bridges of snow with admirable skill, and the mountaineer may seldom do better in such places than to follow their trail, if he can. In the rich Alpine gardens and meadows they find abundance of food, venturing sometimes well down in the prairie openings on the edge of the timber-line, but holding themselves ever alert and watchful, ready to flee to their highland castles at the faintest alarm. When their summer pastures are buried beneath the winter snows, they make haste to the lower ridges, seeking the wind-beaten crags and slopes where the snow cannot lie at any great depth, feeding at times on the leaves and twigs of bushes when grass is beyond reach.

The wild sheep is another admirable Alpine rover, but comparatively rare in the Oregon mountains, choosing rather the drier ridges to the southward on the Cascades and to the eastward among the spurs of the Rocky Mountain chain.

SALMON FISHING ON THE COLUMBIA. FROM PAINTING BY A. HENCKE, AFTER SKETCH BY VICTOR PERARD.

"As the Willamette is one of the most foodful of valleys, so is the Columbia one of the most foodful of rivers. During the fisher's harvest time, salmon from the sea come up in countless millions, urging their way against falls, rapids and shallows, up into the very heart of the Rocky Mountains, supplying every body by the way with the most bountiful masses of delicious food, weighing from twenty to eighty pounds, plump and smooth like loaves of bread ready for the oven. The supply seemed inexhaustible, as well it might. Of late, however, the salmon crop has begun to fail, and millions of young fry are now sown like wheat in the river every year, from the hatching establishments belonging to the government."

Deer give beautiful animation to the forests, harmonizing finely in their color and movements with the grey and brown shafts of the trees and the swaying of the branches as they stand in groups at rest, or move gracefully and noiselessly over the mossy ground about the edges of beaver meadows and flowery glades, daintily culling the leaves and tips of the mints and aromatic bushes on which they feed. There are three species, the black-tailed, white-tailed, and mule-deer; the latter being restricted in its range to the open woods and plains to the eastward of the Cascades. They are nowhere very numerous now, killing for food, for hides, or for mere wanton sport having well nigh exterminated them in the more accessible regions, while elsewhere they are too often at the mercy of the wolves.

Gliding about in their shady forest homes, keeping well out of sight, there is a multitude of sleek, fur-clad animals living and enjoying their clean, beautiful lives—how beautiful and interesting they are is about as difficult for busy mortals to find out as if their homes were beyond sight in the sky. Hence the stories of every wild hunter and trapper are eagerly listened to as being possibly true, or partly so, however thickly clothed in successive folds of exaggeration and fancy. Unsatisfying as these accounts must be, a tourist's frightened rush and scramble through the woods yields far less than the hunter's wildest stories, while in writing we can do but little more than to give a few names, as they come to mind—beaver, squirrel, coon, fox, martin, fisher, otter, ermine, wood-cat—only this instead of full descriptions of the bright-eyed furry throng, their snug home nests, their fears and fights and loves, how they get their food, rear their young, escape their enemies and keep themselves warm and well and exquisitely clean through all the pitiless weather.

For many years before the settlement of the country the fur of the beaver brought a high price, and therefore it was pursued with weariless ardor. Not even in the quest for gold has a more ruthless, desperate energy been developed. It was in those early beaver-days that the striking class of adventurers called "free-trappers" made their appearance. Bold, enterprising men, eager to make money, and inclined at the same time to relish the license of a savage life, would set forth with a few traps and a gun and a hunting knife, content at first to venture only a short distance up the beaver streams nearest to the settlements, and where the Indians were not likely to molest them. There they would set their traps, while the buffalo, antelope, deer, etc., furnished a royal supply of food. In a few months their pack animals would be laden with thousands of dollars' worth of fur. Next season they would venture farther, and again farther, meanwhile growing rapidly wilder, getting acquainted with the Indian tribes, and usually marrying among them. Thenceforward no danger could stay them in their exciting pursuit. Wherever there were beaver they would go, however far or wild, the wilder the better provided their scalps could be saved. Oftentimes they were compelled to set their traps and visit them by night and lie hid during the day, when operating in the neighborhood of hostile Indians. Not then venturing to make a fire or shoot game, they lived on the raw flesh of the beaver, perhaps seasoned with wild cresses or berries. Then returning to the trading stations they would spend their hard earnings in a few weeks of dissipation and "good time," and go again to the bears and beavers until at length a bullet or arrow would end all. One after

STRANNAHAN'S FALLS, MOUNT HOOD.

another would be missed by some friend or trader at the autumn rendezvous, reported killed by the Indians, and—forgotten. Some men of this class have, from superior skill or fortune, escaped every danger, lived to a good old age, earned fame, and by their knowledge of the topography of the vast West then unexplored, have been able to render important service to the country. But most of them laid their bones in the wilderness after a few short, keen seasons. So great were the perils that beset them, the average length of the life of a "free-trapper" has been estimated at less than five years. From the Columbia waters beaver and beaver men have almost wholly passed away, and the men once so striking a part of the view have left scarcely the faintest sign of their existence. On the other hand, a thousand meadows on the mountains tell the story of the beavers, to remain fresh and green for many a century, monuments of their happy, industrious lives.

But there is a little airy, elfin animal in these woods and in all the evergreen woods of the Pacific Coast, that is more influential and interesting than even the beaver. This is the Douglas squirrel (*Sciurus Douglasii*.) Go where you may throughout all these noble forests you everywhere find this little squirrel the master-existence. Though only a few inches long, so intense is his fiery vigor and restlessness, he stirs every grove with wild life, and makes himself more important than the great bears that shuffle through the berry tangles beneath him. Every tree feels the sting of his sharp feet. Nature has made him master-

A FRONTIER CABIN.

INDIAN WIGWAM.

forester, and committed the greater part of the coniferous crops to his management. Probably over half of all the ripe cones of the spruces, firs, and pines are cut off and handled by this busy harvester. Most of them are stored away for food through the winter and spring, but a part is pushed into shallow pits and covered loosely, where some of the seeds are no doubt left to germinate and grow up. All the tree squirrels are more or less bird-like in voice and movements, but the Douglas is pre-eminently so, possessing every squirrelish attribute, fully developed and concentrated. He is the squirrel of squirrels, flashing from branch to branch of his favorite evergreens, crisp and glossy and sound as a sunbeam. He stirs the leaves like a rustling breeze, darting across openings in arrowy lines, launching in curves, glinting deftly from side to side in sudden zigzags and swirling in giddy loops and spirals around the trunks, now on his haunches, now on his head, yet ever graceful and performing all his feats of strength and skill without apparent effort. One never tires of this bright spark of life—the brave little voice crying in the wilderness. His varied piney gossip is as savory to the air as balsam to the palate. Some of his notes are almost flute-like in softness, while others prick and tingle like thistles. He is the mocking-bird of squirrels, barking like a dog, screaming like a hawk, whistling like a blackbird or linnet, while in bluff, audacious noisiness he is a jay. A small thing, but filling and animating all the woods.

Nor is there any lack of wings, notwithstanding few are to be seen on short, noisy rambles. The ouzel sweetens the shady glens and cañons where waterfalls abound, and every grove or forest, however silent it may seem when we chance to pay it a hasty visit, has its singers—thrushes, linnets, warblers,—while humming-birds glint and hover about the fringing masses of bloom around stream and meadow openings. But few of these will show themselves or sing their songs to those who are ever in haste and getting lost, going in gangs formidable in color and accoutrements, laughing, hallooing, breaking limbs off the trees as they pass, awkwardly struggling through briery thickets, entangled like blue bottles in spider webs, and stopping from time to time to fire off their guns and pistols for the sake of the echoes, thus frightening all the life about them for miles. It is this class of hunters and travelers that report that there are "no birds in the woods or game animals of any kind larger than mosquitoes."

Besides the singing birds mentioned above, the handsome Oregon grouse may be found in the thick woods, also the dusky grouse and Franklin's grouse, and in some places the beautiful mountain partridge or quail. The white-tailed ptarmigan lives on the lofty snow peaks above the

SPOKANE FALLS.

timber, and the prairie chicken and sage cock on the broad Columbia plains from the Cascade Range back to the foothills of the Rocky Mountains. The bald eagle is very common along the Columbia River or wherever fish, especially salmon, is plentiful, while swans, herons, cranes, pelicans, geese, ducks of many species, and water birds in general abound in the lake region, on the main streams and along the coast, stirring the waters and sky into fine, lively pictures, greatly to the delight of wandering lovers of wildness.

Turning from the woods and their inhabitants to the rivers, we find that while the former are rarely seen by travelers beyond the immediate borders of the settlements, the great river of Oregon draws crowds of visitors, and is never without enthusiastic admirers to sound its praises. Every summer since the completion of the first overland railroad, tourists have been coming to it in ever increasing numbers, showing that in general estimation the Columbia is one of the chief attractions of the Pacific Coast, and well it deserves the admiration so heartily bestowed upon it. The beauty and majesty of its waters, and the variety and grandeur of the scenery through which it flows, lead many to regard it as the most interesting of all the great rivers of the continent, notwithstanding the claims of the other members of the family to which it belongs and which nobody can measure—the Fraser, McKenzie, Saskatchawan, the Missouri, Yellowstone, Platte, and the

SPOKANE FALLS. FROM AN EARLY SKETCH BY WILLIAM KEITH.

"The famous Spokane Falls are in Washington, about thirty miles below the lake, where the river is outspread and divided and makes a grand descent from a level basaltic plateau, giving rise to one of the most beautiful as well as one of the greatest and most available of water powers in the State." A comparison of the above view with the one on page 488, which shows the city and falls at a later date, will serve to illustrate the wonderful growth in a few years' time.

Colorado, with their glacier and geyser fountains, their famous cañons, lakes, forests, and vast flowery prairies and plains. These great rivers and the Columbia are intimately related. All draw their upper waters from the same high fountains on the broad, rugged uplift of the Rocky Mountains, their branches interlacing like the branches of trees. They sing their first songs together on the heights, then collecting their tributaries they set out on their grand journey to the Atlantic, Pacific or Arctic Ocean.

HUNTER'S LODGE, PEND D'OREILLE LAKE.

The Columbia, viewed as one from the sea to the mountains, is like a rugged, broad-topped picturesque old oak about six hundred miles long and nearly a thousand miles wide measured across the spread of its upper branches, the main limbs gnarled and swollen with lakes and lake-like expansions, while innumerable smaller lakes shine like fruit among the smaller branches. The main trunk extends back through the Coast and Cascade Mountains in a general easterly direction for three hundred miles, when it divides abruptly into two grand branches which bend off to the northeastward and southeastward. The south branch, the longer of the two, called the Snake or Lewis River, extends into the Rocky Mountains as far as the Yellowstone National Park, where its head tributaries interlace with those of the Colorado, Missouri and Yellowstone. The north branch, still called the Columbia, extends through Washington far into British territory, its highest tributaries reaching back through long parallel spurs of the Rockies between and beyond the head waters of the Fraser, Athabasca, and Saskatchawan. Each of these main branches, dividing again and again, spread a network of channels over the vast complicated mass of the great range throughout a section nearly a thousand miles in length, searching every fountain however small or great, and gathering a glorious harvest of crystal water to be rolled through forest and plain in one majestic flood to the sea, reinforced on the way by tributaries that drain the Blue Mountains and more than two hundred miles of the Cascade and Coast Ranges. Though less than half as long as the Mississippi it is said to carry as much water. The amount of its discharge at different seasons, however, has never been exactly measured, but in time of flood its current is sufficiently massive and powerful to penetrate the sea to a distance of fifty or sixty miles from shore, its waters being easily recognized by the difference in color and by the drift of leaves, berries, pine cones, branches, and trunk of trees that they carry.

That so large a river as the Columbia, making a telling current so far from shore, should remain undiscovered while one exploring expedition after another sailed past seems remarkable, even after due allowance is made for the cloudy weather that prevails hereabouts and the broad fence of breakers drawn across the bar. During the last few centuries, when the maps of the world were in great part blank, the search for new worlds was a fashionable business, and when such large game was no longer to be found, islands lying unclaimed in the great oceans, inhabited by useful and profitable people to be converted or enslaved, became attractive objects; also new ways to India, seas, straits, El Dorados, fountains of youth, and rivers that flowed over golden sands. Those early explorers and adventurers were mostly brave, enterprising, and after their fashion, pious men. In their clumsy sailing vessels they dared to go where no chart or light-house

INTERIOR OF HUNTER'S LODGE.

showed the way, where the set of the currents, the location of sunken outlying rocks and shoals were all unknown, facing fate and weather, undaunted however dark the signs, heaving the lead and thrashing the men to their duty and trusting to Providence. When a new shore was found on which they could land, they said their prayers with superb audacity, fought the natives if they cared to fight, erected crosses, and took possession in the names of their sovereigns, establishing claims, such as they were, to everything in sight and beyond, to be quarreled for and battled for, and passed from hand to hand in treaties and settlements made during the intermissions of war.

The branch of the bia all the way to its about ten miles in length range of the Rocky Moun-eighty miles beyond the Upper and Lower Colum-the young river holds a dred and seventy miles in plain called "Boat En-many beautiful affluents Selkirk and main range, Beaver-foot, Blackberry, Gold Rivers. At Boat two large tributaries, the Canoe River from the northwest, a stream about a hundred and twenty miles long; and the Whirlpool River from the north, about a hundred and forty miles in length.

The Whirlpool River takes its rise near the summit of the main axis of the range on the fifty-fourth parallel, and is the northmost of all the Columbia waters. About thirty miles above its confluence with the Columbia it flows through a lake called the

river that bears the name of Colum-head, takes its rise in two lakes that lie between the Selkirk and main tains in British Columbia, about boundary line. They are called the bia Lakes. Issuing from these nearly straight course for a hun-a northwesterly direction to a campment," receiving by the way from the among which are the Spill-e-Mee-Chene and Encampment it receives

DUSKY GROUSE—DOUGLAS SQUIRREL—RUFFLED GROUSE.

Punch-bowl, and thence it passes between Mounts Hooker and Brown, said to be fifteen thousand and sixteen thousand feet high, making magnificent scenery; though the height of the mountains thereabouts has been considerably overestimated. From Boat Encampment the river, now a large clear stream, said to be nearly a third of a mile in width, doubles back on its original course and flows southward as far as its confluence with the Spokane in Washington, a distance of nearly three hundred miles in a direct line, most of the way through a wild, rocky, picturesque mass of mountains, charmingly forested with pine and spruce, though the trees seem strangely small, like second growth saplings, to one familiar with the western forests of Washington, Oregon and California.

About forty-five miles below Boat Encampment are the Upper Dalles or Dalles de Mort, and thirty miles farther the Lower Dalles, where the river makes a magnificent uproar and interrupts navigation About thirty miles below the Lower Dalles the river expands into Upper Arrow Lake, a beautiful sheet of water forty miles long and five miles wide, straight as an arrow and with the beautiful forests of the Selkirk range rising from its east shore, and those of the Gold range from the west. At the foot of the lake are the Narrows, a few miles in length, and after these rapids are passed, the river enters Lower Arrow Lake, which is like the Upper Arrow, but is even longer and not so straight.

A short distance below the Lower Arrow the Columbia receives the Kootenay River, the largest affluent thus far on its course and said to be navigable for small steamers for a hundred and fifty miles. It is an exceedingly crooked stream, heading beyond the upper Columbia Lakes, and in its

mazy course flowing to all points of the compass, it seems lost and baffled in the tangle of mountain spurs and ridges it drains. Measured around its loops and bends it is probably more than five hundred miles in length. It is also rich in lakes, the largest, Kootenay Lake, being upwards of seventy miles in length with an average width of five miles. A short distance below the confluence of the Kootenay, near the boundary line between Washington and British Columbia, another large stream comes in from the east, the Clarke's Fork or Flathead River. Its upper sources are near those of the Missouri and South Saskatchewan, and in its course it flows through two large and beautiful lakes, the Flathead and Pend d'Oreille. All the lakes we have noticed thus far would make charming places of summer resort; but Pend d'Oreille, besides being surpassingly beautiful, has the advantage of being easily accessible, since it is on the main line of the Northern Pacific railroad in the territory of Idaho. In the purity of its waters it reminds one of Tahoe, while its many picturesque islands crowned with evergreens, and its winding shores forming endless variety of bays and promontories lavishly crowded with spirey spruce and cedar, recall some of the best of the island scenery of Alaska.

About thirty-five miles below the mouth of Clarke's Fork the Columbia is joined by the Ne-whoi-al-pit-ku River from the northwest. Here too are the great Chaudiere or Kettle Falls on the main river, with a total descent of about fifty feet. Fifty miles further down, the Spokane River, a clear dashing stream, comes in from the east. It is about one hundred and twenty miles long, and takes its rise in the beautiful lake, Coeur d'Alene, in Idaho, which receives the drainage of nearly a hundred miles of the western slopes of the Bitter Root Mountains, through the St. Joseph and Coeur d'Alene rivers. The lake is about twenty miles long, set in the midst of charming scenery, and like Pend d'Oreille is easy of access and is already attracting attention as a summer place for enjoyment, rest and health.

The famous Spokane Falls are in Washington, about thirty miles below the lake, where the river is outspread and divided and makes a grand descent from a level basaltic plateau, giving rise to one of the most beautiful as well as one of the greatest and most available of water powers in the state. The city of the same name is built on the plateau along both sides of the series of cascades and falls which, rushing and sounding through the midst give singular beauty and animation. The young city is also rushing and booming. It is founded on a rock, leveled and prepared for it, and its streets require no grading or paving. As a power to whirl the machinery of a great city and at the same time to train the people to a love of the sublime and beautiful as displayed in living water, the Spokane Falls are unrivalled, at least as far as my observation has reached. Nowhere else have I seen such lessons given by a river in the streets of a city, such a glad, exulting, abounding outgush, crisp and clear from the mountains, dividing, falling, displaying its wealth, calling aloud in the midst of the busy throng, and making glorious offerings for every use of utility or adornment.

From the mouth of the Spokane the Columbia, now out of the woods, flows to the westward with a broad, stately current for a hundred and twenty miles to receive the Okanagan, a large, generous tributary a hundred and sixty miles long, coming from the north and drawing some of its waters from the Cascade Range. More than half its course is through a chain of lakes, the largest of which at the head of the river is over sixty miles in length. From its confluence with

CRATER LAKE.

MOUNT HOOD AND COLUMBIA RIVER.

the Okanagan the river pursues a southerly course for a hundred and fifty miles, most of the way through a dreary, treeless, parched plain to meet the great south fork. The Lewis or Snake River is nearly a thousand miles long and drains nearly the whole of Idaho, a territory rich in scenery, gold mines, flowery, grassy valleys and deserts, while some of the highest tributaries reach into Wyoming, Utah, and Nevada. Throughout a great part of its course it is countersunk in a black lava plain and shut in by mural precipices a thousand feet high, gloomy, forbidding, and unapproachable, though the gloominess of its cañon is relieved in some manner by its many falls and springs, some of the springs being large enough to appear as the outlets of subterranean rivers. They gush out from the faces of the sheer black walls and descend foaming with brave roar and beauty to swell the flood below. From where the river skirts the base of the Blue Mountains its surroundings are less forbidding. Much of the country is fertile, but its cañon is everywhere deep and almost inaccessible. Steamers make their way up as far as Lewiston, a hundred and fifty miles, and receive cargoes of wheat at different points through shutes that extend down from the tops of the bluffs. But though the Hudson Bay Company navigated the north fork to its sources, they depended altogether on pack animals for the transportation of supplies and furs between the Columbia and Fort Hall on the head of the south fork, which shows how desperately unmanageable a river it must be.

A few miles above the mouth of the Snake the Yakima, which drains a considerable portion of the Cascade Range, enters from the northwest. It is about a hundred and fifty miles long but carries comparatively little water, a great part of what it sets out with from the base of the mountains being consumed in irrigated fields and meadows in passing through the settlements along its course, and by evaporation on the parched desert plains. The grand flood of the Columbia, now from half a mile to a mile wide, sweeps on to the westward, holding a nearly direct course until it reaches the mouth of the Willamette, where it turns to the northward and flows fifty miles along the main valley between the Coast and Cascade ranges ere it again resumes its westward course to the sea. In all its course from the mouth of the Yakima to the sea, a distance of three hundred miles, the only considerable affluent from the northward is the Cowlitz, which heads in the glaciers of Mount Rainier. From the south and east it receives the Walla-Walla and Umatilla, rather short and dreary-looking streams, though the plains they pass through have proved fertile, and their upper tributaries in the Blue Mountains, shaded with tall pines, firs, spruces, and the beautiful Oregon larch (*Larix brevifolia*), lead into a delightful region. The John Day River also heads in the Blue

Mountains and flows into the Columbia sixty miles below the mouth of the Umatilla. Its valley is in great part fertile, and is noted for the interesting fossils discovered in it by Professor Condon in sections cut by the river through the overlying lava beds.

The Deschutes River comes in from the south about twenty miles below the John Day. It is a large, boisterous stream, draining the eastern slope of the Cascade Range for nearly two hundred miles, and from the great number of falls on the main trunk, as well as on its many mountain tributaries, well deserves its name. It enters the Columbia with a grand roar of falls and rapids, and at times seems almost to rival the main stream in the volume of water it carries. Near the mouth of the Deschutes are the Falls of the Columbia, when the river passes a rough bar of lava. The descent is not great, but the immense volume of water makes a grand display. During the flood season the falls are obliterated and skillful boatmen pass over them in safety; while the Dalles, some six or eight miles below, may be passed during low water but are utterly impassible in flood time. At the Dalles the vast river is jammed together into a long narrow slot of unknown depth cut sheer down in the basalt. This slot or trough is about a mile and a half long and about sixty yards wide at the narrowest place. At ordinary times the river seems to be set on edge and runs swiftly but without much noisy surging with a descent of about twenty feet to the mile. But when the snow is melting on the mountains the river rises here sixty feet, or even more during extraordinary freshets, and spreads out over a great breadth of massive rocks through which have been cut several other gorges running parallel with the one usually occupied. All these inferior gorges now come into use, and the huge, roaring torrent, still rising and spreading at length, overwhelms the high jagged rock walls between them, making a tremendous display of chafing, surging, shattered currents, counter-currents, and hollow whirls that no words can be made to describe. A few miles below the Dalles the storm-tossed river gets itself together again, looks like water, becomes silent and with stately, tranquil deliberation goes on its way, out of the gray region of sage and sand into the Oregon woods. Thirty-five or forty miles below the Dalles are the Cascades of the Columbia, where the river in passing through the mountains makes another magnificent display of foaming, surging rapids which form the first obstruction to navigation from the ocean, a hundred and twenty miles distant. This obstruction is to be overcome by locks which are now being made.

BEAVER TRAP.

Between the Dalles and Cascades the river is like a lake a mile or two wide, lying in a valley or cañon about three thousand feet deep. The walls of the cañon lean well back in most places, and leave here and there small strips or bays of level ground along the water's edge. But towards the Cascades, and for some distance below them, the immediate banks are guarded by walls of columnar basalt, which are worn in many places into a great variety of bold and picturesque forms, such as the Castle Rock, Rooster Rock, the Pillars of Hercules, Cape Horn, etc., while back of these rise the sublime mountain walls, forest-crowned and fringed more or less from top to base

ROOSTER ROCK, COLUMBIA RIVER. FROM SKETCH BY E. R. HILL.

"Here again is one of the landmarks of the Columbia, Rooster Rock, a formation not unlike Castle Rock in general contour. This is a column of basalt, strikingly bold in appearance, and forming a picturesque bit as it projects from the background of forest-crowned mountain walls which line the banks of the great river."

with pine, spruce, and shaggy underbrush, especially in the narrow gorges and ravines, where innumerable small streams come dancing and drifting down, misty and white, to join the mighty river. Many of these falls on both sides of the cañon of the Columbia are far larger and more interesting in every way than would be guessed from the slight glimpses one gets of them while sailing past on the river, or from the car-windows. The Multnomah Falls are particularly interesting, and occupy fern-lined gorges of marvelous beauty in the basalt. They are said to be about eight hundred feet in height and, at times of high water when the mountain snows are melting, are well worthy of a place beside the famous falls of the Yosemite Valley.

According to an Indian tradition, the river of the Cascades once flowed through the basalt beneath a natural bridge that was broken down during a mountain war, when the old volcanoes, Hood and St. Helens, on opposite sides of the river, hurled rocks at each other, thus forming a dam. That the river has been dammed here to some extent, and within a comparatively short period, seems probable to say the least, since great numbers of submerged trees standing erect may be found along both shores while, as we have seen, the whole river for thirty miles above the Cascades looks like a lake or mill pond. On the other hand, it is held by some that the submerged groves were carried into their places by immense land slides.

Much of interest in this connection must necessarily be omitted for want of space. About forty miles below the Cascades the river receives the Willamette, the last of its great tributaries. It is navigable for ocean vessels as far as Portland, ten miles above its mouth, and for river steamers a hundred miles farther. The Falls of the Willamette are fifteen miles above Portland, where the river coming out of dense woods breaks its way across a bar of black basalt and falls forty feet in a passion of snowy foam, showing to fine advantage against its background of evergreens. Of the fertility and beauty of the Willamette all the world has heard. It lies between the Cascade and Coast ranges, and is bounded on the south by the Callapooia Mountains, a cross spur that separates it from the valley of the Umpqua. It was here the first settlements for agriculture were made and a provisional government organized, while the settlers, isolated in the far wilderness, numbered only a few thousand and were laboring under the opposition of the British government and the Hudson Bay Company. Eager desire in the acquisition of territory on the part of these pioneer state-builders was more truly boundless than the wilderness they were in, and their unconscionable patriotism was equaled only by their belligerence. For here, while negotiations were pending for the location of the northern boundary, originated the celebrated " 54° 40' or fight," about as reasonable a war-cry as the "North Pole or fight." Yet sad was the day that brought the news of the signing of the treaty fixing their boundary along the forty-ninth parallel, thus leaving the little land-hungry settlement only a mere quarter-million of miles!

As the Willamette is one of the most foodful of valleys, so is the Columbia one of the most foodful of rivers. During the fisher's harvest time salmon from the sea come in countless millions, urging their way against falls, rapids and shallows, up into the very heart of the Rocky Mountains, supplying everybody by the way with most bountiful masses of delicious food, weighing from twenty to eighty pounds, plump and smooth like loaves of bread ready for the oven. The supply seemed inexhaustible, as well it might. Large quantities were used by the Indians as fuel, and by the Hudson Bay people as manure for their gardens at the forts. Used, wasted, canned and sent in shiploads to all the world, a grand harvest was reaped every year while nobody sowed. Of late, however, the salmon crop has begun to fail, and millions of young fry are now sown like wheat in the river every year, from hatching establishments belonging to the government.

All of the Oregon waters that win their way to the sea are tributary to the Columbia, save the short streams of the immediate coast, and the Umpqua and Rogue rivers in southern Oregon. These both head in the Cascade Mountains and find their way to the sea through gaps in the Coast Range, and both drain large and fertile and beautiful valleys. Rogue River valley is peculiarly attractive. With a fine climate, and kindly productive soil, the scenery is delightful. About the main central open portion of the basin, dotted with picturesque groves of oak, there are many smaller valleys charmingly environed, the whole surrounded in the distance by the Siskiyou, Coast, Umpqua and Cascade mountains. Besides the cereals nearly every sort of fruit flourishes here, and large areas are being devoted to peach, apricot, nectarine, and vine culture. To me it seems above all

PEAK GLACIER OF SIR DONALD. FROM PAINTING BY JOHN A. FRASER.

"Presently your eyes will turn away and be led along a lofty crenelated wall up to the noblest peak in British Columbia,—Sir Donald. Its form is that of a prism, a three-sided purple obelisk, sharply apexed and faced by precipices piled six thousand feet above its icy buttress : a sublime peak. America has no grander picture to show than these crowded, glacier-studded, snow-swept heights when the evening light is dyeing them crimson and gold."

others the garden valley of Oregon and the most delightful place for a home. On the eastern rim of the valley in the Cascade Mountains, about sixty miles from Medford in a direct line, is the remarkable Crater Lake, usually regarded as the one grand wonder of the region. It lies in a deep sheer-walled basin about seven thousand feet above the level of the sea, supposed to be the crater of an extinct volcano.

Oregon as it is to-day is a very young country, though most of it seems old. Contemplating the Columbia sweeping from forest to forest, across plain and desert, one is led to say of it as did Byron of the ocean, "Such as Creation's dawn beheld, thou rollest now." How ancient appear the crumbling basaltic monuments along its banks, and the gray plains to the east of the Cascades! Nevertheless, the river as well as its basin in anything like their present condition are comparatively but of yesterday. Looking no further back in the geological records than the tertiary period, the Oregon of that time looks altogether strange in the few suggestive glimpses we may get of it—forests in which palm trees wave their royal crowns, and strange animals roaming beneath them or about the reedy margins of lakes, the Oreodon, Lephiodon, and several extinct species of the horse, the camel, and other animals.

Then came the fire period with its darkening showers of ashes and cinders and its vast floods of molten lava, making quite another Oregon from the fair and fertile land of the preceding era. And again while yet the volcanic fires show signs of action in the smoke and flame of the higher mountains, the whole region passes under the dominion of ice, and from the frost and darkness and death of the Glacial Period, Oregon has but recently emerged to the kindly warmth and life of to-day.

JOHN MUIR.

TWIN PEAKS: BOW RIVER AT BANFF.

THE ROCKIES, FROM ABOVE CANMORE.

The Canadian Rockies

BRITISH Columbia, Canada's Pacific province, embraces the whole breadth of the great western cordillera from the summit of the Rockies to the shore of the "South Sea," and fills the space between the United States and Alaska—an area larger than New England would be, even were its boundaries stretched north to the St. Lawrence.

Scarcely more can be attempted, in the present writing, than a mere outline of its magnificent scenery; of its mines, fisheries, forests and other resources; of its varied peoples savage and civilized, and the political and social conditions and potentialities under which they live and have made an adventurous history. The whole province consists of a series of mountain ranges trending north and south and divided into four main lines. Easternmost lie the Rockies, between the plains and the headwaters of the Columbia River. Next westward stands the Selkirk range, and beside it, west of the Columbia, the Gold or Columbia range, which coalesces with the Rockies in the rough region northward, where through wild cañons and golden gravel the great Fraser gathers its waters from the glaciers that feed the Mackenzie and Saskatchewan. Near the coast runs the lofty sierra known as the Cascades (though not truly a continuation of the Cascades of Oregon,) sending grand spurs down to the sea which penetrates far between them in fiords like those of Norway; and lastly, a half-submerged line of summits, forming the chain of elongated islands along the northwest coast.

This physical configuration causes a variety of climates and produces distinct regions, botanically and zoölogically considered. The prevailing western winds endow the islands and coast-valleys with a warm, wet climate, promoting the growth of forests as dense and gigantic as those of Oregon or New Zealand. The interior, on the contrary, is high and arid. The clouds sweep across it from the crest of the Cascades, letting fall little moisture, so that its summers are hot and very dry, and irrigation is needful for agriculture in the southern half of the province, where alone does any considerable open ground exist and grazing is the principal occupation. Winter there is correspondingly dry and intensely cold, far more so however in the southern than in the northern or more woody part of the interior, where, in the "Cariboo country," a considerable population of miners and farmers is to be found remote from the busy world but not indifferent to it. The rain-clouds striking the Columbia-Selkirk ranges deliver copious showers, clothing their pedestals with heavy forests and loading their uplands with snow and glacial ice which feed such noble rivers as the Columbia, the Thompson and the Okinagan. By this time the greater part of the moisture has been extracted from the clouds, so that the climate of the Rockies, especially on their eastern slope, is dry and in winter intensely cold, while the forests are comparatively small and sparse.

The modern development of the province has taken place altogether along its southern border,— a fact closely connected with the building of the Canadian Pacific Railway. When finally, in 1867, the federation of the Dominion of Canada had been accomplished, a transcontinental railroad became an inevitable corollary of the event—a tie necessary to bind the isolated and somewhat antipathetic provinces together until a natural coherence was developed, and at the same time an artery through which the life-blood of the new political body might circulate to the extremities. British Columbia, theretofore an independent colony of the British Crown, made the construction of this line the price of her adhesion to the Dominion. The government accordingly began work, but in 1881 resigned the affairs to a private company of capitalists, to whom a vast land grant was given and money advanced. This company, under the management of W. C. Van Horne (now its president), proceeded so energetically that by the end of 1883 trains were running from Lake Superior to the base of the Rocky Mountains, and two years later the enormous difficulties of engineering had been surmounted and passengers were daily carried from Montreal to Vancouver, the Pacific terminus, without change of cars. Thus well has British Columbia been paid her price. The railway chose the Bow River Valley—the real head of the South Saskatchewan: and the entrance to the mountains by ascending this stream is a grand introduction to the magnificent beauty of their scenery.

The Rockies in this part show no crystalline or volcanic rocks, but are composed wholly of uplifted beds of limestones and sandstones, which have been heaved aloft in masses of strata thousands of feet thick, sometimes greatly displaced and decaying into such castellated and pinnacle-studded heights as are seen when we approach the central, watershed range, but more usually simply lying at a steep incline, so as to present a broken escarpment on the outward face and a comparatively smooth slope on the inward side, or that next to the central range. These rocks are of the carboniferous age, and on the lower Bow extensive deposits of anthracite coal are mined at Duthil.

As we ascend the Bow an amorphous mass of mountains, loaded with snow down almost to the forest line, fills the scene on the right and ahead; but on the left the valley is overhung by a line of terrific precipices, separated by alcoves in which gorgeous color lies engulfed, transfiguring into a structure of opal the alternate courses of rock and snow that build up these mighty scarps. Twenty miles above the gap the line is broken by the escape of the Bow between Mount Rundle and Cascade Mountain. Turning through this gap we encounter a second but more irregular rank of huge precipices—the faces of mountain strata dipping steeply southwestward. Splintered peaks and saw-edged summits contrast with piles of ledges like Titanic masonry, or with hills round and wooded, while glimpses can be caught far up the Bow of the untrodden heights of the central range.

In the very midst of these serried crags—

> " . . . . imaginative heights that yield far-stretching views into eternity,"

—lies the Canadian National Park. It is a public reservation twenty-six miles long by ten miles wide, and the government has laid out roads and bridle-paths connecting the points of principal interest, and has permitted the growth of a flourishing little village of private hospitals, boarding houses, livery stables and shops, called National Park Post Office. The railway station is Banff, seventy-five miles west of Calgary. Two miles south of the station, prettily surrounded and commanding an amazing cyclorama, stands the great Banff Hotel, a modern and beautiful caravansary, heated by steam, lighted by electricity, richly furnished, and thus far managed in a highly satisfactory manner.

The *raison d'être* of a public park just here was not so much the variety and beauty of the scenery (though I am myself of the opinion, after having seen all the remainder of the range, that no one district of the United States can equal it in this respect) as the presence of copious hot sulphur springs, which gush out along the slope of a mountain-spur. The largest of these supplies

THE GREAT GLACIER.   FROM PAINTING BY W. NOTMAN & SON.

" A path up the valley runs through a beautiful forest, over wreckage of rocks and logs brought down by an avalanche, and along a milky torrent to the foot of one of the grandest glaciers in the whole district. It hides the head of the valley under a silvery curtain of ice, a mile wide at the top and over 2,500 feet in fall, etched with blue and green crevasses, and, in its upper portion, broken into innumerable *séracs*, while the lower part rounds off into a smooth forefoot. Above and beyond its sky-line stretches a vast *névé*, or plateau of compacted snow, which incessantly pushes it on, and which sends off other huge glaciers down other glens beyond the visible heights."

water to the hotel's bath-houses, and to the medicinal rooms of several sanitary establishments, but two others, near the foot of the range, are set apart for public bathing, picturesque cottages being attached, under government control, and a trifling fee charged. One of these springs is a fine open pool, where the water is simply warm; but the other can be taken as hot as you please. Originally it bubbled up in a crater around the edges of which was gradually built up a rim of lime-rock deposited from the overflowing water; and this finally assumed a beehive form, with an opening in the top down which the early visitors would descend by a slippery ladder through a column of steam. Now an entrance has been tunneled through the side on a level with the water. Donning your suit (if you mean to bathe) you pass from the house directly into the interior of this natural dome, which is some sixty feet in diameter, and step into a pool of mineral water, on one side too hot to endure, but on the other more comfortable. The floor is bubbling sand and the atmosphere an equable temperature of sulphurous (yet not offensive) vapor, which escapes through the natural ventilator in the roof, while the overflow of the spring maintains continual freshness in the tank. The medicinal advantages

MOUNT BURGESS—EMERALD LAKE.

HOT SPRINGS AT BANFF.

THE OPEN POOL.

of this bath are highly lauded by physicians and patients alike; and when it is done you may return to your snug dressing-room without contact with the outer air, thus avoiding any danger of a chill. It is an arrangement admirable in every way.

The attractions of this park might furnish material for a long essay and for many years to come a visitor may experience the excitement of a genuine explorer as he wanders among pathless glens and climbs untrodden crags. No shooting is permitted in the park, but game is abundant within a few miles. Trout fishing may be enjoyed in every stream inside the park as well as out. The Bow above its falls is a quiet stream, capital for boating, and in a canoe one may paddle far up its devious course to the Vermilion lakes. Here a long section of the great central range stands in line before him—monarchs of the Rockies, sitting in superb array, robed in a royal ermine of snow, crowned with coronets of ice, and fondled by troops of cloud-maidens. Rising in domes, pyramids, cubes and spires of every shape, barred with lines of palest blue marking their structural ledges,

"Tinted and shaded by pencils of air,"

the sharply cut crags in front firm against the remoter peaks and intersected by opalescent gorges, this wonderful sierra chains the eye and profoundly stirs the imagination. Our fancy flies to explore those blue cañons and sport with the roseate mists upon peak and plateau. They are so ethereal and so harmonious with the brilliant sky, that when our canoe breaks into rippling confusion their reflection in the water, we half expect to see that sublime original in the west totter and fall with instant sympathy. This is only an index of what is to be seen and studied in all directions about Banff. Many of these lesser heights are easily ascended, and the greater ones are such as the Alpine Club would not despise. There is no end to the "things to be done" and the places to go to, and as a rule, the finest weather prevails, especially in autumn. The time will come when Banff Park will be one of the shrines of the world to the pilgrim-worshipers of nature.

VIEW FROM OVER BOW FALLS, BANFF.

Past the enormous blue and white ledges of Pilot and Copper Mountain; past the rust-red towers and splintering pinnacles of Castle Mountain, "torn like battlements of Mars;" past the helmet-shaped head of Mount Lefroy, tallest peak of this part of the range and 7,000 feet above the railroad, skirting by audacious engineering the foot of the gothic pile of cathedral peak and feasting our eyes upon glimpses of majestic heights unnamed and untrodden, we enter the Hector Pass, 5,200 feet above the sea. On our left the noble gray terraces of Mount Stephen form an ice-clad pyramid just a mile in altitude; opposite are the circling summits of the Wahputtek and Van Horne ranges, an amphitheatre of snow rimmed by glistening peaks. Below sinks a narrow forested valley, down which the Kickinghorse (or Wapta) River rushes westward in a series of cascades that drop eleven hundred feet in five miles. The railroad winds down to the bottom of the gorge where the comfortable hotel at Field Station invites mountain lovers to pause, and it then follows the river westward. All these peaks are glacier-clad and the hollows of their summits white with vast stretches of unbroken snow. Range after range, each nobler than the last, one thinks, come into view and are left behind as the train rolls on. Who that has seen the purple and crimson grandeur of the Ottertail range from Leanchoil can ever forget it; or the sapphire heights upholding heaven at the head of the North Wapta? There are no people, no roads, no visible trails, except this iron one. The grandeur of primitive nature, unsoiled by human contact, is before us.

Along the western base of the Rockies flows the Columbia, from its source in Lake Windermere, some fifty miles north of the international boundary. Its course is straight north for one hundred and fifty miles or more. Where the Kickinghorse flows in, giving an outlet through its terrific gorge for the railway, is the village of Golden; and between this point and the lake runs a steamboat, making a round trip once a week. Its service is as a connecting link between the railway and the ranches of the Kootenay Valley, a broad grazing and agricultural region adjoining

CHEOPS,
AND THE HERMIT RANGE.

AT THE SUMMIT OF THE SELKIRKS—HERMIT MOUNTAIN.

Idaho, and drained by the Kootenay River and lakes, which drain the western slope of the Rockies and empty into the Columbia south of the boundary.

Before long, no doubt, a railway through the Crow's Nest or the Kootenay Pass will connect this fine valley with the eastern plains.

Prairie ridges surround Lake Windermere, where there is nothing but a primitive landing for the boats. The river winds through marshes and shallow bars, and navigation is difficult in the season of low water. The Rockies are tame on this side, and the eye turns most often to the west, where the Selkirks recall Thoreau's simile, "solid stacks of hay," so regular and shapely are their white pyramids above the broad foundation of densely forested foothills. Some landings are scattered along this western bank, where short roads lead back to silver mines; and in the summer bands of Shushwap Indians will be found ready to send by the boat and train large packages of wild berries which they formerly carried laboriously over the mountains on horseback. Kootenay Indians, with bark canoes whose bows project under water like a naval ram, race with the boat. Shooting and fishing is always possible, and this pretty trip is a favorite one with sportsmen.

Twenty miles below Golden the Columbia is crossed at Donald, an important railway division point. Here the river is extremely swift and powerful, tearing through a gloomy gorge like the whirlpools of Niagara, and continuing thus until it has turned the head of the Selkirk range, and begun its southward course along their western flank. Many rash voyagers have started down this splendid green torrent, but few of them have ever been heard of again. It was proposed, nevertheless, to carry the railway along the river-cliffs all the way around its "great bend," but Rogers discovered a pass across the then unexplored Selkirks, and crossing the Columbia at Donald, the ascent of these savage mountains begins. Up steep and winding grades, with noble views ahead and behind, so that one is always in fear of losing some fine picture

ON ASULKAN GLACIER.

STANLEY PARK, VANCOUVER. FROM PAINTING BY JULIAN RIX.

"The attractions of this park might furnish material for a long essay, and for many years to come a visitor may experience the excitement of a genuine explorer as he wanders among pathless glens and climbs untrodden crags. Many of these lesser heights are easily ascended, and the greater ones are such as the Alpine Club would not despise. There is no end to the 'things to be done' and the places to go to; and, as a rule, the finest weather prevails, especially in autumn."

VICTORIA.

he would be sorry to miss, the train labors on toward Rogers' Pass. Forests of gigantic trees clothe the lower slopes, but there are few saw-mills, for the cost of shipping the timber would be more than it was worth. There is no mining and no population except a few exiles in charge of telegraph stations and road-bed. Long lines of massive sheds, made to protect the line from avalanches, rather than from the depth or drifting of snow, cover the track. Finally the pass is entered through a narrow cleft in the mountains 3,000 feet deep, and two miles beyond the watershed we come to Glacier Station.

Bodies and cliffs and cornices of blue ice, and wide swaths and blankets of snow have long been familiar sights to the traveler who has been gazing at the mountain tops. Now he may get a nearer view. Here is a hotel where in perfect comfort he may survey the magnificent alps that encircle him. A path up the valley runs through a beautiful forest, over wreckage of rocks and logs brought down by an avalanche, and along a milky torrent to the foot of one of the grandest glaciers in the whole district. It hides the head of the valley under a silvery curtain of ice a mile wide at the top and over 2,500 feet in fall, etched with blue and green crevasses, and, in its upper portion, broken into innumerable *seracs*, while the lower part rounds off into a smooth forefoot. Caves are hollowed into the turquoise of its forefoot, whence rivers white with silt and ice-crystals come rushing over beds of bowlders whose clinking and grinding are audible above the noise of waters. The sides of the ice-fall are strewn with the blocks that slide down from the walls, but no moraine mars the purity of its surface, and in this as well as other respects Swiss travelers will note a resemblance to the Rhone glacier. Above and beyond its sky-line stretches a vast *névé*, or plateau of compacted snow, which incessantly pushes it on, and which sends off other huge glaciers down other glens beyond the visible heights. Several have been mapped by the Rev. W. S. Green, F.R.G.S., whose admirable book "Among the Selkirk Glaciers" (1888) is an intensely interesting story of personal adventure as well as a valuable treatise on local geography and geology. You cannot follow his footsteps without his equipment and skill, but you may easily climb high upon the rocks alongside the glaciers and even venture out a little way upon the ice without fear; but it is not wise to go into the caves, as certain foolish tourists do.

Presently your eyes will turn away and be led along a lofty crenelated wall up to the noblest peak in British Columbia—Sir Donald. Its form is that of a prism, a three-sided purple obelisk, sharply apexed and faced by precipices piled 6,000 feet above its icy buttress—a sublime peak. America has no grander picture to show than these crowded, glacier-studded, snow-swept heights when the evening light is dyeing them crimson and gold.

Down through the vast ravine of the Illecillewaet goes the train on its way to the west. One rough little village shows where mines back in the hills send ore to the trains. At the western base of the Selkirks the Columbia is again crossed, where the little town of Revelstoke is sustained by the railway operations and a few gold mines northward. Here, years ago, passed the canoes of French voyageurs, bringing cargoes of merchandise from Athabasca Pass down Canoe River and the Columbia, and returning perilously and laboriously with bales of precious fur. Now steamboats run southward to Idaho and the Kootenay.

Westward of the river majestic peaks of the Gold Range are lifted above wide belts of forest land. Fifty miles north of here, some forty years ago, miners' villages were planted in the defiles of those dark mountains, but their owners, though their pockets bulged with gold-dust, could get nothing to eat. Those who survived and got away left everything behind, and to-day the jungle overgrows their abandoned cabins, furniture and all.

Through the cliff-walled forest-glens and down past the dark waters of the Shushwap Lakes, the train finds its way out into the South Thompson Valley, where the ranches around Kamloops make a scene of civilization. This is the open interior plateau country of the province. Its rivers unite in one splendid green torrent which cuts its way westward through strangely picturesque "badlands"

SHUSHWAP MISSION AT KAMLOOPS.

and monumental terraces like those along the upper Missouri. The center of this region is at Ash-croft, where the stage-road from the Cariboo country northward meets the railroad, and pack-trains, prairie-schooners and dusty coaches revive memories of California in '49. Then the emerald Thompson plunges into the swirling yellow flood of the Fraser, and in fierce tumult boils down its mighty cañon through the Cascades. With superlative audacity and skill the railway accompanies it. Crossing upon the first cantilever bridge ever built, it pierces a series of tunnels and winds along a gallery cut out of the cliffs. The scenery is upon a gigantic scale, and as black, savage and desolate as that in the alps of the moon. Naked rocks rear themselves hundreds of feet from the water's edge and then in retreating ledges build up mountains capped with snow. The mind is stunned with the evidence of the stupendous agents that have wrought here, and the voice is silenced in attempt-ing to describe it. Lower down the mountains are higher, the gorge more confined and tortuous, the struggle and tumult of the waters greater, but the savagery and loneliness are somewhat mitigated by occasional signs of human presence. Indians stand picturesquely upon jutting rocks, fishing for salmon and smoking the ruddy flesh upon scaffoldings precariously poised among the rocks. Chinamen wash gold in sandy coves. The old stage-road clings firmly to the opposite wall, a monument of the thrilling days of '60 and the Fraser-River gold excitement. Yale and other little towns on the lower river recall still more emphatically those exciting times, and the snow-anchor still shines upon the Hope peaks. Finally we escape into the lowlands. Here are prairies and farms, and quaint hamlets of Chinese and Indians. The view reaches southward to Mount Baker and the mountains along Puget Sound. Northward from Agassiz station runs a short branch-line to Lake Harrison, where, in one of the most beautiful situations on the continent, a hotel and sanitarium stand beside copious springs of hot mineral water. This was a point on the old Harrison trail to the gold diggings, and steamboats passed from the Fraser into Harrison and the chain of lakes beyond it, now reverted almost to their pristine wildness. A little farther on the Fraser is abandoned and the road strikes across to Port Moody and thence runs on to Vancouver, the sea-terminus, at the entrance of Burrard Inlet.

Vancouver in 1885 was a mere clearing in a forest of firs whose impenetrable jungle reached down to the very water's edge. More than half of the trees were six to twelve feet in diameter and from two to three hundred fifty feet in height. In 1886 a town stood there until one day a fire swept it away. A year later it had been rebuilt, largely in brick and stone, and now a full-fledged seaport of 20,000 people, with all the appurtenances of modern civilization, overlooks the broad bay to the beautiful Capriolani Mountains on its northern shore. Spacious hotels, elegant residences, shops, stores, warehouses and bustling streets give evidence of the large business done. Between Vancouver and China and Japan steamships ply in connection with the Canadian Pacific Railway, and half the tea-crop of the Orient passes over these wharves. Steamers run thence to Alaska, Victoria, San Francisco and the Puget Sound ports. The mountains and glens around the inlet afford fine hunting and fishing, while the park among the grand trees and overlooking the Straits of Georgia must not be forgotten. Some day Vancouver will become a most interesting city.

A dozen miles south of Vancouver, on the Fraser, and reached by steamboat or by rail, is New Westminster, the former colonial capital. It is a pretty place, quiet and homelike, noted for its schools and churches, and by no means asleep. Below it are many square miles of the richest delta-lands, whose produce comes to this market. Above are the grazing tracts, forests and mines. Enormous saw mills and planing mills turn out and export timber and manufactured lumber, doors, sash, etc.; and here is concentrated the salmon-canning industry of the Fraser, the product of which amounts to 2,500 tons a year, and which gives employment to a large part of the white population, as well to a motley crowd of Indians and Chinese.

From New Westminster or Vancouver a few hours' sail through the verdant archipelagoes of the Straits of Georgia carries the traveler to Victoria, the most picturesque seaport on the Pacific Coast. Its harbor is a pocket of deep water among shores and islands of granite, around which the quaint little city is grouped—a thoroughly English town. It has now some 15,000 people and a large maritime business. Its suburbs are adorned with fine villas, modeled upon those of England, and its beautiful park commands a view of the Straits of Fuca and the Olympic Mountains south of them—a picture hard to equal anywhere in the New World. Three miles away is the romantic town and harbor of Esquimalt, the British North Pacific naval station, where are arsenals, repair shops, a new stone graving dock, and the germ of an imposing series of fortresses. The Island of Vancouver is a mountainous wilderness almost impenetrable and untamable, and has few harbors on its ocean-front. A railway skirts the eastern shore to the collieries of Nanaimo, which produce the greater part of the domestic coal used on the Pacific Coast, and around which considerable civilization has arisen. Thus year by year British Columbia is growing in wealth and importance.

ERNEST INGERSOLL.

CANADIAN PACIFIC DOCKS, VANCOUVER.